HISTORIES OF TIBET

Studies in Indian and Tibetan Buddhism

This series was conceived to provide a forum for publishing outstanding new contributions to scholarship on Indian and Tibetan Buddhism and also to make accessible seminal research not widely known outside a narrow specialist audience, including translations of appropriate monographs and collections of articles from other languages. The series strives to shed light on the Indic Buddhist traditions by exposing them to historical-critical inquiry, illuminating through contextualization and analysis these traditions' unique heritage and the significance of their contribution to the world's religious and philosophical achievements.

Members of the Editorial Board:

Tom Tillemans (co-chair), Emeritus, University of Lausanne
Leonard van der Kuijp (co-chair), Harvard University
Shrikant Bahulkar, Bhandarkar Oriental Research Institute
José Cabezón, University of California, Santa Barbara
Georges Dreyfus, Williams College, Massachusetts
Vincent Eltschinger, École Pratique des Hautes Études
Janet Gyatso, Harvard University
Paul Harrison, Stanford University
Toni Huber, Humboldt University, Berlin
Pascale Hugon, Austrian Academy of the Sciences
Shoryu Katsura, Ryukoku University, Kyoto
Kataoka Kei, Kyushu University, Fukuoka
Thupten Jinpa Langri, Institute of Tibetan Classics, Montreal
Chenkuo Lin, National Chengchi University, Taipei
Hong Luo, Peking University
Cristina Scherrer-Schaub, University of Lausanne
Ernst Steinkellner, Emeritus, University of Vienna
Jan Westerhoff, Oxford University
Jeson Woo, Dongguk University, Seoul
Shaoyong Ye, Peking University
Chizoku Yoshimizu, Tsukuba University

STUDIES IN INDIAN AND TIBETAN BUDDHISM

Histories of Tibet

Essays in Honor of Leonard W. J. van der Kuijp

Edited by Kurtis R. Schaeffer, Jue Liang,
and William A. McGrath

Wisdom

Wisdom Publications
132 Perry Street
New York, NY 10014 USA
wisdomexperience.org

Library of Congress Cataloging-in-Publication Data
Names: Schaeffer, Kurtis R., editor. | Liang, Jue, editor. |
McGrath, William A., editor. | Kuijp, Leonard W. J. van der, honoree.
Title: Histories of Tibet: essays in honor of Leonard W. J. van der Kuijp /
edited by Kurtis R. Schaeffer, Jue Liang, and William A. McGrath.
Description: First edition. | New York: Wisdom Publications, 2023. |
Series: Studies in Indian and Tibetan Buddhism |
Includes bibliographical references and index.
Identifiers: LCCN 2022036154 (print) | LCCN 2022036155 (ebook) |
ISBN 9781614297840 (hardcover) | ISBN 9781614298083 (ebook)
Subjects: LCSH: Tibet Region—Civilization. | Tibet Region—History. |
Buddhism—Tibet Region—History. | Tibetans—Intellectual life.
Classification: LCC DS786 .H57 2023 (print) | LCC DS786 (ebook) |
DDC 951/.5--dc23/eng/20220729
LC record available at https://lccn.loc.gov/2022036154
LC ebook record available at https://lccn.loc.gov/2022036155

ISBN 978-1-61429-784-0 ebook ISBN 978-1-61429-808-3

27 26 25 24 23
5 4 3 2 1

Cover image: Detail of Sakya Paṇḍita from a mural in Zhidé Lhadé monastery (Gzhi sde lha sde; BDRC: G2249) in Purang, China. Photo provided by Suwen Lu 卢素文, Sichuan University.

Cover and interior design by Gopa & Ted 2. Set in DGP 10.5/13.

Printed on acid-free paper that meets the guidelines for permanence and durability of the Production Guidelines for Book Longevity of the Council on Library Resources.

Printed in the United States of America.

Publisher's Acknowledgment

The publisher gratefully acknowledges the generous help of the Hershey Family Foundation in sponsoring the production of this book.

Contents

Preface and Bibliography of Leonard van der Kuijp's Published Work
Kurtis R. Schaeffer xi

A Note on Transcription, Transliteration, and Bibliography xxix

CULTURAL HISTORY

On *Gtsug-lag khang*, "Monastery, *Vihāra*"
Christopher I. Beckwith 3

Andrade's Mission to Tsaparang, Western Tibet, and the Mystery of the Aftermath
Hubert Decleer 17

The Fourth Khamtrül Tendzin Chökyi Nyima (1730–79) and Excerpts from His Diaries
Franz-Karl Ehrhard 33

Portraying the Lineage Masters of the Path with Its Fruit: Lowo Khenchen's Description of Ngorchen's Commission
Jörg Heimbel and David P. Jackson 55

Lost—and Added—in Translation between India and Tibet: Theories about Drama in Tibetan Buddhist Epistemology
Isabelle Henrion-Dourcy 95

Origin of the *r-* Allomorph of the Tibetan Causative *s-*
Nathan W. Hill 109

Refractions of Lotus Light: The Early Elaboration and Delimitation of Padmasambhava's Eight Names
Daniel A. Hirshberg 115

The Earliest Example of Printing in the Tibetan Script: Remarks on a *Dhāraṇī* Amulet from Dunhuang
Matthew T. Kapstein 133

Pakpa's Epistolary Manual
Christina Kilby 155

Nature and Emotion in Nineteenth-Century Tibetan Lyric Poetry
Kurtis R. Schaeffer 167

The Jonangpa Scholar Künga Drölchok's Oeuvre, Its Xylography Project, and the *Analects of Zhentong*
Michael R. Sheehy 193

Insects Give Advice to the Scholar and Siddha Kalden Gyatso (1607–77)
Victoria Sujata 213

No Stone Unturned: Un-Disciplining Tibetan Buddhist Studies
Ivette Vargas-O'Bryan 235

The Great One: On the Life and Oeuvre of Tibet's Last Great Statue-Maker, Penba Dorjé
Cameron David Warner 253

Tibet Viewed from Kashmir: Some Notes on the Relationship of Kashmir with Ladakh and Other Parts of Tibet
Michael Witzel 267

INTELLECTUAL HISTORY

Chomden Reldri on Dharmakīrti's *Examination of Relations*
Allison Aitken 283

Maintaining Identification with a Buddha: Divine Identity or Simply False?
Yael Bentor 307

Rumblings of *Thunder*: Notes on the Identity and Intellectual Milieu of the Nyingma School Critic Peldzin
James Gentry 323

"Thunderbolt Blaze" or "Armless Hero"? On the Authorship of the *Essence of Debate*
Pascale Hugon 339

Eclipsing the Great Paṇḍita: Śākyaśrībhadra in the Later Biographies of Jetsün Drakpa Gyeltsen
Rory Lindsay 355

Flower Garland: The Transmission of the *Vinayakārikā Mālākāra* in Tibet
Cuilan Liu 367

Subhāṣākīrti's *Sarvabhāṣāpravartana* and Its Relevance to the *Smra sgo*
Zhouyang Ma 387

Some Interesting Passages from the *Noble Noose of Methods, the Lotus Garland Synopsis* and Its *Commentary*
Robert Mayer and Cathy Cantwell 403

Notes on the Tibetan Lexeme *lo rgyus*: Other Than "History"
Sun Penghao 421

Tibetan Expertise on Sanskrit Grammar (6): Dar Lotsāwa Ngawang Püntsok Lhündrup on Pāṇini
Pieter C. Verhagen 435

INSTITUTIONAL HISTORY

All in the Dudjom Family: Overlapping Modes of Authority and Transmission in the Golok Treasure Scene
Holly Gayley 453

Conflicting Views on Kingship between the Tibetan Buddhist World and the Qing Dynasty: The Fifth Dalai Lama's Visit to Beijing
Ishihama Yumiko 473

Newar Merchants in Tibet: Observations on Frontiers of Trade and Buddhist Culture
Todd Lewis 491

A Discourse on Kingship from the Eighth Karmapa
Ian MacCormack 513

Tibetan Medicine under the Mongols: The Emergence of Medical Houses and Official Physicians in Tibet
William A. McGrath 529

Some Remarks on the *Genealogy of the Sakya* (Sa skya gdung rabs) by Taktsang Lotsāwa (Stag tshang lo tsā ba, 1405–77)
Shoko Mekata 543

Who Owned the Land in Tibet?
Peter Schwieger 557

The Institution of the Qinghai Amban
Gray Tuttle 569

Poppy Cultivation, the Opium Trade, and Its Social Harm in Tibetan Regions of Sichuan Province during the Early Twentieth Century
Yudru Tsomu 587

About the Contributors 609

Tabula Gratulatoria 619

Preface and Bibliography of Leonard van der Kuijp's Published Work

Kurtis R. Schaeffer

"This statement will have to be looked into with greater care" (2013c: 186n156).

CRITICISM. Creativity. Care. An appreciative criticism that stands in the most exacting traditions of European philology since the Enlightenment, and that walks alongside the traditions of Tibetan philological work that have proceeded since at least the ninth century. A creative use of all available sources to address a historical question. Care for the words, the works, and the lives of living—lively, alive!—scholars throughout the centuries of Tibetan intellectual tradition. These three modes of engagement suffuse the work of Leonard W. J. van der Kuijp, from his first essays in the late 1970s through his ongoing work in this present moment. Throughout more than forty years and upward of one hundred articles, van der Kuijp has conjoined the tools of philology and historiography with an unquenchable desire to know the many people, places, and themes that form the lifeblood of Tibetan intellectual and cultural history. He has trained generations of students to use these tools of the trade and—more importantly—has imbued his students with the abiding sense of curiosity and discovery that can be experienced through every one of his writings. Born in Holland in 1952, van der Kuijp moved with this family to Canada in 1968. After studying mathematics, science, philosophy, Tibetology, and Sinology, he received a BA in 1975 and an MA in 1976, both from the University of Saskatchewan. After a year at the University of Bonn in 1976–77, he transferred to the University of Hamburg, where he completed his PhD work in 1979. While working as the deputy director of the Nepal Research Centre and Nepal-German Manuscript Preservation Project from 1980 to 1983, he revised his Hamburg dissertation into his first book, *Contributions to the Development of Tibetan Buddhist Epistemology from the Eleventh to the Thirteenth Centuries.*

During the latter years of his education and the initial years of his scholarly career as a researcher and teacher, he also began to write articles, with a particular focus on the intellectual history of the Indian Buddhist logic and epistemology tradition as it developed in Tibet from the twelfth century onward. After further work as a researcher at the Nepal Research Centre in Kathmandu and as a teacher at the Free University of Berlin, in 1987 he moved to the United States to become a professor of Tibetan language and literature in the University of Washington's Department of Asian Languages and Literature, where he worked for eight years. In 1993 van der Kuijp was awarded a MacArthur Fellowship for his work on the cultural history of Tibet. Shortly thereafter he moved to Harvard University as professor of Tibetan studies. He has worked at Harvard since 1995. In 1999 he cofounded, with Gene Smith, the Tibetan Buddhist Resource Center (now the Buddhist Digital Resource Center), where he served as board president for eighteen years. Throughout these decades van der Kuijp has developed an international community of colleagues and students, working equally with scholars from China, Europe, South Asia, and the United States. As he continued to train students at Harvard, he also trained students in China as a visiting professor at both Renmin University's School of Chinese Classics in Beijing for four years (2009–13) and at Sichuan University's Center for Tibetan Studies in Chengdu, starting in 2011. A seemingly tireless teacher throughout the past several decades, van der Kuijp could be found around the globe training students to do what he loves best, to read Tibetan texts with care, creativity, and a critical and appreciative eye.

In the epigraph to his 1983 book, a revision of his dissertation, van der Kuijp quotes Montaigne (by way of Foucault in *The Order of Things*): "There is more work in interpreting interpretations than in interpreting things; and more books about books than on any other subject; we do nothing but write glosses on one another." While one might be tempted to take this as a foreboding pronouncement upon the inevitable descent into some black hole of intellectual nihilism, at the beginning of van der Kuijp's career as a researcher and a writer, Montaigne's aphorism signals the expansiveness of working among Tibetan texts of old, among the writers—the *creators*—of the texts themselves. Much of van der Kuijp's work stations itself here, amid the creative messiness of the scholar's workshop in fourteenth-century Tsang, seventeenth-century Lhasa, eighteenth-century Amdo. For it is here that the very real, very human work of intellectual tradition occurs. With the persistent desire to get into the workshop, into their libraries, their social networks, to the extent that van der Kuijp's scholarship can be characterized as intellectual history, his emphasis is always on the life of the mind, with a preference for the *life*, the living messy reality that constitutes intellectual pursuits. More fundamentally, van der Kuijp's work always presupposes that scholars in Tibet, regardless of time or place, were also acutely cognizant of the messiness of intellectual life, of the vibrancy

Fig. 1. Leonard van der Kuijp at the Fifth Seminar of the International Association for Tibetan Studies in Narita, Japan, 1989. Photo by Pieter Verhagen.

that comes from situatedness, contingency, or chance encounter, from institutional and economic circumstances, or from technological affordances as well as limitations. "There is plenty of evidence that many Tibetan Buddhist intellectuals were very much aware of the fact that the ever-growing literary corpus that they were reading, studying, and interpreting had many serious text-historical and text-critical problems" (2010d, 441), writes van der Kuijp. It is this sort of evidence that van der Kuijp seeks out and works to make ever more apparent in his scholarship. And in this evidence are the signs of life, the details that reveal Tibetan intellectuals throughout the centuries grappling with received tradition and creatively adapting that tradition to forge new traditions. It is in this evidence that we see Tibetan intellectuals living out Montaigne's dictum that there is "more work in interpreting interpretations." And for van der Kuijp this work does not begin and end with abstract ideas; it crucially and necessarily includes the material basis of scholarly work—the texts, the pen, the paper, the ink, the woodblocks, and the manuscripts and prints that formed the physical body of scholarship, the embodiment of the intellectual mind. It is for this reason that philology, the discipline of critically scrutinizing the texts that constitute our primary evidence for living intellectual traditions of the past, is so important for van der Kuijp's research, and so important in his teaching.

Throughout his publishing career, van der Kuijp has employed philology to range widely through themes and topics in Tibetan intellectual, institutional, and cultural history. Even a partial glance at the list of his published work reveals his interests and expertise in the history of most of the major branches of knowledge and knowledge production in Tibet, including logic and epistemology (1977, 1978, 1979a, 1979b, 1983, 1985e, 1986c, 1989, 1993c, 1993e, 1994c, 2003, 2009b, 2013a, 2014c, 2018a, 2020d), belles-lettres (1982, 1986a, 1986b, 1996b, 2009d), iconography (1987b, 2012), calendrical and chronological systems (2016c), medicine (1975, 2010b, 2015c), law (1991c), and tantra (1985c, 1987c, 1994b, 2004a, 2007d, 2013b, 2013e, 2014a, 2018c, 2019, 2020b, 2020c). Often van der Kuijp's inquiries focus on a particular figure and take up the space of several articles to see themselves through. He has, over the years, produced major studies on Khedrup Jé (1985e, 1986d) and Butön Rinchendrup (2013c, 2016b), for instance. Elsewhere he focuses on a particular period of time, as in his ongoing series of articles on "Fourteenth-Century Tibetan Cultural History" (1993d, 1994a, 1994d, 1995a, 2018b). Other themes running throughout his essays include institutional history (1984b, 1986c, 1987c, 1988, 1991a, 1991b, 1992c, 2007b, 2010c, 2013f, 2015d, 2020a), the lives of travelers across Asia (1993a, 1993b, 1994e, 1995b, 2004b, 2015b), and the scholasticism of Indian classics (1982, 1985c, 1985d, 1992a, 2007d, 2009d, 2013d, 2013g, 2014b, 2014d, 2020b, 2020c, 2021).

Finally, the history of the book in Tibet, with a particular focus on Tibetan traditions of philology, linguistics, printing, and manuscript practices, has been a persistent theme in van der Kuijp's work (1986d, 1993c, 1996c, 1999, 2004a, 2006b, 2009a, 2009c, 2010d, 2013c, 2014e, 2015a, 2018a, 2020a, 2020d). Throughout these and other essays, he challenges us to fully collect the earliest evidence for any given historical issue and cautions us to resist jumping to easy conclusions based upon impressionistic readings of that essay. For instance, in an extended introduction to his study on the making of Butön's famous history of Buddhism, he urges care when ascribing too much causal efficacy to the advent of block printing as an agent of social and cultural change:

> It stands to reason that the sociology of knowledge in Tibet was affected with the advent of blockprinting. This technique that allowed for a different way in which knowledge could be disseminated most probably had its inception, albeit on quite local scales, around the turn of the thirteenth century, although this could perhaps be pushed back into the second half of the twelfth century. But

> the precise degree to which printing may have had an impact on and thus changed the Tibetan intellectual landscape when it became more widespread has yet to be determined. In Central Tibet, the carving of printing blocks took off in a respectable but by no means universal way only during the first half of the fifteenth century. Why this should have been so is not at all obvious and is something that, too, still needs to be studied. The economic resources for projects of this kind had already been in place for a long time, so that their putative absence until that period could not have been an inhibiting factor. We may have to consider issues that have to do with developments in the monastic curricula and, what is of course quite related to these, the extent and depth of the demographic shifts that must have taken place from the villages and countryside to the monasteries. In some cases, we have to take into account the felt need to keep certain texts, especially those that have to do with esoteric teachings, away from the public eye. Accordingly, how decisions were made in particular or in general with regards for what text or textual corpus printing blocks were to be carved, and why, are as yet unknown quantities as well. (2013c, 127)

In this passage van der Kuijp offers a challenge to future scholars; can we investigate a sufficiently wide range of evidence—and of types of evidence—to make grounded claims about the sources of processes of change, be it technological, social, or cultural? For his own part, van der Kuijp offers a cautious and severely delimited "yes" to that question; in what follows in that essay he carefully takes the reader through the making of Butön's most famous work—perhaps Tibet's most famous work of historiography—and through the early years of its production as scholars moved between manuscript and print. In this micro-study of the life of a single work, van der Kuijp offers a model of carefully circumscribed historical work, a type of scholarly labor that always employs philology in service of attempting to know, to understand, to *feel* in a grounded way the work of the Tibetan intellectuals who forged that work in all its materiality throughout the decades and centuries following its author's death.

Beyond the research essay itself, van der Kuijp has also written many reviews over the years, and especially throughout the 1990s. Often his reviews are essays on the subject in and of themselves, offering substantial extension or critique of the book under scrutiny. These review essays extend through the full range of topics he has worked on over the years, including Madhyamaka (1985f), the history of the Tibetan imperial period (1984b, 1991b), the Tibetan reception

Fig. 2. Leonard van der Kuijp at the Sixth Seminar of the International Association for Tibetan Studies in Fagernes, Norway, 1992. Photo by Pieter Verhagen.

of Indian logic and epistemology (1999), the lives of late Indian scholars and travelers (1994b), and the life and works of Tibetan literati (Review 1990a).

A unique feature of his reviews is the attention he has paid to both Tibetan-language scholarship (Reviews 1985a, 1985b, 1985c, 1986b) and editions of Tibetan texts produced by Tibetan and Chinese scholars in China. These reviews, while brief, provide valuable insight into scholarship that too often passes by the notice of the global scholarly community. These reviews are in effect works of research in miniature, as for instance the brief yet detailed biography of the Lhasa aristocrat Dokhar Tsering Wangyel (Review 1985c) that begins the review of Zhuang Jing's edition of Dokhar's *Life of Miwang* (*Mi dbang rtogs brjod*). They also focus our attention on the philological labor required to produce useful editions, in this case by walking us through the editor's work: "The Ltag-rgyab print is, as Zhuang (pp. 1–2) laments, not without its philological problems, and he calls the scribe and/or carver 'thoughtless' (*hol-rgvugs*) and wilfull. Fortunately, Zhuang was able to collate this print (*par-ma*) with a handwritten manuscript (494 folia) (*bris-ma*) housed at the Beijing Library, and completed this important edition of one of the most extraordinary Tibetan historical texts under the tutelage of Dung-dkar dge-bshes" (Review 1985c: 322). Van der Kuijp was, in the 1980s, active in synthesizing the scholarship of Tibetan and Chinese scholars with the work of European and

American scholars. In general, with appreciative comments such as "Zhuang's edition of the MDRB is an important contribution to Tibetan historiography. The printing and production is of the high standard that we have now come to expect from all the Tibetan publications issued in China," van der Kuijp's reviews of editions such as this helped to bring together traditions of philological scholarship that were all too often separate. This is a type of review that few scholars have attempted, and few seek today. It represents a model of scholarly communication that takes scholarly work with the utmost seriousness, takes scholars at their words, and respects the work of Tibetan intellectuals over centuries that the work of us moderns is founded upon.

Van der Kuijp has never been naïve about the challenges inherent to historical research that relies so fundamentally on philological persistence and rigor. His seminars over the decades have been workshops in which students train in this sort of scholarship. And he has been a patient trainer who nevertheless holds each student to a high standard. His essays, too, acknowledge the effort that philology requires, with its necessarily slowed pace relative to contemporary academic practices of knowledge production. They recognize that not all scholars may find this type of scholarship sufficiently compelling, yet politely insist that work on Tibetan history is done best when paired with critical and appreciative textual scholarship:

> We now come to the end of my short essay and it remains to be seen whether this exercise was worth its while and useful for future *Lam rim chen mo* studies or whether it is but "blowing in the wind." To be sure, the textual instability of the *Lam rim chen mo* is by no means an isolated case and we will no doubt encounter the same kind of problems with other seminal and much less seminal works when we are in the fortunate position of consulting a reasonable corpus of xylograph edition and manuscripts of one and the same work. Tibetan book culture, like any other traditional book culture, requires that we engage in as detailed and thoroughgoing textual criticism as possible. (2015a: 264)

The essays in this volume, all written by van der Kuijp's students and colleagues, seek to embody the scholarly methods and intellectual curiosity that van der Kuijp's own work has demonstrated over the decades. Many of the topics, texts, times, and places that make up the subjects of these essays were first encountered by their authors in van der Kuijp's seminars. Some of them approach topics that van der Kuijp has not focused on in his published work, while some dive into the waters in which van der Kuijp has been swimming

Fig. 3. Leonard van der Kuijp with Xiage Wangdui 夏格旺堆 at Sichuan University in Chengdu, China, December 2016. Photo extracted from a video by Danzeng Zunzhu 旦增遵珠.

for years. We have divided the contributions of this volume into three broad historiographic rubrics: intellectual history, institutional history, and cultural history. We do this not because these styles of historical research and writing exist as natural kinds, but because these shorthand terms for particular interests within the nearly infinite scope of historical research speak to the interests of van der Kuijp himself over the years. They also are the kinds of broad subjects in historical research in which his colleagues and students have engaged alongside or under the tutelage of van der Kuijp. Throughout this work, I suspect that nearly all of the writers can hear van der Kuijp's words of encouragement and caution echoing through their minds as they continue their work: "This statement will have to be looked into with greater care."

For myself, I can say that Leonard van der Kuijp has positively impacted my life and career in ways I never could have imagined when I first met him in 1991. His scholarship, at first daunting to me in its methodological pyrotechnics, has over the years and decades become for me a model of meticulous, thoughtful humanistic scholarship. And it is this humanistic work, Leonard's overarching humanism—his *humanity*—that has made my own scholarly life possible. The gratefulness that I feel for his lifelong support cannot be conveyed in words alone. Yet words are what we have. So, along with my co-editors Jue Liang and Bill McGrath, we offer this volume to you, Leonard W. J. van der Kuijp, in deep gratitude for your gifts to us—gifts of criticism, creativity, and care.

Leonard W. J. van der Kuijp Publications, Chronological

Books and Articles

1975. "An Index to a Tibeto-Mongolian Materia Medica." *The Canada-Mongolia Review* 1.2: 15–46.

1977. "Phya pa Chos kyi seng ge's Impact on Tibetan Epistemological Theory." In *Tibetan Studies*, edited by Per Kvaerne and Martin Brauen, 163–77. Zürich: Völkerkundemuseum der Universität Zürich.

1978. "Phya pa Chos kyi seng ge's Impact on Tibetan Epistemological Theory" [expanded version of above]. *Journal of Indian Philosophy* 5: 366–79.

1979a. "Introductory Notes to the *Pramāṇavārttika* Based on Tibetan Sources." *The Tibet Journal* 4: 6–28.

1979b. "Tibetan Contributions to the 'Apoha' Theory: The Fourth Chapter of the *Tshad ma rigs pa'i gter*." *Journal of the American Oriental Society* 99: 408–22.

1982. "On the Interpretation of *Kāvyādarśa* II:274." *Studien zur Indologie und Iranistik* 8–9: 69–76.

1983. *Contributions to the Development of Tibetan Buddhist Epistemology from the Eleventh to the Thirteenth Centuries*. Wiesbaden: Franz Steiner.

1984a. "Marginalia on Sa skya Paṇḍita's Oeuvre." *Journal of the International Association of Buddhist Studies* 7: 37–55.

1984b. "Miscellanea to a Recent Contribution to / on the Bsam yas Debate." *Kailash* 9: 149–84.

1985a. "On the Authorship of the *Gzhung lugs legs par bshad pa* Attributed to Sa skya Paṇḍita." *Journal of the Nepal Research Centre* 7: 75–86.

1985b. "Some Recently Recovered Sa skya pa Texts: A Preliminary Report." *Journal of the Nepal Research Centre* 7: 87–94.

1985c. "A Text-Historical Note on *Hevajratantra* II:V:1–2." *Journal of the International Association of Buddhist Studies* 8: 83–89.

1985d. "Notes on the Transmission of Nāgārjuna's *Ratnāvalī* in Tibet." *The Tibet Journal* 10: 3–19.

1985e. "Studies in the Life and Thought of Mkhas grub rje I: Mkhas grub rje's Epistemological Oeuvre and His Philological Remarks on Dignāga's *Pramāṇasamuccaya*." *Berliner Indologische Studien* 1: 75–105.

1985f. "Apropos of a Recent Contribution to the History of Central Way Philosophy in Tibet: Tsong kha pa's *Speech of Gold*." *Berliner Indologische Studien* 1: 47–74.

1985g. "Miscellanea Apropos of the Philosophy of Mind in Tibet: Mind in Tibetan Buddhism." *The Tibet Journal* 10: 32–43.

1986a. "Bhāmaha in Tibet." *Indo-Iranian Journal* 28: 31–39.

1986b. "Sa skya Paṇḍita on the Typology of Literary Genres." *Studien zur Indologie und Iranistik* 11–12: 41–52.

1986c. "On the Sources for Sa skya Paṇḍita's Notes on the Bsam yas Debate." *Journal of the International Association of Buddhist Studies* 9: 147–53.

1986d. "Studies in the Life and Thought of Mkhas grub rje IV: Mkhas grub rje on Regionalisms and Dialects." *Berliner Indologische Studien* 2: 23–49 [Chinese translation: Xiong Wenbin, trans., in *Guowai zangxue yanjiu yiwenji*, edited by Wang Yao, vol. 7, 32–53. Lhasa: Xizang renmin chubanshe, 1990].

1986e. "Ldong ston Shes rab dpal and a Version of the *Tshad ma rigs pa'i gter* in Thirteen Chapters." *Berliner Indologische Studien* 2: 51–64.

1987a. "An Early Tibetan View of the Soteriology of Buddhist Epistemology." *Journal of Indian Philosophy* 15: 57–70.

1987b. "Ngor chen Kun dga' bzang po on the Posture of Hevajra: A Note on the Relationship between Text, Iconography and Spiritual Praxis." *Investigating Indian Art: Proceedings of a Symposium on the Development of Early Buddhist and Hindu Iconography Held by the Museum of India Art Berlin in May 1986*, edited by Marianne Yaldiz and Wibke Lobo, 173–77. Berlin: Staatliche Museen Preseussischer Kulturbesitz.

1987c. "The Abbatial Succession of Gsang phu ne'u thog Monastery from ca. 1073 to 1250." *Berliner Indologische Studien* 3: 103–27 [Chinese translation: Xiong Wenbin, trans., in *Guowai zangxue dongtai* 6 (1992): 120–35].

1987d. "Additional Marginalia to Sa skya Paṇḍita's Oeuvre." *Berliner Indologische Studien* 3: 129–37 [Chinese translation: Chen Qingying, trans., in *Guowai zangxue dongtai* 6 (1992): 15–52].

1988. "Two Early Sources for the History of the House of Sde dge." *Journal of the Tibet Society* 8: 1–20.

1989. "Introduction." In *An Ancient Commentary on Dharmakirti's Pramāṇaviniścaya, Otani University Collection No. 13971*, 1–31. Otani University Tibetan Works Series 2. Kyoto.

1991a. "On the Life and Political Career of Ta'i si tu Byang chub rgyal mtshan (1302–?1364)." *Tibetan History and Language: Studies Dedicated to Uray Géza on His Seventieth Birthday*, edited by Ernst Steinkellner, 277–327. Vienna: Arbeitskreis für Tibetische und Buddhistische Studien.

1991b. "A Recent Contribution on the History of the Tibetan Empire." *Journal of the American Oriental Society* 111: 94–107.

1991c. "The Yoke Is on the Reader: A Recent Attempt at Studying Tibetan Jurisprudence." *Central Asiatic Journal* 43: 266–92.

1992a. "Notes Apropos of the Transmission of the *Sarvadurgatipariśodhanatantra* in Tibet." *Studien zur Indologie und Iranistik* 16–17: 109–25.

1992b. "Dating the Two Lde'u Chronicles of Buddhism in India and Tibet." *Asiatische Studien* [Études Asiatiques] 46: 468–91.

1992c. "Two Courts of the 'Phags pa Era." *Zhongguo Zangxue* [China Tibetology], 278–306 [Note: this is an unauthorized publication of an incomplete paper].
1993a. "Jayānanda: A Twelfth Century Guoshi from Kashmir among the Tangut." *Central Asiatic Journal* 37: 188–97.
1993b. "*Jambhala: An Imperial Envoy to Tibet during the Late Yuan." *Journal of the American Oriental Society* 113.4: 529–38.
1993c. "Two Mongol Xylographs (*hor par ma*) of the Tibetan Text of Sa skya Paṇḍita's Work on Buddhist Logic and Epistemology." *Journal of the International Association of Buddhist Studies* 16: 279–98.
1993d. "Fourteenth Century Tibetan Cultural History III: The Oeuvre of Bla ma dam pa Bsod nams rgyal mtshan (1312–1375), Part One." *Berliner Indologische Studien* 7: 109–47.
1993e. "Apropos of Some Recently Recovered Manuscripts anent Sa skya Paṇḍita's *Tshad ma rigs pa'i gter*." *Berliner Indologische Studien* 7: 149–62.
1994a. "Fourteenth Century Tibetan Cultural History I: Ta'i si tu Byang chub rgyal mtshan as a Man of Religion." *Indo-Iranian Journal* 37.2: 139–49.
1994b. "Apropos of Some Recently Recovered Texts Belonging to the Lam 'bras Teachings of the Sa skya pa and Ko brag pa." *Journal of the International Association of Buddhist Studies* 17: 175–201.
1994c. "On Some Early Tibetan Pramāṇavāda Texts of the China Nationalities Library of the Cultural Palace of Nationalities in Beijing." *Journal of Buddhist and Tibetan Studies* 1: 1–30.
1994d. "Fourteenth Century Tibetan Cultural History IV: The *Tshad ma'i byung tshul 'chad nyan gyi rgyan*: A Tibetan History of Indian Buddhist Pramāṇavāda." In *Festschrift: Klaus Bruhn*, edited by Nalini Balbir and Joachim Bautze, 375–402. Reinbek: Verlag fuer Orientalistische Fachpublikationen.
1994e. "On the Lives of Śākyaśrībhadra (?–?1225)." *Journal of the American Oriental Society* 114: 599–616.
1995a. "Fourteenth Century Tibetan Cultural History VI: The Transmission of Indian Buddhist Pramāṇavāda According to Early Tibetan *gsan yig*." *Asiatische Studien* [Études Asiatiques] 49: 919–41.
1995b. "'*Baghsi*' and *Baghsi*-s in Tibetan Historical, Biographical and Lexicographical Texts." *Central Asiatic Journal* 39: 275–302.
1996a. "Tibetan Belles-Lettres." In *Tibetan Literature: Studies in Genre*, edited by Roger R. Jackson and José I. Cabezón, 393–410. Ithaca, NY: Snow Lion Publications.
1996b. "Tibetan Historiography." In *Tibetan Literature: Studies in Genre*, edited by Roger R. Jackson and José I. Cabezón, 39–56. Ithaca, NY: Snow Lion Publications.
1996c. "The Tibetan Script and Derivatives." In *The World's Writing Systems*, edited by P. T. Daniels and W. Bright, 431–41. New York: Oxford University Press.
1999. "Remarks on the 'Person of Authority' in the Dga' ldan pa / Dge lugs pa School of Tibetan Buddhism." *Journal of the American Oriental Society* 119: 646–72.
2001. "On the Fifteenth Century Lho rong chos 'byung by Rta tshag Tshe dbang rgyal and Its Importance for Tibetan Political and Religious History." *Lungta* 14: 57–76.

2002. "Tibetische Literatur." In *Neues Handbuch der Literaturwissenschaften. Süd- und Zentralasiatische Literaturen*, vol. 24, edited by G. Ehelers, 115–31. Wiebelsheim: Aula-Verlag, Wiesbaden.

2003. "A Treatise on Buddhist Epistemology and Logic Attributed to Klong chen Rab 'byams pa (1308–1364) and Its Place in Indo-Tibetan Intellectual History." *Journal of Indian Philosophy* 31: 381–437.

2004a. *The Kālacakra and the Patronage of Tibetan Buddhism by the Mongol Imperial Family*. Bloomington: Department of Central Eurasian Studies, Indiana University.

2004b. "U rgyan pa Rin chen dpal (1230–1309) Part Two: For Emperor Qubilai? His Garland of Tales about Rivers." In *The Relationship between Religion and State (chos srid zung 'brel) in Traditional Tibet*, edited by Christoph Cüppers, 299–339. Lumbini: Lumbini International Research Institute.

2005. "The Dalai Lamas and the Origins of Reincarnate Lamas." In *The Dalai Lamas: A Visual History*, edited by Martin Brauen, 5–34. Chicago: Serindia.

2006a. "The Earliest Indian Reference to Muslims in a Buddhist Philosophical Text of circa 700." *Journal of Indian Philosophy* 34: 169–202.

2006b. "On the Composition and Printings of the *Deb gter sngon po* by 'Gos lo tsā ba gzhon nu dpal (1392–1481)." *Journal of the International Association of Tibetan Studies* 2: 1–46.

2007a. "The Names of 'Gos Lo tsā ba Gzhon nu dpal (1392–1481)." In *The Paṇḍita and the Siddha: Tibetan Studies in Honor of E. Gene Smith*, edited by R. Prats, 279–85. Dharamsala: Amnye Machen Institute.

2007b. with Rachel M. McCleary. "The Formation of the Rise of the Tibetan State Religion: The Geluk School 1492–1642." Center for International Development, Kennedy School, Harvard University, Working Paper no. 154.

2007c. "On the Authorship and Date of the Ecclesiastic Chronicle *Chos 'byung rin po che'i gter mdzod bstan pa gsal bar byed pa'i nyi 'od*." In *Tibetstudien: Festschrift fuer Dieter Schuh zum 65. Geburtstag*, edited by P. Maurer and P. Schwieger, 127–48. Bonn: Bierische Verlagsanstalt.

2007d. "*Nāgabodhi / Nāgabuddhi: Notes on the Guhyasamāja Literature." In *Pramāṇakīrtiḥ: Papers Dedicated to Ernst Steinkellner on the Occasion of His 70th Birthday*, vol. 2, edited by H. Krasser et al., 1002–22. Vienna: Arbeitskreis für Tibetische und Buddhistische Studien Universität Wien.

2009a. with Kurtis R. Schaeffer. *An Early Tibetan Survey of Buddhist Literature: The Bstan pa rgyas pa nyi 'od of Bcom ldan rig ral*. Harvard Oriental Series 73. Cambridge: Harvard University Press.

2009b. "Classification of Non-Authoritative Cognitive Processes (*tshad min*) in the Ngog and Sakya Traditions." *Buddhist Philosophy: Essential Readings*, edited by W. Edelglass and J. Garfield, 218–23. New York: Oxford University Press.

2009c. "Some Remarks on the Meaning and Use of the Tibetan Word *bam po*." *Zangxue xuekan* 藏学学刊 [Journal of Tibetology] 5: 114–32 [Chinese translation: in *Zangxue xuekan* 5: 133–49].

2009d. "On the Vicissitudes of Subhūticandra's *Kāmadhenu* Commentary on the *Amarakoṣa* in Tibet." *Journal of the International Association of Tibetan Studies* 5: 1–105.

2009e. "Tibet." In *The Oxford International Encyclopedia of Legal History*, edited by S. Katz. New York: Oxford University Press.

2010a. with R. M. McCleary. "The Market Approach to the Rise of the Geluk School, 1419–1642." *Journal of Asian Studies* 69: 149–80.

2010b. "Za hor and Its Contribution to Tibetan Medicine, Part One: Some Names, Places, and Texts." *Zangxue xuekan* 藏学学刊 [Journal of Tibetology] 6: 21–50.

2010c. "The Tibetan Expression '*bod* wooden door' (*bod shing sgo*) and Its Probable Mongol Antecedent." *Xiyu lishi yuyan yanjiu jikan* 西域歷史語言研究集刊 [Historical and Philological Studies of China's Western Regions] 3: 89–134.

2010d. "Faulty Transmissions: Some Notes on Tibetan Textual Criticism and the Impact of Xylography." *Edition, éditions. l'écrit au Tibet, évolution et devenir*, edited by A. Chayet et al., 441–63. Munich: Indus Verlag.

2011. "A Hitherto Unknown Tibetan Religious Chronicle from Probably the Early 14th Century." *Zangxue xuekan* 藏学学刊 [Journal of Tibetology] 7: 69–91.

2012. with Christoph Cüppers, Ulrich Pagel, and Dobis Tsering Gyal. *Handbook of Tibetan Iconometry. A Guide to the Arts of the 17th Century*. Leiden: Brill.

2013a. with Arthur McKeown. *Bcom ldan ral gri (1227–1305) on Buddhist Epistemology and Logic: His Commentary on Dignāga's Pramāṇasamuccaya*. Wiener Studien zur Tibetologie und Buddhismuskunde 80. Vienna: Arbeitskreis für Tibetische und Buddhistische Studien Universität Wien.

2013b. "On the Edge of Myth and History: Za hor, Its Place in the History of Early Indian Buddhist Tantra, and Dalai Lama V and the Genealogy of Its Royal Family." In *Studies on Buddhist Myths: Texts, Pictures, Traditions, and History*, edited by Wang Bangwei, Chen Jinhua, Chen Ming, 114–64. Shanghai: Zhongxi shuju.

2013c. "Some Remarks on the Textual Transmission and Text of Bu ston Rin chen grub's *Chos 'byung*, a Chronicle of Buddhism in India and Tibet." *Revue d'Etudes Tibétaines* 25: 115–93.

2013d. "Notes on Jñānamitra's Commentary on the *Abhidharmasamuccaya*." In *The Foundation of Yoga Practitioners. The Buddhist Yogācārabhūmi Treatise and Its Adaptation in India, East Asia, and Tibet*, edited by Ulrich T. Kragh, 1388–429. Cambridge: Harvard University Press.

2013e. "Further Notes on the *Bodhicittavivaraṇa* and Some Comments on Its Verses 4–5: Apropos of a Non-Buddhist Ontological Commitment." *Xiyu lishi yuyan yanjiu jikan* 西域歷史語言研究集刊 [Historical and Philological Studies of China's Western Regions] 6: 431–50.

2013f. "Gu ge Paṇ chen Grags pa rgyal mtshan dpal bzang po (1415–86) on the *Nyi ma'i rabs* (**Sūryavaṃśa*) and the Tibetan Royal Families." *Nepalica et Tibetica. Festgabe für Christoph Cüppers*, vol. 1, edited by F.-K. Ehrhard and P. Maurer, 325–35. Andiast: International Institute for Tibetan and Buddhist Studies.

2013g. "A Note on Manorathanandin's *Pramāṇavārttikavṛtti* in Tibet." In *Wading into the Stream of Wisdom. Essays in Honor of Leslie S. Kawamura*, edited by S. F. Haynes and M. J. Sorensen, 161–92. Berkeley: Institute of Buddhist Studies and BDK America, Inc.

2014a. "Some Text-Historical Issues with the *Bodhicittavivaraṇa* by a Nāgārjuna and the Tibetan Commentarial Literature." In *Himalayan Passages: Tibetan and*

Newar Studies in Honor of Hubert Decleer, edited by B. Bogin and A. Quintman, 117–41. Boston: Wisdom Publications.

2014b. "The **Madhyamakālokabhāṣyatattvapradīpa*: An Indic Commentary on Kamalaśīla's *Madhyamakāloka* (*Dbu ma snang ba*)." *China Tibetology Journal* 1: 1–3.

2014c. "Studies in Btsun pa Ston gzhon's *Pramāṇavārttika* Commentary of ?1297, Part One: Bibliographical and Biographical Preliminaries." *Revue d'Etudes Tibétaines* 30: 111–98.

2014d. with He Huanhuan. "Further Notes on Bhāviveka and His Oeuvre." *Indo-Iranian Journal* 57: 299–352.

2014e. "A Note on the *hor par ma*-Mongolian Xylograph of the Tibetan Translation of Dharmakīrti's *Pramāṇavārttika* (*Tshad ma rnam 'grel*)." *Zangxue xuekan* [Journal of Tibetology] 14: 235–40.

2014f. with Gray Tuttle. "Altan Qaγan (1507–1582) of the Tümed Mongols and the Stag lung Abbot Kun dga' bkra shis rgyal mtshan (1575–1635)." In *Trails of the Tibetan Tradition: Papers for Elliot Sperling*, edited by Roberto Vitali, with assistance from Gedun Rabsal and Nicole Willock, 461–82. Dharamshala: Amnye Machen Institute. Also available for download as an issue of *Revue d'Etudes Tibétaines* 31 (2017): 461–82. Translated into Chinese by Giigch Borjigin, "Tumotebu Anda han yu Dalong si sizhu Gongge zhashi jiancan 土默特部俺答汗 (1507–1582) 与达隆寺寺主公哥扎石坚灿 (1575–1635)." *Quaestiones Mongolorum Disputatae* 18 (2022): 50–74. https://mp.weixin.qq.com/s/3mwOY0L7z-a0a9CIeMf21Q.

2015a. "May the 'Original' *Lam rim chen mo* Please Stand Up: A Note on Its Indigenous Textual Criticism." *The Illuminating Mirror: Tibetan Studies in Honour of Per K. Sørensen on the Occasion of His 65th Birthday*, edited by O. Czaja and G. Hazod, 253–68. Wiesbaden: Dr. Ludwig Reichelt Verlag.

2015b. "Tibetan Buddhism Meets Protestant Christianity: A Memorandum of Conversations of Mā yang Paṇḍita with Cecil H. Polhill near Xining, Qinghai, on January 13–15, 1890." *Xiyu lishi yuyan yanjiu jikan* 西域歷史語言研究集刊 [Historical and Philological Studies of China's Western Regions] 8: 443–92.

2015c. "Za hor and Its Contribution to Tibetan Medicine, Part Two: Sources of the Tibetan Medical Tradition." *Zangxue xuekan* 藏学学刊 [Journal of Tibetology] 12: 63–108.

2015d. "A Fifteenth Century Biography of Lha bla ma ye shes 'od (947–1019/1024): Its Prolegomenon and Prophecies." In *Tibet in Dialogue with Its Neighbours: History, Culture and Art of Central and Western Tibet, 8th–15th Century*, edited by E. Forte et al., 341–75. Wiener Studien zur Tibetologie und Buddhismuskunde 88. Vienna: Arbeitskreis für Tibetische und Buddhistische Studien.

2016a. with He Huanhuan. "Once Again on the **Hetucakraḍamaru*: Rotating the Wheels." *Journal of Indian Philosophy* 44: 267–302.

2016b. "The Lives of Bu ston Rin chen grub and the Date and Sources of His *Chos 'byung*, a Chronicle of Buddhism in India and Tibet." *Revue d'Etudes Tibétaines* 35: 203–308.

2016c. "From *Chongzhen lishu* 崇禎曆書 to *Tengri-yin udq-a* and *Rgya rtsis chen mo*."

In *Tibetan Printing: Comparison, Continuities and Change*, edited by H. Diemberger et al., 51–71. Leiden: Brill.

2016d. "On the Life and Oeuvre of the Jo nang pa Scholar Zhang ston Rgya bo Bsod nams grags pa (1292–1370)." *Journal of Tibetan and Himalayan Studies* 1: 17–31.

2016e. "Reconsidering the Dates of Dol po pa Shes rab rgyal mtshan's (1292–1361) *Ri chos nges don rgya mtsho* and the *Bka' bsdu bzhi pa'i don*." *Zangxue xuekan* 藏学学刊 [Journal of Tibetology] 14: 115–59.

2018a. "On the 1449 Xylograph of Rgyal tshab Dar ma rin chen's (1364–1432) *Pramāṇavārttika* Commentary." *China Tibetology Journal* 1: 21–27.

2018b. "Fourteenth Century Tibetan Cultural History III: The Oeuvre of Bla ma dam pa Bsod nams rgyal mtshan (1312–1375), Part Two." *Revue d'Etudes Tibétaines* 46: 5–89.

2018c. "The Bird-Faced Monk and the Beginnings of the New Tantric Tradition, Part One." In *Tibetan Genealogies: Studies in Memoriam of Guge Tsering Gyalpo (1961–2015)*, edited by G. Hazod and Shen Weirong, 403–50. Beijing: China Tibetology Publishing House.

2018d. "The Bird-Faced Monk and the Beginnings of the New Tantric Tradition, Part Two." *Zangxue xuekan* 藏学学刊 [Journal of Tibetology] 19: 86–127.

2019a. "What Kind of Animal Is a Tree? Apropos of Some Tibetan Reactions to the *Vimalaprabhā* and *Laghukālacakratantra*, I:4c and 8c, Part One." *Zangxue xuekan* 藏学学刊 [Journal of Tibetology] 20: 196–221.

2019b. "A lag sha Ngag dbang bstan dar (1759–after August 1, 1840): On Some Chinese Lex-emes and the Chinese Language, Part One." In *Unearthing Himalayan Treasures: Festschrift for Franz-Karl Ehrhard*, edited by Volker Caumanns, Marta Sernesi, and Nikolai Solmsdorf, 287–98. Marburg: Indica et Tibetica Verlag.

2019c. "Gyaltsab Darma Rinchen and the Rigs gter dar ṭik, an Exegesis of Sakya Paṇḍita's *Tshad ma rigs pa'i gter**." In *Reasons and Lives in Buddhist Traditions: Studies in Honor of Matthew Kapstein*, edited by Dan Arnold, Cécile Ducher, and Pierre-Julien Harter, 309–24. Somerville, MA: Wisdom Publications.

2020a. "A Note on the 'Old' and the 'New' Tibetan Translations of the *Prasannapadā*." In *Archaeologies of the Written: Indian, Tibetan, and Buddhist Studies in Honour of Cristina Scherrer-Schaub*, edited by V. Tournier, V. Eltschinger, and M. Sernesi, 417–46. Naples: UniorPress.

2020b. "Indo-Tibetan Tantric Buddhist Scholasticism: Bhavyakīrti and His Summary of Sāṁkhya Philosophy (Part I)." *Journal of Tibetan and Himalayan Studies* 5.1: 1–40.

2020c. "Indo-Tibetan Tantric Buddhist Scholasticism: Bhavyakīrti and His Summary of Sāṁkhya Philosophy (Part II)." *Journal of Tibetan and Himalayan Studies* 5.2: 1–62.

2020d. "On the Transmission of the Verse-Text of Sa skya Paṇḍita's *Tshad ma rigs pa'i gter* and the Rang 'grel Autocommentary." *Hualin International Journal of Buddhist Studies* 3.1: 126–69.

2020e. "A Case of Upward Social Mobility in Fourteenth Century Tibet in Text-historical Context: Dol po pa Shes rab rgyal mtshan (1292–1361) in Confidence to Mi nyag Rin chen bzang po (1317–1383)." In *On a Day of a Month of the Fire Bird Year: Festschrift for Peter Schwieger on the Occasion of His 65th Birthday*, edited by Jeannine Bischoff, Charles Ramble, and Petra H. Maurer, 505–22. Lumbini: Lumbini International Research Institute.

2021. "A Brief Note on the Date of Daśabalaśrīmtra and His *Saṃskṛtāsaṃskṛtaviniścaya*." *Zangxue xuekan* 藏学学刊 [Journal of Tibetology] 24: 67–73.

2022a. with Ning Tien 田凝. "A Bout with Smallpox in Beijing: Personal Accounts of the Tibetan Statesman—Dga' bzhi pa Bsod nams bstan 'dzin dpal 'byor (1761–after 1810) and his Struggle with Smallpox." *Revue d'Etudes Tibétaines* 63: 5–48.

2022b. "Studies in Btsun pa Ston gzhon's *Pramāṇavārttika* Commentary of 1297, Part Two(a): 'U yug pa Rigs pa'i seng ge (ca. 1195–after 1267)." *Revue d'Etudes Tibétaines* 64: 307–343.

2022c. "Studies in the Life and Thought of Mkhas grub rje II: Notes on Poetry, Poetics and Other Things in Mkhas grub rje's Oeuvre." *Journal of Tibetan Literature* 1.1: 75–109.

Reviews

1977. *The Practice and Theory of Tibetan Buddhism*. By Geshe Lhundup Sopa and J. Hopkins. *Philosophy East and West* 27: 462–66.

1979. *Verse-Index of Dharmakīrti's Works (Tibetan Version)*. By E. Steinkellner. *Philosphy East and West* 29: 106–7.

1983. *Contributto allo Studio Biografico dei Primi Gter-Ston*. By R. Prats. *Journal of the International Association of Buddhist Studies* 6: 151–54.

1985a. *Dag yig ngag sgron gyi rtsa 'grel*. By Dpal khang Lo tsā ba and Bstan 'dzin rgyal mtshan. *Indo-Iranian Journal* 23: 213–17.

1985b. *Snyan ngag me long gi spyi don sdeb legs rig pa'i 'char sgo*. By Tshe tan Zhabs drung. *Indo-Iranian Journal* 23: 212–13.

1985c. *Mi dbang rtogs brjod*. Edited by Zhuang Jing. *Journal of the American Oriental Society* 105: 321–22.

1986a. *Tibet Bon Religion*. By Per Kvaerne. *Acta Orientalia* 47: 202–208.

1986b. *Dge ldan legs bshad*. By Paṇ chen Bsod nams grags pa. *Journal of the American Oriental Society* 106: 617–21.

1989a. *A Catalogue of the Stog Palace Kanjur*. By T. Skorupski. *Acta Orientalia* 48: 153–56.

1989b. *A Study of Svātantrika*. By D. Lopez. *Bulletin of the School for Oriental and African Studies* 52: 159–60.

1990a. *The Entrance Gate for the Wise (Section III)—Sa skya Paṇḍita on Indian and Tibetan Traditions of Pramāṇa and Philosophical Debate*, 2 vols. By D. Jackson. *Indo-Iranian Journal* 33: 214–21.

1990b. *Nepalese Manuscripts, Part 1: Nevari and Sanskrit*. By S. Lienhard. *Journal of the American Oriental Society* 110: 540–41.

1991a. *Jñānagarbha's Commentary on the Distinction between the Two Truths: An Eighth Century Handbook of Madhyamaka Philosophy*. By M. Eckel. *Journal of the American Oriental Society* 111: 402–5.

1991b. *Rong ston on the Prajñāpāramitā Philosophy of the Abhisamayālaṃkāra. His Subcommmentary on Haribhadra's "Sphuṭārtha": A Facsimile Reproduction of the Earliest Known Blockprint, from an Exemplar Preserved in The Tibet House, New Delhi.* Edited by D. P. Jackson. *Journal of the American Oriental Society* 111: 584–88.

1992. *The Pradumna-Prabhāvati Legend in Nepal and Jagatprakaśamallas Maladevasasidevavyakhyananujaka.* By H. Brinkhaus. *Journal of the American Oriental Society* 112: 668–70.

1993. *A History of Modern Tibet, 1913–1951: The Demise of the Lamaist State.* By M. Goldstein. *Indo-Iranian Journal* 36: 269–72.

1994a. *Udanavarga*, vol. 3, *Tibetischer Text.* By Champa Thupten Zongtse. *Journal of the American Oriental Society* 114: 124–26.

1994b. *Tshad ma sde bdun rgyan gyi me tog.* By Bcom ldan rigs pa'i ral gri. *Journal of the American Oriental Society* 114: 304–6.

1994c. *Xizang Wenwu jingcai* [Bod kyi rig dngos snying btus]. *Journal of the American Oriental Society* 114: 306–8.

1994d. *Studies in the Buddhist Epistemological Tradition.* Edited by E. Steinkellner. *Bulletin of the School of African and Oriental Studies* 57: 604–6.

1995. *Tibetan Buddhism: Reason and Revelation.* Edited by S. D. Goodman and R. M. Davidson. *Bulletin of the School of African and Oriental Studies* 58: 592–93.

1997. *Recognizing Reality: Dharmakīrti's Philosophy and Its Tibetan Interpretations.* By G. B. J. Dreyfus. *Journal of Asian Studies* 56: 1083–86.

1998a. *Chinesischer und Tibetischer Buddhismus im China der Yüanzeit.* By H. Franke. *Journal of Asian Studies* 57: 255–58.

1998b. *Buddhism and Language: A Study of Indo-Tibetan Scholasticism.* By J. I. Cabezón. *Journal of the American Oriental Society* 118: 563–67.

2014. *"Zhongguanxin lun" jiqi guzhu "Sizeyan" yanjiu* [A Study of Madhyamakahṛdayakārikā and Tarkajvālā], 2 vols. By He Huanhuan. *Indo-Iranian Journal* 57: 271–76.

2015. *Śabdālaṃkāradoṣavibhāga. Die Unterscheidung der Lautfiguren und der Fehler*, 2 vols. By D. Dimitrov. *Indo-Iranian Journal* 58: 171–74.

Fig. 4. Leonard van der Kuijp in Nepal (2018). Photo by Kurtis Schaeffer.

A Note on Transcription, Transliteration, and Bibliography

FOR CONVENIENCE and general legibility, this volume uses a system of phonetic transcription developed by David Germano and Nicolas Tournadre, the Tibetan and Himalayan Library's (THL) simplified phonetic transcription of standard Tibetan (2003). The first appearance of a transcribed personal or place name will also typically include THL extended Wylie transliteration in parentheses (2004), which is based on the Wylie transliteration system (1959). Tibetan-language text titles and special terms have also been translated into English whenever possible, followed by transliteration in parentheses after the first use. In a volume such as this one there will inevitably be some terms that resist translation, however, and these terms have been rendered in phonetic transcription or transliteration at the discretion of the authors. These conventions were carefully chosen by the editors in order to ensure that both specialists and nonspecialists are able to understand this volume, while also ensuring that all salient information is concisely conveyed.

References

Germano, David, and Nicolas Tournadre. 2003. "THL Simplified Phonetic Transcription of Standard Tibetan." *Tibetan and Himalayan Library*. http://www.thlib.org/reference/transliteration/#!essay=/thl/phonetics/.

Germano, David, et al. 2004. "THL Extended Wylie Transliteration Scheme." https://www.thlib.org/reference/transliteration/#!essay=/thl/ewts/all/

Wylie, Turrell V. 1959. "A Standard System of Tibetan Transcription." *Harvard Journal of Asiatic Studies* 22: 261–67.

Cultural History

On *Gtsug-lag khang*, “Monastery, *Vihāra*”

Christopher I. Beckwith

To Leonard, with thanks for many years of friendship and good cheer, and best wishes for many more.

THE JOKHANG, “The Lord’s House,” is the oldest and holiest Buddhist monastery (*vihāra*) in Tibet. It was founded during the reign of Khri Srong rtsan (r. ca. 618–649/650), better known under his later traditional name Srong btsan sgam po. The edifice is also one of the earliest two attested in a datable historical source, the Samyé Inscription of circa 764 CE, which begins:

> རཿསཿདང་། བྲག་མར་གྱི་གཙུག་ལག་ཁང་ལས་སྩོགས་པརཿ། ...
> In the monasteries of Rasa, Bragmar, and so on. . . .[1]

The word གཙུག་ལག་ཁང་ *gtsug-lag khang*, ‘monastery, *vihāra*,’ has always been taken to be native Tibetan.[2] The third syllable, *khang*, is of course the well-known native Tibetan nominal used to form words for various kinds of building, house, or hall. The key term *gtsug-lag* is also attested alone in Old

I would like to thank Andrew E. Shimunek for kindly suggesting improvements to this paper. I am responsible for any remaining errors.

1. Text from Li and Coblin 1987, 188; and Iwao et al. 2009, 11. On the dating of the inscriptions see Walter and Beckwith 2010. For transcriptions, I use the standard system for each language that has one. For others, I use the Wylie system for Tibetan; for Chinese, the modified Wade-Giles system (with Pinyin in parentheses).

2. The words *gtsug-lag khang* and *vihāra* equally mean ‘monastery,’ but refer specifically to the cloister. Each could refer by synecdoche to an entire monastery complex, but when the monastery first appeared it consisted only of the cloister; in some surviving early examples the cloister is still nearly all of it. Several other buildings were eventually added to cloisters for various purposes, making them monastery complexes. Archaeologists of South Asia, followed by architectural historians, call the standard core cloister plan the *vihāra* plan (Beckwith 2017, 2020), as it cannot be confused with any other plan. See note 11 for a word on the mistranslation of the term *vihāra* as ‘temple.’

Tibetan as an attribute of the བཙན་པོ་ *btsanpo* (Tibetan emperor). Li and Coblin define *gtsug-lag* as "wisdom; knowledge; the entire body of indigenous, pre-Buddhist beliefs."[3] However, despite these and other doubtful proposals based on later sources,[4] the word *gtsug-lag* so far has no actual etymology and is unexplained, other than by folk etymologies. The same is true of *gtsug-lag khang*, but scholars today are agreed that this Tibetan word, meaning 'Buddhist monastery, *vihāra*,' refers to the actual thing: a specific foreign physical object with a specific design and specific socioreligious functions unprecedented in Tibet.[5] Based on historical accounts, including the Samyé Inscription quoted above, it is accepted to be a foreign introduction to Tibet from the early imperial period (seventh century CE).

As a complex foreign artifact and concept with a foreign word attached to it, the normal, regular, virtually universal procedure for dealing with it is for the receivers or importers to adopt the previously unknown foreign thing *together with the word* for it.[6] Therefore, *gtsug-lag khang* is undoubtedly a loanword from an unidentified language, or an Old Tibetan folk etymologization of that early loanword, or both.

Since all are agreed that the word *khang* is a genuine Tibetan word or compounding form meaning 'building, house, hall,' we are not looking for a word meaning '[*unknown*]' (plus 'building'), but a word meaning specifically 'Buddhist monastery, *vihāra*' (plus 'building'). Thus, the loanword *gtsug-lag* should mean 'Buddhist monastery,' while the native Tibetan word *khang* means 'building,' together making '*vihāra* building' or 'monastery building.' The question

3. See Li and Coblin 1987, 95, 442, for original text citations. Their definition adds 'statecraft' (when referring to the principles underlying the king's rule). However, the entire definition is purely conjectural. We have no glosses or contemporaneous translations in other languages, and the context is vague enough to allow almost any translation. Note that they include several post-imperial texts in their volume, so that many of the items in their glossary and index are from texts that are *not* Imperial Old Tibetan.

4. Surveyed by Walter 2009, 267n15, who concludes that "*gtsug lag* . . . is never presented in a context in which it is opposed to Buddhism. Indeed, it is difficult to understand how [the term] *gtsug-lag khang*, the Tibetan rendering of the Sanskrit Buddhist term *vihāra*, one of the earliest Buddhist terms in Tibet . . . could have been created if the term were in any way antithetical to Buddhism," noting that the "earliest attestations of *gtsug-lag* are during the reign of Khri Srong Lde Brtsan, a ruler who supported Buddhism" (229–30).

5. See Beckwith 2017, which includes architectural plans of ancient *vihāras*.

6. In some cases (not this one) the borrowing culture coins a native word for the borrowed thing.

then is, from what language, ultimately, does the loanword *gtsug-lag* 'Buddhist monastery'[7] derive, and when was it borrowed?

We must first look at languages spoken in regions near the early Tibetan Empire from which the Tibetans might have borrowed the word for 'monastery' along with the thing itself. As a loanword, the donor form should be a word for the same complex thing that was borrowed, the monastery.[8] Phonetically the word obviously cannot be *vihāra*, an Indic word meaning 'Buddhist monastery' (traditionally etymologized as 'a place for spending the night'), which became the classic word for 'Buddhist monastery' in Indic languages and was widely borrowed in medieval Central Asia and elsewhere to the north, west, and south of Tibet in the early medieval period.

However, the word *vihāra* was not borrowed by Tibetan or by attested East Asian languages as the word for 'monastery.' There is a good reason: the word *vihāra* is not firmly attested *anywhere* before the early medieval period in that meaning.[9] Accordingly, when the monastery was introduced to China in the first two centuries CE, the early Parthian and Kushan Buddhist teachers and translators in China introduced it along with their word for it,[10] Aramaic *dērā*, *dayrā* ('monastery').[11]

As a result, to the east of Tibet, Far Eastern languages share the same word for 'monastery,' which does not go back to *vihāra* but rather to Aramaic *dērā*

7. The loanword originally meant 'monastery, *vihāra*' by itself, so it did not need *khang* ('building') or the like.

8. On the invention and early spread of the Buddhist monastery, which is first attested from archaeology in the first century CE, see Beckwith 2014, 2017, and 2020; on its functioning equally as a college, see Beckwith 2012; on the nonexistence of monasteries and monasticism earlier (in attested Early Buddhism), see Beckwith 2015 and 2020. See also note 9 below.

9. Schopen 2004, 77. Stefan Baums (personal communication 2013) reports that, so far, no references have been found to *vihāras* (monasteries) in the Gāndhārī manuscripts; all occurrences in the *Gāndhārī Dictionary* (online) are from inscriptions.

10. They also introduced the Chinese to many other key Buddhist concepts and terms, and produced the first Chinese translations of Buddhist texts (Nattier 2008). On the history of the transmission of Buddhism to China, see the classic work of Zürcher 2007.

11. Beckwith 2014 and 2017. Unfortunately, the traditional words for 'Buddhist monastery, *vihāra*' in Chinese, Korean, Japanese, and Tibetan are almost universally mistranslated as 'temple,' and thus misunderstood (e.g., Li and Coblin 1987, 95, 442). The English term 'temple,' which is often used to refer to the Buddhist monasteries located in these four nations, apparently goes back to Christian missionaries of the colonial period. The colonial misunderstanding is reinforced by its use in English translations of modern Japanese to distinguish Buddhist monasteries (which are called 'temples') from Shinto establishments (which are called 'shrines'). In Japanese itself, the Buddhist monastery is standardly called a *tera* 寺. In Chinese, the standard headword 'monastery' in names is still *ssu*寺 (*si*).

~ *dayrā*, borrowed via Chinese, specifically from 寺 Late Old Chinese (LOC) *dēʁă,[12] now read *ssu* (*sì*), and LOC 祠 *dērā, now read *ssu* 祠 (*sī*).[13] The word *dēʁă ~ *dērā spread from LOC via Koguryo (which like its relative Japanese has the phonological feature of not allowing voiced word-onsets) to Old Japanese *tera* (perhaps earlier *taira), Jurchen (medieval Manchu) *taira* ~ *taira-n*, and Middle Korean *tyer*, all glossed 寺 '(Buddhist) monastery.'[14] To the west of Tibet, Near Eastern languages all share the same Aramaic word for 'monastery,' *dērā* ~ *dairā* (modern *dayro*, *dayr*) from the early centuries of the Common Era on, meaning '(Christian) monastery.' In both cases the *monastery* cloister's functions included those of the early *college* cloister; they have the exact same plan and function.[15] In the beginning they were one and the same edifice and institution.

Old Tibetan *gtsug-lag* bears no obvious resemblance to the attestations and reconstructions of the words for 'Buddhist monastery' above because shortly after the loan of the Aramaic word into LOC, the Chinese language underwent massive phonological change in which it became pre-Middle Chinese, as recently shown.[16] Then as a loanword in Chinese, the word was reinterpreted in many variant forms, so that there are actually two sets of transcriptions in Chinese. The earlier *monocharacter* transcriptions have *one* character transcribing two syllables: *ssu* 祠 (*sī*) 'spring sacrifice' from LOC *dḗră,[17] with *r, and *ssu*

12. The character 寺 is the phonetic of several other ancient characters, such as *tai* 待 (*dài*) from MChi ☆d'ậi$_2$ (Karlgren 1957, 253 #961g), 'to wait (on), serve,' MChi ☆dəj$_2$ (Pulleyblank 1991, 69), etc., from LOC *dēʁă ~ *daiʁă. It is also the phonetic of many other words once pronounced approximately the same as 寺 in one or more ancient dialects, as shown in detail in Beckwith 2014 and again, with further linguistic and archaeological-architectural data, in Beckwith 2017. In the recently excavated Classical texts, these characters are often interchanged, regardless of their supposed meanings, showing they were (nearly) homonymous; what was important was the *sound* of the spoken Chinese word, which conveyed the meaning.

13. MChi ☆zi 'spring sacrifice' (Karlgren 1957, 256 §972h); the character 祠 is not in Pulleyblank 1991; it is misprinted as 祀 'sacrifice' in Beckwith 2014.

14. Beckwith 2007; cf. Beckwith 2014. See also Shimunek 2021.

15. See Beckwith 2012, which also shows how the disputational method used in them is the historical basis for the earliest known 'scientific method,' the rhetorical-logical method used in medieval Latin texts and often called *quaestiones disputatae*.

16. Beckwith and Kiyose 2018.

17. In a poem by the famous historian Pan Ku 班固 (Bān Gù, 32–92 CE) its homophonous phonetic *ssu* 司 (*sī*) 'supervise' (Karlgren 1957, 256 §972) rhymes directly with *ssu* 寺 (*sì*), which still did not mean 'Buddhist monastery' in Pan's time. See Beckwith 2017 for details. Tones had not yet been recognized by the Chinese, because they did not exist—they only came into existence during or after the transition from LOC to pre-MChi. That little fact

寺 (*sì*) 'eunuch, servant' from Middle Chinese (MChi) ☆*zi* from LOC *dḗʁă, with *ʁ.[18] They were followed not long after by a number of *dicharacter* forms (*two* characters representing two syllables).[19] The dicharacter forms, the result of further Chinese internal developments, are key here.

The earliest of the dicharacter words appears to be *ssu-she* 寺舍 (*sìshè*) '(Buddhist) monastery.'[20] Its post-LOC form, *dzeʁla,[21] shows that the onset *d first affricated to *dz (presumably because of the following long vowel *ē), and later, the Old Chinese vowel length was lost, leaving *e ~ ɛ in the first syllable, while the second syllable onset *r in the word's spoken Old Chinese form became *l in post-LOC.[22] In its post-LOC disyllabic form, the word is *dzeʁla ~ *dzeɣla,

seriously undermines the traditional system of Old Chinese reconstruction (which is based on MChi tone categories); it is further undermined by the discovery of hard data on many monocharacter transcriptions (two syllables written with one character) of Chinese and foreign words (Beckwith and Kiyose 2018). On the Chinese discovery of the tones, see the detailed discussion by Knechtges in Knechtges 2014, 11ff.

18. See note 12 above.

19. The early monocharacter transcriptions *ssu* 祠 (*sī*) and *ssu* 寺 (*sì*) both mean 'monastery' and represent LOC *dḗră and *dḗʁă respectively, a loanword directly from Aramaic *dērā* 'monastery.' The transcription 寺 quickly supplanted the earlier transcription 祠, the Chinese meaning of which is 'spring sacrifice,' a sense not congenial to Buddhism. The characters do not, however, *translate* the word. Before the borrowing, the transcriptional characters referred to unrelated things in Chinese (as shown in Beckwith 2014 and 2017). That is the general rule for all transcriptions of foreign words in Chinese. The later dicharacter transcriptions are treated in the long appendix of my 2014 article.

20. This compound word is said to have earlier meant 'government office' (Morohashi 1984, vol. 4, 3407), but this definition is suspect and should be reexamined. The character *she* 舍 (*shè*) [ʂə] was read *lâ or the like in LOC. Its reading changed in the LOC period via a dialect reading *la to what became MChi☆dʑia (Pulleyblank 1991, 278), Mandarin *she*, and then (via a phonetic change discussed below) pre-MChi *tseŋla (Beckwith 2014, 2017); the resulting *ching-she* 精舍 (*jīngshè*) 'monastery' was then partly supplanted by a writing that preserves LOC *lâ, now read *lu*, namely *ching-lu* 精廬 (*jīnglú*) 'monastery.' See the next note.

21. The phonological changes of this word in the pre-MChi period suggest that the onset of the subsequent MChi reading ☆$ɕia_3$ (Pulleyblank 1991, 279) is a dialect reading from an OChi *la- (cf. Baxter 1992, 786). However, the character 舍 (now read *shè*) may well have had two ancient dialect readings, one with an unvoiced fricative onset, the other with a liquid onset.

22. It is well known and accepted that at the end of the Old Chinese period *r syllable onsets regularly underwent canonical unconditioned change to *l. The great phonological changes that ended the Old Chinese period included particularly the thoroughgoing monosyllabicization of all remaining disyllabic morphemes and the appearance of tone, all undoubtedly due to creolization during the Völkerwanderung, the pan-Eurasian migrations that characterize the third and fourth centuries CE.

with the single intervocalic liquid <*r*> of the original Aramaic loan represented doubly, as the first syllable coda *ʁ/*ɣ and as the second syllable onset *l.[23] The onset of this form then devoiced in pre-MChi times, giving *tseʁla ~ *tseɣla.

This reconstruction is supported by the other dicharacter transcriptions of the word for 'monastery' resulting from a regular Syllable Contact Law change characteristic of the Northeast Asian Sprachbund,[24] whereby syllables ending in a voiced velar stop *g or velar-uvular fricative *ɣ/ʁ coda, when in contact with a liquid onset (*r or *l), became a velar nasal coda, *ŋ.[25] The *regular result* in pre-Early Middle Chinese was *tseŋlâ,[26] and eventually Mandarin *ching-lu* 精廬 (*jīnglú*) '(Buddhist) monastery,' the most frequent of several variants.[27] The devoiced first syllable onset *ts is well attested in the dicharacter transcriptions, so reversing the process gives the original post-LOC dialect form, 寺舍 *tseʁla ~ *tseɣla '(Buddhist) monastery.' The chief significance of the nasalized form *tseŋlâ here is that it directly attests the previous existence of the voiced uvular/velar fricative form *tseʁla ~ *tseɣla,[28] the source of the Chinese loan to Old Tibetan.[29]

The main remaining problems are that Old Tibetan *gtsug-lag* contains an

23. The unexplained splitting or doubling of an original single intervocalic continuant phone (based on externally attested linguistic data) occurs in at least one other ancient loanword in Chinese. Such cases are clearly connected to the monosyllabicization of Chinese morphemes that began around the third century CE, but several of the changes involved are also characteristic of the Northeast Asian Sprachbund, which includes East Scythian (Hsiung-nu), Koguryo, Korean, and Northeastern Chinese. This complex issue is currently under study.

24. The Syllable Contact Law requires that for syllables in contact within a word, the preceding syllable coda should be higher in sonority than the following syllable onset (Davis 1998; Gouskova 2004; Özçelik forthcoming).

25. That is, CVg/ɣ+*l*/*r*V(C) > CVŋ+*l*/*r*V(C), where V stands for any vowel and C for any consonant. This particular change affected several languages, so there are many examples, such as *Sugda* 'East Scythian, Sogdian' > *Sugla (*d > *l is a regular, unconditioned Scythian-internal change) > *Suŋla, recorded in Old Chinese as *Hsiung-nu* 匈奴 (*Xiōngnú*); see Beckwith 2018 and forthcoming.

26. Attested MChi *tseng* ཙེང་ (Takata 1988, 406–7); the second syllable *lu* 廬 is not attested in Takata.

27. See the appendix of Beckwith 2014. One of the variants is *ching-she* 精舍 (*jīngshè*), with the post-Old Chinese fricative reading of the second character.

28. And in turn, it attests to the earlier monocharacter forms; see Beckwith 2014 and 2017.

29. The coda of Old Tibetan *gtsug* <ག> regularly represents not only a stop *g* or *k*, as might be expected, but also a fricative [ɣ] or [ʁ] as in Old Tibetan transcriptions of foreign place names with *γ*, and in old loanwords—e.g., སྟག་ *stag* 'tiger,' a loan from *hu* 虎 (*hŭ*), OChi *stâʁă/*stâɣă 'tiger' (Kiyose and Beckwith 2008).

apparent prefix <g-> and an apparent suffix <-g>, neither of them having any certain meaning within Tibetan, and that the vowel of the first syllable is <u> rather than *e or its central neighbor *ə.

For the prefix and suffix, there are very good reasons why Early Old Tibetan speakers, especially the monks, must have found the foreign word *tsuɣla to be *too* foreign, especially considering that it was the word for their home, the monastery, the heart of monastic Normative Buddhism.[30] One reason is that no native Early Old Tibetan word could begin with an unaspirated unvoiced stop or affricate, such as ཙ [ts]. It could be written, but it would normally be pronounced as its aspirated allophone, ཚ [ts^h], as we know from misspellings in Old Tibetan texts. Another reason is that as a conservative Tibeto-Burman language, Early Old Tibetan was heavily prefixing and suffixing in its morphological structure. Taken together, it was all but inevitable that a prefix-imitating prosthetic element would be supplied to make the word look or sound like a good Tibetan word with a *g-* 'prefix.' In this case it makes the first syllable into a native Tibetan word, གཙུག་ *gtsug*, 'crown of the head; vortex.' As soon as that was done, it would have created a postpositional phrase with ལ་ *la*, meaning 'at the crown of the head' or the like. This was odd for the thing named (a monastery). However, adding a *-g* 'suffix' to *la* makes it ལག་ *lag* 'hand, arm,' which apparently made it (the *word* itself) work semantically—as many Tibetans tell us to this day, pointing to the vortex of their head and then stretching out their arms to explain the meaning of གཙུག་ལག་. So is this textbook example of a folk etymology the *actual* etymology of the word? No. The word means 'monastery,' not 'head-arm.'

There is of course another option. An unknown people located somewhere inaccessibly high in the mountains between Tibet and the outside world could have contributed the word for 'monastery' in their own language, complete with prefixes and suffixes, or they could have added their suffixes to the Chinese loanword *tseɣla, as in one or two known examples of loanwords with added non-Tibetan prefixes.[31] However, this approach violates Ockham's razor

30. For the crucial distinction between attested non-monastic *Early* Buddhism, versus later attested monastic *Normative* Buddhism, see Beckwith 2015.

31. Historically a borrowing makes sense theoretically, since the earliest known Tibetan contacts with China during the early T'ang period (seventh century CE) took place via what is now eastern Gansu province and northeastern Tibet (now Amdo, Chinese Qinghai), as well as northern Khams (partly now in Sichuan). Linguistically there is an attested proclivity for prefixing and suffixing in eastern Tibetan dialects (as well as in Old Tibetan itself), and even more so in other Tibeto-Burman languages. The most famous (if not the only) example is the *k* in ཀླུ་ *klu* '*nāga*,' an early loanword into Tibetan from a western Chinese dialect pronunciation of *lung* 龍 (*lóng*), attested MChi *lung*, *long* (Takata 1988, 416–17),

and here substitutes unknown actors and things for known ones, the reverse of what we should do.

We must in any case still solve the vowel problem. It is necessary to note that even within Old Tibetan the cardinal vowel written <u> was not always pronounced [u], as we might expect based on its canonical place in the list of five original vowels (*a i u e o*), where (as an open vowel) /u/ was no doubt pronounced [u], as it is still usually pronounced today, maintaining its Old Tibetan value. However, in a closed syllable <u> is normally pronounced [ʊ], and was evidently pronounced [ʊ] in Old Tibetan too, as shown by the fact that the mid-back rounded vowel written <o> in Old Tibetan transcriptions of MChi corresponds to MChi *ʊ, a vowel usually reconstructed by Pulleyblank as *ɔ (a mid-back rounded vowel, 'half-round o'), and Old Tibetan transcriptions of Old Turkic usually record Turkic /u/ as Old Tibetan <o>, i.e., [ʊ], while Old Turkic /ü/ [y] is usually transcribed as Old Tibetan <u>.[32]

At least one other early foreign transcription of a Chinese dicharacter word renders an unrounded mid-vowel *ə or *e in the first syllable as *u*. It is the Aramaeo-Sogdian transcription <'ḥwmt'n> *ăḥūm(ă)tān(ă)* in the fourth century CE Sogdian Ancient Letter II.[33] Usually read 'Khumdān,'[34] it represents the Chinese city name now read *Hsien-yang* 咸陽 (*Xiányáng*),[35] from attested Late Middle Chinese *hamyaŋ*, from Early Middle Chinese *ɣamyaŋ (based on *hamyaŋ*) ~ traditionally reconstructed ☆ɣəɨmyaŋ,[36] from Old Chi-

---

traditionally reconstructed ☆luawŋ (Pulleyblank 1991, 198). It was also loaned into Old Turkic as *lū* [luː] 'dragon' (Clauson 1972, 763) and into Serbi-Mongolic—e.g., Middle Kitan *lu 'dragon' and Middle Mongol *lu* 'id' (Shimunek 2017, 86). The same word was borrowed earlier into proto-Tibetan and is attested as Old Tibetan འབྲུག་ *ḥbrug* [^{m}brug], from Old Chinese *mruʁă or *mruɣă ~ mruŋă ~ *βruɣă, etc. (Kiyose and Beckwith 2008).

32. Ligeti 1971, 184, 187 passim.

33. Sims-Williams 2001.

34. The widespread rendering of *'ḥwmt'n* as 'Khumdān' or the like is based on transcriptions in other scripts from the Middle Ages, the earliest being the late sixth century. See Takata 2010 for a thorough survey of the sources.

35. The Aramaeo-Sogdian unambiguously represents *aḥūm(ă)tān(ă) ~ *aɣūm(ă)tān(ă). With the exception of the dialectal <w> it is a standard Imperial Aramaic transcription of the name of the capital of Media, 'Ecbatana.' The Imperial Aramaic is *'ḥmt'[n]*, in pointed Biblical Aramaic *Aḥ(ə)mətā[na]*, which transcribes the Median capital city's name, solidly recorded as *Agamatana* in Akkadian. The only difference is the vowel under discussion. 'Khumdān' is regularly identified and translated as 'Ch'ang-an' (i.e., Cháng'ān, now Xi'an). The two cities are in fact located several kilometers apart and across the Wei River from each other.

36. Attested: Takata 1988, 352–53, 390–91; reconstructed: Pulleyblank 1991, 335, 360.

nese *ăgắmădáNă.[37] In literary Sogdian the segment <ḥ> in this word is sometimes written <γ> [g] instead of <ḥ> [χ].[38] Thus Aramaeo-Sogdian <'γwmt'n> evidently records *ăɣum(ă)tān(ă)*.[39] With the exception of <w> for the expected MChi vowel ☆ə ~ ☆ă,[40] this Sogdian transcription is identical to the Imperial Aramaic transcription of the name of the capital of ancient Media, *Aḥ(ə) mətā[na]* (recording the same name as Akkadian *Agamatana*/*Agammatana*, etc.), Greek *Agbatana*,[41] with the reading of <ḥ> as [ɣ] supported (for both Imperial Aramaic and Aramaeo-Sogdian) not only by the Akkadian but also by Old Chinese *g and MChi *ɣ. The Imperial Aramaic form also has schwa (ə) in the Masoretic pointing, corresponding to the vowel ☆ə in Pulleyblank's reconstruction of the pronunciation of the transcriptional first character 咸 in MChi. In addition, the <t>, read in Sogdian as [d], reflects an Old Chinese reading of the character *yang* 陽 (*yáng*), as pointed out by Takata, suggesting that the Aramaeo-Sogdian name is much older than the fourth century CE. In short, the early fourth-century CE Aramaeo-Sogdian transcription essentially preserves an Old Chinese form of the city name *Hsien-yang* 咸陽 (*Xiányáng*).[42] The vowel shift from [ə] to [u] could be due to Sogdian, though (in view of the word for 'monastery') the Sogdian form of the city name may have been influenced by the local Chinese dialect, which the Sogdian traders who lived there surely knew.

Moreover, there is further evidence on the vowel. Ts'en Chung-mien suggests that T'ang Chinese poets write the *foreign* pronunciation of the name of 'the capital' as *Chin-tien* 金殿 (*Jīndiàn*), in which the first syllable is *chin* 金 (*jīn*) 'gold(en),'[43] reconstructed for MChi as ☆ki̯əm (Karlgren 1957, 173

37. See Beckwith (forthcoming) for details on the Scythian (Avestan) name Aɣəmatā-na- and its use for several ancient capital cities.

38. Gharib 1995, 84, who also gives the reading of <'ḥwmt'n> as *'əxumdān*, where [ə] = [ă].

39. Gharib 1995, 84, following whom <'γwmt'n> should be read *'əxumdān*. However, this reading and the one in note 38 must be late, so the initial vowel must have been deleted, as shown by the many foreign transcriptions of *Khumdān*.

40. Takata 2010.

41. Also written Ecbatana; for a detailed discussion of this Median capital city name (now *Hamadān*) and the two Agamatanas in ancient China, see Beckwith (forthcoming).

42. In full, Early MChi ☆ɣăm-i̯ang (Karlgren 1957, 178 #671a, 188 #720e), ☆ɣəɨm-yɨaŋ (Pulleyblank 1991, 335, 360); *attested* Late MChi *ham-yaŋ* (Takata 1988, 352–53, 390–91) from Early MChi *ɣam-yaŋ; Old Chinese *ăɣắmădáɴă ~ *ăɣə́mădáɴă, not *despite* but *because of* the dialect-shifted vowel *u for *ắ ~ *ə́ ~ ɯ. Its existence shows that the Sogdians wrote what they (or their ancestors) had learned from speakers of a dialect of Old Chinese, as pointed out in Takata 2010.

43. Takata 2010 cites Ts'en Chung-mien's comment that Li Po 李白 and Wang Ch'ang-ling

#652a), ☆kïə̣m (Takata 1988, 358); its pronunciation is actually attested in the name *Chin-ch'eng* 金城 (*Jīnchéng*) in the *Old Tibetan Annals*, where it is written *kïm* ཀྀམ་ (710–11 CE).[44] It has long been thought that the reversed writing of the vowel sign <i> in Old Tibetan as <ྀ> in Old Tibetan script is purely a graphical variation. However, the *consonantal* spelling <kïm> is significant. According to pre-Old Tibetan and Early Old Tibetan phonological rules, the high front unrounded vowel <i> and the mid-front unrounded vowel <e> *always palatalize* eligible preceding consonants, one of which is <k>. According to the rule, if this were an Old Tibetan word it should have been written <kyim>, identical to an allophonic transcription of *khyim* 'house.'[45] In Imperial Old Tibetan no native words appear to violate this rule. That alone tells us what was different about the Chinese vowel: the feature [front] is either missing or is replaced with [back], so that the transcriptional vowel represents a vowel close to [ɯ], the unrounded version of [u].

The Aramaeo-Sogdian transcription with <w>, read [u], or [ɯ]," and the Old Tibetan rendering <u> of its Chinese retranscription indicate that in two instances a northwestern pre-MChi dialect regularly rounded a stressed vowel *ă [ə] ~ *e/ɛ ~ *ɯ to [u]. Thus for the first syllable of the name Hsien-yang 咸陽, the expected vowel ă/ə is recorded as <w> [u] or [ɯ] in Aramaeo-Sogdiann script. Similarly, the vowel e/ɛ in the first syllable of *tseɣla 寺舍 'monastery' is recorded in Old Tibetan script as <u> [ʊ] in the attested loanform *tsugla* 'monastery,' *vihāra*.

In sum, the Old Tibetan word གཙུག་ལག་ཁང་ *gtsug-lag khang* is a compound consisting of the Tibetan nominal ཁང་ *khang* 'building' plus the loanword *tsugla* 'monastery,'[46] from the pre-MChi northwestern dialect form *tsɯɣla, from *tseɣla ~ *tsɨɣla, preserved in Chinese in *ssu-she* 寺舍 and *ching-lu* 精廬 'Buddhist monastery,' two writings of the same loanword from Aramaic.

王昌齡 use 金殿 in their poems for 'the capital.' I thank my colleague Fu Ma for kindly checking Ts'en's book, which is unavailable to me.

44. *Old Tibetan Annals*, line 177, and again identically in line 282 (739–40 CE); cf. *kïm* ཀྀམ་ (Takata 1988, 358).

45. Attested in the *Old Tibetan Annals*, line 206 as ཁྱྀམ *khyïm*.

46. With a quasi-prefix and quasi-suffix <g> of unknown origin, but probably added by Early Old Tibetan folk-etymologization of the foreign word.

Abbreviations

C	any Consonant
V	any Vowel
OChi	Old Chinese
LOC	Late Old Chinese
MChi	Middle Chinese

References

Baxter, William H. 1992. *A Handbook of Old Chinese Phonology*. Berlin: Mouton de Gruyter.

Beckwith, Christopher I. 2007 [2004]. *Koguryo, the Language of Japan's Continental Relatives: An Introduction to the Historical-Comparative Study of the Japanese-Koguryoic Languages, with a Preliminary Description of Archaic Northeastern Middle Chinese*. 2nd ed. Leiden: Brill.

———. 2012. *Warriors of the Cloisters: The Central Asian Origins of Science in the Medieval World*. Princeton, NJ: Princeton University Press, 2012.

———. 2014. "The Aramaic Source of the East Asian Word for 'Buddhist Monastery': On the Spread of Central Asian Monasticism in the Kushan Period." *Journal Asiatique* 201.1: 111–38.

———. 2015. *Greek Buddha: Pyrrho's Encounter with Early Buddhism in Central Asia*. Princeton, NJ: Princeton University Press.

———. 2017. "Once Again on the Aramaic Word for 'Monastery' in East Asia." *Journal Asiatique* 305.2: 211–24.

———. 2018. "On the Ethnolinguistic Identity of the Hsiung-nu." In *Language, Government, and Religion in the World of the Turks: Festschrift for Larry Clark at Seventy-Five*, edited by Zsuzsanna Gulacsi, 33–55. Silk Road Studies 19. Turnhout: Brepols.

———. 2020. "Vihāras in the Kushan Empire." In *The Limits of Empire in Ancient Afghanistan: Rule and Resistance in the Hindu Kush, circa 600 BCE–600 CE*, edited by Richard E. Payne and Rhyne King, 157–67. Classica et Orientalia 24. Wiesbaden: Harrassowitz Verlag.

———. Forthcoming. *The Scythian Empire: Central Eurasia and the Birth of the Classical Age from Persia to China*. Princeton, NJ: Princeton University Press.

Beckwith, Christopher I., and Gisaburo N. Kiyose. 2018. "Apocope of Late Old Chinese Short *ă: Early Central Asian Loanword and Old Japanese Evidence for Old Chinese Disyllabic Morphemes." *Acta Orientalia Academiae Scientiarum Hungaricae* 71.2: 145–60.

Clauson, Gerard. 1972. *An Etymological Dictionary of Pre-Thirteenth Century Turkish*. Oxford: Clarendon.

Davis, Stuart. 1998. "Syllable Contact in Optimality Theory." *Korea Journal of Linguistics* 23: 181–211.

Gharib, B. 1995. *Sogdian Dictionary: Sogdian-Persian-English*. Tehran: Ferhangan.

Gouskova, Maria. 2004. "Relational Hierarchies in Optimality Theory: The Case of Syllable Contact." *Phonology* 21.2: 201–50.

Iwao, Kazushi, Nathan Hill, Tsuguhito Takeuchi, Izumi Hoshi, and Yoshiro Imaeda. 2009. *Old Tibetan Inscriptions*. Tokyo: Research Institute for Languages and Cultures of Asia and Africa, Tokyo University of Foreign Studies.

Karlgren, Bernhard. 1957. *Grammata Serica recensa*. Stockholm: Museum of Far Eastern Antiquities.

Kiyose, Gisaburo N., and Christopher I. Beckwith. 2008. "On the Words for Animals in the Japanese Zodiac." *Arutaigo kenkyū – Altaistic Studies* 2: 1–18.

Knechtges, David R., and Xiao Tong. 2014. *Wen xuan, or, Selections of Refined Literature. Volume One, Rhapsodies on Metropolises and Capitals*. Princeton, NJ: Princeton University Press.

Li, Fang Kuei, and W. South Coblin. 1987. *A Study of the Old Tibetan Inscriptions*. Taipei: Institute of History and Philology, Academia Sinica.

Ligeti, Louis. 1971. "À propos du 'Rapport sur les rois demeurant dans le nord.'" In *Études tibétaines, dédiées à la mémoire de Marcelle Lalou*, 166–89. Paris: Maisonneuve.

Morohashi Tetsuji 諸橋轍次. 1984–86. *Dai Kan-Wa jiten* 大漢和辞典. 13 vols. Tokyo: Taishūkan Shoten.

Nattier, Jan. 2008. *A Guide to the Earliest Chinese Buddhist Translations: Texts from the Eastern Han* 東漢 *and Three Kingdoms* 三國 *Periods*. Tokyo: The International Research Institute for Advanced Buddhology, Soka University.

Özçelik, Öner. Forthcoming. "Kazakh Phonology." In *Encyclopedia of Turkic Languages*, edited by Lars Johanson. Leiden: Brill.

Pulleyblank, Edwin G. 1991. *Lexicon of Reconstructed Pronunciation in Early Middle Chinese, Late Middle Chinese, and Early Mandarin*. Vancouver: University of British Columbia Press.

Schopen, Gregory. 2004. *Buddhist Monks and Business Matters: Still More Papers on Monastic Buddhism in India*. Honolulu: University of Hawaii Press.

Shimunek, Andrew. 2017. *Languages of Ancient Southern Mongolia and North China: A Historical-Comparative Study of the Serbi or Xianbei Branch of the Serbi-Mongolic Language Family, with an Analysis of Northeastern Frontier Chinese and Old Tibetan Phonology*. Tunguso-Sibirica 40. Wiesbaden: Harrassowitz.

———. 2021. "Loanwords from the Puyo-Koguryoic Languages of Early Korea and Manchuria in Jurchen-Manchu." *Altai Hakpo* 31: 65–84.

Sims-Williams, Nicholas. 2001. "The Sogdian Ancient Letter II." In *Philologica et Linguistica: Historia, pluralitas, universitas: Festschrift für Helmut Humbach zum 80. Geburtstag am 4. Dezember 2001*, edited by Maria Gabriela Schmidt and Walter Bisang, 267–80. Trier: Wissenschaftlicher Verlag Trier.

Takata Tokio 高田時雄. 1988. *Tonkō Shiryō ni yoru Chūgoku goshi no Kenkyū* 敦煌資料による中国語史の研究. [A Historical Study of the Chinese Language Based on Dunhuang Materials.] Tokyo: Sobunsha.

———. 2000. "Multilingualism in Tun-huang." *Acta Asiatica, Bulletin of the Institute of Eastern Culture* 78: 49–70.

———. 2010. *Khumdan de duiyin Khumdan* 的對音 [The Transcription of *Khumdan*]. In *Chang Kuang-ta hsien-shen pa-shih hua-tan chu-shou lun-wen chi* 張廣達先生八十華誕祝壽論文集, edited by Chu Feng-yü 朱鳳玉 and Wang Chüan 汪娟, 965–73. Taipei: Hsin wen feng ch'u-pan kung-ssu.

Walter, Michael L. 2009. *Buddhism and Empire: The Political and Religious Culture of Early Tibet*. Leiden: Brill.

Walter, Michael L., and Christopher I. Beckwith. 2010. "The Dating and Interpretation of the Old Tibetan Inscriptions." *Central Asiatic Journal* 54.2: 291–319.

Zürcher, Erik. 2007 [1959]. *The Buddhist Conquest of China: The Spread and Adaptation of Buddhism in Early Medieval China*. Leiden: Brill.

Andrade's Mission to Tsaparang, Western Tibet, and the Mystery of the Aftermath

Hubert Decleer

THIS ESSAY is modeled after a van der Kuijp composition that explains: "Thus, in this essay, we have gathered in one place much that is by now fairly well known and uncontroversial, but also added some data that, to our knowledge, have not yet played a role in these various discussions."[1] In a similar vein, a substantial amount of my starting-off information is based on (and was originally conceived as a review article of) *"More Than the Promised Land": Letters and Relations of Tibet by the Jesuit Missionary António de Andrade (1580–1634)*.[2] "Data that have not yet played a role" constitute the mystery of the aftermath.

Change of Plan: From Delhi to the Western Himalayas, and the Kingdoms Beyond

> On March 30, 1624, . . . [we] departed from Agra to attend upon the king [Moghul emperor Jahangir]. . . We arrived at the city of Delhi just when a large number of [Hindu] pagans were departing from there on pilgrimage to [Badrināth,] a famous idol temple that was a month and a half's journey from Agra.
>
> We were already in possession of a great deal of information that convinced us there were Christian kingdoms in that region. . . . Seeing that I was in the company of people who would serve me as guides for the greater part of the way [up to Garhwal, close to the border with Western Tibet], and realizing that if I were to pass up this opportunity it might be a long time before a similar one presented itself, I made up my mind to go and acquaint myself with these countries.[3] . . . I had no doubt that such was Your Reverence's

1. He and van der Kuijp 2014, 300.

2. Sweet 2017.

3. The pilgrimage to Badrināth was and still is an annual affair, so it would not be "a long

will, . . . since the enterprise was demonstrably for the greater glory of God. . . .[4]

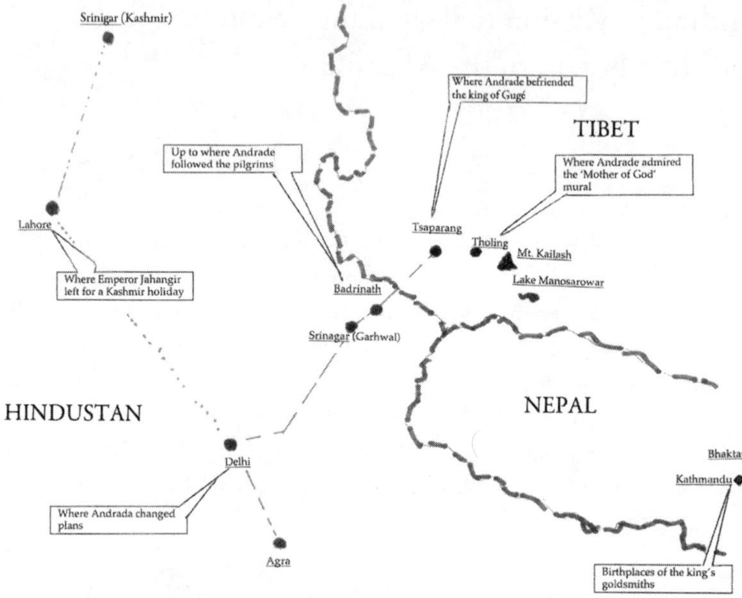

Map. Andrade's 1624 journey to Tsaparang.

Thus begins the Jesuit missionary Andrade's letter to his superiors. The emperor was about to set out for his summer vacation in the vale of Kashmir, mostly to be spent boating, hunting, and carousing, hence with no pressing need for Andrade's presence at the court for the by now customary Thursday evening religious debate sessions.[5]

---

time before a similar [opportunity] presented itself." But on an astrologically more auspicious year, as happens every twelve years, the number of participants used to increase up to fifty thousand, which makes one wonder whether 1624 was such a "twelfth year." If Andrade and his companion hoped to melt into the crowd more easily in their disguise as Armenian merchants, actually that would create *extra* suspicion when crossing the border into Tibet. Fine "merchants" indeed, who were not carrying any wares.

4. Sweet 2017, 62–63, 66.

5. A situation tellingly evoked by Payne 1997, xviii–xix: "It amused Jahangir to listen to disputes between his Mullahs and the Fathers, just as it amused him to watch a fencing match or a cock-fight. . . . He frequently joined in these disputes; and as he usually took the side of the Fathers, and made no effort to conceal his contempt for his own faith, new hopes began to be entertained for his conversion. These were strengthened by the fondness and rever-

Hopes for Christian conversion at the Moghul court, of either the emperor in person or his descendants, had been steadily fading.[6] But perhaps all was not lost. Fresh information about Christian kingdoms up north suddenly revived the possibility of tracing the heir of the elusive King-Priest Prester John, widely said to be "a linear descendant of the Magi"[7] and the author of a mysterious message—soon to appear in translation at courts all over Europe—originally addressed to the Byzantine emperor Manuel Komnenos (r. 1143–80) containing an offer to help stop fast-spreading Islam.

As is clear from the letter extract, Andrade pleads innocence: the idea of a Tibet expedition had never occurred to him, notwithstanding the evidence over the years to the contrary. Joining those travelers in a location close to the western Tibetan kingdom of Gugé happened on the spur of the moment. That left him no choice but to inform his superiors in Goa and Rome of the fait accompli. They at first reacted in a less-than-enthusiastic way: the Portuguese monk had made an "officially unauthorized" move.[8] Would he have the nerve to request funding for it? He would indeed—already in his first letter of 1624, where he pointed out that these lands were far more promising than some of the missions established in places like Madagascar ("San Lorenzo").

As they trace the history of the numerous searches for Prester John that had preceded Andrade's own attempt, Sweet and Zwilling, here and throughout their oeuvre, maintain a tight storyline that never drifts away from the subject matter at hand; yet at every step they also provide detailed annotations and extensive bibliographical references. They call *More Than the Promised Land* a prequel to their earlier magnum opus, *Mission to Tibet: The Extraordinary Eighteenth-Century Account of Father Ippolito Desideri, S. J.* In the course of

ence he displayed for pictures of Christ and the Virgin and the Christian saints, of which he possessed a large number. . . . Jahangir prized the sacred pictures which the Fathers gave him, not, as they imagined, out of veneration for the subjects represented, but because he had a passion for works of art and curios of all kinds." A refined connoisseur, in other words.

6. An extreme case is reported in Gascoigne 1987, 115: "During the next reign, in 1610, three of Akbar's grandsons were even publicly baptized as Christians amid great festivities and were handed over to the Jesuits to be educated. But the fathers' joy was tempered by the subsequent rumor that they had only entered the fold in the hope of acquiring some Christian ladies for the various royal harems, and three or four years later, as a Jesuit writer put it, the princes 'rejected the light and returned to their vomit.'"

7. Sweet 2017, 16.

8. One authority based in Goa, writing to his superior in Rome, is adamant that "Andrade should not have set out along such a distant route without an order of us," but then, to calm the waves, goes on to cite a sympathizer: "Maybe Father Andrade had some revelation from God about this journey" (Sweet 2017, 66n259).

this tremendous research adventure, they left no stone unturned: their unerring command of the mass of data (extending in a hundred directions) is evident on every page. It is simply baffling how they managed to remain in control and withstood being overwhelmed by repeated avalanches of information.

It would be naive to take Jesuit Father Andrade's letters from the field at face value, which is why our scholars weigh the evidence statement by statement and wonder to what extent the author of the missive "really meant it" or had something else up his sleeve. But we cannot doubt his every word, and it would be presumptuous to believe that Andrade's sole motivation was to set up smokescreens. His reports are addressed to the inner circle of the society, so they are likely to be sincere at least much of the time.

Thus we get a grand display of all the available data, annotated by scholars expert in both late-Renaissance Christianity and borderland-Himalayan Buddhism. Already in the choice of their reference works, they offer cogent arguments as to what really happened, and according to what primary and what secondary factors. Even so, *More Than the Promised Land* leaves it to the reader to decipher the finer points of the "plot" (Paul Veyne's *l'intrigue*) and come up with their own interpretation of what, in the end, turned into a total fiasco.

And although the authors inscribe their work within a history of Christian-Buddhist dialogue, I strongly disagree with Richard Sherbourne's earlier appraisal describing the entire Andrade and Desideri episode as Christian missionaries' first attempts at "appreciation of the truth and goodness [t]he[y] perceived in Buddhism."[9] Not only did these missionaries not come anywhere close to "modern levels of sympathetic dialog and ecumenism," but plain God-on-our-side arrogance was the prevalent attitude.

A Portuguese Destiny

> [It was] the widespread hope and belief among many Portuguese of Andrade's time and later . . . that the world would soon be united under the spiritual sway of the pope and the temporal rule of a messianic Portuguese sovereign.[10]

The fascinating chapter on Prester John, alluded to above, is followed by another relevant chapter, "The Tibet Mission and Portuguese Nationalism," which features *The Lusiads*, Portugal's national epic. I have always wondered

9. Sherbourne 1989, 305.

10. Sweet 2017, 61n243.

how anyone today could read *The Lusiads* with a straight face. My previous attempts at perusing it always got stranded before reaching the end of canto I, with nine more cantos to go:

> Vasco de Gama and his men were already sailing across the restless ocean. The winds blew softly, filling their sails. . . . The waters were flecked with their foam.
>
> Up on Olympus . . . Jupiter had sent his summons out by Mercury. . . . And now Jupiter spoke, in a grave and awesome voice:
>
> "Eternal dwellers in the starry heavens, you will not have forgotten the great valor of that great people the Portuguese. You cannot therefore be unaware that it is *the fixed resolve of destiny* that before their achievements those of Assyrians, Persians, Greeks and Romans shall fade into oblivion. . . . Fate has promised them—and its decrees are irrevocable—that they shall for long be supreme on this ocean. . . ."[11]

This time around, it was clear to me that familiarity with *The Lusiads* would provide the indispensable presupposed knowledge for understanding the appeal, to a Portuguese Jesuit like Andrade, of a place like Tsaparang, with—judging by the descriptions of Muslim traders—its idiosyncratic form of Christianity that appeared to have survived in isolation.[12] I now read *The Lusiads* in one go, with the result that even the Baroque pomp of Rome-based Dutch artists like Cornelis Bloemaert (1603–92) fall into place. Witness his portrait in heaven of St. Ignatius of Loyola, the frontispiece of the *Mission to Tibet* volume. The call of the unknown must have been irresistible. As Sweet and Zwilling succinctly put it:

> The potential for profit, *both in souls and commerce*, seemed large. Based on these twin motives, recalling the "search for Christians and spices" which was famously given as the motive for the [earlier] Portuguese explorations, Andrade could have been reasonably con-

11. Camões 1985, 42–43.

12. "The similarities between Tibetan Buddhism and Catholic ritual and religious organization, later remarked upon by so many European visitors, likely convinced the Muslim traders . . . that they were seeing some exotic variation of Christianity" (Sweet 2017, 30). Those traders, in other words, were *not* making things up so that Andrade and friends would hear what they wanted to hear.

> fident that his seemingly impulsive initial trip to Gugé would meet the warm approval of his religious superiors and the viceroy of Goa.[13]

. . . at least in the long run, when the first harvest of souls would come rolling in, followed (who knows?) by a reopening of the overland caravan route to the farther eastern kingdoms, all the way to Cathay.

Reading Padre Andrade's accounts from the field (*relatio*)—the chief subject matter of *More Than the Promised Land*, in finely nuanced translation—one can't help admiring the missionary's courage and determination, whether in negotiating the passes when they're still piled high with snow, dealing with stubborn, greedy border officials, or crossing those dizzying rope bridges above wild mountain rivers.[14]

At this stage, the foreign missionary still believes he is dealing with adherents to a form of Christianity that has gone slightly astray but can be brought back to the fold. Which explains why he isn't entirely surprised by the Tibetan king and queen's eagerness to make a public display of their devotion to the sacred Christian imagery and relics he shows them.

In the course of this twenty-five-day recon, Andrade, for his part, "recognizes" a local image of the "Mother of God," possibly the magnificent White Tārā on a book's cover, although the more likely image identified by him as "a woman seated with her hands raised" (Sweet 2017, 93) is the goddess Prajñāpāramitā. See the famous Tholing (Mtho lding) mural in plate 1.[15]

The Kingdom of Gugé's Precarious Position

Experts agree: the mural paintings at many a site in the Gugé kingdom—at least those not completely vandalized by anti-culture revolutionary zealots—*are* exquisite, among Tibet's finest. Caravans between China and Ladakh would go out of their way to include Tsaparang on their itineraries, for the Gugé kingdom's purchasing power seemed infinite. Full-time employment for four goldsmiths would not have come cheaply either.[16]

13. Sweet 2017, 23.

14. See the well-known mid-twentieth-century photograph by the Swiss geologist Toni Hagen of "the reed bridge over the raging Arun River at Num," https://archive.nepalitimes.com/news.php?id=19173 (consulted August 27, 2019).

15. Reproduced in Rhie and Thurman 1991, 57, fig. 23. This is the four-armed form. Seen from a distance, these outer hands could strike one as those of a Byzantine "Madonna Orante," and Andrade may well have missed the first pair of hands, held close to the body.

16. See Decleer 2019.

In the latter part of his 1624 letter, Andrade was more explicitly descriptive: "However the royal city where we are, which is also the most important in the region, has the most barren land I have ever seen. . . . The Kashmiri Muslims are wont to say that hell lies underneath this region, because of its great barrenness."[17] So how could this rocky desert kingdom, where even the most basic foodstuffs had to be imported, afford all those luxuries? The answer no doubt lies in the wealth generated by its gold mines. Petech casually mentions them, and cites Wessels as his source.[18] The latter has "mines" (*minas*), with the note, "What mines are not specified." Yet Petech was right: western Tibet gold was renowned as the most brilliant of all, simply beyond compare. This is still evident in the Guhyasamāja maṇḍala mural in the Golden Temple (Gser khang) at Tholing, Gugé's religious capital, and on several wall paintings of Dungkar and Piyang (reproduced in Pritzker 1996). When in the early eleventh century the unnamed Qarluq Turco-Mongol king is willing to exchange his prisoner King Yeshé Ö, he asks for the prisoner's weight in gold; the latter had himself been collecting gold for a ceremonial gift to be presented to Jowo Atisha (982–1054), along with an invitation to come to Tibet. And from where? "The regions bordering on Nepal,"[19] which here almost certainly refer to Tsaparang, the capital of Gugé. The Qarluq king knew about the local source of wealth, and from what happened next, it is plain that nearly *every* ruler, in the region and beyond, had their eye on this medieval Himalayan El Dorado.

In the next section of this report from 1624, we learn what occurred soon after Andrade's departure: there was an uprising involving three unnamed "vassal states" and the king of Garhwal took advantage of Tsaparang's vulnerability to invade:

> A little while after we had left his country, great troubles befell the king. Three rajas that were his vassals had joined together and rebelled against him with large forces, compelling the king to call up his troops to deal with this threat, [troops] located many days journey from the city. The raja of Shrinagar (in Garhwal)[20] also suddenly moved to make war against the king, and it appeared he was in league with the three vassals. . . .

17. Sweet 2017, 91–92.

18. Petech 1977, 42; Wessels 1992, 76.

19. Decleer 1997, 164.

20. Not to be confused with the capital of Kashmir with the same name Shrinagara, the town being dedicated to the Wealth Goddess Shri, the Resplendent.

> The main military force [of Garhwal] first reached a certain Tibetan fortress in which there were only thirty soldiers who decided on the first night to attack the enemy army. They killed almost three hundred men and got as far as the tent of the commander whom they sought, capturing the royal insignia. . . . The [Garhwal] enemy army was completely overcome by terror; in fact, the Tibetan soldiers are quite courageous and well-trained in arms, while those from Shrinagar are mountain-dwellers familiar only with farm work. . . . It pleased God that peace was made with Shrinagar and that the other three rajas were defeated and subjugated.[21]

Just previous to this, Andrade had been distributing crosses to nine members of Tsaparang's royal family as protection amulets—including to the king's brother-in-law, "who was leaving that afternoon as general in a very perilous war . . . [and] was quite sure that through it our Lord would deliver him and his soldiers from the dangers of war, *which he did in fact do, granting the general a very easy victory with honor*."[22] We start to see the king's relationship with the Jesuit fathers in a different light. The impression created is that he perceives them first and foremost as holders of a stronger, more trustworthy magic, to be directed against his enemies. All the more since one lama's divination had proved way off the mark:

> On one occasion the king desired to know what had happened to the army he had sent on a certain expedition, and he sent for a lama who is widely esteemed here for being a learned and virtuous man. . . . The lama made his calculations and concluded from them that the army had defeated their adversary that very day and were already returning with much booty from the war. . . . In a few days, accurate news arrived about what had [really] happened on the battlefield, and it turned out the army had never engaged with the enemy, but rather had been avoiding them, as they were much inferior in strength. This news greatly saddened the king, who proceeded to say myriad bad things about the lamas.[23]

21. Sweet 2017, 89–91.

22. Sweet 2017, 89.

23. Sweet 2017, 116. What the Jesuit father here calls "divination" refers in fact to an application of clairvoyance. As explained by Lama Shabkar (1781–1851): "If you just practice calm abiding alone, you will achieve all its qualities, which include clairvoyance and so on." Moreover, "the merit gained in a single day by one with such clairvoyance / Even in a hun-

At this point one thought has been rolling round in my mind. It is possibly a far-fetched one, since it draws information from two sources unmentioned in Sweet and Zwilling's exhaustive bibliography. The first one has no business in any Andrade context, since it deals with eighteenth-century Jesuit involvement in military operations and *materiel* in the service of the Chinese emperor—the "Jesuit cannons" of the title.[24] I only refer to it as a "post-cedent" to secret negotiations that must have occurred in the late 1620s in order to carry out a major operation, which failure to mention I view as *the* black hole in Andrade's *Letters*. The second source is a long note in Michael Aris's *Bhutan*, in which "a group of Portuguese soldiers of fortune (*fidalgos*) of whom no trace remains in western records" suddenly turn up

> with offerings that included muskets, the magical device of cannons (*me'i sgyogs kyi 'khrul 'khor*), gunpowder, . . . also an eye-glass which caused one to see even minute objects at a distance as if they were in front. [Addressing the Zhabdrung Ngawang Namgyel (1594–ca. 1651)] they declared: "Lama, if you have enemies that harass you, we can summon a large army from the country of our king."[25]

Aris—imagining this might have something to do with the earlier visit of that other Jesuit, Estévão Cacella (1585–1630), who intended to bestow gifts of this nature to the ruler of what would become Bhutan—wonders: "The problem largely hinges on the Portuguese gift of guns, which finds no mention in Cacella. Could Cacella have omitted them from his report as being a subject too delicate for the ears of his Provincial?"[26] Yet from the way the freebooters address the Zhabdrung, it seems clear that this is an impromptu offer. The most likely alternative hypothesis would then be that this information was missing from someone else's report—Andrade's—and that the gifts listed were meant for the king of Tsaparang but came too late. Those *fidalgos* arrived in 1634, by which time Gugé had ceased to exist as an independent kingdom.[27]

dred lifetimes cannot be obtained by one without" (Price 2018, 107). Application of clairvoyance for worldly matters—that is, divination proper—is fine for highly realized beings, but practiced by the nonqualified, it easily leads to an obsession with personal power and overconfidence, not to mention blunders such as the one here exposed.

24. Martin 1990.

25. Aris 1980, 289–90n14.

26. Aris 1980, 289–90n14.

27. By 1630 Gugé was no longer an independent kingdom. Someone in extremis must have "redirected" the gifts, which the Zhabdrung politely refused as highly unethical (as contrary

In Memoriam: Tsaparang

It would be such a joy to put ourselves in the shoes of each protagonist and, on the basis of their acts and the snatches of conversation reported by Andrade and others, try to figure out their character and motivation as they faced various dilemmas, and identify among them the bright and the genuine, the *simpatico*, the lost soul, the naïve, the nasty, the unsavory, and the utterly untrustworthy too—taking our inspiration from the way these royals and courtiers are depicted in the masterly panel in Tholing's Red Hall (plate 2).[28] To give one case of character and motivation in action:

> One of the fathers learned to read [= *recite aloud, at a reasonable speed*] their book[s] in the space of five or six days in a manner that astonished them. The king and others asserted many times that their own lamas had not achieved as much despite years of diligent study, and that to learn so much in so short a time was impossible without a great favor from God.[29]

Who, here, is the naïve one? At first sight "the king and others" come across as the simpletons who can't distinguish reading comprehension from parrot-fashion recitation, with only the odd word ringing a bell. But when they go

to "the sacred path of the warrior," one could say), well aware, also, that a barbarian (*kla klo*) army, once invited, sometimes forgets to go back.

28. Dawa Tsering, et al. 2000, 296–97, plate 178, alas, without their individual name tags that elsewhere (Tabo Monastery foremost) are a common feature with donor portraits. Cf. Klimburg-Salter et al. 1997, 25, fig. 2: "*Lha bla ma Ye shes 'od* with his son Deva-rāja"; fig. 3: "Four monks identified by captions"; 87, fig. 50: "The nobleman *'Jig rten mgon*"; and many more. Could it be the case that the main figures were originally identified by name and that their names were at one stage willfully erased? My suspicion is raised by the empty space below the group portrait, with the sole detectable caption (Dawa Tsering 2000, plate 178): *Sbyin bdag rnams min*, "They ain't donors [any more]"—which indeed looks like a graffito added after the king had largely withdrawn state sponsorship from monastic institutions. The *Precious Deposits* authors do not appear to have noticed this inscription, for they tell us the exact opposite in their caption of the photograph: the three main figures *are* the donors, with their attendants and family standing behind them. It also strikes me that on the well-preserved "Gugé Royal Lineage" mural in the same Red Hall, the captions with the names of the early rulers, going back to the times of the empire, are all neatly filled in (*de'i sras khri lde srong btsan la na mo | glang dar ma'i sras 'od srung la na mo |* etc.) but become empty (blacked out?) cartouches starting with the enthroned current king, his "stand in," and their immediate heir.

29. Sweet 2017, 165.

on to insist that local monks are unable to achieve so much even after "years of diligent study," this is pokerfaced Tibetan humor. Only someone grandiosely naïve could take them at their word. From *their* side, if (as I suspect) it is a question of the very survival of the kingdom and its dynasty—a dynasty that is hoping to receive advanced weaponry, along with foreign legion types who will train their men in its use—then no wonder that everyone at court is more than willing to join in the chorus of praise for the Portuguese wunderkind!

Sweet and Zwilling's own approach to this, and to related issues—the Tibetans, especially the monks, invariably being "confused and overwhelmed by Andrade's logic," "dumb struck," and "looking at one another and not knowing what to reply"[30]—is to quote Joan-Pau Rubiès:

> The Jesuits embraced the dialogue [with other religions] as an apologetic genre, and this led them to write many works that successfully fictionalized the raw materials of their dialogic experience and transformed them into literary victories.[31]

Yet I do not find that sort of sophistication reflected in Andrade's diary notes; my overall feeling is that he really believed the impact of his words as described above. But there's more. What happens next is already handily summarized in a note to the authors' *Mission* opus:

> The Buddhist monks from Tsaparang, led by the king's brother, were threatened by the royal family's growing involvement with the Christian missionaries and various measures that the king had taken against them. They[32] turned to the king of Ladakh, who had designs against the region, and offered him the crown; Gugé fell to the invaders, and the king was treacherously taken prisoner, and he and his family led in chains to Leh. The Christians were made captives and slaves, and the church in Tsaparang was sacked.[33]

As Petech makes clear, in this version (1) of the event "treacherously" refers to the fact that the Ladakhi commander of the siege had originally agreed "to accept his submission, on the condition of keeping his kingdom as a tribu-

30. Sweet 2017, 39.

31. Sweet 2017, 37n142. From a 2012 essay that goes by the eloquent title "Real and Imaginary Dialogues in the Jesuit Mission of Sixteenth-Century Japan."

32. They and/or, in the words of Petech 1977, 44, "some influential military commanders."

33. Sweet 2010, 690n558.

tary state"—that is, as a vassal of Ladakh[34]—and his family being granted free passage. Having broken his word immediately after the king's surrender, and sent him off "in chains to Leh," it is hard to believe the Ladakhi ruler Senggé Namgyel's subsequent change of heart, as described in another contemporary source, the sacred biography of the yogin Taktsang Repa Ngawang Gyatso (Stag 'tshang ras pa Ngag dbang rgya mtsho, 1574–1651).[35] Far from being led off in chains, as per "Ladakh's Dynastic History" (*La dwags rgyal rabs*), in this version (2) of the event its author paints a picture of lavish largesse and hospitality, "all sins forgiven." Gugé's king and family

> were sent to Ladakh with a suite of about twenty men and with all their belongings, and were granted a spacious and comfortable residence, where the king and his brother lived till the end of their life and were given state funerals. Later (1647) the prince of Gugé was given as wife a sister of the Ladakhi queen.[36]

Shortly before my own visit to Tsaparang, a discovery was made that may well provide the key to what *actually* happened—that is to say, there's yet another interpretation of the facts. With the melting of the snow, a cave opening had become visible in the mid-1990s. Inside were a dozen or more naturally preserved *headless* corpses, including a number of females (seen with our own eyes). The explanation (version 3), supposedly going back to an oral tradition, has it that upon riding out of the city gates, the

> king and his family were slaughtered [beheaded] immediately in view of the population. . . . The heads were then impaled upon spears, . . . forming a circle around the entire town.[37]

To me, this "tragic testimony" of the cave with the headless corpses sounds much more like the inevitable outcome of the siege of 1630.[38] The main objec-

34. Petech 1977, 44.

35. A famous nearly life-size statue of this "Cottonclad from Tiger's Den" exists in Hemis Gompa in Ladakh, where he is depicted as a mullah, wearing the turban in which he hid his Tibetan texts and an artificial beard, in Fabry and Shahid 1995, 57 (pages not numbered).

36. Petech 1977, 45.

37. Gyurme Dorje 1999, 361.

38. For what it's worth, this version of events is, surprisingly, also the one accepted in the coffee-table book by Dawa Tsering et al. 2000, 8, plate 1, which provides no source for the unexpected assertion: "In the mid-fifteenth [should be mid-seventeenth] century the Ladakh king captured the Gugé Palace and *killed the King Jo-bo bdag-po* leading to the col-

tion would be an eyewitness account. A fellow Jesuit priest, Francisco de Azevedo (1578–1660), allegedly saw, from afar, the imprisoned former king and crown prince in the capital of Leh:

> He tried all possible means to speak to the poor captive king and the prince, but this was impossible due to the many guards and watches that had been placed over them. He only saw the good king from a window, when he and the prince were on their way to obey a summons from the tyrant. When they passed by the door of the house in which the father was staying, the king saw him and displayed a joyous expression, and the prince did the same, showing strong emotion.[39]

It could have been another father and son, made to impersonate the unfortunate king and prince. "Version 2" finds confirmation in the same Andrade letter of 1633, where Azevedo is quoted as saying that "the tyrant [the Ladakhi king] treated them very basely, giving them no more than the bare minimum to eat. The poor queen is suffering even more tribulations, because she was given to the tyrant's brother as a captive."[40] It is not hard to imagine the victorious king humiliating the distraught queen in front of her husband and son and letting his brother treat her as a slave. Any grain of truth in here undermines the likelihood of version 1, whose author would be eager to show that everyone was living "happily ever after," since it was Taktsang Repa who led the negotiations between the kings of Ladakh and Gugé and arranged the deal.

But then in a discreet note, Sweet and Zwilling point out that no such information is to be found in Azevedo's own written report.[41] Was it just hearsay? Did Andrade make it up?

Even after the Gugé king, no doubt on Andrade's advice,[42] decided on a grand cleanup of the monastic institutions and went on to deny state sponsorship to all those who neither studied nor practiced, or else led less than exemplary lives (some 70 percent!), then went on to bestow unending privilege,

lapse of the Gugé kingdom." "Jowo Dakpo" (see Petech 1977, 44) is indeed King Tri Tashi Drakpa's standard honorific title, as referred to in the sacred biography of Taktsang Repa.

39. Sweet 2017, 172.

40. Sweet 2017, 172.

41. Sweet 2017, 172n644.

42. The main argument being that, upon his return to Goa, Andrade embarked on a sort of cleaning-of-the-Augean-stables campaign in his own camp. His strictness resulted in a silent mutiny among the student population at the seminary, some of whom killed him by poisoning (Sweet 2016).

largesse, and adoration to the Jesuit fathers, my own main question remains: *What led the Gugé monastics and army leaders to the extreme move of making overtures to, of all people, the king of Ladakh?*

As Dzongsar Khyentse Rinpoché once said regarding the early Dharma-king rulers of Tibet: guaranteeing the continuity of the Dharma transmission stood "most high in their agenda, possibly 99 percent." And the twentieth-century Tibetan resistance movements, too, blazed that resolve on their banners. It follows that an outright rejection of that transmission was the highest of high treasons, compared to which inviting a foreign invading force from a neighboring Buddhist nation would be a minor evil. Seen from that perspective, it all falls into place.

Postscript: "It is not Christian to proselytize" (Pope Francis, September 25, 2019, this morning on the news).

References

Aris, Michael. 1980. *Bhutan: The Early History of a Himalayan Kingdom*. Ghaziabad: Vikas Publishing.

Camões (Camoens), Luís Vaz de. 1985 [1952]. *The Lusiads*. Translated by William C. Atkinson. Hammondsworth: Penguin Books.

Dawa Tsering [Zla-ba-tshe-ring], et al. 2000. *Precious Deposits—Historical Relics of Tibet, China*, vol. 2, *The Period of Separatist Regimes*. Translated by Xiang Hongjia. Photographed by Yan Zhongyi, et al. Beijing: Morning Glory Publishers; Chicago: Art Media Resources.

Decleer, Hubert. 1997. "Atiśa's Journey to Tibet." In *Religions of Tibet in Practice*, edited by Donald S. Lopez, Jr., 157–77. Princeton: Princeton University Press.

———. 2019. "Which Christian Festivals Were Taking Place in Which Two Himalayan Kingdoms? The Testimony of the Goldsmiths at the Court of Tsaparang, According to Andrade (1626)." Unpublished manuscript.

Fabry, Philippe, and Yousuf Shahid. 1995. *Wandering with the Indus*. Rawalpindi: Ferozsons Publications.

Gascoigne, Bamber. 1987 [1971]. *The Great Moghuls*. Photographs by Christina Gascoigne. New Delhi: Time Books International.

Gyurme Dorje. 1999. *Tibet Handbook (with Bhutan)*. Bath: Footprint Handbooks.

He Huanhuan, and Leonard van der Kuijp. 2014. "Further Notes on Bhāviveka's Principal Oeuvre." *Indo-Iranian Journal* 57: 299–354.

Klimburg-Salter, Deborah E., et al. 1997. *Tabo: A Lamp for the Kingdom: Early Indo-Tibetan Buddhist Art in the Western Himalaya.* Milan: Skira Editore.

Martin, Dan. 1990. "Bönpo Canons and Jesuit Cannons: On Sectarian Factors Involved in the Ch'ien-lung Emperor's Second Goldstream Expedition of 1771–1776, Based Primarily on Tibetan Sources." *The Tibet Journal* 15.2: 3–28.

Payne, C. H., trans. 1997 [1930]. *Jehangir and the Jesuits: With an Account of the Travels of Benedict Goes and the Mission to Pegu, from the Relations of Father Fernão Guerreiro, S. J.* New Delhi: Munshiram Manoharlal.

Petech, Luciano. 1977. *The Kingdom of Ladakh, c. 950–1842 A.D.* Rome: Istituto Italiano per il Medio ed Estremo Oriente.

Price, Sean, trans. 2018. *The Emanated Scripture of Manjushri: Shabkar Tsogdruk Rangdröl's Essential Meditation Instructions.* Boulder, CO: Snow Lion Publications.

Pritzker, Thomas J. 1996. "A Preliminary Report on Early Cave Paintings of Western Tibet." *Orientations* 27.6: 26–47.

Rhie, Marylin, and Robert A. F. Thurman. 1991. *Wisdom and Compassion: The Sacred Art of Tibet.* London: Thames and Hudson.

Sherbourne, Richard. 1989. "A Christian-Buddhist Dialog? Some Notes on Desideri's Tibetan Manuscripts." In *Reflections on Tibetan Culture: Essays in Memory of Turrell V. Wylie*, edited by Lawrence Epstein and Richard Sherbourne, 295–305. Lewiston, NY: The Edwin Mellen Press.

Sweet, Michael J., trans. 2010. *Mission to Tibet: The Extraordinary Eighteenth-Century Account of Father Ippolito Desideri, S. J.* Edited by Leonard Zwilling. Boston: Wisdom Publications.

———. 2016. "Murder in the Refectory: The Death of Fr. António de Andrade, S. J." *Catholic Historical Review* 102.1: 26–45.

———. 2017. *"More Than the Promised Land": Letters and Relations of Tibet by the Jesuit Missionary António de Andrade (1580–1634).* Boston: Institute for Advanced Jesuit Studies, Boston College.

Veyne, Paul. 1971. *Comment on écrit l'histoire.* Paris: Seuil.

Wessels, C., S. J. 1992 [1924]. *Early Jesuit Travels in Central Asia, 1603–1721.* New Delhi: Asian Educational Services.

The Fourth Khamtrül Tendzin Chökyi Nyima (1730–79) and Excerpts from His Diaries

Franz-Karl Ehrhard

This is for Leonard, for many years of friendship since the early days of the 1970s at Hamburg University when we were among the small gang of students of Geshé Gendün Lodrö (Dge bshes Dge 'dun blo gros, 1924–79).

Introduction

KHAMGAR GÖN (Khams sgar dgon), also known as Püntsok Chökhor Ling (Phun tshogs chos 'khor gling), in eastern Tibet is known as the most important Drukpa Kagyüpa ('Brug pa bka' brgyud pa) monastery in the region. It was closely associated with the incarnation lineage of the First Khamtrül Karma Tenpel (Khams sprul Karma bstan 'phel, 1598–1638), who was an important disciple of Ngawang Zangpo (Ngag dbang bzang po, 1546–1615), the First Dechen Chökhor Yongdzin (Bde chen chos 'khor yongs 'dzin), whose incarnation lineage had its seat in the monastery of Dechen Chökhor in Central Tibet. The original foundation of the monastery in Kham was laid by the Third Khamtrül Künga Tendzin (Khams sprul Kun dga' bstan 'dzin, 1680–1729), and this was followed by ambitious building projects, especially under the Fourth Khamtrül Tendzin Chökyi Nyima (Khams sprul Bstan 'dzin chos kyi nyi ma, 1730–79). These began in 1745 and included the establishment of the meditation and teaching convents Sangchen Tongdröl Ling (Gsang chen mthong grol gling) and Tsennyi Dratsang Namgyel Chökhor Ling (Mtshan nyid grwa tshang Rnam rgyal chos 'khor gling).[1]

The Fourth Khamtrül counted among his teachers the Eighth Situ Chökyi Jungné (Si tu Chos kyi 'byung gnas, 1700–74), the Seventh Drukchen Kagyü

1. Concerning Khamgar Gön as the head monastery of the Drukpa Kagyüpas in eastern Tibet and for a description of its teaching convents, see Gruschke 2004, vol. 1, 59–61. See Akester 2016, 260–62, on Dechen Chökhor, located in Gongkar (Gong dkar) near Lhasa and its founding by the Second Dechen Yongdzin Ngawang Lhündrup (Bde chen yongs 'dzin Ngag dbang lhun grub, 1616–75).

Trinlé Shingta ('Brug chen Bka' brgyud 'phrin las shing rta, 1718–67), the Fourth Chögön Jamgön Gyepé Wangchuk (Chos mgon 'Jam mgon dgyes pa'i dbang phyug, 1705–61), and the Fourth Dechen Chökhor Yongdzin Jampel Pawo (Bde chen chos 'khor yongs 'dzin 'Jam dpal dpa' bo, 1720–80). He is famous for his exhaustive work on Daṇḍin's *Kāvyādarśa*, which offers ample proof of his interest in Sanskrit aesthetic theories, an interest acquired during his studies under Situ Paṇchen. As is well known, the latter was very productive in the area of Sanskrit studies, having translated the *Kāmadhenu* almost in its entirety, the Sanskrit-Tibetan text of the *Amarakośa*, and other works. He paid two visits to the Nepal Valley in the years 1723/24 and 1748, and in the course of them acquired Sanskrit manuscripts, including the *Svayaṃbhūpurāṇa*, a translation of which he made during the second sojourn. Tendzin Chökyi Nyima followed in the footsteps of his teacher and visited Nepal a few years later, in 1756, where he composed a pilgrimage guidebook to the sacred Buddhist sites of the valley.[2]

The sojourn of Tendzin Chökyi Nyima in Nepal was part of a longer journey from Kham to Central Tibet and pilgrimages to southwestern Tibet during the years 1755–57. This follows from an account of the life of Tendzin Chökyi Nyima, written by the latter's successor, the Fifth Khamtrül Drupgyü Nyima (Khams sprul Sgrub brgyud nyi ma, 1781–1847):

> From [the age of] twenty-six, a wood-pig year [= 1755], up to [the age of] twenty-eight, a fire-ox year [= 1757], he traveled to the foremost sacred sites: Gang Tisé, Mapam Lake, the two stūpas of Nepal [i.e., Svayaṃbhū and Bodhnāth], the Wati [Zangpo] of Kyirong, and most of the sites of Milarepa's spiritual realization, including the six well-known outer fortresses, the six unknown inner fortresses and the six secret fortresses—eighteen [sites in total]—the two further fortresses—twenty [sites in total]—the four well-known large caves, and the four [caves] that are not well known.

2. See van der Kuijp 1982, 71n10, on the Fourth Khamtrül's commentary of Daṇḍin's *Kāvyādarśa*, apparently first written when he was just twenty-five years old until it was completed in 1770. Consult van der Kuijp 1986, 31–32, and 1996, 396, for six or seven phases of philological scholarship of the *Kāvyādarśa* in Tibet, the last one being marked by Situ Paṇchen and his disciple. The dates of the *Kāmadhenu* and *Amarakośa*—finalized in the years 1757 and 1764, respectively—are given in van der Kuijp 2009, 47–49. The visits of Situ Paṇchen to Nepal, his search for Sanskrit manuscripts, and the translation of the *Svayaṃbhūpurāṇa* in the year 1748 are treated in Verhagen 2013, 322–28. For an edition and translation of the pilgrimage guide to the Nepal Valley, see Macdonald 1975, 89–122; and Macdonald and Dvags-po Rin-po-che 1981, 238–73.

He spread extensively in a hundred directions the doctrine of the Jina in general and the uncorrupted glorious doctrine of the Drukpa [Kagyüpas] in particular and created a retinue [that formed] a connection with all living beings. The magnificence of his sublime virtue produced a rumor that the sound of the words of [his] aspirational prayers for the final attainment of virtue would grant wishes immediately [to those who heard them]. He was able to perform anything in the way of external appearances, such as letting the lotuses [that were] his hands and feet sink into stone. From this period [of his life] onward he was a great lord of yogins who dissolved objects, appearances, and mind into one.

Many men and spirits of these regions, and in particular the great and minor kings of Nepal, bowed down [before him] with respect. The acts through which he guided them on the excellent path of the highest maturation and liberation cannot be expressed in words. After he had completed his journey to all the great sacred sites of the western region [of Tibet,] he went on pilgrimage to the Üru [district] of Central Tibet, and when he had reached his twenty-ninth year [i.e., 1758] he went on to encounter the Upachandoha Mahāpīṭha Himālaya together with the [site called] "New Yongdzö" [in Tsāri].[3]

3. Sgrub brgyud nyi ma 1985, 328.4–29.5: *dgung lo nyer drug shing phag lo nas nyer brgyad me glang yan du / gnas mchog gangs ti se / mtsho ma pham bal yul mchod rten rnam gnyis / skyid grong wa ti sogs dang / yongs su grags pa phyi'i rdzong drug dang ma grags pa nang gi rdzong drug / gsang ba'i rdzong drug dang bco brgyad / yang rdzong gnyis dang nyi shu / yongs grags gi phug chen bzhi / ma grags pa'i bzhi sogs / rje btsun mi la ras pa'i sgrub gnas de dag phal cher zhabs kyis bcag / rgyal bstan spyi dang / khyad par dpal ldan 'brug bstan nyams med phyogs brgyar rab tu rgyas pa dang / 'gro ba kun dang 'brel thog [= thogs] ltos byed la / 'di yi dge legs mchog gi dpal yon nyer thob tu smon pa'i gsung dbyangs re 'bras myur ster du grags pa mdzad / phyag zhabs kyi padmo rdo ba la dim pa sogs phyi rol gyi snang ba la gang byas bya gtub pa / yul snang sems gsum gcig tu 'dres pa'i rnal 'byor gyi dbang phyug chen por 'di skabs nas gyur / yul phyogs de'i mi dang mi ma yin du ma dang / khyad par bal yul gyi rgyal po che phras gus par btud / de dag smin grol mchog gi lam bzang la dkri bar mdzad pa dag smos kyi [= kyis] mi lang / stod phyogs gnas chen kun zhabs kyi bcag grub nas / dbus ljongs sbus ri'i [= ru'i] zhabs skor la du phebs / dgung lo nyer dgu bzhes pa na / nye ba'i gnas chen / tshandho ha himalaya [= chandoha himālaya] / gsar ma yang [= yongs] mdzod dang bcas pa mjal du byon/*. According to the Fourth Drukchen Pema Karpo ('Brug chen Padma dkar po, 1527–92), Tsāri is considered to be the Upachandohapīṭha Himālaya if the mountain Dakpa Shelri (Dag pa shel ri) is taken as primary; see Huber 1990, 146–47. It is also claimed to be the Upapīlavapīṭha Devīkoṭa; see Chos kyi snang ba 1976, 4.1–5.7; and Huber 2008, 114–15.

The Diaries of Tendzin Chökyi Nyima

In addition to this hagiographical account, it is possible to consult the personal descriptions of the Fourth Khamtrül and look in more detail at this phase in his life and his travels. The text in question is a manuscript of 368 folios with the title *A Prose Exposition of My Own Situation: Self-Liberation into the Uncontrived Original State* (*Rang tshul lhug por smra pa ma bcos gnyug ma'i rang grol*). It provides year-to-year entries in chronological order over the whole life of the Fourth Khamtrül and can be compared to a similar work by Situ Paṇchen, the importance of which for the intellectual history of eighteenth-century Tibet has already been assessed. Although the former work, in contrast to the latter, never circulated as a xylograph, the two texts share the same two-section structure: an autobiography proper covering the early years, and a diary of the following period distilled from the entries into yearly packets. At the end of the diaries an editor wrote an account of the death and funeral ceremonies, together with a colophon listing the literary sources used; in the case of the Fourth Khamtrül, the editor can be identified as one Mipam Chömpel (Mi pham chos 'phel, eighteenth/nineteenth centuries), a close disciple of Tendzin Chökyi Nyima.[4]

Special mention is made in this section of the entire journey to Central Tibet, and that the yearly compendiums started at the departure and were regularly maintained up to the return trip to Kham:

> So, at the beginning of spring in the earth-snake year, called *śukla* [= 1749], when this noble one reached his twentieth year, he went to Jalung Monastery in Ling following an invitation to the site where [his] teacher Ngawang Jungné [17th/18th c.] had passed away, and when he had shown kindness in discussing the philosophical view [of other emptiness (*gzhan stong*)] in a conversation with the teacher Tamdrin, the noble precious one himself composed some 183 pages in small format [of a biography], [thereby] manifesting the [same] kindness [as] his actual [spoken] words.

4. See Smith 2001, 89–95, for the intellectual climate of Situ Paṇchen's age and the importance of his diaries. The editor was Belo Tsewang Künkhyap ('Be lo Tshe dbang kun khyab, eighteenth century), a disciple of Situ Paṇchen, who completed the work in the sixth Tibetan month of the year 1774 in the monastery of Pelpung; see Chos kyi 'byung gnas 1968, 740.2–41.5. The work of the Fourth Khamtrül is also available in a typeset version, based on the *umé* (*dbu med*) manuscript; I will quote these two versions as ed. A and ed. B (see references). For the name of the editor see Bstan 'dzin chos kyi nyi ma (n.d.), [ed. A:] fol. 369.3, and [ed. B:] 457.3.

But of everything that was left over by way of remaining topics [there exist] some scattered notes in a rough general notebook. At the beginning of his twenty-fifth year, and for [a period of] eight years [from that time] onward, when he broke encampment at [his monastery] Pün[tsok Chökhor] Ling on the eighth day of the fifth month of the wood-dog [year, 1754,] and left for Central Tibet, up to the tenth day of the tenth month of the iron-snake year called *vṛṣa* [1761], when he returned from the monastery De[chen] Chö[khor in Central Tibet] to the region of Kham, there exists a notebook of a diary kept with passion day by day.

And afterward, [for the time] up to when his excellency was absorbed into the dharmadhātu [i.e., passed away] on the tenth day of the third month of the earth-pig [year, 1779,] there exists a tattered notebook. When the noble father [i.e., the Thirteenth Karmapa Dündül Dorjé (Karma pa Bdud 'dul rdo rje, 1733–97)] and son [i.e., the Tenth Zhamarpa Chödrup Gyamtso (Zhwa dmar pa Chos grub rgya mtsho, 1742–92)] asked for clarification whether I would not provide some words summing up what was left over from among what he himself had composed—an account of himself in the form of a last teaching—the protector, the most precious Vajradhāra [i.e., the Fifth Chögön Tuchen Jampel Dorjé (Chos mgon Mthu chen 'jam dpal rdo rje, 1761–98)] spoke:

> The scattered papers and scrolls of a notebook [making up] the starting point for writing the remaining part of the biography of this precious one have not developed into a text, a collection of well-articulated words. To be sure, the noble precious one himself had sped along [composing] the first part of the sequence of [his] meaningful acts, condensed natural prose in flowing phrases, explained in uniform amounts [of text]—exquisite, well analyzed, dignified—without [self-] exaggeration or [self-]deprecation.
>
> And again, what is right for the father and the son, [taking as] a basis what [the master] had composed, with the corrected adjustments, [if necessary] for a while mediating between two possibilities, it should be written by you, the one who possesses the knowledge of having stayed close to the lotus feet of the noble one![5]

5. Bstan 'dzin chos kyi nyi ma (n.d.), [ed. A:] 367b/3–68a/5, and [ed. B:] 455.4–22: *de ltar*

In the following I will treat only that part of the edited diaries of Tendzin Chökyi Nyima that describes the journey to the Nepal Valley, and in particular the encounters with the kings, already highlighted in the hagiographical account above. Also, in the case of the first assessment of the diaries of Situ Paṇchen, the reception at the fortress in Gorkha by Pṛthvīnārāyaṇ Shah (1722–75) was singled out among the day-to-day happenings, as were his encounters with the Kathmandu kings Jagajjaya Malla (r. 1722–34) and Jayaprakāśa Malla (r. 1735–68). This is due to the fact that these records contain fascinating accounts of the contacts between the Tibetan scholar and the exponents of Sanskrit learning associated with the royal courts.[6]

---

rje de nyid dgung lo nyi shu'i thog tu slebs pa'i dkar po zhes pa sa sbrul lo'i sos thog bla ma ngag dbang 'byung gnas gshegs sar gdan drangs kyis byon nas gling bya lung dgon du phyag phebs nas bla ma rta mgrin dang lta ba'i skor la gsung 'phros 'dri bshad bka' drin gnang ba'i shog chung 'di yi brgya dang gya gsum yan rje rin po che nyid kyis ljags brtsams zhal gsung ma dngos bka' 'drin gnang nas / de 'phros 'phro lus su gyur 'dug pa 'on kyang rtsa ba'i zin tho rag [= rags] rim gyis phyag bris tho re ba 'ga' re dang dgung lo nyer lnga'i thog shing khyi zla ba lnga pa'i tshes brgyad la phun gling nas sgar btegs ste dbus su chibs bskyod pa nas brtsams bod du lo brgyad kyis khyu mchog zhes pa lcags sbrul lo'i zla ba bcu pa'i yar tshes la bde chos nas khams phyogs su chibs bskyod pa'i bar der phyag thor nyin ltar chags kyis zin tho 'dug pa dang / de nas sa phag zla ba gsum pa'i tshes bcur dgongs [= gong] sa chos dbyings su gzhol ba tshun gyis [= gyi] zin tho hral pa [= hrul po] zhig 'dug pa bka' chems su rang gi lo rgyus kho bos brtsams pa'i 'phros sdoms gsung rtsoms gnang min rje yab sras nas bab gzigs zhu zer ba gnang 'dug par / des na skyabs mgon rdo rje 'dzin pa rin po che mchog gi bka' las / rje rin po che'i rnam thar 'phros bri gzhi zin tho shog byang shog gril kha 'thor 'dug pa 'di rnams tshigs [= tshig] tshogs brjod legs bstan bcos su 'gyur ba ma byung kyang / mdzad pa don ldan rag [= rags] bsdus rnams rim bzhin khyon cig tu 'doms pa phul byung rab brtags gzengs bstod kyi sgro bskur ma yin pa'i stod cha rje nyid kyis lcags brtsoms [= brtsams] ma bcos lhug brjod gnang ba'i dkyus 'gro zhig slar rje yab sras gang rigs nas 'phri bsnan [= snon] bcos bsgyur [= 'gyur] gi lcags rtsoms gnang ba'i gzhi zhig re zhig bar gnas pa rje nyid kyi zhabs pad du bcar sdod kyis rgyus yod bcas khyod kyis bri dgos/. The teacher Tamdrin, whose actual name was Gyurmé Tenpel ('Gyur med bstan 'phel, seventeenth/eighteenth centuries), was a disciple of Rindzin Terdak Lingpa (Rig 'dzin Gter bdag gling pa, 1646–1714). He was responsible for the funeral ceremonies for the teacher Ngawang Jungné (Ngag dbang 'byung gnas); for these events, see Bstan 'dzin chos kyi nyi ma (n.d.), [ed. A:] 136b/1–39a/4, and [ed. B:] 171.8–74.14. The Fifth Chögön Tuchen (Chos mgon mthu chen), not the first one of his lineage, can also be identified as the Drukpa Kagyüpa teacher who accompanied the Tenth Zhamarpa on the latter's momentous pilgrimage to Nepal in 1784; see Ehrhard 2007, 119–20.

6. For the reception of Situ Paṇchen at the fortress of Gorkha and his encounters with the Kathmandu kings, see Smith 2001, 93–95. During the stay at Gorkha, which occurred during his return trip after the second visit to the Nepal Valley, he met Jayamaṅgala, a scholar from Benares; see Chos kyi 'byung gnas 1968, 270.1–4; and Verhagen 2013, 331–32. During the first visit to the Kathmandu court, Bachur-Ojā, alias Viṣṇumati, a Tirthutiya brahmin

The Descent from Mangyül Gungtang

The description of the Gang Tisé region that is dated in the hagiographical account to the year 1755 sets in on the second day of the eighth Tibetan month. On the twentieth day of the tenth month the Fourth Khamtrül continued his journey, heading this time to Ngari Dzongkar (Mnga' ris rdzong dkar), the capital of Mangyül Gungtang. Two days later he was able to meet the Seventh Drukchen, who was then residing at the Gawo Lhading (Dga' bo lha sdings) hermitage in Gungtang. After another three days he began a rather short stay in Dzongkar, where he called upon the local governor. On the twenty-eighth day of the month he, together with a group of fellow travelers, reached Orma ('Or ma), the first village on the descent to the south. By then a heavy snowfall had set in, and verses from the *Bsam pa lhun grub ma* were intoned to counter this obstacle, especially ones for the pacification of local deities when approaching a "hidden land" (*sbas yul*). Once the weather had cleared, the journey continued to Günda (Dgun mda'), and after further difficulties they arrived in Gro-thang. One of the "stewards" (*mgron gnyer*) of the Seventh Drukchen, Damchö (Dam chos) by name, had acted as guide and had suffered light frostbite of his feet. The third day of the twelfth Tibetan month was marked by the arrival at Jampa Trin, one of Tibet's twelve royal temples of the Yarlung dynasty. The Fourth Khamtrül stayed four days at the site and met further members of the Seventh Drukchen's entourage, special mention being made of his disciple Lori Trülku Künzik Chökyi Gyatso (Lo ri sprul sku Kun gzigs chos kyi rgya mtsho, eighteenth century). This group was engaged in preparing for a pending renovation of the Svayaṃbhū stūpa in Kathmandu set in motion by Kaḥtok Rindzin Tsewang Norbu (Kaḥ thog rig 'dzin Tshe dbang nor bu, 1698–1755) and followed up on by the Seventh Drukchen.[7]

who taught Situ Paṇchen Sanskrit, is mentioned, and during the second visit he had several meetings with the renowned Tirthutiya Brahmin Pradhumna/Pradyumna; see Chos kyi 'byung gnas 1968, 120.7–21.3, 125.2–4, and 269.3–5. Consult Verhagen 2013, 320–25, for these individuals, who brought along manuscripts, including grammatical and lexicographical works and the **Vāmanābhidhāna*.

7. Consult Bstan 'dzin chos kyi nyi ma (n.d., [ed. A:] 193a/6–98b/5, and [ed. B:] 141.19–48.2) for the description of the pilgrimage to the Gang Tisé region. The journey to Ngari Dzongkar and the initial descent to the south is contained in ibid., [ed. A:] 198b/5–200b/5, and [ed. B:] 248.2–50.15. The transport of the *yaṣṭi* had already started in 1754, but there were long delays before it arrived it Kathmandu; for these details, and the fact that it was the Gorkha king's responsibility to arrange for the transport within the area controlled by him, see von Rospatt 2001, 229.

The subsequent itinerary of the Fourth Khamtrül has been described elsewhere, where it is noted that the diaries identify the successive ethnic groups, including the Magars (*rma gar*), Nyishangpas (*gnyi shang pa*), and Newars (*bal po*), along the route further south. On the seventeenth day of the twelfth Tibetan month he arrived at Drezhing ('Bras zhing), the place name referring to the open rice paddies on the banks of the Trishuli River below Nuwakot. There Tendzin Chökyi Nyima rested for four days, during which time he met Pṛthvīnārayāṇ Śāha. Before the actual audience the diaries highlight the warfare between the kings of Gorkha and Kathmandu and the trouble caused to Tibetan traders and pilgrims by tax collectors and guards stationed on the Kathmandu border. The transport of the *yaṣṭi* for the renovation of Svayaṃbhū stūpa is mentioned again, along with a group from the entourage of the Seventh Drukchen who acted as donors for this project. The main person was another of the latter's stewards called Chödzin (Chos 'dzin), who found himself under constant surveillance by heavily armed soldiers. The military camp was guarded at night along an outer fence by regular watches. It was not possible to meet the ruler in the daytime, so that the actual encounter took place at night:

> Although there were two not very brightly shining torches, I could not see clearly the interior of the main room on either side. In its inner part, on a not very large throne, [were] the rulers [Pṛthvīnārayāṇ Śāha and Pratāp Siṃha (1751–77)], father [and] son, and after the others got up I took my place on a seat, a cushion of satin [placed] on a cushion stuffed with velvet, woolen cloth, and silk, in front of [and] to the right of the rulers and three or four [other] seated persons.
>
> With the help of the steward Chödzin as translator such questions were raised as: "From what places in Tibet have you come, and for what purpose?" I gave the corresponding answers. Then I conveyed my thanks for [their] service on behalf of the spiritual masters, father [and] son, and [to] the Mahācaitya, [including] the transport of the *yaṣṭi* and so forth. And I requested once more [on their behalf] that the final completion [of the renovation] should be viewed [by the rulers (i.e., father and son)], and also that I myself was in need of an official document allowing me to travel freely without being hindered by tax collectors during my travels in Nepal. The answer came back that this would [all] be done accordingly. Then I returned up to my encampment."[8]

8. The itinerary of the descent from Kyirong to the Nepal Valley according to the diaries of

Various gifts were received from the Gorkha ruler on the following day, and the journey resumed on the twenty-second of the month, once the travel pass with the seal of Pṛthvīnārāyaṇ Śāha had come through. One day later, the Fourth Khamtrül joined the vast group of people tasked with dragging the *yaṣṭi* from the Nuwakot area to the south, the number of Magars, Nyishangpas, and Newars employed being given as 1,500 individuals. They were led by *kāji* Kalu Pande, Pṛthvīnārayāṇ Śāha's right-hand man, and the above-mentioned steward Chödzin. The arrival of the *yaṣṭi* at its destination is not reported, but Tendzin Chökyi Nyima reached the Nepal Valley without incident and set his eyes on the Bodhnāth stūpa on the twenty-fifth day of the twelfth Tibetan month.[9]

It was thus in difficult times that the Fourth Khamtrül arrived in Kathmandu. Military clashes between the armies of the Gorkha and the Kathmandu kings are mentioned several times in the diaries. At the same time, Kathmandu and Patan were engaged in warfare of their own, as will be seen below.

The Sojourn in the Nepal Valley

During the five weeks that Tendzin Chökyi Nyima stayed in Kathmandu, Bhaktapur, and Patan, the base of his travels around the valley was Drepung ('Bras spungs) vihāra in present-day Kimdol in the vicinity of the Svayaṃbhū stūpa. A description of the valley—including the Buddhist and non-Buddhist

---

the Fourth Khamtrül is described in Quintman 2014, 89–90. For the translated passage, see Bstan 'dzin chos kyi nyi ma (n.d.), [ed. A:] fol. 201b/2–6, and [ed. B:] 251.16–252.2: *sgron me mdangs tshar [= 'tsher] mi gsal ba gnyis 'dug kyang rtsa khang nang phan tshun gsal bar ma mthong yang / sbugs su khri gdan yang [= yangs] cher med pa'i khong pa rgyal po pha bu gnyis / gzhan ldang nas sdod mkhan gsum bzhi dang / khong rgyal po'i g.yas mdun de nas nged sdod sar gos phrug spu ma'i sab [= bsabs] gdan khar gos chen gyi gdan kha ma zhig 'dug pa der bsdad / mgron gnyer chos 'dzin lo tshar brgyud / bod sa chas gang gang nas yin byon don ci yin tsam 'dri ba byed 'dug / de yi len zhus / de nas bla ma yab sras dang mchod rten chen po'i zhabs phyi srog shing 'dren pa sogs bka' drin che 'dug tshul dang / slar yang mthar grub gzigs pa gang dgos tshul dang / nged kyang bal por bsgrod bsgrod pa'i lam bar khral pa rnams nas gegs med nyer bsgrod chog pa'i bka' 'dzin yi ge gang dgos tshul zhus pa / de de bzhin yongs tshul len byung / de nas yar sgar du log song /*. In 1752 Gorkha forces under Pṛthvīnārāyan Śāha had begun campaigns to cut off the approaches to the Nepal Valley from the north and west, in part to disrupt the Newar trade with Tibet; see the more detailed reference in Huber 2008, 403n63.

9. For the final leg of the journey to the Nepal Valley, see Bstan 'dzin chos kyi nyi ma (n.d.), [ed. A:] fols. 201b/6–202a/5, and [ed. B:] 252.2–14. The *yaṣṭi* was finally erected according to the Newar sources at the end of May of the following year—i.e., 1757; see von Rospatt 2001, 231–33. This took place under dramatic circumstances, when the forces of the Gorkha king had set out yet again to conquer the valley from the west; during one of the military clashes, the famous *kāji* Kalu Pande was killed.

traditions of its inhabitants and the valley's own natural (fauna, flora, etc.) and spiritual qualities—stands at the beginning of his guidebook, together with a verbatim quotation from a song of Marpa Chökyi Lodrö (Chos kyi blo gros). This section is followed by the history of the Self-Manifested Mahācaitya, which was under repair at the time of his arrival. The Fourth Khamtrül reports on the persons responsible for the gilded copper shields and the Newar craftsmen engaged in the renovation. They were led by Kaḥtok Rindzin Tsewang Norbu's "ceremony master" (*mchod dpon*) and a representative of the Kathmandu king Jayaprakāśa Malla named Jamyang ('Jam dbyangs). On the twenty-seventh day of the twelfth month a note on the religious beliefs of the Newars as followers of Viṣṇu and Śiva was penned, along with the fact that Tendzin Chökyi Nyima had become further involved in the ongoing renovation of the Svayaṃbhū stūpa.[10]

As the ceremony master was busy with supervising the ongoing work, it was the Fourth Khamtrül who stood in for him in following up on an invitation to the royal palace in Kathmandu. He declined an offer to ride there on an elephant and was joined by the above-mentioned Jamyang, who is described as a Newar Buddhist who had visited Tibet and was well versed in its language. The audience took place on the twenty-eighth day and is introduced with a vividly painted picture of the Hanuman Dhoka palace in the center of the city just south of the traditional trans-Himalayan trade route. The actual encounter with the king is described in the following words:

> Then [came] the courtyard of the royal palace in the middle of it, surrounded by fully armed infantry troops, one of the four branches [of the royal army]. Afterward I passed through the inner door of the palace into its interior, where the king came occasionally in order to witness spectacles—dances and the like. The floor of [its] vestibule and corridors was as spacious as the earth, and immacu-

10. The first two days of the stay at Drepung vihāra in Kimdol can be found in Bstan 'dzin chos kyi nyi ma (n.d.), [ed. A:] 202a/5–204a/2, and [ed. B:] 252.14–55.7. For the description of Nepal, see ibid., [ed. A:] 202a/6–203a/5, [ed. B:] 252.15–53.18; and the verbatim quotation in Bstan 'dzin chos kyi nyi ma 1978, 163.1–165.3; for a translation, see Macdonald and Dvags-po Rin-po-che 1981, 239–41. The work adds quotations from the *Kāvyādarśa* and the *Bodhisattvāvadānakalpalatā* concerning the *tsampaka* flower (genus *Magnolia*). The name of the ceremony master was Tendzin Dorjé (Bstan 'dzin rdo rje); for his role in the five-year-long renovation of Svayaṃbhū, see Chos kyi dbang phyug 2006, 139.10–15. The concluding consecration was performed in 1758 by the Seventh Pawo Tsuklak Gawa (Dpa' bo Gtsug lag dga' ba, d. 1781); see Ehrhard 2013, 61.

late. As soon as I entered, a group of eighty royal servants emerged from inside the palace toward me. The members of this entourage were wearing beautiful ornaments and clothing and bore knives and shields. The retinue attending this entourage all had the bodily marks of Indian *atsaras*; they were decked out with golden bangles on hands and feet.

The king himself [i.e., Jayaprakāśa Malla, was wearing] religious dress like [that worn by] Newars in general, including a two-tiered turban of white cotton adorned by bands studded with pearls. His hands and feet were decked out with golden bangles. Two small iron chains encircled his neck one above the other, and at his waist he was wearing a small Nepalese knife, the upper part of its handle and its case made of gold, and [the rest of] its handle of pearl. He was draped in what had the form of a printed cotton shawl, its [one] end placed in the crook of his left arm. He was holding in his right hand a Kashmiri battle-ax, its broad-surfaced golden top ornamented with the head of a *makara*. In the interior, [off] the corridors and vestibule, was a high throne on an earthen platform, on which there was a square satin mat on top of a cushion of black woolen cloth and silk; my seat was on it. In front of it to the right, on a lower level, was a throne of gilded copper with [images of] the Six Ornaments and so forth, and on a square silk mat on this throne was seated the king in the pose of [Buddha] Maitreya.

The officers of his entourage, [still] holding their knives and shields, went [and] stood in front [of him]. Then, with the help of the translator Jamyang, questions were posed, such as: "O respected teacher, what is your birthplace? From where in the upper [or] lower [parts of Tibet] [have you come]? Did nothing occur because of obstacles along the way? And what is the purpose of your visit?" And I answered [accordingly]. Then I conveyed in all ways possible my thanks that [the king] had provided necessary materials to the honorable father [and] son and for the renovation of the Mahācaitya toward increasing the happiness and prosperity of Tibet—the whole country in general and its parts in particular. And once more I beseeched him, with quite a big show of praise, that he should, given his noble love of giving [and] supporting [it], witness the final completion [of the renovation]. He said that the meaning [for him] of whatever had come [from it,] including the joy that had entered his heart, being such as it was, it would not change again from [what] it [was]—[that he] by all means planned to do

> [as requested]. As soon as the audience was over, everyone having dispersed, the king went to [his] vehicle outside of the royal palace.[11]

On the following day the Fourth Khamtrül received various gifts from the Kathmandu court through one *kāji* Rula Rabhal. His trip around the valley then got underway. Setting off from the Kimdol vihāra, he visited first the Lokeśvara statues of Jowo Akham (Jo bo A kham) and Jowo Bhukham (Jo bo Bhu kham) in Patan. It was there that he celebrated the Tibetan "female fire-mouse new year" (*me mo byi pa'i gnam lo gsar*), which corresponds to the first of February 1756. On that day he also visited the Śākyamuni statue of the Kva Bahal and the replica of the Mahābodhi temple. This was followed by a pilgrimage to Yanglé Shö (Yang le shod) on the southern rim of the valley and nearby sacred sites, especially ones associated with Padmasambhava, whose descriptions can be found in both the diaries and the guidebook. He headed

11. See Bstan 'dzin chos kyi nyi ma (n.d.), [ed. A:] 205a/3–206a/2, and [ed. B:] 255.23–257.2: *de nas rgyal po'i pho brang gyi 'khor sa bar mar yan lag bzhi pa'i dpung las bu chung zhes pa'i dpung mtshon cha sna tshogs dang ldan pas bskor ba / de nas pho brang gis [= gi] sgo nang du slebs pa dang / skabs skabs su rgyal po zlos gar la sogs pa'i sgyu rtsed la gzigs mor phebs pa'i gnas sbugs su khang pa sgo khang ka phibs rnams sa ltar gyi mthil shin tu yangs shing dag pa zhig 'dug pa nged der slebs pa dang thogs mnyam du rgyal po g.yog brgyad cu skor pho brang nas tshur der thon pa / de yang 'khor rnams rgyan gos bzang pos klubs te lag tu gri phub 'dzin bzhin pa 'khor ltos che ba [= bcas pa] rnams rgya gar ba'i a tsa ra sha stag pa / de dag ni gser las byas pa'i rkang gdub lag gdab [= gdub] gyis mdzes pa / rgyal po dngos chos gos bal po spyi 'gro ltar la ras dkar gyi thod gnyis rim la mu tig* [205b] *zhag pas [= zhags pas] phra tshoms su brgyan pa / gser gyi gdub bus phyag zhabs mdzes pa / mgrin par lcag thag chung ngu gnyis rim su dkris pa / bal po lugs kyi gri chung yu ba'i tog dang shub [= shubs] gser las byas pa / mu tig gi yu ba can sked la gzer ba / ras khra'i bzan [= gzan] gyis [= gyi] rnam pa zhig gyon pas sne mo gru mo g.yon pa'i mchan khungs su bcug pa / lag g.yas su dgra sta kha che tog gser gyi chu srin mgo bos mtshan pa zhig bzung bzhin par / ka phibs sgo khang gis [= gi] sbugs su sa stegs gyi khri mtho ba zhig 'dug pa'i steng du gos phrug nag po'i sab gdan gyis khar gos chen gyis [= gyi] gdan kha gang zhig la nged sdad sa dang / de'i mdun g.yas ngos su zangs gser gyi khri rgyan drug sogs yod pa chung ngu'i khar gos can gdan kha gang ma'i steng khri thog der byams bzhin lta bus rgyal po bsdad / 'khor rnams mdun gyis phyi rol tu gri phub 'dzin par ldang nas bsdad song / de bas lo tsā ba bla ma 'jams dbyangs brgyud / bla ma gus 'khrungs yul lo stod smad ga nas yin / lam bar du gegs rkyen las ma byung ngam / 'byon don yi yin sogs 'dri bar gnang 'dug pa'i len dang / yul khams spyi bye brag kun tu bod skyid dpal 'byor rgyas phyir sku zhabs yab sras dang rang byung mchod rten chen po'i zhig gsos mthun rkyen gnang ba ci nas bka'i drin che tshul dang / slar yang mthar grub kyi gnang skyongs thugs rje'i rtse bas gzigs dgos kyis [= kyi] ngo bstod che se ba'i sgro btags kyis zhus par / kho rang thugs la bab pa'i dgyes mo dangs [= dang] bcas ji phebs kyi don de de bzhin yin par slar yang de las ma gyur ba zhig ci nas kyang bya rtsis yod gsung / de nas mjal phrad grub pa dang so sor gyes pas rgyal po pho brang du phar theg song ba dang /*. For the term *atsara* as a general term for mendicant Indian trader pilgrims who visited Tibet in large numbers during the eighteenth century, see Huber 2008, 404n72.

back on the fourth day of the first Tibetan month, stopping in at the Ramadoli charnel ground along the way, and upon arriving in Kathmandu paying his respects to the Mahākala statue known as Protector of the Tibetan Plain (Bod thang Mgon po). An ascent of Nāgārjun Hill (Ri bo 'bigs byed) to the northwest of Svayaṃbhū took place on the fifth day; Tendzin Chökyi Nyima inspected various caves, stories relating to which he later recounts. He also reports on certain prognostic practices associated with funerals on the top of the hill as described to him by a *vajrācārya* named Samantabhadra, who appears to have accompanied him. However, there were some problems in communicating with each other.[12]

The next part of the trip brought the Fourth Khamtrül to Cangu Narayan and Sankhu, followed by a visit to the Milarepa cave near Bhaktapur and a stay at Takmo Lüjin (Stag mo lus sbyin) on the eastern rim of the valley; the route to these sites was covered in a period of four days.[13]

The entry for the fourteenth day of the first Tibetan month describes the Vasubandhu and Mañjuśrī stūpas on Svayaṃbhū hill, referring in the latter case to narratives in the *Svayaṃbhūpurāṇa.* For the first time the diaries also refer to military activities of the Gorkha king. About fifty people, among them children without any clothes, are depicted fleeing from the approaching troops, seeking shelter in the Kimdol vihāra. The army of the Kathmandu king was able to drive back the attack, but the sound of fighting echoed for a long time through the night. On the fifteenth (a full moon) day a great offering was made to the Mahācaitya, the diaries containing a long passage on the "five

12. For these first travels in the valley, see Bstan 'dzin chos kyi nyi ma (n.d.), [ed. A:] 206a/3–208b/5, and [ed. B:] 257.5–60.12. The descriptions of the individual sites in Patan, Yanglé Shö, and Kathmandu can be compared with the respective sections in the pilgrimage guidebook; see Bstan 'dzin chos kyi nyi ma 1978, 197.5–99.3, 200.4–203.4, 208.6–14.4, 206.3–4, and 228.2–30.6; and Macdonald and Dvags-po Rin-po-che 1981, 256–57, 258–59, 260, 261–64, and 265–66. The Vajracārya Samantabhadra (Kun [tu] bzang [po]) was acquainted with Situ Paṇchen and is mentioned by the latter in his account of his second journey to the Nepal Valley, in connection with a manuscript of the **Vāmanābhidhāna.* He was also the one from whom Situ Paṇchen received the manuscript of the *Svayaṃbhūpurāṇa* translated later (in 1748) into Tibetan; see Chos kyi 'byung gnas 1968, 269.3–5 and 267.6; and Verhagen 2013, 324–25.

13. For this part of the pilgrimage, see Bstan 'dzin chos kyi nyi ma (n.d.), [ed. A:] 208b/5–10a/6, and [ed. B:] 260.12–62.7; the corresponding sections in the guidebook can be found in Bstan 'dzin chos kyi nyi ma 1978, 188.6–93.6 and 193.6–95.2; and Macdonald and Dvags-po Rin-po-che 1981, 252–55. The latter source not only describes the main sacred item at Cangu Narayan, a Garuda statue, but also points out that it had been brought to the royal palace of Kathmandu due to a local war that had started in the Nepal Valley in the previous year—i.e., 1755; for the military conflict between Patan and Kathmandu, see note 16.

towns" (*grong khyer lnga*) around Svayaṃbhū, the temple of Śāntipur and the shrine of the goddess Haritī, and, most particularly, the religious practices of the Newars. Two days later the pilgrimage continued to Stham vihāra in Kathmandu, and in the night of the seventeenth day another attack by the Gorkha troops is recorded; on that occasion three regiments, bearing wooden barriers, swooped into the suburbs of the city like a swarm of birds.[14]

The nineteenth day of the month is given as the date when Khamtrül paid his respects to the Lokeśvara statue of the Jowo Jamali Karpo (Jo bo 'Ja' ma li dkar po) in the center of Kathmandu and to an Aśoka stūpa in the courtyard of a nearby Buddhist vihāra, a monastic complex under the charge of the previously mentioned Vajrācārya Samantabhadra. In the night, three regiments once again showed up, the time units of the king of Kathmandu. After describing a visit to Buḍhanīlkaṇṭha, known to Tibetans as the "Supine Nāga" (Klu gan rkyal), a longer section of the diaries treats the details of an attack in this area by the Kathmandu king's army, headed by a general with the name *kāji* Dolir. His forces were able to drive back the Gorkha invaders, as personally witnessed by Tendzin Chökyi Nyima. On the twenty-second day he arrived in Bodhnāth and remained there for three days, making extensive offerings, including a whitewash of the stūpa.[15]

Side visits to nearby Guhyeśvarī and Gulang (i.e., Paśupati) were made, the local customs at these non-Buddhist sites being observed and later recorded in the diaries. A long section deals with the Heruka myth, and it is in this context that the land of Nepal is identified as a major site for religious practice called Upacchandoha Himālaya *pīṭha*. As the kings of Kathmandu and Patan had had a "slight disagreement" (*cung ma 'tshams pa*), localized fighting broke out at Guhyeśvarī, again in front of the Fourth Khamtrül's eyes. He reports that after a minister of Patan had surrendered himself to the Kathmandu troops but then managed to trick his way out of confinement, many people were killed around the sacred realm.

14. For this week of the sojourn in Kathmandu, see Bstan 'dzin chos kyi nyi ma (n.d.), [ed. A:] 210a/6–13a/5, and [ed. B:] 262.7–66.8. On the two mentioned stūpas at Svayaṃbhū, compare Bstan 'dzin chos kyi nyi ma 1978, 216.1–6 and 179.5–80.4; on the Mahācaitya and the religious practices of the Newars, ibid., 219.6–25.4; and on Stham vihāra, ibid., 199.3–200.2. The corresponding translations can be found in Macdonald and Dvags-po Rin-po-che 1981, 245–46, 257–58, 266–67, and 267–68.

15. These events once again cover the period of a week; see Bstan 'dzin chos kyi nyi ma (n.d.), [ed. A:] 213a/5–14b/5, and [ed. B:] 266.8–68.6. For the visits to the Jowo Jamali Karpo, the Aśoka stūpa, and the two sites, the Buḍhanīlkaṇṭha and the Bodhnāth stūpa, see Bstan 'dzin chos kyi nyi ma 1978, 182.5–84.2, 197.1–4, 200.2–4, and 225.4–26.2; cf. Macdonald and Dvags-po Rin-po-che 1981, 249–50, 256–58, and 268.

In the early morning of the twenty-fourth day of the first Tibetan month the Gorkha army attacked the valley again with great force. The soldiers of the king of Kathmandu were able to drive back the invaders and burn their wooden barriers, but many deaths occurred and the suffering was great. The last stages of the pilgrimage followed the next day on the way back to Svayaṃbhū as he passed through a tantric Catuḥpīṭha site of Yogāmbara and at the Vajravārāhī charnel ground paid his respects to a special statue of the latter deity.[16]

Returning to the Kimdol vihāra, now described as a property of the Kathmandu king, the Fourth Khamtrül remained for nine days in strict seclusion. On the fourth day of the second Tibetan month, he left for the Svayaṃbhū stūpa, and during the next three days offerings were made at Śāntipur and the Vasubandhu stūpa and Mañjuśrī stūpas. An account of the state of Buddhism at the time is given, and although he was not able to visit all the sacred sites, he lists the sacred objects in Gobicandra vihāra in Patan based on the biography of Mahāpaṇḍita Vanaratna (1384–1468) and regrets that he was not able to see further Buddhist vihāras in that city or a distinctive Tārā image in the royal palace of Bhaktapur. After mentioning the main literary sources available to him, he states that he wrote his guidebook during his sojourn in the valley for the benefit of future pilgrims.[17]

The final version of this work was obviously not completed during the sojourn in the Nepal Valley. Further entries on sacred sites were added later on, based on entries in the diaries made on the way back to the Tibetan plateau.

The Return Journey

On the eighth day of the second Tibetan month the Fourth Khamtrül departed for the journey back. He was accompanied by the *vajrācārya* Samantabhadra,

16. These last travels in the valley, including details of the military conflict between Kathmandu and Patan and the attack of the Gorkha army, are described in Bstan 'dzin chos kyi nyi ma (n.d.), [ed. A:] 214b/5–17a/6, and [ed. B:] 268.6–71.7. The pilgrimage guidebook includes Guhyeśvarī and Gulang as well, and devotes particular space to the Heruka myth and Nepal's status as the Upacchandoha Himālaya *pīṭha*; see Bstan 'dzin chos kyi nyi ma 1978, 184.2–88.2; and the translation in Macdonald and Dvags-po Rin-po-che 1981, 250–52. For the Catuḥpīṭha site and the Vajravārāhī charnel ground, see ibid., 226.2–27.3 and 195.2–97.1.

17. For the final days in the Kimdol vihāra and at Svayaṃbhū, including the literary sources (the newly translated *Svayaṃbhūpurāṇa* by Situ Paṇchen and the register of the Bodhnāth stūpa), see Bstan 'dzin chos kyi nyi ma (n.d.), [ed. A:] 217a/6–18b/1, and [ed. B:] 271.1–72.13. The register itself, the *Bya rung kha shor dkar chag*, had already been circulating as a xylograph for exactly two centuries; on the original xylograph, dated 1556, see Ehrhard 2018, 75–87.

the latter only for the first leg of the journey. Particular attention is paid in the account to the beautiful landscape before reaching the first stopover. The different localities on the way north have been noted elsewhere, and I will name only the main ones up to Mangyül Gungtang. Nuwakot (Bal po rdzong) is mentioned and described as the site where Milarepa and Dharmabodhi had met. Tsawé Tsashö (Tsha ba'i tsha shod), the region from which the *yaṣṭi* for the renovation of the Mahācaitya had been transported, follows. Once again Tendzin Chökyi Nyima received a travel pass from the king of Gorkha for the onward journey, this time in the northern direction. He also met a brahmin scholar highly versed in Sanskrit grammar, but since neither knew the other's *spoken* language very well, it is stated that not much benefit was gained from this encounter.

The village of Dommang ('Dom mang) was reached on the fourteenth day of the month, and Lake Nīlakaṇṭha (i.e., Gosainkund) is mentioned, located further up in the hills. The Fourth Khamtrül did not take the path to the lake, nor did he visit Yölmo or Landhe, Himalayan valleys identified in the text, respectively, as the birthplaces of the Eighth Zhamarpa Chökyi Döndrup (Zhwa dmar pa Chos kyi don grub, 1695–1732), and the Third Karmapa Rangjung Dorjé (Karma pa Rang byung rdo rje, 1284–1339). On the seventeenth day of the month he arrived in Kyirong, where he stayed for four days, paying reverence to Ārya Wati Zangpo while chanting spiritual songs of Milarepa devoted to that statue. After a meeting with the local governor, he went on to further sites in the Kyirong region, the list of which corresponds to the one in the pilgrimage guidebook.[18]

Jampa Trin temple was reached on the twenty-first day of the month. The Zarong River was in flood, allowing the Fourth Khamtrül to remain for a week at this place and its surroundings for a needed break. The diaries enumerate the sacred objects of the old site, including an effigy of Buddha Śākyamuni said to have been brought from India by the legendary Bhikṣu Akaramatiśīla. The twenty-third day records the arrival of the Seventh Drukchen Kagyü Trinlé Shingta from Gawo Lhading. The two men's discussion focused on the successful pilgrimage to the Nepal Valley. The ongoing renovation of the Svāyaṃbhū stūpa came up, in particular Kaḥtok Rindzin Tsewang Norbu's efforts to urge the king of Gorkha to hasten its completion. As the master had recently passed

18. For the journey from Kathmandu to Kyirong, passing through Nuwakot, see Bstan 'dzin chos kyi nyi ma (n.d.), [ed. A:] 218b/1–220a/2, and [ed. B:] 272.13–74.9. Consult Quintman (2014, 90) for more details of this itinerary. The sections on Nuwakot, Nīlakaṇṭha, and the various sites in Kyirong are also contained in Bstan 'dzin chos kyi nyi ma 1978, 228.2–30.6, 231.1–32.2, and 232.3–33.3; cf. Macdonald and Dvags-po Rin-po-che 1981, 269–72.

away and a reliquary shrine of his was located at the nearby Ngödrup cave, the Fourth Khamtrül was able to spend part of the following day in its presence. There he met the deceased's previously mentioned disciple and representative, Lori Trülku. On the twenty-eighth day he left the Ngödrup cave and traveled on to Riwo Pembar (Ri bo dpal 'bar) Mountain. The following week was taken up with excursions to Milarepa sites in Mangyül, starting with Jangchup Dzong (Byang chub rdzong) in Rakma (Rag ma) and leading via Drakkar Taso (Brag dkar rta so) and Kyarnga Tsa (Skya rnga rtsa), the birthplace of the great yogin, up to Lingwa Drakmar Dzong (Ling ba brag dmar rdzong).[19]

On the sixth day of the third Tibetan month the Fourth Khamtrül returned to Ngari Dzongkar, this time to visit the monastery Pelgyé Ling ('Phel rgyas gling), also known as Dzongkar Chödé (Rdzong dkar chos sde). Among the sacred items kept there are mentioned the copy of the *Ratnakuṭasūtra* once owned by Milarepa and his meditation belt. On the eighth day he proceeded to Gawo Lhading and once again met the Seventh Drukchen. For a period of about three weeks he remained in the latter's company, receiving various teaching transmissions. During that stay he completed his guidebook to the Nepal Valley and presented it to Kagyü Trinlé Shingta. Without going into the further details of this sojourn—for example, his time with another student of Situ Paṇchen and an expert in Sanskrit grammar by the name of Sanggyé Chokdrup (Sangs rgyas mchog grub)—I shall just refer to his visit to a Milarepa site called the Rala Zaok (Ra la za 'og) cave, the last place noted in the pilgrimage guidebook. The date of his departure from Gawo Lhading is given as the first day of the fourth Tibetan month. After reaching the shore of Pelkhü (Dpal khud) Lake in upper Gungtang, he venerated three further Milarepa sites from afar; another group of three—Langgo Ludü Dzong (Glang sgo Klu bdud rdzong), Lapuk Pema Dzong (La phug Padma rdzong), and Bepuk Mamo Dzong (Sbas phug Ma mo rdzong)—were afterward visited in person.[20]

19. The visit to Jampa Trin, the meeting with the Seventh Drukchen, and the pilgrimage to the Milarepa sites are contained in Bstan 'dzin chos kyi nyi ma (n.d.), [ed. A:] 220a/5–22a/2, and [ed. B:] 275.3–77.6. For the parallel description of the temple and the list of the various caves, see Bstan 'dzin chos kyi nyi ma 1978, 233.4–34.3; and Macdonald and Dvags-po Rinpo-che 1981, 272. Kaḥtok Rindzin Tsewang Norbu had passed away in the eighth Tibetan month of the previous year; concerning the funeral ceremonies and the reliquary shrine, see Chos kyi dbang phyug 2006, 137.4–18. The Milarepa sites visited in Mangyül are the six "well-known outer fortresses" mentioned in the hagiographical account of Bstan 'dzin chos kyi nyi ma above; for their location see the map in Quintman 2008, 386.

20. For the arrival in Ngari Dzongkar, the sojourn in Gawo Lhading, and the pilgrimage to the Milarepa sites in Gungtang, see Bstan 'dzin chos kyi nyi ma (n.d.), [ed. A:] 222a/8–25a/4, and [ed. B:] 277.15–80.23. The Rala Zaok cave is described in both the diaries and

Conclusion

According to the hagiographical account, further travels brought the Fourth Khamtrül back to Central Tibet, and he also later completed a pilgrimage to Tsāri. It was on that pilgrimage that he heard about the successful completion of work on the Svayaṃbhū *caitya* by the Seventh Drukchen while staying in the latter's monastery, Sangngak Chöling (Gsang sngags chos gling) in Jar (Byar). As noted above, he visited various sacred sites and identified Tsāri—as he had the Nepal Valley—as the Upacchandoha Himālaya *pīṭha*. It would be worthwhile to track these further travels and pilgrimages in the following years before he finally embarked on his return trip to Kham. I conclude, though, by simply drawing attention to the figure Kagyü Trinlé Shingta and his activities. Like Situ Paṇchen and Tendzin Chökyi Nyima, the Seventh Drukchen shared an interest in the Sanskritized Buddhist cultural milieu of the Nepal Valley, where he had also stayed before the visit of his disciple. It is known that Kagyü Trinlé Shingta dispatched Sönam Rapgyé (Bsod nams rab rgyas, eighteenth century), another one of his disciples, from Garsha in western Tibet on a pilgrimage to India, resulting in a travel account whose description of Bodh Gayā and further sites of Buddhist India has been assessed elsewhere. The journey took place in the year 1752 and can be characterized as one of knowledge gathering combined with pilgrimage activity. The same holds true for Tendzin Chökyi Nyima's journey, which took place shortly afterward, although not confronted with similar obstacles due to the control of trade and travel between Tibet and the Nepal Valley.[21]

The exhaustive text of the Fourth Khamtrül on Daṇḍin's *Kāvyādarśa* was

the guidebook as being located in the home region of Rechungpa Dorjé Drak (Ras chung pa Rdo rje grags, 1084–1161) and as the site where Milarepa met his disciple for the first time; see Bstan 'dzin chos kyi nyi ma 1978, 234.3–5; and Macdonald and Dvags-po Rin-po-che 1981, 272–73. For a map of the six sites along the shore of Pelkhü Lake—the so-called unknown secret fortresses—see Quintman 2008, 388; instead of Takpuk Senggé Dzong (Stag phug seng ge rdzong) on this map, one finds in the diaries Kyipuk Nyima Dzong (Skyid phug nyi ma rdzong).

21. The pilgrimage to Tsāri started from Dechen Chökhor on the fifth day of the sixth Tibetan month of 1757 and lasted up to the first day of the eleventh Tibetan month of the same year, when he returned to the monastery. The identification of Tsāri as Upacchandoha Himālaya is mentioned during the description of his arrival at the sacred site; see Bstan 'dzin chos kyi nyi ma (n.d.), [ed. A:] 243b/3–48b/3, and [ed. B:] 303.5–308.18. The mission to Bodh Gayā dispatched by the Seventh Drukchen is described in Bsod nams rab rgyas 1752. See Huber (2008, 177–92) for the difficult transit through Nepal and the significance of this work for the description of Buddhist India; cf. Bsod nams rab rgyas 2013, 626–29. A teacher bearing this name is mentioned by the Fourth Khamtrül in an entry dating from the tenth

initially written upon his arrival in Central Tibet. This was after studies with Situ Paṇchen in Pelpung and before embarking on the journeys to southwestern Tibet and Nepal. After a period of eight years and further travels, the Fourth Khamtrül returned to Kham, starting from the monastery of Dechen Chökhor, in the autumn of 1761. As mentioned in the colophon of his diaries, up to that point regular records had been kept listing day-to-day events. After further studies of poetics with Situ Paṇchen, Tendzin Chökyi Nyima completed his commentary on the *Kāvyādarśa* in the year 1770, and at the beginning of the year 1773 the diaries note that he also supervised a first print of the text at his monastery, Püntsok Chökhor Ling.[22]

References

Tibetan Texts

Sgrub brgyud nyi ma, Khams sprul V. 1985. *Rje btsun kun gzigs phrin las 'gro 'dul rtsal gyi skyes rabs rnam thar dang bcas pa ngo mtshar grub gyis 'dod 'jo'i nor phreng*. In *Biographies of the Predecessors in the Khams Sprul Incarnation Lineage from the Great Yogis of India through the Fourth Khams-sprul bsTan-'dzin chos-kyi ñi-ma*, 1–355. Tashijong, Parola Dist., Kangra, H.P.: Tibetan Craft Community.

Chos kyi snang ba, 'Brug chen VIII. 1976. *Tsa ri gnas bshad rgyas par bshad pa'i le'u*. In *Rare Tibetan Texts from Nepal: A Collection of Guides to Holy Places, Lives of Religious Masters, and Khrid yig by the Famed Rdza Roṅ-phu Bla-ma*, 1–59. Dolanji, P.O. Ochghat, H.P.: Tibetan Bonpo Monastic Centre.

Chos kyi dbang phyug, Brag dkar rta so sprul sku. 2006. *Dpal rig 'dzin chen po rdo rje tshe dbang nor bu'i zhabs kyis [= kyi] rnam par thar pa'i cha shas brjod pa ngo mtshar*

month of 1760 when he had returned from a further trip to Sangngak Chöling in Jar to Dechen Chökhor; see Bstan 'dzin chos kyi nyi ma (n.d.), [ed. A:] 269a/6, and [ed. B:] 333.7.

22. For this print of the commentary on Daṇḍin's *Kāvyādarśa* see Bstan 'dzin chos kyi nyi ma (n.d.), [ed. A:] fol. 325a/4–5, and [ed. B:] 402.4–8. Although no copy of this original is available, a manuscript version contains the printing colophon; see Bstan 'dzin chos kyi nyi ma 1976, [ed. A:] 704.4–705.3. A "new xylograph" (*par gsar*) was printed in the year 1933 at Pelpung by Jamyang Chökyi Gyentsen ('Jam dbyangs chos kyi rgyal mtshan, nineteenth/twentieth centuries), a scholar who taught grammar and poetics to the Eleventh Situ Pema Wangchuk Gyelpo (Si tu Padma dbang phyug rgyal po, 1886–1952); for the benedictory verses see Bstan 'dzin chos kyi nyi ma 1976, [ed. B:] 430a/4–31a/5; and for the latter teacher, Bayer 2019, 92–94 and 331–32.

dad pa'i rol mtsho. In *Kaḥ thog rig 'dzin tshe dbang nor bu'i bka' 'bum*, vol. 1, 1–158. Beijing: Krung go'i bod yig dpe skrun khang.

Chos kyi 'byung gnas, Si tu VIII. 1968. *Ta'i si tu 'bod pa karma bstan pa'i nyin byed kyi rang tshul drangs par brjod pa dri bral shel gyi me long*. In *The Autobiography and Diaries of Si-tu Paṇ-chen*. Śata Piṭaka Series 77. New Delhi: International Academy of Indian Culture.

Bstan 'dzin chos kyi nyi ma, Khams sprul IV. n.d. *Rang tshul lhug par smras pa ma bcos gnyug ma'i rang grol*. 1–368 [manuscript = ed. A]; and n.d. 1–457 [BDRC W4CZ346624 = ed. B]. [n.p.]: Zla 'od gzhon nu rtsom sgrig khang.

———. 1976. *Rgyan gyi bstan bcos me long paṇ chen bla ma'i gsung bzhin bkral ba dbyangs can ngag gi rol mtsho legs bshad nor bu'i byung khungs*. 1–704 [manuscript = ed. A]. Thimphu; and 1–431 [BDRC W2PD9561, blockprint = ed. B].

———. 1978. "Yul chen po nye ba'i tshandhoha bal po'i gnas kyi dkar chag gangs can rna ba'i bdud rtsi." In *Collected Writings of the Fourth Khamtrul Tenzin Chökyi Nyima and His Disciple Khedrup Sonam Rabpel*, 307–79. Tashijong, Palampur, U.P.: Sungrab Nyamso Parkhang. Also published in Macdonald 1975, 123–44.

Bsod nams rab rgyas. 1752. *'Phags pa'i yul dbus dpal rdo rje gdan du garsha'i rnal 'byor pa bsod nams rab rgyas gyis legs par mjal ba lam yig dad pa'i snye ma*, 1–7. Toyo Bunko, no. 285–2446.

———. 2013. "Cluster of Fait: Travelogue of Garsha Yogin Sönam Rabgyé's Good Encounter with Glorious Vajrāsana, Center of the Noble Land." In *Sources of Tibetan Tradition*, edited by Kurtis R. Schaeffer, Matthew T. Kapstein, and Gray Tuttle, 626–29. New York: Columbia University Press

Western Literature

Akester, Matthew. 2016. *Jamyang Khyentsé Wangpo's Guide to Central Tibet*. Chicago: Serindia Publications.

Bayer, Achim. 2019. *The Life and Works of mKhan-po gZhan-dga' (1871–1927). rDzogs-chen Master and Educational Reformer of Eastern Tibet*. Hamburg Buddhist Studies 11. Freiburg: Projekt Verlag.

Ehrhard, Franz-Karl. 2007. "The Biography of sMan-bsgom Chos-rje Kun-dga' dpal-ldan (1735–1804) as a Source for the Sino-Nepalese War." In *Pramāṇakīrtiḥ: Papers Dedicated to Ernst Steinkellner on the Occasion of His 70th Birthday*, edited by Birgit Kellner, Helmut Krasser, Horst Lasic, Michael Torsten Much, and Helmut Tauscher, vol. 1, 115–33. Wiener Studien zur Tibetologie und Buddhismuskunde 70.1. Vienna: Arbeitskreis für Tibetische und Buddhistische Studien Universität Wien.

———. 2013. *Buddhism in Tibet & the Himalayas: Texts and Traditions*. Kathmandu: Vajra Publications.

———. 2018. "Printing a Treasure Text: The 1556 Edition of the *Bya rung kha shor lo rgyus*." In *Saddharmāmṛtam: Festschrift für Jens-Uwe Hartmann zum 65. Geburtstag*, edited by Oliver von Criegern, Gudrun Melzer, and Johannes Schneider,

75–94. Wiener Studien zur Tibetologie und Buddhismuskunde 93. Vienna: Arbeitskreis für Tibetische und Buddhistische Studien Universität Wien.

Gruschke, Andreas. 2004. *The Cultural Monuments of Tibet's Outer Provinces: Khams.* 2 vols. Bangkok: White Orchid Press.

Huber, Toni. 1990. "Where Exactly Are Cāritra, Devikoṭa and Himavat? A Sacred Geography Controversy and the Development of Tantric Buddhist Pilgrimage Sites in Tibet." *Kailash: A Journal of Himalayan Studies* 16.3–4: 121–64.

———. 2008. *The Holy Land Reborn: Pilgrimage and the Tibetan Reinvention of Buddhist India.* Chicago: The University of Chicago Press.

van der Kuijp, Leonard W. J. 1982. "On the Interpretation of *Kāvyādarśa* II:274." *Studien zur Indologie und Iranistik* 8–9: 69–76.

———. 1986. "Bhāmaha in Tibet." *Indo-Iranian Journal* 29: 31–39.

———. 1996. "Tibetan Belles-Lettres: The Influence of Dandin and Kṣemendra." In *Tibetan Literature: Studies in Genre,* edited by José I. Cabezón and Roger R. Jackson, 393–410. Ithaca, NY: Snow Lion Publications.

———. 2009. "On the Vicissitudes of Subhūticandra's *Kāmadhenu Commentary* on the *Amarakośa* in Tibet." *Journal of the International Association of Tibetan Studies* 5: 1–105.

Macdonald, Alexander W. 1975. "A Little-Read Guide to the Holy Places of Nepal, Part I." *Kailash: A Journal of Himalayan Studies* 3.2: 89–144.

Macdonald, A. W., and Dvags-po Rin-po-che. 1981. "Un guide peu-lu des Lieux-saints du Népal (IIe partie)." In *Tantric and Taoist Studies in Honour of R. A. Stein,* edited by Michel Strickmann, vol. 1, 237–73. Mélanges Chinois et Bouddhiques 20. Brussels: Institut Belge des Hautes Études Chinoises.

Quintman, Andrew. 2008. "Towards a Geographic Biography: Mi la ras pa in the Tibetan Landscape." *Numen: International Revue for the History of Religion* 55: 363–410.

———. 2014. "Redacting Sacred Landscape in Nepal: The Vicissitudes of Yolmo's Tiger Cave Lion Fortress." In *Himalayan Passages: Tibetan and Newar Studies in Honor of Hubert Decleer,* edited by Benjamin Bogin and Andrew Quintman, 69–96. Boston: Wisdom Publications.

von Rospatt, Alexander. 2001. "A Historical Overview of the Renovations of the *Svayambhūcaitya* at Kathmandu." *Journal of the Nepal Research Centre* 12: 195–241.

Smith, E. Gene. 2001. *Among Tibetan Texts: History and Literature of the Himalayan Plateau.* Boston: Wisdom Publications.

———. 2013. "Notes Apropos to the Oeuvre of Si tu paṇ chen Chos kyi 'byung gnas (1699–1774) (4): A Tibetan Sanskritist in Nepal." *Journal of the International Association of Tibetan Studies* 7: 316–39.

Portraying the Lineage Masters of the Path with Its Fruit: Lowo Khenchen's Description of Ngorchen's Commission

Jörg Heimbel and David P. Jackson

To fulfill the last wishes of two of his deceased masters, the Sakya tantric expert Ngorchen Künga Zangpo (Ngor chen Kun dga' bzang po, 1382–1456) commissioned two outstanding sets of scroll paintings, which, however, only survive in fragments.[1] Ngorchen ordered paintings directly linked with the teachings he had received from his revered masters: an eleven-painting set portraying the chief lineage masters of the Path with Its Fruit (Lam 'bras) instructions in memory of Drupchen Buddhaśrī (Grub chen Buddhaśrī, 1399–1420) and a fourteen-painting set depicting the forty-two maṇḍalas of the *Vajrāvalī* cycle (with three additional maṇḍalas from the *Kriyāsamuccaya*) in memory of Sapzang Pakpa Zhönnu Lodrö (Sa bzang 'Phags pa Gzhon nu blo gros, 1346–1412). Though the first set might possibly have already been painted in the early 1420s when Ngorchen was still based at his original home monastery of Sakya (Sa skya), he had the latter set painted by Newar artists at his new monastic seat of Ngor Ewaṃ Chöden (Ngor E waṃ chos ldan), the important center of Sakyapa tantric teaching and training that he founded in 1429 in the remote Ngor Valley, about thirty kilometers southwest of present-day Zhikatsé (Gzhis ka rtse) in Tsang province (Gtsang).[2]

In his research on sacred art connected to Ngor Monastery, David Jackson was able to identify three existing paintings from Ngorchen's Lamdré (Lam

1. For better readability, we have refrained in our translations (with few exceptions) from using square brackets to supply any additional explanatory words or phrases that are implicit in the original works.

2. On Ngorchen and his monastery, see Heimbel 2017. On the set depicting the maṇḍalas of the *Vajrāvalī* cycle, see Heimbel 2017, 193–205; Jackson 1996, 78, 82; Jackson 2010b, 186–87; Mori 2008; and Mori 2009, vol. 2, 711–15.

'bras) lineage set (nos. 1, 2, and 7).[3] An indispensable source enabling that identification was the set's iconographic description written by Lowo Khenchen Sönam Lhündrup (Glo bo Mkhan chen Bsod nams lhun grub, 1456–1532), a royal monk from Lowo (Glo bo, i.e., Mustang in present-day northwestern Nepal) who had very close relations with the greatest lamas of the Sakya and Ngor traditions. Lowo Khenchen paid remarkably great attention to many historical details, even such relatively minor things as the exact layout of some of the most important paintings of both traditions. During two extended sojourns in central Tibet (from 1489 to 1497 and 1506 to mid-1509), he paid several study visits to Ngor. During one of these visits, he must have had the opportunity to examine the Lamdré lineage set in situ and decided to write down its description, thus providing us with an invaluable overview of the set. In the colophon of that work, he specifies his motive for doing so as that he hoped to make the arrangement of the figures on the paintings comprehensible for faithful followers of the tradition, as well as to ascertain their layout for himself. From his brief remarks on the historical circumstances of commissioning the set, we also learn that Lowo Khenchen highly appreciated the fact that the great master Ngorchen himself had designed, consecrated, and used these paintings for his own spiritual practice.

During his two sojourns in central Tibet, Lowo Khenchen examined two other important paintings for which he also noted down descriptions. The first account describes a realistic and nearly contemporaneous portrait thangka (*yin thang*) of Sachen Künga Nyingpo (Sa chen Kun dga' snying po, 1092–1158) that was commissioned by his son Jetsün Drakpa Gyeltsen (Rje btsun Grags pa rgyal mtshan, 1147–1216).[4] The second outlines a thangka depicting Pañjaranātha Mahākāla that was owned by Künga Wangchuk (Kun dga' dbang phyug, 1424–78), the fourth abbot of Ngor who was Lowo Khenchen's revered guru, as an object of his spiritual practice.[5] All three of Lowo Khenchen's descriptions can be classified as examples of the relatively rare subtype of the *driyik* (*bri yig*) genre in which the text is an actual description of paintings and

3. See Jackson 1986, 181–84, 189–91; Jackson 1996, 78, 81 (fig. 24), 82; Jackson 2010b, 182–86 (figs. 8.4–5); and Jackson 2011, 83–85 (fig. 3.12).

4. For a manuscript witness of this work, see, for instance, Glo bo Mkhan chen Bsod nams lhun grub, *Rje tsun sa skya pa'i yin thang dngos la zhib tu gzigs tshul.*

5. For a manuscript witness of this work, see, for instance, Glo bo Mkhan chen Bsod nams lhun grub, *Bla ma rdo rje 'chang kun dga' dbang phyug pa'i thugs dam thang ka mgon po'i bri yig.*

not the plan or written guide for executing them (which was the more common subgenre).[6]

To make this less-studied Tibetan genre of written or iconographic descriptions better known, we shall in the following pages present a first complete translation of Lowo Khenchen's work. The translation will be preceded by an introduction to Ngorchen's commission and a brief discussion of the three existing paintings of the set, which will also introduce and identify a fourth painting of the set (no. 3).

Ngorchen's Commissions to Fulfill the Last Wishes of Buddhaśrī

Some of the best sources on early sacred art at Ngor are the two available biographies of the monastery's founder, Ngorchen Künga Zangpo. One was written by Müchen Könchok Gyeltsen (Mus chen Dkon mchog rgyal mtshan, 1388–1469), his direct disciple and successor as abbot of Ngor, and another by Sanggyé Püntsok (Sangs rgyas phun tshogs, 1649–1705), the twenty-fifth abbot of Ngor, who compiled early Ngorchen biographies into a single extensive summary in 1688.[7] Both biographies describe the major sets of paintings, statues, and murals that Ngorchen commissioned in memory of his teachers. They also mention his commissioning of numerous other scroll paintings (depicting maṇḍalas and pure realms) and present a fairly detailed description of the murals of Ngor's assembly hall (that is, the Dbang khang chen mo).

Sanggyé Püntsok, whose account is slightly more detailed than Müchen's, describes the following major sets of paintings, statues, and murals that Ngorchen commissioned in honor of his late Lamdré master Buddhaśrī:

> As a means to fulfil the intentions of Drupchen Buddhawa, Ngorchen commissioned eleven great paintings of the complete lineage masters of the Oral Instructions [that is, the Lamdré]. Furthermore, he commissioned in the upper inner sanctum, which is nowadays known as the Lamdré Chapel, a set of statues of the Lamdré lineage beginning with a magnificent gilt image of Vajradhara and large magnificent clay images of the subsequent lineage

6. On such written descriptions of paintings, see Jackson 1996, 369–71. One finds the Tibetan term for the *driyik* genre also written with the past tense form (i.e., *bris*). However, the proper spelling can be assumed to have the future form (i.e., *bri*) expressing, in this context, the necessitative aspect of the future—that is, a written guide for how a painting should be executed.

7. On Ngorchen's biographies, see Heimbel 2017, 23–67.

> from Nairātmyā until Drupchen Buddhapa; small clay images of the entire lineage from Vajradhara until Drupchen Buddhapa, which are housed in the Lamzap Chapel; and as murals of the inner sanctum of the lamas' residence, depictions of the lineage masters of Hevajra, Cakrasaṃvara, Guhyasamāja, as well as innumerable depictions of buddhas and bodhisattvas.[8]

As his biographers do not provide dates for Ngorchen's commissions, scholars have so far dated them to between 1429 and 1456, the period from Ngorchen's founding of Ngor until his passing away. However, that this was most likely not the case for commissioning the set portraying the Lamdré lineage masters can be learned from the biography of Buddhaśrī that Ngorchen wrote himself at Sakya, as he reveals in its colophon, which he wrote probably not long after his master's death in 1420. Since Ngorchen mentions commissioning that very set in Buddhaśrī's biography, we can conclude that he had the set painted in the early 1420s, when still based at Sakya and before shifting to his new monastic seat of Ngor after its founding in 1429:

> To infuse with the blessings of that Sublime One himself and in order to fulfill his intentions, I commissioned eleven paintings of the lineage masters of the Precious Oral Instructions [that is, the Lamdré] from the Buddha Vajradhara until the Lord Buddhaśrī himself, which are the painting set's central figures, and the lineage masters are surrounded by many *yidam* deities. For preparing the cloth for that painting set, by pulverizing the Lord's cremated

8. Sangs rgyas phun tshogs 1983, 548.4–49.1: *grub chen buddha ba'i thugs dgongs rdzogs pa'i thabs su| gsung ngag gi bla ma brgyud pa yongs su rdzogs pa'i bris sku chen mo bcu gcig dang| gzhan yang gtsang khang steng ma da lta lam 'bras lha khang du grags par| rdo rje 'chang gi gser sku khyad par du 'phags pa dang| bdag med ma nas grub chen buddha pa'i bar lder sku khyad par du 'phags pa che ba rnams dang| rdo rje 'chang nas grub chen buddha pa'i bar du brgyud pa yongs su rdzogs pa'i lder sku chung ba rnams lam bzang* [= *zab*?] *lha khang du bzhugs pa dang| bla ma rnams bzhugs pa'i gtsang khang gi logs bris la| kye rdo rje dang| 'khor lo bde mchog dang| gsang ba 'dus pa rnams kyi bla ma brgyud pa dang| sangs rgyas dang byang chub sems dpa' dpag tu med pa bzhengs|*. For this passage, see also Mus chen Dkon mchog rgyal mtshan 1983, 464.3–5. The Lamdré Chapel was located on the first floor of Ngor's assembly hall (that is, the Dbang khang chen mo). The Lamzang Chapel is most probably a reference to the famous Lamzap Chapel, which was located on the first floor of the Zimkhang Kadrukma. Initially, it served as Ngorchen's living quarters. According to Luding Khenchen Rinpoche (Klu lding Mkhan chen Rin po che; Ngor ma dgon, 24 September 2012), the "inner sanctum of the lamas' residence" (*bla ma rnams bzhugs pa'i gtsang khang*) might refer to the Lamdré Chapel on the first floor of Ngor's assembly hall.

> remains together with some fragrant aroma, I grinded the remains to divide them. From within them, two extraordinary relics appeared.[9]

The fact that Buddhaśrī's ashes were used in preparing the cloth for the paintings suggests that Ngorchen commissioned that set not long after Buddhaśrī's death in 1420. Furthermore, since Ngorchen does not mention any other commission recorded by his biographers—such as the two sets of Lamdré lineage master clay statues and some murals—it seems very likely that the painting set was the first of his commissions and that he sponsored it while he was still based at Sakya, and that his other commissions were executed later, while at Ngor.[10]

However, after founding Ngor, he obviously took the set to his new monastic seat, where it was displayed during the annual bestowal of the Lamdré, and where Lowo Khenchen also saw it. This can be inferred from Ngorchen's detailed biography by Sanggyé Püntsok, who also provides some further information about other later Lamdré lineage paintings at Ngor:

> The eleven Lamdré thangkas made as a means to fulfil the intentions of Drupchen Buddhawa, together with the supplement thangkas of subsequent lamas, are this very set that is displayed during the Hevajra path initiation of the Oral Instructions [that is, the Lamdré] in annual alternation with the set of golden thangkas commissioned by Lord Könchok Penden. The continuation of the golden thangkas has been commissioned by Jampa Künga Tashi. All these thangkas are kept in the erstwhile Zimchung Kanyima that is nowadays known as the Lamzap Chapel. If they are forcibly taken from this place of storage to somewhere else, the adamantine Dharma protectors will perform activities for stopping such attempts.[11]

9. Ngor chen Kun dga' bzang po 1983, 431.4–5: *dam pa de nyid kyi byin rlabs 'jug cing thugs kyi dgongs pa rdzogs pa'i ched du bdag gis rgyal ba rdo rje 'chang nas rje nyid kyi bar gyi gsung ngag rin po che'i bla ma brgyud pa rnams gtso bor gyur ba la| bla ma brgyud pa la yi dam mang pos bskor ba'i bris sku bcu gcig bzhengs te| de'i ras 'dul la rje nyid kyi gdung dri bzang po dang lhan cig phye mar byas te bgo ba'i ched du gdung btags pa'i gseb nas ring bsrel khyad 'phags gnyis byon to|.*

10. For an account of Ngorchen's commissioning of clay statues of the Lamdré lineage masters at Ngor, see Sangs rgyas phun tshogs 1983, 552.6–53.1.

11. Sangs rgyas phun tshogs 1983, 549.2–4: *grub chen buddha ba'i dgongs rdzogs thabs lam 'bras thang ka bcu gcig| bla ma phyi ma'i kha skong dang bcas| gsung ngag gi lam dbang skabs su| rje dkon mchog dpal ldan pas bzhengs pa'i gser thang rnams dang res mos su 'grems pa 'di yin| gser thang 'phros rnams byams pa kun dga' bkra shis kyis bzhengs par 'dug| bzhugs sa sngar*

In addition to those written mentions of the set's commission that we find in Ngorchen's biographies and its description by Lowo Khenchen, each of the existing paintings bears an important inscription clarifying the purpose of its commissioning that allows for linking it with Ngorchen and his commission. This inscription is written with golden letters at the center of the blue bottom strip directly below the vase from which the undulating lotus vines encircling the minor figures originate, and it reads (as transcribed from the first painting depicting Vajradhara):[12] "May the extraordinary intentions of Drupchen Buddhaśrī be ever more and completely fulfilled."

The existing paintings also feature two additional kinds of inscriptions. One type is an invocation prayer written with small golden letters in the red bottom cartouche of each painting. It consists of one verse invoking each depicted central figure, the last hemistich of which mentions the name of the master to whom the prayer is addressed. These are prayers commonly found in written supplications to the Lamdré lineage, and those invocation prayers with their corresponding written equivalents we have provided below, in the appendix "Invocational Prayers." Another type of inscription is the small naming label written directly below each depicted minor figure, providing the names of each depicted deity or lineage master.

According to Lowo Khenchen's description, the complete set of paintings consisted of eleven pieces, whose twenty-one main figures were the successive Lamdré masters. The central masters were portrayed in successive pairs facing each other, except for the three paintings of Vajradhara, Sachen Künga Nyingpo, and Buddhaśrī, which have single main figures (such pairing of masters facing each other was merely a convention of placement and does not show them "in conversation," as some have speculated):

1. Vajradhara, with standing Vajragarbha and Nairātmyā to his right and left
2. Virūpa and Kāṇha
3. Ḍamarūpa and Avadhūtipa

gyi gzims chung ka gnyis ma da lta lam zab lha khang du grags par bzhugs| 'di las gzhan du 'khyer bcom byed na rdo rje chos skyong rnams kyis tshar gcod kyi las mdzad par 'gyur ro|. Könchok Penden (Dkon mchog dpal ldan, 1526–90) was the twelfth abbot of Ngor and Jampa Künga Tashi (Byams pa Kun dga' bkra shis, 1558–1615), the fourteenth abbot; see Heimbel 2017, 520–21.

12. Inscription: *grub chen bud dha shri pa'i thugs kyi dgongs pa khyad par can gong nas gong du yongs su rdzogs par gyur cig*. This inscription can be clearly seen in the photos of the other paintings from the set but cannot be read in full due to the poor quality of those photos.

4. Gayādhara and Drokmi Lotsawa Śākya Yeshé ('Brog mi Lo tsā ba Śākya ye shes, 993–1077?)
5. Setön Künrik (Se ston Kun rig, 1025–1122) and Zhangtön Chöbar (Zhang ston Chos 'bar, 1053–1135)
6. Sachen Künga Nyingpo (1092–1158), with standing Maitreya and Mañjuśrī to his right and left
7. Loppön Sönam Tsemo (Slob dpon Bsod nams rtse mo, 1142–82) and Jetsün Drakpa Gyeltsen (1147–1216)
8. Sakya Paṇḍita (Sa skya Paṇḍi ta, 1182–1251) and Chögyel Pakpa (Chos rgyal 'Phags pa, 1235–80)
9. Zhangtön Könchokpel (Zhang ston Dkon mchog dpal, b. 1240) and Napza Drakpukpa Sönampel (Na bza' Brag phug pa Bsod nams dpal, 1277–1350)
10. Ritröpa Lodrö Tenpa (Ri khrod pa Blo gros brtan pa, 1316–58) and Penden Tsültrim (Dpal ldan tshul khrims, 1333–99)
11. Buddhaśrī (1339–1420), with standing Avalokiteśvara and Maitreya to his right and left

According to Lowo Khenchen's description, these central masters were framed by minor figures portraying various main tantric deities, accompanying minor deities of their maṇḍalas, the eighty-four siddhas, or lineal masters from other lineages received by Ngorchen. In addition to identifying each main figure, Lowo Khenchen names some of these minor figures, and those that he does not name individually he at least describes or classifies clearly enough that we can identify them if we know the relevant iconography.

Regarding the central masters, it is noteworthy that Ngorchen did not depict Lama Dampa Sönam Gyeltsen (Bla ma dam pa Bsod nams rgyal mtshan, 1312–75) as a central lineage master. This is surprising, since the main Lamdré lineage passed down through him, and thus he would have been expected on painting number 10 as the lineage master of Penden Tsültrim. However, since the latter had received the entire Lamdré instructions from three different masters—Ritröpa Lodrö Tenpa, Shang Karpo Drakpa Khedrup Rinchen Senggé (Shangs dkar po brag pa mKhas grub Rin chen seng ge, fl. fourteenth c.), and Lama Dampa—it seems that Ngorchen wanted to stress the teaching line of Lodrö Tenpa.

In addition, Ngorchen evidently also wanted to depict such major alternative forks in the Lamdré lineage by including two alternative lineage masters among the minor figures of paintings 9 and 10. Without explaining their function within the structure of either painting, Lowo Khenchen records the depiction of four important masters in the viewer's left and right corners of the second upper row. All four were major Lamdré masters: Tsokgom Küngapel (Tshogs sgom Kun dga' dpal, 1210–1307) and Nyenchenpa Sönam Tenpa (Nyan chen pa Bsod nams brtan pa, 1222–1317) in painting number 9, and Lama Dampa and Rinchen Senggé in painting number 10.

In the last painting of the set, number 11, Sharchen Yeshé Gyeltsen (Shar chen Ye shes rgyal mtshan, 1359–1406) and Sapzang Pakpa are depicted in the viewer's left and right corners of the second upper row. However, unlike in paintings 9 and 10, they are not depicted as members of a Lamdré lineage alternative fork but simply as crucial teachers of Ngorchen, who appears at the viewer's bottom left of the same painting.

The First Painting

The first painting of the set portrays the primordial Buddha Vajradhara as its main figure, while two minor figures are shown standing to his proper right and left: Vajragarbha and Nairātmyā (see fig. 1). In the red bottom cartouche, however, only two invocation prayers are written—namely, for Vajradhara and Nairātmyā. This clarifies that, in addition to the main figure, Vajradhara, just one of the minor figures, Nairātmyā, should also be counted as a main lineal guru of the Lamdré lineage, as is also confirmed by written supplications and lineage records.

For us, that Vajragarbha suddenly appears here in iconographically such a crucial place and role is very puzzling. We used to count him as an alternative lineage guru for that reason (in the *Nepalese Legacy* catalogue). We now guess that he is meant to be the enlightened bodhisattva Vajragarbha who composed a famous Hevajra commentary (but who was not an actual transmitter of the lineage).

The arrangement of the minor figures on the first painting, as well as on the following ones, would be impossible to understand without Lowo Khenchen's help. As he described it:

> First, the Buddha Vajradhara: He is surrounded by a group of deities, according to the yoga tantric system, whose "three seats" are complete. In the corners above and diagonally out from his right and left shoulders are two figures of Dharma Lord Yeshé Gyeltsen, symbolizing learning and meditative practice. Of these, the first holds a scripture on top of a *padma* flower at his right shoulder, the stem of which emerges from between the hands he has in Dharma-teaching gesture. The second performs the gesture of meditative concentration.
>
> To the right and left of Vajradhara stand two main figures: Vajragarbha and Nairātmyā. Vajragarbha's right hand holds a *vajra* on top of an *utpala* flower, the stem of which emerges from between the

Fig. 1. Vajradhara as the Original Teacher of the Lamdré instructions flanked by Vajragarbha and Nairātmyā (the latter as second lineal master). For the full caption and color plate of this and the other paintings, see the color section, plates 3–6.

thumb and index finger of his right hand performing at his heart the Dharma-teaching gesture. His left hand holds a *ghaṇṭa* on top of an *utpala* flower, the stem of which emerges from between the thumb and index finger of his left hand, which is extended as in the gesture of highest giving. As for Vajranairātmyā, her right hand is outstretched downward holding a curved knife, and her left hand is in the manner of offering nectar with a skull-cup to the central figure.[13]

13. This passage has been cited from the translation of the entire iconographic description provided below.

The painting depicts thirty-four minor figures that include, according to this description, the groups of maṇḍala deities who together constitute the three main "seats" or types of deities according to the yoga tantric system. These three are: type 1, the five buddhas and eight bodhisattvas; type 2, the five female buddha consorts (*rig ma*) and six goddesses (*lha mo*); and type 3, male and female wrathful deities (*khro bo, khro mo*). In this painting, one can see the five buddhas of the maṇḍala on the top row, the second through sixth figures (d1–d5). Next to them and downward in both columns are the bodhisattvas (d6–d13), and next to and below the five buddhas, the buddha consorts (d14–18) and goddesses (d29–d34). The third "seat" or class is represented by the ten wrathful deities (d19–d28).

In addition, a Tibetan lama is depicted twice above and to the right and left shoulders (t1 and t2 in the following chart) of the main figure (1 in the following chart). With the help of Lowo Khenchen's description, he can be identified as Ngorchen's late master Sharchen Yeshé Gyeltsen, who is shown in two different aspects as a religious master.[14] (He did not give Ngorchen the Lamdré instructions, but Ngorchen still recalled his spiritual inspiration with great gratitude here, at the beginning of the thangka series.)

The structure of the painting can thus be diagrammed:

d6	d1	d2	d3		d4	d5	d14	d7
d8		d15				d16		d9
	t1						t2	
d10								d11
	d17			1			d18	
d12								d13
d19		**2a**				**2b**		d20
d21								d22
d23								d24
d25								d26
d27	d29	d30	d31		d32	d33	d34	d28

(Abbreviations: "d" stands for "deity," while "t" is short for "teacher.")

14. Sharchen is also identified by labels written directly below his depiction. However, these two labels are not legible on the available photos.

Fig. 2. Virūpa and Kāṇha as third and fourth lineal masters.

The Second Painting

The second painting portrays as main figures the Indian siddhas Virūpa and Kāṇha as third and fourth lineal masters of the Lamdré instructions (see fig. 2). Since the arrangement of the minor figures on paintings two through five is thematically related, Lowo Khenchen introduces their general composition together, adding to the above description:

> The second scroll painting depicts as main figures Virūpa and Kāṇha facing each other. The third painting will depict Ḍamarūpa and Avadhūtipa; the fourth, Gayādhara and the Great Lama Drokmi; and the fifth, Setön Künrik and Zhangtön Chöbar. In

> those successive paintings the top row and the right and left columns framing each pair of main figures will be taken up by twenty-one great siddhas per painting—that is, by eighty-four siddhas in all. At the lower ends of the right columns are found in each one of the four main figures of Hevajra of the *Vajrapañjara Tantra*, together with each of their respective group of eight goddesses in the bottom rows—namely, Dorjé Chen (Rdo rje can) in the second scroll painting, Penpa (Phan pa) in the third, Dorjé Nyima (Rdo rje nyi ma) in the fourth, and Padma Garwang (Padma gar dbang) in the fifth.[15]

Moreover, Lowo Khenchen provides other important details specific just to the second painting:

> Further, in the center above the ornamental roof over the two main figures of the second painting Bhagavān Hevajra abides standing on a stacked seat of reclining deities. To his right is the Nairātmyā of the *Saṃpuṭa Tantra*. In the first of her two right hands she brandishes a *vajra* and her first left hand holds a skull-cup to her heart. Her lower two hands have a curved knife and skull-cup.[16] She abides in a half crossed-leg dancing posture with her left leg extended. To Hevajra's left is the Nairātmyā of the *Mūlatantra* of Hevajra.[17]

We can thus see that Ngorchen has ordered the great siddhas depicted following the traditional order of Vajrāsana.[18] As Rob Linrothe established, the twenty-one siddhas (s1–s21) shown on the painting depict the siddhas Nāgārjuna through Kantipa or Śāntipa.[19] Mahāsiddhas number 7 and 8 in Vajrāsana's list have changed positions, with Virūpa (s7) moving ahead of Ḍombi Heruka (s8). Virūpa thus appears twice in the painting: as the first main lineal master of the painting (and thus number 3 of the series) and as seventh of eighty-four siddhas.

According to Lowo Khenchen, in this painting near the bottom of the "right" column (which is, from the viewer's perspective, on the left) is pic-

15. This passage has been cited from the translation of the entire iconographic description provided below.

16. Note that Nairātmyā is actually depicted holding an arrow in her second lower hand.

17. This passage has been cited from the translation of the entire iconographic description provided below.

18. On Vajrāsana's list and his versified praise, see Linrothe 2006, 423 and 427–32, respectively.

19. See Linrothe 2006, 296, no. 49.

tured one of the four main forms of Hevajra (d4) according to the *Vajrapañjara Tantra*—that is, blue Akṣobhya Hevajra—while beneath him is his own special group of eight goddesses (g1–g8)—namely, those of the class called Possessing Vajras (Rdo rje can).

This painting can thus be diagrammed as follows:

s1	s2	s3	s4		s5	s6	s7	s8
s9								s10
s11		d2		d1		d3		s12
s13								s14
s15			3		4			s16
s17								s18
s19								s20
d4								s21
g1	g2	g3	g4		g5	g6	g7	g8

(Abbreviations: "s" stands for "siddha," "d" stands for "deity," and "g" is short for "goddess.")

The Third Painting

The third painting continues the Lamdré lineage, portraying as its main figures the two Indian siddhas Ḍamarūpa and Avadhūtipa as the fifth and sixth lineal masters (see fig. 3). Moreover, the minor figures surrounding the two central masters on all four sides also continue the thematic composition arranged on paintings two through five. Following Lowo Khenchen's description, the third painting shows the second set of twenty-one siddhas, and we would thus expect that they depict the siddhas Atiśa through Tampaka of Vajrāsana's list (nos. 22–42). However, since after Tampaka, who is shown as a blacksmith working metal (s41), an additional siddha is shown—number 43 from Vajrāsana's list, the musician Bhinasa playing the *vīṅa* (s42)—one of the siddhas 22 to 42 from Vajrāsana's list is apparently missing. He might have changed position with Bhinasa and thus be found on the fourth painting of the set, which is not available. The identity of the missing siddha should be relatively easy to establish as soon

Fig. 3. Ḍamarūpa and Avadhūtipa as fifth and sixth lineal masters.

as we obtain photos of the labeling inscriptions written below the depiction of each siddha. Otherwise, an iconographical comparison with other siddha depictions might also solve the question.

The other theme continued near the bottom of the proper right column is a depiction of the second of four main Hevajra forms (d4) according to the *Vajrapañjara Tantra*—that is, white Vairocana Hevajra. He is accompanied by his own special group of eight goddesses (g1–g8), called Helpful Ones (Phan pa), in the bottom row. On the further specifics of the third painting, Lowo Khenchen adds:

> In the center above the ornamental roof over the two main figures of the third painting Kāyavajra is shown with one face and two hands. His right hand holds a *vajra* and his left a skull-cup. He stands in a

dancing posture with extended right leg. He holds a *khaṭvāṅga* staff in his left elbow. [Gloss: This figure lacks a consort.]

To his right is Cittavajra with three faces and six hands. His basic face is blue, the right white, and the left red. His first pair of hands embraces his consort. The two beneath them hold a curved knife and trident. The next two below them hold a *vajra* and *ghaṇṭa*. The female consort, who holds a curved knife and skull-cup, embraces her male consort.[20] Cittavajra stands in a half crossed-legged posture with extended right leg.

To Kāyavajra's left is Vākvajra with three faces and four hands. His faces are like the previous deity [that is, Cittavajra], and his first two hands embrace his consort. His two lower hands hold a *vajra* and skull-cup. He abides in a half crossed-leg dancing posture with right leg extended.[21]

The diagram of this painting would thus be:

s22	s23	s24	s25		s26	s27	s28	s29
s30								s31
s32		d2		d1		d3		s33
s34								s35
s36			5		6			s37
s38								s39
s40								s41
d4								s42
g1	g2	g3	g4		g5	g6	g7	g8

(Abbreviations: "s" stands for "siddha," "d" stands for "deity," and "g" is short for "goddess.")

20. The description of the consort differs from her appearance on the painting. Since she is apparently embracing Cittavajra with her left hand, which is thus not visible, only her right hand is depicted, and this hand does not seem to hold any implement. The description continues with Vākvajra. Though he also has a consort, the implement she holds in her right hand (a curved knife?) is not mentioned by Lowo Khenchen.

21. This passage has been cited from the translation of the entire iconographic description provided below.

Fig. 4. Sönam Tsemo and Drakpa Gyeltsen as twelfth and thirteenth lineal masters.

The Seventh Painting

On the seventh painting, Ngorchen had depicted Sachen's two great sons Loppön Sönam Tsemo (1142–82) and Jetsün Drakpa Gyeltsen (1147–1216), as twelfth and thirteenth lineal masters of the Lamdré instructions (see fig. 4). The two main figures are framed by minor figures representing another lineage that Ngorchen had received. In his description, Lowo Khenchen identifies it as the Sakya tradition (*sa lugs*) of the lineage of Cakrasaṃvara descending through the siddha Kṛṣṇācārya—a lineage that Ngorchen had received from Sharchen Yeshé Gyeltsen—and continues to enumerate the names of the depicted lineal masters:

> The seventh painting depicts the two Jetsün Brothers [that is, Loppön Sönam Tsemo and Jetsün Drakpa Gyeltsen] facing each other. In the center above the ornamental roof over them is Cakrasaṃvara Saṃvarodaya; to his right, Cakrasaṃvara in the tradition of Kṛṣṇācārya; and to his left, Cakrasaṃvara in the tradition of Lūhipa, together with Pañjaranātha at the end of the lineage [below at the proper far left of the bottom row].
>
> The lineage of the Sakya tradition of Cakrasaṃvara in the tradition of Kṛṣṇācārya surrounding these figures on all sides is: [. . .].[22]

The lineage begins on the far left of the top row for the viewer and goes straight across to the right, continues then by alternating on left and right columns, before ending in the bottom row with Ngorchen's master Sharchen (no. 29). Thus the arrangement is:

1	2	3	4		5	6	7	8
9	d2			d1			d3	10
11								12
13								14
15			**12**		**13**			16
17								18
19								20
21								22
23	24	25	26		27	28	29	d4

(Abbreviation: "d" stands for "deity.")

Textual Witnesses of Lowo Khenchen's Description

Lowo Khenchen's description of the painting set is available in four different manuscript versions: three textual witnesses (*Bri yig* 1–3) are preserved among three different collections of his collected writings housed in the Nationalities

22. This passage has been cited from the translation of the entire iconographic description provided below.

Library of the Cultural Palace of Nationalities (Beijing, China) and another one (*Bri yig* 4) in a manuscript collection of his works from Geling, Mustang (Glo bo).[23]

Moreover, there is a fifth witness from Mustang surviving in Lowo Khenchen's collected writings, a late-seventeenth-century manuscript commissioned by the Lowo ruler Samdrup Pembar (Bsam grub dpal 'bar) now preserved in the Tōyō Bunko library, Tokyo. Though the manuscript itself is presently not possible to consult, there exists a transliterated version as a Word file (*Bri yig* 5) prepared by David Jackson, who used it in his previous studies.[24]

There is also a modern digital-input version in Western book format (*Bri yig* 6), which was edited as part of Lowo Khenchen's collected writings by the Mönzang Penying Tsöldu Khang (Smon bzang dpe rnying 'tshol bsdu khang) in Lhasa (2018), and which has been input on the basis of the fourth textual witness (*Bri yig* 4).[25]

Lowo Khenchen's description most likely also forms part of another recent collection of his writings that was edited in Chengdu (2016), which is, however, unavailable to the authors at present.[26]

Interestingly, these textual witnesses refer to Lowo Khenchen's description by two slightly varying titles:

- *A Written Description of the Lineage Masters of the Path with Its Fruit* (*Lam 'bras bu dang bcas pa'i bla ma brgyud pa rnams kyi bri yig*)[27]
- *A Written Description of the Lamas of the Path with Its Fruit, Together with Lineages* (*Lam 'bras bu dang bcas pa'i bla ma brgyud pa dang bcas pa rnams kyi bri yig*)[28]

23. For the table of contents (*dkar chag*) of this four-volume set, which is missing from the scan available from BDRC, see Jackson 1987, 546–54.

24. On this incomplete collection of Lowo Khenchen's writings, see Jackson 1987, 212–13, 555–65.

25. The Geling manuscript of Lowo Khenchen's writings was edited some years ago by the Mönzang Penying Tsöldukhang and printed for local distribution in Nepal; see Smon bzang dpe rnying 'tshol bsdu khang 2017. The digital-input version of his writings edited by the Monzang Penying Tsöldukhang in Western book format, in 2018, is mainly based on the Geling manuscript; see Spang rdzong Skal bzang chos ldan 2018. However, this editorial preface mistakenly states that the manuscript is not housed at Geling but at Lowo Möntang or Möntang Gön.

26. See Si khron bod yig dpe rnying bsdu sgrig khang 2016.

27. See Glo bo Mkhan chen Bsod nams lhun grub, *Bri yig* 1–2.

28. See Glo bo Mkhan chen Bsod nams lhun grub, *Bri yig* 3–6.

Moreover, the different textual witnesses contain slight variations in the use of case suffixes as well as in spellings. Regarding the latter, we encounter, for instance, variations in how the personal names of lineage masters or their titles are written (such as *lo tstsha ba* or *lo tsā ba* and Rje btsun chen po or Rje btsun chen mo). Since the limited scope of our present contribution did not allow a critical edition of Lowo Khenchen's description, the translation follows in the case of such variations the most correct syntax and also provides the most common forms of names or titles. The very few important content-related variations we have recorded in footnotes.

Tibetan names occurring in the following translation are transcribed phonetically, and their Wylie spelling equivalents are transliterated below in a "Transliteration Table Translation." Only for the Sanskrit names of Indian gurus have the Tibetan equivalents been given directly in Wylie in brackets.

Translation

A Written Description of the Lineage Masters of the Path with Its Fruit
or
A Written Description of the Lamas of the Path with Its Fruit, Together with Lineages

Oṃ svāsti siddhaṃ!

> I bow to the Immaculate Master together with his lineage,
> the supreme sun of the wisdom and kindness of all buddhas,
> whose compassion, dawning throughout the sky,
> opens wide all the doors of well-maintained tantric scriptures.[29]

Here is the plan of the eleven painted scrolls preserved at [Ngor] Ewaṃ Chöden of the Lamdré lineage, which were made as an object of spiritual practice of the Great Buddha Vajradhara Künga Zangpo himself and the arrangement of the divine figures of which he designed in detail.

29. An alternative translation of this verse may read:

> I bow to the Excellent Master together with his lineage,
> who is the supreme sun of the wisdom and kindness of all buddhas,
> and who causes the well-maintained media of tantric scriptures to flourish
> across the vast space-like domain of his compassion.

The Immaculate Master or Excellent Master (Kun bzang) is a reference to Ngorchen, whose personal name was Künga Zangpo (Kun dga' bzang po).

[*The First Painting*]

First, the Buddha Vajradhara: He is surrounded by a group of deities, according to the yoga tantric system, whose "three seats" are complete. In the corners above and diagonally out from his right and left shoulders are two figures of Dharma Lord Yeshé Gyeltsen, symbolizing learning and meditative practice. Of these, the first holds a scripture on top of a *padma* flower at his right shoulder, the stem of which emerges from between the hands he has in Dharma-teaching gesture. The second performs the gesture of meditative concentration.

To the right and left of Vajradhara stand two main figures: Vajragarbha and Nairātmyā. Vajragarbha's right hand holds a *vajra* on top of an *utpala* flower, the stem of which emerges from between the thumb and index finger of his right hand performing at his heart the Dharma-teaching gesture. His left hand holds a *ghaṇṭa* on top of an *utpala* flower, the stem of which emerges from between the thumb and index finger of his left hand, which is extended as in the gesture of highest giving. As for Vajranairātmyā, her right hand is outstretched downward holding a curved knife, and her left hand is held in the manner of offering nectar with a skull-cup to the central figure.

[*Description of the Next Four Paintings*]

The second scroll painting depicts as main figures Virūpa and Kāṇha facing each other. The third painting will depict Ḍamarūpa and Avadhūtipa; the fourth, Gayādhara and the Great Lama Drokmi; and the fifth, Setön Künrik and Zhangtön Chöbar. In those successive paintings the top row and the right and left columns framing each pair of main figures will be taken up by twenty-one great siddhas per painting—that is, by eighty-four siddhas in all. At the lower ends of the right columns are found in each one of the four main figures of Hevajra of the *Vajrapañjara Tantra*, together with each of their respective group of eight goddesses in the bottom rows—namely, Dorjé Chen in the second scroll painting, Penpa in the third, Dorjé Nyima in the fourth, and Padma Garwang in the fifth.

[*The Second Painting*]

[As just mentioned, the second painting depicts as main figures Virūpa and Kāṇha, and also twenty-one great adepts, and one of the four main figures of Hevajra from the *Vajrapañjara Tantra*, together with one group of eight associated goddesses below—namely, those called Dorjé Chen.]

Further, in the center above the ornamental roof over the two main figures of the second painting Bhagavān Hevajra abides standing on a stacked seat of reclining deities. To his right is the Nairātmyā of the *Saṃpuṭa Tantra*. In the first of her two right hands she brandishes a *vajra* and her first left hand holds a skull-cup to her heart. Her lower two hands have a curved knife and skull-cup.[30] She abides in a half crossed-leg dancing posture with her left leg extended. To Hevajra's left is the Nairātmyā of the *Mūlatantra* of Hevajra.

[*The Third Painting*]

[As mentioned above, the third painting depicts as main figures Ḍamarūpa and Avadhūtipa, with twenty-one great adepts and one of the four main figures of Hevajra of the *Vajrapañjara Tantra*, along with a group of eight associated goddesses below—namely, those called Penpa.]

In the center above the ornamental roof over the two main figures of the third painting Kāyavajra is shown with one face and two hands. His right hand holds a *vajra* and his left a skull-cup. He stands in a dancing posture with extended right leg. He holds a *khaṭvāṅga* staff in his left elbow. [Gloss: This figure lacks a consort.]

To his right is Cittavajra with three faces and six hands. His basic face is blue, the right white, and the left red. His first pair of hands embraces his consort. The two beneath them hold a curved knife and trident. The next two below them hold a *vajra* and *ghaṇṭa*. The female consort, who holds a curved knife and skull-cup, embraces her male consort.[31] Cittavajra stands in a half crossed-legged posture with extended right leg.

To Kāyavajra's left is Vākvajra with three faces and four hands. His faces are like the previous deity [that is, Cittavajra] and his first two hands embrace his consort. His two lower hands hold a *vajra* and skull-cup. He abides in a half crossed-leg dancing posture with the right leg extended.

[*The Fourth Painting*]

[As mentioned above, the fourth painting depicts as main figures Gayādhara and the Great Lama Drokmi, with twenty-one great adepts, one of the four main figures of Hevajra of the *Vajrapañjara Tantra*, together with an associated group of eight goddesses below—namely, those called Dorjé Nyima.]

In the center above the ornamental roof over the two main figures of the fourth painting is shown Vajradhātu of the *Saṃpuṭa Tantra*. To his right is

30. Note that Nairātmyā is actually depicted holding an arrow in her second lower hand.

31. The description of the consort differs from her appearance on the painting. Since she is apparently embracing Cittavajra with her left hand, which is thus not visible, only her right hand is depicted, and this hand does not seem to hold any implement. The description continues with Vākvajra. Though he also has a consort, the implement she holds in her right hand (a curved knife?) is not mentioned by Lowo Khenchen.

Caturpītha with blue skin, three faces, and six hands.[32] His three faces are blue, white, and red. His first two hands, which hold a *vajra* and *ghaṇṭa*, embrace his consort. The second of his right hands holds the breast of his consort. The third right hand holds a curved knife. In the second of his left hands he holds a skull-cup, and in the third one a bow and arrow. The female consort—with red skin, her right hand holding a *khaṭvāṅga* staff, and the left a skull-cup—embraces her male consort. Caturpītha sits on a lion-mat with legs folded in the posture of a *sattva*.

To Vajradhātu's left side is Jñānaḍākinī with blue skin, three faces, and six hands. Those three faces are like the previous deity [that is, like Caturpītha]. In the first of the right ones of her six hands, she holds a battle-axe, in the second a *vajra*, and in the third a *vajra* staff. In the first of her left hands she holds a *ghaṇṭa*, in the second a skull-cup, and in the third a sword. She sits on a lion with legs folded in the posture of a *sattva*.

[*The Fifth Painting*]

[As mentioned above, the fifth painting depicts Setön Künrik and Zhangtön Chöbar, with as minor figures twenty-one great adepts, and one of the four main figures of Hevajra of the *Vajrapañjara Tantra*, accompanied by their associated groups of eight goddesses below—namely, those called Padma Garwang.]

In the center above the ornamental roof over the two main figures of the fifth painting Red Yamāri is depicted. To his right is Vajrāmṛta with three faces that are green, white, and red, and with six hands. With his first two hands holding a *vajra* and *ghaṇṭa* he embraces his consort. In the second of his right hands he holds a sword, and in the third a jewel. In the second of his left hands he holds a *patākā* banner, and in his third a noose. The female consort's skin is green with three faces and six hands. Her facial colors are like those of her male consort, and with her first two hands she embraces her male consort. Her two hands below them hold a jewel and noose. Her final two hands hold a sword and *patākā* banner. The legs of the male consort [that is, Vajrāmṛta] are in *vajra* posture. To Raktayamāri's left is Vajratārā with four faces, eight hands, and yellow skin, as taught in the *Vajrapañjara Tantra*.

[*The Sixth Painting*]

In the sixth painting the Great Sakyapa [that is, Sachen Künga Nyingpo] is

32. Some versions of Lowo Khenchen's description—*Bri yig* 3, 3a3; *Bri yig* 4, 2b1; *Bri yig* 5, 137b; and *Bri yig* 6, 126.19–20—begin this passage with a misplaced phrase that has to be deleted: *g.yas su ~~rdo rje dbyings| g.yon du~~ rdo rje gdan bzhi|*.

present as central figure. To his right and left are the two [great bodhisattvas] Maitreya and Mañjuśrī, in standing posture.

In the right and left corners above and diagonally out from Sachen's shoulders are the two figures Lama Penden Tsültrim and Dharma Lord Yeshé Gyeltsen. Above these two are two figures of Hevajra standing on spread-out seats.

To the right and left of the central jewel at the top of the ornamental roof are the two figures of Khyin Lotsāwa and Khön Könchok Gyelpo.

At the bottom end of the right column is Aśvarāja, who continues the previously mentioned [four main figures of Hevajra as depicted in paintings two through five], and his group of eight goddesses in the bottom row beneath.

In the surrounding area on all sides are the lineage masters of the commentarial tradition of Hevajra. Their names have been written in front of each:[33]

1. Vajradhara (Rdo rje 'chang)
2. Nairātmyā (Bdag med ma)
3. Virūpa (Birwa pa)
4. Ḍombi Heruka (Ḍom bhi he ru ka)
5. Alalavajra (A la la badzra)
6. Araṇyavāsin or Vanavāsin? (Nags khrod pa)
7. Garbharīpāda (Garbha ri pa)
8. Jayaśrījñāna (Bsod snyoms pa)
9. Durjayacandra (Mi thub zla ba)
10. Vīravajra (Dpa' bo rdo rje)
11. Drokmi Lotsawa [Śākya Yeshé]
12. Ngaripa Selwé Nyingpo
13. Khön Gechuwa [Dralhabar]
14. Lama Sachen [Künga Nyingpo]
15. Jetsün Sönam Tsemo
16. Jetsün Chenpo [Drakpa Gyeltsen]
17. Chöjepa [Sakya Paṇḍita]
18. Chögyel Pakpa
19. Tashipel
20. Drakpukpa [Sönampel]
21. Lodrö Tenpa
22. Penden Tsültrim
23. Lama Dampa Yeshé Gyeltsen

33. On this lineage and its forks, see Ngor chen Kun dga' bzang po 1993, 196.6–98.2. See also Jackson 1986, 190–91. Here and in the following cases, the numbering of the lineage masters was added by the authors.

[*The Seventh Painting*]

The seventh painting depicts the two Jetsün Brothers [that is, Loppön Sönam Tsemo and Jetsün Drakpa Gyeltsen] facing each other. In the center above the ornamental roof over them is Cakrasaṃvara Saṃvarodaya; to his right, Cakrasaṃvara in the tradition of Kṛṣṇācārya; and to his left, Cakrasaṃvara in the tradition of Lūhipa, together with Pañjaranātha at the end of the lineage [below at the proper far left of the bottom row].

The lineage of the Sakya tradition of Cakrasaṃvara in the tradition of Kṛṣṇācārya that surrounds these figures on all sides is:[34]

1. Vajradhara (Rdo rje 'chang)
2. Vajrapāṇi (Phyag na rdo rje)
3. Saraha (Sa ra ha)
4. Nāgārjuna ('Phags pa Klu sgrub)
5. Sabaripāda (Shwa wa ri dbang phyug)
6. Lūhipāda (Lo hi pa)
7. Dārikapāda (Dhā ri ka pa)
8. Vajraghaṇṭāpāda (Rdo rje dril bu pa)
9. Kūrmapāda (Rus sbal zhabs)
10. Jālandharapāda (Shrī dza landha ri pa)
11. Kṛṣṇācārya (Nag po spyod pa)
12. Guhyapāda? (Gu hya pa)
13. Vijayapāda (Rnam rgyal zhabs)
14. Tailopa (Ti lo pa)
15. Nāropāda or Nāḍapāda (Nā ro pa)
16. Pamtingpa, the elder brother [Jikmé Drakpa; Abhayakīrti]
17. Pamtingpa, the younger brother [Ngakgi Wangchuk; Vāgīśvara]
18. Lokya Sheraptsek
19. Melgyo Lodrö Drakpa
20. Jé Sachen [Künga Nyingpo]
21. Jetsün [Sönam] Tsemo
22. Jetsün Chenpo [Drakpa Gyeltsen]
23. Sakya Paṇḍita

34. As described by Ngorchen, this is the lineage of initiation for Cakrasaṃvara associated with Kṛṣṇācārya (*bde mchog nag po pa'i dbang gyi brgyud pa*); see Ngor chen Kun dga' bzang po 1993, 204.6–5.3. See also Blo gter dbang po 1972, 107.1–8.3, 113.4–6; Jackson 1986, 183; and Jackson 2011, 209nn227–28. Note that there is a lineage record of the Sakya tradition (*sa lugs*) that begins similarly—that is, the one associated with Lūhipāda—but differs after Sakya Paṇḍita; see Ngor chen Kun dga' bzang po 1993, 201.3–6.

24. Chögyel Pakpa
25. Zhang Könchokpel
26. Chöjé Drakpukpa [Sönampel]
27. Lodrö Tenpa
28. Penden Tsültrim
29. Chöjé Yeshé Gyeltsen

[*The Eighth Painting*]

The eighth painting depicts the two central figures Dharma Lord, the uncle [that is, Sakya Paṇḍita] and [his] nephew [that is, Chögyel Pakpa].

In the center and to its right and left above the ornamental roof over those two central masters are as main deities the Three Guhyasamāja Families.

In the surrounding area on all sides are the lineage masters of the Ngok tradition of Guhyasamāja, together with Wrathful Takkirāja as final support below. The names of the lineage masters are:[35]

1. Vajradhara (Rdo rje 'chang)
2. Vajradharma (Rdo rje chos)
3. Jñānaḍākinī (Ye shes kyi mkha' 'gro ma)
4. Visukalpa (Bi su kalpa)
5. Saraha (Sa ra ha)
6. Nāgārjuna ('Phags pa Klu sgrub)
7. Āryadeva (Ārya de ba)
8. Śākyamitra (Shākya bshes gnyen)
9. Nāgabodhi (Klu'i byang chub)
10. Candrakīrti (Zla ba grags pa)
11. Śiṣyavajra (Slob pa'i rdo rje)
12. Kāṇha (Nag po pa)
13. Gomiśra (Slob dpon Sa 'dres pa)
14. Abhijña (Mngon shes can)
15. Yoṣa (Btsun mo can)
16. Kṛṣṇasamayavajra (Dam tshig rdo rje)
17. Gö Lotsāwa [Khukpa Lhetsé]
18. Mangra Senggyel
19. [Ngok] Yeshé Senggé
20. [Ngok] Nyima Senggé

35. On this lineage and its forks, see Ngor chen Kun dga' bzang po 1993, 183.5–85.3. Note that in this lineage record Saraha is referred to as Brahmin Rāhulabhadra (Bram ze Sgra gcan 'dzin bzang po) and Nāgārjuna by his ordination name (Dge slong Dpal ldan).

21. [Len Tsetsa] Nyimacham
22. Dok Āryadeva [that is, 'Phags pa lha]
23. [Gyakhar Tangbewa] Pakpakyap
24. Serdingpa [Zhönnu Ö]
25. Chöku Özer
26. Künkhyen Pakö
27. Butön Khaché [Rinchendrup]
28. [Khyungpo Lhepa] Zhönnu Sönam
29. Lama Dampa Yeshé Gyeltsen

[*The Ninth Painting*]

The ninth painting depicts as its two central figures Zhangtön [Könchokpel] and Dharma Lord Drakpukpa [Sönampel]. In the center, above the ornamental roof over them, is Buddha Amitāyus; to his right, Tsokgom [Küngapel]; and to his left, Nyenchenpa [Sönam Tenpa].

In the bottom row are successively from right to left: the five Mahāmāyā deities [that is, Mahāmāyā with four retinue deities], Siṃhanāda, Vasudhārā, Gaṇapati, and Mahācakra Vajrapāṇi. In the surrounding columns to the right and left are the lineage masters for the initiation of the Ngok tradition for the maṇḍala of the five Mahāmāyā deities, which Ngorchen received from Sapzang Pakpa, namely:[36]

1. Vajradhara (Rdo rje 'chang)
2. Jñānaḍākinī (Ye shes kyi mkha' 'gro)
3. Kukuripa (Ku ku ri pa)
4. Saroruhavajra (Mtsho skyes rdo rje)
5. Ḍombipa (Ḍoṃ bhi pa)
6. Tailopa (Ti lo pa)
7. Nāropāda or Nāḍapāda (Nā ro pa)

36. On this lineage and its forks, see Ngor chen Kun dga' bzang po 1993, 326.6–27.5. Note that after the entry for Ngok Chökyi Dorjé (*rngog gzhung pa chos rdor|*), the lineage record confusingly reads: *sras jo sras mdo sde|*, which might refer to both Ngok José and Ngok Dodé. When recording the lineage for the third chapter of the *Mahāmāyā Tantra*, these two Ngok masters are clearly separated; see Ngor chen Kun dga' bzang po 1993, 359.5: *rngog chos rdor| rngog jo sras| rngog mdo sde|*. Note also that the lineage record gives an additional master between Drakpapel and Sapzang Paṇchen called Künkhyen Gangpa; see Ngor chen Kun dga' bzang po 1993, 327.2–3: *bla ma kīrti shrī| kun mkhyen gangs pa| paṇ chen ma ti|*. However, by comparison with BDRC (P0RK410, P3830), Drakpapel (Bla ma Kīrtiśrī) and Künkhyen Gangpa might actually be one and the same person: Künkhyen Gangpa Drakpapel.

8. Śāntibhadra (Zhi ba bzang po)
9. Marpa Lotsāwa [Chökyi Lodrö]
10. [Ngok] Chökyi Dorjé
11. Ngok José
12. Ngok Dodé
13. Ngo[tsa] Chöku
14. [Ngotsa] Könchokpel
15. [Lokya] Wangchukdrak
16. [Dongtön] Sherappel
17. Chögyel Pakpa
18. Zhönnubum
19. Drakpapel
20. Sapzang Paṇchen [Lodrö Gyeltsen]
21. Sapzang Pakpa [Zhönnu Lodrö]

[*The Tenth Painting*]
The tenth painting depicts the two central figures Lodrö Tenpa and Penden Tsültrim. In the center, above the ornamental roof over them, is Mañjuśrī; to his right, Dharma Lord Sönam Gyeltsen; and to his left, Rinchen Senggé.

In the bottom row are from right to left: Bhūtaḍāmara, Mahābala, Yellow Tārā with three faces and eight hands, White Prajñāpāramitā, Vajrānaṅga, Kurukullā, Ekavīrā Amoghapāśa, and Yellow Mañjuśrī.

As for Mahābala, his body is blue color with four faces and eight hands. His central face is blue, the right white, the left yellow, and the back red. In his successive right hands, he holds snakes that are white, green, red, and yellow.[37] In his left ones, he holds snakes that are red, green, white, and blue. He sits on top of a *garuḍa* with legs folded in *sattva* posture.

Regarding that Vajrānaṅga, his body is yellow with one face and six hands. In his first two hands he holds a bow and arrow, in the second two a white and green *padma* flower, and in his third two a *vajra* staff and *utpala* flower. He wears a skirt of tiger skin. His right leg is extended and the left bent. He is bejeweled.

That Yellow Mañjuśrī, who is taught in the *Vajrapañjara Tantra*, holds his right hand in the gesture of highest giving and with his left an *utpala* flower. He sits with legs crossed in *vajra* posture.

37. Glo bo Mkhan chen Bsod nams lhun grub, *Bri yig* 1, 4b7 reads "yellow" (*ser po*), whereas all other textual witnesses have for a second time "white" (*dkar po*); see Glo bo Mkhan chen Bsod nams lhun grub, *Bri yig* 2, 6a5; *Bri yig* 3, 5a5; *Bri yig* 4, 4b1; *Bri yig* 5, 141b; and *Bri yig* 6, 130.5–6.

In the surrounding area [in the upper row and right and left columns] those masters and deities are framed by the lineage masters of the Dro tradition of the practical instructions for the *ṣaḍaṅgayoga* of Kālacakra, the profound *vajra-yoga*, which Ngorchen received from Drupchen Buddhaśrī. Their names are:[38]

1. Primordial Buddha (Dang po'i sangs rgyas; Ādibuddha) [Gloss: With blue skin and a white head, his two hands in the gesture of meditative concentration, legs crossed in *vajra* posture, with crown protuberance of his head, and bejeweled.]
2. Kālacakra (Dus kyi 'khor lo)
3. Sucandra (Zla ba bzang po)
4. Mañjuśrīkirti ('Jam dbyangs grags pa)
5. Puṇḍarīka (Padma dkar po)
6. Kālacakrapāda, the Senior (Dus zhabs pa che ba)
7. Kālacakrapāda, the Second (Dus zhabs pa gnyis pa)
8. Somanātha (Kha che Zla ba mgon po)
9. Dro Lotsāwa [Sherap Drakpa]
10. Könchoksung
11. Namlatsek
12. Druptop Yumo [Depa Gyelpo]
13. Dharmeśvara (Dharme shwa ra) [that is, Chökyi Wangchuk]
14. Namkha Ö
15. Semo Chepa [Namkha Gyeltsen]
16. Jamyang Sarma [Sherap Özer]
17. Chöku Özer
18. Künpang Küntu Zangpo [that is, Tukjé Tsöndrü]
19. Künkhyen Pakö
20. Butön Khaché [Rinchendrup]
21. [add: Lama Dampa Sönam Gyeltsen]
22. [add: Penden Tsültrim][39]
23. Buddhaśrī (Buddha shrī pa)

38. On this lineage, see Ngor chen Kun dga' bzang po 1993, 288.3–6, the beginning of which varies, however: *yang de nyid las| dpal dus kyi 'khor lo'i rdzogs rim| zab lam rdo rje'i rnal 'byor sbyor ba yan lag drug pa'i khrid thob pa'i 'bro lugs kyi brgyud pa ni| dus kyi 'khor lo| chos rgyal so gnyis| dus zhabs pa chen po| dus zhabs chung ba gnyis pa|* [...].

39. In line with Ngorchen's record of teachings received, Lama Dampa Sönam Gyeltsen and Penden Tsültrim have to be added to the lineage; see Ngor chen Kun dga' bzang po 1993, 188.5–6. Since these two masters are already shown in the painting in other positions (as translated above)—Lama Dampa to the right of Mañjuśrī and Penden Tsültrim as second central master—Lowo Khenchen did not list them here. Yet they have to be counted as lineage masters.

[*The Eleventh Painting*]
In the eleventh painting Drupchen Buddhaśrī abides in the center. To his right and left are [the two bodhisattvas] Avalokiteśvara and Maitreya, in standing posture. To the right and left of the jewel at the top center of the ornamental roof over Buddhaśrī are Asaṅga and his brother [that is, Vasubandhu]. To their right and left are the pair Dharma Lord Yeshé Gyeltsen and Sapzang Pakpa.

To the right and left, directly next to the *makara* on each side of the ornamental roof, are the pair Śāntideva and the Great Scholar of Kashmir [that is, Śākyaśrībhadra]. At the beginning of the bottom row is a figure of the Lord [that is, Ngorchen] himself, and above him the figure of Uṣṇīṣavijayā. In the bottom row following the figure of the Lord are from right to left, Black Yamāri, Green Tārā, Mārīcī, Yellow Jambhala, Pañjaranātha with consort, and Vaiśravaṇa.

In the top row and the right and left columns are in their entirety the lineage masters of the vow for generating bodhicitta of the Madhyamaka tradition, namely:[40]

1. Buddha, the Teacher (Ston pa Sangs rgyas)
2. Mañjuśrī ('Jam dbyangs)
3. Nāgārjuna ('Phags pa Klu sgrub)
4. Āryadeva (Ārya de ba)
5. Nāgabodhi (Klu'i byang chub)
6. Candrakīrti (Zla ba grags pa)
7. Śiṣyavajra (Slob pa'i rdo rje)
8. Jitāri or Jetāri (Dze tā ri)
9. Vajrāsana, the Senior (rDo rje gdan pa che ba)
10. Vajrāsana, the Second (rDo rje gdan pa gnyis pa)
11. Puṇyaśrī (Puṇya shrī)
12. Bari Lotsāwa [Rinchendrak]
13. Jé Sachen [Künga Nyingpo]
14. Lobpön Rinpoche [Sönam Tsemo]
15. Jetsün Chenpo [Drakpa Gyeltsen]
16. Sakya Paṇḍita
17. Drogön Pakpa [Lodrö Gyeltsen]

40. On this lineage, see Ngor chen Kun dga' bzang po 1993, 183.1–4. Note that the lineage record lists Nāgārjuna and Āryadeva together as "Nāgārjuna, father and son" (*klu sgrub yab sras*) and continues next with Candrakīrti. Between them, it does not make mention of Nāgabodhi, though. Should Nāgabodhi thus be included as another "son" into the above-mentioned group? On the depiction of this lineage, see also the discussion by Heimbel 2021, 322–23, 349–51.

18. [Jamyang] Khöntön
19. Jangsem Rinchengön
20. Gyelsé Tokmé [Zangpo]
21. Lochen Jangchup Tsemo
22. Lama Dampa Yeshé Gyeltsen Pelzangpo

[*Final Remark on All Paintings*]
All central figures sit on a lotus seat on top of a throne of jewels supported by lions and are represented precisely according to their respective physical characteristics, within an ornamental roof decorated with a blazing jewel crest.

[*Concluding Verses and Colophon*]
The quintessence of all immaculate scriptural traditions [that is, the Lamdré] came from an authentic transmission lineage, which is like a snow mountain. For the fortunate followers, who are like fertile soil of the earth, I have here and now set down the magical display of the well-arranged paintings of those upholding its excellent path.

By the merit of having written this description, may the excellent path, together with its lineage, which is the victory banner of the unwaning teachings, be very stable. And may at all places and times the river current of enlightened activities flow into its destination, the ocean of the minds of intelligent ones.

As for the present eleven paintings of the Lamdré lineage, which were an object of spiritual practice of Buddha Vajradhara Künga Zangpo, the Lord himself had designed the arrangement of their divine figures and properly performed their consecration.

While they are present at Pel Ewaṃ Chöden, so that I myself develop certainty about them, and hoping that the arrangement of the divine figures may help other devout persons, I, Gelong Sönam Lhündrup Gyeltsen Lekpé Jungné Pelzangpo, wrote this description at Pel Ewaṃ Chöden, the source of numerous precious qualities. Once again, I corrected it at Tsedong Pelgyi Podrang. The scribe was Bhikṣu Śrīmatikīrti. *Maṅgalaṃ bhavantu!*

Appendix: Invocational Prayers

Here we would like to present the invocational prayers written in the red bottom cartouche of each existing painting. For each depicted central figure, one such verse was added in golden lettering, the last hemistich of which mentions in these present cases the name of the master to whom the prayer is addressed.

Since not all prayers were legible on the available images, they had to be partly reconstructed from liturgies of the lineage masters of the Lamdré.

Verses from these liturgies are regularly found in paintings written at the bottom strip below the central figure (or central figures) and are thus important sources for their identification. An early ritual text in which the first versified prayers from Ngorchen's painting set can be found was written by Pakpa Lodrö Gyeltsen ('Phags pa Blo gros rgyal mtshan, 1235–80)—*Worship of the Lamdré Lineage by Reciting Verses of Homage* (*Lam 'bras brgyud pa'i phyag mchod*)—and it contains prayers from Vajradhara down to the author's uncle and teacher, Sakya Paṇḍita (1182–1251). (The latter's prayer is much longer than those of most other masters, which usually comprise only one verse with four metrical lines.)

The work by Pakpa was supplemented over time by masters from different Sakya sub-schools updating the prayers in accord with their respective Lamdré lineages. The verses by Pakpa, together with later supplements for the main masters of the Lamdré lineage of Ngor, were integrated into a guru-worship ritual compiled by Künga Chöpel (Kun dga' chos 'phel; *Lam 'bras bla ma mchod pa'i cho ga khrigs chags su bkod pa tshogs gnyis rab rgyas*). This work contains the supplementary verses for Pakpa through Ngorchen, along with those for the successive abbots of Ngor down to Tsültrim Lhündrup (Tshul khrims lhun grub, 1676–1730), the thirty-second abbot.[41]

We know that Ngorchen contributed some prayers to Pakpa's work, such as for his teacher Penden Tsültrim.[42] We could thus expect that Ngorchen also wrote the prayer for his Lamdré teacher, Buddhaśrī, and that he had these prayers written below the portraits of those masters in the Lamdré set that he commissioned. But this hypothesis awaits further confirmation until Ngorchen's work—*Supplement to Worship of the Lamdré Lineage by Reciting Verses of Homage* (*Lam 'bras phyag mchod kyi kha skong*)—or other paintings from the set (such as the one of Penden Tsültrim) become available.

Finally, we should note that though these prayers are mainly found written on Lamdré lineage master portraits, which can form part of a larger set or series of supplementary paintings, they were also added to other individual paintings that did not portray the central master as a proponent of the Lamdré lineage.[43]

41. The text does not contain a prayer for Ngakwang Sönam Gyeltsen (Ngag dbang bsod nams rgyal mtshan, 1598–1674), the twentieth abbot of Ngor. On his omission when counting the abbots of Ngor, see Heimbel 2017, 513n1.

42. See Sangs rgyas phun tshogs 1983, 496.5–6. See also Heimbel 2017, 447, Comparative Table, no. 10.

43. On a thirty-plus Lamdré set commissioned in the late sixteenth century—the individual

The First Painting

Vajradhara (written at the bottom left)

Homage to Vajradhara, who fully completed the accumulations of merit and wisdom, master of emptiness and compassion, and the glory of both worldly existence and nirvana!

bsod nams ye shes rab rdzogs pa|| stong pa dang ni snying rje'i bdag|| srid dang mya ngan 'das pa'i dpal|| rdo rje 'chang la phyag 'tshal lo||

Nairātmyā (written at the bottom right)

Homage to Nairātmyā, who perfected insight and the dharmadhātu, whose illusory body is undefiled bliss, and who is the mother of all tathāgatas!

chos dbyings shes rab pha rol phyin|| zag med bde chen sgyu ma'i sku| |bde gshegs thams cad bskyed pa'i yum|| bdag med ma la phyag 'tshal lo[||]

The Second Painting

Virūpa (written at the bottom left)

Homage to Virūpa, who after studying all objects of knowledge reached the highest stage through diligence, and out of loving kindness benefitted others!

shes bya kun la rab sbyangs nas| |brtson pas go 'phang mchog brnyes te| |brtse bas gzhan gyi don mdzad pa| |'bir wa pa la phyag 'tshal lo||

Kāṇha (written at the bottom right)

Homage to Kāṇha, whose mind through profound instructions became liberated and achieved the weal of others by practicing tantric behavior!

rjes su gdams pa zab mo yis| |nyid kyi thugs ni rnam grol nas| |brtul zhugs spyod pas gzhan don mdzad| |nag po pa la phyag 'tshal lo||

The Third Painting

Ḍāmarupa (written at the bottom left, partly reconstructed)

Homage to Ḍāmarupa, who was completely liberated from worldly behavior by seeing ultimate reality and abided in the tantric behavior of paranormal yogic powers!

---

paintings of which feature those verses and the last master of which might have been Drangti Paṇchen Namkha Pelzang (Brang ti Paṇ chen Nam mkha' dpal bzang, 1535–1602), the thirteenth abbot of Ngor—see, for instance, Jackson 2010b, 206–8 (fig. 8.19); Jackson 2010a, 94–95 (fig. 1); and Linrothe 2006, 298–301, nos. 50–51. For images of individual paintings from this set, see also the Himalayan Art Resources website (https://www.himalayanart.org/search/set.cfm?setID=385). On paintings unrelated to this set, see, for instance, Heimbel 2021, 324n74; Heller 2019, 146; Jackson 2003, 96; Jackson 2010b, 192–93 (fig. 8.9); Jackson 2011, 19, 22 (fig. 1.21); Jackson 2012, 215n150; and Jackson 2016, 312–13 (fig. 13.9).

dam pa'i de nyid don gzigs pas| |'jig rten spyod las rnam grol zhing| |grub pa'i brtul zhugs la gnas pa| |ḍa ma ru pa la phyag 'tshal||

Avadhūtīpa (written at the bottom right, partly reconstructed)
Homage to Avadhūtīpa, who through extreme diligence for the profound path obtained paranormal yogic powers and engaged in the practice of nonduality in the manner of a child!
zab mo'i lam la rab brtson pas| |dngos grub brnyes nas byis pa yi| |tshul gyis gnyis med spyod pa mdzad| |a wa dhū tī la phyag 'tshal||

The Seventh Painting
Loppön Sönam Tsemo (written at the bottom left, partly reconstructed)
Homage to Sönam Tsemo, who by achieving immeasurable virtue, and by the vastness of his all-knowing wisdom, became the highest friend of all living beings!
bsod nams dpag med las grub cing| |mkhyen pa'i ye shes rab rgyas pas| |'gro ba'i rtsa lag mchog gyur pa| |bsod nams rtse mo la phyag 'tshal||

Jetsün Drakpa Gyeltsen (written at the bottom right, partly reconstructed)
Homage to Drakpa Gyeltsen, who perceived the reality of all phenomena and went to the far side of the ocean of the Secret Mantra, the lord of all tantric masters!
chos rnams kun gyi de nyid gzigs| |gsang sngags rgya mtsho'i pha rol son| |rdo rje 'dzin pa kun gyi rje| |grags pa rgyal mtshan la phyag 'tshal||[44]

Transliteration Table

THL Phonetic Transcription	Wylie Transliteration
Bari Lotsāwa Rinchendrak	Ba ri Lo tsā ba Rin chen grags
Butön Khaché Rinchendrup	Bu ston Kha che Rin chen grub
Chöjé Drakpukpa	Chos rje Brag phug pa

44. For all these verses translated above, see also 'Phags pa Blo gros rgyal mtshan 1993, 72.3–4, 72.4, 72.4–5, 72.5, 72.5–6, 72.6, 73.4, 73.4–5; and Kun dga' chos 'phel 1971, 852.6, 852.6–7, 852.7–53.1, 853.1, 853.1–2, 853.2–3, 853.7, 853.7–54.1.

Chöjé Yeshé Gyeltsen	Chos rje Ye shes rgyal mtshan
Chöjepa Sakya Paṇḍita	Chos rje pa Sa skya Paṇḍi ta
Chöku Özer	Chos sku 'od zer
Chökyi Wangchuk	Chos kyi dbang phyug
Dok Āryadeva	Rdog Ārya de ba/wa
Dongtön Sherappel	Ldong ston Shes rab dpal
Dorjé Chen	Rdo rje can
Dorjé Nyima	Rdo rje nyi ma
Drakpapel	Grags pa dpal
Drakpukpa Sönampel	Brag phug pa Bsod nams dpal
Dro	'Bro
Dro Lotsāwa Sherap Drakpa	'Bro Lo tsā ba Shes rab grags pa
Drogön Pakpa Lodrö Gyeltsen	'Gro mgon 'Phags pa Blo gros rgyal mtshan
Drokmi	'Brog mi
Drokmi Lotsawa Śākya Yeshé	'Brog mi Lo tsā ba Śākya ye shes
Druptop Yumo Depa Gyelpo	Grub thob Yu mo Dad pa rgyal po
Gelong Sönam Lhündrup Gyeltsen Lekpé Jungné Pelzangpo	Dge slong Bsod nams lhun grub rgyal mtshan legs pa'i 'byung gnas dpal bzang po
Gö Lotsāwa Khukpa Lhetsé	'Gos Lo tsā ba Khug pa lhas rtse
Gyakhar Tangbewa Pakpakyap	Rgya mkhar Thang dpe/sbe ba 'Phags pa skyabs
Gyelsé Tokmé Zangpo	Rgyal sras Thogs med bzang po
Jamyang Khöntön	'Jam dbyangs 'Khon ston
Jamyang Sarma Sherap Özer	'Jam dbyangs gsar ma Shes rab 'od zer
Jangsem Rinchengön	Byang sems Rin chen mgon

Jé Sachen	Rje Sa chen
Jetsün	Rje btsun
Jetsün Chenpo Drakpa Gyeltsen	Rje btsun chen po Grags pa rgyal mtshan
Jetsün Sönam Tsemo	Rje btsun Bsod nams rtse mo
Khön Gechuwa Dralhabar	'Khon Dge [= Sgyi] chu ba Dgra lha 'bar
Khön Könchok Gyelpo	'Khon Dkon mchog rgyal po
Khyin Lotsāwa	'Khyin Lo tsā ba
Khyungpo Lhepa Zhönnu Sönam	Khyung po Lhas pa Gzhon nu bsod nams
Könchoksung	Dkon mchog bsrung
Künga Zangpo	Kun dga' bzang po
Künkhyen Gangpa Drakpapel	Kun mkhyen Gangs pa Grags pa dpal
Künkhyen Pakö	Kun mkhyen 'Phags 'od
Künpang Küntu Zangpo	Kun spangs Kun tu bzang po
Lama Sachen Künga Nyingpo	Bla ma Sa chen Kun dga' snying po
Len Tsetsa Nyimacham	Glan rtsad tsha Nyi ma lcam
Lochen Jangchup Tsemo	Lo chen Byang chub rtse mo
Lodrö Tenpa	Blo gros brtan pa
Lokya Sheraptsek	Klog skya Shes rab brtsegs
Lokya Wangchukdrak	Klog skya Dbang phyug grags
Loppön Rinpoche Sönam Tsemo	Slob dpon Rin po che Bsod nams rtse mo
Lowo Möntang	Glo bo Smon thang
Mangra Senggyel	Mang ra Seng rgyal
Marpa Lotsāwa Chökyi Lodrö	Mar pa Lo tsā ba Chos kyi blo gros

Melgyo Lodrö Drakpa	Mal gyo Blo gros grags pa
Möntang Gön	Smon thang dgon
Namkha Ö	Nam mkha' 'od
Namlatsek	Gnam la brtsegs
Ngaripa Selwé Nyingpo	Mnga' ris pa Gsal ba'i snying po
Ngok	Rngog
Ngok Chökyi Dorjé	Rngog Chos kyi rdo rje
Ngok Dodé	Rngog mdo sde
Ngok José	Rngog Jo sras
Ngok Nyima Senggé	Rngog Nyi ma seng ge
Ngok Yeshé Senggé	Rngog Ye shes seng ge
Ngotsa Chöku	Sngo tsha Chos sku
Ngotsa Könchokpel	Sngo tsha Dkon mchog dpal
Padma Garwang	Padma gar dbang
Pamtingpa Jikmé Drakpa	Pham mthing pa 'Jigs med grags pa
Pamtingpa Ngakgi Wangchuk	Pham mthing pa Ngag gi dbang phyug
Pel Ewaṃ Chöden	Dpal E waṃ chos ldan
Penpa	Phan pa
Rinchen Senggé	Rin chen seng ge
Samdrup Pempar	Bsam grub dpal 'bar
Sapzang Paṇchen	Sa bzang Paṇ chen
Sapzang Paṇchen Lodrö Gyeltsen	Sa bzang Paṇ chen Blo gros rgyal mtshan
Semo Chepa Namkha Gyeltsen	Se mo che pa Nam mkha' rgyal mtshan

Serdingpa Zhönnu Ö	Gser sdings pa Gzhon nu 'od
Sönam Gyeltsen	Bsod nams rgyal mtshan
Tashipel	Bkra shis dpal
Tsedong Pelgyi Podrang	Rtse gdong dpal gyi pho brang
Tukjé Tsöndrü	Thugs rje brtson 'grus
Zhang Könchokpel	Zhang Dkon mchog dpal
Zhönnubum	Gzhon nu 'bum

References

Tibetan-Language Sources

Kun dga' chos 'phel. 1971. *Lam 'bras bla ma mchod pa'i cho ga khrigs chags su bkod pa tshogs gnyis rab rgyas*. In *Gdams ṅag mdzod: A Treasury of Instructions and Techniques for Spiritual Realization*, compiled by 'Jam-mgon Koṅ-sprul Blo-gros-mtha'-yas, vol. 4 (*ga*), 846–74.4. Reproduced from a xylographic print from the Dpal-spuṅs blocks. Delhi: N. Lungtok and N. Gyaltsen.

Glo bo Mkhan chen Bsod nams lhun grub. *Rje tsun sa skya pa'i yin thang dngos la zhib tu gzigs tshul. Dbu med* manuscript, 2 fols., volume number in margin: *ka*. In *Glo bo mkhan chen bsod nams lhun grub kyi gsung rtsom bris ma phyogs bsdus*, vol. 1, 99a7–100b6. BDRC W3CN2634.

———. *Bri yig 1* = *Lam 'bras bu dang bcas pa'i bla ma brgyud pa rnams kyi bri yig. Dbu med* manuscript, 6 fols., volume number in margin: *ka*. In *Glo bo mkhan chen bsod nams lhun grub kyi gsung 'bum*, vol. 1, 99a–104a. BDRC W00KG01660.

———. *Bri yig 2* = *Lam 'bras bu dang bcas pa'i bla ma brgyud pa rnams kyi bri yig. Dbu med* manuscript, 8 fols. In *Glo bo mkhan chen bsod nams lhun grub kyi gsung 'bum*, vol. 4, 1021–35 (of the PDF document; Tibetan volume pagination illegible). BDRC W00KG01660.

———. *Bri yig 3* = *Lam 'bras bu dang bcas pa'i bla ma brgyud pa dang bcas pa rnams kyi bri yig. Dbu med* manuscript, 5 fols., volume number in margin: *ka*. In *Glo bo mkhan chen bsod nams lhun grub kyi gsung 'bum*, vol. 5, 102a–106b. BDRC: W00KG01660.

———. *Bri yig 4* = *Lam 'bras bu dang bcas pa'i bla ma brgyud pa dang bcas pa rnams kyi bri yig. Dbu med* manuscript, 5 fols., volume number in margin: *ka*. In *Glo bo mkhan chen bsod nams lhun grub kyi gsung rtsom bris ma phyogs bsdus*, vol. 1, 94a–98b. BDRC W3CN2634.

———. *Bri yig 5* = *Lam 'bras bu dang bcas pa'i bla ma brgyud pa dang bcas pa rnams kyi bris yig*. Gold and silver letters on black paper, *dbu can* script, Tōyō Bunko library,

Tokyo, Tibetan manuscript no. 44, vol. *ka* in a collection of an incomplete collection of Glo bo Mkhan chen's writings, 136b2–43b1.

———. 2018. *Bri yig 6 = Lam 'bras bu dang bcas pa'i bla ma brgyud pa dang bcas pa rnams kyi bri yig*. In *Glo bo mkhan chen bsod nams lhun grub kyi gsung 'bum*, edited by the Smon bzang dpe rnying 'tshol bsdu khang, vol. 1, 125–32. Lhasa: Bod ljongs bod yig dpe rnying dpe skrung khang.

———. *Bla ma rdo rje 'chang kun dga' dbang phyug pa'i thugs dam thang ka mgon po'i bri yig. Dbu med* manuscript, 1 fol., volume number in margin: *ka*. In *Glo bo mkhan chen bsod nams lhun grub kyi gsung rtsom bris ma phyogs bsdus*, vol. 1, 99a1–6. BDRC W3CN2634.

Ngor chen Kun dga' bzang po. 1983. *Grub chen buddha shrī pa'i rnam par thar pa*. In *Lam 'bras slob bśad: The Sa-skya pa Teachings of the Path and the Fruit, according to the Tshar-pa transmission*, vol. 1 (*ka*), 413.5–31.6. Reproduced from prints from the Sde-dge redaction from the library of the Ven. Klu-sdiṅs Mkhan Rin-po-che of Ṅor. Dehra Dun: Sakya Centre.

———. 1993. *Thob yig rgya mtsho*. In *Ngor chen kun dga' bzang po'i bka' 'bum*, vol. 1 (*ka*), 179–433. Dehra Dun: Ngor Pal E-Wam Cho Dan.

Spang rdzong Skal bzang chos ldan. 2018. *Bsdu sgrig pa'i gtam*. In *Glo bo mkhan chen bsod nams lhun grub kyi gsung 'bum*, edited by the Smon bzang dpe rnying 'tshol bsdu khang, vol. 1, 1–2. Lhasa: Bod ljongs bod yig dpe rnying dpe skrung khang.

'Phags pa Blo gros rgyal mtshan. 1993. *Lam 'bras brgyud pa'i phyag mchod*. In *dPal ldan sa skya pa'i bka' 'bum: The Collected Works of the Founding Masters of Sa-skya*, vol. 13 (*pa*), 71–80.5. Reproduced from the 1736 Derge edition. Dehra Dun: Sakya Centre and Nagwang Topgyal.

Blo gter dbang po. 1972. *Rgyud sde rin po che kun las btus pa'i thob yig de bzhin gshegs pa thams cad kyi gsang ba ma lus pa gcig tu 'dus pa rdo rje rin po che'i za ma tog*. In *Rgyud sde kun btus: Texts Explaining the Significance, Techniques, and Initiations of a Collection of One Hundred and Thirty Two* [sic] *Mandalas of the Sa-skya-pa Tradition*, edited by 'Jam-dbyangs Blo-gter-dbang-po under the inspiration of his guru 'Jam-dbyangs Mkhyen-brtse'i-dbang-po, vol. 30 (*a*), 1–237. Reproduced photographically from the xylograph set of the Sde-dge edition belonging to Thartse Rimpoche of Ngor. Delhi: N. Lungtok and N. Gyaltsan.

Mus chen Dkon mchog rgyal mtshan. 1983. *Snyigs dus kyi rdo rje 'chang chen po chos kyi rje kun dga' bzang po'i rnam par thar pa mdor bsdus pa*. In *Lam 'bras slob bśad: The Sa-skya pa Teachings of the Path and the Fruit, according to the Tshar-pa transmission*, vol. 1 (*ka*), 432–73. Reproduced from prints from the Sde-dge redaction from the library of the Ven. Klu-sdiṅs Mkhan Rin-po-che of Ṅor. Dehra Dun: Sakya Centre.

Smon bzang dpe rnying 'tshol bsdu khang, ed. 2017(?). *Glo bo mkhan chen bsod nams lhun grub kyi gsung 'bum*. Kathmandu: 2nd Executive Committee of Mustang Sakya Buddhist Association.

Sangs rgyas phun tshogs. 1983. *Rdo rje 'chang kun dga' bzang po'i rnam par thar pa legs bshad chu bo 'dus pa'i rgya mtsho*. In *Lam 'bras slob bśad: The Sa-skya pa Teachings of the Path and the Fruit, according to the Tshar-pa transmission*, vol. 1 (*ka*), 475–585. Reproduced from prints from the Sde-dge redaction from the library of the Ven. Klu-sdiṅs Mkhan Rin-po-che of Ṅor. Dehra Dun: Sakya Centre.

Si khron bod yig dpe rnying bsdu sgrig khang, ed. 2016. *Glo bo mkhan chen bsod nams lhun grub kyi gsung 'bum*. Lhasa: Bod ljongs bod yig dpe rnying dpe skrun khang.

Works in European Languages

Béguin, Gilles, ed. 1977. *Dieux et demons de l'Himâlaya: Art du Bouddhisme lamaïque*. Paris: Secrétariat d'État à la Culture, Editions des Musées Nationaux.

BDRC = Buddhist Digital Resource Center. www.tbrc.org (accessed May 28, 2021).

Galerie Koller Zürich. 1992. *Asiatica: Tibet, Nepal, China, Japan, Südostasien; Asiatische Keramik*. Auktion 85/3. 20./21. November 1992. Zürich: Galerie Koller Zürich.

HAR = Himalayan Art Resources. www.himalayanart.org (accessed May 28, 2021).

Heimbel, Jörg. 2017. *Vajradhara in Human Form: The Life and Times of Ngor chen Kun dga' bzang po*. Lumbini: Lumbini International Research Institute.

———. 2021. "Portraits of the Great Abbots of Ngor: The Memorial or Death Anniversary Thangka (*dus thang*)." In *Gateways to Tibetan Studies: A Collection of Essays in Honour of David P. Jackson on the Occasion of his 70th Birthday*, edited by Volker Caumanns, Jörg Heimbel, Kazuo Kano, and Alexander Schiller, vol. 1, 301–79. Indian and Tibetan Studies 12.1–2. Hamburg: Department of Indian and Tibetan Studies, Universität Hamburg.

Heller, Amy. 2019. "Historic and Iconographic Identification of a Thangka of the Ngor Lineage." In *Reasons and Lives in Buddhist Traditions: Studies in Honor of Matthew Kapstein*, edited by Dan Arnold, Cécile Ducher, and Pierre-Julien Harter, 143–48. Studies in Indian and Tibetan Buddhism. Somerville, MA: Wisdom Publications.

Jackson, David P. 1986. "A Painting of Sa-Skya-Pa Masters from an Old Ngor-Pa Series of Lam 'Bras Thangkas." *Berliner Indologische Studien* 2: 181–91.

———. 1987. *The Entrance Gate for the Wise (Section III): Sa-skya Paṇḍita on Indian and Tibetan Traditions of Pramāṇa and Philosophical Debate*. Wiener Studien zur Tibetologie und Buddhismuskunde 17. Vienna: Arbeitskreis für Tibetische und Buddhistische Studien, Universität Wien.

———. 1996. *A History of Tibetan Painting: The Great Tibetan Painters and Their Traditions*. Österreichische Akademie der Wissenschaften, Philosophisch-Historische Klasse, Denkschriften 242. Beiträge zur Kultur- und Geistesgeschichte Asiens 15. Vienna: Verlag der Österreichischen Akademie der Wissenschaften.

———. 2003. "The Dating of Tibetan Paintings is Perfectly Possible—Though Not Always Perfectly Exact." In *Dating Tibetan Art: Essays on the Possibilities and Impossibilities of Chronology from the Lempertz Symposium, Cologne*, edited by Ingrid Kreide-Damani, 91–112. Contributions to Tibetan Studies 3. Wiesbaden: Dr. Ludwig Reichert Verlag.

———. 2010a. "Four Tibetan Paintings Linked with Ngor: Stylistic Diversity in the 16th Century." *Arts of Asia* (Commemorative 40th Anniversary Issue) 40.2: 93–102.

———. 2010b. *The Nepalese Legacy in Tibetan Painting*. Masterworks of Tibetan Painting Series. New York: Rubin Museum of Art.

———. 2011. *Mirror of the Buddha: Early Portraits from Tibet*. Masterworks of Tibetan Painting Series. New York: Rubin Museum of Art.

———. 2012. *The Place of Provenance: Regional Styles in Tibetan Painting*. Masterworks of Tibetan Painting Series. New York: Rubin Museum of Art.

———. 2016. *A Revolutionary Artist of Tibet: Khyentse Chenmo of Gongkar*. Masterworks of Tibetan Painting Series. New York: Rubin Museum of Art.

Kramrisch, Stella. 1964. *The Art of Nepal: Catalogue of the Exhibition presented under the Patronage of His Majesty King Mahendra Bir Bikram Shah Deva*. New York: The Asia Society.

Linrothe, Rob, ed. 2006. *Holy Madness: Portraits of Tantric Siddhas*. New York: Rubin Museum of Art.

Mori, Mahaside. 2008. "The *Vajrāvalī* Maṇḍala Series in Tibet." In *Esoteric Buddhist Studies: Identity and Diversity. Proceedings of the International Conference on Esoteric Buddhist Studies, Koyasan University, 5 Sept.–8 Sept. 2006*, edited by Editorial Board, ICEBS, 223–41. Koyāsan: Koyāsan University.

———. 2009. *Vajrāvalī of Abhayākaragupta: Edition of Sanskrit and Tibetan Versions*. Buddhica Britannica, Series Continua 11. Tring: The Institute of Buddhist Studies.

Pal, Pratapaditya, and Hsien-ch'i Tseng. 1969. *Lamaist Art: The Aesthetics of Harmony*. Boston: Museum of Fine Arts.

Lost—and Added—in Translation between India and Tibet: Theories about Drama in Tibetan Buddhist Epistemology

Isabelle Henrion-Dourcy

I met Leonard van der Kuijp in the last stages of my training as a postdoctoral student, yet the two-and-a-half years (2005–7) at Harvard University under his caring guidance were formative, even transformative. Having a focus on contemporary Tibet and anthropology, my profile was not exactly attuned to his lifelong research interests. But without ever having seen me, he welcomed me at his department with exceptional generosity, granting me a wonderful workspace, allowing me in his classes, and dispensing advice on my research. Between his native Holland and my native Belgium, we shared a language (Dutch/Flemish) in which we occasionally exchanged jokes and small talk to start or end the day with a smile. His rigorousness and the trust he bestowed on his students have been a truly empowering experience.

This modest contribution is an attempt to bridge both of our research worlds: Buddhist epistemology and Tibetan drama. I hope that as a scholar who so thoroughly detailed the Tibetan reception and creative reformulation of Indian thought and literary arts, Leonard will enjoy these brief reflections on the Tibetan imaginative reception of Indian drama theories. With a touch of academic humor, he has repeatedly described the "vicissitudes"[1] of cultural translation and adaptation between India and Tibet as he scrutinized how Tibetans have translated Indian tantras (*Sarvadurgatipariśodhanatantra*),[2] poetic treatises (*Kāvyādarśa* and *Bodhisattvāvadānakalpalatā*),[3] treatises on Buddhist epistemology and logic (by Dignāga and Dharmakīrti),[4] or treatises on poetics and lexicog-

1. van der Kuijp 2009.
2. van der Kuijp 1992.
3. van der Kuijp 1996.
4. van der Kuijp 2003.

raphy (*Amarakoṣa* and its commentary).[5] In this chapter, I will consider similar, if not more curious, "vicissitudes," related to dramaturgy. Unsurprisingly, since he is a favorite author of Leonard's, I will start and end with quotations by the great scholar Sakya Paṇḍita (1182–1251), whom we discussed during the very first of his lectures that I attended at Harvard University.

DURING THE SECOND diffusion of Buddhism into Tibet, from the eleventh century onward, India was considered the absolute model of spiritual, philosophical, and cultural perfection. This led to extensive translations from Sanskrit into Tibetan, carried out mostly by monks. Among the immense body of texts that Tibetans found in India were writings about drama, the acme of classical Sanskrit literature. Drama had given rise in India to prolific and celebrated works on aesthetic theory, the most famous treatise being the *Nāṭyaśāstra*, commonly considered as having been compiled in the second century CE, though it was probably older. When Tibetan translators encountered this Indian drama literature and related theoretical writings, they must have felt just as bewildered as the Arab philosopher Averroes (Ibn Rushd, 1126–98) when he came across the words "tragedy" and "comedy" in his translation of Aristotle's *Poetics* from Greek into Arabic. There were then no such performances in Arabic culture. In his essay "Averroes' Search," Jorge Luis Borges (1947) vividly described the Arab philosopher's attempts to make sense of spectacles that he had never seen and his confusion in finding a suitable translation in his native language. We can imagine a similar perplexity among Tibetan translators because we know that in the early thirteenth century, shows such as those described in the Indian literature did not exist in Tibet. The polymath Sakya Paṇḍita, a pivotal figure in the importation of Indian thought into Tibet, noted in his famous *Treatise on Music* (*Rol mo'i bstan bcos*) in 1204:

> In the forested central regions [i.e. India],
> [one can see] everywhere actors playing spoken-and-dance shows [*dögar*] staging stories.
> In these barbaric confines [i.e. Tibet],
> it is rare to have seen this type of actors, even to have heard about them.[6]

Drama was thus (then) absent from the Tibetan cultural world, but that did

5. van der Kuijp 2009.

6. *Dbus 'gyur tshal na gtam rgyud kyi/ zlos gar byed pa thams cad sbyor/ mtha' 'khob 'di na de lta bu / byed pa lta zhog thos pa'ang dkon //* (in Canzio 2019, 130 [fol. 9]). I slightly diverge from Canzio's translation (Canzio 2019, 67).

not deter monks from translating Indian plays and integrating drama into their model of the perfect bodhisattvic knowledge. Imagining what "drama" could be gave rise to Tibetan idiosyncratic developments in dramaturgy. These were neither faithful translations from original Sanskrit texts nor Buddhicized transformations of local Tibetan pre-Buddhist notions to be fitted into the Indian model. They were close to what Leonard van der Kuijp called "a hybrid Tibskrit,"[7] a fictive and purely literary production, neither Indian nor Tibetan, that is rather opaque.

In this chapter I shall review the various meanings of *dögar* (*zlos gar*) in literary Tibetan,[8] which is often translated as "drama" but used in a variety of ways to allude to drama as a text to read, drama as a field of Buddhist knowledge, and drama as a tangible spectacle to watch. The final section of the paper will be devoted to the surprising popularity of the old literary Indic dramaturgic theories among contemporary Tibetan scholars, especially when these theories are held to have been instrumental in the development of Tibetan opera (*a lce lha mo*, often simply called *lha mo*)—a suggestion that holds neither historically not ethnographically but that may adroitly fulfill other purposes.

When exactly was the neologism *dögar* coined in literary Tibetan, meaning literally "repeating (words)" (*zlos*) and "dancing" (*gar*)? What exact Sanskrit term or terms did it translate (Skt. *nāṭya*; *nāṭaka, natana*)?[9] At least one classical Buddhist Sanskrit drama had been translated during Tibet's imperial period[10], but it was not called a *dögar*: Aśvaghoṣa's *Śāriputraprakaraṇa*, describing how the Buddha converted Śāriputra and Maudgalyayāna. We definitely find the word *dögar* in 1204, in Sakya Paṇḍita's quote above, where it refers to actual shows that are to be watched. It is difficult to ascertain if he created the term or if it was in use before him. It is sometimes found in writings of subsequent centuries, especially from the sixteenth century onward, with the same connotation of an actual show to be watched.

7. van der Kuijp 2009, 22.

8. The use of the term *dögar* in colloquial Tibetan started only in the mid-twentieth century, but it shifted to mean, first, "modern" shows remote in style from traditional performances and mixing all sorts of techniques, and subsequently, the whole range of Tibetan performing arts as a type of cultural production. This happened in both Tibet and in exile in South Asia, in a dynamic that I have not fully understood yet. For example, the Tibetan Institute of Performing Arts is called Böshung Dögar (Bod gzhung zlos gar) in Tibetan, and the Tibet Autonomous Region Spoken Theatre Troupe is called Tamjö Dögar Tsokpa (Gtam brjod zlos gar tshogs pa).

9. See Henrion-Dourcy 2017a, 163–90, for a detailed discussion of the evolving meaning and usage of *dögar* and theories about drama by Tibetan premodern and contemporary scholars.

10. Lha mkhar tshe ring 2001, 37.

During the thirteenth century, as translations from the Sanskrit were extensive, including under Sakya Paṇḍita's tutelage, *dögar* was predominantly used to translate the Sanskrit term *nāṭaka* and referred to drama as a text to read—again, as such spectacles were absent in Tibet. *Dögar* was used in the titles of the two most important Buddhist Sanskrit plays translated in Tibet during the thirteenth century and included in the Tengyur (Bstan 'gyur) a century later: Harṣa Śīlāditya's *Play to Please All the Nāgas*[11] and Candragomin's *Play to Please All the Worldly Beings*.[12] The first one is quoted by Sakya Paṇḍita as a compulsory reading for monks in his *Entrance Gate for the Wise* (*Mkhas pa rnams 'jug pa'i sgo*). And about the second one, Leonard van der Kuijp sums up the consensus opinion in the following assessment related to the quality of the translation: "These translations were unmitigated philological disasters (. . .). Singularly unimpressed by (the) translation, Michael Hahn (1974) came to the well-nigh unavoidable conclusion that the philological quality of their rendition of the play was by no means beyond reproach in that 'it teems with clumsy, semantically ambiguous, or even wrong passages.'[13] Similarly, Ryugen Tanemura came to the same conclusion, but his assessment needs to be set against the background of an insufficient appreciation of the changes that can and often do occur in the transmissive history of a Tibetan text, from handwritten manuscript to blockprint to copies thereof."[14] These stories couched in dramatic style were mere edification literature with no onstage counterpart, a literary genre confined to monastic education that probably did not trickle down into lay society.

Let us now move over to the body of literature under which *dögar* is most well known in Tibetan studies: *dögar* as one of the five minor "fields of knowledge" (Skt. *vidyāsthāna* = Tib. *rig gnas*). These are organized bodies of knowledge that the bodhisattva needs to master to help all beings toward enlightenment. I shall make here three remarks: First, it is unclear whether the *Nāṭyaśāstra* was ever translated into Tibetan, but if it was and if it was lost, it has not left any trace in Tibetan theoretical ponderings about dramaturgy. Second, considerations about the relationship between drama and the cosmic illusion (Skt. *māyā*), so important in Indian theories, are absent in Tibet. Third, Tibetan reflections about drama have not been compiled into a single text but are scattered in short sections of various encyclopedias, mostly devoted

11. Skt. *Nāgānanda-nāṭaka* = Tib. *Klu kun tu dga ba'i zlos gar.*

12. Skt. *Lokānanda-nāṭaka* = Tib. *'Jigs rten kun tu dga' ba'i zlos gar.*

13. van der Kuijp 2009, 22.

14. van der Kuijp 2009, 23.

to the fields of knowledge. An important part of these reflections is actually made up of indigenous developments based on another famous Indian literary treatise translated in part by Sakya Paṇḍita, Daṇḍin's *Mirror of Poetry* (Skt. *Kāvyādarśa* = Tib. *Snyan ngag me long*). That treatise left such a deep mark on Tibetan belles-lettres and literary theory up to this day, and facilitated to such an extent the enculturation of Tibetans with Indian mores, that we can speak of an effective "Indian literary identity of Tibet."[15]

The Buddhist organization of all learning into "fields of knowledge" (a literal translation that I prefer to the commonly found "sciences") was imported from India during the first diffusion of Buddhism, but its systematic use in organizing the monastic curriculum is usually credited to Sakya Paṇḍita. The five "major" fields of knowledge are of Indian origin (though with Tibetan inflections), but the five "minor" fields of knowledge are later Tibetan additions (based on Indian conceptions). The number, names, and hierarchy of these fields of knowledge have varied over time, with important reconfigurations in the fifteenth and sixteenth centuries, but by the eighteenth century, Longdöl Lama's (Klong rdol bla ma Ngag dbang blo bzang, 1719–94) classification seems to have become the standard in monastic education. A brief mention will suffice here, as these classifications are abundantly analyzed in Tibetan studies.[16] The five major fields comprise first and foremost the "inner" field, or Buddhist contemplative praxis, and four "outer" fields (not belonging to Buddhism proper): grammar (also translated as "phonology," or the "science of sound"), logic (or dialectics), healing (or medicine), and craftsmanship (or technology). The five minor fields of knowledge comprise calendrical computation (or astrology) and four sub-sections of the major field of grammar that can be dubbed "literary arts" and that all add to the persuasive power of the Buddhist teacher: poetics, metrics, lexicography, and drama (*dögar*). The addition of the literary arts started as early as Pang Lotsāwa (Dpang lo tsā ba blo gros brtan pa, 1276–1342), but grew especially after Narthang Lotsāwa (fifteenth century).[17] Some religious schools, such as the Nyingmapa (Rnying ma pa), have shown more interest in the literary arts, inscribing them in the monastic curriculum, whereas other schools, such as the Gelugpa (Dge lugs pa), have neglected these skills as mere distractions. The two most quoted commentators about the five minor fields of knowledge are contemporaries of Longdöl Lama in the eighteenth century: First, the Fourth Khamtrül (Khams sprul Bstan 'dzin chos kyi nyi ma, 1730–79), a Nyingma scholar who wrote the most well-

15. Kapstein 2003. See also van der Kuijp 1996 and 2009.

16. See among others Gold 2007.

17. Tenzin Tsepak 2021, 404.

known commentary on the *Mirror of Poetry*, "The Treatise on Ornamentation, Ocean of Melodious Speech," in which we find a short discussion on *dögar*.[18] Most of his remarks on the minor fields of knowledge actually stemmed from oral instructions received from his master Situ Paṇchen (1699/1700–1774),[19] the accomplished Sanskritist and greatest Tibetan scholar of his time. The second is Zhuchen (Zhu chen Tshul khrims rin chen, 1698–1774), who penned "The Classification of the Five Tibetan Fields of Knowledge."[20] As Tenzin Tsepak notes, "the historiography of the five minor fields of learning is far more complicated and convoluted compared to the five major sciences."[21] It has also attracted a lot less attention in Tibetan studies than has the five major fields of knowledge.[22] Moreover, among the five minor fields of knowledge, when we compare the body of Tibetological literature devoted to poetics to that devoted to *dögar* (which is barely existent), it is fair to assess that drama is a very marginal subject of inquiry for Tibetan scholars—to come back to Sakya Paṇḍita's quote, probably due to the relative irrelevance of these reflections for actual Tibetan culture until recently.

Taking now a peek at Longdöl Lama's model of the fields of knowledge,[23] the minor field of *dögar* appears in the unique position of being both a sub-section of the major field of grammar and a sub-section of the major field of craftsmanship. Indeed, drama plays have, at least in theory, both literary and tangible performative dimensions. A bodhisattvic performance is understood to encompass crafts of the body (dancing, making and using masks, playing musical instruments), speech (narrating and singing), and mind (studying and memorizing texts, meditating on the meaning of the words). The contribution of the field of craftsmanship is best visible when considering the "limbs" (*yan lag*) of *dögar* that are the sub-sub-sections into which *dögar* itself is divided. *Dögar* is here closer to the Sanskrit term *nāṭya* and *natana* than to *nāṭaka* evoked above. It is worthwhile to note here that *dögar* is the only field of knowledge with this detailed arborescence. The number of limbs vary accord-

18. Khams sprul Bstan 'dzin chos kyi nyi ma 1986, 13–14, for a discussion on *dögar*. I thank Tashi Tsering (Amnye Machen Institute) for this reference and the next one.

19. Information from Tashi Tsering.

20. Zhu chen btsun pa Tshul khrims rin chen 1981, 40–41, for his comments on *dögar*.

21. Tenzin Tsepak 2021, 417.

22. See especially Eppling 1989; Kapstein 2003; Gold 2007; Townsend 2016; Tenzin Tsepak 2021.

23. Ellingson 1979, 374, fig. 15, has provided a helpful drawing to visualize Longdöl Lama's model of the fields of knowledge on a single page. See also Snyder 1979, 36, and Henrion-Dourcy 2017b, 193, for adaptations of Ellingson's figure.

ing to scholars (four for Khamtrül, five for Longdöl Lama, six or seven for others),[24] but, to give an example, Longdöl Lama's model mentions the skills of narrating the story (*mdo 'dzin*), music (*rol mo*), costumes (*chas zhugs*), laughter (*bzhad gad*), and finally the reduplication of *dögar* (*zlos gar*), understood here as dance. It is remarkable that this entirely Tibetan development about drama in Buddhist epistemology appears close to what dramatic shows are in real life. It is unclear whether Longdöl Lama had any personal experience of watching a performance, and if so, what it may have been. There is no such mention in his writings, as he was certainly more interested in ideal classifications than in documenting popular customs. It is not impossible, but somewhat unlikely, that he had Tibetan opera in mind: at his time, opera was a small affair played by a few local troupes, not yet the popular full-blown performance style that it would become in the late nineteenth century after the boom of the Yoghurt Festival (*zho ston*) in the Norbulingka gardens in Lhasa (after 1848).[25]

Two further idiosyncrasies of Tibetan drama theory have led to a much larger volume of commentaries and discussions, because they hail from the literary side of drama (as a sub-section of grammar; thus *dögar* here is closer to Skt. *nāṭaka*) and because they both originated from the *Mirror of Poetry* and its Tibetan commentaries: the idea that *dögar* is fundamentally a play on language categories, and the attempts at making sense of the Indian quintessential aesthetic theorization about "primary emotions" and "aesthetic pleasures/tastes" (Skt. *sthāyibhāva/rasa* = Tib. *nyams 'gyur/'gyur* ba). For lack of space, I will only discuss here, and quite succinctly, the former. The latter ponderings are technical and, in my eyes, confusing; it seems that the aesthetic speculation was lost on Tibetan commentators, who merely used the *rasa* theory as a way to classify emotions.[26] As for the former, the Fourth Khamtrül had evoked the specific purpose of *dögar* among all the literary arts (one major and four minor fields of knowledge) as follows:

> Knowing grammar is to be not ignoring the meaning (of sentences).
> Knowing *alamkāra* is to be not ignoring ornate poetry.
> Knowing lexicography is to be not ignoring names(' usage).
> Knowing metrics is not to be ignoring prosody.

24. Chorus (*ram 'degs*); auspiscious narrations (*shis brjod*). Zhol khang Bsod nams dar rgyas 1992, 22.

25. For the historic development of Tibetan opera, and its quite late expansion, see Henrion-Dourcy 2017a, chap. 2.

26. See Eppling 1989, 1450; Kapstein 2003, 780–81. See Henrion-Dourcy 2017a, 646–58, for a longer examination of the tribulations of the notion of *rasa* in Tibet.

Knowing *dögar* is to be not ignoring the categories of languages.[27]

To be an accomplished dramaturgist or actor, one must then be a sort of polyglot—a distant echo to the rich linguistic fabric of Indian plays, where characters speak in a variety of dialects according to their region, social rank, profession, the person they are addressing, and the requirements of the situation. But the Tibetan sociolinguistic makeup is very different from the medieval Indian one. Whereas Indian dramaturgy could comprise up to fifty different topolects/sociolects, the Tibetan theorists of *dögar* adapted the model to retain only four such "categories of languages" (*skad rigs bzhi*), perhaps having in mind the four varnas. This quadripartition is held to correspond to differences in social uses between Sanskrit (for kings), Prākrit (for ladies), *apabramśa* (for commoners), and *paiśācī* (for jesters and lowly beings),[28] but this shows how shallow was the Tibetan knowledge about language use in India. All Tibetan commentators emphasize how necessary the four categories of languages are for a good composition, but there is some degree of confusion between authors as to their hierarchies and their effective use. This had led the Third Gungtang (Gung thang dkon mchog bstan pa'i sgron me, 1762–1823) to playfully write in 1814 his "Treatise on Drama, or An Entertainment Leading to the Pure Path" (*Zlos gar gyi bstan bcos yang dag lam du bkri ba'i rol rtsed*). He literally applied the rule of the four categories of language to four completely different languages with different writing systems.[29] The play is meant to be read, not performed, and features four monks (an Indian, a Tibetan, a Mongolian, and a Chinese monk), each speaking in his language, with a subsequent transcription and translation into the four languages. The result is a tedious and abstruse read, and the three non-Tibetan languages are, at best, approximations.[30]

Now, rounding off this discussion on *dögar*, one may wonder: Was this theorization about drama, quite abstract and confined to the ivory tower of select monastic curriculums, ever implemented to make sense of actual performances in Tibet? Have these theories had any social life? Have they even inspired or sustained dramatic production in Tibet—when drama eventually emerged and developed in the Land of Snows? The overall answer to all these questions

27. Khams sprul Bstan 'dzin chos kyi nyi ma 1986, 13: *sgra shes na don la mi rmongs/ tshig rgyan shes na snyan-ngag la mi rmongs/ mngon brjod shes na ming la mi rmongs/ sdeb sbyor shes na tshigs bcad la mi rmongs / zlos gar shes na skad rigs la mi rmongs//.*

28. See Kapstein 2003, 769.

29. Ligeti 1933, 40.

30. Ibid.

is "no," but it begs for nuance and fine-tuning. Surprisingly, all contemporary Tibetan (this is important) scholars on the performing arts, especially *ache lhamo* (Tibetan opera), do not merely mention the Buddhist epistemological perspective on *dögar*, they actually open their writings with this theoretical model and imply that these theories have been instrumental in the development and shaping of Tibetan opera. How did we get there, since Tibetan opera is a folk tradition that developed independently from this erudite and arcane Indic literature? This point hardly needs to be proven, since an ethnography with actors of Tibetan opera will show that their art and skills, their techniques of learning and transmission, and finally their values have no common ground with these abstract theories, not even in vocabulary.[31] Most actors were illiterate, or barely literate, in premodern Tibet. Although most actors today are somewhat literate, none of them would be able to name, let alone understand, the Indic model of *dögar*, especially the more convoluted *rasa* theory. Clearly, the Indic model never intersected with the production of Tibetan opera.

The association between these two unconnected aspects of drama in Tibet is not, however, a mere invention by contemporary scholars out of what could possibly be ignorance or confusion. The exact genealogy of this correlation is at this point of my studies difficult to trace. But it is likely to have happened after the boom of *ache lhamo* in both popularity and onstage amplification in the late nineteenth century. In any case, the connection was made before the twentieth century by a very prominent Tibetan scholar, Jamyang Khyentse Wangpo ('Jam dbyangs mkhyen brtse'i dbang po, 1820–92), a great Nyingma master who was among the spearheads of the ecumenical *rimè* (*ris med*) religious movement. The following excerpt is set in a series of comments about *dögar* as a lesser field of knowledge:

> Generally, the types of shows that are actually known in India and Nepal, even if they have not spread over here to Tibet, if I adopt an ordinary point of view, (I cannot say that) performing *a lce lha mo* (Tibetan opera) etc.[32] does not belong to *dögar* (as a minor field of knowledge).[33]

31. See Henrion-Dourcy 2017b.

32. The "etc." here probably refers to a particular cham (*'chams*), or monastic dance, that he was discussing in the previous section.

33. 'Jam dbyangs mkhyen brtse'i dbang po 1977, 457–58: *Lar zlos gar gyi rigs rgya bal du grags pa dngos ni bod 'dir ma dar na'ng/ thun mong gi dbang du byas na a lce lha mo rtse ba sogs kyang zlos gar las ma 'das /*. I thank Tashi Tsering for sharing this reference.

So contemporary scholars' assertions are not totally groundless: there has been at least one precedent in premodern Tibet—a precedent that they actually do not quote. But what is remarkable is the lengths to which they go to hypostasize a posteriori a historical connection between *dögar* and *lhamo*, spreading over a few pages. An older generation of twentieth-century scholars stick to traditional presentations congruent with the theories that I have exposed above: *lhamo* is *dögar*, and *dögar* is one of the five minor fields of knowledge, has sub-sections, and puts forth language categories and emotions.[34] Jeanette Snyder, an American anthropologist who authored one of the first and still authoritative synthesis on *lhamo*, who carried out fieldwork in the 1960s and 1970s in Dharamsala among actors and the local intellectual elite, also uses the Indic and scholarly subdivisions of *dögar* as an organizing principle of her general presentation of *lhamo*.[35] A slightly younger generation of Tibetan scholars takes the matter further and engages with wider theoretical ideas from Indian philosophy, trying to really fathom what this theory may offer to analyze *lhamo* in new ways.[36]

Whether relying on a traditional understanding of *dögar* or on a newer, more inquisitive search for Indian aesthetic philosophy, claims that *lhamo* is intimately connected with Indian ancient aesthetics and epistemology have become very popular among Tibetan intellectuals. It may appear quite disconcerting that this partially digested exogenous cultural model serves to introduce their own folk tradition. But it is impossible to ignore how completely at odds this presentation falls with People's Republic of China's propaganda and Chinese folklorists' views—that is, claiming that Tibetan opera is a mere sub-example of the vast umbrella of Chinese opera, without any significant cultural distinctiveness, and that it needs to be developed according to the central government's aesthetics. These Tibetan scholars' assertions put *lhamo* in a very different light from the rewriting of folk culture that has been going on for decades. Here *lhamo* appears as a noble, highbrow, religious part of Tibetan culture that deserves the utmost respect. And of course Tibetan opera's historical roots are plunged not in the Chinese cultural world but in ancient India at the time when it inspired Tibet's most precious culture.

34. Zhol khang Bsod nams dar rgyas 1992, 1, 21–24; Hor khang Bsod nams dpal 'bar 1989, 65; Hor khang Bsod nams dpal 'bar 1992; and 'Jam dbyangs rgyal mtshan 1980–81, 26–27.

35. Snyder 1979, 35.

36. The most elaborate texts are by Dga' ba pa sangs 1994 and Rdo rje thar 1999, esp. 457–58. See also Dge 'dun 'phel rgyas 2011, 138–39; Phun tshogs bkra shis 1990; Rin chen rdo rje and Tshe dbang rdo rje 1996; and finally, writing in Chinese, Qiangba qujie (Jampa Choegyal) 2020.

In closing, this brief contribution has shown once again that the predicament of academics who research Tibetan intellectual history is to be footed in shifting sands. Over the centuries, Tibetan scholars and commentators have borrowed from multiple neighbors, and these sources of inspiration have often been selective and partially digested. Given the tendency of Tibetan authors to copy their predecessors mostly without quoting their sources, untangling the history of Tibetan ideas is a daunting task. Tibetans' cultural creativity in "localizing" foreign abstract ideas onto their cultural ground is indeed endearing, but it implies countless layers of complexity, with shifting terminologies and/or meanings, puzzling hybrids, and fragmentary accounts. As Tibetologists chronicle the vicissitudes of cultural changes throughout the last millennium and into the tragic twentieth and twenty-first centuries, it is of utmost importance to rely on solid sources to ground interpretations. As Sakya Paṇḍita wrote in one of his *Good Sayings*:

> You know a fine horse by its pace,
> you know gold and silver by their melting points,
> you know an elephant by its conduct in battle,
> and you know the wise by the good sayings they compose.[37]

Leonard van der Kuijp leaves for the next generation of Tibetologists, both in the West and in Asia, a dense collection of erudite writings that will help navigate through these vicissitudes for many years to come.

37. From Sakya Paṇḍita's *Good Sayings*, chap. 9, verse 57: *Rta mchog 'gro ba'i tshe na shes / gser dngul bzhu na shes par 'gyur / glang chen g.yul ngor shes 'gyur te / mkhas pa legs bshad rtsom na shes//* (Lozang Jamspal 2003, no. 455). My translation.

References

Borges, Jorge Luis. 1964 [1947]. "Averroes' Search." Translated by James E. Irby. In *Labyrinths: Selected Stories and Other Writings*, edited by Donald A. Yates and James E. Irby, 148–55. New York: New Directions.

Canzio, Ricardo. 2019. *Sakya Pandita's Treatise on Music, Rol-mo'i bstan bcos, with a Commentary by Kunga Sonam*. Kathmandu: Vajra Books.

Dga' ba pa sangs. 1994. "Gna' bo'i rgya gar gyi sgyu rtsal gzhung lugs dang bod kyi sgyu rtsal gzhung lugs dbar gyi 'brel bar brtag pa" [An Examination of the Relationship Between Ancient Indian Artistic Theory and Tibetan Artistic Theory]. *Krung go'i bod kyi shes rig* [China Tibetology] 1: 117–26.

Dge 'dun 'phel rgyas. 2011. *Bod kyi rol dbyangs lo rgyus bsdus gsal dpyid kyi pho nya* [A Concise History of Tibetan Music: A Messenger of Spring]. Lhasa: Bod ljongs mi dmangs dpe skrun khang [Tibetan People's Publishing House].

Ellingson, Terry Jay. 1979. *The Mandala of Sound: Concepts and Sound Structures in Tibetan Ritual Music*. PhD diss., University of Wisconsin–Madison.

Eppling, John. 1989. *A Calculus of Creative Expression: The Central Chapter of Daṇḍin's Kāvyādarśa*. PhD diss., University of Wisconsin–Madison.

Gold, Jonathan. 2007. *The Dharma's Gatekeepers: Sakya Pandita on Buddhist Scholarship in Tibet*. Albany: State University of New York Press.

Hahn, Michael. 1974. *Candragomin's Lokānandanāṭaka. Ein Beitrag zur klassischen indischen Schauspieldichtung*. Asiatische Forschungen 39. Wiesbaden: Otto Harrassowitz.

Henrion-Dourcy, Isabelle. 2017a. *Le théâtre ache lhamo: Jeux et enjeux d'une tradition tibétaine*. Mélanges Chinois et Bouddhiques 33. Leuven: Peeters.

———. 2017b. "The Art of the Tibetan Actor: *A lce lha mo* in the Gaze of Western Performance Theories." *Revue d'Etudes Tibétaines* 40: 179–215.

Hor khang Bsod nams dpal 'bar. 1989. "A lce lha mo'i rnam thar las 'phros te skyor lung dge rgan Mig dmar rGyal mtshan gyi sgyu rtsal 'gro lam skor lam tsam gleng ba" [Short Discussion on the Kyormolung Teacher Migmar Gyaltsen's Artistic Evolution from the *Namtar*s of Tibetan opera]. *Bod ljongs sgyu rtsal zhib 'jug* [Tibetan Arts Research] 12: 65–70.

———. 1992. "Lha mo'i gzhung brgyad kyi khungs bstan pa 'phrul gyi rgyangs shel" [Looking Closely at the Origins of the Tibetan Opera Stories]. *Bod ljongs sgyu rtsal zhib 'jug* 2: 1–13.

'Jam dbyangs mkhyen brtse'i dbang po. 1977. *Gsang chen rdo rje theg pa phyi 'gyur gsar ma gtso bor ston pa'i zin bris sna tshogs dang mdo rgyud lung btus bcas bzhugs so* [The Collected Works of the Great 'Jam dbyangs mkhyen brtse'i dbang po], vol. 4. Gangtok, printed by author.

'Jam dbyangs rgyal mtshan. 1980–81. "La dwags su zlos gar byung tshul" [The Origin of Drama in Ladakh]. *La dwags kyi shes ra za* [Ladakh studies] 2.2: 26–36.

Kapstein, Matthew. 2003. "The Indian Literary Identity in Tibet." In *Literary Cultures in History: Reconstructions from South Asia*, edited by Sheldon Pollock, 747–804. Berkeley: University of California Press.

Khams sprul Bstan 'dzin chos kyi nyi ma. 1986. *Rgyan gyi bstan bcos dbyang can ngag gi rol mtsho* [The Treatise on Ornamentation, Ocean of Melodious Speech]. Lhasa: Bod ljongs mi dmangs dpe skrunkhang [Tibet People's Publishing House].

van der Kuijp, Leonard W. J. 1992. "Notes Apropos of the Transmission of the *Sarvadurgatipariśodhanatantra* in Tibet." *Studien zur Indologie und Iranistik* 16: 109–25.

———. 1996. "Tibetan Belles-Lettres: The Influence of Daṇḍin and Kṣemendra." In *Tibetan Literature: Studies in Genre*, edited by José I. Cabezón and Roger R. Jackson, 393–410. Ithaca, NY: Snow Lion Publications.

———. 2003. "A Treatise on Buddhist Epistemology and Logic Attributed to Klong Chen Rab 'Byams Pa (1308–1364), and Its Place In Indo-Tibetan Intellectual History." *Journal of Indian Philosophy* 31: 381–437.

———. 2009. "On the Vicissitudes of Subhūticandra's Kāmadhenu Commentary on the *Amarakoṣa* in Tibet." *Journal of the International Association for Tibetan Studies* 5: 1–105.

Lha mkhar tshe ring. 2001. "Zlos gar gyi rnam bshad nying bsdus" [Brief Commentary on Drama]. *Bod ljongs sgyu rtsal zhib 'jug* 1: 37–41.

Ligeti, Louis. 1933. *Rapport préliminaire d'un voyage d'exploration fait en Mongolie chinoise 1928–1931*. Budapest: Société Körosi-Csoma.

Lozang Jamspal, ed. 2003. *The Treasury of Good Sayings of Sa skya Paṇḍita the Eminent Tibetan Lama, 1182–1251, Translated during the Summer of 1966 in Mussoorie, India, by Lozang Jamspal and Ngawang Sonam Tenzin / Legs par bshad pa rin po che'i gter bzhes bya ba'i bstan bcos.* Bilingual edition. Leh: Ladakhratnashridipika.

Phun tshogs bkra shis. 1990. "Lha mo'i rnam thar gyi mi sna'i gzugs brnyan khyad chos lam tsam gleng ba" [Short Discussion on the Characteristics of the Images of the Characters of Tibetan Opera]. *Krung go'i Bod kyi shes rig* [China Tibetology] 4: 107–21.

Qiangba qujie 强巴曲杰 [= Byams pas chos rgyal]. 2020. "Zangzu 'shi ming xue' dui zangxi yishu xingcheng, fazhan ji zangxi lilun chansheng de yingxiang 藏族 '十明学' 对藏戏艺术形成、发展及藏戏理论产生的影响" [On the Influence of the Tibetan "Ten Fields of Knowledge" on the Formation and Development of Tibetan Opera Art and Tibetan Opera Theory]. *Xizang daxue xuebao*: *Shehui kexue ban* 西藏大学学报:社会科学版 [Journal of Tibet University: Social Science Edition] 4: 88–95.

Rdo rje thar. 1999. "Zlos gar rig pa" [The Field of Knowledge of Drama]. In *Krung go bod kyi rig gnas sgyu rtsal kun 'dus zhal thang chen mo'i rnam bshad mthong grol kun gsal me long* [The Illuminating Mirror, Liberating upon Seeing, the Explanation about the Great *Thangka* Assembling All the Tibetan Culture and Arts of China's Tibet], edited by Brtson 'grus Rab rgyas, 457–78. Beijing: Mi rigs dpe skrun khang.

Rin chen bkra shis. 1998. "Zlos gar dang zlos gar rtsom rig gi khyad chos" [On the Characteristics of Drama and Drama Literature]. *Bod ljongs zhib 'jug* 4: 75–81.

Rin chen rdo rje and Tshe dbang rdo rje. 1996. "Bod kyi lha mo'i bstan bcos khag gi byung rim gyi khyad chos skor rags tsam gleng ba" [Short Discussion on the Origin and Characteristics of Some Treatises about Tibetan Opera]. *Rtser snyeg* 4: 56–68.

Snyder, Jeanette. 1979. "Preliminary Study of the Lhamo." *Asian Music, Journal of the Society for Asian Music* 10.2: 23–62.

Tenzin Tsepak. 2021. "A Tibetan History of Lesser Knowledge: The Coming of Poetry in the Five Minor Fields of Learning." *Revue d'Etudes Tibétaines* 61: 403–20.

Townsend, Dominique. 2016. "Buddhism's Worldly Other: Secular Subjects of Tibetan Learning." *Himalaya, the Journal of the Association for Nepal and Himalayan Studies* 36.1: 130–44.

Zhol khang Bsod nams dar rgyas. 1992. *Glu gar tshangs pa'i chab rgyun* [The Pure Tradition of Songs and Dances]. Lhasa: Bod ljongs mi dmangs dpe skrun khang.

Zhu chen btsun pa Tshul khrims rin chen. 1981. *Bod kyi rig gnas lnga'i rnam gzhag* [The Classification of the Five Tibetan Fields of Knowledge]. Beijing: Mi rigs dpe skrun khang.

Origin of the *r-* Allomorph of the Tibetan Causative *s-*

Nathan W. Hill

THE BEST-KNOWN morpheme in the Tibetan language, and indeed in the entire trans-Himalayan language family, is the causative and denominative prefix *s-*,[1] for example, Tibetan *'khol* "boil" versus *skol* "set to boil." This prefix shows very little morphophonemic variation, but before laterals may have the forms *s-*, *z-*, and *r-*. Michael Hahn argues that the variation between *s-* and *z-* is a spelling convention reflecting the distinction between the phonemically distinct voiced and voiceless lateral—that is, orthographic *zl-* reflects morphophonemic /sl/, whereas orthographic *sl-* reflects morphophonemic /sl̥/.[2] However, it appears that no researcher has addressed the *r-* allomorph.

At least two lateral initial verbs have both a *z-* and an *r-* causative.

ldug, blugs, blug, lhugs, "pour"[3]
zlug, bzlugs, bzlug, zlugs, "pour, caste"
rlug, brlugs, brlug, rlugs, "purge"

ldog, log, ldog, log, "turn, return"
zlog, bzlogs, bzlog, zlogs, "make turn, make return"
rlog, brlags, brlag, rlogs, "destroy, overturn"

According to Kuryłowicz's fourth law of analogy, when a language presents a doublet the inherited form has the more specialized meaning—for example, *lost* versus (*for*)*lorn*, *melted* versus *molten*.[4] According to this principle the forms with *r-* are inherited.

1. Among many possible citations, see Conrady 1896; LaPolla 2003; and Hill 2014.

2. Hahn 1999; see also Hill 2010b.

3. All verb paradigms may be confirmed in Hill 2010a.

4. Kuryłowicz 1949.

One way to explain the *rl-* ~ *zl-* alternation is to suggest that *sl- > *rl-* was a regular change and that the new *zl-* forms were analogically created on the basis of pairs like *'gyel* "fall" and *sgyel* /zgyel/ "throw down"—that is, *'gyel* : *'log > *ldog* :: /zgyel/ :: X, X = *zlog*. However, this explanation predicts that the word "moon" should be **rla-ba* rather than the attested *zla-ba* "moon." Since "moon" is outside of the verbal system there is no mechanism by which to propose the analogical reinstatement of *zl-* in this word. Thus an unconditioned change *sl- > *rl-* is not an acceptable explanation; instead, it is necessary to isolate a conditioning environment for *sl- > *rl-* that permits "moon" to remain unaffected.

The paradigm of *zlog, bzlogs, bzlog, zlogs* has an invariant *o*-grade throughout its paradigm. The ex hypothesi more archaic paradigm *rlog, brlags, brlag, rlogs* instead shows the normal *o*-ablaut in the present and in the imperative, as generally witnessed in verbs with an etymological root with an *a* vocalism (√sad "kill," *gsod, bsad, gsad, sod*; cf. Burmese *sat* and Chinese 殺 *sreat* < *rsat). In order for *zlog, bzlogs, bzlog, zlogs* to have obtained a present stem *-o-* in all four of its stems, the entire paradigm must have been generalized from the present stem (e.g., with the verb *sgrub, bsgrubs, bsgrub, sgrubs* "accomplish" as a possible model—*sgrub* : *bsgrubs* :: *zlog* : X, X = *bzlogs*). In turn, for this verb to be generalized from the present stem the present stem of the original paradigm must have been *zlog*. If the present tense of the verb was originally *zlog*, then the present *rlog* must be back-formed from another stem, either the past or the future (e.g., with the verb *sgrog, bsgrags, bsgrag, sgrogs* "proclaim" as a possible model—*bsgrags* : *brlags* :: *sgrog* : X, X = *rlog*). This reasoning suggests the inherited paradigm was *zlog, brlags, brlag, zlogs*. The lack of ablaut in the paradigm of the causative of "pour" forbids the formulation of the same argument. Nonetheless, parallel developments from an inherited paradigm *zlug, brlugs, brlug, zlugs* are certainly possible. The opacity of such paradigms clearly motivates their splitting into better-behaved offspring.

The argument so far has been based entirely on possible analogical models for explaining the attested forms but has the side benefit of motivating a context for the sound change *zl- > *rl-*, namely, that it occurred only after b-, that is, *bzl > *brl-*. This conditioning for the sound changes accounts for the retention of *zl-* in *zla-ba* "moon," but also for the lack of the cluster *bzl- in nominal forms. The change *bzl > *brl-* also raises the possibility that some nouns with initial *brl-* originate from *bsl-.[5] In contrast, according to the condition-

5. Cognates, such as Chinese 魄 *phaek* < *p^{hʕ}rak, written Burmese *prā*, and Japhug Gyalrong *tɯ-rla* suggest that *r-* is original in Old Tibetan *brla* "soul."

ing of this sound change the cluster *rl-* in nouns such as *rlig* "testicle" cannot derive from *zl-.

In sum, the sound change *bzl > *brl-* and a few plausible analogical developments explain both the causative doublets *zlug* "pour, caste," *rlug* "purge," and *zlog* "make turn, make return," *zlog* "destroy overturn," and also the presence of initial *zl-* and *brl-* but not *bzl-* in nominal forms. The inherited paradigms of the two verbs discussed so far were *zlog, brlags, brlag, zlogs* "make turn" and *zlug, brlugs, brlug, zlugs* "make pour."[6]

There is some evidence for an analogous change *bsn- > *brn-*. Joanna Bialek draws attention to the spelling variation between *bsnan bskyed* "extended," on the east face of the inscription at Zhwa'i lha-khang (lines 38 and 45), and *brnan bskyed*, on the west face of the same inscription (line 58).[7] The version with *s-* can, as she points out, be easily etymologized as a combination of the past stems of the verbs *snon* "add" and *skyed* "increase." Facing the variants *bsnan* and *brnad*, she writes that whether "this alternation is grammatically motivated or resulted from a misspelling or a damage to the text has to be left unanswered."[8] The foregoing argument would instead suggest that *brnan* is the older spelling and *bsnan* is its analogical replacement. The east face, with *bsnan*, was inscribed in 812 CE, somewhat after the west face (with *brnan*), which was inscribed in 800–810 CE.[9] This chronology is at least consistent with the diachronic explanation of the spelling variation proposed here. In her analysis of the phrase *gtsigs brnand-pa'i yi-ge zhib-mo* "detailed text of the extended edict," on line 55 of the Skar-chung inscription, Bialek similarly understands *brnand* as equivalent to *bsnand*.[10] It would be convenient for my analysis if the Skar-chung inscription were inscribed before 812 CE, and perhaps it was, but Iwao et al. are able only to date to within the reign of Khri lde srong brtsan (779?–815).[11]

6. The root grade *-a-* in the inherited causative *zlog, brlags, brlag, zlogs* suggests that the *-o-* seen in *ldog* is also explainable as part of the present formation. If so, the past *log* is an analogical creation; the inherited past is *lags*. There is the copula verb *lags*, which is the wayward past of "turn." This seems reasonable to suggest for two reasons. First, *lags* is only negated with *ma*, the negation prefix typically used for past stems. Second, the semantics of "turn" > "become" > "be" is plausible; compare German *werden*, Latin *vertō* "turn," Sanskrit *vártate* "id.," etc. I owe this argument to a conversation with Abel Zadoks from circa 2015. I also take this opportunity to thank Abel for sending me down the path that led to this article.

7. Bialek 2018, 252–53.

8. Bialek 2018, 252–53.

9. Iwao, Hill, and Tsuguhito 2009, 17–20.

10. Bialek 2018, 338n1.

11. Iwao, Hill, and Tsuguhito 2009, 22.

Implicitly Bialek also proposes a second instance of *bsn- > *brn-* in a past-tense verb stem. She connects the first syllable of *brnal-khab* "sewing needle" to the verb *snol* "unite,"[12] a proposal that I can only interpret as the suggestion that *snol* is the present stem and *brnal* the past.

One can also point to limited evidence for a change *bsny- > *brny-*. In a passage concerning shaving in the *Vinayakṣudrakavastu* (D Kangyur, vol. 3) one finds the phrase *des skabs de dge-slong dag-la bsnyad-pa-dang/* "he at that time conferred with the bhikṣus" (D Kangyur, vol. 10, 200b), but the Pukdrak (F), Ulan Bator (U) and Narthang (N) Kangyurs agree on the alternative reading *brnyad-pa-dang*. The high quality of these three Kangyurs in general, the agreement of the "independent" Pukdrak with Kangyurs from the Them spangs ma branch, and the principle of *lectio difficilior* all weigh in favor of taking *brnyad-pa-dang* as the original reading. Although the matter certainly requires more investigation, there is thus some reason to believe that this verb "tell, confer" originally had a conjugation such as *snyod, brnyad, brnyad, snyod.*

The combined evidence for the changes *bsl- > *brl-*, *bsn- > *brn-*, and *bsny- > *brny-* lends credibility to an overall change of *bs- to *br-* before voiced resonant root initials.[13]

12. Bialek 2018, 250–51.

13. Since labial prefixes are not compatible with labial roots, the lack of any evidence for *bsm- > *brm- poses no problem.

References

Bialek, Joanna. 2018. *Compounds and Compounding in Old Tibetan: A Corpus-Based Approach*, vol. 2. Marburg: Indica et Tibetica Verlag.

Conrady, August. 1896. *Eine indochinesische Causativ-Denominativ-Bildung und ihr Zusammenhang mit den Tonaccenten*. Leipzig: O. Harrassowitz

Hahn, Michael. 1999. "Blags und Verwandtes (Miscellanea etymologica tibetica, VI)." In *Studia Tibetica et Mongolica (Festschrift Manfred Taube)*, edited by Helmut Eimer et al., 123–25. Swisttal-Odendorf: Indica et Tibetica Verlag.

Hill, Nathan W. 2010a. *A Lexicon of Tibetan Verb Stems as Reported by the Grammatical Tradition*. Munich: Bayerische Akademie der Wissenschaften.

———. 2010b. "An Overview of Old Tibetan Synchronic Phonology." *Transactions of the Philological Society* 108.2: 110–25.

———. 2014. "Sino-Tibetan: Part 2 Tibetan." In *The Oxford Handbook of Derivational Morphology*, edited by Rochelle Lieber and Pavol Štekauer, 620–30. Oxford: Oxford University Press.

Iwao, Kazushi, Nathan W. Hill, and Takeuchi Tsuguhito. 2009. *Old Tibetan Inscriptions*. Tokyo: Research Institute for Languages and Cultures of Asia and Africa, Tokyo University of Foreign Studies.

Kuryłowicz, Jerzy. 1949. "La nature des procès dit analogiques." *Acta Linguistica* 5: 17–34.

LaPolla, Randy J. 2003. "Overview of Sino-Tibetan Morphosyntax." In *The Sino-Tibetan Languages*, edited by Graham Thurgood and Randy J. LaPolla, 22–42. London: Routledge.

Refractions of Lotus Light: The Early Elaboration and Delimitation of Padmasambhava's Eight Names

Daniel A. Hirshberg

Padmasambhava (eighth century CE), the "lotus-born" tantric master credited as the catalyst for establishing Buddhism in Tibet, has been known by several names since his earliest documentation. Various Dunhuang manuscripts reference him as Padmasambhava, Sambhava, and Pema Gyelpo (Padma rgyal po), the "lotus king." He is also celebrated as a master (*ācārya*), a fourth-level knowledge-holder of the great seal (*māhāmudrā vidyādhara*), and a "second buddha."[1] It is generally accepted that these names and distinctions were shared by a single historical individual whose apotheosis significantly expanded his role and renown in the centuries that followed the ninth-century collapse of the Tibetan empire, though it cannot be completely ruled out that some number of Indian Buddhists sharing a similar time, tantric aptitude, range of activity, and/or nomenclature were later conflated.[2]

Building off the character traits and appellations recorded in early sources, a vibrant biographical tradition coalesced from the twelfth century, as Padmasambhava's brilliant potential was acutely focused through the creative matrix of the Tibetan *imaginaire*. Ngadak Nyangrel Nyima Özer (Mnga' bdag Nyang ral nyi ma 'od zer, 1124–92) composed *The Copper Island* (*Zangs gling ma*) as the first complete, autonomous biography of Padmasambhava's activities in India and Tibet. Like clear light passing through a crystal, Nyangrel refracts Padmasambhava into a spectrum of aliases, titles, and epithets that serve as episodic signposts in the narrative progression of his life. Eventually among his most definitive details, a selection became normative as the "eight names of the guru" (*gu ru mtshan brgyad*). These were further enhanced, envisioned, and popularized by their iconography, which has been remarkably stable throughout Himalayan Buddhism for centuries.[3] And yet such high degrees

1. See Dalton 2020. For Padma rgyal po, see Mayer 2020, 82–83n101.

2. On the topic of Padmasambhava's historicity, see Kapstein 2000, 155–60; Cantwell and Mayer 2013, 27; Hirshberg 2016, 1–18; Mayer 2020, 68; Doney 2020, 110.

3. Cf. Cantwell 2020b, 137–38, who highlights variance in their iconography. HAR 160

of consistency and ubiquity belie how little has been known about the introduction, elaboration, and delimitation of this revered rubric, both textually and iconographically.

Copper Island has long been recognized as the font of Padmasambhava's names and epithets, aggregating and elaborating but not delimiting them. As recollected at the end of his *Stainless Proclamations* biography (*Dri ma med pa bka' rgya*),[4] Nyangrel first discerned a restricted set of eight Padmasambhavas during a meditative vision late in life, apparently after *Copper Island* was complete. He encounters eight distinct aspects of and names for Padmasambhava, which are positioned in the maṇḍalic array of the cardinal and intermediate directions. Nyangrel's vision appears to be the earliest application of the eightfold framework that would come to define Padmasambhava for subsequent treasure revealers, such as Guru Chöwang (Gu ru chos kyi dbang phyug, 1212–70), and eventually the entire Tibetan tradition.

Naming Padmasambhava in Copper Island

As with every inquiry concerning the elaboration of Padmasambhava lore, we must turn to its wellspring, the twelfth-century treasure revealer Nyangrel and his first complete biography of Padmasambhava, *Copper Island*.[5] In it Nyangrel compiles diverse appellations for Padmasambhava, which are neither delimited by number nor defined as a set: the multiplicity of his names lacks any organizing principle. Padmasambhava simply receives them in accordance

(https://www.himalayanart.org/items/160), a fourteenth-century painting referenced by Cantwell, may very well preserve an early depiction of the eight names' iconography, reflecting the idiosyncrasy of textual sources that predate standardization, as evidenced by the present discussion. It appears to be an exception rather than the rule among surviving examples, however—including the earliest ones. A maṇḍala of Hayagrīva from the same era (https://www.himalayanart.org/items/30911) and attributed to the lineages of Nyangrel and Chöwang already depicts each of the eight names with their standard iconography. Likewise, a fifteenth-century painting of the Fierce Guru (*Gu ru drag po*) features the normative eight names and iconography in its top register (see Hirshberg 2018, 94; and https://www.himalayanart.org/items/65125). While some variation persists among specific iconographic details, it appears that each of the eight names became visually identifiable, distinguishable, and quite consistent within just two or three centuries of their introduction.

4. While not committed to the page by Nyangrel, his direct disciples attest that they compiled *Stainless* based on Nyangrel's oral testimony, which is often reproduced in the first person. Hirshberg 2016, 35.

5. For an extended discussion of Nyangrel's life, treasure recoveries, and contributions to Padmasambhava lore, see Hirshberg 2016.

with key moments in his life, especially in the first five chapters that describe his early years in greater India. The procession of new epithets ebbs during his Tibetan sojourn—a precedent replicated in most Padmasambhava biographies thereafter.

Even when the circumstances that inspire a new name for Padmasambhava are extraordinary, the basic context of its bestowal is not: new names, epithets, and titles are offered in contexts of enthronement, ordination, empowerment, praise, and other forms of tribute, as is customary. As evidenced by the chapter headings from an exemplar of *Copper Island*'s earliest recension, his most generic designation is Master Pema (Slob dpon Padma).[6] When discovered on the pistil of a lotus and adopted by King Indrabodhi, he receives the royal title Prince Tsokyé Dorjé, Lake-Born Vajra (Rgyal bu mtsho skyes rdo rje), where lake-born is a synonym for lotus or *padma*. While this name is unattested in Dunhuang manuscripts, it is cited as the author of a commentary in the Tibetan canon (Bstan 'gyur), translated during the imperium. Moreover, this commentary is placed before another text sometimes attributed to Padmasambhava, *A Noble Noose of Methods* (*Thabs kyi zhags pa*), a version of which was recovered from Dunhuang. The commentary's colophon forwards an alias for Tsokyé Dorjé, the "skull garlanded" Pema Tötreng (Padma thod 'phreng),[7] who emanates a powerful influence upon Nyangrel, Chöwang, and subsequent treasure revealers. Pema Tötreng also makes an appearance in *Copper Island* (see below), yet he is not counted among most standard sets of Padmasambhava's eight names.

Proceeding from Padmasambhava's birth into another famous episode, not long after his glorious anointment as heir to his adoptive father's kingdom, the prince flings his trident, which karma carries down into the skull of a minister's infant son, killing him instantly. Padmasambhava is banished to the charnel grounds, where he subsists on human corpses for both sustenance and attire while engaged in meditation. The local population fearfully designates this grotesque, terrifying aspect as the "human-devouring demon" (*srin*) Śāntarakṣita. The taxonomy is cogent and yet the name is curious: a contemporary by the same name is Nālānda's venerable abbot, renowned for his monastic purity, who proposes Padmasambhava's invitation to Tibet later in the same narrative. Welcomed by the ḍākinīs, Padmasambhava in demonic aspect cavorts across the charnel grounds and gains empowerment under the

6. For the stemmatic analysis of *Zangs gling ma*, see Doney 2014, whose recensional designations are followed here.

7. Cantwell and Mayer 2012, 92n2.

secret name Dorjé Drakpo Tsel (Rdo rje gra [*sic*] po rtsal), the first of Padmasambhava's explicitly "fierce" aspects.[8]

As *Copper Island*'s plot progresses, Padmasambhava traverses the Indian subcontinent to Bodh Gayā for a brief foray onto a conventional path: he goes forth as a monk (albeit under Prabhāhasti, a tantric master of the fierce deity Vajrakīlaya), and receives the ordination name Śākya Senggé (Shākya seng ge).[9] This conflicts with later hagiographies where Śākya Senggé trains in Vinaya under the historical Buddha's attendant Ānanda, circa the fifth century BCE—an anachronism that inserts Padmasambhava into prophecies that predict his arrival as a direct emanation of Śākyamuni Buddha.[10] While Nyangrel encapsulates Padmasambhava's activities within the span of a single human lifetime, subsequent biographers employ this prophecy to assert his immortality. In their accounts, Padmasambhava appears soon after the death of the Buddha and still resides, even today, on Cāmara, the southwestern subcontinent of our world in the idealized Buddhist universe. As Padmasambhava's lore develops, it weaves elements from diverse and sometimes conflicting sources into single narratives, extending his life from a time into the timeless.

Despite a brief engagement with exoteric Buddhism as Śākya Senggé, Padmasambhava swiftly shifts, in the same chapter, back into hardcore esoterica, receiving both outer and inner yoga tantra transmissions from various masters. An ordained ḍākinī blesses him to attain the *vidyādhara* level of mahāmudrā, replicating a detail evidenced in a Dunhuang manuscript.[11] Then, having received numerous transmissions, including each of the *Eight Instructions* (*Bka' brgyad*) from their designated lineage holders, the reinvigorated tantrika is empowered under the secret name Loden Choksé (Blo ldan mchog sred).[12]

As the tantrika Loden Choksé, Padmasambhava sets off for the kingdom of Zahor in search of a consort,[13] where he is condemned for seducing the local princess, Mandāravā. Bound and burned at the stake together, the master and Mandāravā are soon revealed unscathed atop a lotus at the center of a lake. Thus born again, Padmasambhava is praised by the king of Zahor as Padmasambhava (Padma 'byung gnas) and Tsokyé Dorjé, his original birth name

8. *Zangs gling ma* h, 10a5.

9. *Zangs gling ma* h, 10b5, 11a2.

10. Several prophecies are gathered and reproduced by Tsele Natsok Rangdrol (b. 1608). See Kunzang 1991, 8–9.

11. *Zangs gling ma* h, 12a.2–3; Dalton 2020, 34. For an accounting of Dunhuang details echoed in *Zangs gling ma*, see Doney 2020, 99, 103–9.

12. *Zangs gling ma* h, 13a.2.

13. On Zahor, see van der Kuijp 2010.

acquired upon discovery by King Indrabodhi.[14] Although *Copper Island* provides few descriptors for iconographical inspiration, these two aliases come to share his most definitive iconography as a mustachioed, lotus-crowned tantrika, who is featured as the central figure in many compositions.

Padmasambhava then returns to his homeland, Uḍḍiyāna, from which he had been expelled for infanticide.[15] Having transgressed the terms of his sentence, Padmasambhava again is burned at the stake, survives, and regains his line to the throne as Pema Gyelpo, the "lotus king."[16] He is noted here for his primary adornment, a garland of skulls, and so receives the name Pema Tötreng (Padma thod 'phreng), Lotus Skull Garland, though this item is excluded from visual depictions of Pema Gyelpo. In standard compositions of the eight names, Pema Gyelpo is the iconographical pairing for Loden Choksé: they parallel each other on opposite sides of the central figure, both clothed in the billowing robes of royal attire. While this is consistent with Pema Gyelpo's narrative arc, it is incongruent for Loden Choksé, whose story singularly underscores his tantric acumen in the charnel grounds. His royal vestments are derived from an artistic preference for symmetry and balance in the visual depiction of the eight names as a single composition, where his robes mimic and balance those of his pairing across from him. Pema Gyelpo is to inherit the throne at the epicenter of his father's kingdom; thus his royal attire is cogent. Conversely Loden Choksé thrives in the liminality of the charnel grounds, at the fringes of society and beyond mundane law.

Having converted the kingdoms of northwestern India, Pema Gyelpo/Tötreng journeys east once again to debate the Hindu ascetics at Bodh Gayā. In reverence of his logical and theurgical victories, the Buddhist paṇḍitas praise him as Senggé Dradrok (Seng ge sgra sgrog),[17] the "lion's roar" proclaiming the supremacy of Buddhism over competing sects. This is the second of his two fierce aspects, consistently depicted as a monstrous dark-blue buddha engulfed in flames. These characteristics extend from the force of his victory rather than any explicit visual cues in *Copper Island*.

Elsewhere in the early recension of *Copper Island*, Padmasambhava is identified as a magically emanated buddha-body (*sprul pa'i sku, nirmāṇakāya*) and, later in Tibet, Emperor Tri Songdetsen equates him with the celestial bodhisattva Avalokiteśvara, the Great Compassionate One. While later editions of

14. *Zangs gling ma* h, 14b.2, 14b.4.

15. On Uḍḍiyāna, see Hirshberg 2016, 6–9.

16. *Zangs gling ma* h, 16b.1–3.

17. *Zangs gling ma* h, 17a.4.

Copper Island include even more names and details, this covers the range of about a dozen names and epithets for Padmasambhava in its earliest recension.[18] Nowhere does it list them as a set or suggest a limit. Six of these names would become normative in the eight-name rubric: Tsokyé Dorjé, Śākya Senggé, Loden Choksé, Padmasambhava, Pema Gyelpo, and Senggé Dradrok. Dorjé Drolö is absent; this name was unknown to Nyangrel, but his place is held by an explicitly "fierce" antecedent, Guru Drakpo Tsel.

Precisely one aspect, uniformly included across all iterations of Padmasambhava's eight names, is conspicuously absent here: Nyima Özer, which is none other than the given name of Padmasambhava's original biographer, Nyangrel.

Table 1: Padmasambhava's names, the episodic contexts of their bestowal, and any visually relevant details from the earliest surviving recension of Nyangrel's *Copper Island Biography of Padmasambhava.* Later recensions of the same text, most especially the widely distributed nineteenth-century *Rin chen gter mdzod* edition (cited as *Zangs gling ma* a; translated in Tsogyal 1993), feature a significant elaboration of his names and details, thus indicating and incorporating the expansion of Padmasambhava lore over the eight centuries since Nyangrel's initial formulation of the text.

Name	Episode	Iconographical Descriptors
Tsokyé Dorjé	a. Birth/discovery b. Surviving the stake in Zahor	a. Beautiful eight-year-old boy, immaculate and excellent body b. Accompanied by Mandāravā
Srin Śāntarakṣita => Guru Drakpo Tsel	Exile from Uḍḍiyāna and empowerment	Demonic; human body parts as attire

18. Urgyen Dorjé Chang (U rgyan rdo rje 'chang, Uḍḍiyāna Vajradhāra) is an alternate among the eight names. Depicted as a deep-blue figure holding a vajra and bell, the signature attributes of the buddha Vajradhāra, and embraced by his consort, he is absent from *Copper Island*, but Nyangrel's *Stainless* biography attests that he encountered Guru Pema Dorjé Chang (Gu ru padma rdo rje 'chang) in union with Yeshé Tsogyel (Ye shes mtsho rgyal) during a meditative vision at Samyé Chimphu (Bsam yas mchims phu; Chos kyi 'od zer et al. 1978, 104.6–106.1). He also appears as one of the eight names in a fourteenth-century maṇḍala of Hayagrīva (https://www.himalayanart.org/items/30911), one of the earliest surviving examples of the eight.

Name	Episode	Iconographical Descriptors
Śākya Senggé	Monastic ordination	Shaved head and monk's robes (implied)
Loden Choksé	Empowerment and attainment	None
Padmasambhava/ Pemajungné	Surviving the stake in Zahor	Accompanied by Mandāravā
Pema Gyelpo => Pema Tötreng	Enthronement in Uḍḍiyāna	Skull garland
Senggé Dradrok	Defeat of competing sects in Bodh Gayā	None

Nyangrel's Maṇḍalic Vision in Stainless Proclamations

Nyangrel Nyima Özer's elaboration of Padmasambhava lore and literature is among his most celebrated contributions, but the eight-names rubric itself does not stem from *Copper Island*. Instead, he envisioned an octet of Padmasambhavas very late in life, apparently after that text was complete. Corroborated by Nyangrel's two biographies, he elected to retire from his treasure-seeking peregrinations and public duties in his forties to spend the final two to three decades of his life in meditative retreat, primarily above his home base and hermitage, Mawochok (Smra bo lcog), in south-central Tibet's Lodrak (Lho brag) region. While Nyangrel's most cited biography, *Clear Mirror* (*Gsal ba'i me long*), scarcely describes this period, the last third of Nyangrel's *Stainless Proclamations* presents detailed, first-person accounts of his meditative experiences during his final decades in retreat.[19]

In the vision most relevant to the present discussion, Nyangrel recounts that one evening he witnessed countless karmic and gnostic ḍākinīs gather. One among them steps forward to declare that she and Nyangrel share a profound connection. She declares:

> Karmically endowed, magically emanated yogin:
> you and I are bound by the same oath!
> The eight abodes of the great charnel grounds
> are the eight positions (*bkod pa*) of Guru Padma.

19. Myang ston rig 'dzin lhun grub 'od zer 1979 and Chos kyi 'od zer et al. 1978.

In practicing yogic discipline,
let's proceed [there] to request an introduction to the signs and
meanings.[20]

While *bkod pa* can be interpreted as "expression" or "manifestation," the appositive sentence construction equates the eight charnel grounds as Padmasambhava's eight "positions." The context here refers to his placements in the charnel grounds rather than his names, thereby structuring a maṇḍala in reliance upon the cardinal and intermediate directions. While Padmasambhava's epithets in *Copper Island* are restricted only by the number of nameworthy events, Nyangrel's vision spatially defines and delimits a set of eight in accordance with the maṇḍala's directional architecture.

Nyangrel accepts the samaya-bound ḍākinī's invitation, then they merge indivisibly and arrive at the first of the eight charnel grounds to the east, as is customary. Proceeding from charnel ground to charnel ground, tracing a clockwise circumambulation from the east to the southeast and so on, a formula is repeated: Nyangrel encounters a yogin for whom he provides terse visual cues that hint at his identity as one of the Indian mahāsiddhas,[21] then he requests instructions. In response the yogin introduces himself by name, thereby confirming his status as an enlightened master, but defers Nyangrel toward an emanation of Padmasambhava a short distance away, who comfortably abides in the cool shade of a tree, each of its own variety. Gazing over as directed by the siddha, Nyangrel describes his first impression of each Padmasambhava before the master intones a mantra and states his name as preface to three lines of esoteric instruction.

Progressing around the maṇḍala to each Padmasambhava, all but the final one finds precedent in Nyangrel's *Copper Island*. The first, the eastern aspect, introduces himself as Pemajungné, and his siddha-attendant is Indrabodhi/Indrabhūti, the mahāsiddha sometimes conflated with Padmasambhava's adoptive father. None of Pemajungné's now iconic vestments or implements are described; Nyangrel only notes a jeweled *uṣṇīṣa*-bump upon the crown of his head, a mark of the "Great Man" (*mahāpuruṣa*) that is absent in the iconography of this particular aspect, who dons a lotus-shaped crown that would thus conceal it. Nyangrel's first encounter concludes with Pemajungné symbolically instructing the ḍākinīs by silently raising a lotus.

As Nyangrel proceeds around the maṇḍala, each siddha-attendant introduces him to a distinct aspect of Padmasambhava, who is formulaically

20. Chos kyi 'od zer et al. 1978, 151–52.

21. See Robinson 1998, 57.

introduced by name, head ornament, and a hand implement that serves as a pedagogical device.

Table 2: Sequence and details of Nyangrel's visionary encounter with eight Padmasambhavas (Chos kyi 'od zer et al. 1978, 151–60).

Seq.	Direction	Attending Siddha	Aspect's Name	Head Ornament	Hand Implement
1.	East	Indrabhūti	Pemajungné	Jeweled protuberance	Lotus
2.	Southeast	Ḍombi Heruka	Pema Gyelpo	Jeweled helmet	Egg-shaped jewel
3.	South	Nāgārjuna-garbha	Pema Tötreng	Wreath of skulls	Trident
4.	Southwest	Vajra Ghaṇḍhapa	Padmasam-bhava	Crown of flowers	Conch
5.	West	Padma Vajra	Loden Choksé	Hovering parasol	Wooden scepter[22]
6.	Northwest	Lūhipa	Shākya Senggé	Saffron scholar's hat	Walking stick
7.	North	Kukkuripa	Senggé Dradrok	Vipers	Skull staff
8.	Northeast	Sarahapa	Nyima Özer	Red silk turban	Wood-handled mirror

While seven of these eight aspects are named in *Copper Island* as well, few of their features relate to their normative iconography. The only one bearing a hand implement that may have contributed to later depictions is the eighth and final Padmasambhava, Nyima Özer.

It is intriguing that one of Nyangrel's Padmasambhavas shares his given name of Nyima Özer, who retains a certain pride of place at the conclusion

22. *Chags shing*. The first syllable is likely a homonymal misspelling of *phyag* or *lcag*, which would then indicate a wooden scepter or switch. Chos kyi 'od zer et al. 1978, 156.

of the visionary tour. Bearing a wood-handled mirror beneath the shade of a bodhi tree, this aspect of Padmasambhava may be the perfected reflection of Nyangrel himself. At the end of Nyangrel's journey—both in terms of this brief visionary experience as well as his entire life's progression to becoming the great treasure revealer—he finally confronts his own enlightened analog. This Padmasambhava sings:

> *Sūrya smṛti dharma āḥ*
> I am Nyima Özer.
> The lamp of luminous primordial gnosis
> dispels the darkness of the afflictions and ignorance
> and discerns bliss-emptiness as a wish-fulfilling jewel.[23]

While Nyangrel inserts prophecies into *Copper Island* that presage Tri Songdetsen's reincarnation as a great treasure revealer (with precise biodata that can only specify Nyangrel as their fulfillment), nowhere do he and Padmasambhava share the same name. Among the dozen names that Padmasambhava acquires in the earliest recension of *Copper Island*, Nyima Özer is not among them—even when seven of the eight Padmasambhava names that become normative find strong precedent if not explicit mention. Instead, Nyangrel's nominal conflation with the ultimate object of his devotion, Padmasambhava as the cipher of complete buddhahood, is reserved for a final vision in the final section of his biography that features first-person journal entries of his meditative experiences.

Here Padmasambhava as Nyima Özer bears a mirror fixed to a wood handle or staff, an object that extends back to the Iron Age on the Tibetan plateau.[24] This circular object may have been re-envisioned and revised due to the name of the one who bears it: later descriptions of Padmasambhava as Nyima Özer center upon a defining event where he halts the progression of the sun in the sky. This offers a cogent narrative context for Padmasambhava to receive the epithet Nyima Özer, "rays of the sun." In his iconography, the disc suspended above his left hand is commonly explained as the sun tethered by its rays, though some sources describe these closed spheres as lassoes, which function as implements in the magical action of binding the sun.[25]

23. Chos kyi 'od zer et al. 1978, 156, 159–60.

24. Bellezza 2014.

25. Jeff Watt 2000, https://www.himalayanart.org/items/675. Also see Hirshberg 2018, 107, and figure 3.23, a detail of https://www.himalayanart.org/items/1093. Fixing the sun is a *siddhi* featured in the story of the mahāsiddha Virūpa (Robinson 1979, 29). In Nyangrel's

In this we may discern the symbiosis of narrative and iconography, as when the webbed digits of Buddha statues, functionally introduced to maintain the structural integrity of the icon, became textually integrated as one of the marks of the Great Man.[26] Perhaps Guru Nyima Özer's disc operates in the inverse: what originally was described as a mirror came to be understood as a sun in deference to his name, then an iconographical detail and narrative episode developed that directly incorporated it. By means of his inclusion here as Nyima Özer, Nyangrel Nyima Özer inscribes himself into the legacy of what becomes Padmasambhava's foremost organizing principle. As the architect of Padmasambhava's apotheosis, Nyangrel's vision of the "eight positions of Padmasambhava" is certainly among the earliest examples of Padmasambhava in a restricted set of eight names and aspects, and is quite likely the original.

Guru Chöwang and the "Guru's Eight Names"

In claiming to be Nyangrel's reincarnation, Guru Chöwang, a disciple of Nyangrel's second son and designated heir, Namkhapel (Nam mkha' dpal, 1169?–1235?),[27] picks up where Nyangrel left off in the devotional elaboration of Padmasambhava. With the first documented revelation of the renowned "Seven Line Supplication" (*Tshig bdun gsols 'debs*) among them, Chöwang's contributions to Padmasambhava's popularization and articulation are extensive and permeate much of his surviving literature.[28]

After Nyangrel's "eight positions" of Padmasambhava, it is Chöwang who introduces the "guru's eight names" (*guru mtshan brgyad*), his foremost rubric, in the vivid recollection of his visions and dreams. In his *Eight Chapter Biography* (*Rnam thar skabs brgyad ma*), Chöwang notes a vision in which he "met face to face the completely liberated arrangement (*bkod*) of the guru's eight names set upon eight lotus petals, with a secret name making nine."[29] Here we find the terminological confluence of Nyangrel's original "eight positions" (*bkod pa brgyad*) with Chöwang's "eight names." None are specified here, but

Copper Island this feat is accomplished by Padmasambhava's disciple, Namkhai Nyingpo (Nam mkha'i snying po; *Zangs gling ma* h, 48b.1–2; Kunzang 1991, 88).

26. Strong 2001, 8–9.

27. For a synopsis of Namkhapel's life, see Hirshberg 2013.

28. For a précis of Padmasambhava's names in Chöwang's *Great History of the Treasures* (*Gter 'byung chen mo*), which are limited to variants of Padmākara/Padmasambhava, see Mayer 2020, 73n.87.

29. Chos kyi dbang phyug 1979b, I.48.1: *ghu ru padma'i mtshan brgyad/ gsang mtshan dang dgu'i rnam thar gyi bkod pa'i zhal gzigs pa . . .*

Chöwang's *Dream Journal* (*Rnam thar rnal lam ma*) centers upon eidetic encounters with nine Padmasambhavas, each in their own locale.[30] These occur in the spring of 1234 while he is practicing the liturgy (*thugs sgrub*) of Pema Tötreng Tsel,[31] whom he frames as a ninth Padmasambhava distinct from the eight-name rubric.

Table 3: List of the eight names, plus Pema Tötreng Tsel, presented in Chöwang's *Dream Journal.*

Seq.	Name	Location
1.	Guru Dorjé Drolö	Samyé Monastery (Bsam yas)
2.	Guru Śakya Senggé	Jokhang Temple (Lha sa 'khrul snang)
3.	Guru Padmasambha	Nepal (Bel yul)
4.	Guru Pema Gyelpo	Asura Cave (A su ra'i brag phug, Nepal) and Vajrāsana (Rdo rje gdan, Mahābodhi Temple, Bodh Gayā, India)
5.	Guru Pemajungné	Uḍḍiyāna (U rgyan)
6.	Guru Senggé Dradrok	Land of Heretics (Mu stegs kyi yul)
7.	Guru Nyima Özer	Cāmara (southwestern subcontinent, Rnga yab)
8.	Guru Loden Choksé	Laṅkā, Land of Demons (Srin yul lang ka)
9.	Jétsun/Loppön chenpo/ Guru Pema Tötreng Tsel	Copper-Colored Mountain (Zangs mdog dpal ri)

Although the names and sequence of Chöwang's oneiric Padmasambhavas differ slightly from Nyangrel's vision, seven of the eight names match, and Chöwang relies on a similar formula at the time of each introduction. Padmasambhava states his name, intones a mantra, and then introduces the signs and meanings with a four-line stanza. As reflected by Chöwang's designation of a ninth name, Pema Tötreng Tsel often retains an autonomy just outside the

30. Chos kyi dbang phyug 1979b, I.315–39.

31. Chos kyi dbang phyug 1979b, I.320.7.

standard sets of Padmasambhava's eight names. While his final full mention in the *Dream Journal* reveres him as Guru, aligning him with the other Padmasambhavas, prior to this Pema Tötreng alone is distinguished as Exalted One and Great Master (*Rje btsun, Slob dpon chen po*).

Chöwang's biographical literature is replete with accounts of his dreams and visions. In a distinct application, Chöwang legitimates his claim to Nyangrel's reincarnation through a visionary encounter with Padmasambhava, which is found in multiple versions at various stages of refinement in his surviving auto/biographies.[32] It is possible (if not likely) that Chöwang encounters eight Padmasambhavas in additional versions, visions, and dreams scattered throughout this literature, and he adopts the rubric in his devotional and ritual texts, such as *Secret Embodiment of the Guru* (*Bla ma gsang 'dus*), greatly aiding its swift renown in the century to come.[33]

Rapid Popularization in the Fourteenth Century

The fourteenth century marks a new era in the apotheosis and popularization of Padmasambhava and his eight names. After Nyangrel's *Copper Island*, Padmasambhava's most famed *Testament* (*Bka' thang*) hagiographies emerge just decades apart: Urgyen Lingpa (U rgyan gling pa, 1323–60?) recovers the *Crystal Cave* (*Shel brag ma*), and Sangyé Lingpa (Sangs rgyas gling pa, 1340–96) reveals the *Golden Rosary* (*Gser 'phreng*). Padmasambhava accumulates additional names throughout the first half of *Crystal Cave* especially, but *Golden Rosary* multiplies them throughout, with Padmasambhava receiving name after name, epithet after epithet as the narrative progresses.

Crystal Cave makes several references to the "guru's eight names" and includes at least two supplications to them. The first appears in chapter 19, which excludes any narrative content and instead stacks a series of devotional songs, presumably from various sources. Here the praise to the "eight names in one exalted body" features five-line stanzas for each of the eight, which are sung by a chorus of sixteen gnostic ḍākinīs.[34] Another is sung by the king of Zahor in chapter 41 and proves to be excerpted from Guru Chöwang's *Secret Embodiment of the Guru*, with some variance in the sequence of names.[35]

In addition to their embedment within these two influential hagiographies,

32. Hirshberg 2017.

33. Phillips 2004, 305, references numerous encounters with Padmasambhava in Chöwang's biographical *Ma ṇi bka' 'bum chen mo.*

34. U rgyan gling pa 1987, 126–27.

35. U rgyan gling pa 1987, 263–64; Chos kyi dbang phyug 1979a, 33–34; Cantwell 2020b, 138–39; also translated in Helffer 2012, 147–48.

we also find autonomous treasure texts centered exclusively upon the eight names emerging in the fourteenth century. Dorjé Lingpa (Rdo rje gling pa, 1346–1405) recovered *Eight Names in Detail* (*Bye brag mtshan brgyad rnams*).[36] Rikdzin Gödem (Rig 'dzin rgod ldem, 1337–1409), the third of the most celebrated revealers after Nyangrel and Chöwang, recovered the same text under a similar title: *Sādhana for Each of the Eight Names* (*Mtshan brgyad bye brag gi sgrub thabs*).[37] Included among his Northern Treasures collection (*Byang gter*), this liturgy is more elaborate and refined than the version recovered by Dorjé Lingpa.

The guru's eight names are replicated among the works of the most celebrated treasure revealers of the fourteenth century and, eventually, of all time. It is common if not standard practice for revealers to mine the works of those who preceded them, occasionally with explicit citation by name, but most often simply by embedding elements of prior works within their own.[38] As a neighbor of Nyangrel's hermitage, close disciple of his son and chosen heir, claimant to his reincarnation, and intimately familiar admirer of his oeuvre, Chöwang served as a critical bridge between Nyangrel's original elaboration and delimitation of Padmasambhava's names and their broader popularization in the fourteenth century. Nyangrel's contribution to the delimitation of eight names may have passed relatively unnoticed, but Chöwang's innovations ensured its continuity. It is Chöwang's supplication that is incorporated into what remains the preeminent biography of Padmasambhava, Urgyen Lingpa's *Crystal Cave Testament*, and this excerpt continues to be replicated in many liturgies, rituals, dances (*'cham*), and traditions all the way to the present. The inherent tension of such tradency, between the fidelity of authoritative sources and their innovation for new contexts, defines the entire *terma* (*gter ma*) or treasure tradition. At its very core is the figure of Padmasambhava, whose eight names, and with them his lore and iconography, became revered throughout all the sects of Tibetan Buddhism, both in Tibet and now abroad.

36. Rdo rje gling pa 1984, 185–208.

37. Rig 'dzin rgod ldem 1981, 129–47.

38. For an illuminating analysis of how one of the modern tradition's most revered masters, Dudjom Rinpoche (1904–87), compiled treasures foremost based on lineal resources, see Cantwell 2020a.

References

Primary Sources

Chos kyi dbang phyug (1212–70). 1979a. *Gsang 'dus bla ma'i thugs sgrub kyi skor: A Collection of Rare Teachings from the Revelations of Gu-ru Chos-kyi-dbang-phyug.* Paro, Bhutan: Ugyen Tempai Gyaltsen.

———. 1979b. *Gu ru chos dbang gi rang rnam dang zhal gdams.* 2 vols. Paro, Bhutan: Ugyen Tempai Gyaltsen.

Chos kyi 'od zer, Myang ston bsod nams seng ge, and Mi 'gyur rdo rje (twelfth–thirteenth centuries). 1978. "Sprul sku mnga' bdag chen po'i skyes rabs rnam thar dri ma med pa'i bka' rgya can la ldeb." In *Bka' brgyad bder gshegs 'dus pa'i chos skor*, vol. 1, 1–163. Gangtok: Lama Sonam Tobgay Kazi.

Mnga' bdag Nyang ral Nyi ma 'od zer (1124–92). n.d. *Pad ma bka' chems brgyas pa.* NGMCP E 2703/10 (=*Zangs gling ma* h).

———. 2007–2008. *Bka' thang zangs gling ma.* In *Rin chen gter mdzod chen mo*, vol. 1, 17–206. New Delhi: Shechen Publications (=*Zangs gling ma* a).

Myang ston rig 'dzin lhun grub 'od zer (twelfth–thirteenth centuries). 1979. "Bka' brgyad bde gshegs 'dus pa'i gter ston myang sprul sku nyi ma 'od zer gyi rnam thar gsal ba'i me long." In *Bka' brgyad bde gshegs 'dus pa'i chos skor*, vol. 2, 199–381. Paro, Bhutan: Lama Ngodrup.

Rdo rje gling pa (1346–1405). 1984. "Bye brag mtshan brgyad rnams." In *Bla ma zhi ba bka' 'dus kyi chos skor*, vol. 3, 185–208. Thimphu: Drug Sherig Press.

Rig 'dzin rgod ldem (1337–1408). 1981. "Mtshan brgyad bye brag gi sgrub thabs." In *[Byang gter nang sgrub] rig 'dzin gdung sgrub kyi chos skor*, 129–47. Gangtok: Bari Longsal Lama.

Sangs rgyas gling pa (1340–96). 2007. *Gu ru'i rnam thar rgyas pa gser gyi phreng ba thar lam gsal byed.* Lhasa: Bod ljongs mi dmangs dpe skrun khang.

U rgyan gling pa (1323–60?). 1987. *Padma bka' thang.* Lhasa: Si khron mi rigs dpe skrun khang.

Secondary Sources

Bellezza, John Vincent. 2014. *Flight of the Khyung.* http://www.tibetarchaeology.com/december-2014/.

Cantwell, Cathy. 2020a. *Dudjom Rinpoche's Vajrakīlaya Works: A Study in Authoring, Compiling, and Editing Texts in the Tibetan Revelatory Tradition.* Sheffield: Equinox Publishing.

———. 2020b. "The Formative Impact of Guru Chöwang's Secret Embodiment of the Lama on the Padmasambhava Ritual Traditions." In Samuel and Oliphant, *About Padmasambhava*, 123–46.

Cantwell, Cathy, and Robert Mayer. 2012. *A Noble Noose of Methods, the Lotus Garland Synopsis: A Mahāyoga Tantra and Its Commentary.* Vienna: Österreichische Akademie der Wissenschaften.

———. 2013. "Representations of Padmasambhava in Early Post-Imperial Tibet." In

Tibet After Empire: Culture, Society and Religion between 850–1000, edited by Christoph Cüppers, Robert Mayer, and Michael Walter, 19–50. Lumbini: Lumbini International Research Institute.

Dalton, Jacob P. 2020. "The Early Development of the Padmasambhava Legend in Tibet: A Second Look at the Evidence from Dunhuang." In Samuel and Oliphant, *About Padmasambhava*, 29–64.

Doney, Lewis. 2014. *The Zangs gling ma: The First Padmasambhava Biography. Two Exemplars of Its Earliest Attested Recension.* Andiast: International Institute for Tibetan and Buddhist Studies.

———. 2020. "The Lotus-Born in Nepal: A Dunhuang Narrative and the Later Biographical Tradition." In Samuel and Oliphant, *About Padmasambhava*, 97–118.

Helffer, Mireille. 2012. "Preservation and Transformations of Liturgical Traditions in Exile: The Case of Zhe chen Monastery in Bodhnath (Nepal)." In *Revisiting Rituals in a Changing Tibetan World*, edited by Katia Buffetrille, 137–62. Leiden: Brill.

Hirshberg, Daniel A. 2013. "Namkha Pel." https://treasuryoflives.org/biographies/view/Namkha-Pel/6010.

———. 2016. *Remembering the Lotus-Born: Padmasambhava in the History of Tibet's Golden Age.* Boston: Wisdom Publications.

———. 2017. "A Post-Incarnate Usurper? Inheritance at the Dawn of Catenate Reincarnation in Tibet." *Revue d'Etudes Tibétaines* 38 (February): 65–83.

———. 2018. "The Guru beyond Time: Padmasambhava's Eight Names and Three Exalted Bodies. In *The Second Buddha: Master of Time*, edited by Elena Pakhoutova, 86–117. New York: Prestel.

Kapstein, Matthew T. 2000. *The Tibetan Assimilation of Buddhism: Conversion, Contestation and Memory.* New York: Oxford University Press.

van der Kuijp, Leonard W. J. 2010. "On the Edge of Myth and History: Za hor, Its Place in the History of Early Indian Buddhist Tantra, and Dalai Lama V and the Genealogy of Its Royal Family." In *Studies on Buddhist Myths: Texts, Pictures, Traditions and History*, edited by Wang Bangwei, Chen Jinhua, and Chen Ming, 114–64. Shanghai: Zhongxi Book Company.

Kunsang, Erik Pema, trans. 1991. *Advice from the Lotus Born.* Hong Kong: Rangjung Yeshe Publications.

Mayer, Robert. 2020. "Geographical and Other Borders in the Symbolism of Padmasambhava." In Samuel and Oliphant, *About Padmasambhava*, 65–96.

Phillips, Bradford Lyman. 2004. *Consummation and Compassion in Medieval Tibet: The* Maṇi bka'-'bum chen mo *of Guru Chos-kyi dbang-phyug*. PhD dissertation at the University of Virginia.

Robinson, James B. 1979. *Buddha's Lions: The Lives of the Eighty-Four Siddhas* (*Caturaśīta-siddha-pravṛtti* by Abhayadatta). Berkeley, CA: Dharma Publishing.

———. 1998. "The Lives of Indian Buddhist Saints: Biography, Hagiography and Myth." In *Tibetan Literature: Studies in Genre*, 57–69. Ithaca, NY: Snow Lion Publications.

Samuel, Geoffrey, and Jamyang Oliphant, eds. *About Padmasambhava: Historical*

Narratives and Later Transformations of Guru Rinpoche. Switzerland: Garuda Verlag.

Strong, John S. 2001. *The Buddha: A Brief Biography*. Oxford: OneWorld Publications.

Tsogyal, Yeshe. 1993. *The Lotus-Born: The Life Story of Padmasambhava*. Translated by Erik Pema Kunsang. Boston: Shambhala Publications.

The Earliest Example of Printing in the Tibetan Script: Remarks on a *Dhāraṇī* Amulet from Dunhuang[1]

Matthew T. Kapstein

I first became acquainted with Leonard van der Kuijp, to whom this modest essay is offered, when he was studying for his Master's degree under the late Herbert V. Guenther at the University of Saskatchewan in 1975. I was then living in Nepal, where, to support myself, I had created a small mail-order bookshop, Shedrup Books, distributing out-of-the-way Tibetan publications. Leonard was one of my first customers. Unfortunately, the present pandemic does not allow me to access my files in storage, in which his correspondence with Shedrup Books is preserved.

We only met for the first time in person, however, a decade later at the Fourth Seminar of the International Association for Tibetan Studies at the Schloss Hohenkammer outside of Munich. My more vivid memory of Leonard dates to just a few months afterward, when, soaked by monsoon rain as I trudged up a muddy slope at the Nepal-Tibet border near Kodari—the road, of course, being washed out—I was hailed from the mists by a figure gliding down the slippery trail toward me with the news that it might at last be possible to obtain permission to visit Sakya. In our shared passion for the Tibetan book and its history, few destinations loomed so large. Although the present offering does not concern Sakya, I hope that, as a small stone raised onto

1. I am grateful to Irina Popova, Director of the Institute of Oriental Manuscripts of the Russian Academy of Sciences, St. Petersburg, for her kind invitation to present a preliminary version of this research to the conference "The Written Legacy of Dunhuang" in September 2016. The comments of several of the participants, especially Kuo Liying, Kirill Solonin, and Takata Tokio, contributed much to its revision. Nathalie Monnet, of the Bibliothèque nationale de France, has my profound thanks for her constant interest in and support of this project, first calling my attention to the object studied here, Pelliot tibétain 4216, through its appearance in Cohen and Monnet 1992, and subsequently facilitating my examination of the actual artifact in the collections of the BnF and signaling to me the documentation of a closely similar object in Matsumoto 1937 (see fig. 18). Without this, the present work could not have been undertaken. I extend my thanks, too, to Alexander Zorin for his observations when we examined P.T. 4216 together at the BnF in May 2018.

the growing *maṇi*-wall of our knowledge of early Tibetan printing, an area in which Leonard's contributions loom particularly large, it will serve as a small way of honoring his impact on Tibetan studies in the decades that have since passed.

Introduction

THE LONG HISTORY of Tibetan printing has often been traced back to the Xixia kingdom, where in 1149 a little book of prayers was published. This work, discovered at Khara-Khoto and preserved in the Institute of Oriental Manuscripts of the Russian Academy of Sciences in St. Petersburg, together with a number of other fragments probably dating to the same period, remains our earliest evidence for the reproduction of texts in the Tibetan language in print.[2] However, as I will show here, the antecedents of Tibetan printing may have emerged almost two centuries earlier and further to the west, in the region of Dunhuang.

Among the remarkable documents preserved among the Tibetan Dunhuang manuscripts acquired in 1908 by the sinologist Paul Pelliot (and bearing the shelf mark P.T., "Pelliot tibétain," at the BnF, the Bibliothèque nationale de France), one of particular interest that has received only slight attention to date is P.T. 4216 (fig. 1 and plate 7), a large *dhāraṇī* sheet that, with the exception of a number of early Tibetan seal impressions, is perhaps the earliest example of printed Tibetan characters so far found.[3] It seems to have first been brought to public attention as part of a 1992 exhibition of Chinese prints preserved at the BnF and curated by Monique Cohen and Nathalie Monnet. In their published catalogue, where it is reproduced as entry no. 38, we find this description:

> This text printed in Tibetan, found in the walled cave of Dunhuang, was probably printed in this town during the period of Tibetan occupation between 787 and 848. The unprinted central circle has been filled with a handwritten inscription in Chinese, of which the

2. Schaeffer 2009, 9, gives the date 1153 on the basis of a lecture delivered by Shen Weirong. However, in the published version of the talk in question (Shen 2010), the precise year is not given, though Shen states that the identification of the Chinese version of the text "provides the exact date when the XT 67 was printed" (357). Be that as it may, the recent publication of Hamanaka and Sizova (2020) establishes the year of publication to have in fact been 1149. For a detailed description of this booklet, see Piotrovsky et al. 1993, 278 (entry 87); and for its physical description, see Helman-Ważny 2014, 69, 121–22.

3. On the use of engraved personal seals (*sug rgya*) in Old Tibetan documents, see Takeuchi 1995, 108–10.

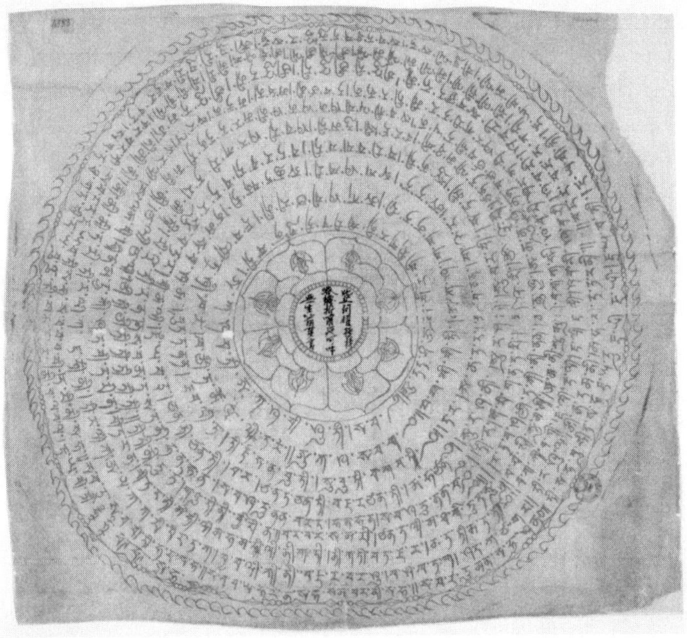

Fig. 1 and plate 7. P.T. 4216. A printed dhāraṇī from Dunhuang in Tibetan script, with handwritten Chinese in the center. Source gallica.bnf.fr / Bibliothèque nationale de France. All details of P.T. 4216 in the following figures are derived from the same source, except for fig. 13.

reconstructed title in Tibetan is *Mi skye bahi mdahi* (*sic!*) and *Anutpada isu dhâranî* (*sic!*) in Sanskrit. Petals are printed around this circle and then a text arranged in ten concentric circles. The print, produced in red ink, was made with one block of very large dimensions on two sheets of very fine paper that had been first glued together. The use of red pigments goes back to the very beginning of Chinese writing. . . .[4]

4. The full entry (Cohen and Monnet 1992, 59) reads as follows:

Dhâranî tibétaine imprimée en rouge
Fin VIIIe siècle—milieu IXe siècle ?
bois 52 cm de diamètre, 10 lignes concentriques
2 feuilles collées (47 x 53)
Pelliot tibétain 4216

Ce texte imprimé en tibétain, trouvé dans la grotte murée de Dunhuang, fut probablement imprimé dans cette ville durant la période d'occupation tibétaine entre 787 et 848. Le cercle central non imprimé a été rempli par une inscription manuscrite en chinois

The remainder of the entry, which describes the use of red ink in China, provides no further discussion of the document P.T. 4216 itself.

A decade after Cohen and Monnet's publication, the dhāraṇī sheet received a second brief notice in Françoise Wang-Toutain's catalogue of Chinese fragments found in the Pelliot tibétain collection. Her description of it reads in part:

> P. tib. 4216
> *Maṇḍala*
> Xylograph. *Dhāraṇī* in Tibetan spiraling in 10 concentric circles, encircled by flame and *vajra* designs. In red ink.
> Chinese inscription mentioning the *dhāraṇī* of the arrow of immortality: *Wu sheng jian zhen yan/ an ? zhe le tuo he ti/ bi qiu he que shou chi* 無生箭真言/ 唵 ? 折羅陀呵啼/ 比丘何確授持. In dark, black ink in the center, in the midst of eight red petals.[5]

---

dont le titre restitué en tibétain est "*Mi skye bahi mdahi*" et "*Anutpada isu dhâranî*" en sanscrit. Autour de ce cercle sont imprimés des pétales puis un texte disposé en dix cercles concentriques. L'impression produite à l'encre rouge, a été obtenue à partir d'un bois de très grande dimension sur deux feuilles de papier très fin préalablement collées. L'emploi de pigments rouge remonte au tout début de l'ecriture chinoise. En effet, des signes découverts sur des poteries néolithiques sont de cette couleur. Lors de leur mise au jour en septembre 1991, à Yinxu dans la province du Henan, il a été possible d'observer que les incisions d'inscriptions oraculaires gravées sur os conservaient un enduit fait d'un pigment rouge encore brillant. Les sceaux, d'abord imprimés sur l'argile, fur aux Ve et VIe siècles appliqués à l'encre rouge, les caractères gravés en creux apparaissant en blanc sur un fond vermillon. Très probablement, les prêtres taoïstes employaient aussi pour apposer leurs sceaux à usage magique, une encre fabriquée à partir d'une mixture de vermillon et de plomb. Les bouddhistes en firent aussi usage pour les impressions de rouleaux aux "mille bouddhas."

This entry is briefly mentioned too in Fraser 2004, 277n26.

5. The full entry (Wang-Toutain 2001, 125) reads as follows:

> P. tib. 4216
> *Maṇḍala*
> Xylographie. *Dhāraṇī* en tibétain enroulée sur 10 cercles concentriques, encerclés par des dessins de flammes et de *vajra.* À l'encre rouge.
> Inscription chinoise mentionnant la *dhārani* [*sic*!] de la flèche d'immortalité: *Wou cheng tsien tshen yen/ ngan ? tche lo t'o ho t'i/ pi ts'ieou ho kiue cheou tch'e* 無生箭真言/ 唵? 折羅陀呵啼/ 比丘何確授持. À l'encre noire, foncée au centre, au milieu de huit pétales rouges.
> Repr. in M. Cohen, N. Monnet, *Impressions de Chine*, Paris, BNF, 1992, p. 99 [*sic*!].
> *Maṇḍala* de 50 cm de diamètre. L'impression du noyau central (texte chinois entouré

Wang-Toutain's significant contribution to the study of the document lies in her decipherment of the central Chinese inscription, only one character remaining still obscure. Nevertheless, as we shall see, the interpretation of the inscription still poses some problems. The approximate dating proposed by Wang-Toutain for P.T. 4216 is the ninth century.

The contributions of Cohen and Monnet and of Wang-Toutain generally agree in their characterization of the sheet as a printed dhāraṇī in Tibetan produced in about the ninth century and bearing a title written in Chinese that mentions a "*dhāraṇī* of the unborn (or immortal) arrow." While these observations provide a useful point of departure, it will be seen that a closer examination reveals a number of interesting puzzles.

Identification

Let us begin with the statement that the dhāraṇī that appears here is Tibetan. Neither of the notices of our learned colleagues makes clear whether it is a question of the Tibetan language, or the Tibetan script, or both. The language and the text contained here, however, can both be readily identified. To illustrate this, let us consider just the first line inscribed within the innermost circle (fig. 2):

Fig. 2. The beginning of the first line of text: u tat tha a ma gi ra gI rI ga.

u tat tha a ma gi ra gI rI ga ra nI gI rI ba tI gu na ba tI | a ka sha ba tI
a ka sha bI shu tI | sa ba

What we find here is a very approximate transcription of a work in Sanskrit, in which some expressions are readily recognizable (e.g., gu na ba tI < Skt. *guṇavati*). Fortunately, the work in question is quite well known: it is the

de cercles rouges) apparaît en filigrane dans la partie inf. du texte tibétain. Traces de régl. horizantales et verticales de 2,5 cm.

2 ff. (f. 1: 25,5 cm; f. 2: 23,4 cm). Pap. assez irrégulier, chamois clair (10 YR 8/3). Verg. 5 par cm. Ép. 0,14 à 0, 17 mm. Montage dans cadre cartonné (réserve).

IXe siècle. [49 x 54,5 cm]

second of the dhāraṇīs of the *Mahāpratisarāmahāvidyārajñī*, the "Great Amulet, the Great Queen of Spells," or, in Chinese, the *Da suiqiu tuoluoni* 大隨求陀羅尼.[6] The relationship between the two will be seen clearly when we compare them:

P.T. 4216	*Mahāpratisarāmahāvidyārajñī*
u tat tha a ma gi ra gI rI	*tadyathā. Oṃ giri giri*
ga ra nI gI rI ba tI gu na ba tI |	*giriṇi girivati guṇavati*
a ka sha ba tI a ka sha bI shu tI |	*ākāśavati ākāśa viśuddhe*
sa ba	*sarva*

Those familiar with the standard Tibetan conventions for the transcription of Sanskrit will at once perceive some problems here. For, as is well known, the Tibetans developed a system for the exact transcription of Sanskrit that was in use by the beginning of the ninth century at the latest and for which we have substantial evidence in Dunhuang documents, including a version of the *Mahāpratisarāmahāvidyārajñī* (though one that does not include the portion of the text that concerns us here).[7] The transcription of the dhāraṇī we find in P.T. 4216, however, mostly ignores that system. It is in fact remarkably imprecise with respect to Indic phonology and provides only a very approximate representation. Some of the significant departures from standard usage are as follows:

- *ca* and *tsa* are used indifferently (fig. 3), suggesting that, for the creators of the document, there was no relevant distinction between

6. This scripture has a long history of study in modern Buddhology. For the most comprehensive treatment to date, including discussion of earlier work and critical editions of the Sanskrit versions, refer to Hidas 2012.

7. The Dunhuang manuscript of the *Mahāpratisarā* in question is IOL Tib J 397 of the Stein Collection at the British Library, London. Like certain other Dunhuang Tibetan documents that include "correct" transcriptions of Sanskrit, there are many errors in the text as given there, though the distinctions of voiced/unvoiced, aspirated/unaspirated, and simple/conjunct consonants, as well as long and short vowels, are all recognized and often correct. (On the other hand, the difference between dental and retroflex consonants is generally overlooked.) The manuscript, which is just one of the surviving parts of a larger collection of *Pañcarakṣā* texts, is described in the catalogue of Dalton and van Schaik 2006, 131–33, but without reference to the question of Sanskrit usage within it.

them. Similarly, it seems to have been unclear to them whether Tibetan *ja* or *dza* was to be used to render Sanskrit *ja* (figs. 4a–b).

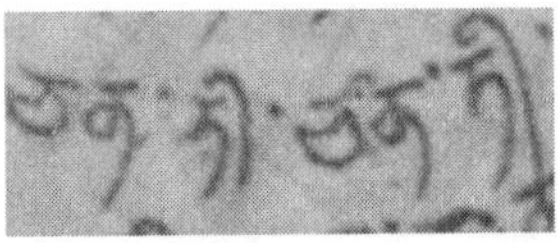

Fig. 3. From line 4: can tI tsan tI = Skt. *caṇḍi caṇḍi*

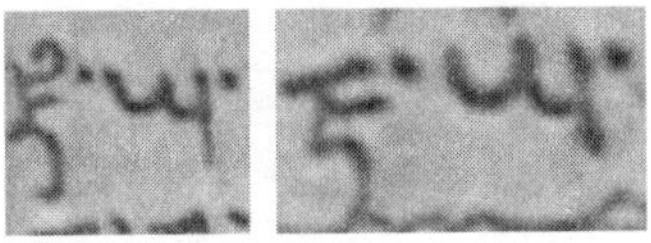

Fig. 4a–b. dza ya (line 4) and ja ya (line 10), both for Skt. *jaya*. Note, too, the peculiar form of the syllable ya.

- Although both *ta* and *tha* are represented, there is no definite occurrence of *da* (fig. 5).[8] More generally, the important distinctions of unvoiced/voiced and unaspirated/aspirated stops seem to be treated quite carelessly (fig. 6).

Fig. 5. From line 3: but ta nan = Skt. *buddhānām*.

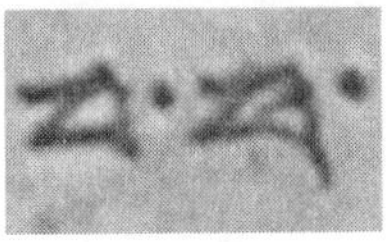

Fig. 6. From line 2: ba pha = Skt. *pāpa*.

- Conjunct consonants are rarely used, and some conjuncts occurring in the Sanskrit have been resolved into polysyllabic groups—e.g., for Skt. *tri-* we find *ti ra* (fig. 7). The conjunct *tra*, however, also occurs on some occasions, and conjuncts with *ya* affixed in the form of the Tibetan *ya btags* as well. But as a general rule, syllables are reduced to simple consonant + vowel combinations.

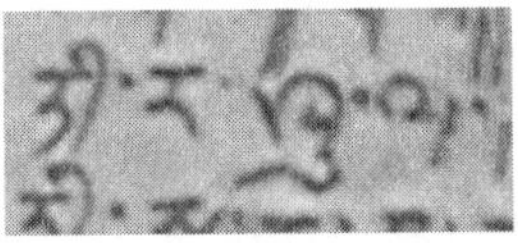

Fig. 7. From line 9: tI ra shu la = Skt. *triśūla*.

8. Note, in the example given—*but ta nan*—besides the treatment of the dental stops, the final syllable *nan* as the transcription of the Sanskrit genitive plural ending *-ānām*. This frequently occurs in Old Tibetan transcriptions of Sanskrit; refer to Kapstein 2019, 263.

- Vowel length is usually ignored, and Sanskrit diphthongs only sometimes approximated. However, some polysyllabic groups are due to the treatment of long vowels and diphthongs—e.g., for Skt. *cū* we have *ci u* (fig. 8), and for Skt. *gau* we see *ga 'u* (fig. 9). Note also the unusual treatment of the syllable *hūṃ* (resembling *ha* + *'a chung* + *M*, with just a trace of what might be *u* attached to the right of the *'a chung*) toward the end of the dhāraṇī (fig. 10).

Fig. 8. From line 8: tsI 'u ti = Skt. *cūḍi*.

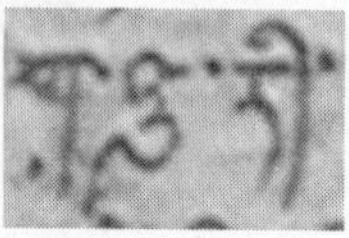

Fig. 9. From line 6: ga 'u rI = Skt. *gaurī*.

- The Sanskrit retroflex series is mostly ignored, the sole exception being in the case of *ṭ* in the seed-syllable *phaṭ* (fig. 10).

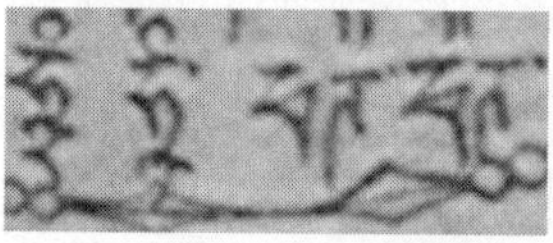

Fig. 10. From line 10: *hūṃ hūṃ phaṭ phaṭ*

- In a small number of cases (see notes 33 and 36), it is possible that letterforms are borrowed from the Siddhaṃ script.

Of course, with the exception of the last mentioned, similar features are known from Tibetan tantric documents from Dunhuang and elsewhere that seem to have emanated from outside of circles familiar with learned conventions for the treatment of Sanskrit.[9] However, the *ca/tsa* confusion seems not at all evident, so far as I am aware, in materials of undoubted Tibetan provenance—for this reflects not just lack of familiarity with Indic phonology but with Tibetan itself. Moreover, the treatment of the mantra-syllable *oṃ* as *a ma* (fig. 11) seems not plausibly to emanate from a Tibetan linguistic milieu, learned or popular. More likely, it reflects the Chinese representation of the sacred syllable as 唵 *an*.

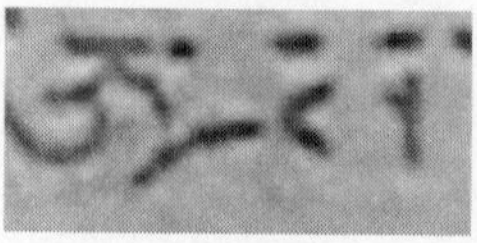

Fig. 11. From line 1: *a ma* = *oṃ*, probably on the basis of Ch. 唵 *an*.

Several features of the script used here further suggest that the origin of the document was not at all Tibetan. Although it closely resembles and is certainly

9. A well-known example is P.T. 849, studied in Kapstein 2006.

based upon the Tibetan *dbu can* script, it also deviates from it in some striking ways. These include:

- The common occurrence of the vowel *i*, the *gi gu*, with an elongated "tail" that does not appear in other Tibetan sources that are known to me (fig. 12). Although in form this closely resembles the long vowel *ī* in the Devanāgarī and related scripts (such as the Siddhaṃ script that was often used for printed dharaṇīs in China, fig. 13), there is no evidence that the particular form of the *i* we find here is phonetically relevant. It is possible, of course, that it is merely a graphic affectation, perhaps intending to suggest the appearance of Indic texts.

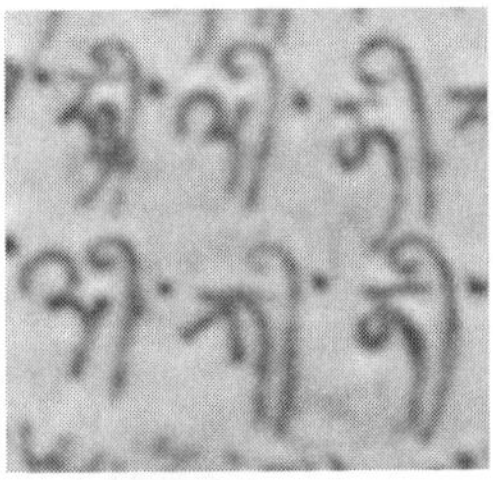

Fig. 12. From line 7 and 8: Examples of the elongated *i* (transcribed as I):
hI lI nI = Skt. *hīle ni* (in the phrase *mahīle nigaḍe*);
lI kI nI = Skt. *lokani* (in the phrase *vyavalokani*).

Fig. 13. The syllable *rkī* in the Siddhaṃ script, with the vowel *ī* represented by an elongated stroke affixed to the right side of the consonant cluster.

- The form of the *ya*, though clearly based on standard Tibetan, noticeably deviates from known models in the execution of the abrupt vertical stroke at the right (figs. 4a–b).
- A few very oddly formed characters may be noted too, such as a variant of *ts-* (fig. 14) or of *'u* (fig. 15, resembling also the Siddhaṃ *u*), both of which appear on a number of occasions.

Fig. 14. From line 6: ba sha tsI = Skt. *piśācī.*

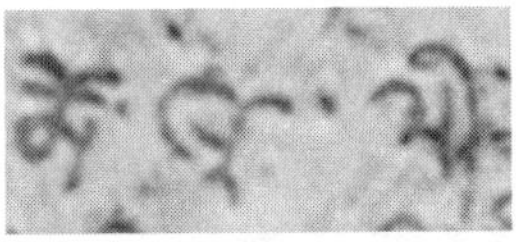

Fig. 15. From line 2: mo 'u lI = Skt. *mauli.*

These features, taken altogether, suggest to me that Tibetans had no role in the creation of P.T. 4216. How, then, to account for it?

Interpretation

A number of clues shed some light on the milieu in which P.T. 4216 was probably executed and the period during which this took place. First, we must consider the general design and layout of the sheet. Wang-Toutain has described it as a "maṇḍala," and certainly it does exhibit some iconographic elements that are widely associated with maṇḍalas of various kinds. Particularly noteworthy, in this regard, are the concentric lotuses and vajras in the center (fig. 16)

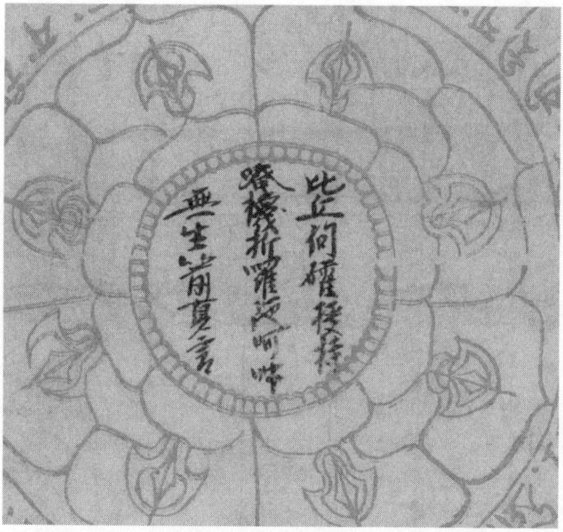

Fig. 16. "Maṇḍala" features: lotus and three- (or five- ?) pronged vajra design of center.

and the vajra and flame patterns of the outer border (fig. 17). Nevertheless, it is probably not to be considered a maṇḍala in the strict sense of a cosmogram—that is, a symbolic representation of a three-dimensional divine realm conceived as isomorphic with the Mount Meru world system. Compared with

Fig. 17. Flame and single-pronged vajra design of the border.

later Tibetan conventions, it most closely resembles the printed diagrams referred to as *tsak ra*, from Sanskrit *cakra*, "wheel," or as *srung ba*, "protection," both of these being terms for protective amulets,[10] which is also one of the meanings of the Sanskrit word *pratisara*. And we know, in particular, that the amulet of the *Mahāpratisarādhāraṇī* was very widely promoted in China during the Tang dynasty and for some time thereafter. Indeed, printed copies of this dhāraṇī stemming from tenth–twelfth century China, and often giving the text in Siddhaṃ script, conform with P.T. 4216 in the spiraling concentric layout of the dhāraṇī itself.[11] Moreover, although the *Mahāpratisarādhāraṇī* was available in a Tibetan version from about the early ninth century on, we do not so far have evidence for such a well-developed cult of it from Tibetan sources as we do from Chinese.[12]

A second clue may be seen in the Chinese inscription. Here, however, a word of caution is required, for although it seems likely that this inscription reflects the milieu in which the dhāraṇī itself was manufactured, we cannot assume this to be so. It remains a possibility that the inscription was added to a recuperated print with which it had no fundamental relation, and as such sheds no light on the print itself. As will be seen below, however, this was almost certainly not the case; the inscription was in essence the dedicatory inscription that accompanied the bestowal of the protective amulet that had been expressly prepared.

The inscribed Chinese text is arranged in three vertical lines. As each line appears to be syntactically independent of the others, it is not quite clear whether we should read them from right to left or vice versa, though I believe that Wang-Toutain's decision to take them, perhaps exceptionally, in the left to right order in this case makes better sense. The first line reads *wusheng jian zhenyan* 無生箭真言, which means "mantra of the unborn arrow, or archer." (In Wang-Toutain's interpretation, the "unborn arrow" is taken to mean the "arrow of immortality," perhaps with a nod to Tibetan longevity rites in which an arrow is employed as a ritual instrument, though there is no evidence to

10. In this context, both of these terms are probably to be derived from Skt. *rakṣacakra*, Tib. *srung ba'i 'khor lo*, "protective circle." For a broad survey of modern *srung ba*, see Skorupski 1983.

11. Among pertinent studies, see Copp 2014, chap. 2; Drège 1999; Hidas 2014; Tsiang 2010.

12. The Chinese evidence is reviewed in Copp 2014 and, with reference to Korea as well, McBride 2018. Although it may not have been so prominent in early Tibetan Buddhism, the *Mahāpratisarādhāraṇī* was by no means unknown, as Tibetan copies from Dunhuang demonstrate (see note 7 above).

connect these with our dhāraṇī.) Cohen and Monnet have proposed that the underlying Tibetan and Sanskrit titles may be reconstructed on the basis of this phrase—*Mi skye bahi mdahi* and *Anutpada isu dhâranî*—but I know of no titles that are at all similar to these suggestions, neither of which, in any case, is plausible as given. A distant possibility is that the syllables *sa ra* in the title *Mahāpratisarā* have been taken out of context and treated as equivalent to Skt. *śara*, "arrow" (Prakrit *sara*), though this speculation may be merely an exercise in grasping at straws.

The second line—*an (?) zhe le tuo he ti* 唵 (?) 折羅陀呵啼—must be the transcription of an otherwise unidentified mantra, for the first syllable, *an*, regularly stands for the initial mantra-syllable *oṃ*. The second character has not yet been conclusively deciphered and may be defective, though the context, followed as it is by *zhe le*, convincingly argues for reading it as *wa* (perhaps 襪), so that the whole—*wa zhe le*—would form a somewhat unusual but not implausible transcription of Sanskrit *vajra*.[13] Although *oṃ vajra* is a typical opening formula in Buddhist mantras, the concluding phrase *tuo he ti* has proven elusive.[14] Further, we can neither discount nor confirm the possibility that it is this in fact, and not the printed dhāraṇī, that represents the "mantra of the unborn arrow" mentioned in the previous line.

The last line reads *biqiu he que shouchi* 比丘何確授持. This appears to name a particular Buddhist monk, Bhikṣu He Que, as the bestower or recipient of the mantra, or perhaps of the dhāraṇī amulet. If it is indeed the amulet that is referenced, it may be most plausible to see him as the donor, for the custom of inscribing donors' names in copies of the *Mahāpratisarā* is known to have been widespread. Although this particular dhāraṇī was specifically associated with ensuring fertility and the birth of male offspring, it offered broad protection

13. *Vajra* is most often transcribed in Chinese as *ba zhe le* 跋折羅 or *fa zhe le* 伐折羅, in either case with the final two syllables as we find them here. For suggesting the reading *wa* for the first syllable of the word in our dhāraṇī sheet, I am indebted to Kuo Liying and Kirill Solonin.

14. I am grateful to Mingyuan Gao and Dan Lusthaus for their reflections about this. They have independently suggested to me the possibility that *tuo he ti* represents a derivative of Skt. √*dah*, "to burn." I have found the phrase *vajra daha* in the dhāraṇī of the divinity Vajravidāraṇa (Tib. Rdo rje rnam 'joms), who is frequently invoked in Tibetan Buddhism in connection with purification and healing, but I can see no reason to suppose that its occurrence there might have been familiar to the creators of P.T. 4216 and lifted out of context to form the brief mantra we find in the document considered here. However, *dahanī* ("she who burns," vocative *dahani*) does occur as an epithet of the divinity in the present dhāraṇī, as seen in the Sanskrit text of line 7 in the appendix. See, as well, note 16 below.

as well, and the inscriptions of monk-donors are by no means unknown.[15] In China, it was often placed in tombs.[16]

In sum, then, the Chinese inscription names a mantra or dhāraṇī that may or may not be the *Mahāpratisarā* itself; it transcribes a brief mantra whose interpretation remains uncertain and that may be defective; and it names a bhikṣu, possibly in the role of donor or beneficiary.[17]

Implications

Adding to the mystery surrounding this Chinese-inscribed dhāraṇī printed in the Tibetan script is the existence of a twin. As Nathalie Monnet kindly indicated to me, the Japanese art historian Matsumoto Eiichi, in his pioneering work on Dunhuang painting published in 1937, reproduced a nearly identical single-sheet print (fig. 18).[18] Although the quality of the reproduction there presents an obstacle to very close comparison, neither the print nor the Chinese inscription in its center appear to differ substantially from P.T. 4216, with but one telltale exception: the name of the monk entered into the third line of the inscription. Though it is not, unfortunately, clearly legible, it is quite certain that the two-character name given there is not He Que 何確, as in our example.[19] It seems possible, therefore, that the dhāraṇī was printed in series on behalf of a particular community, whose members were registered as the

15. Hidas 2012, 31–33, reviews the question of the dhāraṇī's users, as known from both inscribed examples and literary sources, noting that the donor inscriptions from East Asia "contain the names of various *śramaṇa*s and *bhikṣu*s."

16. Tsiang 2010. The funerary association perhaps lends support to a suggestion from Mingyuan Gao (note 14 above) that the "burning" possibly referenced in the mantra may allude to cremation.

17. One further point that suggests that the amulet was prepared for actual use is the presence of traces of a faint double impression of both the red-print and black-ink inscription in reverse, showing that the sheet had been folded before the ink had dried. It would seem that it was intended to be quickly inserted into an amulet case of some kind.

18. Matsumoto 1937 gives the location of the artifact as Delhi, so that it may well be conserved today in the collection of the National Museum of India. I have not yet been able to examine a copy of Matsumoto 2019, the Chinese translation of the original work, to determine whether the dhāraṇī he presented has been located and rephotographed for that publication.

19. Although it has not yet been possible to make out the monk's name, the inscription as reproduced in Matsumoto 1937 is sufficiently clear so as to be certain that the remaining characters are identical to what we find in P.T. 4216.

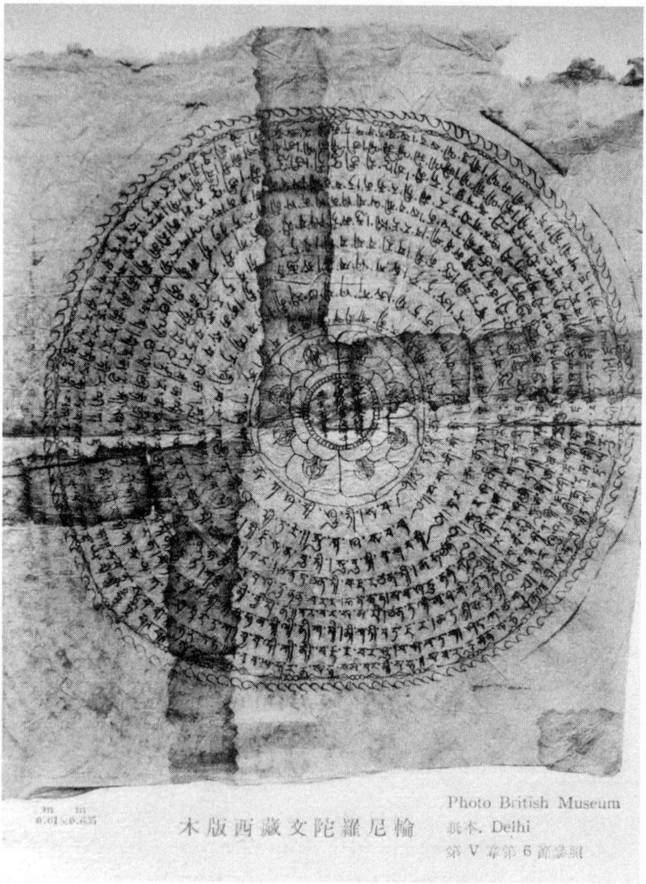

Fig. 18. Printed dhāraṇī from Dunhuang, after Matsumoto 1937, plate V.6.

donors or beneficiaries of individual sheets. The prints, therefore, were intended to receive such inscriptions; they were not ex post facto additions.

If we are thus entitled to suppose that the central inscription, notwithstanding its several obscurities, did issue from the same circle as that which produced the printed dhāraṇī, and that this was not a case in which recuperated images were employed,[20] and taking account too of the many departures in the text of the dhāraṇī from proper Tibetan conventions, we may propose that P.T. 4216 was the product of one of the tenth-century Buddhist communities in the Dunhuang region that Takata Tokio has character-

20. For examples of such recuperation of images at Dunhuang, see Mollier 2014, 2015.

ized as "Tibeto-Chinese."[21] That is to say, it was created by Chinese speakers who were to some extent Tibetanized and made use of Tibetan writing to varying degrees, often as a kind of "Pinyin" with which to represent Chinese phonetically.

It may be possible to advance this hypothesis by comparing the *Mahāpratisarādhāraṇī* as given in P.T. 4216 with the versions in the Siddhaṃ script known from Chinese prints of about the same period. A further desideratum is the careful comparison of the text of our dhāraṇī with Chinese character transcriptions of the Sanskrit for the phonological evidence that this may afford. These, however, remain tasks for future research. In all events, among the communities of which we have some knowledge, Sino-Tibetan Buddhists of the Guiyijun period in and around Dunhuang seem the votaries most likely to have attempted a rendering of the *Mahāpratisarādhāraṇī* in Tibetan script following not the regular rules for the transcription of Sanskrit but the pronunciation as they took it to be. These same Sino-Tibetan Buddhists, it seems, were also the first to experiment with the reproduction of Tibetan characters in print.

Appendix: The Mahāpratisarādhāraṇī *and Its Transcription in P.T. 4216*

Following is the text of the *Mahāpratisarādhāraṇī* as it appears in the printed sheet P.T. 4216, beginning from the center, with each of the ten rings of text numbered successively. Following each line is the corresponding Sanskrit text, in *italics*, given according to the edition of the East Indian and Nepalese recensions, Hidas 2012, 177–82. The CBETA online edition (https://tripitaka.cbeta.org/T20n1153_002), which follows the Taishō Tripiṭaka, has also been consulted. The portion of the Sanskrit text given below will be found there on page 0633a30.

- Majuscule *I*, in the transcribed text of the Dunhuang print, stands for the extended vowel *i*, graphically resembling the long *ī* of Indic scripts, as discussed above.

21. Takata 2000, who writes that "with the increasing penetration of the Tibetan script and language in the Han-Chinese society during the period of Tibetan rule, there gradually developed the practice among some Chinese of using the Tibetan script, rather than Chinese . . . [C]hronologically speaking, it is worth noting that these texts were written not only during the T'u-po period, but up until the period of the Return-to-Allegiance Army under the Ts'ao in the tenth century" (58).

- Doubtful readings are indicated by an interrogation point (?), sometimes with the addition of an alternative reading.
- A syllable that cannot be read is marked X.
- Square brackets [ ] in the Sanskrit are used to bracket phrases not at all represented in P.T. 4216. (Where portions of the text were dropped, it is usually not clear whether this was due to differences in the exemplar, eye-skip, or a decision to abridge.) Square brackets are also used to mark off passages discussed in an accompanying note.
- Round brackets ( ) in the Sanskrit signify emendations to the Sanskrit text suggested by P.T. 4216. In some cases, these correspond to possible readings given by Hidas in his critical apparatus, but this is by no means always the case. Evidently, such emendations, if warranted, would apply only to the texts posited as the immediate sources of P.T. 4216. In some cases, however, they may merely reflect idiosyncratic readings in P.T. 4216 alone.
- @ = the Tibetan "head-letter" (*mgo yig*).
- In Sanskrit text, the numeral 2 indicates the repetition of the word that precedes it; e.g., *hana 2 = hana hana.*

It should be noted that, because the correspondences between P.T. 4216 and the available Sanskrit versions are at best approximate, I have not attempted to comment upon each point of difference between them; that would require a gloss on virtually every syllable. Accordingly, the issues noted in the following are only a selection of those points that appeared most prominent in preparing this transcription.

1. @ || u tat tha a ma gi ra gI rI ga ra nI gI rI ba tI gu na ba tI | a ka sha ba tI a ka sha bI shu tI | sa ba
tadyathā. Oṃ giri 2 giriṇi girivati guṇavati ākāśavati ākāśa(vi)śuddhe, (sarva)

2. @ || ba pha gi gI tI | a ka sha | ga ga na ta lI | a ka sha bI tsa rI nI | ja ba lI ta shI kha re | kha tsI ta mo u lI ta re || u ka sha sa ba ga
pāpa vigate, ākāśe gaganatale, ākāśavicāriṇi, jvalitaśikhare. [maṇi mauktika]khacitamaulidhare sukeśe suvaktre

3. @ || ta ra | a na ta ra | a ba nan | ga u ra | a ta ta | a ka sha kha rI | a chu ta ban tI | na ma sa ba sha ma | but ta nan | jab lI ta | tI dza sa na bu tI | su bu ti ba ga ba tI
[sunetre suvarṇe, suvarṇagaure, atīte, anutpanne,][22] *pratyut-*

22. The correspondence between P.T. 4216 and the Sanskrit text is particularly problematic

panne. namaḥ sarveṣāṃ buddhānāṃ jvalitatejasāṃ, buddhe subuddhe bhagavati

4. @ || su ra sha nI | su ra sha nI | sa ba ra bI | sa ta mI | su na tI | pa rI ba ga ba tI | ba ta ra ba ta | ba ta ra su ba ta ra | gi ma lI | dza ya ba tra | can tI tsan tI | ba ra | tsa na ta can tI | ba ja ra tsan tI | ma ha tsan

surakṣaṇi. [sukṣame][23] *suprabhe sudame sudānte vare bhagavati bhadravati, bhadre subhadre vimale. jayabhadre*[24] *pracaṇḍe, caṇḍe, vajracaṇḍe mahācaṇ*

5. @ || tI ra | go rI ga na ta rI | ga? u rI | tso u rI | tsan ta lI ma tha gI | ba ra ja | sI | su? ma tI | sha ba rI sha ra ka rI ta ra | mI tI | rI u tI ra na | nas ba a ta sa ta nI ha na ha na | sa ba sha tru nan ba rat | ha na ha na | sa ba sha tru nan ba

ḍe ghori gandhāri gauri, (cauri),[25] *caṇḍāli, mātaṅgi, varcasi, sumati, [pukkasi,] śavari [śāvari] śaṅkari, dramiḍi, raudriṇi, sarvārthasādhani hana 2 sarvaśatrūnām [daha 2, sarva duṣṭānām]*[26] *p-*

6. @ || ra ta ba sha tsi ta kI nI nan | ma nu shya | a ma nu shya nan ba tsa tsa ba[27] hI ta ya na | sa ba kI la bI sha na sha na[28] sha nI ma ra ta tan tI ma nI nI | ca lI ca lI | tsI tI ci tI tI tI tI tI || tI tI nI tu te | ga 'u rI nI byi rI na || ba ra ba ra sa ma rI | tsan ta lI ma tha gi tru(?) ta su

retapiśācaḍakinīnāṃ manuṣyāmanuṣyāṇām paca 2 hṛdayaṃ [vidhvasaya jīvitaṃ sarvaduṣṭagrahāṇāṃ nāśaya 2 sarva pāpāni me bhagavati rakṣa 2 māṃ sarvasattvānāṃ ca sarvatra sarvabhayopadravebhyaḥ sarvaduṣṭānāṃ bandhanaṃ kuru 2] sarvakilbiṣanāśanī, mārtaṇḍe, [mṛtyudaṇḍanivāraṇi mānadaṇḍe] mānini [mahāmānini] cale

---

here. In P.T. 4216 ta ra may be the *tre* of *sunetre*, but a na ta ra seems more likely to represent *sunetre*, with *suvarṇe* left out. Skt. *suvarṇagaure* is transcribed as a ba nan ga u ra, *atīte* is evidently a ta ta, but there is no correspondence between *anutpanne* and a ka sha kha rI.

23. For *sukṣame*, P.T. 4216 repeats su ra sha nI, i.e., *surakṣaṇi.*

24. Following *jayabhadre* (dza ya ba tra), P.T. 4216 adds can tI tsan tI before its transcriptions of *pracaṇḍe* (ba ra tsa na ta), probably by dittography.

25. Though *cauri* is not found in Hidas's apparatus, it was perhaps found in the exemplar followed by the creators of P.T. 4216, whose text reads tso u rI at this point.

26. It appears that, in this section, P.T. 4216 departs from the Sanskrit owing to eyeskip, whether in the course of the preparation of the print or in its ancestry. Following *sarvaśatrūnām* (P.T. 4216: sa ba sha tru nan), it jumps ahead to *preta* (ba rat/ba ra ta) and then skips back to repeat hana 2 *sarvaśatrūnām* (ha na ha na sa ba sha tru nan), before resuming once more with *preta* (ba ra ta) at the end of line 5 and beginning of line 6.

27. tsa ba is no doubt to be taken as an instance of metathesis.

28. sha na added by dittography.

(cale) ciṭi 2 [viṭi 2 niṭi 2 niṭini][29] *tuṭe ghoriṇī vīriṇi pravarasamare caṅḍāli mātaṅgi rundhasi*

7. @ || ba ba(?rba) sI su ma nI | a ma nI su mu X[30] ba ga ka sI sha ba rI shar ka rI sha ra ka rI ta ra mI tI ra ha na | ta ba tsa ni | ma tha na | | ma rta na | sa ra la | sa ra lI | sa lam bI | hI na ma tya kI sha ta bI ta rI na | bI ta ra na | bI ta ra nI[31] ma hI lI ma ha ma hI lI nI ga tI | nI ga tI ba ta ja ra | ma ta tI ma ta tI

[sarasi,] varcasi, sumati, pukkasi, śavari, [śāvari,] śaṅkari, (śaṅkari), dramiḍi, [drāmiḍi,] dahani, pacani, [mardani,][32] *sarale 2, saralambhe, hīnamadhyonkr̥ṣṭavidāriṇi vidhāriṇi, mahile [2] mahāmahīle, nigaḍe, nigaḍabhañje, matte, mattini*

8. @ || ba ga kI ga kI | ja lI ja lI | ja lI ja lI | sha ba rI sha ba rI | sha ba rI | sha ba rI sa ba X[33] ta ha nI ˡ gi 'u rI tsI'u ti | ci 'u ta nI | tsi 'u ta ma na | nI mI nI | mI nI mI ta rI tI ra lI ka ju hI nI | tI ra lI kaṃ(?) | a la ka ka rI tI ra ta ka | bya ba lI kI nI ba ja ra ba ra shu | ba sha kha ta ga shang ka tsa ga ra

[dānte, cakre,] cakravākini,[34] *jvale 2, jvāle 2, [jvalini,] śavari, śāvari, (śavari, śāvari), sarvavyādhiharaṇi, (gauri) cūḍi [2], cūḍini [2] (cūḍāmaṇe?), nimi 2 nimindhari, trilokajanani, trilokālokakari, traidhātukavyavalokani, vajraparaśupāṣa[mudgara] khaḍgaśaṅkhacakra-*

9. || tI ra shu la | tshI na tam nI | ma ha bI ta ta ranI || || ba ja ra ba ja ra ba tI | hI lI hI lI | mI lI mI lI mI lI | tsI lI tsI lI | cI bI lI sI mI rI | bI lI bI lI | ba ra ba ra tI sa ba ta ra ja ya ba tI sa ha sa ba ba ba bI | ta rI nI sa ha || sa ba tra sa ba bI tI ha ra sa ha || sa ba ba ya ha ra na sa ha sam bar nI sa ha || sa ba ra tu man sa ha shan

triśūlacintāmaṇimahāvidyādhāriṇi [rakṣa 2 māṃ sarvasattvānāṃ ca sarvatra sarvasthānagataṃ sarvaduṣṭabhayebhyaḥ sarvamanuṣyāmanuṣyabhayebhyaḥ sarvavyādhibhyaḥ.] vajre, vajravati,

29. Represented as tI tI tI tI || tI tI nI in P.T. 4216.

30. a ma nI su mu X has no clear counterpart in the Sanskrit text.

31. bi ta ra nI by dittography.

32. ma tha na || ma rta na in P.T. 4216 corresponds to the variant *mathani mardani* in the Sanskrit text.

33. As the lower part of this syllable resembles the Tibetan *ya btags*, the syllable as a whole may be taken to stand for the *vy-* of Skt. *vyādhi*. It is possible that the upper part is the consonant *wa*, but as this would be a hapax in the present context, it remains uncertain. Another possibility is that it is based on Siddhaṃ *vvy-*.

34. This would appear to be represented in P.T. 4216 in part by ba ga kI ga kI.

[vajrapāṇidhare,] hili 2 mili 2 [kili 2] (mili) cili 2 [sili 2][35] *(bhili bhili* or *vili vili) vara [2] varade sarvatra [jayalabdhe] (jayavati) svāhā. (sarva)pāpavidāriṇi svāhā. (sarvatra) sarvavyādhiharaṇī svāhā. [sarvatra] (sarva)bhayaharaṇi svāhā. (saṃbharaṇi svāhā.) svastir bhavatu mama [sarvasattvānāṃ ca] svāhā. śān-*

10. @ || ti sa ha bu sI ta sa ha ja ya tu ja ya tu ja yI ja yI | ja ya ba tI | ja ya bI tI | ja ya bI ma lI | bI bu lI sa ha | sa ba ta tha ga ta mu ñtsa[36] ra sa ha | I[37] bu rI bu rI ba jar ba ta | sa ba ta tha ga ta hI ra ya bu u nI sa na ta ra nI ba la ba la | ja ya bI tI hūṃ hūṃ phaṭ phaṭ sa ha

ti svāhā. puṣṭi svāhā. jayatu (jayatu) jaye (jaye), jayavati (jayavati), jaya vimale, vipule svāhā. sarvatathāgatamūrte svāhā, Oṃ bhūri 2 vajravati, (sarva)tathāgatahṛdayapūraṇi, sandhāraṇi, bala 2, jayavidye hūṃ 2 phaṭ 2 svāhā.

References

Cohen, Monique, and Nathalie Monnet. 1992. *Impressions de Chine.* Paris: Bibliothèque Nationale.

Copp, Paul. 2014. *The Body Incantatory: Spells and the Ritual Imagination in Medieval Chinese Buddhism.* New York: Columbia University Press.

Dalton, Jacob, and Sam van Schaik. 2006. *Tibetan Tantric Manuscripts from Dunhuang: A Descriptive Catalogue of the Stein Collection at the British Library.* Leiden: Brill.

Drège, Jean-Pierre. 1999. "Les premières impressions des *dhāraṇī* de Mahāpratisarā." *Cahiers d'Extrême-Asie* 11 (Nouvelles études de Dunhuang. Centenaire de l'École française d'Extrême-Orient): 25–44.

Fraser, Sarah E. 2004. *Performing the Visual: The Practice of Buddhist Wall Painting in China and Central Asia, 618–960.* Stanford, CA: Stanford University Press.

Hamanaka, Saya, and Alla Sizova. 2020. "Imperial Postscript to the Tangut, Chinese and Tibetan Editions of the Dhāraṇī-sūtras in the Collection of the IOM, RAS." *Written Monuments of the Orient* 6.2: 65–92.

35. In place of *sili sili*, P.T. 4216 reads cI bI lI sI mI rI.

36. Possibly following Siddhaṃ *ñc-*. It is not clear how the phrase mu ñtsa ra here is to be reconciled with Skt. *-mūrte.*

37. There appears to be no other possible reading of the letterform, though no doubt *oṃ* is what was intended.

Helman-Ważny, Agnieszka. 2014. *The Archaeology of Tibetan Books*. Leiden: Brill.

Hidas, Gergely. 2012. *Mahāpratisarā-mahāvidyārajñī: The Great Amulet, Great Queen of Spells*. New Delhi: Aditya Prakashan.

———. 2014. "Two Dhāraṇī Prints in the Stein Collection at the British Museum." *Bulletin of the School of Oriental and African Studies* 77: 105–17.

Kapstein, Matthew T. 2006. "New Light on an Old Friend: PT 849 Revisited." In *Tibetan Buddhist Literature and Praxis: Studies in Its Formative Period, 900–1400*, edited by Ronald Davidson and Christian Wedemeyer, 9–30. Leiden: Brill.

———. 2019. "*The All-Encompassing Lamp of Awareness*: A Forgotten Treasure of the Great Perfection, Its Authorship and Historical Significance." In *Unearthing Himalayan Treasures: Festschrift for Franz-Karl Ehrhard*, edited by Volker Caumanns, Marta Sernesi, and Nikolai Solmsdorf, 259–86. Indica et Tibetica 59. Marburg: Indica et Tibetica Verlag..

Matsumoto, Eiichi 松本榮一. 1937. *Tonkōga no Kenkyū* 燉煌畫の研究. Tōkyō: Tōhō Bunka Gakuin Tōkyō Kenkyūjo: Hatsubaijo Bunkyūdō Shoten.

———. 2019. *Dunhuang Hua Yanjiu* 敦煌画研究. (Chinese translation of Matsumoto 1937 by Lin Baoyao, Zhao Shengliang, and Li Mei.) Hangzhou: Zhejiang daxue chubanshe.

McBride, Richard D., II. 2018. "Wish-Fulfilling Spells and Talismans, Efficacious Resonance, and Trilingual Spell Books: The *Mahāpratisarā-dhāraṇī* in Chosŏn Buddhism." *Pacific World* 3.20: 55–93.

Mollier, Christine. 2014. "Un talisman-*dhāraṇī*." In *La fabrique de lisible: La mise en texte de manuscrits de la Chine ancienne et médiévale*, edited by Jean-Pierre Drège, 273–78. Paris: Collège de France.

———. 2015. "Astrological Talismans and Paper Amulets from Dunhuang: Typology and Function." *Journal of Dunhuang and Turfan Studies* 敦煌吐魯番研究 15: 505–19.

Piotrovsky, Mikhail, et al. 1993. *Lost Empire of the Silk Road: Buddhist Art from Khara Khoto (X–XIIIth Century)*. Milan: Electa and Thyssen-Bornemisza Foundation.

Schaeffer, Kurtis R. 2009. *The Culture of the Book in Tibet*. New York: Columbia University Press.

Shen Weirong. 2010. "Reconstructing the History of Buddhism in Central Eurasia (11th–14th Centuries): An Interdisciplinary and Multilingual Approach to the Khara Khoto Texts." In *Editions, éditions: L'écrit au Tibet, évolution et devenir*, edited by A. Chayet, C. A. Scherrer-Schaub, F. Robin, and J.-L. Achard, 337–62. Munich: Indus Verlag.

Skorupski, Tadeusz. 1983. *Tibetan Amulets*. Bangkok: White Orchid Books.

Takata, Tokio. 2000. "Multilingualism in Tun-huang." *Acta Asiatica* 78: 49–70.

Takeuchi, Tsuguhito. 1995. *Old Tibetan Contracts from Central Asia*. Tokyo: Daizo Shuppan.

Tsiang, Katherine R. 2010. "Buddhist Printed Images and Texts of the Eighth–Tenth Centuries: Typologies of Replication and Representation." In *Esoteric Buddhism at Dunhuang: Rites for This Life and Beyond*, edited by Matthew T. Kapstein and Sam van Schaik, 201–52. Leiden: Brill.

Wang-Toutain, Françoise. 2001. *Catalogue des manuscrits chinois de Touen-houang*, vol. 6, *Fragments chinois du fonds Pelliot tibétain de la Bibliothèque nationale de France*. Paris: École française d'Extrême-Orient.

Leonard van der Kuijp (2022). Photo by Ning Tien.

Plate 1. Tholing mural.

Plate 2. Tholing Red Hall panel.

Plate 3. Vajradhara as the Original Teacher of the Lamdré instructions, flanked by Vajragarbha and Nairātmyā (the latter as second lineal master).
First painting of the set; 1420s; made in Sakya?
Image: 86.4 x 78.7 cm, Mount: 137.2 x 92.7 cm
Philadelphia Museum of Art, Philadelphia; Stella Kramrisch Collection, 1994; 1994-148-634
Literature: HAR 87083; Heimbel 2017: pl. 5; Kramrisch 1964: pl. 83; Jackson 2010a: fig. 8.4

Plate 4. Virūpa and Kāṇha as third and fourth lineal masters.
Second painting of the set; 1420s; made in Sakya?
Image: 86.40 x 80 cm
The Collection of Mr. and Mrs. Gilbert H. Kinney
Literature: HAR 81552; Heimbel 2017: pl. 6; Jackson 2010a: fig. 8.5; Linrothe, ed., 2006: no. 49

Plate 5. Ḍamarūpa and Avadhūtipa as fifth and sixth lineal masters.
Third painting of the set; 1420s; made in Sakya?
Image: 87.50 x 80 cm
Private Collection?
Literature: Galerie Koller Zürich 1992: pl. 5; HAR 204009
After Galerie Koller Zürich 1992: pl. 5

Plate 6. Sönam Tsemo and Drakpa Gyeltsen as twelfth and thirteenth lineal masters.
Seventh painting of the set; 1420s; made in Sakya?
Image: 84 x 78.2 cm
Museum of Fine Arts, Boston; Gift of John Goelet; 67.831
Literature: Béguin (ed.) 1977, no. 121; HAR 87230; Heimbel 2017: p. 7; Jackson 1986: Painting 1; Jackson 1996: fig. 24; Jackson 2011: fig. 3.12; Pal and Tseng 1969: no. 24

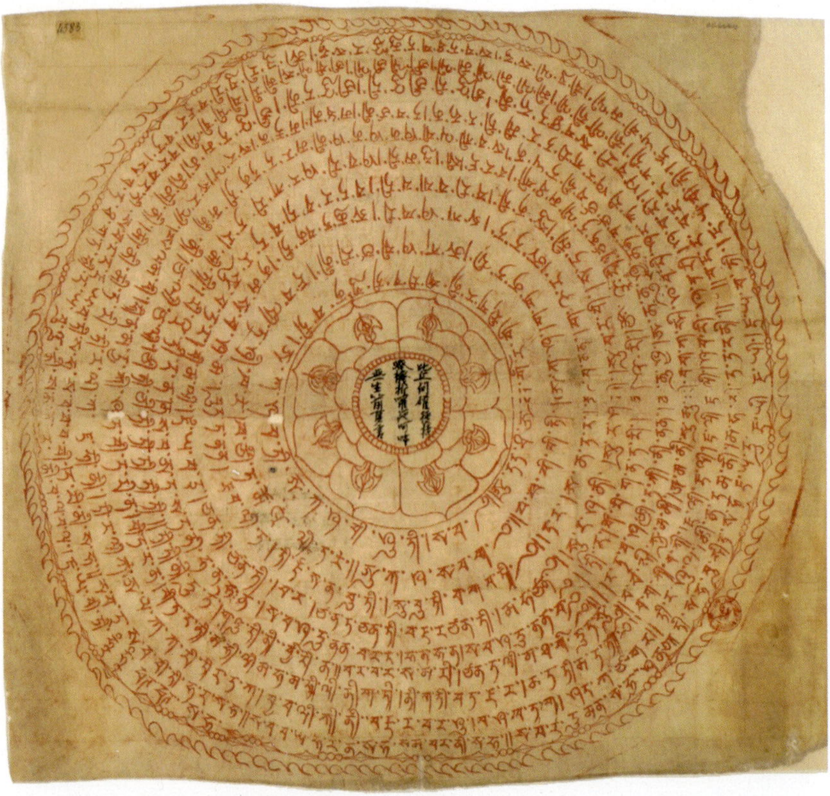

Plate 7. P.T. 4216. A printed dhāraṇī from Dunhuang in Tibetan script, with handwritten Chinese in the center. Source gallica.bnf.fr / Bibliothèque nationale de France.

Pakpa's Epistolary Manual

Christina Kilby

I studied with Leonard van der Kuijp while a graduate student in Buddhist studies at Harvard Divinity School. A few years ago, Leonard generously shared with me his notes on a newly surfaced edition of the epistolary manual by Pakpa Lodrö Gyeltsen ('Phags pa Blo gros rgyal mtshan, 1235–80) as well as two letters by the Sakya (Sa skya) scholar Lama Dampa Sönam Gyeltsen (Bla ma dam pa Bsod nams rgyal mtshan, 1312–75), which Leonard had found in an unpublished manuscript collection.[1] This essay is no match for Leonard's gifts, but perhaps it will bring some pleasure by introducing Pakpa's fascinating manual to a wider readership and by answering a question raised in Leonard's notes about possible Indian sources for Pakpa's work.

Pakpa's Epistolary Manual: The Vessel

PAKPA LODRÖ GYELTSEN is the attributed author of our earliest known Tibetan epistolary manual. Pakpa was both a lama and a powerful official, the nephew of Sakya Paṇḍita Künga Gyeltsen (Sa skya paṇḍi ta Kun dga' rgyal mtshan, 1182–1251) and chaplain to Kublai, the fifth Mongol *khagan* and founder of the Yuan dynasty in China. That Pakpa might compose a manual of epistolary instructions is not surprising, because the standardization of writing in general, and correspondence in particular, was a potent tool of premodern statecraft.[2] Letters, especially in their modes of address, illustrate particular visions of the social order that are hierarchically arranged and attuned to the authority of rank. In its close attention to mapping a system of

1. The *Condensed Presentation on Correspondence* (*Yig bskur rnam bzhag 'gag sdom*) that is attributed to Pakpa has recently surfaced in a fifteen-folio collection of grammatical works, which includes 'Jam dbyangs ral gri's (1360–ca. 1430) *Yi ge'i rnam bzhag yid bzhin nor bu* and other short texts. 'Jam dbyangs ral gri, alias Paṇḍita Nam mkha' smon lam, was a scholar affiliated with Bo dong E monastery. According to Leonard's notes, the work was filmed by the Nepal-German Manuscript Preservation Project, Kathmandu, under reel no. L 731/9.

2. Jha 2019, 106.

ranks and offices, establishing an official epistolary protocol is not so different from organizing a military or creating a maṇḍala.

Pakpa played a prominent role in the development of official correspondence during the Yuan. In addition to the official letters that he issued as chief of the Bureau of Tibetan and Buddhist Affairs, he served as emissary to Tibet on several occasions, carrying Kublai's edicts that outlined protections for Tibetan monasteries and relieved them from the burdens of taxation, military conscription, and corvée service. Kublai also charged Pakpa with creating a new script based on the Tibetan alphabet to serve as a transliterative vehicle for seals and official documents in Chinese, Mongolian, Tibetan, and Sanskrit. In 1269 Pakpa's script was adopted for use in all Yuan dynasty official documents, often in parallel with the local script, and was also used on coins, banknotes, and badges. Pakpa was awarded the title of imperial preceptor soon thereafter, marking the height of his political career.

Pakpa's manual is less than a full folio long and composed in verse, comprising four sections of several stanzas each. The text, *A Condensed Presentation on Correspondence* (*Yig bskur rnam bzhag 'gag sdom*), gives practical instructions about the proper vocabulary and formatting to employ when sending letters to recipients of various stations, applying seals, identifying letters as replies (important for acknowledging the receipt of official correspondence), and formatting envelopes. The manual was previously known in an appendix to the much later epistolary manual by Welmang Paṇḍita (Dbal mang Dkon mchog rgyal mtshan, 1764–1853).[3] It was also excerpted in epistolary manuals by Jamyang Zhepa ('Jam dbyangs bzhad pa'i Rdo rje ngag dbang brtson 'grus, 1648–1721/22), Sumpa Khenpo (Sum pa mkhan po Ye shes dpal 'byor, 1704–88), Bipa Mipam Dawa (Bis pa Mi pham zla ba, 1767–1807), and Ju Mipam Gyatso ('Ju Mi pham rgya mtsho, 1846–1912). Leonard van der Kuijp located an additional witness of Pakpa's text in the archives of the Nepal-German Manuscript Preservation Project in a fifteen-folio collection of grammatical works, which includes the *Presentation on Writing: A Wish-Fulfilling Jewel* (*Yi ge'i rnam gzhag yid bzhin nor bu*) by Jamyang Reldri ('Jam dbyangs ral gri, 1360–ca. 1430), among other texts.[4] I share Leonard's eagerness that a critical edition of Pakpa's text might be undertaken, although regrettably I do not provide one here.

Pakpa's epistolary manual is historically significant for several reasons. This short text provides the earliest known foundation for the classical Tibetan epistolary style that has been refined over the past eight centuries; two early

3. 'Phags pa 1974.

4. Again, according to Leonard's notes, under reel no. L 731/9.

modern manuals that draw on Pakpa's text continue to be printed and taught in Tibetan-language schools in Amdo today.[5] Not only is Pakpa's manual the seminal contribution to Tibet's epistolary arts, but it is also an important source for the history of Tibetan governmental administration. The manual helps us interpret official documents from the Yuan period and beyond, including cues of hierarchy that reveal political posturing and position taking.[6] Even into the twentieth century, ex-officials of the Ganden government have testified that Pakpa's letter-writing manual was the main text studied in the Ganden Accounting Office (Rtsis khang), which attests to the historical importance of letter writing and diplomatics for the official bureaucracy.[7] In short, Pakpa's manual has influenced almost the entire history of formal Tibetan letter writing in both official and private contexts.

We have several indications that the manual's attribution to Pakpa may be correct. First, Pakpa's manual includes several terms relevant to the Yuan period: commanders of one hundred thousand (*brgya stong* for the Mongolian *orlok*), ten thousand, and one thousand, and the likely Chinese loan words for "stamp" (*then tse* = [?] Chi. *qianji* 鈐記)[8] and "official letter" (*tsa ho* = [?] Chi. *zhafu* 札付).[9] This terminology reflects the military structure of the Yuan as well as its multilingual and multicultural position between the Mongol and Chinese imperial traditions. Additionally, the two letters by Lama Dampa that Leonard shared with me, which postdate Pakpa by less than a century, use vocabulary that conforms relatively well to Pakpa's instructions (although I cannot verify their conformity with Pakpa's formatting, folding, or sealing instructions because those aspects of the original documents are lost when edited).[10]

An even more convincing validation of Pakpa's authorship, however, is the fact that Pakpa's instructions conform closely to original Yuan dynasty edicts

5. These are the manuals by Bis pa Mi pham zla ba (*Phrin yig gi rnam bzhag dper brjod dang bcas pa padma dkar po'i phreng mdzes, A Beautiful Garland of White Lotuses*) and Tshe tan zhabs drung (*'Phrin yig spel tshul lhag bsam pad mo 'dzum pa'i nyin byed, How Letters Spread*).

6. Ishihama 1998 has used careful attention to epistolary style in order to decipher diplomatic posturing in the relationships among the Fifth Dalai Lama and his regent Sanggyé Gyatso, the Qing Emperor Kangxi, and the Mongol Khan Galdan.

7. Personal communication in February 2014 with Tsering Gyel (Tshe ring rgyal) of the Lhasa Archives, who has conducted many interviews with former Ganden government officials in Lhasa.

8. Leonard van der Kuijp kindly provided this suggestion in his notes.

9. Christopher Atwood kindly provided this suggestion in a personal correspondence.

10. Kilby 2020.

that have been preserved in the archives of the Tibetan Autonomous Region.[11] This collection, published as a *Collection of Historical Archives of Tibet*, is particularly valuable because it includes facsimile images of original archival documents, enabling the reader to examine the material constitution and formatting features of the texts and not merely their verbal content. In the Yuan period documents in Tibetan script, not only do the imperial edicts employ the verb "to declare" (*zlo ba*; reflecting Pakpa's instructions that "Mongolian kings put 'declared' [*blzo ba*]" when addressing their edicts), but they also employ the vertical spacing requirements that Pakpa describes. A fuller study of the *Collection of Historical Archives of Tibet* in light of Pakpa's manual would be a welcome contribution to the field.

The Vessel's Contents

Pakpa's manual attends carefully to the hierarchical difference between the letter writer and the addressee. It should be noted that this short manual does not make a distinction in kind between official correspondence ("political letters" or "official letters" [*chab shog*] are not included here) and private or personal correspondence. Those various modes of epistolary writing are integrated here, where religious preceptors, military commanders, and parents are all listed in the same set of instructions for reverential address. Here I offer a translation of the first of the manual's four short chapters, this one on "letters":

> Chinese and Mongolian kings put "declared" (*bzlo ba*).
> Tibetan kings put "sent" (*springs pa*).
> Yogis put "thus" (*'di lta*).
> Commanders of hundreds of thousands put "dispatched" (*bskur ba*).
>
> To religious persons: lamas and preceptors,
> commanders of tens of thousands, commanders of thousands, and lords,
> chiefs of Ü Tsang, parents, and so forth—
> those to whom you offer reverence—
> put "before the honorable feet" (*zhabs drung du*) and "submitted" (*zhu ba*).
> Put a vertical space (*gong 'og*) of eight finger breadths (*sor*).

11. Bod rang skyong ljongs yig tshags khang 1995.

To those who are definitely greater than you,
as well as elder relatives, put "submitted before the feet" (*drung zhu*).
Put a vertical space of six finger breadths.
To those slightly greater than you,
put "submitted before the honorable eyes" (*spyan sngar zhu*).
Put a vertical space of about two finger breadths.
To those lower than you—to inferiors—
put "submitted before the ears" (*snyan du zhu*).
Put a vertical space of four finger breadths.

The properly composed letter establishes a hierarchical relationship between the imagined bodies of the letter writer and recipient. This physical positioning is accomplished not only through word choice (the phrase "offered before the feet" evokes a prostration) but also through the material formatting of the document (a larger vertical space indicates a greater difference in rank between the two parties). When writing to inferiors, the vertical space of four finger breadths should be understood to place the recipient decidedly below the sender. Ju Mipam Gyatso interprets the instruction to put "submitted before the ears" (*snyan du zhu*) as "like hearing a command."[12] In this context, the ears are metaphorically lower than the eyes because the invocation of oral rather than visual receipt of the letter is a mark of inferior status.

Tibetan letter writing is a coded genre that requires specialized knowledge for its interpretation; epistolary manuals grant us that specialized knowledge. I have previously discussed ritual dimensions of the embodied prostration that is encoded into letters to superiors;[13] here, I wish to emphasize that the intricate mapping of bodies onto Tibetan letters is very different from the Old Tibetan epistolary conventions we encounter in the Dunhuang archives. In the Dunhuang documents, dating from the late imperial period to the eleventh century, Tibetan letter writing already followed highly formalized protocol that was specialized according to the context of writing and the hierarchical relationship between the sender and the recipient, but this attention to hierarchy and differentiation did not result in the same conventions of embodied hierarchies that Pakpa introduces. Takeuchi, who made invaluable contributions to our understanding of Old Tibetan letters, characterized the Dunhuang Tibetan letters as falling into three major types: formal-official, informal-official, and letters of courtesy.[14]

12. 'Ju Mi pham rgya mtsho 2007, 1b4.

13. Kilby 2019.

14. Takeuchi 1990, 183.

1. *Formal-official*: The letter begins with the name of the official and the governing body dispatching the letter; the date is listed and the placement of a seal of dispatch is stated; the addressee is sometimes omitted. Honorific language denotes "an epistle conferred" (*mchid stsal pa*) from someone higher to someone lower.

2. *Informal-official*: The letter begins with the sender's name (although this may be omitted); the date is omitted; and the addressee is designated with the language of "sent to" (*la spring ngo*), which is neutral in terms of the hierarchical relationship between sender and recipient. Most examples of these letters are invoices and receipts.

3. *Letters of courtesy*: More than three-quarters of the Tibetan letters from Dunhuang fall into this category, by Takeuchi's estimate.[15] The addressee is listed first, along with a title of office or of respect; the date is usually omitted; humilific language indicates "an epistle offered" (*mchid gsol pa*) from someone lower to someone higher.

Takeuchi further identified two subtypes to the category of letters of courtesy. In both subtypes, the body of the letter begins with an inquiry after health along with other formalized niceties. In the first subtype, which we will call 3A, they consist of inquiring after the addressee's "peacefulness of mind" (*thugs bde*). In type 3B, they refer instead to the fatigue (*'o rgyal*) that religious activities may have caused the addressee. Type 3B letters also introduce a new formatting feature: the inclusion of several lines of vertical space after the name of the addressee and before the self-identification of the sender and the body of the letter. This vertical space is the only major link between Old Tibetan epistolary practice at Dunhuang and the epistolary style of hierarchically mapped bodies that Pakpa details. The sending verbs that Pakpa prescribes are new, with the sole exception of *springs pa*; these terms of address betray no hints of bodily positioning. Furthermore, Pakpa indicates the use of a carefully measured vertical space in all correspondence, whereas in Dunhuang documents a vertical space is reserved only for letters of personal courtesy and does not appear to vary in scale for different recipients.

Following the Thread: Sources for Pakpa's Manual

Pakpa's manual presents an artful vision of epistolary style that differs from the conventions in use at Dunhuang. Whence might Pakpa have drawn this vision? Bipa Mipam Dawa, who wrote two epistolary treatises drawing on Pakpa's manual, presents a hypothesis about the origins of Pakpa's epistolary style.

15. Takeuchi 1990, 181.

In the *Beautiful Garland of White Lotuses*, he offers a brief history of Tibetan epistolography, in which he narrates:

> In later times, when the haughty kings of Greater Mongolia came to power in the snow land of Tibet, "By the king's own decree" (*rgyal po nged kyi lung*) began to be written, and under it was inserted a large vertical space. Then the names of whoever the recipients were—kings or vassals or ministers or subjects—were written, along with "to this one and this one: a summons." And so, because of their obviously high level of conceit and arrogance due to their might, letters of official decree (*bka' lung gi yi ge*) emerged. Thus, when writing letters to superiors, the name of that recipient is written above, connected with words of praise. Beneath that is a large vertical space and then, with words conveying one's own great respect in gentle and euphonic phrasing, the inquiry about the recipient's health, and so on—this method spread.[16]

According to Mipam Dawa, Kublai's lust for power was the basis for the stratified hierarchies written into Pakpa's manual, expressed both in vocabulary and in the carefully measured spacing of text on the page. If we seek a less moralistic explanation, we might turn to Leonard's notes on Lama Dampa's two letters to the Mongol heir-apparent, where he speculates about possible Indian sources for Pakpa's epistolary instructions. Admittedly, the canonical Indian epistles are of little help in providing a link between Pakpa's epistolary style and possible Indian precedents. Whatever epistolary framing originally surrounded these epistles—the address, standardized spacing, words of closing, listing of gifts, the place and date of dispatch, seal impressions, and so forth—was stripped away long ago, if indeed it ever existed.

Thanks to several rare examples of Indian epistolary manuals, however, I can confirm Leonard's speculations of Indian links to Pakpa's epistolary style. The *Patra Kaumudī* is a short work attributed to one Vararuci, whose identity is not settled and whose text is not easy to date. Sures Chandra Banerji provides an overview of the work along with translated excerpts. Most relevant to our purposes is his discussion of the instructions about how letters are to be carried when they are received. He writes, "On the head should be carried a royal despatch, a letter from the preceptor, a Brāhmana, a recluse and the husband. Forehead is the proper place for ministerial communications. . . . A letter from

16. Bis pa Mi pham zla ba 1986 [1806], 3.

a foe should be carried in the throat."[17] These instructions for receiving letters at different parts of the body complement Pakpa's map of bodily postures for sending letters. In a full prostration of respect, a letter is offered before the feet of the superior, or in turn, received upon one's head. In a slight bow of courtesy to a near equal, a letter is offered before the eyes of the recipient or received at the forehead. In a posture of strength before an enemy, orality rather than literacy is invoked, as the epistolary exchange is located between the throat and the ears. As noted above, the conceit of uttering a command places the hearer (the enemy) in an inferior position.

Whereas Pakpa prescribes precise measurements for a vertical space after the salutation in order to indicate status, the *Patra Kaumudī* indicates status by using the honorific title *śrī* a prescribed number of times: "As regards the number of the word *śrī*, it varies with the kind of the addressee. To a preceptor, there should be six *śrīs*, to a husband five, to a servant two, to a foe four, to a friend three, and one each to son and wife."[18] These instructions seem remarkably like Pakpa's measurements of the vertical space after the salutation: six for religious preceptors, four for a foe or clear inferior. Although not an exact match for Pakpa's text, this work illuminates a world of embodied epistolary imaginings in which Pakpa's manual also participates.

Our second Indian source is the *Lekhapaddhati*, a collection of "documents of state and everyday life from ancient and early medieval Gujarat, ninth to fifteenth centuries."[19] This offers instructions similar to those in the *Patra Kaumudī* about using *śrī* a certain number of times to indicate the level of respect:

> 5. The writer should use the word *Śri* set in the tablet before commencing to write the names of kings, ministers, as well as officers.
> 6. Such use [of *Śri*] is also appropriate before the names of the lords of the *mandala*, queens and sons of kings, and such like, and those who have the grace of the teacher and the ritual-prescribing masters.
> 7. The word *Śri* thrice is to be used for friend, one each for son, six times for teacher, five times for lord (*svāmi*), twice for servant, and four times for an enemy [. . .]
> 12. Those who are respectable, such as maternal uncle, father-in-law,

17. Banerji 1960, 5.

18. Banerji 1960, 6.

19. Prasad 2007. I thank Jason Neelis for referring me to this excellent source.

> mother-in-law and master (*svāmi*), their names should be suffixed with the term *pāda* (respectable).[20]

The Tibetan translation for Sanskrit *pāda* is *zhabs*, an honorific for "foot" in both languages that by extension refers to the person. This requirement echoes Pakpa's instructions that for "those to whom you offer reverence" (*phyag 'phul*), put "before the honorable feet" (*zhabs drung du*). Furthermore, in a model letter to a guru, the *Lekhapaddhati* provides the reference to bodily prostration that Pakpa does: the writer, "saluting, in reverential prostration of body with most respect and modesty, made this petition."[21]

Finally, the *Likhanāvalī* of Vidyapati (d. 1413) is a theoretical treatise that stems from an influential Maithili poet-priest from eastern India (present-day Bihar).[22] This text includes four parts: writing letters to superiors, inferiors, equals, and then model documents of business transactions.[23] Jha's analysis of this text gestures all the way back to the *Arthaśāstra* of Kautilya, which prescribes that "after having considered the caste, lineage, position, age, learning, work/occupation, character, time, place, and blood-kinship [*yaunānubandha*] of the man [that is, the addressee], the writer should be committed to writing accordingly."[24] Jha links this detailed concern with the rank and identity of the addressee to the Persian *insha* (composition manuals, primarily for guiding secretarial correspondence), and also emphasizes that the *Likhanāvalī* includes words of "Perso-Arabic stock."[25] Jha observes that

> a text on "how to write letters and frame documents" was certainly not common in Sanskrit literature, classical or otherwise. In Arabic and Persian, however, compiling model documents/letters into a text or composing a manual for scribes was already a literary achievement to be proud of, even by the thirteenth century, if not earlier. Such compositions were known as *insha*, and their most "representative form" in Persian came to be regarded as *rasail* (literally, letters).[26]

20. Prasad 2007, 195, for paragraphs numbered 5 through 12.

21. Prasad 2007, 129.

22. Jha 2019.

23. Jha 2019, 86.

24. Jha 2019, 107.

25. Jha 2019, 104.

26. Jha 2019, 113.

Here Jha provides an important link between Indian epistolary traditions and the Persianate influences circulating in India from the thirteenth century onward. This point, taken along with the documented historical connections between Tibetans and the Mongolian kings of Persia known as the Ilkhans,[27] is a strong invitation for further research on Persian epistolary practice and possible connections to the epistolary style that Pakpa's manual details.

Final Musings

The three Indian epistolary manuals listed above exhibit several salient resonances with Pakpa's manual, though none of these sources matches Pakpa's system perfectly. Instead, these texts point to a shared world of evolving epistolary forms and an increasing sophistication of the scribal profession. Yet Jha makes a final point in his reading of the *Likhanāvalī*: that Buddhist literary sources are particularly interested in the epistolary genre. "We do come across references to letters (being written, sent, received, read, and replied to) occasionally in Sanskrit dramas, mostly in passing, and in Buddhist literature, frequently, particularly in the Jatakas."[28] Not only had the Jātakas been translated in Tibet by Pakpa's time, but Pakpa also sponsored the translation of Kṣemendra's *Wish-Fulfilling Vine of Bodhisattva Avadānas*, which includes several narratives about letter writing in the lifetime of the Buddha and his early followers. In some cases, the content of those letters is presented in quotation and the epistolary medium is directly discussed. Perhaps these literary influences further spurred Pakpa to contemplate the importance of the epistolary form for the flourishing of both religion and state—and to turn to India for inspiration in standardizing a Tibetan epistolary style.

The most direct link between Pakpa and Indian epistolary practices may not have been a text, however, but a person. Pakpa corresponded with the paṇḍita Lakṣmīkāra, who worked with Shongtön (Shong ston) to translate the *Wish-Fulfilling Vine* under Pakpa's sponsorship. In the letter to Lakṣmīkāra preserved in his collected works, Pakpa displays full mastery of the bodily metaphors that emerge in his manual. He writes:

> *OM swasti siddam.*
> I prostrate to the lama and the three jewels.
>
> By the monk with the name of "understanding" (*blo gros*, the first of Pakpa's given names):

27. Jampa Samten and Martin 2015; Sperling 1990.

28. Jha 2019, 112.

> To one whose body of understanding is thoroughly pure,
> endowed with the two eyes of grammar and epistemology,
> and whose sweet voice of poetry and tongue faculty of prosody
> make manifold melodies resound everywhere, in myriad forms,
> delighting the wise among beings, the paṇḍita of Brahmins, Lakṣmīkāra,
> offered before the ears:

Here, Pakpa offers his letter "before the ears" of Lakṣmīkāra, placing the esteemed translator decidedly lower than Pakpa in rank.[29] Still, we may forgive Pakpa for this posturing because he shows such respect to the translator in his effusive lines of address, not to mention his sending a full ounce of gold dust as a gift along with his letter. How much did these two writers correspond? Pakpa's letter to Lakṣmīkāra goes on to mention that he would like to meet Lakṣmīkāra, but in the meantime, "isn't seeing the letters sent back and forth between us the same as meeting and conversing?"[30] I conclude with a suggestion that Lakṣmīkāra's erudite letters provided models for Pakpa as he crafted Tibet's foundational epistolary manual; Lakṣmīkāra may have served as the most salient link between Pakpa and India's rich epistolary culture.

References

Banerji, Sures Chandra. 1960. "Patra-Kaumudī of Vararuci." *Bulletin of the Deccan College Research Institute* 20.1: 3–18.

Bis pa Mi pham zla ba. 1986 [1806]. *Phrin yig gi rnam bzhag dper brjod dang bcas pa padma dkar po'i phreng mdzes*. Xining: Mtsho sngon mi rigs dpe skrun khang.

Bod rang skyong ljongs yig tshags khang. 1995. *Bod kyi lo rgyus yig tshags gces btus*. Beijing: Rig dngos dpe skrun khang.

Ishihama, Yumiko. 1998. "An Aspect of the Tibet, Mongol, and China Relationship in the Late 17th Century from the View of Tibetan Letter Format. Based on the Letters of the Fifth Dalai Lama, the Regent Sangs-rgyas-rgya-mtsho and the Mongolian Prince Galdan." *Ajia Afurika gengo bunka kenkyū* アジア・アフリカ言語文化研究 [Journal of Asian and African Studies] 55: 165–89 [in Japanese with English summary].

Jampa Samten, and Dan Martin. 2015. "Letters to the Khans: Six Tibetan Epistles of Togdugpa Addressed to the Mongol Rulers Hulegu and Khubilai, as Well as to the Tibetan Lama Pagpa." *Revue d'Etudes Tibétaines* 31: 297–331.

29. 'Phags pa 2006, 558.

30. 'Phags pa 2006, 559.

'Jam dbyangs bzhad pa'i Rdo rje ngag dbang brtson 'grus. 1997 [?] [18th c.]. *'Phrin yig gi rnam par bzhag pa blo gsal rna rgyan sindu wā ra'i 'phreng mdzes*. In the author's *Collected Works* (*Gsung 'bum*), vol. 1, 363–430. Labrang Monastery block print.

Jha, Pankaj. 2019. *A Political History of Literature: Vidyapati and the Fifteenth Century*. Oxford: Oxford University Press.

'Ju Mi pham rgya mtsho. 2007 [nineteenth century]. *Yig bskur gyi rnam bzhag mdo tsam brjod pa me tog nor bu'i phreng ba*. In the author's *Collected Works* (*Gsung 'bum*), vol. 2, 677–90. Chengdu: Gangs can rig gzhung dpe rnying myur skyobs lhan tshogs.

Kilby, Christina. 2019. "Bowing with Words: Paper, Ink, and Bodies in Tibetan Buddhist Epistles." *Journal of the American Academy of Religion* 87.1: 260–81.

———. 2020. "Printing Tibetan Epistolaria: A Bibliographical Analysis of Epistolary Transformations from Manuscript to Xylograph." *The Journal of Epistolary Studies* 2.1: 19–33.

'Phags pa Blo gros rgyal mtshan. 1974 [thirteenth century]. *Yig bskur rnam bzhag 'gag sdom*. In *Yig bskur rnam bzhag nyung nyu rnam gsal*. In the *Collected Works* (*Gsung 'bum)* of Dkon mchog rgyal mtshan, vol. 4, 383–406 [Dga' ldan chos 'khor gling, fols. 11b.3–12a.7]. New Delhi: Gyalten Gelek Namgyal.

———. 2006. *Paṇḍi ta lakṣi ma ka ra la spring ba*. In *Sa skya bka' 'bum*, vol. 15, 572–73. Kathmandu: Sachen International.

Prasad, Pushpa. 2007. *Lekhapaddhati: Documents of State and Everyday Life from Ancient and Early Medieval Gujarat, 9th to 15th Centuries*. New York: Oxford University Press.

Sperling, Elliot. 1990. "Hülegü and Tibet." *Acta Orientalia Academiae Scientiarum Hungaricae* 44.1–2: 145–57.

Sum pa mkhan po Ye shes dpal 'byor. 1975 [eighteenth century]. *Yig skur sogs kyi rnam bzhag blo gsar dga' ston sgo 'byed*. In the author's *Collected Works* (*Gsung 'bum*), vol. 7, 819–958. New Delhi: International Academy of Indian Culture.

Takeuchi, Tsuguhito. 1990. "A Group of Old Tibetan Letters Written under Kuei-I-Chun: A Preliminary Study for the Classification of Old Tibetan Letters." *Acta Orientalia Academiae Scientiarum Hungaricae* 44.1–2: 175–90.

Tshe tan zhabs drung 'Jigs med rig pa'i blo gros. 2007 [twentieth century]. *'Phrin yig spel tshul lhag bsam pad mo 'dzum pa'i nyin byed*. In the author's *Collected Works* (*Gsung 'bum*), vol. 4, 459–79. Beijing: Nationalities Publishing House.

Nature and Emotion in Nineteenth-Century Tibetan Lyric Poetry

Kurtis R. Schaeffer

Leonard van der Kuijp introduced me to Tibetan poetry. He pointed me to Shabkar's *Collected Lyrics* in 1992 or so, suggesting that I look to Shabkar's prefaces to each of the two volumes for comments about the history and purpose of *mgur* and *glu*. Shabkar's historical sketch of the lyric begins with Saraha and ends with Kalden Gyatso and, of course, his own poetry. Over the past thirty years this brief sketch has marked out the full historical range of Tibetan poetry—and the particular types of poetry, *mgur* and *glu*—that has captivated me again and again. In seminars throughout the 1990s Leonard had us read *mgur* and *glu* from various eras, from the early songs of the Sakya hierarchs through songs of sorrow such as Barawa Gyeltsen Pelzangpo's laments at the coming of the Mongol armies, all the way to Shabkar's poetry itself. He also introduced me to Don grub rgyal's *History and Features of Tibetan Poetry* (*Bod kyi mgur glu'i byung 'phel gyi lo rgyus dang khyad chos*), a book that has oriented me to the finer points of Tibetan meter ever since. Leonard graciously agreed to serve as supervisor on a dissertation treating the songs of Saraha, a topic in which he was of course (as he was in all things Tibetological!) interested, though had not expended much ink upon it himself. This project oriented many of my interests in Tibetan culture ever since. I would like to offer thanks to Leonard for bestowing this beautiful world of literature upon me; in doing so he gave me a gift that has continued to offer renewed riches throughout my life.

> Critics know that in the end they cannot account adequately for the power of either poetry or music. But this side of complete enlightenment, there remains much to learn.
> — Robert von Hallberg, *Lyric Powers*

"It was summertime," the Tibetan poet Shabkar tells us at the close of one of his poems. He is staying at a small hermitage located on Lake Heart Island in the middle of Tso Ngönpo—Blue Lake—in the Amdo region of northeast Tibet (which today also happens to be the largest lake in China). He is likely there for the season; Blue Lake sits at ten-thousand-feet elevation and freezes in the winter. Visitors to the island typically walked there from the shore across the frozen lake, and boats were a rarity on the water.[1] Shabkar is explaining his reasons for singing a song about the island, its flora and its fauna.

"I went outside to take a break," he writes, "and the outside was overflowing with appearances." In this simple scene he brings the reader from the confines of his dwelling into the wide natural world, abundant with all the signs of life—"overflowing." And no sooner are we in the open with Shabkar than the outer world transforms into a malleable reality where the inner world of perception and the cosmic energy implicit in Buddhist cosmology interweave: "Waves emitted from the power of these appearances. They pulsated. They vibrated. The waterfowl were wailing plaintively here upon the southern cliff of the Lake Heart Hermitage."[2] What did he do in response to this vibration? How did he react—interact—with this effervescent wilderness scene? He sang joy. He sang idleness. He sang animals. He sang the sun. He spoke back to the natural world that was singing to him. He spoke the language of the lyric poem:

།ཕྱོགས་རྣམས་ཀུན་གསལ་གྱི་རིན་ཆེན་བྲག་སྟེང་ན།
།བྱ་བཏང་རྣལ་འབྱོར་ངས་དགའ་སྤྲོ་རྒྱང་གླུ་འཛིན།

།ས་ཆུ་རབ་ཏུ་དྲོས་སྨྱུ་གུ་འཁྲུངས་པ་ཡིས།
།སྐྱེ་འགྲོ་ཐམས་ཅད་ལ་དགའ་སྤྲོའི་ཉི་མ་ཤར།

།གཡུ་འབྲུག་སྔོན་མོ་ཡིས་གསུང་སྙན་བསྒྲགས་པ་ཡིས།
།རྨ་བྱ་ཐམས་ཅད་ལ་དགའ་སྤྲོའི་ཉི་མ་ཤར།

།ཟིམ་བུའི་སྦྲང་ཆར་དེ་དལ་བུས་བབས་པ་ཡིས།
།ཁུ་བྱུག་ཐམས་ཅད་ལ་དགའ་སྤྲོའི་ཉི་མ་ཤར།

།ཁུ་བྱུག་སྐད་སྙན་དེ་ལྷང་ལྷང་བསྒྲགས་པ་ཡིས།
།མི་རྣམས་ཐམས་ཅད་ལ་དགའ་སྤྲོའི་ཉི་མ་ཤར།

1. Buffetrille 1999, 105.

2. Zhabs dkar 1987–88, vol. 2, p. 242, line 8 (hereafter 2.242.8, etc.): *'di yang tshogs drug rang grol gyis dbyar dus shig tu phyi rol du khams gseng byas pas snang ba spro'i shugs kyi rba rlabs chal chil g.yo zhing chu bya dar dir sgrog pa'i mtsho snying dben pa'i dga' tshal lho yi brag steng zhig nas blangs pa'o //.*

།འཇའ་ཚོན་རི་མོ་དེ་ལམ་ལམ་ཤར་བའི་ཚེ།
།བྱིས་པ་ཐམས་ཅད་ལ་དགའ་སྤྲོའི་ཉི་མ་ཤར།

།སྔོ་ལྗང་རྩི་ཤིང་དང་མེ་ཏོག་རྒྱས་པ་ཡིས།
།འབྲོག་པ་ཐམས་ཅད་ལ་དགའ་སྤྲོའི་ཉི་མ་ཤར།

ལོ་ལེགས་ཕུན་ཚོགས་ཀྱི་སྙེ་མ་འཁྲུངས་པ་ཡིས།
།ཞིང་བ་ཐམས་ཅད་ལ་དགའ་སྤྲོའི་ཉི་མ་ཤར།

།དབྱར་ཟས་ཟྭ་ཚོད་དང་ཤིང་འབྲས་སྨིན་པ་ཡིས།
།རིབ་ཨ་ཐམས་ཅད་ལ་དགའ་སྤྲོའི་ཉི་མ་ཤར།

Atop this cliff of jewels that shines all around,
this lazy yogin sings a song of joy.

Earth and water are warm. The seedlings sprout.
And sun shines on, with joy for all creatures.

Bluegreen dragon cries its lovely song.
And sun shines on, with joy for all peacocks.

Gentle summer rain falls softly down.
And sun shines on, with joy for all cuckoos.

Cuckoo sounds, resounds its lovely song.
And sun shines on, with joy for all people.

Rainbows arc and glitter, shine, and then,
the sun shines on, with joy for all children.

Bluegrass, fruits, and flowers bloom, and so,
the sun shines on, with joy for all nomads.

A bumper crop yields perfect ears of corn.
The sun shines on, with joy for all farmers.

Summer foods are here, ripe fruits and nettles.
The sun shines on, with joy for mountain folk.

The published corpus of the nineteenth-century figure Shabkar (Zhabs dkar Sna tshogs rang grol, 1781–1851) offers a wide vantage point from which to view the history, form, and function of Tibetan lyric poetry. With an estimated poetic catalog of two thousand poems, Shabkar likely stands as the most prolific poet in Tibetan history. The autobiography of his early years (1781–1837), available in English translation,[3] alone contains over 330 poems. The second volume of the autobiography (covering the years 1838–51) contains a like number. The *Collected Lyrics*, from which all the poems presented here are taken, boasts over nine hundred works, and his scattered autobiographical and didactic writings include many other poems not assembled in either the major autobiography or the poetic anthology. His poems range in length from a few lines to over a hundred verses, while their metrical and rhythmic forms represent a broad range of both popular and learned prosody in Tibet.

Shabkar was a poet and performer first, but he was also at times a theorist of poetry, its performance and its history. In several poems, he prescribes the proper settings in which poetry should be performed before an audience, the way the poet should perform, and the usefulness of poetry for both performer and audience. He also deftly constructs a literary history of Indian and Tibetan Buddhist poetry that places him at the zenith of an illustrious and multi-sectarian past and allows him to claim equal place in the institutional and anchoritic Buddhist communities of nineteenth-century Tibet.[4]

In what follows I briefly survey Shabkar's comments on the function of poetry and then turn to a favorite subject of his poems, human emotion, and a favorite source with which to express the emotions, imagery of the natural world. As will become obvious, my principal goal is simply to present a handful of Shabkar's poems in order to provide a basis for further investigation and appreciation of Shabkar's lyric output, its precedents, and its impact up to the present day.[5] I also take this occasion to suggest that reflection upon how we construct the genre and history of the "lyric" in Tibetan literature can productively go hand in hand with attention to major poets such as Shabkar.

3. Ricard 1994, a translation of volume 1 of Zhabs dkar, *Zhabs dkar pa'i rnam thar*.

4. Zhabs dkar 1987–88, 1.4.1–1.5.10. For a translation of part of this passage, see Schaeffer 2005, 3.

5. Variant translations of several of the thirteen poems presented here are in Schaeffer, Kapstein, and Tuttle 2013, 669–72; and Schaeffer, forthcoming. Generally I find that my understanding of a given poem increases with each attempt at translation.

Shabkar's *Collected Lyrics* opens with three poems about poetry, and we may follow his lead and begin with these, even if their directives seem somewhat at odds with the evidence of performance that we might glean from the many concluding statements appended to his poems. These introductory poems treat the occasions for performing poetry, the ways to perform it, and poetry's benefits. The first draws on Indian Buddhist tantric literature and its Tibetan exegesis, and quickly lists the situations in which one might sing a "diamond song," an old style of song favored by the Indian siddhas and well represented in the Tibetan Buddhist canon. These occasions include when a large tantric gathering is convened; when one is engaged in the ritual contemplative practice of "distinguishing between saṃsāra and nirvāṇa"; when a maṇḍala is created for a ritual initiation; when one walks through cremation grounds, island lakes, or forests; and to encourage others toward the Dharma. "If," Shabkar suggests, "at these occasions one knows one's own diamond song, one should sing it. If one does not, one should perform a song sung by the great people of old."

The potential benefits that arise from performing songs include a range of Buddhist tropes, from the cultivation of basic ethics and the accumulation of merit and wisdom to no less than the transmutation of primordial unknowing into pure awareness and the attainment of buddhahood. Shabkar describes the benefits of poetry in similarly transcendent terms as well in a passage that is worth reading in full:

> The fortunate yogin forsakes the goals of this life. If the yogin gains enlightenment on the path of liberation, and thereupon sings diamond songs, the mind of all buddhas dissolves in the yogin. The yogin captivates the hearts of the muses, and virtuous gods flock to renew their faith and renunciation. The minds of disciples turn toward the Dharma. One's own awareness meets with peace and clarity, and one's body, speech, and mind are purified.
>
> In particular, songs are the best for overcoming a loss of faith. They are the best teachers for encouraging virtue. They are best friends when one is living alone. They activate the blessing of buddhas everywhere. Songs bestow the spiritual powers of one's personal deities and muses. They activate the work of Dharma protectors and guardians. They establish favorable conditions for the gods, the spirits, and the people. Songs sever the bonds of the existentially repetitive life, and quickly bring awakening. So that fortunate disciples of the future may forsake the labors of this life,

> cultivate spiritual experience in solitude, and from time to time sing a diamond song. The virtue of this will instantly benefit everyone, both you and others. Just as Master Milarepa did, please perform songs at great length.[6]

Here Shabkar extolls the soteriological benefits of poetry, though elsewhere he praises the more mundane benefits of poetry. At times at the beginning of his collection he argues for the primacy of poetic language itself: "All, all people, whose extent is no different than the sky, express doubt at the same time, and [Buddha] shows the best, the best body for each," he writes. "Still, song, song sweetly spoken, cuts at once the doubts of those limitless people, in speech. In speech!"[7] The body of the Buddha is an instrument of skillful means, a mechanism that can be reconfigured to meet different needs. But the body of the Buddha is not the primary means with which the Buddha addresses the human predicament. For this he uses speech, and as Shabkar would have it, the primary mode of speech is poetry. Elsewhere Shabkar argues for the importance of poetry in more prosaic terms, suggesting that poetry is simply the most effective way to encourage regular people to practice Buddhist ethics and mental training, much more so than scholastic treatises.[8]

Shabkar's advocacy of poetry can take on a defensive tone. In one poem he contrasts his life as a mountain poet with that of the mountain hunter, making a clear ethical division that entails grave consequences:

> །མི་སྡིག་ཅན་རྔོན་པས་རི་ནས།
> །མར་དམྱལ་བར་དུ་བཞིན་འགྲོ་བའི།
> །རྒྱུ་རི་དྭགས་མང་པོ་གསོད་ཚེ།
> །དགའ་བཞིན་གླུ་དབྱངས་ལེན་ན།
> །ངས་དབེན་པའི་དགའ་ཚལ་ཉམས་དགར།
> །ཡར་ཐར་བར་དགོད་བཞིན་འགྲོ་བའི།[9]

6. Zhabs dkar 1987–88, 1.11.1.
7. Zhabs dkar 1987–88, 1.1.10.
8. Zhabs dkar 1987–88, 2.3.
9. Zhabs dkar 1987–88, 1.481.2.

Hunter kills game in sin,
and plummets from the peak,
weeping, down to hell.
I sing my songs with joy,
I keep the holy Dharma,
I rise from this good forest,
laughing, up to heaven.

The latter half of this poem is an out-and-out defense of poetry, making up what it lacks in finesse with sheer vehemence:

> Why wouldn't I sing songs? Were I to remain silent, were I to sing no songs at all, I still would not avert adversity. To perform poems now and then is the way of mountain people. It's okay if they do not have the qualities of spiritual experience and realization. I delight in poems, and through the force of this others might be encouraged to practice the Dharma. So, I have performed many poems in the past.[10]

Two persistent and intertwining themes of Shabkar's poetry are, as I suggested earlier, the natural world and human emotion. While nature imagery can be found in Tibetan religious lyric poetry stretching back to the famous twelfth-century poet Milarepa, Shabkar uses flora and fauna to an unprecedented degree (or rather the precedents for his extensive and elaborate use of nature imagery remain to be studied in detail; certainly nature imagery is present in the works of his more immediate predecessor, Kalden Gyatso, yet Shabkar's poetry exceeds even this in variety and extent). And while Shabkar's use of poetry to convey doctrine links him with almost every other Tibetan Buddhist writer who has composed a verse since the twelfth century, the extent to which he uses poetry to discuss, evoke, provoke, and react to emotional states seems to set him apart from many poets. Nature and emotion are best spoken of together rather than separately, for they most often appear together in the poems. That is, if Shabkar is working on an emotional effect or describing an emotion in verse, he is most often employing natural imagery, and if he is using natural imagery he is, more likely than not, crafting a poem on the

10. Zhabs dkar 1987–88, 1.481.6.

emotions. But we can begin with a few poems that highlight his repertoire of natural imagery.

Emotions are often, perhaps nearly always, thematized in Shabkar's lyrics. Songs of sadness, of joy, of excitement, of frustration, of boredom, fear, anger, bemusement—the range of emotions and the resources of poetic language he employs to articulate them has yet to be explored with any comprehensiveness. Here we can highlight just a few, beginning with reactions to the basic axiom of Buddhist thought: life is suffering. Shabkar's typical response to human suffering and to errant activity in the face of its palpable consequences is pity. Pity often drives him to poetry, for poetry may be the one thing that can encourage people to practice the Dharma. He touches upon the issue of pity in a poem featuring the Indian cuckoo:

།དབྱངས་སྙན་ཀ་ལ་པིངཀ་འི་ཕྲུ་གུ་དང་།
།ཐོས་བསམ་སྒོམ་གསུམ་འདབ་གཤོག་ལེགས་བསྐྱངས་ནས།
།ཡིད་འོང་དབེན་པའི་དཔག་བསམ་ལྗོན་ཤིང་རྩེར།
།འཕུར་ནས་ལེགས་བཤད་ཆོས་ཀྱི་སྒྲ་དབྱངས་དེ།
།སྙང་སྙང་ཕྱོགས་བཅུར་ཡོངས་སུ་སྒྲོན་པ་ཡིན།
།ཡིད་འཕྲོག་ཤིན་ཏུ་སྙན་པའི་དབྱངས་སྙན་འདིས།
།གཞན་ཡིད་འཕྲོག་ནས་ལྗོན་ཤིང་རྩེར་འཛེག་ཤོག །[11]

A sweet-voiced Kalapinga cuckoo,
wings wide to learn, to think, to pray,
alone atop the wishing tree—
you fly! And lilting Dharma songs,
sound, resound, across the land.
Enchanting melodies entice
others to scale these forested heights.

At the poem's conclusion he tells us something of its rationale: "I look out upon the [people] and feel pity. Even the children, the little ones, act in ways that land them back in this repetitive life again. And I hope that this [song] may lead them to me, that they may act without desire in retreat, that they may work on spiritual skills."

Animals abound in Shabkar's poetry, appearing variously as examples, audiences, or advisers. Blue cuckoos, dark eagles, gold-eyed fish, and wild yak

11. Zhabs dkar 1987–88, 1.166.8.

inhabit Shabkar's lyrics. Bees frequently sing to Shabkar of their free-floating life, and Shabkar sings back about the dangers of having one's wings clipped, like a monk stuck in the monastery. Sun, moon, sky, and sea, valley, meadow, and rocky peak all form the landscape of his lyrics, at times serving individually as simile or metaphor, at times as the concrete world in which Shabkar's interior musings come to life. In one poem he offers a list of plants, animals, and geographic and atmospheric images, ending with one possible response to nature's rich pageant:

།ཉམས་དགའ་མཚོ་སྙིང་རི་བོ་ན།
།སྤོས་དང་དྲི་བཟང་ཆེ་ལི་ལི།
།ལྗོན་ཤིང་ལོ་འདབ་ཁྲི་ལི་ལི།
།མེ་ཏོག་སྣ་ཚོགས་ཁྲ་ལམ་ལམ།
།བུང་བ་གླུ་ལེན་དི་རི་རི།
།ཁོར་ཡུག་རྒྱ་མཚོ་མེ་རེ་རེ།
།ཉ་མོ་ཟས་འཚོལ་ཤ་ར་ར།
།རྦ་རླབས་སྣ་ཚོགས་ཉེ་ལི་ལི།
།ཆུ་བྱ་སྐད་སྙན་ཀྱུ་རུ་རུ།
།སྤྲིང་ན་ནམ་མཁའ་ས་ལ་ལ།
།དྲི་མེད་ཉེ་ཟླ་འོད་ལམ་ལམ།
།ཟིམ་བུའི་སྦྲང་ཆར་སི་ལི་ལི།
།འཇའ་ཚོན་རི་མོ་ཡ་ལ་ལ།
།དེ་ལྟར་ངོ་མཚར་མཐའ་ཡས་པའི།
།ཡིད་འོང་རང་བྱུང་བྲག་ཕུག་ཏུ།
།སྒོམས་ལས་མཁས་ང་ཉལ་ཉལ་ནས།[12]

Incense aromatic,
trees and leaves abundant,
flowers varied and vivid,
bees singing, buzzing,
land a shimmering sea.
Fish feeding, flittering,
waves all whistling,

12. Zhabs dkar 1987–88, 1.539.8.

ducks pleasantly droning.
Sky atop the earth,
sunlight trailing moonlight,
rains quietly chime,
rainbows brightly flash.
Such wonders without end
lull me, a lazy man,
to sleep in this fine cave.

Landscape features such as the green meadow or the rocky cave, or signs of seasonal change such as the first snowfall, often are linked to strong feelings of nostalgia, loss, and sadness, and these emotions are in turn linked to long-standing Buddhist perspectives on the human condition. Sadness, lamentation, and even depression are for Shabkar natural responses to the acute pain experienced by humans and other animals, and to the generalized state of existential unease plotted out in Buddhism's first truth as the location of all human action this side of Buddhist utopia, be it nirvāṇa, the pure land, or the nebulous dharma realm.

Death, the most potent sign of human suffering, receives lengthy treatment in Shabkar's poems, and the precarious lives of animals often serve to highlight the fragility of human life. In this poem the young buck and the fish make up the audience for admonitions to practice the Dharma before it is too late. This poem was written as Shabkar learned that a young friend of his had unexpectedly passed away:

།ནམ་འཆི་ཆ་མེད་མ་དྲན།
།ཚེ་འདིའི་བྱ་བས་གཡེངས་པའི།
།སྙིང་མེད་སྨྱོན་པ་བདག་ལ།
།བླ་མའི་ཐུགས་རྗེས་གཟིགས་ཤིག།

།ཤ་བ་སྨུག་པོ་གཞོན་ཆུང་།
།སྔོ་ཐུར་སྟོན་པས་བསད་ཐལ།
།ཤུལ་ན་ལུས་པའི་ཡུ་མོ།
།ཤོད་དུ་མ་འབབ་རྫ་ཟུངས།

།སྟོན་པ་ནམ་འོང་མི་ཤེས།
།རྒྱུན་དུ་བཙན་ས་ཟུངས་ཡ།

།བསླིབས་ཚེ་བྲོས་ན་འདོད་ཀྱང་།
།རྔོན་པས་འབྲོས་དབང་མི་སྟེར།

།ཤ་མོ་གསེར་མིག་གཞོན་ཙུང་།
།གློ་བུར་ཤ་བདས་བསད་ཐལ།
།ཤུལ་ནས་ལུས་པའི་ཤ་ཆུང་།
།མཚོ་མཐའ་མ་བསྐོར་དཀྱིལ་ཟུངས།

།ཤ་བདའ་ནམ་འོང་མི་ཤེས།
།རྒྱུན་དུ་བཙན་ས་ཟུངས་ཡ།
།བསླིབས་ཚེ་བྲོས་ན་འདོད་ཀྱང་།
།ཤ་འདས་འབྲོས་དབང་མི་སྟེར།

།གྲོགས་པོ་ན་ཚོད་གཞོན་ཙུང་།
།གློ་བུར་ཉིད་དེ་ཤི་ཐལ།
།ཤུལ་ན་ལུས་པའི་བྱ་བཏང་།
།གྲོང་དུ་མ་འཁྱམས་རི་ཟུངས།

།འཆི་བདག་ནམ་འོང་མི་ཤེས།
།རྒྱུན་དུ་ལྷ་ཆོས་མཛོད་ཡ།
།འཆི་ཚེ་ཆོས་བྱེད་འདོད་ཀྱང་།
།འཆི་བས་བྱེད་དབང་མི་སྟེར།[13]

A buck, dark red, youthful and strong,
the hunter kills him, just like that.
Left standing in his tracks, a doe—
don't flee downhill, just keep to ground.

When will the hunter come? Don't know.
Keep to your hiding place always.
He comes. And now you want to run.
But hunter gives no chance to run.

13. Zhabs dkar 1987–88, 1.496.3.

A fish, gold-eyed, youthful and strong,
fisherman kills him, just like that.
Left swimming in his wake, a small fish—
don't circle the shore, keep to the deep.

When will the fisherman come? Don't know.
Keep to your hiding place always.
He comes. And now you seek escape.
Fisherman gives no chance to flee.

A friend, young, in the prime of life.
Died suddenly. Just like that.
Left in his path, an old beggar—
don't wander in town, keep to the hills.

When will the Death Lord come? Don't know.
Practice the gods' faith always.
Death comes. And now you long for faith.
But Death will give no chance to act.

Another frequent subject in the *Collected Lyrics* is the death of Shabkar's master, Ngagi Wangpo (d. 1807). This singular event in Shabkar's life provides an occasion to reflect more generally, yet also more poignantly, on the first truth. In this brief poem two pairs of natural phenomena, sun and lotus, cloud and cuckoo, establish the relationship between the two subjects of the third verse, the master and disciple. The master has died, and the disciple is at a loss to continue in the wake of his master's passing:

།འོད་གསལ་འཛམ་གླིང་ཉི་མ།
།ཤར་ནས་ནུབ་རིར་ཡིབས་སོང་།
།ཉམ་ཆུང་པད་དཀར་ལུས་པོ།
།གྲང་རེག་བ་མོས་མནན་བྱུང་།

།དབྱར་སྐྱེས་ཆུ་འཛིན་སྟོན་མོ།
།འཁྱུར་ནས་ནམ་མཁར་ཡལ་སོང་།
།ཉམ་ཆུང་ཁུ་བྱུག་ལུས་པོ།
།སྐྱོམ་ཚད་དྲག་པོས་གདུང་བྱུང་།

།དྲིན་ཅན་རྗེ་བའི་བླ་མ།
།བྱོན་ནས་ཞིང་གཞན་གཤེགས་སོང་།
།ཉམ་ཆུང་སློབ་བུའི་ལུས་པོ།
།རྒས་པའི་མཚན་མས་མནན་སོང་།[14]

The sunlight breaks on land,
to set on mountains west.
It leaves a fragile lotus,
cold and crushed by frost.

Summer cloud swells blue,
to fade into the sky.
It leaves a fragile cuckoo,
wracked by fearsome thirst.

My kindly master's gone,
set out for other realms.
He leaves a frail pupil,
depressed by signs of age.

Shabkar also links the sorrow felt at the passing of a loved one to memory, perhaps transforming sorrow into something more akin to productive melancholy, and through natural imagery he breaks memory down into distinct experiences in which each feature of the landscape relates to a particular recollection of his deceased master. The setting is his favorite hermitage in Amdo, the island in the middle of Blue Lake:

།གནས་ཡིད་འོང་མཚོ་སྙིང་ཁོར་ཡུག་གི།
།ཤིང་སྡོ་ལྗང་མེ་ཏོག་འདབ་རྒྱས་ཆེ།
།ཕ་བླ་མའི་སྐུ་མཛེས་ཡང་ཡང་དྲན།

།ཡིད་བག་ཕེབས་ཆུ་བྱ་སྣ་ཚོགས་ཀྱིས།
།སྐད་སྙན་མོ་དར་དིར་སྒྲོག་པའི་ཆེ།
།ཕ་བླ་མའི་གསུང་སྙན་ཡང་ཡང་འདྲ།

14. Zhabs dkar 1987–88, 2.346.2.

།སྙིང་མཐོ་ལ་ཡངས་པའི་ནམ་མཁ་ལ།
།སྤྲིན་མེད་པར་ས་ཞེར་འདུག་པའི་ཚེ།
།ཕ་བླ་མའི་ཐུགས་དགོངས་ཡིད་ལ་དྲན།

།ཆུ་དྭངས་བསིལ་རྙོག་མེད་མཚོ་སྔོན་ལ།
།རླབས་ཆུ་གཉེར་རི་མོ་གཡོ་བའི་ཚེ།
།ཕ་བླ་མའི་ཡོན་ཏན་ཡང་ཡང་དྲན།

།ཤར་རི་བོའི་རྩེ་ནས་ནམ་མཁའ་ལ།
།འོད་ལམ་ལམ་ཉི་མ་ཤར་བའི་ཚེ།
ཕ་བླ་མའི་འཕྲིན་ལས་ཡང་ཡང་དྲན།[15]

Lake Heart, stunning,
flowers bloom bluegreen.
I remember Father Master's look.

Carefree birds
shouting for joy.
I remember Father Master's voice.

Sky-wide heavens
cloudless and clear.
I remember Father Master's love.

Blue lake, spotless,
shimmering, rippling.
I remember Father Master's way.

In some cases, the emotional experience portrayed in the poem is entirely shifted away from Shabkar to the natural feature itself, as in the case of this cloud song. The heavens form a favorite element in Shabkar's repertoire. Sky, sun, moon, wind, clouds, and rain all feature prominently in the poems. Clouds in particular lend themselves to talk of impermanence, and here a song of sadness is sung in the voice of the evening cloud:

15. Zhabs dkar 1987–88, 2.246.19.

།ཡུལ་གངས་ཅན་ལྷ་ལམ་ཡངས་པ་ཡི།
།ང་ཆུ་འཛིན་དགའ་བའི་དཀར་མདངས་ཅན།
།མགོན་ཆོས་རྒྱལ་ཉི་མས་བོར་སྐབས་ཀྱིས།
།མདོག་གནས་འགྱུར་མྱ་ངན་སྨུག་པོར་གྱུར།

།གདོང་མཆི་མའི་ཆར་པ་འབབ་ལ་ཁད།
།ཚུགས་མ་ཐུབ་ཕན་ཚུན་ཕང་ཕུང་གཡོ།
།མཐར་ན་འཆིའི་རླུང་གིས་མ་གཏོར་བར།
།ཆར་ཟམ་ཟིམ་སྐབས་སྐབས་འབབ་འབབ་འདུག།[16]

Big-sky trails across the snowy land,
brilliant white with joy, I am a cloud!
Dharma Master Sun has set, and so,
I've now become a dark and dismal hue.

Rain tears ready to fall upon my face,
shifting shapeless here, there, up and down.
Until ill winds of death break me apart,
at times the rain sprinkles, at times it pours.

The rich variety of the natural world can also serve as cause for joy, particularly when embedded in the idealized landscape of the hermitage, the lonely setting of contemplative practice. In mountain retreats Shabkar laughs as much as he laments, as short poems such as the following illustrate. This poem, he tells us, he wrote when he was out on begging rounds and was overcome with joy for the mountains.

།ཨེ་མ་རི་ཁྲོད་དབེན་པ་ན།
།དབྱར་དང་སྟོན་གྱི་དུས་སྐབས་སུ།
།ཉེའུ་ཐང་མེ་ཏོག་སྣ་ཚོགས་བཀྲ།
།བུང་བའི་གླུ་བརྙན་སྙན་པ་འབྱིན།

།ལྗོན་ཤིང་ཡལ་འདབ་མཛེས་པར་རྒྱས།
།བྱ་བྱིའུ་སྒྲ་འབྱིན་འཕུར་ལྡིང་གཡོ།

16. Zhabs dkar 1987–88, 2.257.8.

།ཆུ་མིག་རྫིང་བུ་བསིལ་ངད་ལྡང་།
།སུས་འཐུང་སྐོམ་པའི་གདུང་བ་སེལ།

།མཚོ་དང་རྫིང་བུའི་ནང་ན་ཡང་།
།ངང་པ་སྐད་སྙན་ཡིད་འོང་འགྲོ།
།བདེ་འཇམ་ཡངས་པའི་སྤང་གཞོངས་ན།
།རི་དྭགས་དུ་མ་བག་ཕེབས་རྒྱུ།

།དེ་ལྟར་ངོ་མཚར་མཐའ་ཡས་པའི།
།ཡིད་འོང་དབེན་པའི་གནས་མཆོག་ཏུ།
།སྔོ་ལྡང་རྩྭ་ཡི་གདན་འཇམ་སྟེང་།
།ནམ་ཞིག་བདག་ནི་ཉལ་བར་འགྱུར།[17]

Lonely mountain hermitage,
through the summer into fall.
Meadow flowers, many shades,
sweet support for swarms of bees.

Branches budding, lovely trees,
birds give voice and flap their wings.
Fountain pools fragrant and cool,
quenching pangs for all who thirst.

On the lakes and in the ponds
float sweet-voiced and lovely geese.
On these vast, these gentle fields,
deer at ease roam all around—

In this supreme and lonely place,
so infinitely wonderful,
on a gentle bluegrass seat,
at times I just lie down to sleep.

At other times he thematizes naturalness as a positive state, a state of contentedness and ease likened to the stages of advanced contemplative practice

17. Zhabs dkar 1987–88, 1.181.2.

and contrasted with the everyday business of life. Here he offers what he calls a "playful" song to an audience of patrons, gently prodding them to reflect on their current social practices:

།སེང་གེ་གངས་དཀར་སྟོངས་ན་བདེ།
།རྒོད་པོ་བྲག་དམར་ཀླད་ན་བདེ།
།རི་དྭགས་སྤང་གཞོངས་འཇམ་པོར་བདེ།
།ཉ་མོ་མཚོ་ཡི་ནང་ན་བདེ།
།སྟག་མོ་ནགས་ཀྱི་གསེབ་ན་བདེ།
།ང་རྣལ་འབྱོར་དབེན་པའི་རི་ན་བདེ།

།སྟེང་ན་སྲ་བའི་བྲག་ཕུག་བདེ།
།འོག་ན་སྔོ་ལྡང་རྩྭ་གདན་བདེ།
།བར་ན་རྣལ་འབྱོར་སྒྱུ་ལུས་བདེ།
།ངག་ནས་གླུ་དབྱངས་བླངས་པས་བདེ།
།སེམས་ལ་ཉམས་རྟོགས་ཤར་བས་བདེ།

།ཡོན་བདག་འཁོར་བཅས་བདེ་ལགས་སམ།[18]

Lion on white snow, at ease
Vulture above red rock, at ease
Deer on gentle plains, at ease
Fish under the stream, at ease
Tigress in deep woods, at ease.

Me on lonely mountains, at ease
A sturdy cave above, at ease
Bluegrass seat below, at ease
Phantom being at center, at ease
Voice calls out in song, at ease
Mind is skilled, aware, at ease—
Patrons and your clique, are you at ease?

18. Zhabs dkar 1987–88, 1.180.12.

Other poems may not deal overtly with the emotions, yet they do serve to extol the joys of the hermit's life in wilderness retreat and pass negative judgment on the trials of social life in towns and in monasteries:

།གཡུ་འབྲུག་སྔོན་མོ་དེ་ཡང་།
།ས་ལ་བབས་ན་མི་མཛེས།
།ཆུ་འཛིན་གསེབ་ཏུ་བསྡད་ནས།
།སྒྲ་དབྱངས་བསྒྲགས་ན་མཛེས་སོ།

།དར་སེང་དཀར་མོ་དེ་ཡང་།
།ཤོད་དུ་བབས་ན་མི་མཛེས།
།གངས་དཀར་ལྗོངས་སུ་འཁྱིངས་ནས།
།ང་རོ་བསྒྲགས་ན་མཛེས་སོ།

།བྱ་བཏང་རྣལ་འབྱོར་དེ་ཡང་།
།གྲོང་དུ་འཁྱམས་ན་མི་མཛེས།
།དབེན་པར་ཉམས་ལེན་བྱས་ནས།
།མགུར་དབྱངས་བླངས་ན་མཛེས་སོ།[19]

If bluegreen dragon falls
to earth, he terrifies.
Floating on rain clouds,
he sings. How beautiful.

If young white lion drops
to the vale, he terrifies.
Perched high above the snow,
he sounds a lovely roar.

If Yogin Jatang wanders
to town, he horrifies.
In solitary practice,
he sings. How beautiful.

19. Zhabs dkar 1987–88, 1.152.18.

Still other poems employ natural images to humorous effect as they offer advice on ethics and contemplative practice. In such poems Shabkar personifies animals or objects in the natural world and speaks directly to them. In this song the poet admonishes a fish, the sun, the moon, and a pomegranate to maintain a state of constant vigilance as they move through a world of all-too-human foibles:

།དད་གུས་ཀྱི་ཉ་མོ།
།མཁས་མང་མཚོར་ཕྱིན་པས།
།ཆོས་གཏམ་གྱི་གཉེར་མ།
།སྣ་ཚོགས་པ་གཡོས་ཐལ།
།ཕྲག་དོག་གི་ལྷགས་ཀྱུས།
།མ་བཟུང་བ་སྐྱིད་དོ།

།ཐོས་བསམ་གྱི་ཉི་ཟླ།
།གསུང་རབ་མཁར་ཤར་བས།
།མི་ཤེས་ཀྱི་མུན་པ།
།མཐུག་པོ་དེ་སངས་ཐལ།
།ཉེ་སྒྱོད་ཀྱི་གཟའ་ཡིས།
།མ་བཟུང་བ་སྐྱིད་དོ།

།དམ་ཆོས་ཀྱི་སེ་འབྲུ།
།ཡོན་ཚོད་ལ་ཟློས་པས།
།བདག་བློའི་ཕོ་སྟོང་བ།
།ཅུང་ཟད་ཅིག་འགྲངས་ཐལ།
།གདམས་ངག་གི་མུ་གེ།
།མ་བྱུང་བ་སྐྱིད་དོ།[20]

Gone, big faithful fish,
set out for the sea of scholars.
Religious currents
flow where they will.

20. Zhabs dkar 1987–88, 1.153.16.

Be glad if jealousy's hook
does not catch up with you.

Learning sun, thinking moon,
shine on the fortress of scripture.
Ignorant shadows,
gloomy, blot you out.
Be glad a wicked star
does not catch up with you.

Holy Dharma pomegranate,
eaten when mature, so
empty stomach self
is somewhat satisfied.
Be glad a teaching famine,
does not catch up with you.

Shabkar laments that he lives in a fallen world—a complaint familiar to all who read Buddhist literature. He complains that the great teachers are gone, that the glory days of Buddhism are past. He expresses regret that he is a poor teacher. But in the wake of a corrupted tradition, in the face even of death, Shabkar offers poetry as a defense, however tragic, against the passage of time, as a chance for renewal. He writes again:

།བྱ་རྒྱལ་རྒོད་པོའི་ཚོགས་རྣམས།
།མི་མཐོང་དགུང་དུ་འཕུར་ཐལ།
།ལྕུམ་བུ་མག་པོའི་གསེབ་ན།
།བུང་བས་ཀུ་ཅོ་སྒྲོག་བྱུང་།

།ཆུ་བོ་ཆེན་པོའི་ཚོགས་རྣམས།
།རྒྱ་མཚོའི་ནང་དུ་འདྲེས་ཐལ།
།རྫ་རིགས་མང་པོའི་གསེབ་ན།
།ཆུ་ཕྲན་ཀུ་ཅོག་སྒྲོག་བྱུང་།

།སྔོན་གྱི་རྒྱལ་བའི་ཚོགས་རྣམས།
།དག་པའི་ཞིང་དུ་བཞུད་ཐལ།

།བྲག་ཁུང་སྐམ་པོའི་ནང་ན།
།སྤྲང་ཀན་ཀུན་ཅོ་སྒྲོག་བྱུང་།

།བུང་བ་ལུས་པོ་ཆུང་ཡང་།
།བུང་སྒྲ་ཁོ་ལས་ལྷག་སྣང་།
།རྒྱུན་དུ་སྒྲ་དབྱངས་སྒྲོག་པ།
།བུང་བའི་རང་གཤིས་ཡིན་ནོ།

།ལུང་ཕྲན་ཆུ་བོ་ཆུང་ཡང་།
།ཀུ་ཅོ་ཁོ་ལས་ལྷག་སྣང་།
།རྒྱུན་དུ་ཙ་ཅོ་སྒྲོག་པ།
།ཆུ་ཕྲན་རང་གཤིས་ཡིན་ནོ།

།ཀད་པོ་ཉམས་རྟོགས་མེད་ཙང་།
།ལེགས་བཤད་ཁོ་ལས་ལྷང་སྣང་།
།རྒྱུན་དུ་མགུར་དབྱངས་འཐེན་པ།
།སྤྲང་ཀན་རང་གཤིས་ཡིན་ནོ།[21]

Now all the eagle kings,
have vanished into space.
Amidst the forest trees,
the bees still babble on.

Now all the grand rivers,
have drained into the sea.
Amidst the river rocks,
the brook still babbles on.

Now bygone champions,
have left for other realms.
Inside a barren cave,
the beggar babbles on.

21. Zhabs dkar 1987–88, 1.191.3.

Small, forgotten, and yet,
the buzz transcends the bee,
to hum the tune forever is,
the spirit of the bee.

Small, so narrow, and yet,
the babble transcends the brook.
To babble on forever is,
the spirit of the brook.

Old, unwise, and yet,
teachings transcend the man.
To sing a song forever is,
the old man beggar's way.

The study of Tibetan lyrics is wide open for historical exploration and literary interpretation. There have been several sketches of a history of one sort of poetic literature or another.[22] When Döndrup Gyel's essential survey of Tibetan poetry—*mgur* and *glu*—was published in 1985, global scholarship did take note.[23] Since then studies of select major writers have appeared.[24] Nevertheless, few contemporary scholars have dedicated sustained attention to the formal and stylistic features of Shabkar's poetry, or for that matter, of any other Tibetan poet. A study of the history of Tibetan poetry from its origins to the present, or indeed of any extended period, remains to be written. As important, the field lacks any extended exploration of the ways we employ terms such as "poem," "song," "lyric," etc.—genre terms, in short—to define and refine bodies of literature and areas of inquiry. Descriptions of traditional and contemporary accounts of literary types and genres are crucial, though global scholars can and should use the interpretive resources at their disposal.

It is not enough to reduce *mgur* and *glu* to a fuzzy category such as "reli-

22. Sorensen 1990, 11–22; Jackson 1996; van der Kuijp 1996.

23. Jackson 1996, 374; Sujata 2005, chap. 7, "Metrics," and elsewhere. The development of literary history in Tibet is surveyed in Hartley 2003, 244–53.

24. Sujata 2005 is the most sustained study to date. This is also the best place to start for a bibliography of scholarship on *mgur* and *glu*. See also Sujata 2012 for translations of some of Shabkar's poems.

gious poems,"[25] which does not speak to their formal features but rather to a limited notion of their content.[26] To consider *mgur* and *glu* foremost as "religious" literature turns our attention away from the plethora of subjects that such literature does treat and the ways in which it does this. "Religion" here is an overdetermined category whose boundaries are both too vast and too stalwart, regardless of whether it is maintained by critics or caretakers. Shabkar's lyrics offer a perfect example; if we consider his poetry to be expressive of, for instance, emotional experience, or even as instances of aesthetically heightened representations (or even constructions) of experience rather than "Buddhist experience," we open up interpretive possibilities, possibilities that not only expand our sense of what literature is and does in Tibetan contexts but also turn back around to offer new perspectives on what "Buddhism" is when considered through the lens of literary aesthetics.

It is also not advantageous to leave such issues as prosody, melody, or more general issues of performance and performativity to specific fields such as ethnomusicology because poems are "songs" from a certain perspective,[27] or performance studies because they are "ritual" or "oral performance." These categories are, for their better part, constructions of the inquiry and not first-order defining features of the objects of inquiry. At the social level, the field of Tibetan studies in general is too small to give over to stark disciplinary compartmentalization—not to speak of the smaller subset of scholars within that field who are actively interested in Tibetan poetic studies. Of course, the unique perspectives and the types of expert inquiry provided by methodologies within distinct disciplines are essential to gain knowledge that is both wide and deep; yet this should not deter attempts to generate a more generalized or more synthetic knowledge of lyric poetry.

Beyond the issue of the relative size of a given field or a given interest group, the material we might include within the genre of lyric poetry itself is hybrid, cutting across disciplines by its very nature. In terms of distribution media alone, poetry collections might be oral, handwritten, or printed, or some simultaneous combination of any of these. A lyric may be meant to be sung—or it may not be. "Performance" may mean different things at different times and in different places, as the very existence of anthologies such as Shabkar's *Collected Lyrics* makes possible.

25. Sorensen 1990, 14–17.

26. Döndrup Gyel also reduces *mgur* and *glu* to "religion," though within a distinct cultural and political context compared with, say, European or American scholars; see Lin 2008, 95.

27. As suggested in Sorensen 1990, 11.

It is from within this history of interpretation of Tibetan poetry that I consider the notion of the "lyric" useful for examining the nature and scope of *mgur* and *glu*. As a broad-viewed orientation, the lyric offers poets "a repertoire of discursive possibilities: complaint, praise, hope, and suffering, relating inner and outer worlds."[28] As a genre, lyric poetry offers critics a useful tool for both historical and interpretive work. The lyric is typically characterized as a brief-to-mid-length verse that presents itself as compactly expressing the subject's innermost sentiments or experiences. Of course, the term has a long history of shifting meanings and a vibrant recent history of debate about its scope and value, which makes it more valuable for a field such as Tibetan literary studies. Its compactness—its density—makes it useful for considering Shabkar's verse. Like English or Chinese lyric poetry, Shabkar's poetry could be said to be "compelled by the centrality of [the] poet's thoughts and emotions as the chief focus of attention." In Shabkar's verse, "This is done with but minimal reference to how such feelings and reflections come into being, how they evolve, and how they are resolved or not resolved. It is usually through subtle hints dropped by the poet that we infer the context of the lyric. The nature of the content delivered in the lyric is thus one of sheer presence of the thoughts and emotions themselves."[29]

If Earl Miner's contention that the "lyric is the foundation genre for the poetics or systematic literary assumptions of cultures throughout the world"[30] offers us any insight, then the category of "lyric" offers a powerful viewpoint from which to investigate the history of literature in Tibet broadly. At the very least, it provides a means to consider *mgur* and *glu* together with *snyan ngag* (*kāvya*).

I sketch Shabkar's own comments on poetic intention and audience as well as his construction of the natural world, emotions, and their interrelations in his poems and their paratexts primarily to develop a sense of informed appreciation of his lyric poetry, but also to better understand the history of literary form and style in Tibet. These two aims are commensurate: attention to both the aesthetic scope of a given poet's work in comparison to a generalized model of genre and to the distinctive examples of poetry in history are necessary to contribute to a poetics that gives equal attention to poetic subject, style, and social context across regional and temporal divides. The ways in which we construct a genre such as the lyric and the ways we construct the history of works that fall within that genre are intimately linked: "[A] broad conception of lyric

28. Culler 2015, 21.

29. Sun 2011, 216.

30. Miner 2000, 579.

as genre is helpful for thinking about short, nonnarrative poetry, permitting exploration of its historical tradition, making salient its discursive strategies and possibilities in a range of periods and languages."[31]

If Shabkar's poetry provides a cue to do this, I suggest that it is in his claim that notions of life's transience and the rich pageant of emotions that accompanies the central insight of his tradition (i.e., the first noble truth) are well, or even perhaps best, expressed through poetry, and that poetry is an especially effective form of literature with which to inculcate attitudes, feelings, and practices. In other words, Shabkar's claims might encourage us to treat poetry as a good place to study relationships between aesthetics, emotion, philosophy, and practice across the centuries in Tibet, and throughout different regions of the Buddhist world.

References

Buffetrille, Katia. 1999. "The Blue Lake of A-mdo and Its Island: Legends and Pilgrimage Guide." In *Sacred Spaces and Powerful Places in Tibetan Culture*, edited by Toni Huber, 105–24. Dharamsala: Library of Tibetan Works and Archives.

Cabezón, José Ignacio, and Roger R. Jackson, eds. 1996. *Tibetan Literature: Studies in Genre*. Ithaca, NY: Snow Lion Publications.

Culler, Jonathan. 2015. *Theory of the Lyric*. Cambridge, MA: Harvard University Press.

Don grub rgyal. 1985. *Bod kyi mgur glu'i byung 'phel gyi lo rgyus dang khyad chos bsdus par ston pa rig pa'i khye'i rnam par rtsen pa'i skyed tshal*. Beijing: Mi rigs dpe skrun khang.

Hartley, Lauran. 2003. "Contextually Speaking: Tibetan Literary Discourse and Social Change in the People's Republic of China (1980–2000)." PhD diss., Indiana University.

Jackson, Roger. 1996. "'Poetry' in Tibet: Glu, mGur, sNyan ngag and 'Songs of Experience.'" In Cabezón and Jackson, *Tibetan Literature*, 368–92.

van der Kuijp, Leonard W. J. 1996. "Tibetan Belles-Lettres: The Influence of Daṇḍin and Kṣemendra." In Cabezón and Jackson, *Tibetan Literature*, 393–410.

Lin, Nancy G. 2008. "Döndrup Gyel and the Remaking of the Tibetan Ramayana." In *Modern Tibetan Literature and Social Change*, edited by Lauran R. Hartley and Patricia Schiaffini-Vedani, 86–111. Durham: Duke University Press.

Miner, Earl. 2000. *The Renewal of Song: Renovation in Lyric Conception and Practice*. Calcutta: Seagull Books.

Ricard, Mattheiu, trans. 1994. *The Life of Shabkar: The Autobiography of a Tibetan Yogin*.

31. Culler 2015, 90.

Albany: State University of New York Press. [A translation of Zhabs dkar, *Zhabs dkar pa'i rnam thar*, vol. 1.]

Schaeffer, Kurtis R. 2005. *Dreaming the Great Brahmin: Tibetan Traditions of the Buddhist Poet-Saint Saraha*. New York: Oxford University Press.

———. Forthcoming. *Buddhist Meditation: Classic Teachings from Tibet*. New York: Penguin Classics.

Schaeffer, Kurtis R., Matthew T. Kapstein, and Gray Tuttle. 2013. *Sources of Tibetan Tradition*. New York: Columbia University Press.

Sorensen, Per K. 1990. *Divinity Secularized: An Inquiry into the Nature and Form of the Songs Ascribed to the Sixth Dalai Lama*. Vienna: Arbetskreis für Tibetische und Buddhistische Studien Universität Wien.

Sujata, Victoria. 2005. *Tibetan Songs of Realization: Echoes from a Seventeenth-Century Scholar and Siddha in Amdo*. Leiden: Brill.

———. 2012. *Songs of Shabkar: The Path of a Tibetan Yogi Inspired by Nature*. Berkeley, CA: Dharma Publishing.

Sun, Cecile Chu-chin. 2011. *The Poetics of Repetition in English and Chinese Lyric Poetry*. Chicago: The University of Chicago Press.

von Hallberg, Robert. 2008. *Lyric Powers*. Chicago: University of Chicago Press.

Zhabs dkar Tshogs drug rang grol (1781–1851). 1985. *Zhabs dkar pa'i rnam thar* [The Life of Shabkar]. 2 vols. Xining: Mtsho sngon mi rigs dpe skrun khang.

———. 1987–88. *Zhabs dkar pa'i mgur 'bum* [Collected Lyrics of Shabkar]. 2 vols. Xining: Mtsho sngon mi rigs dpe skrun khang.

The Jonangpa Scholar Künga Drölchok's Oeuvre, Its Xylography Project, and the *Analects of Zhentong*

Michael R. Sheehy

THE JONANGPA SCHOLAR Künga Drölchok (Kun dga' grol mchog, 1507–66) was one of the most eclectic thinkers and authors of sixteenth-century Tibet. He was born in Lo Möntang (Glo smon thang) in Mustang, Nepal, to a family with strong ties to the Sakya order.[1] When he was thirteen, he traveled to Tibet and studied at Sakya Monastery and at Serdokchen (Gser mdog can) Monastery, the monastic seat of Shākya Chokden (Shākya mchog ldan), and later in the 1530s at Ngor, Ngamring, and Tsurpu monasteries. Throughout his life, he taught the Six Dharmas of Niguma (Ni gu chos drug) from the Shangpa order (Shangs pa), the Lamdré (Lam 'bras) teachings on the Path and Its Result from the Sakya order, and the Sixfold Vajrayoga (Rdo rje rnal 'byor ba yan lag drug) from the Jonang Kālacakra tradition.[2] A true itinerant scholar-yogi (though he held several administrative appointments as abbot at different monasteries), he traveled extensively across the highlands of the northern Himalayas and throughout central and southwestern Tibet. For instance, as his autobiography details, while serving as abbot of a small monastery in Mustang, he traveled to the pilgrimage site of Muktinath in Nepal, where he amazed the Hindu ascetics by speaking to them in their local vernacular. During his travels, he sought out and received rare Buddhist transmissions that he compiled into an anthology, the *One Hundred and Eight Guidebooks of the Jonang*.[3] Starting in 1546, he served as the twenty-fourth throneholder at Jonang, an appointment that he held until his death in 1566.[4]

1. Blo gros grags pa 1992, 49–52.

2. On Künga Drölchok's transmission of the Shangpa Kagyü, see Smith 2001a, 55; and Sheehy 2019b, 117–18.

3. Grol mchog, *Jo nang*. For a translation, see Kongtrul Lodrö Taye 2020.

4. Künga Drölchok passed away on the eighth day of the first month during the fire-tiger year (*me stag*), which was 1566.

My quest for the writings of Künga Drölchok began during fieldwork in the summer of 2006 while in south-central Tibet. The Jonangpa Tulku Künga Tsültrim Zangpo (Kun dga' tshul khrims bzang po) and I spent several weeks camping at Takten Damchö Püntsok Ling (Rtag brtan dam chos phun tshogs gling) Monastery, the fortress citadel monastic complex that was constructed by Tāranātha in 1615 on the lip of the Jomonang (Jo mo nang) Valley, where the Great Stūpa at the Richö Chenmo (Ri chos chen mo) mountain retreat is situated. Located in the Lhatsé district, Takten Ling Monastery served as headquarters for the Jonangpas until its confiscation by the Ganden Podrang government. From base camp at Takten Ling, we made excursions to Jonang sites within the radius of a few miles. One site that we visited was Chölung Jangtsé (Chos lung byang rtse dgon), Künga Drölchok's home monastery. A day's trip by horseback over a mountain adjacent to Takten Ling Monastery, Chölung Jangtsé is a humble monastery built into the mountainside, nestled deep in the Chölung hollow along the Takcho River (Rtag cho).[5] Künga Drölchok served as the abbot at Chölung Jangtsé during the latter days of his life, and Tāranātha was later formally conferred as his incarnation at the monastery.[6] Soon after we arrived and exchanged greetings with the head lama, Tulku Zangpo and I began to inquire about writings by Künga Drölchok. Bemused that we were asking about Künga Drölchok, the elderly lama leaned toward me and, with a sorrowful face, said that he believed Künga Drölchok's writings were no longer available. Though we expected that books were seized during the Ganden Podrang's confiscation of Jonang monasteries in the mid-seventeenth century, I found it striking that the abbot at Künga Drölchok's home monastery believed that his works no longer existed.

As homage to Leonard van der Kuijp's contributions to the history of xylography in Tibet, the study of Jonang thought, and the writing on Shākya Chokden, and his lifelong effort to preserve rare Tibetan texts, this chapter discusses the recompiled *oeuvre* (as Leonard would put it!) of the Sakya, Shangpa, and Jonangpa scholar Künga Drölchok and his writing on Zhentong (*gzhan stong*; "extrinsic emptiness").[7] Given that an intact *Collected Works* (*Bka' 'bum* or *Gsung 'bum*) is not extant, the first part asks, Were Künga Drölchok's collected

5. The Takcho River, a tributary of the Yarlung Tsangpo (Yar klungs gtsang po), is located adjacent to the Tokzhung (Rtog gzhung) region in the minor Chölung (Chos lung) Valley.

6. Tāranātha wrote on the Kālacakra while at Chölung Jangtsé.

7. For instance, on xylography, see van der Kuijp 2010; on Jonang thought, see 2016a and 2016b; and on Shākya Chokden, see 1983. For an introduction to Zhentong philosophical thought and literary history, see Mathes and Sheehy 2019.

writings printed in Tibet?[8] To address this, and to provide a history of the author's literary oeuvre, we discuss extant xylographic prints and manuscripts of Künga Drölchok's writings. References draw from recent efforts to relocate and recompile Künga Drölchok's writings from scattered bundles in private and monastery libraries and in state-run collections in Tibet, Nepal, Bhutan, Ladakh, China, and Europe—an effort that owes a debt of gratitude to Leonard van der Kuijp.[9] As an example of Künga Drölchok's reconstituted oeuvre, the second part introduces excerpts from the recently unearthed manuscript instruction on the Zhentong philosophy of emptiness written by Künga Drölchok titled the *Analects of Zhentong*. Since a work on Zhentong by Künga Drölchok was not known to exist until recently, these philosophical extracts provide a sample of Künga Drölchok's writings and a critical missing piece in the puzzle of the history of Zhentong philosophy in Tibet.

The Oeuvre of Künga Drölchok

With the requisition of Takten Ling Monastery in 1650, the printery was sealed, and writings by Jonang authors were banned from being printed in Central Tibet, confiscated from Jonang monastery libraries, and rendered inaccessible.[10] As the lack of access to Künga Drölchok's works demonstrates, prohibition and censorship of Jonang books from the mid-seventeenth century had a traumatic impact on the literary archive of the tradition. During the centuries that ensued after the requisition, several unsuccessful attempts were made to rescue the books at Takten Ling, most notably by Situ Paṇchen Chökyi Jungné (Si tu paṇ chen Chos kyi 'byung gnas, 1699/1700–1774) during his visit in 1723 and by his compeer Rindzin Tsewang Norbu (Rig 'dzin tshe dbang nor bu, 1698–1755) during a diplomatic attempt in 1734.[11] It wasn't until over 215 years after the Ganden Podrang official lockdown that the Takten Ling printery

8. For preliminary catalogs, see Hor rgyal sogs kyis sgrig bsgyur byas 2000, 23–35; and *Gdan sa chen po*, 2: 1412–26.

9. A recompilation of Künga Drölchok's works as well as works by his primary Kālacakra teacher, Ratnabhadra (Ratna bha dra), are under preparation to be published in the "Jonang Publication Series" (Jo nang dpe tshogs) by the Nationalities Publishing House (Mi rigs dpe skrun khang), Beijing. See Sheehy 2020, 266, 4. A special thanks to Leonard van der Kuijp for gifting a copy of Künga Drölchok's travelogue, *Lam yig dpyod ldan snying gi mun sel* (44 folios), to the recompilation project, which he acquired at the Cultural Palace of Nationalities in Beijing.

10. Smith 2004, 188–92; and on the censorship of Jonang books and the controversy of Zhentong philosophy in seventeenth-century Tibet, see Sheehy 2010, 10 and 17–21.

11. Chos kyi 'bung gnas 1990, 104–5; and Smith 2001b, 95n235.

was reopened to print Jonang books, thanks to the Zhalu scholar and close collaborator in the nineteenth-century nonsectarian (*ris med*) project, Losel Tenkyong (Blo gsal Bstan skyong, b. 1804), who had Jonang works printed at both the Takten Ling and Jang Ngamring printeries.[12] Writing about lifting the ban and unsealing the printeries, Losel Tenkyong wrote in 1874:[13]

> At Ganden Püntsok Ling, I was sincerely hoping to gain permission from the authorities. Eventually, by petitioning the administrator at the great [Trashi Lhünpo] monastic complex, impressions were printed from the maltreated woodblocks, starting with [Tāranātha's] commentary on the great praise to Cakrasaṃvara.
>
> While at Ngamring, I requested what they possessed that was composed by Jé Künga Drölchok, and in particular, I was interested in the *One Hundred and Eight Guidebooks of the Jonang*. At the Püntsok Ling printery, I gained the necessary permissions and was also able to produce a useful catalog of Jetsun Tāranātha's *Collected Works*.[14]

At Takten Ling printery, Losel Tenkyong was able to print works by Tāranātha from woodblocks and record a full catalog (*dkar chag*) of his writings.[15] Takten Ling Monastery, which he refers to by its converted name, Ganden Püntsok Ling, was under the jurisdiction of authorities at Trashi Lhünpo Monastery, so Losel Tenkyong petitioned the official (*skyabs dbyings*) at Trashi Lhünpo for permission.[16]

12. *Byang ngam ring gi par khang*. Smith 2001c, 250; and Sheehy 2019a, 352–53.

13. Losel Tenkyong's visit to Takten Ling was during a wood-horse (*shing khyi*) year, which would have been 1874 or early 1875. Tenkyong's handwritten preface to his catalog reads, *dga' ldan phun tshogs gling gi par tho zhu dag pa blo gros brtan pas bkod pa'i mgor/ rab byung nyi ma'i shing khyi yan chad du*. See Chandra 1963, 98.

14. Blo gsal Bstan skyong 1971, 675.

15. Chandra 1963, 86–101; and Ngawang Gelek Demo 1970, 214.

16. Trashi Lhünpo Monastery being the administrative seat of Takten Ling appears to have started in 1650, the year writings were confiscated from Jonang Monastery libraries. Tenkyong's catalog colophon reads, "Completed by the retreatant from Zhalu, Losel Tenkyong, after petitioning the great monastic headquarters" (*ces pa 'di ni zha lu ri khrod pa blo gsal bstan skyong gis bla brang chen por gsol ba btabs nas bsgrubs pa'o*). Chandra 1963, 20, states this was "derived from the xylographed karchag in the Ganden Monastery at Ulanbator"; however, this was compiled by Blo gsal Bstan skyong. Smith 2001c, 250, 333–34n847, notes that the official at Trashi Lhünpo was Sengchen Lozang Tendzin Penjor (Seng chen Blo bzang bstan 'dzin dpal 'byor), patron of Sarat Chandra Das.

At the end of Losel Tenkyong's catalog, there is a brief list of works by Künga Drölchok along with his notes that indicate several blocks were broken or missing. This includes Künga Drölchok's biography of Jangdak Namgyel Drakzang (1395–1475), the physician, Jonang Kālacakra adept, and ruler of the Jang principality;[17] his record of teachings received (*thob yig*), titled *A Bounty of Teachings*;[18] lineage supplications (*brgyud 'debs*) along with manuals for the preliminary and main practices (*sngon 'gro dngos gzhi*) associated with the *One Hundred and Eight Guidebooks of the Jonang*; instructions on the five stages according to the Buddhajñānapāda tradition of the Guhyasamāja;[19] an explanation of difficult points in the Lamdré system;[20] his autobiography, *A Floral Garland of Experience*;[21] as well as instruction manuals (*khrid yig*) and miscellaneous works.[22] Though xylographic prints of Künga Drölchok's works printed at Takten Ling printery have yet to be identified, Losel Tenkyong's catalog records that works were printed at Takten Ling up to the sealing of the printery.

At the Ngamring printery, Losel Tenkyong printed the *One Hundred and Eight Guidebooks of the Jonang* anthology of guidance instructions, demonstrating that this important work was carved at Ngamring and that blocks survived up until the late nineteenth century. Losel Tenkyong brought the Ngamring print of the anthology of guidebooks to his collaborator, Jamgön Kongtrül (1813–99), who regarded the work to be exemplary of an early

17. Chandra 1963, 100; and see Grol mchog 1985.

18. Chandra 1963, 100. Regent Stag brag's catalog distinguishes the *rnam thar* and *thob yig*. See Ngawang Gelek Demo 1970, 215. Several witnesses of the *thob yig* have become available, including a handwritten *dbu can* manuscript that we acquired in Amdo, Grol mchog, *Dam pa'i chos* (W1KG18291), and a block print that we acquired from Giuseppe Tucci's collection in Rome, Grol mchog, *Dam pa'i chos* (W1KG18290), which is possibly a Takten print. On "*gsan yig*-ology," see van der Kuijp 1995, 920.

19. Chandra 1963, 100. This work follows the tradition of the Buddhajñānapāda (Sangs rgyas Ye shes zhabs) transmission of the Guhyasamāja. See Grol mchog, *Dpal gsang*. Tāranātha wrote related works.

20. Chandra 1963, 100. See Grol mchog, *Lam 'bras*. An interlinear note in the catalog reads, *'di nang shing par gnyis chad*, suggesting that two blocks were missing.

21. Chandra 1963, 100. See Grol mchog, *Myong ba* and *'Jam dbyangs*, and Grol mchog 2005, 320–404 (however, there are significant corruptions in this publication).

22. Other works include *Tshe sgrub grub rgyal ma'i 'khrid yig la*; *Bla ma lam 'khyer sogs la*; *Sbas ba'i tshig 'byed thar ba'i them skas la*; *Byang bdag rnam rgyal grags bzang gi mdzad gras/ dus 'khor sgrub thabs dngos grub gter mdzod la*, with a note that four blocks were missing; *Bdag 'jug la*, with a note that one block was missing; and *Dus 'khor sgrub thabs yid nor la*. See Chandra 1963, 100.

ecumenical (*ris med*) vision. The xylographic print that Losel Tenkyong gifted Jamgön Kongtrül served as the source for Kongtrül to model his extensive collection, the *Treasury of Precious Instructions*.[23] Künga Drölchok's anthology, along with supplemental historical and liturgical materials that were composed by Tāranātha and Losel Tenkyong, were slated as the final volume of the *Treasury of Precious Instructions*.

Losel Tenkyong prefaces his record of the biography of Namgyel Drakzang with an annotation that indicates the provenance to be from Ngamring.[24] This prefatory note is recorded virtually verbatim in the survey of extant blocks at the Takten Ling printery made by the Takdrak Regent, Ngawang Sungrap Tutop (Stag brag Ngag dbang gsung rab mthu stobs, 1874–1952), completed in 1957.[25] The Takdrak Regent's survey is nearly identical to Losel Tenkyong's catalog over eighty years earlier, confirming that the printery remained intact during this period.[26] These clues locate the provenance of at least two of Künga Drölchok's works—the biography of Namgyel Drakzang and the anthology of guidebooks—from Ngamring, suggesting they were printed from Jang Ngamring blocks.

Until recently, only a few witnesses of xylographic prints of Künga Drölchok's works were available. This included the prints of Künga Drölchok's biography of Jowo Atiśa as well as his biography of Shākya Chokden.[27] A comparison of observable codicological features from these two block prints suggest that they were both derived from blocks at Ngamring printery.

Fig. 1. Title page, biography of Jowo Atiśa by Künga Drölchok, Ngamring print, in Grol mchog, *Jo bo rje*.

23. Grol mchog 1999.

24. Chandra 1963, 100. The interlinear note on the catalog states that it was taken from Ngamring, suggesting it was printed there.

25. Chandra 1963, 100. Ngawang Sungrap Tutop's team cataloged 114 printeries, and a source for a pre-1959 inventory of printeries in Central Tibet. See Ngawang Gelek Demo 1970, 172–243.

26. Ngawang Gelek Demo 1970, 214–16. There are minor emendations to titles; otherwise, it's the same list. Based on the preface of Losel Tenkyong's catalog, it is plausible that Takdrak copied his catalog.

27. Grol mchog, *Jo bo rje, Paṇḍi ta* (W25586 and W1NLM555), and Grol mchog 1995. On Künga Drölchok's biography of Shākya Chokden, see Komarovski 2011, 24–25.

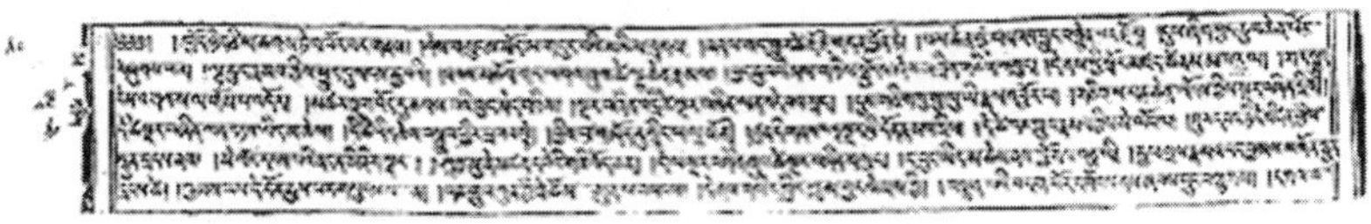

Fig. 2. Second folio, biography of Jowo Atiśa by Künga Drölchok, Ngamring print, in Grol mchog, *Jo bo rje*.

Print features of Jowo Atiśa's biography closely resemble the biography of Shākya Chokden, including title-page layouts, indentation and distinct double-cut lines on the margins (*mtha' thig*), signature triple-curl headers (*dbu khyud*) to start a work (double curlers are more common), similar glyph configurations, and so forth.

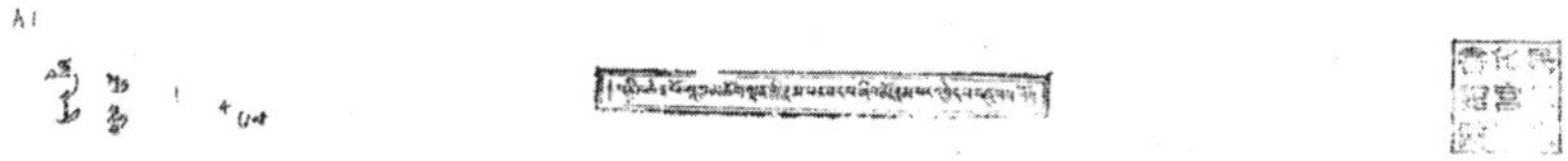

Fig. 3. Title page, biography of Shākya Chokden by Künga Drölchok, Ngamring print, in Grol mchog, *Paṇḍi ta*.

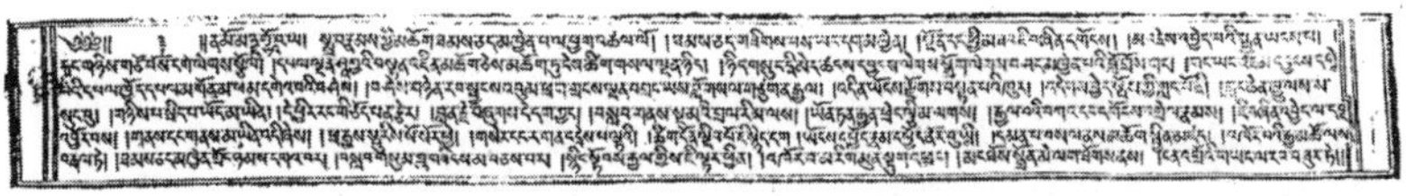

Fig. 4. First folio, biography of Shākya Chokden by Künga Drölchok, Ngamring print, in Grol mchog, *Paṇḍi ta*.

Observable evidence from these prints is compounded by the synchronized marginalia that have identical enumerations, block shapes, carved labels, and handwritten annotations by a cataloger.[28] Both prints bear the same official Chinese stamp that declares the prints were cataloged at a national cultural office library.[29] The prints were likely stamped at the library during the cataloging process after these block prints were acquired, and though the stamp does

28. For instance, Grol mchog, *Jo bo rje*, starts with the enumeration *la gcig*, and Grol mchog, *Paṇḍi ta*, starts with the enumeration *gi gcig*. Both are labeled with "A'" on the margins.

29. The Chinese stamp reads "Nationalities Cultural Palace Library Collection" (Min[zu] wenhua gong [tu]shuguan zang 民[族]文化宮[圖]書館藏). The second and sixth characters are unidentifiable.

not indicate a provenance, this detail suggests that these were collected as part of a larger batch. Putting these pieces together, in the aggregate—Losel Tenkyong's record of findings, observable evidence on the xylographic prints, and the cataloging information—we can infer that several of Künga Drölchok's works were printed at Jang Ngamring printery.[30] Given the strong multigenerational ties of Jonangpas to Ngamring, starting with Choklé Namgyel (Phyogs las rnam rgyal, 1306–86), and the fact that Künga Drölchok spent a good portion of his life in Ngamring, this makes total sense.[31]

That a *Collected Works* was printed at Ngamring printery is further confirmed with new evidence from works that have emerged from library archives in Tibet. A set of xylographic prints, several with markings that indicate they came from Drepung Monastery, show identical codicological features to the Jowo Atiśa and Shākya Chokden biographies printed at Ngamring.[32] The smoking gun, however, is a copy of the three-page catalog of the *Collected Works* titled *Exquisite Goodness* (*Dge legs phul byung ba*); bundled with miscellaneous writings by Künga Drölchok from Drepung, this catalog sheds new light on his printed works. The colophon of *Exquisite Goodness* reads:

> Departed Jamgön Lama, sovereign of siddhas, matchless holder of the extended tradition of the Sakyapa; to the extent that he set forth scholarship, he was none other than a hero who vanquishes a host of demons.[33]

30. Evidence of xylographic works printed elsewhere include Grol mchog, *Paṇḍi ta*, printed in Beijing (Pe cin par khang), identified in the National Library of Mongolia; and Grol mchog 1982, a two-volume set that is a reproduction of the autobiographies printed at Gyantsé printery (Rgyal rtse par khang). These prints were among the earliest writings by Künga Drölchok to circulate outside Tibet. The cover title is a *gsung 'bum*; however, this is an imputation by the publisher: these texts do not indicate being part of a larger collection. Each biography is labeled by a syllable, according to the arrangement: volume 1: a, ā, i, ā'i, u, ū, ri, rā'i, li, lā'i, e, and volume 2: nga, ca, cha, ja. This set was likely a standalone production. Similar Gyantsé prints were produced of other Jonang authors, most notably, printings of Dölpopa's *Ri chos*; see Ngawang Gelek Demo 1970, 212.

31. Ngamring was historically a center of Jonangpa activity from when Dölpopa's disciple Choklé Namgyel was appointed the seat at Ngamring Chödé Monastery in 1347/48, an appointment he held until he went to Jonang in 1354. Works by other Jonang authors were printed at the Jang Ngamring printery (Byang ngam ring gi par khang).

32. *'Bras spungs dpe rnying dkar chag* 2004; and Ducher 2020.

33. Grol mchog, *Rje btsun thams cad mkhen pa'i bka' 'bum*, 2b: *'jam mgon bla mar byon pa sa skya pa'i/ ring lugs zla bral 'dzin la grub pa'i dbang / mkhas pa'i tshad du bzhag pa 'di lta bu/ bdud sde 'joms pa'i dpa' bo min na su.*

Commenting on the meaning of each syllable of Künga Drölchok's name, the colophon continues:

> "Kün" means the whole aggregation of dharmas everywhere.
> "Ga" means being adept at creating joy from bondage.
> "Dröl" means to bestow freedom through the power of Tārā.
> "Chok" means the ingredients of ambrosia that complete one's highest aspirations.
>
> His intelligence is the sun that entirely illuminates a lotus grove. An ocean of the Buddha's teachings, he is the orb of the moon that brings joy! Like a wheel-turning monarch amid his troops, his sublimity among Jetsuns commands admiration.[34]

The colophon details the history of this lost collection:

> Just as white lotuses on a shore come from a lake, Künga Rinchen's aspirations were for all the written volumes to be arranged and produced flawlessly. The Dharma King of Jang [Ngamring] thought, "We must accomplish this without reservation." When the first books were brought from distant places in every direction, the faithful said this "made the sound of a melodious bell ringing." Ngamring provided the requisite tools, which was Rājagṛha. The learned rishi scribes prepared and compiled [the texts] in the area known as "Nyel," which was Vaiśālī.[35] Among them was Tsojang Pakchokpa, chieftain of seven tribes, and there were the rishi scribes, Gong and Sam, and so forth. As for the printing, there was a group of forty master [carvers] who produced, including Tashi Tsewang, Tsewang Dar, and so forth. Prints were made according to the templates.
>
> Through this merit, may the Buddha's teachings flourish, the wishes of the illustrious lama be perfected, the temporal powers

34. Grol mchog, *Rje btsun thams cad mkhen pa'i bka' 'bum*, 2b: *kun tu kun la chos kyi tshogs mang po/ dga' bas dga' bar mdzad mkhan 'ching ba las/ grol de grol ba ster la sgrol ma'i mthus/ mchog la mchog gi bsam rdzogs bdud rtsir sbyar/ blo gros pad tshal yongs kyi gsal byed nyi/ thub bstan rgya mtsho'i dga' byed zla ba'i snying/ sde bcas dbus na 'khor lo sgyur ba bzhin/ bsngags 'os rje btsun nang na dam pa de'i.*

35. Though the blocks were printed in Ngamring, preparations occurred in Nyelyül (Gnyal yul) in southeastern Tibet, along the border of Bhutan, which may have been because of Pema Karpo's ('Brug chen Padma dkar po) involvement.

of the Dharma king and his brother flourish, and the splendor of Amitāyus be fostered!

All the hardship of arranging these [block prints] was cleared away by the one with the name Dragon, who acted with the nature of a supreme ruler and likewise executed with reason to make everything understood.[36]

Ngakwang Künga Rinchen was the Twenty-Third Sakya Trichen (1517–84), a student of Künga Drölchok's, and his efforts brought together the scattered writings to publish a *Collected Works*. The king of Ngamring sponsored the project by providing the requisite tools, equipment, and resources. Written in poetic (*snyan ngag*) style, the colophon alludes to places and episodes in Indian Buddhist history, paralleling Ngamring with Rājagṛha and Nyel with Vaiśālī, and referring to the master scribes as learned rishis (*rig byed mkhas pa*).[37] The one named Dragon is the Fourth Drukchen, Pema Karpo (1527–92), who encouraged Künga Rinchen to undertake the xylography project. This history is confirmed by a passage in the autobiography of Drukchen Pema Karpo where he writes about his relationship with the Sakya Trichen, stating that Künga Rinchen was instrumental in assembling and printing Künga Drölchok's *Collected Works*.[38]

Xylographic prints of Künga Drölchok's works, however, remain scarce, and the lion's share of his extant works are handwritten. Among these extant manuscripts, there is little evidence of an attempt to reproduce by hand a full

36. Grol mchog, *Rje btsun thams cad mkhen pa'i bka' 'bum*, 2b: *bka' yig glegs bam 'khod pa kun/ mi nyams par du sgrub bo zhes/ kun dga' rin chen bzhed pa'i mtsho/ brten la pad dkar 'jug ngogs bzhin/ chos kyi rgyal bo byang pa des bsam pa/ ma lus 'grub bo zhes la pu sta ka/ dang po 'ong 'di yangs pa'i sa phyogs kun/ snyan pa'i dril bsgrags byas zhes dad pa gleng / ngams ring rgyal po'i khab kyi yo byad dang / gnyal zhes bya ba yangs pa can gyi yul/ rig byed mkhas pa'i 'du byed sgrig pa la/ mtsho byang 'phags mchog pa zhes sde bdun pa/ de yi yi ge'i rig byed gong sam sogs/ par la mkhas pa bkra shis tshe dbang dang / tshe dbang dar sogs bcu phrag bzhi yis bsgrubs/ ma phyi bzhin du dag par bgyis pa yin/ gang gi dge bas thub bstan rgyas pa dang / dpal ldan bla ma'i dgongs pa rdzogs pa dang / chos kyi rgyal po mched bcas srid rgyas nas/ tshe dpag med pa'i dpal gyi 'tsho gyur cig / gang gi bkod sogs ngal ba 'di thams cad/ sa la 'brug ba zhes bya ming gsal de/ mi dbang mchog da'i ngo bor byas so zhes/ kun la go bar byed 'di rtags sbyor bzhin.*

37. The phrase, "learned rishi" (*rig byed mkhas pa*), in this context, does not literally mean those learned in Vedic knowledge, per se. The phrase is used as an analogy to acknowledge the high level of learning of these scribes while making a poetic allusion that parallels them with the past scribes of Rājagṛha and Vaiśāli, who were learned in Vedic knowledge and a range of Indic fields of knowledge, as well as exclusively Buddhist knowledge.

38. Padma dkar po 1974, 593 (f. 130).

Collected Works, but rather the witnesses that have emerged are reproductions of select individual writings.[39] One significant finding of Künga Drölchok's handwritten works was made in the Dzamtang Valley of southern Amdo. After our visit to Chölung Jangtsé, later that summer Künga Zangpo and I accrued a cache of rare manuscripts from the private library of the late monk Lama Ngakwang Püntsok.[40] Within the fifteen volumes acquired, two volumes were writings attributed to Künga Drölchok, including manuscripts that show the eclecticism of his oeuvre.[41] Included in this cache are works on tantric ritual and liturgy concerning Hevajra, Vajrayoginī, and the special form of black Cakrasaṃvara that was transmitted via Künga Drölchok and Tāranātha; instructions on the Sixfold Vajrayoga of the Kālacakra; as well as several additional biographies, two Mahāmudra works, miscellaneous poetic songs and praises, a guidebook to nooks at Chölung Jangtsé, a mind-training (*blo sbyong*) manual, and two significant works on Lamdré.[42]

The Analects of Zhentong

The Dzamtang cache of handwritten manuscripts included a work by Künga Drölchok on the Zhentong philosophy of emptiness titled *Analects of Profound Points of the Zhentong View* or, simply, the *Analects of Zhentong*.[43] Throughout the history of Buddhist thought in Tibet, one of the most pervasive doctrinal tensions is that between a view of emptiness as being empty of an intrinsic nature (*svabhāva, rang bzhin*), which is known as Rangtong

39. There are several miscellaneous manuscript compilations in circulation titled *Gsung 'bum* or *Gsung thor bu*; however, none replicate Künga Drölchok's full *Collected Works*. See, for instance, Grol mchog, *Kun dga' grol mchog gi gsung 'bum*, which includes his biographies; Grol mchog, *Kun dga' grol mchog gi gsung thor bu'i skor*, from Central Tibet; and Grol mchog, *Kun dga' grol mchog gi gsung thor bu*, collected by the author from Dzamtang ('Dzam thang).

40. For a fuller account, see Sheehy 2020, 265–66.

41. For some works, see Grol mchog, *Kun dga' grol mchog gi gsung thor bu*.

42. *Theg chen po blo sbyong gi gdams pa* (f. 30); *Bde mchog nag po'i sgrub thabs kyi ngag 'don* (f. 30); *Chos lung byang chub rtse mo'i gnas bshad* (f. 3); *Lta ba'i gnas la mos nyi yis/ 'phyang mor spyod pa las bzlog nas/ 'di nyid rje btsun dgongs pa ces/ mngon sum gsal ba'i nges gsang* (f. 14); *Lam 'bras dka' 'grel sbas don gnad kyi lde mig skal ldan yid kyi nga las 'jam dbyangs bla ma dges pa'i zhal lung sogs bzhugs/ rnal 'byor ba sems kyi mdud grol gyis* (f. 93). A *mgur 'bum* was printed at Ngamring printery; for a listing of songs, see *Gdan sa chen po*, 2: 1419–26. Colophons of these works indicate the places where he wrote, including Serdokchen Monastery, Richö Chenmo hermitage at Jomonang, and Chölung Jangtsé Monastery.

43. Grol mchog, *Gzhan stong*, 1–15.

(*rang stong*, "intrinsic emptiness") on the one hand; and a view of emptiness as being empty of everything other than the continual luminous buddha-nature (*tathāgatagarbha, de bzhin gshes pa'i snying po*), which is known as Zhentong.[44] The Jonangpa scholar Dölpopa Sherab Gyeltsen (Dol po pa Shes rab rgyal mtshan, 1292–1361) posited a Zhentong view and opposed an exclusive Rangtong interpretation of emptiness. Contemporary scholarship has suggested that Jonangpa authors after Dölpopa Sherab Gyeltsen's immediate students did not compose works on Zhentong, until Tāranātha, and that a lack of works by Künga Drölchok on this hallmark Jonangpa view is notable.[45] An exception is the Sakya scholar Shākya Chokden (1428–1507), who wrote extensively on Zhentong. Künga Drölchok was heir to Shākya Chokden's intellectual tradition, making him scholastically prepared and historically situated to author Zhentong works.[46] The proposed logic for a lack of writing on Zhentong by Künga Drölchok was that he was more interested in fostering social tolerance than prioritizing a single view or tradition, which is indicative of the historical circumstances of the Jonangpas after the highly polemicized fifteenth century. Given that Künga Drölchok's Zhentong work is not well cited in later Jonang writings or by other Zhentong exegetes, until this finding, it is reasonable to infer that he did not write on Zhentong. An analysis of his *Analects of Zhentong*, however, confirms that Künga Drölchok favored the Jonang philosophical position of Zhentong over normative views of Rangtong adherents.[47]

Written in a pithy style, the *Analects of Zhentong* fits within the genre of analects (*khol byung*), which compile key philosophical excerpts using syllogisms, declaratives, references to Buddhist canonical works, and poetic allusions. As an example of a work from Künga Drölchok's lost oeuvre, which was recently found, here are a few select stanzas in translation to provide a sense of his writing style and this important philosophical work:[48]

44. On the philosophy of Zhentong, see Mathes and Sheehy 2019, 1–2 and 7–16.

45. Stearns 2010, 67, writes about Künga Drölchok, "What is striking is the apparent lack of any strong attempt to spread the shentong view of Dolpopa." See also Stearns 2010, 60; and for discussion of Zhentong after Dölpopa, see Nyingcha 2019.

46. In the supplication to the Zhentong lineage, Tāranātha cites Künga Drölchok after his teacher Serdok Paṇchen Dönyö Druppa (Gser mdog Paṇ chen Don yod grub pa), who was a disciple of Shākya Chokden. Tāranātha, *Zab mo*, 4: 487. On Shākya Chokden, see Komarovski 2011, 127–36.

47. Another philosophical work by Künga Drölchok has also recently become available that demonstrates his Zhentong position, and specifically his critique of Sakya Rangtong exegetes. See Grol mchog, *Rang gzhan*, 7–8.

48. The colophon reads, "These discursive ideas were brought together by the monk of pro-

From without beginning, while arriving, there is going without end—
nothing comes nor goes; nothing is unbound nor unfree.
Because stains are adventitious, supports for bondage and freedom are even devoid of roots in the ground.
This is the ground of all saṃsāra and nirvāṇa.[49]

The opening stanza evokes the paradox of movement analyzed in Nāgārjuna's *Verses of the Middle Way*, the *Mūlamadhyamkakakārikā*: "If there is coming and going along a path, there must be the act of moving; however, nothing moves on a path already traversed, since movement has already occurred, yet on a path not traversed, no movement has occurred."[50]

The *Analects of Zhentong* continues:

Everything that appears and anything that cannot be observed
is the body of phenomena—radiant, intrinsically cognizant pristine awareness.
Because it's devoid of arising and ceasing,
it's the fact that relies on the single constant.

Immutable, everlasting spontaneity—
because it's indivisible from every facet, it's singular.
Invincible to others, it's the sovereign of independence.
Not touched by origin stains, it's utter quiescence.

When its manifold capacities and marvelous qualities are realized,
it brings forth the fruits of manifest longing.
A wish-fulfilling jewel,
it's as natural as one's own face.[51]

---

digious learning, Künga Drölchok Losel Gyatso" (*zhes mang du thos pa'i btsun pa kun dga' grol mchog blo gsal rgya mtsho'i sdes yid dpyod du bsdebs pa'o*). Grol mchog, *Gzhan stong*, 85b.

49. Grol mchog, *Gzhan stong*, 84a: *thog med las 'ongs tha ma med 'gro yang / 'gro 'ong med cing ma bcings ma grol med/ glo bur dri mas bcings dang grol ba'i brtan/ gzhi rtsa bral yang 'khor 'das kun gyi gzhi.*

50. Siderits and Katsura 2013, 32–33.

51. Grol mchog, *Gzhan stong*, 84a–84b: *cir yang snang zhing gang du'ang ma dmigs pa/ rang rig ye shes 'od gsal chos kyi sku/ skye 'gag bral bas rtag gcig brtan pa'i don/ 'gyur med lhun gyis grub pa'i g.yung drung ni/ kun du rnam dbyer med pas gcig pu ste/ gzhan gyis gzhom med rang dbang can gyi bdag / dri mas ma reg gdod nas rnam par zhi/ ngo mtshar yon tan du ma'i nus par brtan/ gang gis rtogs na mngon 'dod 'bras ster ba'i/ yid bzhin nor bu gnyug ma'i rang zhal 'di.*

These stanzas introduce key Zhentong concepts and vocabulary—namely, that the body of phenomena (Skt. *dharmakaya* = Tib. *chos kyi sku*) is inseparable from reflexive, intrinsically cognizant pristine awareness (*rang rig ye shes*). Künga Drölchok states that these are a single constant (*rtag gcig*), not subject to transient fluctuations. Identified by Tāranātha as one of the critical distinctions between the Zhentong views of Dölpopa and Shākya Chokden in his *Twenty-One Distinctions of the Profound Meaning*, the stance that pristine awareness (Skt. *jñāna* = Tib. *ye shes*) is ontologically continuous follows that of Dölpopa.[52] From the onset, Künga Drölchok's interpretation that pristine awareness is constant aligns him with the prevailing Jonang view of Zhentong. Without naming it, Künga Drölchok alludes to the cardinal doctrine of Zhentong—that of buddha-nature, an indwelling heart of buddhahood—stating that it's as natural as one's own face.

The *Analects of Zhentong* continues:

> The expanse and awareness, distinctly, are not nothingness—
> and while their own inherent nature is not contrived,
> like hues and angles of a variegated crystal,
> types of the three vehicles are distinguished
> without diminishing each type.[53]

Künga Drölchok asserts a double negation to affirm that the expanse (*dbyings*) and awareness (*rig*), key concepts for understanding Zhentong, are not nothingness. Retorting a critique of nihilism, he pivots to repurpose a key Rangtong concept—the axial insight of Rangtong Madhyamaka philosophy that all conditioned phenomena are devoid of an inherent nature (Skt. *svabhāva* = Tib. *rang bzhin*)—stating that unlike the inherent nature of phenomena, the inherent nature of the expanse and awareness are not contrived. With the simile of a variegated crystal refracted by light, he affirms that the "single constant" is manifold. Making a hermeneutical point about difference, he holds true to a Zhentong view, a proto-nonsectarian commentarial point. To illustrate, he writes:

52. The colophon title is *Zab don khyad par nyer gcig pa*, Tāranātha, *Zab don*, 795. This is the sixth of Tāranātha's twenty-one points of comparison between these two scholars. See also Mathes 2019, 204 and 210.

53. Grol mchog, *Gzhan stong*, 84b: *dbyings rig so sor chad pa ma yin zhing / rang gi rang bzhin bcos su med na yang / chu shel sna tshogs tshon dang 'phrad pa ltar / rigs su ma chad theg gsum rigs dbye byas.*

For instance, according to venerable types of desireless *śrāvaka*
and Yogācārins, particulars of the sense fields of mind
and capacities of an undissipated universal substrate
are explained by some types to be the expanse of phenomena.
Distinct vehicles have distinct presentations.

Zhentong is isolated from the stain of concepts.
Rangtong is free from elaborations of an inherent nature.[54]

The example draws from Indian Buddhist doctrinal discourses that dispute the origins of the mental faculty, referencing how *śrāvaka*, adherents of early Abhidharma tenets, posit the sense fields of mind (Skt. *mano-āyatana* = Tib. *yid kyi skye mched*) to be the source of cognition, while adherents of the Yogācāra school posit the universal substrate (Skt. *ālaya* = Tib. *kun gzhi*).[55] Both, however, reference the expanse of phenomena (Skt. *dharmadhātu* = Tib. *chos dbyings*) to be the source, applying the technical term distinctly.[56] Künga Drölchok cites this example to make the point that, like Rangtong and Zhentong, discourses within Buddhism are contextually situated. The *Analects of Zhentong* continues:

To cease the mind is manifestation of the body [of phenomena] –
Without everlasting pure awareness, manifestation would be totally amazing!
The stainless body of phenomena is endowed with fivefold pristine awareness.[57]

The first line in this stanza paraphrases Candrakīrti's *Entry to the Middle Way*, the *Madhyamakāvatāra*, that asserts by ceasing the mind, the body

54. Grol mchog, *Gzhan stong*, 84b: *'on kyang nyan thos ma chags 'phags rigs dang / rnal 'byor spyod pas yid kyi skye mched kyi/ khyad par kun gzhi zag med nus pa dang / la lar chos dbyings rig(s) su gsungs pa ni/ theg pa so so'i rnam bzhag so so yin/ rnam rtog dri mas dben pa gzhan stong ste/ rang bzhin spros dang bral ba rang stong yin.*

55. On the meaning of *āyatana* in early Buddhism and arguments made by Sautāntrikas and Vijñānavādins, see Guenther 1976, 16 and 172.

56. In the *Abhidharmasamuccaya*, Vijñānavādins also apply the term *dharmāyatana*, meaning a phenomenally experiential field, distinct from the field of tangible sense perceptions (*rūpāyatana*). See Guenther 1976, 161.

57. Grol mchog, *Gzhan stong*, 85b: *sems 'gags sku yi mngon sum mdzad pa 'di/ rig pa gtan med mngon sum ngo mtshar che/ chos sku dri med ye shes lnga ldan 'di.*

of phenomena manifests.[58] Künga Drölchok refutes Candrakīrti's assertion, stating that without everlasting awareness, manifestation of the body of phenomena would be truly amazing, meaning that the body of phenomena cannot manifest without awareness. He juxtaposes the distinction between the mind (*sems*) and pure awareness (*rig pa*) to contrast Rangtong with Zhentong; while the mind is temporary, awareness is everlasting. The body of phenomena, which he synthesized in his opening stanzas with intrinsically cognizant pristine awareness, is moreover endowed with the five displays of pristine awareness.[59] With this, Künga Drölchok retorts a canonical Rangtong Madhyamaka source to articulate the manifold effulgence of Zhentong.

To Fill a Lacuna

Künga Drölchok's literary oeuvre is wide ranging, and with his writing on Zhentong, it's truly eclectic. Works by Künga Drölchok, both prints and manuscripts, were scattered in libraries around the world, without a clear indication that a coherent *Collected Works* was printed in Tibet. An analysis of the extant block prints, including prints newly available from inside Tibet, provide evidence to conclude that a *Collected Works* of Künga Drölchok's writings was printed at the Jang Ngamring printery. The xylography project to print his *Collected Works* was undertaken by his student Künga Rinchen, the Sakya Trichen, with the support of Drukchen Pema Karpo, under the patronage of the king of Ngamring. That Künga Drölchok's works were printed by the efforts of his Sakya and Drukpa Kagyü contemporaries, and not Jonangpas, shows that Jonangpas were not in the position to undertake this grand production at that moment in their history. Among the recently unearthed works by Künga Drölchok is his *Analects of Zhentong*. Though writings on Zhentong by Jonang authors are scarce during the sixteenth century, Künga Drölchok's work fills a long-standing lacuna in the intellectual and literary history of the Zhentong philosophy of emptiness in Tibet. Using philosophical argumentation and poetic allusion, Künga Drölchok makes vivid his dexterity as an author and fluency in Zhentong thinking to assert a Zhentong view that aligns with his Jonangpa forebearer Dölpopa.

58. Candrakīrti 1985, 432, 11.17–18: *bsregs pas zhi de rgyal rnams chos sku ste/ de tshe skye ba med cing 'gag pa med/ sems 'gags pas de sku yis mngon sum mdzad/ zhi sku dpag bsam shing ltar gsal gyur zhing / yid bzhin nor bu ji bzhin rnam mi rtog / 'go grol bar du 'jig rten 'byor slad rtag / 'di nis pros dang bral la sang bar 'gyur.*

59. These five displays of pristine awareness (*ye shes lnga*) are: (1) *chos dbyings kyi ye shes*, (2) *me long lta ba'i ye shes*, (3) *mnyam pa nyid kyi ye shes*, (4) *so sor rtog pa'i ye shes*, and (5) *bya ba grub pa'i ye shes*.

References

Tibetan Works

Blo gros grags pa, Ngag dbang. 1992. *Jo nang chos 'byung ba'i sgron me*. Beijing: Khrung go'i bod kyi shes rig dpe skrun khang.

Blo gsal Bstan skyong. 1971. *Rang gi rnam thar du byas pa shel dkar me long*. In *Dpal ldan zhwa lu pa'i bstan pa la bka' drin chen ba'i skyes bu dam pa rnams kyi rnam thar lo rgyus ngo mtshar dad pa'i 'jug ngogs*, 473–678. Leh: S. W. Tashigangpa.

'Bras spungs dpe rnying dkar chag, vols. 1–2. 2004. Edited by Dpal brtegs bod yig dpe rnying zhib 'jug khang. Beijing: Mi rigs dpe skrun khang.

Candrakīrti. 1985. *Dbu ma la 'jug pa*. In *Bstan 'gyur*. Reproduced by Delhi Karmapae Choedhey. Sde dge: Sde dge par khang. BDRC W23703.

Chos kyi 'bung gnas, Si tu Paṇ chen. 1990. *Ta'i si tu'bod pa karma bstan pa'i nyin byed kyi rang tshul drangs por brjod pa dri bral shel gyi me long*. In *Ta'i si tiu pa kun mkhyen chos kyi 'byung gnas bstan pa'i nyin byed kyi bka' 'bum*, vol. 14, 1–741. Sansal: Palpung Sungrab Nyamso Khang.

Gdan sa chen po dpal ldan sa skya dgon gyi dpe rnying dkar chag. 2018. Vols. 1–5. Sakya: Sa skya sgo rum rig gnas rtsom sgrig khang. BDRC W3CN8601.

Grol mchog, Kun dga'. 1982. *Dpal ldan kun dga' grol mchog blo gsal rgya mtsho'i sde'i gsung 'bum*, vol. 2. Block print, Rgyal rtse par khang. New Delhi: Tibet House.

———. 1985. *Rigs ldan chos kyi rgyal po byang bdag rnam rgyal grags bzang gi rnam par thar pa rab bsngags snyan pa'i 'brug sgra*. Kansu: Kan su'u zhing chen grangs nyung mi rigs kyi gna' dpe dag sgrib gzhung las khang and Kan lho bod sman zhib 'jug khang.

———. 1995. *Shākya mchog ldan gyi rnam thar zhib mo rnam par 'byed pa*. In *The Complete Works (Gsung 'bum) of Gśer-mdog paṇ-chen śākya-mchog-ldan*. Reproduced from the unique manuscript prepared in the eighteenth century at the order of Rje Sakya-rin-chen, the Ninth Rje Mkhan-po Bhutan. Preserved at Pha-jo-sdins 'og-min-gnyis-pa Monastery. Bhutan: Ngawang Topgyal.

———. 1999. *Zab khrid brgya dang brgyad kyi yi ge*. In *Gdams ngag rin po che'i mdzod*, vol. 18, edited by 'Jam mgon Kong sprul, 127–354. Block print. Delhi: Shechen Publications.

———. 2005. *Rje btsun kun dga' grol mchog gi phyi nang gsang gsum gyi rnam thar*. Beijing: Mi rigs dpe skrun khang.

———. *Dam pa'i chos kyi thob yig bstan pa'i nor rdzas*. Handwritten manuscript. BDRC W1KG18291.

———. *Dam pa'i chos kyi thob yig bstan pa'i nor rdzas*. Block print. Library of the Istituto Italiano per l'Africa e l'Oriente. BDRC W1KG18290.

———. *Dpal gsang ba 'dus pa ye shes zhabs lugs kyi rim lnga'i khrid*. In *Kun dga' grol mchog gi gsung thor bu*. Handwritten manuscript, 'Dzam thang. Collected by Jonang Foundation. BDRC W2MS2257.

———. *Gzhan stong lta ba'i zab gnad khol byung*. Unpublished manuscript. Collected by Jonang Foundation.

———. *'Jam dbyangs kun dga' grol mchog gi thun mongs ma yin pa'i rnam par thar pa myong rgyan gyi me tog*. Unpublished manuscript. BDRC W3CN2594.

———. *Jo bo rje dpal ldan ā ti sha'i rnam thar don bsdu*. Block print. Ngam ring: Byang ngam ring par khang. BDRC W26572.

———. *Kun dga' grol mchog gi gsung 'bum*. Handwritten manuscript. BDRC W00KG04004.

———. *Kun dga' grol mchog gi gsung thor bu*. Handwritten manuscript, 'Dzam thang. Collected by Jonang Foundation. BDRC W2MS2257.

———. *Kun dga' grol mchog gi gsung thor bu'i skor*. Handwritten manuscript. BDRC W1CZ1130.

———. *Lam 'bras dka' 'grel sbas don gnad kyi lde mig skal ldan yid kyi nga las 'jam dbyangs bla ma dges pa'i zhal lung sogs*. Unpublished manuscript. Collected by Jonang Foundation. BDRC W2MS2257.

———. *Myong ba rgyan gyi me tog*. Unpublished manuscript. Collected by Jonang Foundation. BDRC W00KG0638.

———. *Paṇdi ta 'bar ba'i gsto bo'i rtogs pa brjod pa'i yal 'dab sogs*. Block print. National Library of Mongolia. BDRC W1NLM555.

———. *Paṇḍi ta chen po shākya mchog ldan gyi rnam par thar pa zhib mo rnam par 'byed pa*. Block print. Ngam ring: Byang ngam ring par khang. BDRC W25586.

———. *Rang gzhan gyi lta ba'i gnas mgnon sum ston pa'i rab byed*. Handwritten manuscript. BDRC W8LS29186.

———. *Rje btsun thams cad mkhen pa'i bka' 'bum par du bsgrubs pa'i dkar chag dge legs phul byung ba*. Block print. Ngam ring: Byang ngam ring par khang.

Hor rgyal sogs kyis sgrig bsgyur byas. 2000. *Jo nang dkar chag shel dkar phreng mdzes*. Beijing: Mi rigs dpe skrun khang.

Ngawang Gelek Demo. 1970. *Three Dkar chag's*. New Delhi: Gedan Sungrab Minyam Gyunphel.

Padma dkar po, 'Brug chen. 1974. *Sems dpa'i chen po padma dkar po'i rnam thar thugs rje chen po'i zlos gar*. In *Kun mkhyen padma dkar po'i gsung 'bum*, vol. 3, 1–597. Darjeeling: Kargyud Sungrab Nyamso Khang.

Tāranātha. 1985. *Zab don nyer gcig pa*. In *Rje btsun tā ra nā tha'i gsung 'bum*, vol. 4, 781–95. Leh: Namgyal and Tsewang Taru.

———. 1985. *Zab mo gzhan stong dbu ma'i brgyud 'debs*. In *Rje btsun tā ra nā tha'i gsung 'bum*, vol. 4, 483–89. Leh: Namgyal and Tsewang Taru.

Secondary Sources

Chandra, Lokesh. 1963. *Materials for a History of Tibetan Literature*. New Delhi: International Academy of Indian Culture.

Ducher, Cécile. 2020. "Goldmine of Knowledge: The Collections of the Gnas bcu lha khang in 'Bras spungs Monastery." *Revue d'Etudes Tibétaines* 55: 121–39.

Guenther, Herbert V. 1976. *Philosophy and Psychology in the Abhidharma*. Berkeley, CA: Shambhala Publications.

Komarovski, Yaroslav. 2011. *Vision of Unity: The Golden Paṇḍita Shakya Chokden's New Interpretation of Yogācāra and Madhyamaka*. Albany: State University of New York Press.

Kongtrul Lodrö Taye, Jamgön. 2020. *Jonang: The One Hundred and Eight Teaching Manuals*. Translated by Gyurme Dorje. Boulder, CO: Snow Lion Publications.

van der Kuijp, Leonard W. J. 1983. *Contributions to the Development of Tibetan Buddhist Epistemology: From the Eleventh to the Thirteenth Century*. Alt-und Neuindische Studien 26. Wiesbaden: F. Steiner.

———. 1995. "Fourteenth Century Tibetan Cultural History VI: The Transmission of Indian Buddhist Pramāṇavāda according to the Early Tibetan *Gsan yig-s**." *Asiatische Studien: Zeitschrift der Schweizerischen Asiengesellschaft. Études Asiatiques: Revue de la Société Suisse-Asie* 49.4: 919–41.

———. 2010. "Faulty Transmissions: Some Notes on Tibetan Textual Criticism and the Impact of Xylography." In *Edition, éditions: L'écrit au Tibet, évolution et devenir*, edited by Anne Chayet, Cristina Scherrer-Schaub, Françoise Robin, and Jean-Luc Achard, 442–64. Munich: Indus Verlag.

———. 2016a. "Reconsidering the Dates of Dol po pa Shes rab rgyal mtshan's (1292–1361) *Ri chos nges don rgya mtsho* and the *Bka' bsdu bzhi pa'i don*." *Journal of Tibetology* 14: 115–59.

———. 2016b. "On the Life and Oeuvre of the Jo nang pa Scholar Zhang ston Rgya bo Bsod nams grags pa (1292–1370)." *Journal of Tibetan and Himalayan Studies* 1.1: 17–31.

Mathes, Klaus-Dieter. 2019. "Tāranātha's *Twenty-One Differences with Regard to the Profound Meaning*: Comparing the Views of the Two Zhentong Masters Dolpopa and Shakya Chokden." In Sheehy and Mathes, *The Other Emptiness*, 197–233.

Mathes, Klaus-Dieter, and Michael R. Sheehy. 2019. "*The Philosophical Grounds and Literary History of Zhentong*." In Sheehy and Mathes, *The Other Emptiness*, 1–27.

Nyingcha, Dorje. 2019. "Buddha-Nature in Garungpa Lhai Gyaltsen's *Lamp That Illuminates the Expanse of Reality* and among Tibetan Intellectuals." In Sheehy and Mathes, *The Other Emptiness*, 95–113.

Sheehy, Michael R. 2010. "The Jonangpa after Tāranātha: Auto/biographical Writings on the Transmission of Esoteric Buddhist Knowledge in Seventeenth Century Tibet." *The Bulletin of Tibetology* 45.1: 9–24. Sikkim: Namgyal Institute.

———. 2019a. "The Zhentong Lion Roars: Dzamtang Khenpo Lodro Drakpa and the Jonang Scholastic Renaissance." In Sheehy and Mathes, *The Other Emptiness*, 351–77.

———. 2019b. "The Case of the Missing Shangpa in Tibet." In *Reasons and Lives in Buddhist Traditions: Studies in Honor of Matthew Kapstein*, edited by Daniel Arnold, Cecile Ducher, and Pierre-Julien Harter, 113–28. Boston: Wisdom Publications.

———. 2020. "Materializing Dreams and Omens: The Autobiographical Subjectivity of the Tibetan Yoginī Kun dga' 'Phrin las dbang mo (1585–1668)." *Revue d'Etudes Tibétaines* 56: 263–92.

Sheehy, Michael R., and Klaus-Dieter Mathes, eds. 2019. *The Other Emptiness: Rethinking the Zhentong Buddhist Discourse in Tibet*. Albany: State University of New York Press.

Siderits, Mark, and Shōryū Katsura. 2013. *Nāgārjuna's Middle Way: Mūlamadhyamakakārikā*. Boston: Wisdom Publications.

Smith, E. Gene. 2001. *Among Tibetan Texts: History of Literature of the Himalayan Plateau*. Edited by Kurtis R. Schaeffer. Studies in Indian and Tibetan Buddhism. Boston: Wisdom Publications.

———. 2001a. "The Shangs pa Bka' brgyud Tradition." In *Among Tibetan Texts*, 53–57.

———. 2001b. "The Diaries of Si tu Paṇ chen." In *Among Tibetan Texts,* 87–96.
———. 2001c. "'Jam mgon Kong sprul and the Nonsectarian Movement." In *Among Tibetan Texts,* 235–72.
———. 2004. "Banned Books in the Tibetan Speaking Lands." In *Symposium on Contemporary Tibetan Studies Collected Papers: 21st Century Tibet Issue,* 186–96. Taipei: Mongolian and Tibetan Affairs Commission.
Stearns, Cyrus. 2010. *The Buddha from Dolpo: A Study of the Life and Thought of the Tibetan Master Dölpopa Sherab Gyaltsen.* Ithaca, NY: Snow Lion Publications.

Insects Give Advice to the Scholar and Siddha Kalden Gyatso (1607–77)

Victoria Sujata

THE ANIMAL REALM is considered among the dreaded lowest three of the six realms of existence for sentient beings, just above the realms of hell beings and hungry ghosts. The physical level of suffering of animals is great because they eat one another, they are stupid, they feel hot or cold, they have hunger and thirst, and they are exploited or forced to work. But most objectionable about the animal state is that they are not able to understand the Dharma or possess virtues such as faith, wisdom, or renunciation; and it has been lamented that they cannot even recite *Oṃ maṇi padme hūṃ*. This means that they tend to wander from lower realm to lower realm and don't have the means to consciously elevate themselves into one of the higher states to move toward enlightenment.[1] For these reasons, rebirth in the animal realm is thought to be terribly unfortunate. The most desirable realm of existence into which to be reborn is the human realm, since it affords one the possibility of making spiritual gains and attaining enlightenment.[2]

It is in contradiction to this context that the seventeenth-century scholar and siddha-to-be Kalden Gyatso (Skal ldan rgya mtsho) wrote two dialogues with insects in the form of cycles of *gur* (*mgur*)—or songs of realization—in 1633 when he was twenty-seven,[3] playfully portraying the insects as articulate, patient spiritual masters, and himself as a haughty, resistant student, slow to learn but finally convinced by their teachings. In the dialogues, the insects,

I thank Lobsang Chödrak of Repgong and K. E. Duffin for offering many helpful suggestions for the creation of this paper.

1. Richards 2006, 272; for more about the suffering of animals, see 346–51; and Ohnuma 2017, 5–23.

2. I use the terms "animal" and "human" in the conventional way here. Obviously, humans are animals too, and many authors correctly use terms like "nonhuman animals" to refer to animals other than humans. However, in Tibetan distinctions between "animal" (*dud 'gro*) and "human being" (*mi*) are well understood, and I will comply with that tradition.

3. Byang chub mi la 1990, 23–24.

though in animal bodies, seem unexpectedly content, and are intelligent, strong-willed, and articulate. They have faith in the Dharma, the wisdom to understand and preach it, and an appreciation of the benefits of renunciation.[4]

In one of the two *gur* cycles, bees approach Kalden Gyatso spontaneously and lecture him because all he cares about is gain and esteem and his life has been senseless. The bees state boldly that they know more. They go on to criticize him and other corrupt clergy and tell him that although he knows something about the Dharma, he does not know how to practice it, and is therefore a terrible teacher. They advise him to pray to the lama daily, to stringently follow the lama's oral instructions, and to be rigid with his vows. The bees tell him that if he does so, he will receive the lama's blessings and be led to the city of liberation and paradise. Kalden Gyatso depicts himself as gradually being convinced by the bees. The dialogue closes as he enthusiastically tells them that they are right, and that he's going to go off to a hermitage to meditate. Thus he sets off in a new direction in life thanks to the bees' crucial advice.

The other dialogue is between Kalden Gyatso and lice, fleas, and lice eggs. He reacts angrily to them being on his robe, and tells them he wants to kill them. The overall theme of the insects' advice is karma, and they respond that he should not eat slaughtered animals or funeral repasts, and should soar on up above saṃsāra. As in the other *gur* cycle, he decides to change the course of his life and behavior based on what he has learned from the insects, and goes off to a hermitage to perform deep Dharma practice.

Kalden Gyatso's dialogues depict the insects as his teachers.[5] This is especially surprising since by the time he composed the dialogues he had already undergone rigorous traditional training for nine years at the prestigious Ganden (Dga' ldan) Monastery near Lhasa;[6] had received numerous instructions, textual transmissions, and empowerments from lamas and scholars; and had been fully ordained by the First Paṇchen Lama in the Jokhang, the most sacred temple in all of Tibet.[7] Moreover, after returning home to Amdo he founded a philosophical college,[8] and was growing in fame as a teacher and lama in his

4. This two-pronged approach on how animals are presented in Buddhist literature—negative and positive—has been remarked on by Schmithausen and Maithrimurthi 2009, 100; Ohnuma 2017, 41–42; and Chapple 1992, 53.

5. Some 170 years or so later, Shabkar (Zhabs dkar, 1781–1851) wrote a *gur* that imitates Kalden Gyatso's conversation with bees, but Shabkar's bees pay homage to him rather than instructing him. Ricard 1994, 162–63.

6. Byang chub mi la 1990, 6–9.

7. Byang chub mi la 1990, 10.

8. Thösamling (Thos bsam gling) at Rongwo Monastery was founded in 1630 when Kalden Gyatso was twenty-four. Byang chub mi la 1990, 66.

own right. So what was he doing following spiritual instructions given to him by insects?

In *Tibetan Songs of Realization*, I provided a stylistic analysis of how the form of these dialogues, along with their prosody and stanza patterns, enhances the basic message of going to a solitary place to practice the Dharma.[9] In this paper, I provide updated translations of the two dialogues,[10] and expand our understanding of them by exploring what might have attracted Kalden Gyatso to write them.[11] Obviously, we can never know his intentions, but I explore six possibilities.

I began my search for clues by looking at other writings up through Kalden Gyatso's time related to *gur*—such as songs and verse by Indian and Tibetan siddhas and teachers, biographies, and Indian classical verse. My aim was to see how they refer to bees, fleas, lice, and lice eggs, and what we can learn from that.

Bees are frequently used as a motif to express beauty. For example, in the *Kāvyādarśa*, the influential treatise on Indian poetics, poetic figures sometimes use bees to symbolize women's (or men's) eyes and promiscuity because of their attraction to many flowers. Buddhist songwriters also frequently employ bee imagery to express beauty: bees are in descriptions of exquisitely lovely hermitages, and are used for didactic purposes—the frailty of bees and flowers illustrates teachings on impermanence, and the attraction of bees to honey demonstrates the downfalls of attachment. While references to bees for various reasons are plentiful up through Kalden Gyatso's time, references to lice and insects in general are rare, and when they do appear it is clear that they are disliked. For instance, after Milarepa had been cheated out of his father's fortune by his wicked aunt and uncle, he has to resort to begging. He finds himself at the entrance to his wicked aunt's tent and describes himself as being "like an insect dying at the opening to an anthill."[12] In the dialogues the insects are anthropomorphic and articulate. I have not in my preliminary search of the periods up through Kalden Gyatso's time found any other anthropomorphic insects.[13]

9. Sujata 2005, 97, 103, 108–11.

10. I thank Brill for the right to reuse my translations of the two dialogues in Sujata 2005, which in any case appear here in a much-updated form.

11. They are very different from anything else in his 242 collected *gur*, in which bees and lice are mentioned briefly only a few times, fleas are hardly mentioned, if at all, and lice eggs are not present.

12. Lhalungpa 1985, 18, 109.

13. For fascinating tales in Chinese literature about anthropomorphic insects speaking back and forth, see Idema 2019. These seem numerous when compiled in a book, being from all literary periods and suggested by many people, but they are actually very rare.

When I expanded my search to include all animals in the genres mentioned so far, I discovered some examples of unusual interactions with humans. A starving dog is saved by Kukkuripa and they live together in a cave for years. When he shows exceptional selflessness to her, she suddenly turns into a ḍākinī and gives him some crucial teachings that facilitate his enlightenment.[14] A pigeon into which Marpa's dying son has transferred his consciousness then follows Marpa's instructions to fly to India and makes a second transference into the corpse of a young boy.[15] A flock of pigeons bow and circumambulate Milarepa and then turn into devas to receive his teachings.[16] But unlike the insects in the dialogues, these animals turn into their *real* forms—a ḍākinī, a human, and devas—before speaking.[17]

But there is another genre in which anthropomorphic, articulate animals are actually the norm: Tibetan folktales.[18] Among them are inspiring stories of animals rescuing other animals, such as the story of the seven sheep carrying the body of their beloved, deceased master to Lhasa to say the proper prayers for him. On the way, a wolf announces that he is going to eat them, but they plead for the wolf to wait for some months until they are on their return trip, and they make a firm promise to meet him at the very same spot, where he can eat them and their yet-to-be-born seven lambs. On the way home, though terribly sad, they firmly intend to keep their word, but a hare intervenes and tricks the wolf. The wolf ends up dead, and the sheep and lambs are saved.[19]

There are also some folktales of animals causing humans to reform, such as the story of the clever rabbit. A very corrupt husband and wife are about to kill a rabbit in revenge for having exposed an earlier crime of theirs. The rabbit confuses the couple so they mistakenly break all the earthen pots in their kitchen and, out of frustration, end up deciding that it would be easier to reform.[20] These stories differ from those of Kalden Gyatso; here, wicked humans who reform seem to do it because of punishment rather than inspiration, and animal perpetrators usually end up dead.

A related genre in which anthropomorphic, articulate animals frequently

14. Dowman 1985, 199–200.

15. Nālandā 1995, 162–76.

16. Chang 1989, 88–93.

17. Animals speaking in divinations are beyond the scope of this paper.

18. I thank Per Sørenson for pointing this out to me.

19. Norbu Chöphel 1984, 76–80. See also a story about a hare who rescues a deer from a tiger, and a story about a hare who rescues a wild donkey (*rkyang*) from a wolf and a fox. O'Connor 1992, 19–25, 48–52.

20. Sherab Gyatso n.d.

feature is the Jātaka tales, stories of the Buddha's previous lives as a bodhisattva. Oral antecedents of the Jātaka tales have been hypothesized to be pre-Buddhist, possibly originating in folktales or fairy tales, and later appropriated by Buddhism as teaching tools.[21] Frozen in writing, they have come down to us in sources such as the Pāli collection of over five hundred tales;[22] and the *Jātakamālā*,[23] a small collection of rewritten, elaborated tales composed by Āryaśūra around the fourth century.[24]

Among the Jātaka tales, there are many stories in which humans are inspired to reform their corrupt ways through interaction with articulate, anthropomorphic, ethical animals who teach them verbally and through their behavior.[25] For example, there once was a golden goose-king who was caught in a snare by a hunter through lure and deceit. The goose-king's general—albeit free—nevertheless insists on staying with him. By their actions they inspire the hunter to repent and free the goose-king. They are then resolute about accompanying the hunter unfettered back to the royal palace so they can meet the king who had ordered their capture, and the hunter can receive the promised reward. The king, in turn, is so inspired by their behavior and the teachings the goose-king imparts to him about ruling with virtue and justice for the common good that he reforms his ways.[26]

The *Jātakamālā* was translated from Sanskrit into Tibetan before the early ninth century, and by the eleventh century came to be relied upon by the Kadampa school as one of its prestigious six fundamental treatises (Bka' gdams pa gzhung drug) at that very decisive period of Tibetan Buddhist history.[27] It continues to be highly revered in formal monastic writings and sermons. Moreover,

21. Schmithausen and Maithrimurthi 2009, 100; Ohnuma 2017, 43; Khoroche 1989, vii, xiv.

22. For an English translation, see Cowell 1994.

23. This was translated into Tibetan. For an English translation, see Khoroche 1989.

24. Kapstein 2020, 438.

25. For more examples of animals who inspire humans to reform, see Cowell 1994, 1:36–42 (#12: deer); 1:51–53 (#18: goat); 1:58–61 (#22: dog); 1:61–63 (#23: horse); 1:63–64 (#24, similar to #23); 1:300–302 (#140: crow); 2:23–26 (#159: peacock); 3:120–23 (#359: stag); 4:210–16 (#491: peacock, similar to #159 but with a different beginning); 4:257–63 (#501: deer); 5:59–64 (#521: owl, mynah, and parrot); 5:175–86 (#533: goose); and 5:186–202 (#534, similar to #533).

26. Khoroche 1989, 140–52 (#22 in Khoroche's numbering, which does not reflect the original order). For a very similar story in the Pāli collection, see Cowell 1994, 4:264–67 (#502). For another tale about an animal inspiring a human to reform that is in both collections, see the story of the deer who saved the life of a king who had fallen into a chasm while chasing the deer to kill it. Khoroche 1989, 173–77 (#25); Cowell 1994, 4:166–74 (#483).

27. Kapstein 2020, 438–39; Kapstein 2013, 102.

the tales may well have been enjoyed informally in Tibet, since sharing folktales socially has been, until recently, "one of the main sources of recreation and pastime."[28] The Buddhist-appropriated, charming animal stories, described as "highly sophisticated doctrinal medicine with the sweet coating of entertainment," are known to have crucial didactic purposes.[29] Since Kalden Gyatso's dialogues share important aspects with this popular genre, we can assume that his dialogues were also written with the aim of ethical education in mind.

Another reason why Kalden Gyatso may have chosen to write the dialogues was his interest in experimenting with different literary styles. His songs show a wide range of influences from Tibetan folk songs all the way to the *Kāvyādarśa*.[30] He wrote verse in at least fourteen meters, some that traditional classical verse most frequently employs, and some that clearly have the beats of folk music. He also experimented with a variety of stanza patterns and poetic figures—both formal and seemingly indigenous.[31] These were two challenging literary puzzles he solved in writing the dialogues.

The *gur* cycles demonstrate interesting approaches to pairing basic Buddhist teachings with specific types of insects. Since lice and fleas bite and it is so easy for an insensitive person to kill them with a casual slap, it is ideal to depict lice and fleas as lecturers on karma. Kalden Gyatso sees the lice and fleas biting him and lice eggs burrowing into his clothes, and he threatens the lice eggs:

> You dazzling white and smiling lice eggs,
> you look like pearls.
> But when I see my damaged garments,
> being unmindful of my next life, I want to kill you.

His threat sets the lice, fleas, and lice eggs off, and the lice respond:

> You old monk who knows the karma of virtue and vice!
> In previous lives you ate others.
> Because of that, we are eating you.

The insects use a carrot-and-stick approach, first threatening him with more bites, and later making alluring promises not to bite him again if he mends his ways. The fleas tell him:

28. Norbu Chöphel 1984, ix.

29. Forsthoefel 2007, 28. See also Schmithausen and Maithrimurthi 2009, 104.

30. For a summary of influences of Kalden Gyatso's songs, see Sujata 2005, 261–62.

31. Sujata 2005, 112–38, 139–61, 162–84, 185–246.

We fleas who dwell here
don't eat yogis who dwell on mountain peaks.

The insects as a group encourage him to reap the benefits of good karma by changing his ways. Separately or together, they work to really hammer home the reality that his actions will have consequences.

Furthermore, the dialogues use the insects' habits in real life metaphorically for the teachings they are imparting. The fleas recommend:

You listen, our watchman.
Sometimes we soar up and sometimes we drift down.
You, in this ocean of the three realms of cyclical existence,
sometimes soar up and sometimes drift down.

Don't stay there, don't stay there—soar on up!
Soar up to a solitary, delightful mountain peak.
The nature of mind soars in the expanse of the sky.
Don't threaten us—soar up like us!

Here the fleas' habit of jumping up and down is a metaphor for Kalden Gyatso's going up and down within the realms of saṃsāra. And their rising up is a metaphor for Kalden Gyatso's physical rising to a mountain peak, and spiritual rising to recognize the nature of mind above the extremes of saṃsāra. The lice eggs recommend that Kalden Gyatso meditate as they do in their cozy homes within peoples' clothes:

In our meditation huts within the weave of your clothes,
we will meditate in samādhi without wavering.
If you delight in meditating in solitude,
don't harm us. Just dwell as we dwell.

The lice eggs dwelling blissfully in peoples' clothes is a metaphor for Kalden Gyatso residing peacefully in a solitary hermitage. The lice eggs not needing to move away from their homes is a metaphor for Kalden Gyatso's staying fast in a hermitage retreat.

In addition to being drawn to the literary challenge, Kalden Gyatso may have written dialogues with insects as spiritual masters in order to put criticism in the mouths of others. The bees are even more intolerant of other monks and nuns than they are of him, attacking their corrupt ways. This allows Kalden Gyatso to be outspoken in criticizing other people's faults, since the bees are saying those things:

> A bee speaking human language is a bad omen!?
> All the monks and novices who took monastic vows
> in front of preceptors and instructors
> yet indulge in such things as women, drinking, fighting, and robbery
> are bad omens![32]

These are critiques that Kalden Gyatso may have liked to make directly, but it's much more diplomatic to articulate them as the words of others, especially one of the smallest of all animals, bees.

The dialogues with insects may also have been a way for Kalden Gyatso to demonstrate immeasurable equanimity, a method for increasing one's humility.[33] In literature, bees are frequently liked, and nuisance insects are typically despised or ignored. Though Kalden Gyatso's relationships with the two sets of insects are initially very different, he gradually listens to both of them and ultimately comes to respect the advice of lice, fleas, lice eggs, and bees.

In many Jātaka tales in which an animal inspires a human to reform and become more ethical, that human is a king. Just as the contrast between the apparent status of a king and an animal in the Jātaka tales is extreme, so is the contrast between the apparent status of Kalden Gyatso and the insects. Yet both the kings and Kalden Gyatso are able to let go of their presumptions of status, gain humility, and learn important lessons from those traditionally thought to be inferior.

Interestingly, among all the tales in the *Jātakamālā* or the Pāli collections, there is not one in which the Buddha in former lives was an insect.[34] Conceiving of or including any stories of the bodhisattva as an insect may have gone farther than others were willing to go. Yet in Kalden Gyatso's dialogues, he does dig that deep, and we have the lowliest of tiny animals—even nuisance animals—advising someone already renowned as a lama and a founder of a philosophical college!

The dialogues also allow Kalden Gyatso to demonstrate the strictest interpretation of the fundamental rules and vows regarding animals. The first precept—the most important precept to be obeyed by both monks and lay-

32. For the monastic disciplinary rules (*prātimokṣa*) concerning women (loss of celibacy?), drinking alcohol, and theft, see Chandra 1915, 40 (#1), 59 (#79), and 40 (#2), respectively. I thank Shayne Clarke for his guidance.

33. For more about developing immeasurable equanimity of mind with all sentient beings, see Richards 2006, 519–20.

34. Ohnuma 2017, 183–85. Insects in the Pāli collection occasionally play minor roles in the plots.

people alike—prohibits the taking of life. It is sometimes more widely interpreted to prohibit harming any being.[35] The softening of the prohibition to include only intentional killing seems to be for the purpose of enabling trades and livelihoods to proceed without the need to be unreasonably careful, even when some unintentional killing of insects is inevitable, such as in agriculture.[36]

According to the *Mūlasarvāstivādavinaya*, which presents the rules of monastic discipline that dictate proper behavior, killing is forbidden—though punishment depends on the details of the crime. Killing a human is a *pārājika* offence, punishable by expulsion from the monastery; whereas killing an animal is a *pācittika* offence, with a much less severe punishment and for which guilt can be expiated through confession. And to be practical, there is a distinction made between intentional and unintentional killing,[37] starting with the issues related to just walking about. These loopholes result in a relative lack of punishment for killing animals. However, the *Mūlasarvāstivādavinaya* does demonstrate concern for protecting animals. As for insects, it makes recommendations such as how to deal with annoying ones,[38] how to deal with insects that may be in one's water,[39] and how to choose a site for a home without insects around or how to construct it so that they cannot enter.[40]

Kalden Gyatso, in elevating the insects to the status of his teachers, extends the precept of nonharm to encompass ultimate love and respect. This is in harmony with the strictest interpretations of the first precept, the *Mūlasarvāstivādavinaya*, and the bodhisattva ideal of compassion for all beings.

As I have suggested, Kalden Gyatso may have been motivated to write his dialogues in order to teach, to take on literary challenges, to use the opportunity to criticize indirectly, to cultivate immeasurable equanimity, and to extend the strictest interpretation of nonharm to insects. The dialogues also enact in brief one of the most crucial concerns of Kalden Gyatso's life—how to have time for practice so that he could progress spiritually. This theme comes up often. Yet his older half brother had left him for some nine years at Ganden Monastery for rigorous study, and after he returned to Amdo his older

35. Chapple 1992, 54.

36. For difficulties that laypeople have in keeping the first precept, see Schmithausen and Maithrimurthi 2009, 62–68. As for sericulture, see Heirman 2020, 39–40. I for one feel that it would be best for temples to use silk made exclusively from wild, discarded cocoons.

37. Heirman 2019, 4n13.

38. Heirman 2019; Heirman 2020, 45–47.

39. Heirman 2019, 5, 14–15; Heirman 2020, 29–30.

40. Heirman 2019, 10.

brother encouraged him to found and care for the philosophical college in Rongwo (Rong bo), and later on yet another school.[41] Though he took numerous shorter retreats to many beautiful places around Repgong, he always had the ongoing responsibilities of teaching an increasing number of disciples into the hundreds, of engaging with patrons, including Mongols for sponsorship of the two schools, and of running the schools.

At the end of each *gur* cycle Kalden Gyatso makes it seem like he is following the advice of the insects immediately by going off to meditate and do deep Dharma practices in a solitary place. The bees speak their approval at the time of Kalden Gyatso's retreat:

> We bees and other winged creatures
> will offer songs when you are joyfully in retreat.

And Kalden Gyatso requests this enthusiastically as he departs to meditate:

> Bee friends,
> Kalden Gyatso
> is going to meditate!
> Please sing a mellifluous song!

Only in 1670 was he finally able to resign from his monastic responsibilities and move to a hermitage, where he mostly remained for the last seven years of his life.[42] At last he fully embraced the advice the bees, lice, fleas, and lice eggs had given him thirty-seven years earlier. He may have had it in mind all along.

Bees Give Advice to Kalden Gyatso[43]

Moreover, on one occasion I was sitting under the seku trees that were drooping from the weight of their fruits, flowers, and lush leaves, while sunbeams shone up above through the trees in various shapes and sizes, adorning the ground where I was sitting with various patterns, like phases of the moon and twisted swastikas, and at this time in which I was in a carefree mood of jesting and laughter,

41. In 1648 he founded a seminary for tantric studies named Kadam Podrang (Bka' gdams pho brang). Byang chub mi la 1990, 33.

42. Byang chub mi la 1990, 66.

43. Skal ldan rgya mtsho 1994, 64–67; Skal ldan rgya mtsho 1999, 58–61. For my former critical edition, see Sujata 2005, 276–81. My current critical edition, unpublished, is based on yet one more source. I thank Lobsang Chödrak of Repgong for help with both.

many bees, dancing with their wings, buzzed through their windpipes singing this poetic song.

Hey, hey, listen, "learned one" under the tree!
As you have been carelessly joking around, playing games, and so forth,
in lives from beginningless time up to now,
you have been passing days and nights wandering about in this cyclical
saṃsāric existence.

Given how your deeds keep violating the Dharma,
it seems that from now on you will be bidding farewell
to the perpetual bliss of higher rebirths and liberation.

As for truth and falsehood, make sure that your thoughts
are in accord with the Dharma.
Take note of this!
The root of the Dharma reaches into one's own mind.

No matter how much you have attempted to expound
the holy teachings,
you have done so like a parrot.
Until you have tamed your mind itself,
your hollow talk will always miss its target.

If the elephant of your mind, which has been straying capriciously,
is not bound by the rope of a lama's oral instructions
to an absolutely firm pole in a solitary place,
there's no doubt that it will roam the dense forest of riches and esteem.

The holy lama, whose kindness exceeds that of all Buddhas
and bodhisattvas,
brings benefits to you continually
through the nectar of the Dharma.
Therefore continually make prayers to the lama, and his blessing
will enter into you.

Once you have received his blessings,
then profound experiences and realization, spiritual qualities,
and so forth
will instantaneously gather in you, just as we instantly gather

in a grove of lotuses without even summoning one another,
and you will be led to the village of higher realms and liberation.

If you have not received the essence of the profound, holy Dharma
in these times when a free, well-favored human form
is very hard to obtain, like a wish-fulfilling jewel,
although you repent at death, would it not be too late to change?

You have not made any use of your life up to now.
If you continue to make yourself stay in your homeland,
this demonic prison,
consuming the remainder of your life senselessly,
you would not be considered a human being.

You ask why? You are meaninglessly squandering your life
with senseless singing, dancing, eating, drinking and so on,
but we swarm of animals are much more prudent than you.

As for that human who, frightened by the dangers of the three
evil rebirths,
takes refuge wholeheartedly in the Three Jewels,
renounces evil and strives to attain virtue,
wherever he goes and wherever he stays
he will later be reborn in a higher realm.

But the lama who clings to all these saṃsāric places, fiery pits—
earthly goods and pleasures like honey on the blade of a knife—
has abandoned altruistic aspiration for enlightenment,
the central vow of training of all Victorious Ones and their sons.
And since he merely pretends to benefit others,
we have no faith in his actions.

Many doctrines that do not reject grasping at a self,
and even oppose the teaching of a lack of self,
have been appearing in this region.

Alas! How pitiful for most Dharma practitioners
in these evil times, when what is is postulated as what is not.
Though they receive empowerments and meditate through
the Generation and Completion Stages,

if they do not observe the vows, the benefits are like a castle built
  on water,
unworthy of trust.
So study the path from its foundation!

So they said, to which in response I spoke these words:

A bee speaking human language is a bad omen!
Although we humans engage in activities such as joking, playing,
  and so forth,
we realize that is not all there is to life!
Your yakking is contemptuous of life!

In response to what I had said they said:

A bee speaking human language is a bad omen!?
All the monks and novices who took monastic vows
in front of preceptors and instructors
yet indulge in such things as women, drinking, fighting, and robbery
  are bad omens!

A bee speaking human language is a bad omen!?
All those "learned" ones who studied the words of the Victorious One
  properly
but sell the Dharma and perform village rites
in order to obtain the wealth of others are bad omens!

A bee speaking human language is a bad omen!?
All those disciples who received many Dharma teachings due to
  a lama's kindness
yet after a brief while sully their vows
and completely abandon the lama are bad omens!

A bee speaking human language is a bad omen!?
Most lineage holders who do not know much about religion
yet pretend to be authentic lamas and do the majority of
  Dharma talks,
bringing harm to the doctrine of the Buddha, are bad omens!

A bee speaking human language is a bad omen!?
Ordained ones make bows, arrows, and other weapons.

"Exalted" ones commit shameless acts.
But where we bees dwell there are no bad omens at all.

A bee speaking human language is a bad omen!?
Especially you, who have knowledge of the Dharma,
skillfully deceiving others by expounding religion
while not practicing it—
this is a bad omen!

So they said. Then, in response I said these words:

Although I have seen the faces of a hundred lamas,
I have not heard a teaching deeper than that!

You're right, bees, right! You bees are right!
Now I'll remain solitary in order not to deceive others!

Since I said thus, the bees said these words:

Do not discard your vows. Be strict with vows.
Do not discard your oaths. Be strict with oaths.
Do not discard your promises. Be strict with promises.
If you don't value those three directives, you are not in
the human family.

If you want to value them,
without a doubt go into retreat.

We bees and other winged creatures
will offer songs when you are joyfully in retreat.

There are not many things to be mindful of.
Roll them into one.
The Dharma to strive for, as one condensed act,
is preserving the intent to renounce secular life.

If you understand that, it is the king of instructions!

Based on what the bees had said, rejoicing, delight, and sadness simultaneously arose in me. I decided to go and practice the Dharma, and moreover, at that time made this request:

Bee friends,
Kalden Gyatso
is going to meditate!
Please sing a mellifluous song!

I requested.
This also was composed by Kalden.

Lice, Fleas, and Lice Eggs Give Advice to Kalden Gyatso[44]

Also at one time I saw on my robes and other things that there were lots of lice calmly meandering, many fleas hopping about, and many lice eggs smiling and hanging around, and I advised them as follows:

Listen, you lice who are roaming about—
you lice have been consuming my body!
You are happy now while you eat and drink,
but when you realize I can see you, what will you think?

You reckless fleas, skilled in flight,
when young you feared being killed by someone.
If now you think there are no karmic consequences to your actions—
keep on eating and the truth will become clear.

You dazzling white and smiling lice eggs,
you look like pearls.
But when I see my damaged garments,
being unmindful of my next life, I want to kill you.

Because I said that, an aged louse assembled his friends and counseled them as follows:

Since I, an elderly louse, am skilled at eating and drinking,
up till now I have been peaceful and happy.
You youngsters have been eating inappropriately.
Will I now also enter death for the sake of a smell?

44. Skal ldan rgya mtsho 1994, 67–71; Skal ldan rgya mtsho 1999, 61–64; Sujata 2005, 282–87.

Based on what he said, all the young and old lice huddled and carefully deliberated, replying unanimously to me as follows:

You old monk who knows the karma of virtue and vice!
In previous lives you ate others.
Because of that, we are eating you.

Now you have trouble replying.
Above all, don't lecture us! Be mindful of karma!

Earlier, when you human noticed us you were moved to tears.
Though you saw where we were hiding,
we still didn't believe you would kill us with fingernail and tooth.
If you murder some of us, we'll keep biting you!

Otherwise, the patron and we recipients
will need one another forevermore.
Now whether we eat or not eat, it's your call.

So they said. Also the fleas unanimously said:

You listen, our watchman.
Sometimes we soar up and sometimes we drift down.
You, in this ocean of the three realms of cyclical existence,
sometimes soar up and sometimes drift down.

Don't stay there, don't stay there—soar on up!
Soar up to a solitary, delightful mountain peak.
The nature of mind soars in the expanse of the sky.
Don't threaten us—soar up like us!

So they said. Also the lice eggs, smiling, said this:

In our meditation huts within the weave of your clothes,
we will meditate in samādhi without wavering.
If you delight in meditating in solitude,
don't harm us. Just dwell as we dwell.

So they said. Then I advised the lice, fleas, and lice eggs as follows:

You stupid and foolish insects—
among humans, I am a venerable, pious monk.
Among insects, you are the lowest!
For you to give me advice! Ha! Ridiculous!

Because I said that, the lice, fleas, and lice eggs scolded me this way:

Even though we lice, fleas, and lice eggs
act under the power of religious convention,
we pervade the entire range of clergy, from lamas and Dharma lords
to mendicant monks.

Although we act under the power of worldly convention,
there is no one—whether exalted kings, queens, ministers,
or subjects, rich persons, warriors, powerful orators, and so on—
whom we don't eat or drink.

A faction of lice from our group here
who are dark and very hot mouthed
consider you an offering of rich food.

Because you have eaten funeral repasts for so long,
it is natural for you to be eaten by us.

We fleas who dwell here
don't eat yogis who dwell on mountain peaks.
You village priests, who wander about towns saying,
"Performing village rites is food for my mouth"—
soar and be!

Also, listen, listen, old monk, listen!
Don't eat funeral repasts
and the dark lice won't eat you!

Don't rove about towns, but wander among mountain hermitages.
On green grass in a solitary and pleasant place,
you will dwell in peace,
and the fleas as a group
will make a solemn vow never to bother you.

Again—focus your earhole for a moment!
Don't judge other people. Judge yourself!
Judging others is simply chasing after your own self-interest.

By benefiting the Dharma and sentient beings,
and breaking away from concern for yourself,
you will not be eaten by beguiling demons when you die.

Each and every one of us lice, fleas, and lice eggs
has the same idea—
namely, that we don't have to counsel you,
who eat flesh and drink blood.

Likewise, you old monks
who have renounced concern for this life through the teaching
and who practice the holy Dharma
feel it is unnecessary to counsel us!

Be harmonious with everyone!
Don't despair because you have no entourage!
Strive for perfect Buddhahood,
and when one day you attain enlightenment,
we will also be in your retinue!

Moreover, listen! When you are sitting in meditation
and we eat you,
be mindful of your karma of past lives.
Becoming liberated from evil karma,
you will strive to perform virtuous deeds.

Based on what the insects said to me, I decided to go meditate, and said these words:

Because I received the blessing of a lord lama,
lice, fleas, and lice eggs have expounded the Dharma.
Because the Dharma is profound, I have steered my mind to it.
In order to practice the Dharma, I am going to a solitary place!

Because I said that, the insects said this:

Don't cast your words to the wind.
Carry out your intent. Hey!
It doesn't suffice to know about the Dharma—you must practice it.
Now, in order to practice it, go to a solitary place!

Thus they discoursed.
This also was composed by Kalden.

References

Tibetan-Language Sources

Byang chub mi la Ngag dbang bsod nams. 1990. *Grub chen skal ldan rgya mtsho'i rnam thar yid bzhin dbang gi rgyal po.* Xining: Mtsho sngon mi rigs dpe skrun khang.

Skal ldan rgya mtsho. 1994. *Shar skal ldan rgya mtsho'i mgur 'bum.* Xining: Mtsho sngon mi rigs dpe skrun khang.

———. 1999. *Yab rje bla ma skal ldan rgya mtsho'i mgur 'bum.* In *Yab rje bla ma skal ldan rgya mtsho'i gsung 'bum*, vol. 4, 1–320. Xining: Kan su'u mi rigs dpe skrun khang.

Western-Language Sources

Chandra Vidyabhusana, S., ed., trans. 1915. "So-sor-thar-pa, or, a Code of Buddhist Monastic Laws: Being the Tibetan Version of Prātimokṣa of the Mūla-Sarvāstivāda School." *Journal of the Asiatic Society of Bengal* 11: 29–139.

Chang, Garma C. C., ed., trans. 1989. *The Hundred Thousand Songs of Milarepa.* Boston: Shambhala.

Chapple, Christopher. 1992. "Nonviolence to Animals in Buddhism and Jainism." In *Inner Peace, World Peace: Essays on Buddhism and Nonviolence*, edited by Kenneth Kraft, 49–62. Albany: State University of New York Press.

Clarke, Shayne. 2015. "Vinayas." In *Brill's Encyclopedia of Buddhism: Literature and Languages*, edited by Jonathan A. Silk, vol. 1, 60–87. Leiden: Brill.

Cowell, Edward B., ed. 1994 [1895–1913]. Six volumes, plus index volume, reprinted in 3 vols. *The Jātaka, or Stories of the Buddha's Former Births.* Delhi: Motilal Banarsidass Publishers Private Limited.

Dowman, Keith, ed., trans. 1985. *Masters of Mahāmudrā: Songs and Histories of the Eighty-Four Buddhist Siddhas.* Albany: State University of New York Press.

Forsthoefel, Thomas A. 2007. "Jataka, Pancatantra, and the Rhetoric of Animalia in South Asia." In *Buddha Nature and Animality*, edited by David Jones, 23–39. Fremont, CA: Jain Publishing Company.

Heirman, Ann. 2019. "How to Deal with Dangerous and Annoying Animals: A *Vinaya* Perspective." *Religions* 10.2: 1–18.

———. 2020. "Protecting Insects in Medieval Chinese Buddhism: Daoxuan's *Vinaya* Commentaries." *Buddhist Studies Review* 37.1: 27–52.

Idema, Wilt L. 2019. *Insects in Chinese Literature: A Study and Anthology*. Amherst, NY: Cambria Press.

Kapstein, Matthew. 2013. "Stoics and Bodhisattvas." In *Philosophy as a Way of Life*, edited by Stephen R. L. Clark, Michael McGhee, and Michael Chase, 99–115. Oxford: Blackwell.

———. 2020. "The *Jātakamālā* of Āryaśūra with the Supplement of the Third Rgyal dbang Karma pa Rang byung rdo rje: The 1430 Dalongshan Xylographic Edition Conserved in the Berthold Laufer Collection of the Field Museum of Natural History, Chicago." In *On a Day of a Month of the Fire Bird Year: Festschrift for Peter Schwieger on his 65th Birthday*, edited by J. Bischoff, P. Maurer, and C. Ramble, 437–51. Kathmandu: Lumbini International Research Institute.

Khoroche, Peter. 1989. *Once the Buddha Was a Monkey: Ārya Śūra's Jātakamālā*. Chicago: University of Chicago Press.

Lhalungpa, Lobsang P., trans. 1985. *The Life of Milarepa*. Boston: Shambhala.

McDermott, J. P. 1989. "Animals and Humans in Early Buddhism." *Indo-Iranian Journal* 32.4: 269–80.

Nālandā Translation Committee under the direction of Chögyam Trungpa, trans. 1995. *The Life of Marpa the Translator: Seeing Accomplishes All*. Boston: Shambhala.

Norbu Chöphel. 1984. *Folk Tales of Tibet*. Dharamsala: Library of Tibetan Works and Archives.

O'Connor, W. F. 1992 [1979]. *Folk Tales of Tibet*. Delhi: Sterling Publishers Private Limited.

Ohnuma, Reiko. 2017. *Unfortunate Destiny: Animals in the Indian Buddhist Imagination*. Oxford: Oxford University Press.

Ricard, Matthieu, ed., trans. 1994. *The Life of Shabkar: The Autobiography of a Tibetan Yogin*. Albany: State University of New York Press.

Richards, Michael, trans. 2006. *Liberation in the Palm of Your Hand, Pabongka Rinpoche: A Concise Discourse on the Path to Enlightenment*. Edited by Trijang Rinpoche. Boston: Wisdom Publications.

Schmithausen, Lambert. 1991. *Buddhism and Nature: The Lecture Delivered on the Occasion of the EXPO 1990: An Enlarged Version with Notes.* Tokyo: The International Institute for Buddhist Studies.

Schmithausen, Lambert, and Mudagamuwe Maithrimurthi. 2009. "Attitudes Towards Animals in Early Buddhism." In *Penser, dire et représenter l'animal dans le monde indien*, edited by Nalini Balbir and Georges-Jean Pinault, 47–121. Paris: Librairie Honoré Champion.

Sherab Gyatso. n.d. *The Clever Rabbit: A Tibetan Folk Tale*. Dharamsala: Tibetan Children's Villages.

Sujata, Victoria. 2005. *Tibetan Songs of Realization: Echoes from a Seventeenth-Century Scholar and Siddha in Amdo*. Brill's Tibetan Studies Library 7. Edited by Henk Blezer, Alex McKay, and Charles Ramble. Leiden: Brill.

———. 2008. "Relationships between Inner Life and Solitary Places: The *Mgur* of Two *Siddha*s in Amdo." In *Contributions to Tibetan Buddhist Literature: Proceedings of* *the Eleventh Seminar of the International Association for Tibetan Studies, Königswinter 2006*, edited by Orna Almogi, 549–69. Halle: International Institute for Tibetan and Buddhist Studies.

———. 2011. *Songs of Shabkar: The Path of a Tibetan Yogi Inspired by Nature*. Cazadero, CA: Dharma Publishing.

———. 2019. *Journey to Distant Groves: Profound Songs of the Tibetan Siddha Kälden Gyatso*. Kathmandu: Vajra Books.

No Stone Unturned: Un-Disciplining Tibetan Buddhist Studies

Ivette Vargas-O'Bryan

I REMEMBER SITTING in Leonard's office musing over my dissertation topic as I was preparing for my research trip to Nepal. He surprised me by saying, "Just hang out." Instead of a list of expectations, he advised me to simply receive rather than demand, to let go and learn from the experience. It was rather liberating. These formative years were marked by balancing my personal needs and interests in anthropologically based methods with the institutional pressures to conduct text-based, historical studies and pursue research in intellectual history and Buddhist philosophy. During my career as an academic, an interdisciplinary approach had considerably expanded the scope of Tibetan Buddhist studies. As Leonard has shown, history is a journey of perspectives replete with encounters and unexpected collaborations.[1] Leonard's meticulous attention to detail and historical context in order to draw out the meaning of a text influenced my own work on Indo-Tibetan Buddhist thought. However, for one long-term project, I had to go one step further. Given the complexity of the content and transmission history of the Tibetan Buddhist tantric tradition of the Gelongma Pelmo (Dge slong ma Dpal mo) meditational system and biographies (*Dpal mo lugs*), my research required more than the selectivity and synthesis offered in interdisciplinary studies that only presented part of her story. By applying the transdisciplinary research strategies of disability and feminist studies, the integration of materials from the Tibetan medical sciences and Western medical anthropology was made more accessible, uncovering the tradition's surprising networks of influence and philosophical possibilities.[2] This brief study explores how the application of a transdisciplinary approach further expands our understanding of the significance of the Pelmo tradition in terms of Buddhist and Tibetan notions of the body and contemporary applications for gender equity.

1. See van der Kuijp 2006, 169–202, and 2016, 51–71.

2. A historical study of *Dpal mo lugs* is forthcoming in 2023.

Research Methods and Tibetan Religious Traditions

For over a decade, diverse research methods and approaches have advanced the field of Tibetan Buddhist studies. *The Tibetan History Reader*[3] represents one of the pinnacles of this advancement, demonstrating that Tibetan studies as a global endeavor demands discussion across geographical, cultural, and disciplinary borders. Moreover, *Sources of Tibetan Tradition*,[4] which provides translations of Tibetan literary works, continued the longstanding Tibetan tradition of textual translation and hermeneutics. Research in the disciplines of religious studies, folklore, anthropology, philosophy, and medicine have expanded our knowledge of Tibetan culture and history.[5] Interdisciplinarity and multidisciplinarity have predominantly been the hallmark of Tibetan studies (and religious studies) methods as a whole. However, with the diversity of Tibetan Buddhist perspectives (that often transcend Western categories of culture and religion) and regional (as well as translocal) views, these traditional methods that either maintain disciplinary boundaries (multidisciplinarity) or attempt to synthesize or harmonize disciplinary approaches into a coherent whole using common themes, topics, or issues (interdisciplinarity) can potentially have disciplinary (and Western-based) limitations. Research in Tibetan Buddhist studies does not always fit into neat compartments; it requires a comprehensive study of topics that affect different areas of Tibetan religious life, culture, and identity, and that strategically should embody some versatility and creative envisioning.

The research strategy of transdisciplinarity integrates the natural, social, and health sciences (and transcends their traditional boundaries) to provide new avenues for interpretation and collaboration in a humanities context.[6] A term originally chosen in the context of the philosophy of science and the organization of the sciences, and expanded upon since the 1970s, transdisciplinarity indicates an engagement with different disciplines to come up with more comprehensive and reliable solutions. This research method allowed the social, natural, and health sciences to solve problems that could not be solved by isolated efforts; an example of this new strategy is solving problems through science, technology, and society. Unlike interdisciplinarity, which utilizes, for exam-

3. Tuttle and Schaeffer, 2013.

4. Schaeffer, Kapstein, and Tuttle, 2013.

5. Flood 1999, 40; Mortensen 2019, 115–39.

6. Coined by the philosopher and psychologist Jean Piaget (1896–1980), the word "transdisciplinarity" first appeared in France in 1970, referring to a new stage of interdisciplinarity, or beyond the disciplines. See Nicolescu 1996 and 2006, 142–66.

ple, anthropological methods and still maintains disciplinary integrity, this research strategy facilitates the emergence of new perspectives resulting from the merging of different disciplines. With the integration of feminist studies, gender studies, and medical studies, intrepid Tibetan scholars[7] have already to some extent applied the research strategy of transdisciplinarity to address gaps in conclusions made in past Tibetan studies research.

One promising area of research to expand this trend in Tibetan Buddhist studies is incorporating the field of disability studies inclusive of both medical and social paradigms, thus creating a network of conversations across different fields of study and disciplines (gender studies, feminist studies, body studies, medicine, anthropology) that could address gaps in Tibetan studies research and bring to the fore previously ignored topic areas. One of the major contributions disability studies scholars have made is developing contrasting models that define disability in terms of physical and mental impairments. One way to think about theorizing disability is through three modes[8]—the medical, social, and human-variation model—providing alternative platforms to think about notions of the body, gender, and illness prominent in the current study.

Transdisciplining the Pelmo Tradition: Applying Disability and Feminist Studies

One of the Tibetan cultural traditions that has held my attention throughout the years is that of Nun Pelmo. Although Western scholarship still does not consider the Pelmo tradition to be a robust subject worthy of major critical studies,[9] in contrast, throughout South Asian and Tibetan history, there exists a rich transmission of texts from this lineage by key religious and political figures across several geographic areas, not to mention its proliferation in contemporary times.[10] Spanning several regions (India, Nepal, Bhutan, Tibet,

7. Gyatso 2003, 89–115; Makley 2007; Fjeld and Hofer 2011, 175–216; Padma'tsho and Jacoby 2020, 1–19.

8. Disability studies also provides a variety of models to think about, including the inspirational/religious model and the tragedy/charity model, both clearly exemplified in Robert Orsi's work on Catholicism (2006). Other models in conjunction with feminist and Buddhist studies include Schumm 2010 and Harris 2016, 25–45.

9. I am one of the only academics who have worked on this tradition and will soon publish a comprehensive study. See Vargas-O'Bryan 2001, 157–87, an article based on my dissertation.

10. See the references section for notable works. A cursory search in the Buddhist Digital Resource Center website yields 175 entries for *dpal mo lugs* and 412 for *smyung gnas* (the latter does include non-Pelmo traditions). https://library.bdrc.io/.

China, and Mongolia), the Nun Pelmo tradition, a collection of fasting rituals (*smyung gnas sgrub thabs*), praise prayers or eulogies (*bstod pa*), and biographies (*rnam thar*), is one of the central Great Compassionate (Mahākāruṇika) Avalokiteśvara meditational lineages in Indo-Tibetan Buddhist history and modern Tibetan Buddhist practices.

The main biographies are dedicated to the founder of the practices, Gelongma Pelmo, the early tenth-century Indian or Central Asian[11] Buddhist nun of high-caste royalty who was disfigured by a skin disease (*mdze nad*) inflicted by local spirits, healed by a fasting practice taught by the bodhisattva Avalokiteśvara, and revealed as a tantric ḍākinī and trülku (*sprul sku*, incarnate buddha).[12] The tradition also includes the biographies of the lineage holders who transmitted the fasting practice. Her disease and the subsequent fasting ritual became a platform for Nun Pelmo to assert her compassionate qualities.[13] The Nun Pelmo tradition proposes that one can transform adverse conditions into the path of enlightenment.

Throughout the centuries, there were many notable lineage holders.[14] The earliest lineage holders of the tradition in Indian and Tibetan regions include prominent names such as Yeshé Zangpo (Ye shes bzang po, Jñānabhadra, 1000?–1077?), Rinchen Zangpo (Rin chen bzang po, 958–1055), and Atiśa Dīpaṃkara Śrījñāna. The latter actively promoted the tradition of Nun Pelmo as well as two other systems of the Avalokiteśvara meditational lineages in the Tibetan region.[15]

11. Some scholars and local practitioners dispute Nun Pelmo's historical identity. See Dimitrov 2000, 9–27; Ujeed 2016, 128–66; and Wangdi Rinpoche 2009, 1.

12. See Jo gdan Bsod nams bzang po (n.d.), 7a.1–5.

13. This correlates with a Tibetan Buddhist practitioner Chekawa Yeshé Dorjé's ('Chad kha pa Ye shes rdo rje, 1102–76) mind-training (*blo sbyong*) and giving-and-taking meditation practice (*gtong len*). See Braitstein and Shamar Rinpoche 2011.

14. The list of prominent scholars includes the fourteenth-century scholar Joden Sönam Zangpo (Jo gdan Bsod nams bzang po Mtshal min pa, 1341–1433), the fifteenth-century Mongolian scholar Dzaya Paṇḍita Lozang Trinlé (Dza ya Paṇḍi ta Blo bzang 'phrin las, 1642–1715), and, in the eighteenth-to-nineteenth centuries, the Seventh Dalai Lama Kelzang Gyatso (Skal bzang rgya mtsho, 1708–57) and Shabkar Tsokdruk Rangdröl (Zhabs dkar Tshogs drug rang grol, 1781–1851). According to an inscription, the Sixth Paṇchen Lama Lozang Pelden Yeshé (Blo bzang Dpal ldan Ye shes, 1738–80) offered in 1780, right before he died of smallpox, a nine-paneled painting to the Qianlong emperor on behalf of his seventieth birthday celebration, one of which was a curious painting depicting Hari Hari Hari Lokeśvara with Nun Pelmo on the upper lefthand corner. See Zhang 2014, 25–26, 157.

15. Atiśa's (Dīpaṃkara-Śrījñāna, 982–1054) three systems include *Dpal mo lugs kyi spyan ras gzigs*, *Bka' gdams lha bzhi'i spyan ras gzigs*, and *Skyer sgang lugs kyi spyan ras gzigs*. See also 'Gos Lo tsā ba 1988, 1006–46.

In addition, the Pelmo tradition is practiced in modern Tibetan monasteries and nunneries.[16] In Nepal and India, for example, Nun Pelmo is often taken as a model for Tibetan nuns. In Bhutan, Nun Pelmo is placed on a pedestal, comparable to a postmortem Saint Francis of Assisi. Marked miracle-laden pilgrimage sites and images of her flanking Avalokiteśvara are prominent in temples.[17] The first English-language novel in Bhutan written by a female Bhutanese novelist memorializes Nun Pelmo as a healer of not just people but also mangy, homeless dogs.[18]

Overall, these central features of the Pelmo tradition are critical to address: (1) the presence of illness (understood under both Buddhist and non-Buddhist terms) as instrumental for spiritual development; (2) the connections between body, gender, and perfection; (3) healing via an Avalokiteśvara fasting practice; and (4) cultural identity. After I had collected information on Tibetan medicine and monasticism on the textual and ethnographic level for several years, disability studies, in conjunction with gender and feminist studies, provided a compass to address the nuances in the intersections of these areas in the contemporary context.

The Nun Pelmo Tradition as an Enabling Feminist Model

One way of understanding the use of the Nun Pelmo tradition in modern Tibetan Buddhism is through the exploration of assertions for gender equity by Tibetan nuns. There are several female Tibetan monastic institutions in India, Nepal, and Tibet that endorse and embrace the practice of the Nun Pelmo tradition, often more so than their male counterparts. As cited earlier, feminist and disability studies provide rich tools for analysis of modern Tibetan nunneries advocating feminist values.

One view asserts that the practice of the Nun Pelmo tradition has been implicated as a means through which to maintain the persistent patriarchal hegemony of Buddhist monasticism that Tibetan nunneries often operate under. For example, in the case of nuns in Ladakh, India, the anthropologist Kim Gutschow has noted that the endorsement of the fasting ritual in nunneries is representative of women's continued oppression in Tibetan Buddhist monastic institutions. There are two claims for this: (1) Tibetan nuns' ritual restrictions to non-tantric or lower tantric Buddhist practices like the

16. See Gutschow 2004, 51–62, 66–78, and 115–16.

17. Wangdi 2008, 116–20, and 292–93.

18. Choden 2004.

tradition of Nun Pelmo, [19] and (2) textual descriptions that include derogatory terms and misogynistic passages in the biographies themselves.[20] There are several examples in the Pelmo tradition's biographies that support this latter view particularly; for example, drawing attention to the female body in relation to impurity:

> When she [Gelongma Pelmo] stayed there five days,
> in an experiential vision in which sleep and light were mixed,
> she saw many tadpoles, fish, frogs, snakes, and so forth
> come out of her vagina and anus
> and glide into the earth
> while she recited the six-syllable mantra without distraction.[21]

In this passage, the specific water animals (referred to collectively as the *lu* spirits, implicated in different genres, such as medical texts for skin diseases)[22] are dispelled out of specifically gendered or sexual body parts through ritual means, thus equating disease and female impurities. However, the analysis cannot stop here. Because of the inclusion of sickness and obvious disabling dismemberment in the story, the misogynistic attitude is extended to the disabled body.[23] Several examples from the biographies note that Nun Pelmo, when identified as having a skin condition stigmatized in Indian society, is thrown out of sacred spaces like temples and is considered too impure to continue as a monastic person and even as an abbess in her monastery. One biography of

19. The tradition of Gelongma Pelmo is considered a lower-level *kriyātantra* (*bya rgyud*), although there is evidence of higher levels in descriptions of Nun Pelmo's consortial relationship with her brother (or father).

20. See Gutschow 2004, 51–62, 66–78, 115–16.

21. *Dge slong ma dpal mo'i rnam thar nges 'byung rgyud la skye ba'i chos gtam* 1953, 13.14–14.6.

22. As I explained in an earlier study, the presence of spirits such as *lu* (a *klu*, a serpentine spirit in some cases equated with the Indian *nāga*) in diverse Tibetan contexts points to the concern over the preservation of religious teachings, the maintenance of moral or social order, or the rise of a political crisis mapped onto an embodied natural environment. Consultations of a variety of sources, including Indian and Tibetan medical texts and anthropological findings, provide critical comparative lenses and a deeper understanding of this tradition's preoccupations with a shared cultural and ecological environment underlying a moral framework. As in the tradition of Nun Pelmo, the serpentine spirits are most often implicated as the pathogens of skin diseases. Vargas-O'Bryan 2013, 110–35. See also DeCaroli 2004. The Tibetan tradition's Bonpo text, the *Collected Works of the Serpentine Spirits* (*Klu 'bum*), is also useful in describing rituals that help against their attacks.

23. See Schriempf 2001, 53–79.

Nun Pelmo shows that after a custodian notices twitching of an almost leper-like woman with a missing finger in his temple, he explicitly states:

> "You beggar woman, who is a disfigured, sick beggar, came inside my temple. I myself cannot do offerings of incense to the deities and ablutions in the temple. If the crops fail, hail strikes, and so forth, it is certain that [all] will come to my head." With the key handle, he beat her from the crown of her head to the soles of her feet. Having pulled the nun from her feet, he brought her to the back of the temple.[24]

The second passage from the same biography states:

> When the nun was afflicted and consumed with a severe skin condition, suffering arose like an arrow into the mind of that very servant, Sampelma. Although she offered whatever services were possible [to Nun Pelmo], it had no effect. About three months later, the ten toes of the lama's feet fell off. Then five months later the ten fingers of her hands fell off. At that time, severe suffering arose in the minds of both master and servant. Sampelma enclosed the lama with a curtain. During this time, it was as if her body was not seen by anyone. . . . After all [in the temple] noticed the pus and blood, [Nun Pelmo and Sampelma] were thrown out after the end of the year.[25]

Passages such as these clearly support the misogynistic claim about the gendered body and are comparable with medical and social models pointed out in disability studies. According to the medical model, disability is identified with physical or mental impairment that gives rise to disadvantages and barriers in society. As such, based on physical impairments, the disabled person is seen as impure and inferior compared with a normative and able-bodied person. As a monastic, Nun Pelmo had to abide by the rules of the sangha into which she was ordained. Any deviation from what was considered a normative, "healthy," able-bodied (or perfect) woman—that is, missing parts or gendered parts, organs not in perfect working order, suffering from specific diseases, or having excessive or stigmatized bodily discharges—automatically

24. *Dge slong ma dpal mo'i rnam thar nges 'byung rgyud la skye ba'i chos gtam* 1953, 16.7–17.3.
25. *Dge slong ma dpal mo'i rnam thar nges 'byung rgyud la skye ba'i chos gtam* 1953, 7.16–8.4.

disqualified her from ordination and continuation in the monastic order.[26] Furthermore, fitting specifically within the social model,[27] such a stigmatized person as Nun Pelmo is believed to desecrate sacred spaces and directly violate Buddhist monastic rules for "perfect" bodies in a model Buddhist sangha—as was the case for female monastics in medieval Europe, whose leper bodies were interpreted as a reflection of their internal corrupted or sinful nature. In the Pelmo tradition, gender and a stigmatized leper-like body are linked and connected to moral and karmic teachings, views widespread in society.[28] The stigmatized diseased female body is pathologized as a condition of alterity, of crossing boundaries, in a predominantly male monastic institution.

What is also implied in such passages, based on the close study of Tibetan medical texts, is the fact that this disease arises from a non-Buddhist source that requires Buddhist ritual to appease and transform it into a viable vessel for Buddhism. The twelfth-century Tibetan medical text *Secret Essence of Ambrosia in Eight Branches: An Instructional Tantra* (*Bdud rtsi snying po yan lag brgyad pa gsang ba man ngag gi rgyud*), commonly known as the *Four Tantras* (*Rgyud bzhi*), provides a comparative context through which to understand the significance of disease deities in the Pelmo tradition. Prophetic proclamations about an epidemic in the form of somatic-ecological-moral disruptions are described in the eighty-first chapter of the third volume, the *Instructional Tantra* (*Man ngag gi rgyud*), titled *Cure for the Gdon Disease of the Malevolent Klu* (*Gdud pa klu'i gdon nad gso ba*). This section makes critical connections

26. According to José Ignacio Cabezón's landmark study, *Sexuality in Classical South Asian Buddhism*, often the monastic rules note that the physical body was ultimately a barrier to ordination into and continuance in the monastic institution. Both men and women specifically had to meet certain criteria for ordination, including not being a leper, and women in particular could not be a female *paṇḍaka* (*ma ning mo*), a complex term for queer or sexless persons. Even if a monastic was found to have desires that did not fit into societal norms of heterosexuality, he or she must have had an inclination to particularly interfere with monastic discipline and celibacy, a problem thought to be specific to intersex and queer persons. Cabezón 2017, 409–11, 433.

27. The social model specifically addresses the negative effects of discrimination and marginalization affecting the disabled person.

28. Skin diseases like leprosy have historically gendered implications and were often believed to have been sexually transmitted. In the Catholic monastic context, the bodies of lepers and women were often equated, both considered corrupt due to original "sexual" sin and the crossing of boundaries as a result of corporeality. See Gilchrist 1994, 59; and Brody 1974. For studies about leprosy in Asia, see De Bruin 1998 on India, and Angela Ki Che Leung's *Leprosy in China*, 114–24, which indicates the gendered, sexual nature of this disease or related skin conditions in the Chinese context.

between spiritual, moral, and ecological environments particularly during the degenerate age (*snyigs ma'i dus*):[29]

> Then again Brahman Rikpé Yeshé spoke: "Kyé! Great Brahman, listen! In the time of the last five hundred degenerate years, when the degenerate *age* arises, human beings are in poverty as their provisions decline. Having ploughed arid grassland for farming, earth demon-gods (*sa gnyan*) are turned up. Water demon-gods (*chu gnyan*) are disturbed by transforming natural bodies of water into artificial lakes and ponds. Tree demon-gods (*shing gnyan*) are deforested and stone demon-gods (*rdo gnyan*) are uprooted or overturned. Contaminating the hearth, burning impure substances, the reckless slaughtering of animals in (spirit homes), and disturbing *gnyan sa* with the hope to subdue enemies by Buddhist and Bön priests who have no time to practice in the proper manner all result in agitating *nāgas*, demon-gods, and earth spirits, and gods and *rākṣasah*. Poisons merely spread through touch, sight, breath, and thought. The time comes for the rise of *tsi ti dzva la.*[30] It is disconcerting to see and fearful to think about. Merely hearing about these [events] causes sadness, a vision of one's own corpse, and separation from loved ones."[31]

In summary, the disruption of the ecological balance affects several embodied landscapes: nature (spirit world), human, and society. The rest of the chapter prescribes rituals of appeasement, typical of what is commonly seen in tantric ritual. In the Pelmo passage, the water spirits are transformed into protectors of the Dharma-like Nun Pelmo, who after practicing the fasting ritual (*smyung gnas*) is purified and transformed into a ḍākinī.[32]

Alternatively, my own studies have shown that although there is endorsement of the tradition by male monastic leaders who oversee Tibetan nunneries, endorsement does not necessarily mean supporting the subordination of wom-

29. Descriptions of crises such as these are also common in another Avalokiteśvara text, the *Great Chronicle of the Mani Kabum*. See Kapstein 2013, 96.

30. Amchi Thinley Gyatso and Phuntsok Gyaltsen of the Men Tsee Khang, the Tibetan Medical and Astro-Science Institute, in Dharamsala, India, equated this term with the more common Tibetan medical term *mdze nad* (which could be equated with leprosy but is also inclusive of other skin conditions). I am indebted to them for assistance on this translation.

31. G.yu thog Yon tan mgon po 2002, 392–93. My translation.

32. Jo gdan Bsod nams bzang po (n.d.), 5b.5–6a.6.

en.[33] The Pelmo tradition has been seen as both asserting marginalized Tibetan cultural identity as well as providing a feminist model for a nun's ordination and education in the sangha.

In my recent studies of the Nun Pelmo tradition in Tibetan areas of the People's Republic of China, the annual practice of fasting, the recitation of the biographies of Nun Pelmo, and the Buddhist appeasement rituals aimed at *lu* during the holiest day of the Tibetan calendar, Sagadawa (Sa ga zla ba, the fourth month), as well as when there is a crisis, like a disease outbreak, reveal Tibetans' inclination to assert their cultural identity through embodied practices and to express a stewardship toward the natural environment. In studies of modern-day Gyelthang (Rgyal thang; Chi. Xianggelila) in northwestern Yunnan Province, the Pelmo tradition is practiced by both male and female monastics and laypeople and is often linked with a stewardship of the natural environment too.[34] Furthermore, in practicing their religion through an Avalokiteśvara system in the peripheral regions, Tibetans are representative of a culture in which place and their embodied selves are critical, while expressing resistance and transgression of state-sanctioned cultural norms.

More directly pertinent to this study is how the Pelmo tradition stands as a dynamic model for modern female renunciant Tibetans to express their identity and hope for inclusion in institutions of power, like the monastery. For instance, since 2005 Dolma Ling Nunnery near Dharamsala, India, under the jurisdiction of the Tibetan Nuns Project (a nonprofit organization dedicated to educating female Buddhist monastics in India in higher education) and the Institute of Buddhist Dialectics, has been central to female Tibetan monastic institutions, representing the changing status of women in Buddhist monastic life in India. Dolma Ling has enabled nuns to take higher Buddhist academic degrees, like the *geshema* (*dge bshes ma*) examination, and has offered other innovations in practice and study. As is common in other Tibetan cultural areas in Asia, at Dolma Ling the fasting ritual is practiced and the biographies are recited annually. In contrast to anthropological interpretations like that of Kim Gutschow,[35] the male abbot directly promotes the figure of Nun Pelmo as a model for Tibetan renunciant women by hanging thangkas of her in the main prayer hall, reciting prayers of the Pelmo tradition, and hosting the fasting ritual in order to support the nuns' aspirations to access higher levels of monastic

33. Forthcoming in Vargas-O'Bryan 2023.

34. Vargas-O'Bryan 2015, 122–45. As in Tibetan communities in Lhasa, the performance of *lu* rituals at lakes and mountains by Tibetans is an opportunity to both preserve their culture and protest local conditions. See Yeh 2008, 103–37; and Yeh 2013.

35. Gutschow 2004.

education and reach spiritual advancement. During my fieldwork, nuns spoke about women's access to education and full ordination as a woman's right to participate in a monastic structure like "Nun Pelmo."[36]

In connection with Tibetan nuns' experiences, the Nun Pelmo tradition as a Buddhist tradition does offer some different avenues for understanding embodiment and transcendence. In the study of Western Catholic medieval hagiographies from feminist and disability perspectives, male monastic-generated hagiographies of female saints relied on patriarchal, socially constructed, and marginalized identities,[37] including disabled identities, to represent the position of their female subjects. In such an analysis, disability is extended to include marginalized identities that do not fit into the dominant norm or ableist framework. As the disability theorists Sharon Snyder and David Mitchell noted in their discussion of "narrative prosthesis," disability becomes a device of characterization in literature, accentuating the marginality of disabled people.[38] In comparison, throughout the centuries, male monastic and yogic practitioners composed and transmitted textual representations of Nun Pelmo as a marginalized, disabled female and divine figure, while visual images never represented her as diseased but rather as a healthy empowered nun or divine deity. In the modern context, Tibetan nuns in a predominantly patriarchal monastic institution embraced this dualistic model and often internalized it. As Robert Orsi has shown through his studies of disability in modern Catholicism,[39] marginalized religious practitioners often seek out hagiographic models that they can relate to and that can empower them, often subverting the theologies and static models presented by the monastic and political institutions of their time. In the writings describing Nun Pelmo's embodiment, a diseased body and a gendered body operate not just within patriarchal worldviews but within normative Buddhist notions of impermanence and buddha nature and the Mahāyāna view of re-embodiments through skillful means. A female dis-abled renunciant displays her agency through theodicy, soteriological inclusiveness, and embodied empowerment.[40]

36. Based on my research on the nunnery in 2009–11. An interesting comparison would be to review the Larung Gar nuns studied in Padma'tsho and Jacoby 2020.

37. Kafer 2013, 129–48.

38. See Mitchell and Snyder 2000, 49.

39. Orsi 2006.

40. These claims are elaborated in my chapter titled "Disablement for Enlightenment in the Hagiographies of Gelongma Palmo," in the forthcoming volume edited by Stephanie Grace-Petinos, Leah Pope Parker, and Alicia Spencer-Hall (Vargas-O'Bryan forthcoming).

For example, Nun Pelmo's embodiment as a woman with a stigmatized skin condition is often described in the hagiographies as having a higher purpose—to liberate others: "Gelongma Pelmo said, 'I am sick for the sake of sentient beings who are as vast as the sky.'"[41] This leper-like renunciant woman, often described as a learned abbess of a predominantly male institution, surpasses the expectations of her parents, gurus, and male monastics and takes on the responsibility of suffering because of, rather than despite, her embodied condition as diseased and female—both marks of impurity and marginality in a medieval Indian context. The fact that disease is described as an opportunity and not as an affliction is a powerful hermeneutic in the writings.

In addition, Nun Pelmo's intercession on behalf of others as a female diseased (or marginalized disabled) person represents empathy toward the suffering of real others. As the feminist disability scholar Susan Stocker makes us aware in her work on disability and embodiment, there is a possibility of what she calls "mutuality" in our "biological vulnerability" that enables empathic connections.[42]

Moreover, transcendence through the bodily performance of fasting (that includes ecstatic visionary experiences with Avalokiteśvara) and re-embodiment as a divine being represent agency and control over the environment; transcendence does not disable her or reduce her physically to an emaciated state. Buddhist notions of transcendence or liberation reinforce a bodily re-engagement as a divine being displaying agency despite public critique:

> Then, moreover, she practiced the fasting ritual
> for three months more for the sake of all sentient beings.
>
> When she went to Magadha, people said,
> "Since the cause for this nun's illness subsided,
> she became lax in her instructions and vows. How is that?"
> In order to reverse their disbelief,
> at a congregation for a worship service for Khasarpāṇi,
> [Nun Pelmo] cut off her own head.
> Since she placed it on her monastic staff [*mkhar bsil*] and danced,
> now the people,
> realizing that she was one who attained spiritual realization,
> all requested a blessing and obtained a realization as well.[43]

41. *Dge slong ma dpal mo'i rnam thar nges 'byung rgyud la skye ba'i chos gtam* 1953, 7.12–7.13. See also another use of the Nun Pelmo tradition as embodiment in Zivkovic 2013, 45–63.

42. Susan Stocker 2001, 53–79.

43. Jo gdan Bsod nams bzang po (n.d.), 7a.3–6.

The body as a site of conflict is also a site of constructive discourse, as in the case of Western analyses of diseased bodies.[44] As a Buddha figure, there is transcendence of a dualistic body with binary characteristics (well/sick, able/disabled) that includes moral and social constructions of marginality and disability.[45] Transformation depends on what is needed. Nun Pelmo's responsibility in her manifestations is to help others realize that ultimately the body can never lack; her manifestation is a tool to overcome any preconceived limitations or societal biases. This is a critical issue too because Nun Pelmo has never been depicted in visual media as a disabled, sick, or "leper" nun, or even with lepers, but most often as a "healthy" nun or as a Buddhist deity, in keeping with the Buddhist notion of enlightenment as being a state of perfect equilibrium on all levels and to the tantric hermeneutics in which the texts operate.

In the modern Tibetan context, the tradition of Nun Pelmo offers a reframing of embodiment within a much more inclusive category, reversing stigma from a mark of disgrace to a mark of virtue. Ultimately, what Dolma Ling and other similar female monastic institutions have discovered is that rather than being limited by the body as a site of conflict, and rather than reductively interpreting Nun Pelmo's experience with her body according to abelist binary norms that result in a marginalized status, the female diseased and liberated body instead represents an empowered embodiment for the modern Tibetan Buddhist nun. Nun Pelmo's performative materializations take on a positive light—in other words, illness and gender are necessary for embodied spiritual elevation and revelation. The body is in reality not a boundary, because it is porous—it has the ability to transform restrictive interpretations and be transgressive and transcending. The gendered, differently abled embodied subject is an alternative corporeality, a tool that has agency to liberate all bodies from oppressive attitudes about the body.[46] So in this alternative function of the Pelmo tradition, rather than representing nuns as having limited access and powers in a Buddhist community in contrast to male monks, the tantric tradition of Nun Pelmo provides a female monastic deity who is able to perform ritual activities of a soteriological, instrumental, and proprietary nature. Tibetan nuns harness the energies of local spirits connected with their native traditions, which are said to ward off disease, danger, and natural disaster. Feminist disability theory introduces this as a "universalizing view" of disability that will replace an often persisting "minoritizing view." Understanding how disability operates as an identity category and cultural concept will enhance how we

44. See Susannah Mintz's study of Nancy Mairs; Mintz 2011, 161–82.

45. See Scully 2014, 204–21.

46. See McRuer 2004, 48–78; and Erevelles 2001, 92–111.

understand what it is to be human, our relationships with one another, and the experiences of embodiment.[47] Therefore, through the lens of resistance to normativity and the reversal of liminality and disability to centrality and ableness, the Nun Pelmo tradition reminds the reader about our shared humanness, empowered identity, compassion, and capacity for greatness despite obstacles.

Transdisciplinarity research, through the lens of feminist and disability theories, provides a new compass to uncover uncharted territories in the popular Tibetan Buddhist tradition of Nun Pelmo, undisciplining the boundaries often encountered in understanding modern applications. The legacy of this tradition in the modern context supports monastic gender equity and reveals the struggles for cultural representation.

References

Tibetan Sources

Dge slong ma dpal mo'i rnam thar nges 'byung rgyud la skye ba'i chos gtam [The Biography of Kamala Bhikshuni, Princess of King Dharma Pal, an Ancient King of Kashmir, India]. 1953. Kalimpong: Tibet Mirror Press.

G.yu thog Yon tan mgon po. 2002. *Bdud rtsi snying po yan lag brgyud pa gsang ba man ngag gi rgyud* [The Secret Essence of Ambrosia in Eight Branches: The Secret Upadesha Section of the Tantra]. Lhasa: Nationalities Languages Press.

Jo gdan Bsod nams bzang po. n.d. *Smyung gnas bla ma brgyud pa'i rnam thar* [Hagiographies of the Lineage Gurus of the Fasting Ritual]. Block print. Lhasa: Dpal ldan par khang.

Western Sources

Braitstein, Lara, and Shamar Rinpoche. 2011. *The Path to Awakening: A Commentary on Ja Chekawa Yeshe Dorje's Seven Points of Mind Training.* Delhi: Motilal Banarsidass.

Brody, Saul Nathanial. 1974. *The Disease of the Soul: Leprosy in Medieval Literature.* Ithaca, NY: Cornell University Press.

Cabezén, José Ignacio. 2017. *Sexuality in Classical South Asian Buddhism.* Somerville, MA: Wisdom Publications.

Choden, Kunzang. 2004. *Dawa: The Story of a Stray Dog in Bhutan.* Bhutan: Riyang Books.

47. Garland-Thomson 2002, 5; and Porter 1997, xiv.

De Bruin, Hanne. 1998. *Leprosy in South India: Stigma and Strategies of Coping.* Pondicherry: Institut Français de Pondicherry.

DeCaroli, Robert. 2004. *Haunting the Buddha: Indian Popular Religions and the Formation of Buddhism*. Oxford: Oxford University Press.

Dimitrov, Dragomir. 2000. "Lakṣmī—On the Identity of Some Indo-Tibetan Scholars of the 9th–13th Centuries." *Zentralasiatische Studien* 30: 9–27.

Erevelles, Nirmala. 2001. "In Search of the Disabled Subject." In *Embodied Rhetoric: Disability in Language and Culture*, edited by James C. Wilson and Cynthia Wilson-Lewiecki, 92–111. Carbondale: Southern Illinois University Press.

Fjeld, Heidi, and Theresia Hofer. 2011. "Women and Gender in Tibetan Medicine." *Asian Medicine* 6: 175–216.

Flood, Gavin. 1999. *Beyond Phenomenology. Rethinking the Study of Religion*. London: Cassell.

Garland-Thomson, Rosemarie. 2002. "Integrating Disability: Transforming Feminist Theory." *NWSA Journal* 14.3: 1–32.

Gilchrist, Roberta. 1994. *Medieval Bodies in the Material World: Gender, Stigma and the Body.* Manchester: Manchester University Press.

'Gos Lo tsā ba Gzhon nu dpal. 1988. *The Blue Annals.* Translated by George Roerich. Delhi: Motilal Barnarsidass.

Gutschow, Kim. 2004. *Being a Buddhist Nun: The Struggle for Enlightenment in the Himalaya.* Cambridge, MA: Harvard University Press.

Gyatso, Janet. 2003. "One Plus One Makes Three: Buddhist Gender, Monasticism, and the Law of the Non-Excluded Middle." *History of Religions* 43.2: 89–115.

Harris, Stephen E. 2016. "Buddhism and Disability." In *Disability and World Religions: An Introduction*, edited by Darla Y. Schumm and Michael Stoltzfus, 25–45. Waco, TX: Baylor University Press.

Kafer, Alison. 2013. *Feminist, Queer, Crip*. Bloomington: Indiana University Press.

Kapstein, Matthew T. 2013. "Remarks of the Mani Kabum and the Cult of Avalokiteśvara in Tibet." In Tuttle and Schaeffer, *Tibetan History Reader*, 90–107.

van der Kuijp, Leonard W. J. 2006. "The Earliest Indian Reference to Muslims in a Buddhist Philosophical Text of 'circa' 700." *Journal of Indian Philosophy* 34.3: 169–202.

———. 2016. "From Chongzhen lishu 崇禎曆書 to Tengri-yin udq-a and Rgya rtsis chen mo." In *Tibetan Printing: Comparison, Continuities, and Change*, edited by Hildegard Diemberger, Franz-Karl Ehrhard, and Peter Kornicki, 51–71. Leiden: Brill.

Leung, Angela Ki Che. 2009. *Leprosy in China: A History*. New York: Columbia University Press.

Makley, Charlene E. 2007. *The Violence of Liberation: Gender and Tibetan Buddhist Revival in Post-Mao China*. Berkeley: University of California Press.

McRuer, Robert. 2004. "Composing Bodies; or, De-Composition: Queer Theory, Disability Studies, and Alternative Corporealities." *JAC: A Quarterly Journal for the Interdisciplinary Study of Rhetoric, Culture, Literacy, and Politics* 24.1: 48–78.

Mintz, Susannah B. 2011. "Transforming the Tale: The Auto/body/ographies of Nancy Mairs." In *On the Literary Nonfiction of Nancy Mairs*, edited by M. Johnson and S.

Mintz, 161–82. Critical Studies in Gender, Sexuality, and Culture 14. New York: Palgrave Macmillan.

Mitchell, David, and Sharon Snyder. 2000. *Narrative Prosthesis: Disability and the Dependencies of Discourse*. Ann Arbor: University of Michigan Press.

Mortensen, Eric. 2019. "Boundaries of the Borderlands Mapping Gyelthang." In *Frontier Tibet: Patterns of Change in the Sino-Tibetan Borderlands*, edited by Stéphane Gros, 115–39. Amsterdam: Amsterdam University Press.

Nicolescu, Basarab. 1996. *La transdisciplinarité: Manifeste*. Monaco: Éditions du Rocher.

———. 2006. "Transdisciplinarity: Past, Present and Future." In *Moving Worldviews: Reshaping Sciences, Policies, and Practices for Endogenous Sustainable Development*, edited by Bertus Haverkort and Coen Reijntjes, 142–66. Holland: Compas Editions.

Orsi, Robert. 2006. *Between Heaven and Earth: The Religious Worlds People Make and the Scholars Who Study Them*. Princeton, NJ: Princeton University Press.

Padma'tsho (Baimacuo), and Sarah Jacoby. 2020. "Gender Equality in and on Tibetan Buddhist Nuns' Terms." *Religions* 11: 1–19.

Porter, James. 1997. "Foreword." In *The Body and Physical Difference: Discourses of Disability in the Humanities*, edited by David T. Mitchell and Sharon L. Snyder, xiii–xciv. Ann Arbor: University of Michigan Press.

Schaeffer, Kurtis, Matthew Kapstein, and Gray Tuttle, eds. 2013. *Sources of Tibetan Tradition*. New York: Columbia University Press.

Schriempf, Alexa. 2001. "(Re) fusing the Amputated Body: An Interactionist Bridge for Feminism and Disability." *Hypatia* 16.4: 53–79.

Schumm, Darla Y. 2010. "Reimagining Disability." *Journal of Feminist Studies in Religion* 26.2: 132–37.

Scully, Jackie Leach. 2014. "Disability and Vulnerability: On Bodies, Dependence, and Power." In *Vulnerability: New Essays in Ethics and Feminist Philosophy*, edited by Catriona Mackenzie, Wendy Rogers, and Susan Dodds, 204–21. London: Oxford University Press.

Stocker, Susan S. 2001. "Disability and Identity: Overcoming Perfectionism." *Frontiers: A Journal of Women Studies* 22, no. 2: 154–73.

Tuttle, Gray, and Kurtis Schaeffer, eds. 2013. *The Tibetan History Reader*. New York: Columbia University Press.

Ujeed, Sangseraima. 2016. "Dge-slong-ma dpal-mo, the Princess, the Mahasiddha, the Nun and the Lineage Holder: As Presented in the *thob yig* of Za-ya Paṇḍita Blo-bzang 'phrin-las (1642–1715)." *Journal of the Oxford Centre for Buddhist Studies* 10: 128–66.

Vargas-O'Bryan, Ivette. 2001. "The Life of dGe-slong ma dPal mo: The Experience of a Leper, Founder of a Fasting Ritual, a Transmitter of Buddhist Teachings on Suffering and Renunciation in Tibetan Religious History." *Journal of the International Association of Buddhist Studies* 24.2: 157–87.

———. 2013. "Falling Reign, Raining Power in Reptilian Affairs: The Balancing of Religion and the Environment." In *Non-Human Animals in South Asian Religions: Myth, Ritual and Folklore, Religions of South Asia*, edited by Fabrizio Ferrari and Thomas Dähnhardt, 110–25. Sheffield: Equinox Publishing.

———. 2015. "Balancing Tradition Alongside a Progressively Scientific Tibetan Medical System." In *Disease, Religion and Healing in Asia: Collaborations and Collisions*, edited by Ivette Vargas-O'Bryan and Zhou Xun, 122–45. London: Routledge.

———. Forthcoming [2023]. "Disablement for Enlightenment in the Hagiographies of Gelongma Palmo." In *Disability and Medieval Cult of Saints: Interdisciplinary and Intersectional Approaches*, edited by Stephanie Grace-Petinos, Leah Pope Parker, and Alicia Spencer-Hall. Amsterdam: Amsterdam University Press.

Wangchen Rinpoche. 2009. *Buddhist Fasting Practice: The Nyungne Method of Thousand-Armed Chenrezig.* Ithaca, NY: Snow Lion Publications.

Wangdi, Pema. 2008. *Seeds of Faith: A Comprehensive Guide to the Sacred Places of Bhutan.* Thimphu, Bhutan: KMT Publishers.

Yeh, Emily. 2008. "From Wasteland to Wetland?: Nature and Nation in China's Tibet." *Environmental History* 14.2: 103–37.

———. 2013. *Taming Tibet: Landscape Transformation and the Gift of Chinese Development.* Ithaca, NY: Cornell University Press.

Zhang, Yajing. 2014. "Halihalihali Guanyin tuxiang chutan 哈里哈里哈里观音图像初探" [An Iconographical Study of Harihariharivāhanodbhavalokeśvara (Harihari-hari Guanyin) Image]. *Palace Museum Journal* [故宫博物院院刊] 1: 25–26.

Zivkovic, Tanya. 2013. "Embodying the Past: Gelongma Palmo and the Tibetan Nyungne Rituals." *Journal of Ritual Studies* 27.2: 45–63.

The Great One: On the Life and Oeuvre of Tibet's Last Great Statue-Maker, Penba Dorjé

Cameron David Warner

Few teachers end up changing the actual subject they teach ontologically and epistemologically. What I mean is that few teachers change the population of people who enter a discipline and the types of questions that discipline asks of its subject. Leonard W. J. van der Kuijp, who was my PhD supervisor, is that kind of teacher. Though he spent the majority of his career at Harvard, Leonard always struck me as almost radically non-hierarchical or non-elitist. He did not place much value on where a graduate student had done their undergraduate training, nor on their family background. He judged all of his students by the same measure: how well they performed in class, week after week. Because of these principles, Leonard oversaw generations of American students like me who came from middle-class backgrounds, which was once uncommon at the Harvard Graduate School of Arts and Sciences, as well as many Tibetan and Chinese students from the People's Republic of China (PRC). His drive to share his fascination with Tibetan history and philosophy led Leonard to offer a course on Tibet to the Bachelor of Liberal Arts students at the Harvard Extension School, to train high school teachers through the National Endowment for the Humanities summer institutes, and to teach many courses at Renmin University and Sichuan University in the PRC.

Many online biographies mention Leonard's time working in Kathmandu with the Nepal-German Manuscript Preservation Project. But few mention his pioneering effort to access rare Tibetan manuscripts first in Beijing and later in Lhasa. Leonard's focus on manuscripts helped to foster an epistemological revolution in Tibetan studies. Certainly Leonard was not alone in this endeavor. Elliott Sperling, Gene Smith, as well as many of their colleagues in the PRC and elsewhere understood the direct correlation between the quality of our understanding of Tibetan literature and the materials available. In his many publications on often obscure or unknown historical figures, texts, and social movements, Leonard created a methodological foundation, a body of knowledge, and material resources that would benefit others for many generations to come. Reflecting on this brief biography of Leonard drew me back to my graduate school days and my interest in the oeuvre of a Tibetan master with qualities similar to Leonard—Penba Dorjé.

Brief Biography of Chenmola Penba Dorjé

Penba Dorjé (Spen ba rdo rje, 1930–2011) served as one of the chief craftsmen (*dbu che*) or, in this case, chief sculptor for the Ganden Podrang and later as the chief craftsman of the Central Tibetan Administration.[1] In his own words, Penba Dorjé and his closest colleagues labored as experts in the "crafting" (*bzo bo*) of sculptures (*rten*).[2] After his education and early career in Tsang and Ü, Penba Dorjé fled Tibet in 1963. In 1967 the Dalai Lama requested that Penba Dorjé help construct a new geomantic imperial temple (*gtsug lag khang*) for the exile community and a new Norbulingka for the education of future Tibetan artists. Based on a very fortunate suggestion from Tashi Tsering of the Amnye Machen Institute, I had the opportunity to interview Penba Dorjé in 2006. The subject of that interview formed the basis for a chapter of my dissertation on the history and practice of the Jowo Śākyamuni, part of which was later published in English (Warner 2011) and translated into

I would like to acknowledge and thank Kim Yeshi from the Norbulingka Institute for her kind help in sending me her interview with Penba Dorjé; the financial support of the Danish Council for Independent Research, Culture and Communication (Grant number DFF 4180-00326); the editors of this volume; Tashi Tsering of the Amnye Machen Institute; and Penba Dorjé himself for meeting with me so many years ago and gifting me his two-volume book on which this chapter is based.

1. In my experience, people in Dharamsala referred to him as Chenmola Penba Dorjé (Chen mo lags Spen ba rdo rje), or simply Chenmola, a term of both affection and deep respect that indexes a person's status as being officially employed as a type of craftsman for the Dalai Lama and his government. For example, another great statue-maker, and a colleague of Penba Dorjé, was Chenmola Shilok (Chen mo lags Shi logs).

2. Though of course it is normally insufficient to translate *rten* as "statue," I have decided to do so here to place our focus on Penba Dorjé more than the *rten* he produced. Literally meaning "support," *rten* contextually refer to statues, books, and stūpas, but not in the modern European sense of "statue." In this context, *rten* means specifically "Body-supports" (*sku rten*), in the sense that these objects exist in an ontological continuity with other Bodies of the Buddha. In his own writings, Penba Dorjé almost exclusively refers to the three-dimensional metal images of Buddhist deities that he made as either *rten* or by the name of the deity. Only in relation to one particularly special Padmsambhava statue does he use the term of art "proxy" (*sku tshab*). This is in variance to much of Tibetan writing, for which I once documented over twenty-six potential words for the English word "statue" (Warner 2011).

Tibetan (Warner 2016). At the time of the interview, Penba Dorjé gave me his two-volume work on Tibetan craftmanship and manufacturing, the *Book of the Seven Precious Possessions* (*Deb ther rin chen sna bdun*). Passages from volume 1 of that work form the primary empirical basis for this chapter. Like Leonard, Penba Dorjé spent the majority of his working life changing his craft through pathbreaking research and passing his knowledge on to a new generation.

The Book of the Seven Precious Possessions *and Related Titles*

The full title of Penba Dorjé's two-volume work is *Bod kyi mchog gi lus bzo 'bur sku'i mdo rgyud thig yig gis brgyad cing rtse gdong rig pa'i 'byung gnas kyi bzo rtsal gyi byung brjod mthong brgyud lag len man ngag gcig tu bkod pa'i deb ther rin chen sna bdun gyi khra tshom*, written by Btsan byol bod gzhung rten bzhengs dge che'i ming 'dzin rtse gdong khang chung ltag pa'i mi ngo Spen pa rdo rje, with the abbreviated title *Book of the Seven Precious Possessions* (*Deb ther rin chen sna bdun*). The second volume consists of passages of important Tibetan texts on crafting from luminaries such as Bodong Paṇchen Choklé Namgyel (Bo dong paṇ chen Phyogs las rnam rgyal, 1376–1451), the great scholar of Tibetan iconometry Menla Döndrup (Sman bla don grub, mid-fifteenth century),[3] and others.[4] I will not discuss volume 2 in further detail.

The first volume consists of an introduction followed by six sections: (1) India, (2) the earliest diffusion of the Dharma in Tibet, (3) the later diffusion of the Dharma in Tibet, (4) Tsedong Mönkarling (Rtse gdong smon dkar gling), (5) regarding manufacturing and its benefactors,[5] and (6) "ancillary items" (which consists mainly of a catalogue of native and foreign sources on Tibetan statuary available between 1982 and 1999). There are many fascinating chapters within all six sections, but for the sake of brevity, I will focus my discussion on various chapters in sections three and four.

Section three, "The Later Diffusion of the Dharma in Tibet," consists of fourteen chapters covering the main headings one would expect in an over-

3. For more on Menla Döndrup, see Denwood 1996.

4. For an overview of sources on iconometry and Tibetan statue-making, a good place to begin is the oeuvre of Erberto Lo Bue 1990, 1991, 1997.

5. The majority of this section focuses on various rituals important to the tradition of Tibetan Buddhist statuary, such as the *sems bkyed cho go*, the *gsol 'debs smon lam*, the *rab tu gnas pa*, the *tshon gyi cho ga* (the "method of [creating] pigments"), and so forth, drawn from Dil [De'u] dmar dge bshes bstan 'dzin phun tshog's *A Flower That Reflects the Full Spectrum of the Rainbow: A Clear Explanation of the Process of Preparing Pigments* (*Kun gsal tshon gyi las rim me tog mdangs ster 'ja' 'od 'bum byin*).

view of Tibetan statue-making. For example, Penba Dorjé guides the reader from the origin of the renovation of Tibetan manufactured items and buildings at the beginning of the second diffusion of the Dharma in Tibet through the Lhasa Döpel ('Dod dpal), the artistic practices of Repgong (Reb gong), and the techniques of the Royal House of Bhutan. The first few chapters, for example, concern Lachenpo Gongpa Rapsel (Bla chen po Dgongs pa rab sal, 832?–915?), Sapaṇ Künga Gyeltsen (Sa paṇ Kun dga' rgyal mtshan, 1182–1251), Butön Rinchendrup (Bu ston rin chen grub, 1290–1364), and Tsongkhapa's *An Ocean of Sacrificial Cakes* (*Zhal zas rgya mtsho*). The choice of these chapters and their order closely resembles that of the celebrated *The Fine Arts: A Drop of Water on the Tip of a Hair* (*Bzo gnas skra rtse'i chu thigs*) by Könchok Tendzin (Dkon mchog bstan 'dzin), which was published seven years before Penba Dorjé's *Book of the Seven Precious Possessions*.[6] Specifically, section three, chapters 1–11 of *Book of the Seven Precious Possessions* closely resemble chapters 18–29 of Könchok Tendzin's *A Drop of Water* (*Chu thigs*). Penba Dorjé consistently marks which sections of his book derive from *A Drop of Water*. However, he does not follow *A Drop of Water* exactly in either content or order. For example, *Book of the Seven Precious Possessions* reverses chapters 18 and 19 of *A Drop of Water* and does not include chapter 20 on Pakmodrupa (Phag mo gru pa), "The Vajra-King Pakmodrupa and His Knowledge and Training in Painting" (Ri mo ma bslab par mkhyen cing phul byung phag mo gru pa rdo rje rgyal po). For the most part, the differences between these sections of the two works are minor until we reach chapter 30 of *A Drop of Water* and section three, chapter 12, of *Book of the Seven Precious Possessions*. Whereas *A Drop of Water* continues with chapters on particular artists or schools of art that arose during and after the mid-seventeenth century, *Book of the Seven Precious Possessions* begins to turn its attention to particular local people, traditions, and schools of art that either interest Penba Dorjé or will serve as a backstory for his own autobiography. Of these, the most notable chapters are a paragraph on a female painter from his natal district of Tsedong (*Rtse gdong bud med lha bris jo mo chos sgron*)[7] and an overview of the Döpel goldsmith workshop at the

6. Future work could productively compare the contents of *A Drop of Water* and *Book of the Seven Precious Possessions* with *The Precious Casket: A Collection of Writings on the Fine Arts* (*Bzo rig phyogs bsgrigs rin chen sgrom bu*), a collection of early writings by famous scholars on technological aspects of Tibetan arts and crafts (*śilpaśāstra*), including iconography, the manufacturing of incense, the construction of maṇḍalas, and so forth (Dkon mchog bstan 'dzin 2011).

7. Further information on the Tsedong tradition of metal sculpture is available in volume 23 of *Selected Materials for an Analysis of Tibetan History and Culture* (*Bod kyi rig gnas lo rgyus dpyad gzhi'i rgyu cha bdams bsgrigs*), *A History of Copper and Other Crafts of the Peo-*

foot of the Potala (*'Dod dpal bzo las kyi tshogs pa rtsa 'dzugs dang de'i 'gan nus skor*).[8] In later chapters on the Tsedong sculptural tradition and its most honored practitioners, many further references to the Döpel also occur.

The fourth section of *Book of the Seven Precious Possessions* contains the most valuable historical information on the Tsedong district, its unique artistic tradition, and the autobiography of Penba Dorjé. The section begins with a concise summary of the Sakya Khön ('Khon) family lineage, the lineage of the Tsedong Labrang, the monastic seat, and wealthy families. Penba Dorjé recounts his personal experiences of learning and teaching the specific skills needed in the Tsedong manufacturing tradition, he covers Tsedong songs, and finally he turns his attention to his own autobiography. He writes about his ancestors and how he paid reverence to them through constructing Tibetan Buddhist images with his own hands and his crafting education in Tibet. After some pages on his journey into exile and his time in a Tibetan refugee camp in Siliguri, he recounts how the Dalai Lama requested he erect a series of statues for the newly constructed Tekchen Chöling Tsuklakhang (Theg chen chos gling gtsug lag khang) in order to correct the mistake of an unfulfilled prophecy by Dzongsar Khyentsé Jamyang Chökyi Lodrö (Rdzong gsar mkhyen brtse 'Jam dbyangs chos kyi blo gros, 1893–1959). Penba Dorjé is best known for those images and for his crucial role in founding a statue-making workshop at the Norbulingka Institute in Sidhpur and educating a new generation of artisans. Additionally, Penba Dorjé includes two sets of images in volume 1. The first is a series of photographs of his family in exile, together with line drawings of Tibetan artistic details and examples of iconometric measurements. Volume 1 ends with a second series of photographs of the most important statues of Penba Dorjé's career.

Notes on the History of the Tsedong Tradition

In his excellent *A History of Tibetan Painting: The Great Tibetan Painters and Their Traditions*, David Jackson presents an overview of the artistic traditions of Tsedong with a focus, unsurprisingly, on the painters from that region.[9] In the course of his research, Jackson uncovered some information about another chief craftsman, Shilok (*dbu che* Shi logs, 1919–92), who was a painter, but he

ple of Tsedong District (Rtse gdong khul gyi mi rigs lag shes zangs bzo'i lo rgyus skor 2003), but unfortunately I was not able to consult it for this chapter. For more information on the history of Tsedong, see Jeshong 2009.

8. Alexander 2002.

9. Jackson 1996.

also interviewed the sculptor Shilok (Shi logs, 1921–?) in 1995, the same sculptor I later interviewed in 2006. According to the sculptor Shilok, Tsedong is near to the Tsangdram Jema Lhakhang (Gtsang 'gram Bye ma lha khang; one of the ancient demon-suppressing temples). He also told Jackson that famous painters from Tsedong included Chemo Künga Döndrup (Che mo Kun dga' don 'grub) of the Mönkyi (Smon skyid) family and his son, Tsewang Wangdü (Tshe dbang dbang 'dus, 1915–73), each of whom painted at Sakya. In fact, Shilok's own father was the great painter Yudrung (G.yu drung, ca. 1897–1959) of the Changra (Lcang rwa) family, who served as the *chemo* of both Sakya and Lhasa and died in Lhasa. His first son was Püntsok Wangdü (Phun tshogs dbang 'dus, 1916–64), who was a member of the Döpel ('Dod dpal) in Lhasa and, as we will see, a teacher to Penba Dorjé.

Section four, chapter 6 of *Book of the Seven Precious Possessions* is titled *Rtse gdong gi bzo rig rten bgzhengs phyag rtsal dar lugs sogs rang gi myong tshor ngo ma* and outlines how the Tsedong tradition of Tibetan statuary arose over a period of four generations. According to Penba Dorjé, there were three traditions of metal statuary in Tibet: the Chinese tradition in the Kham region, the Newari tradition, and the Tsedong tradition in Ü and Tsang. The Tsedong tradition was particularly influential at Trashikhyil (Bra shis khyil) in Zhikatsé, Sakya, and in Lhasa through the Döpel goldsmith workshop. The Tsedong practitioners produced distinctive "offering utensils" (*mchod chas*), "ritual objects" (*mgron chas*), and "statuary" (*sku rten*). Centered at Tsedong Mönkarling (Rtse gdong smon dkar gling), Penba Dorjé roots the beginning of his lineage in a series of miracles and prophecies at the time of the third generation of the Sakya Dakchen Drölma Podrang (Sa skya bdag chen sgrol ma pho brang); the Tenth Dalai Lama Tsültrim Gyatso (Tshul khrims rgya mtsho, 1816–37); and the Thirty-Fifth Sakya Trindzin Trashi Rinchen (Bkra shis rin chen).[10] As the tradition grew, their lineage passed on the oral instructions for line drawings in the *Dgongs rgyan bshad khrid zab nan* written by Lhodrak Mentang Yizhin Norbu (Lho brag sman thang Yid bzhin nor bu) "based on the underlying meaning of the sutras and tantras." Among the second generation of the Tsedong Dekyi Khangsar (Rtse dgong bde skyid khang gsar), there were artists such as Wangdü Norbu (Dbang 'dud nor bu) and Tsedong Trashi Dargyé (Rtse gdong Bkra shis dar rgyas). In the third generation, some of the prominent artists were Tsedong Dekhanggi Jolak Drandül (Rtse gdong bde khang gi Jo lags Dgra 'dul), Tsedong Changsharpé Yap Yungdrung (Rtse gdong lcang shar pa'i Yab G.yung drung), Dzongpönpé Jolak Norgyé (Rdzong dpon pa'i Jo lags Nor

10. The Thirty-Fifth Sa skya Bdag khri khri rabs, Nga dbang kun dga' theg chen bkra shis rin chen grags pa rgyal mtshan dpal bzang po.

rgyas), and Khewang Shatak (Mkhas dbang sha stag), who served as the official chief craftsman for the construction of images at Sakya. Penba Dorjé offers particular praise for the work of the fourth generation under whom he trained and whom he worked with in Tibet: Dekyikhang Sarpé Jolak Dzamlhala (Bde skyid khang gsar pa'i Jo lags 'Dzam lha lags), Changshargyi Jolak Kudrepa Püntsok Wangdüla (Lcang shar gyi Jo lags sku bgres pa Phun tshogs dbang 'dus lags), Drenpönpé Jolak Wanggyella ('Dren dpon pa'i Jo lags Dbang rgyal lags), Khangtakgi Jolak Dzamlha Dorjela (Khang ltag gi Jo lags 'Dzam lha rdo rje lags), and Changshargyi Jolak Kuzhön Shilokla (Lcang shar gyi Jo lags sku gzhon Shi logs lags). The fourth generation Tsedong masters worked closely on a number of the Thirteenth Dalai Lama's well-known renovation projects. For example, Püntsok Wangdü was an integral part of the renovations of Samyé in 1936.

Penba Dorjé's Work in Tibet

It is difficult to provide a complete chronological account of Penba Dorjé's life. I consulted three sources: the current website of the Norbulingka Institute, a translation of an interview with Penba Dorjé sent to me by Kim Yeshi, one of the cofounders of the Norbulingka, and the *Book of the Seven Precious Possessions*. The biography on the Norbulingka's website is clearly based on the translated interview. In both of those sources, Penba Dorjé states that he can only remember a small fraction of the statues he erected; he admitted to being especially forgetful of his time in Tibet.[11] The account of his work life in *Book of the Seven Precious Possessions* is much more complete, but his recollections are not always presented in chronological order. In bringing the three sources together, I have erred on the side of caution, making special note of projects I expect will be of interest to most historians of Tibet.

Born into the Tsedong Mönkarling Khangchung Takpa (Rtse gdong smon dkar gling khang chung ltag pa), which was an "estate owned by a monastery" (*chos gzhi mi rtsa*) of Sakya, his family had around twenty-five members (counting the servants), of which there were five older brothers, two older sisters, and one younger brother. Penba Dorjé began his education as a statue-maker at age fourteen in an apprenticeship with his older brother, Dzamlha Dorjé ('Dzam lha rdo rje). At that time, there were around forty people from

11. When I interviewed Penba Dorjé in 2006 regarding Dzongsar Khyentsé's prophecy of the Chinese invasion of Tibet, his memory was entirely clear. Unfortunately, Shilok said he could not remember those events, though I do not know whether that was due to his advanced age or his reticence in divulging sensitive historical details to me.

Tsedong employed as statue-makers in Ü and Tsang. From around 1948 to 1950, he assisted in the construction of a private chamber in the Rasa Trülnang Tsuklakhang (Ra sa 'Phrul snang gtsug lag khang) for the Fourteenth Dalai Lama. In 1950 he worked on the Three Long-Life Deities (Tshe lha rnam gsum), the Tsongkhapa and His Five Main Disciples (Rje yab sras cha tshang lnga), two One-Thousand-Armed and One-Thousand-Eyed Avalokitas (Phyag stong spyan stong), the Lords of the Three Families (Rigs gsum dgon po), and the Three Main Gelukpa Tantric Deities: Guhyasamāja, Cakrasaṃvara, and Vajrabhairava (Gsang bde 'jigs gsum) for Lho Shelkar Chödé (Lho Shel dkar chos sde) Monastery. Many of the projects he worked on took multiple years to complete. For example, he labored for two years on the creation of a new set of ritual implements and traditional ornaments for the renovation of the Great Temple at Sakya and the refurbishment of the statues therein. Penba Dorjé also participated in the manufacture of three thousand of the Three Long-Life Deities—including Amitāyus (Tshe dpag med), Sitatārā (Sgrol dkar), and Uṣṇīṣavijayā (Rnam rgyal ma)—that were offered to the Dalai Lama when he was eight years old. In a team of seven, he worked for two years on the construction of large statues such as Vajrabhairava (Rdo rje 'jigs byed), Heruka (Khrag 'thung), and Guhyasamāja (Gsang ba 'dus pa) for wealthy families, and on colossal statues for the two principal Bön monasteries in Central Tibet, Menri Gön (Sman ri dgon) and Yungdrungling (G.yung drung gling). Later, he spent a year and four months constructing a number of large statues for the Khangsar Labrang (Khang gsar bla brang) at Ngor Monastery. He also reports that he worked on the Fourteenth Dalai Lama's new summer palace in Lhasa, the Norling Takten Mingyur Podrang (Nor gling rtag brtan mi 'gyur pho brang).[12]

Unsurprisingly, the rate of his work declined after the People's Liberation Army (PLA) invaded Central Tibet, but his work did not stop completely, even after the Dalai Lama fled into exile. His team completed another three thousand of the Three Long-Life Deities for the Desi Podrang (Sde srid pho brang) of Trashi Lhünpo (Bkra shis lhun po). In 1952 he made new statues of gold and copper for the assembly hall at Tingkyé Trashi Chödé (Gting skyes bkra shis chos sde; in present-day Dingjie County 定结县). In 1955 he and Shilok built a Tön Shenrap (Ston gshen rab) chief image for the newly constructed assembly hall at Menri Gön. In 1957 he erected the chief Buddha image with two attendants and other images for Shang Ganden Chökhor Gön (Shangs Dga' ldan chos 'khor dgon). And in 1959 Penba Dorjé and three subordinates took responsibility for building the statues needed for the Nyangtö Pökhang

12. Blo gros chos 'dzin 2009.

Dratsang (Nyang stod spos khang grwa tshang). Despite increasing restrictions on the practice of religion and rapid changes to Tibetan agriculture and economics, the Beijing government continued to support the Tenth Paṇchen Lama, Lobzang Trinlé Lhündrup Chökyi Gyentsen (Blo bzang phrin las lhun grub chos kyi rgyal mtshan, 1938–89), after the Dalai Lama fled to India in March 1959. For a chief sculptor like Penba Dorjé, this meant some orders for new statuary and other metalworks continued to come in. For example, in 1961, in service of the express wishes of the Tenth Paṇchen Lama, Penba Dorjé, his elder brother, Chenpo Jolak Dzamlha Dorjé (Gcen po Jo lags 'Dzam lha rdo rje), and Tsedong Drenpön Jolak Wanggyel Chok (Rtse gdong 'Dren dpon Jo lags Dbang rgyal mchog), together with ten other people from Tsedong and twelve people from Trashikyil Tselpa (Bkra shis dkyil tshal pa), formed a coalition in order to rebuild and restock the Trashi Lhünpo Dechen Podrang (Bde chen pho brang).[13] The newly constructed complete set of three thousand of the Three Long-Life Deities were the last sculptures that he ever constructed in Tibet.

In Tibet he collaborated with a different team on each project, but the majority of time was with three of his teachers: he spent his first ten years with his close relative Dzamlha Dorjé (1944–54), for two years Shilok "corrected his work," after which he "touched the feet" of the "second Viśvakarmā," Drenpönpé Jolak Wanggyel ('Dren dpon pa'i Jo lags dbang rgyal). In general, Penba Dorjé's career overlapped with primarily difficult times in Tibet for a craftsman of Buddhist statuary. Practices were changing, traditions were being lost. His autobiography offers specific praise for the Tsedong Changra Sharpé Uché (Rtse gdong lcang ra shar pa'i dbu che), Püntsok Wangdü (Phun tshogs dbang 'dus; the older brother of Shilok), and the Dekyi Khangsargyi Uché (Bde skyid khang gsar gyi dbu che), Dzamlha, for doing their best to uphold the traditions of the Döpel office in Lhasa, which they had inherited from the official administrator, the Chikhyap Uché (Spyi khyab dbu che).

13. With only the name to go on, the exact building is unclear. This could be either the Dechen Kelzang (Bde chen skal bzang) Palace built in Zhikatsé (Gzhis ka rtse) to replace the summer palace destroyed in a flood in 1954, or the Lhasa residence constructed for the Tenth Paṇchen Lama, but properly called the Dorjé Podrang (Rdo rje pho brang). It is my hunch that it is the Dechen Kelzang, as the Dorjé Podrang appears to have been built in the mid-1950s.

The Beginning of His Life in Exile

Beginning on March 4, 1963, Penba Dorjé, his father, and six others fled Tibet at night, hiding in the daytime. By March 24 they arrived at Samdrong (Sa 'brong) in Sikkim. Not long after, they ended up in the Tibetan refugee camp in Siliguri, which Penba Dorjé likened to a life-threatening prison. At the time there were 180 Tibetans who arrived in stages but were prevented from leaving the camp. Many possessed chronic illnesses, difficulties of all kinds, or were simply ill-suited for life in a relatively low-altitude, humid environment. Penba Dorjé summed up the experience of the Siliguri camp in the following way:

> The people who had abided in the cool snow ranges [of the Himālaya] became refugees, forced to stay in the hot district of Siliguri with no way to tolerate hardship, like a big fish who falls into hot sand.[14]

Many of those in the camp were accused of crimes, such as stealing from Indians. Some Tibetan officials attempted to negotiate on behalf of the refugees. When he finally left Siliguri, Penba Dorjé traveled to Bylakuppe in the Mysore district of Karnataka. There he received teachings from Nyoshül Khenpo Jamyang Dorjé (Myo shul mkhan po 'Jam dbyangs rdo rje, 1931–99) on the *Abhisamayālaṃkāra*, the *Madhyamakāvatāra*, the *Bodhisattvacaryāvatāra*, and *The Words of My Perfect Teacher* (*Kun bzang bla ma'i zhal lung*), all from the point of view of the *Khrid yig ye shes bla ma*, an esoteric Dzogchen text written by Jikmé Lingpa (1730–98), and other teachings. He resumed his life's work constructing three new sculptures for the Namling Dratsanggi Tsuklakhang (Rnam gling grwa tshang gi gtsug lag khang): a chief image of the Buddha, an image of Tsepakmé, and an image of a Guru Nangsi Zilnön (Gu ru snang srid zil gnon), which measured eight feet high, together with a long trumpet (*dung chen*), Chinese flute (*rgya gling*), leg flute (*rkang gling*) and sundry other items.

14. Spen pa rdo rje 2001, 198: *bsil ldan gangs khrod du gnas pa'i mi rigs skyabs bcol rnams tsha yul shi li gu rir lo zla bstud mar do dam 'og gnas dgos 'di/ nya mo bye tshan du lhung 'dra'i dka' ngal bzod thabs bral nas/.*

In Service of the Expressed Wishes of Gongsa Kyapgön Chenpo (Gong sa skyabs mgon chen po), the Dalai Lama

In October 1967, in accordance with the underlying intentions granted by the general order of the private office of the Dalai Lama, housed in the original temporary dwelling of the government in Dharamsala, Penba Dorjé began to erect the statues for the newly constructed Tekchen Chöling Tsuklakhang (Theg chen chos gling Gtsug lag khang), the temple that would serve as the "national cathedral," the equivalent of the Rasa Trülnang Tsuklakhang (Ra sa 'Phrul snang Gtsug lag khang), in exile.[15] I have already dealt with the origin of those sculptures at length in my dissertation and a previous article.[16] In short, around 1950 Dzongsar Jamyang Khyentsé Chökyi Lodrö recovered a treasure text that predicted the PLA would invade Tibet unless a Guru Nangsi Zilnön statue was erected in the Rasa Trülnang Tsuklakhang. On the surface, the purpose of the statue was to repel any invading forces, in the same way Guru Nangsi Zilnön statues had been used for centuries. But as Penba Dorjé explained to me in 2006, anti-Nyingmapa aristocrats intervened. They insisted a Guru Rinpoché statue with an *añjali mudra* that was less than life size be constructed and installed directly in front of the Jowo Śākyamuni. The purpose of the placement of the statue derives from a long-running controversy that the crown Tsongkhapa put on the head of the Jowo blocked the light rays from his *uṣṇīṣa*, which previously pinned down a group of demons called the seven Damsi brothers (*dam srid spun bdun*). The Guru Nangsi Zilnön recommended by Jamyang Khyentsé Chökyi Lodrö would counteract Tsongkhapa's crown, retrapping the demons. Of course, the *añjali mudra* Guru Rinpoché failed and the PLA captured Tibet. Therefore the Dalai Lama was particularly keen to ensure that the mistake would not be repeated a second time. He personally conveyed his orders to Penba Dorjé. Later when I repeated this story to other learned Tibetans in Dharamsala, some would claim they had repeatedly heard the Dalai Lama tell this story in monasteries in exile.[17] Penba Dorjé was well placed to know this story well. Not only was he responsible for the statues for the Tekchen Chöling Tsuklakhang, but his relatives and close colleagues worked for the Döpel, the office presumably tasked with erecting a

15. For an alternative account of the Dalai Lama's orders regarding the construction of the Tsuklakhang, see Rwa rgya dpal ldan 2019.

16. Warner 2008, 2011, 2016.

17. For an alternative early account of the history of Tibetans in Dharamsala, see Fürer-Haimendorf 1990.

new Padmasambhava for the Rasa Trülnang Tsuklakhang. In fact, according to Penba Dorjé, it was his colleague Shilok and Shilok's older brother, Püntsok Wangdü, who were forced to make the failed *añjāli mudra* Guru Rinpoché. Unfortunately, when I asked Shilok about that image in 2006, he said he did not remember its origin and I never had a second chance to interview him after hearing Penba Dorjé's recollection of this controversy.

The account of the construction of the statues for the Tekchen Chöling Tsuklakhang in *Book of the Seven Precious Possessions* repeats this story in detail, but carefully avoids mentioning the aristocrats' intervention and anti-Nyingmapa biases. Rather it states that Chokteng Kungo (Lcog steng sku ngo),[18] Tālama Tupten Norzang Chok (Tā bla ma thub bstan nor bzang mchog, 1904–?), and Kugerkyap Ngowo Dampa Tupten Nyima (Sku sger skyabs bsngo do dam pa Thub bstan nyi ma) and he were all summoned into the presence of the Dalai Lama, who was seated on his throne, for the purpose of receiving instructions on the design and layout of the new *tsuklakhang*. It was to be "a place for the Tibetan people to accumulate merit" and "an indispensable *tsuklakhang* on which they could rely." And since the one-story-high Guru Nangsi Zilnön facing east proscribed in Jamyang Khyentsé Chökyi Lodrö's prophecy to be erected in the Rasa Trülnang Tsuklakhang "was never realized," and "because of the very quick compassion and spiritual activity of Guru Rinpoché for human beings in this degenerate age," the Dalai Lama ordered that it be done in exile. The Dalai Lama also ordered the construction of the One-Thousand-Armed and One-Thousand-Eyed Avalokita (Spyan ras gzigs phyag stong spyan stong), and that it sit alongside the Guru Nangsi Zilnön so that in the future independence would be brought to Tibet.[19] These pages of *Book of the Seven Precious Possessions* deserve a closer reading in relation to other sources on this time period, especially the construction of the proxy (*sku tshab*) of the Rangjung Ngaden (Rang byung lnga ldan). Penba Dorjé's work on the Tekchen Chöling Tsuklakhang ended in 1970.

In the pages that follow, *Book of the Seven Precious Possessions* recounts some of Penba Dorjé's efforts to support the construction of the temples and monasteries that served to house the Buddhas, books, and ordained nuns and monks that embody Tibetan Buddhism in exile. In 1972 the Dalai Lama's tutor, Trijang Rinpoché (Khri byang rin po che, 1901–81) and Chopgyé Trichen Rinpoché Ngawang Khyenrap Tupten Lekshé Gyatso (Bco brgyad khri chen rin po che Ngag dbang mkhyen rab thub bstan legs bshad rgya mtsho, 1920–2007), the highly esteemed Sakya lama who once played a role in Leonard's life,

18. A title for a government official.

19. Spen pa rdo rje 2001, 202.15.

requested Penba Dorjé's help with erecting images for new monastic colleges. Penba Dorjé constructed new sculptures for Trijang's Genden Shartsé Dratsang (Dga' ldan shar rtse grwa tshang) and an eight-foot-high Buddha for Chopgyé Trichen Rinpoché's new monastery in Lumbini. After accounts of other work completed in exile in the 1970s, the fourth section of the first volume of *Book of the Seven Precious Possessions* continues with an elucidation of the statues that Penba Dorjé erected for the new Norbulingka Institute in the 1980s and his efforts to pass on the Tsedongpa tradition to a new generation of students who studied at the Norbulingka.

In conclusion, *Book of the Seven Precious Possessions* provides a wealth of information on the working lives of artists in Central Tibet in the late nineteenth and early twentieth centuries. It is also an important document of the early experience of exile and crucial for a history of the construction of the Tekchen Tsuklakhang, arguably the most important building for the ritual life of Tibetan refugees and converted pilgrims. A future study could fruitfully compare Penba Dorjé's notes on the training and education of Tibetan artists with that of Konchog Lhadrepa's *Art of Awakening*.[20] With the Dalai Lama in an advanced age and an increasing number of Tibetan exiles leaving South Asia for North America and Europe, we can see how a period of "exile" is transitioning to a period of diaspora. Not only has most of the first generation to leave Tibet passed away, but the way of life they recreated for themselves outside of Tibet is also declining. In sum, Penba Dorjé's firsthand perspective in the *Book of Seven Precious Possessions* offers two invaluable contributions to Tibetan history. First, he provides a fascinating account of the social relations and institutional organization of sculpture production in Tibet before 1959. Second, his account of the construction of sculptures for Tibetan temples in South Asia will serve as a window into the motivations and practices behind the construction of the exquisite Tibetan monuments that will hopefully survive in South Asia for centuries to come.

References

Alexander, André. 2002. "Zhol Village and a Mural Painting in the Potala: Observations Concerning Tibetan Architecture." *The Tibet Journal* 27.3–4: 109–11, 113–20.

Blo gros chos 'dzin. 2009. *Nor gling rtag brtan mi 'gyur pho brang gsar skrun skor*. In *Bod*

20. Konchog Lhadrepa and Davis 2017.

kyi lo rgyus rig gnas dpyad gzhi'i rgyu cha bdams bsgrigs, vol. 2, 214–25. Chengdu: Si khron dpe skrun tshogs pa si khron mi rigs dpe skrun khang.

Denwood, Philip. 1996. "The Artist's Treatise of sMan bla don grub." *The Tibet Journal* 21.2: 24–30.

Dkon mchog bstan 'dzin, ed. 2011. *Bzo rig phyogs bsgrigs rin chen sgrom bu*. Beijing: Krung go'i bod rig pa'i dpe skrun khang.

Fürer-Haimendorf, Christoph von. 1990. *The Renaissance of Tibetan Civilization*. Delhi: Oxford University Press.

Jackson, David Paul. 1996. *A History of Tibetan Painting: The Great Tibetan Painters and Their Traditions*. Beiträge zur Kultur- und Geistesgeschichte Asiens 15. Vienna: Verlag der Österreichischen Akademie der Wissenschaften.

Jeshong, Tashi Wangyal. 2009. *A Short Historical Account of Tsedong in Tsang Province, Tibet* [Gtsang g.yas ru rtse gdong gi phyi nang snod bcud kyi ngo sprod lo rgyus gzhon nu'i mgul rgyan]. Edited by Tashi Tsering. Historial Materials of Dbus gtsang Series 1. Dharamsala: Amyne Machen Institute.

Konchog Lhadrepa and Charlotte Davis. 2017. *The Art of Awakening: A User's Guide to Tibetan Buddhist Art and Practice*. Ithaca, NY: Snow Lion Publications.

Lo Bue, Erberto. 1990. "Iconographic Sources and Iconometric Literature in Tibetan and Himalayan Art." In *Indo-Tibetan Studies: Papers in Honour and Appreciation of Professor David L. Snellgrove's Contribution to Indo-Tibetan Studies*, edited by Tadeusz Skorupski, 171–97. Tring, UK: The Institute of Buddhist Studies.

———. 1991. "Statuary Metals in Tibet and the Himālayas: History, Tradition and Modern Use." *Bulletin of Tibetology* 1–3: 7–42.

———. 1997. "Érudits, artistes et fêtes de Lhasa." In *Lhasa: Lieu du Divin*, edited by Françoise Pommaret, 217–34. Geneva: Éditions Olizane.

Rtse gdong khul gyi mi rigs lag shes zangs bzo'i lo rgyus skor. 2003. In *Bod kyi rig gnas lo rgyus dpyad gzhi'i rgyu cha bdams bsgrigs*, edited by Bod rang skyong ljong srid gros lo rgyus rig gnas dpyad bzhi'i rgyu cha u yon lhan khang gis rtsom sgrig byas pa. Beijing: Mi rigs dpe skrun khang.

Rwa rgya dpal ldan. 2019. *Rda sa theg chen gtsug lag khang ngo sprod*. https://www.khabdha.org/?p=96748 (accessed May 1, 2021).

Spen pa rdo rje [Btsan byol bod gzhung rten bzhengs dge che'i ming 'dzin rtse gdong khang chung ltag pa'i mi ngo Spen pa rdo rje]. 2001. *Bod kyi mchog gi lus bzo 'bur sku'i mdo rgyud thig yig gis brgyad cing rtse gdong rig pa'i 'byung gnas kyi bzo rtsal gyi byung brjod mthong brgyud lag len man ngag gcig tu bkod pa'i deb ther rin chen sna bdun gyi khra tshom zhes bya ba deb dang po*. Sidhpur, HP: Norbulingka Institute.

Warner, Cameron David. 2008. "The Precious Lord: The History and Practice of the Cult of the Jowo Śākyamuni in Lhasa, Tibet." PhD diss., Harvard University.

———. 2011. "Re/crowning the Jowo Śākyamuni: Texts, Photographs, and Memories." *History of Religions* 51.1: 1–30.

———. 2016. "Jo bo śākya mu ne la dbu rgyan gsar du bsgron bskyar du bskron pa gang zhig yin nam 'brel yod yig cha dang/ dra dpar/ dran 'char bcas." *Dus babs*. http://tibettimes.net/2016/08/03/150319.

Tibet Viewed from Kashmir: Some Notes on the Relationship of Kashmir with Ladakh and Other Parts of Tibet

Michael Witzel

KASHMIR IS a close neighbor of the western parts of Tibet, just as Nepal is of Tibet's southern provinces. The inscriptions and texts of both areas contain scattered data on Tibet, though both regions (*maṇḍala*) have been largely focused on themselves.[1] Here a selection of data on Tibet will be presented that have been preserved in various medieval texts from Kashmir,[2] especially in the various Rājataraṅgiṇīs, starting with that of Kalhaṇa (composed in 1151 CE). Unfortunately, unlike Nepal, we have only about a dozen inscriptions from the Kashmir valley. They do not contribute much to the current endeavor.[3]

Bhoṭa and Bhoṭṭa

The country of Tibet is called *bhoṭa* or *bhoṭṭa*, both in Kashmir and Nepal. The term is based on Tibetan *bod*. Its inhabitants are the Bhoṭṭa, Bhoṭ(i)ya,[4] or Bhauṭṭa. The country and its people are mentioned frequently[5] from the mid-first millennium BCE onward. In Kalhaṇa's *Rājataraṅgiṇī* (1151 CE) they occur as Bhoṭṭa at 1.312, 4.168, as Bhuṭṭa[6] at 2.408, 435, or as Bhauṭṭa at 8.2287; Kṣemandra's *Lokaprakāśa* (ca. 1050 CE), or rather the additions made to it during Muslim rule (1339 CE), has *bhoṭiya* ("Tibetan [blankets]") at LPr.

1. Slaje 2012; Gutschow 1974.

2. See Sahnī and Francke 1908, 181–92.

3. Deambi 1982. The early modern period (Afghan, Sikh, Jammu reigns) is neglected here.

4. Note also Mahābhoṭa. Bhautya refers to one of the various *manus* called Bhūti (*Harivaṃśa*).

5. See the detailed discussion by Sahnī and Francke 1908, 181.

6. The vowels *o* and *u* are interchangeable in Kashmiri texts; see Witzel 2020, chap. 11.

2.40.[7] Bhoṭa appears a few times in Nepalese inscriptions (Vajrācārya 1974, 515–18)[8] and texts (*Gopālarājavaṃśāvali*, Vajrācārya and Malla 1985)[9] of the first and early second millennium CE.

The western part of Tibet and its population appear under the name Cīna as an undefined area (Chatterji 1951). In the *Mahābhārata*[10] and the *Manu Smṛti* (10.44), the Cīna[11] appear together with the Kirāta,[12] Khaśa, etc. In the *Mahābhārata* and *Rāmāyaṇa*, the Kirātas and Cīnas are described as "golden colored."[13] A late Pāli text of ca. 150 BCE, the *Milindapañha*[14] (The Questions of [the Indo-Greek king] Menandros) mentions Kashmir in a list of countries arranged in a rare spiral order.[15] The list starts with the Yavana (Greek) and Saka[16] in the center (i.e., the Panjab). It then continues clockwise, with the Cīna (W. Tibet), Vilāta (Virāṭa, Madhya Pradesh), Alasanda (Alexandria on the Indus, or in Arachosia), Kāsi (Benares)/Kosala (N. Bihar), and finally Kasmīra/Gandhāra.[17]

Another region and population of western Tibet is Zhangzhung; it is not mentioned in Kashmiri sources under this or a similar name. It probably over-

7. See Gopāl 2008, 121; cf. *Lokaprakāśa*.

8. Śivadeva's Lagantol inscription, no. 139, p. 411; with *bhoṭṭaviṣṭi*, a kind of yearly forced service by five people, as discussed by Vajrācārya 1974.

9. "The king of Bhoṭa ruled Nepal" (Vajrācārya 1974). This occurred some time after Amśūvarman (605 CE), but the exact year is unclear due to the overlap of the royal Licchavi and Gupta lines, at Manadeva Samvat 48–65 (624–41 CE), see Witzel 1990, 198.

10. Usually as eastern Himalayan people: see Mbh. *Sabhāparvan* 26.32; 52.8–10; 4.35.2; 5.584.

11. Cf. Chatterji, 1951: 20. While Cīna was originally thought to be located in western Tibet, later on Mahācīna refers to China itself. There is some confusion of the two areas.

12. First found in the *Atharvaveda* 10.4.14 (as girls digging up Himalayan herbs, just like today); further in *Vājasaneyi Saṃhitā* 30.16 and *Taittirīya Brāhmaṇa* 3.4.12.1 (see Chatterji 1951, 16 ff.); cf. also Rönnow 1936. The Kirātas were later on regarded as degraded Kṣatriyas; see *Manu Smṛti* 10.44.

13. *Kiṣkindya Kāṇḍa* 40, 27–28; Mbh. 5.584; 2.1836.

14. *Milindapañha* 4.8.88; see Witzel 1980 and 2000.

15. *Sacred Books of the East* 36, p. 204; see Witzel 1980, 206n26. For other schemes of geographic organization—clockwise *pradakṣiṇa,* anticlockwise *apasalavi*—see Witzel 2000; this is evident in the order of "provinces" in Old Persian inscriptions.

16. Then the land of the Indo-Greeks and of the newly arrived Central Asian Sakas.

17. Cf. Chatterji 1951, 21, who takes "Vilāta" as "Kirāta." On such lists, see my forthcoming detailed discussion "The 600 Nāgas of Kashmir." The list in the *Mahāmāyurī* seems to be equally complex, shifting between the extremes in the east and west, north, and south, and back. See the discussion by Lévi 1915 (who does not treat the actual arrangement).

laps with the Cīna area. It has recently been investigated by archaeologists who connect it with the Iron Age culture of the Changtang plateau of northwestern Tibet.[18] Zhangzhung was conquered by the Tibetan empire in 625 CE. Interestingly, this is the same time[19] that the new Hindu-oriented Kārkoṭa dynasty emerged in Kashmir. Was it a reaction to the expanding Tibetan influence and dominance in Central Asia and the Himalayas?

Also to be compared, though of unclear location in (western) Tibet, is the area of Strīrājya, "the realm of women." Its background may be quite ancient. The mid-/late Vedic *Jaiminīya Brāhmaṇa* 2.299 (definitely composed before 500 BCE) mentions the female hunters (*vyādhinī*)[20] of the Trigarta (Jammu) area. Similarly, the *Suishu* (seventh century) and Xuanzang mention a Strīrājya: "to the north of the country [of Kashmir] in the great snow mountain was the Suvarnagotra [golden people] country . . . the eastern 'Women Country,' so called because it was reigned by a succession of women. The husband of the queen was the king, but he did not administer the government."[21]

The country of Strīrājya is also mentioned in a legendary account at RT 4.587 as having been conquered by the Kashmiri king Jayāpīḍa. Further quotes are found in the *Kāmasūtra*, Varāhamihira's *Bṛhatsaṃhitā* (ca. 550 CE), and Bāṇa's *Harṣacarita* (seventh century CE).[22] This is reminiscent of an extensive belt of matriarchal societies, extending farther to Arunachal Pradesh (Khasi), Burma, Yunnan (Nakhi, Bei), central south China (Yao, Miao), and all the way to early Japan.[23] For Kashmir and the surrounding Himalayan/Hindukush areas, one may also compare the concept of "high mountain fairies" (hence, the new term "Peristan" for the area). The RT 3.468 records that the Kashmiri king Raṇāditya, who reigned shortly before the emergence of the Kārkoṭa dynasty (625–855 CE), is given the incredibly long reign of three hundred years, at the

18. Zhangzhung texts and bilingual Tibetan documents (eleventh century). Their language is closely related to the non-Indo-Aryan—i.e., Tibeto-Burman version—of Kinnauri. See the update by Martin 2013. The religion of the area was an early form of Bön.

19. Based on the recalculation of the *Rājataraṅgiṇī* dates by twenty-five years, corresponding to Chinese data (see Witzel 2020).

20. *Jaiminīya Brāhmaṇa* 2.299; cf. various Amazon legends, starting with Herodot and see below, note 22, on *strīrājya.*

21. Cf. Stein 1900, vol. 1, 330.

22. See also *Kāmasūtra* 2.6.45: *grāmanārī-viṣaye strīrājye ca bāhlīke* . . . ; Varāhamihira's *Bṛhatsaṃhitā* 14.22: *diśi paścimottarasyāṃ tuṣāra [tukhāra] . . . madrā aśmaka-kulūta . . . strīrājya* . . . ; Bāṇa's *Harṣacarita* 130: *sarvābhyo digbhyaḥ strī-rājyānīvâvarjitāni*. . . .

23. For which, note the description of Yamatai and its queen "Himiko" in the Chinese *Weishi* history (220–65 CE), a part of the histories of the Three Kingdoms.

end of which he disappeared, Barbarossa-like,[24] in Namuci's mountain cave along with some Daitya women—that is, fairies.

Geography

Returning to Tibet proper, Bhoṭa as such is not mentioned early on.[25] However, one of the local spirits, the Yakṣa Pāñcika, is located at the eastern border of Kashmir. This Yakṣa is mentioned in the *Mahāmāyurī*,[26] which was compiled in the third or fourth century CE[27] and has several layers.[28] This text mentions (no. 77) Kāśmīra and its surroundings, such as the neighboring populations of Darada, Khaśa, and Haimavata, several times.[29] The Yakṣa of Kashmir is the otherwise unknown Prabhaṃkara. Entry 78, however, has "Kāśmīrasaṃdhi," "the borders of Kashmir," mentioning the five hundred sons of the Yakṣa Pāñcika, who reside in Cīna.

Another feature of that area is Haṃsadvāra, "the gate of the geese," situated in the eastern Kashmir mountains. At the beginning of spring the geese fly from their winter quarters in India through several Himalayan passes bearing this name toward Tibet and northern Asia. For example, at *Mahābhārata* 2.48.13, the Kashmiris appear next to those people who follow the "goose path" (*haṃsakāyanāḥ*).[30] The latter is a feature of the Himalayan landscape known also from Kālidāsa's *Meghadūta* and from central Nepal (Kali Gaṇḍakī gorge, north of Pokhara),[31] where it was photographed in the 1960s. The Kashmirian *haṃsadvāra* appears in the *Nīlamata Purāṇa* near the mountain Muṇḍapṛṣṭhagiri: it is one of the "gates" that the birds make use of when cross-

24. The twelfth-century German emperor who suddenly died during a crusade in south Turkey, but who, according to legend, still lives on in the central German mountain Kyffhäuser.

25. See RT, in Stein 1900, index; and Sahnī and Francke 1908: mentioned next to Cīna and Zhangzhung.

26. The Sanskrit version, published in 1897–98, has several layers, discussed in Lévi 1915, 20–21, 24–25, 26, 121.

27. Its first Chinese translation dates to 516 CE.

28. Lévi 1915.

29. Discussion in Lévi 1915, 101.

30. Mentioned next to other populations of the northwest: Mbh. 2.48.13: *kāśmīrāḥ kundamānāś ca paurakā haṃsakāyanāḥ śibi-trigarta-yaudheyā rājanyā madra-kekayāḥ.*

31. Ved Kumari 1968, 39; de Vreese 1936, *Nīlamata*, SR 1069 = LR 1109; SR 1250 = LR 1299. In Nepal the geese fly into Tibet starting from approximately an 800 meter-/2400 feet-high elevation around Pokhara, through the Kali Gaṇḍakī gorge, surrounded by 8,000 meter-/24,000 feet-high peaks.

ing the Himalayas on their seasonal flights.[32] Indian texts in general know of the central Tibetan lake Mānasarovara and of Mount Kailāsa;[33] the latter has been known since the Vedic text *Kaṭha Brāhmaṇa* (Caland 1920, 486). Unlike in later texts, a pilgrimage to Kailāsa is not yet mentioned. However, the region north of Kashmir, the Takla Makan Desert (*sikatāsindhu*, "the ocean of sand") in eastern Central Asia (Xinjiang), appears in RT 4.277, 294. From there, the Central Asian Turks appear in Kashmir and leave it, just like the mythical Piśācas, at the beginning of winter. The cruel invasion of Kashmir by Ḍalaca (Ḍu'l-Qadr) is related at JRT 142 sqq. Ḍalaca was a Turkish chief from eastern Turkistan, which was ruled by the descendants of Chagatay, the son of Chingiz Khan. Ḍalaca invaded Kashmir with a Turko-Mongol army of 60,000–70,000 soldiers and committed many atrocities.[34] Earlier, the Hindu king Kalaśa (1063–89 CE), infamous for plundering temples,[35] was called *Turuṣka*, a "Turk" (Muslim foreigner). The first one so named was King Harṣa, "the Turk" (JRT 598). Kalhaṇa also reports an invasion of Muslim Turks from the north under Salāra Vismaya during the time of Sussala and Bhikṣācara (1020/21 CE, RT 8.885, 919, 923, 965). They also appear as allies of the Dards at RT 8.2843 during the reign of King Jayasiṃha (ca. 1144 CE). However, just as seen in the frequently repeated Eurasian pattern of border tribes growing in significance and power, Muslim Turks are mentioned as Kashmirian soldiers during Harṣa's reign, ca. 1100 CE, and then expand their influence steadily.

32. Though geese actually fly across the Pamirs at some 8,000 meters (24,000 feet) as well, as recently documented. Cf. Sanderson 2009, 103. He mentions seeing the sacred sites of Kālodaka, Nandikuṇḍa, and Uttaramānasa, as well as the image of Nandīśvara on the Haramukuṭa Mountain (at the northern border of the Kashmir valley). He adds a note on the "unpublished *Śarvāvatāra*, one of the few surviving texts in praise of Kashmir's sacred sites that appears to pre-date the advent of Islam."

33. Mentioned as Meru/Sineru; cf. the Tirich Mir mountain at the northern end of the Chitral Valley, derived from *Meru*; and the Diamer Mountain further east, derived from **Devameru*; cf. Mayrhofer 1986, 3:416: Khowar *mēr*, "mountain." The Aruṇaketuka section of the *Taittirīya Āraṇyaka* 1 is a particularly late Vedic text that includes Purāṇic names of mountains such as Meru and Kailāsa, as well as other unusual data (Caland 1920, 485 sqq.; Witzel 1972).

34. Cf. Bamzai 1973, 308ff.

35. Stein 1900, 113.

Historical Notes

It is remarkable that the historical accounts of both Kashmir[36] and Nepal "neglect" the Tibetan dominance or overlordship during the heyday of the Tibetan empire. The history of Kashmir before the Kārkoṭa dynasty (625 CE)[37] remains vague, but the documents of the well-attested early Kārkoṭa kings do not indicate a contemporary Tibetan dominance. This is to be expected for the seventh to ninth centuries, the heyday of the empire, with its apex around 790 CE.

In about 634 CE, the Tibetan emperor Songtsen Gampo added Zhangzhung to his empire. On the southern front, in 641 CE, he sent back the Licchavi royal Narendradeva[38] with an army and thus subjugated Nepal. Additionally, the *Gopālarājavaṃśāvalī* (ca. 1380 CE) reports that "the king of Bhoṭa ruled Nepal."[39] Unlike Kashmir, Nepal was thus for some time under the indirect rule of Tibet. In Nepalese records, Bhoṭa ("Tibet") has to be separated from Bho(ṃ)ṭa, an area in the eastern Kathmandu Valley. In 723 CE the Tang princess Jincheng married the Tibetan emperor Tride Tsuktsen, but she wrote to the Kārkoṭa king Lalitāditya Muktāpīḍa asking for asylum. In response, Muktāpīḍa formed an alliance against the Tibetan empire.

As pointed out, the Tibetan dominance over much of Central Asia and the Himalayas during the seventh to ninth centuries is not mentioned in Kashmiri sources. At the same time, the Kārkoṭas, in their own heyday (625–ca. 800 CE), briefly extended southward[40] and even eastward to western Nepal. King Lalitāditya Muktāpīḍa[41] (Chi. Mu-to-pi) reigned during the time of the Chinese emperor Xuanzong (r. 712–56 CE), at the time of the Chinese expedition

36. The Kashmiris report about the famous Gupta dynasty of northern India, who are supposed to have sent a viceroy, Mātṛgupta (RT 3.207–89), with his royal coronation *abhiṣeka* (3.239). Both Kashmir and Nepal, however, were never parts of Indian realms. The local Kashmir *Mahātmya*, the *Nīlamata* (*Purāṇa*), fends off the charge that the king of Kashmir did not take part in the (mythical) *Mahābhārata* battle: he "was too young then."

37. See Witzel 1990 and 2020 for the correct dating in the various books of the RT (such as book 6: Kalhaṇa's dates plus twenty-five years).

38. Note the continuation of a double monarchy after Aṃśuvarman (605 CE); see Witzel 1980 and 1990.

39. *Bhoṭarājena māyātiḥ nepālamaṇḍala rājya karoti*, in the typical Tibeto-Burman influenced Sanskrit of the period, see Vajrācārya and Malla 1985, fol. 21.

40. In Haripāla's commentary on the *Gāüḍavāho*, a drama written on the occasion of the Kashmiri king Lalitāditya Muktāpīḍa's victory (736 CE) over Yaśovarman, the king of Kanauj and Bengal (RT 4.175).

41. Kalhaṇa's dates correspond to 701–37 CE.

to Baltistan (ca. 736 CE).[42] As reported by Kalhaṇa, RT 731–579, Lalitāditya Jayāpīḍa carried out an expedition to western Nepal up to the Kālagaṇḍikā fortress (modern [Gaṇḍa]Gulmi), where he fought an otherwise unknown king, Aramudi. The latter is not mentioned in the Nepalese chronicles or inscriptions. He may have been a local Magar chieftain whose name probably is taken from the area he reigned in.[43] Another Kārkoṭa king, Lalitāditya Muktāpīḍa, carried out an expedition to the north, to the sand ocean (*sikatāsindhu*),[44] where—as the legend says—he dug up water for his soldiers. Unfortunately, no details in this account are given about the Tibetan areas north of Kashmir.

However, perishing in ice and snow in these northern areas is mentioned elsewhere. There was a disaster in 1517 CE when Kashmiris went to the Gaṅgā (a local river in northern Kashmir) to dispose of the bones and ashes of their departed ancestors, where they perished by the thousands in snow (Śuka, RT 109). This reminds of the little-discussed evidence at Roopkund Lake in the high Himalayan area of Uttarakhand, where many skeleton remains have been found strewn over a wide area around the lake. The deceased are said to have been killed by large-size hailstones. Recent investigations (Harney et al. 2019), based on genetic studies, indicate that the deaths were not due to a single event but several events extending over about a thousand years. Curiously, the remains belonged to several genetically different groups, one related to South Asian haplogroups, the other to western Asian ones. The purpose of these excursions into the Himalayan mountains remains a mystery.

As for further Kashmiri connections with Central Asia and Turkic peoples emanating from there, the first influences of Turkic Islam in the Kashmir valley began long before actual Islamization in the fourteenth century. Muslim Turks first occur as soldiers in the Kashmiri army during the reign of King Harṣa as *centurios*, (1089–1101 CE, RT 7.1091). They were leaders of companies (*centurias*, RT 7.1149, ca. 1100 CE). Harṣa was called a Turk, *Turuṣka*, due to his behavior of robbing temple property.[45]

There is, however, one clear Tibetan impact on Kashmir in 1323 CE. The

42. See Kuwayama 1994, 13.

43. In the Tibeto-Burmese languages of western Nepal *di* means "river"; the local river will have been called *mu-di* and may have designated "Aramudi's" area as well. Also possible is *mud* ("river") from another Tibetan-Burmese language; however, *ara-* remains enigmatic. The area could have been *Gaṇḍa-gulmi* in the modern Gulmī area in the Lumbini zone, Nepal (see Witzel 1993); *gulma* signifies a troop of soldiers, an army division, or a fort (see Mbh. 1, 290).

44. RT 4.277ff., 294.

45. Cf. Chattopadhyaya 1998.

Ladakhi adventurer Rinchen (Riñcana)[46] entered the valley under King Sūhadeva (r. 1301–20 CE) as a refugee, but was soon made an official. He then ousted the successor, King Rāmacandra (r. 1320 CE), a former minister of King Sūhadeva, and thus became the first non-Kashmiri king for many centuries to come. He reigned from just 1320 to 1323. This would look like the typical incursion by one of the many neighbors of Kashmir under weak kings (especially by the Dards and Khaśa).[47] However, the outcome of this incursion differs from the standard recurring pattern that saw a quick reestablishment of the Hindu Kashmiri monarchy. Instead, due to Rinchen's conversion to Islam it led to the beginnings of the establishment of Islam in Kashmir.[48]

Riñcana married Koṭā, the powerful daughter of King Sūhadeva, and tried to adapt to local Hinduism. However, the narrow-minded brahmin Śrī Devasvāmin refused to initiate the king into the Śaiva religion on the grounds that as a Tibetan (Bhoṭṭa), and thus a Buddhist, he could not be initiated (JRT verse 193). This led to the conversion of Riñcana to Islam. No one at the time would have imagined what serious and long-lasting consequences this move would create. Under Udyānadeva, the second husband of Queen Koṭā, a Turkish invasion by one Acala (RT 232) occurred, but this time from the south. There were other Turkish raids from the north, from eastern Central Asia, notably that of Ḍalaca,[49] and, vice versa, occasional conquests of Ladakh by Kashmiri kings and sultans, continuing up to the Sikhs and Dogras, who established the pre-1947 extent of the state of Jammu and Kashmir. One invasion that is well reported was the invasion of Ladakh by Sultan Zain ul-Abidin (1418–1470 CE).[50] There, he saved the statue of the golden Buddha (JRT 834). He also appointed a Buddhist minister, Tilaka, one of the last Buddhists mentioned in the Kashmir histories.

46. Jonarāja's RT 157–254; see the detailed discussion by Sahnī and Francke 1908, 182ff.

47. Some of them moved eastward to western Nepal and founded the western Malla kingdom, and later the state of Gorkha in central Nepal; the rest is recent Nepali history.

48. The Sufi missionary Bulbul Śāh, who had visited the valley earlier, exerted a strong influence on this first Muslim king of Kashmir.

49. Jonarāja's RT 170–94; see detailed discussion by Sahnī and Francke 1908; and Slaje 2014.

50. Jonarāja's RT; Śrīvara's RT 1.5.51 (see Sahnī and Francke 1908, 188ff.). For the expedition by Zain's son Ādam Khān (ŚRT 5.71, 82), see Sahnī and Francke 1908, 189; and King Hasan Khān (ŚRT 5.32, 190). See also ŚRT 5.440; and Prajyabhaṭṭa's RT 5.28, 191.

The People, Their Language, and Their Religion

Remarkably, RT 4.168 refers to the Tibetans as "originally white faced," but they then are compared to red-faced monkeys, echoing the Tibetan origin myth, according to which they had devolved from the union of a monkey and a female demon and their six sons, as detailed in a legend in the *Maṇi Kambum* (*Maṇi bka' 'bum*). Had this myth been transmitted to medieval Kashmir (by 1150 CE) via commercial contacts? This tale is unlike those in Indian texts (like the *Mahābhārata*, see above) that refer to the Tibetans and Chinese as "golden colored" (Chatterji 1951).

Other references to local and neighboring populations refer to the Nāga and Piśāca, both mythological people—for example, in the *Nīlamata Purāṇa* (Ved Kumari 1968)—however, without any direct references to the Ladakhis and Tibetans. The Piśācas probably are pastoral transhumants who each year retreat to the northern Kashmir mountains, though not to Ladakh.

The Tibetan language is not referred to in Kashmiri texts. There is, however, one instance where the term *lotsāba* has been misunderstood as a personal name, though it means "the translator."[51]

A number of references to Buddhist texts in the Burushaski (Tib. Bruža) language of northernmost Kashmir (Gilgit, Hunza, etc.) are not relevant here, as Burushaski is thought to be an isolated language[52] whose early texts have been almost completely lost.[53] It is often difficult to establish a one-to-one relationship between the Burushaski and Sanskrit titles of the Buddhist texts quoted in Tibetan texts; Poucha (1960) has succeeded in a number of them. The Burusho are also referred to in inscriptions and early colophons of manuscripts of the Gilgit area as *Puruṣa*.[54]

The origin of the Tibetan script from a form of the Gupta-era script of Kashmir (pre-Śāradā) is well known, and some aspects of Tibetan pronunciation of Sanskrit words point in the same direction.[55] This is certainly substantiated by the history of the transmission of Buddhism into Tibet. Details

51. Cf. Lo-stunpā RT 1.310 with Stein's note on this verse.

52. Unless it is related, as likely, to the Northern Caucasian, Yenesseian, Basque languages (Bengtson 1997).

53. Poucha 1960, with the identification of some meanings of words in the corresponding Sanskrit/Tibetan/Bruža titles.

54. See Hinüber 1989 on *Pruṣa/Puruṣa*, etc. (Tibetan *Bruzha*, etc.) in Gilgit data; see also Hinüber 2009, 738.

55. Liu 2006, 334–53.

about its history in Tibet have been collected by J. Naudou,[56] which therefore is not necessary to repeat here. There are numerous instances of Kashmirian monks and scholars traveling to Tibet, many of them becoming translators of Sanskrit texts that are mentioned in the colophons of the canon. Some Buddhist converts from Hinduism are mentioned;[57] the well-known data in the *Blue Annals*[58] are not repeated here. According to Tāranātha, Dharmakīrti was converted to Buddhism by three Kashmiri brahmins: Vidyāsiṃha, Devasīmha, and Devavidyākara (Naudou 1980, 65). Śaṅkarānanda, a logician (*paramōpasaka mahāpaṇḍita brāhmaṇa*), is another convert (Naudou 1980, 126). Ratnavajra converted a Śaiva brahmin called the "red ācārya" or Guhyaprajña (Naudou 1980, 169, 172). A brahmin called Śrībhadra or Sūryaketu was the teacher of Sajjana, grandson of Ratnavajra (Naudou 1980, 188). Somanātha (or Candranātha), of the early eleventh century, was converted by his mother. He studied together with Sonasati, Lakṣmīkara, Dānaśrī/Dānaśīla, and Candrarāhula (Naudou 1980, 198).

As mentioned, Sultan Zain ul-Abidin (Zayn al-'Ābidīn, 1418–70) saved the great Buddha of Ladakh (see Jonarāja's JRT 834).

Pilgrimages are not yet mentioned in medieval texts, such as to Śiva's Amaranātha ice liṅgam in northeastern Kashmir. A pilgrimage under late sultans to the Haramukuṭa Mountain at the northern border of the valley occurs, but it does not concern Tibet. We can only imagine similar travel to Lake Mānasarovara and Mount Kailāsa, whose name is attested since a late part of the KaṭhB (Caland 1920).

Unfortunately, Kashmiri sources do not tell much about direct Kashmiri Buddhist influence on Tibet, outside of what is mentioned in the numerous colophons of the Tibetan canon (Naudou 1980) or in the *Blue Annals*. In contrast, the Tibetan translation from Sanskrit of Kuladatta's *Kriyāsaṃgraha* manual (1215 CE) of the prominent *Homa* fire ritual goes back to a Nepalese tradition, of which a Nepalese manuscript of 1530 has been preserved.[59] The dearth of such Kashmiri ritual materials is certainly due to the fact that after circa 1500 CE there is no evidence of Buddhist persons and, therefore, of their manuscripts in Kashmir. The last prominent Kashmiri Buddhist mentioned is Tilaka, a minister of Sultan Zain ul-Abidin (JRT 823), while some merchants under his grandson Hassan (1472–85) still built a Buddhist *vihāra*.

56. Naudou 1968, and cf. also the less reliable English translation of 1980.

57. See Witzel 2016.

58. Such as Roerich 1976, 68, 72.

59. Bajracharya 1972; he claims that his text is based on a manuscript dated 1530 CE.

These relatively sparse Kashmiri data about Ladakh and Tibet underline the self-centeredness of the inhabitants of the two large Himalayan valleys, that of Kashmir (Slaje 2012) and that of Nepal (Gutschow 1974). In fact, Kashmir was independent until the Mughal conquest in 1586, and even after that, under the Afghans, Sikhs, and even the Dogras of Jammu, it was not part of India until 1947. Under the Mughals and Afghans, it was part of an administrative unit based in Kabul. The outside world is only noticed in the texts if outside forces directly impact the valley, or if an important Kashmir king undertakes an expedition to India or Ladakh. Otherwise, the Kashmiris (like the Nepalese, Sikkimese, Bhutanese—and Tibetans) prefer to be left alone. Unfortunately, this no longer occurred after 1947, when the last king of Kashmir joined the Indian Union, with dire consequences that have persisted to today.

Abbreviations of Translated Primary Sources

JRT	*Jainarājataraṇgiṇī*, in Slaje 2014
KaṭhB	*Kaṭha Brāhmaṇa*, in Caland 1920
LPr	*Lokaprakāśa*
Mbh	*Mahābhārata*
RT	*Rājataraṇgiṇī* (Kalhaṇa), in Stein 1900
SP	*Sambandhaparīkṣā* (Dharmakīrti), in Steinkellner 2022
ŚRT	*Rājataraṅgiṇī of Śrīvara and Śuka*, in Kaul 1966

References

Bajracharya, Amoghabajra. 1972. *Kalaśārcanādi homavidhāna-pustakam*. Kathmandu: Nandakumari Bajracharya.

Bamzai, P. N. Kaul. 1973 [1962]. *A History of Kashmir, Political, Social, and Cultural, from the Earliest Times to the Present Day*. New Delhi: Metropolitan Book Co.

Bengtson, J. 1997. "Ein Vergleich von Buruschaski und Nordkaukasisch." *Georgica* 20: 88–94.

Caland, William. 1920. "Brāhmaṇa en Sūtra aanwinsten." In *Verslagen en mededeelingen der Koningklijke Akademie van Wetenschappen, Afdeeling Letterkunde*, 461–98. Amsterdam: Koninklijke Nederlandse Akademie van Wetenschappen.

Chatterji, S. K. 1951. *Kirāta-jana-kṛti: The Indo-Mongoloids: Their Contribution to the History and Culture of India*. Calcutta: Royal Asiatic Society of Bengal.

Chattopadhyaya, B. 1998. *Representing the Other? Sanskrit Sources and the Muslims.* New Delhi: Manohar.

Deambi, B. K. Kaul. 1982. *Corpus of Śāradā Inscriptions of Kashmir, with Special Reference to Origin and Development of Śāradā Script.* Delhi: Agam Kala Prakashan.

Gopāl, Lallanji. 2008. *Lokaprakāśa of Śrīkṣemendra with the English Translation.* Varanasi: Sampurnanand Sanskrit University.

Gutschow, N. 1974. *Bhaktapur; Gestalt, Funktionen und religiöse Symbolik einer nepalischen Stadt im vorindustriellen Entwicklungsstadium: Aufgezeichnet und interpretiert von Gerhard Auer und Niels Gutschow.* Darmstadt: Technische Hochschule.

Harney, E., et al. 2019. "Ancient DNA from the Skeletons of Roopkund Lake Reveals Mediterranean Migrants in India." *Nature Communications* 10, article no. 3670: 1–10.

Hinüber, O. von. 1989. *Antiquities of Northern Pakistan: Reports and Studies,* vol. 5, *Palola Sāhis.* Edited by Karl Jettmar et al. Mainz: P. von Zabern.

———. 2009. *Kleine Schriften,* vol. 2. Edited by H. Falk and W. Slaje. Wiesbaden: Harrassowitz.

Kaul, Srikanth. 1966. *Rājataraṅgiṇī of Śrīvara and Śuka.* Hoshiarpur: VVRI.

Kumari, Ved. 1968. *The Nīlamata Purāṇa.* vol.1, *A Cultural and Literary Study of a Kaśmīrī Purāṇa.* Srinagar: J & K Academy of Art, Culture and Languages. [Long recension, LR]

Kuwayama, S. 1994. *Dating Yaśovarman of Kanauj on the Evidence of Huichao. Zinbun.* Annals of the Institute for Research in Humanities 29. Kyoto: Kyoto University.

Lévi, Sylvain. 1915. "Le catalogue géographique des Yakṣa dans la Mahāmāyurī." *Journal Asiatique* 51: n.p.

Liu, Kuowei 劉國威. 2006. "Xizang fojiaozhong de *Zhouyu niantong* wenxian 西藏佛教中的「咒語念誦」（Sngags kyi bklag thabs）文獻" [The *Sngags kyi bklag thabs* in Tibetan Buddhism]. In *Cong Indu dao Xizang: Renwu yu sixiang* 從印度到西藏: 人物與思想 [From India to Tibet: Characters and Thoughts], 334–53. Taipei: Puti changqing chubanshe.

Lokaprakāśa. 2018. Edited by M. Witzel. Harvard Oriental Series 85. Cambridge: Harvard.

Mahāmāyurī. 1899. Edited by Sergey F. Oldenburg. St. Peterburg.

Martin, Dan. 2013. "Knowing Zhang-zhung: The Very Idea." *Journal of the International Association for Bon Research* 1: 175–97.

Mayrhofer, M. 1986–2001. *Etymologisches Wörterbuch des Altindoarischen.* 3 vols. Heidelberg: Winter.

Naudou, J. 1968. *Bouddhistes Kasmiriens du moyen age.* Paris: Presses universitaires de France.

———. 1980. *Buddhists of Kaśmīr.* Delhi: Agam Kala Prakashan.

Poucha, P. 1960. "Bruža—Burušaski?" *Central Asiatic Journal* 5.4: 295–300.

Roerich, G. N., trans. 1976. *The Blue Annals.* New Delhi: Motilal.

Rönnow, K. 1936 "*Kirāta.* A Study on Some Ancient Indian Tribes." *Le Monde Oriental* 30: 99–170.

Sacred Books of the East. 1879–1910. Edited by Max Müller. Oxford: Clarendon Press.

Sahnī, Dayā, and A. H. Francke. 1908. "References to the Bhoṭṭas or Bhauṭṭas in the Rājataraṅgiṇī." *Indian Antiquary* 37: 181–92.

Sanderson, A. 2009. "Kashmir." In *Brill's Encyclopedia of Hinduism*, edited by K. A. Jacobsen et al., 99–126. Leiden: Brill.

Slaje, W. 2012. "Kashmir Minimundus: India's Sacred Geography en Miniature." In *Highland Philology: Results of a Text-Related Kashmir Panel at the 31st DOT, Marburg 2010*, edited by Roland Steiner, 9–32. Halle: Universitätsverlag Halle-Wittenberg.

———, ed. 2014. *Kingship in Kaśmīr (AD 1148–1459): From the Pen of Jonarāja, Court Paṇḍit of Sulṭān Zayn al-'Ābidīn.* Critically edited by Walter Slaje, with an annotated translation, indexes, and maps. Halle: Universitätsverlag Halle-Wittenberg.

Stein, M. A. 1900. *Kalhaṇa's Rājataraṅgiṇī, a Chronicle of the Kings of Kaśmīr*, 2 vols. Westminster: Archibald Constable and Company.

Steinkellner, E. 2022. *Dharmakīrti's Sambandhaparīkṣā and Devendrabuddhi's Sambandhaparīṭṣāvṛtti.* Vienna: Verlag Oesterreichischen Akademie der Wissenschaften.

Vajrācārya, Dh. 1974. *Licchavi Kāla.kā Abhile*kh. Kathmandu: Tribhuvan University.

Vajrācārya, Dh., and K. P. Malla, eds. and trans. 1985. *Gopālarājavaṃśāvalī.* Wiesbaden: Franz Steiner Verlag.

de Vreese, K. 1936. *Nīlamata, or, Teachings of Nīla. Sanskrit Text with Critical Notes.* Leiden: Brill. [Short recension, SR]

Witzel 1972. "jav. *apāxəδra-* im System der avestischen Himmelsrichtungsbezeichnungen." *MünchenerStudien zur Sprachwissenschaft* 30: 163–91.

———. 1980. "On the Location of the Licchavi Capital of Nepal." *Festschrift für P. Thieme. Studien zur Indologie und Iranistik* 5.6: 311–37.

———. 1990. "On Indian Historical Writing: The Case of the Vaṃśāvalis." *Journal of the Japanese Association for South Asian Studies* 2: 1–57

———. 1993. "Nepalese Hydronomy: Towards a History of Settlement in the Himalayas." In *Nepal Past and Present: Proceedings of the Franco-German Conference at Arc-et-Senans, June 1990*, edited by G. Toffin, 217–66. New Delhi: Sterling Publishers.

———. 2000. "The Home of the Aryans." In *Anusantatyai. Festschrift für Johanna Narten zum 70. Geburtstag*, edited by A. Hintze and E. Tichy, 283–338. Dettelbach: J. H. Roell.

———. 2016. "Kashmiri Brahmins under the Kārkoṭa, Utpala and Lohara Dynasties, 625–1151 CE." In *Around Abhinavagupta: Aspects of the Intellectual History of Kashmir from the Ninth to the Eleventh Century*, edited by Eli Franco and Isabelle Ratié, 609–44. Berlin: LIT Verlag Dr. Hopf.

———. 2020. *The Veda in Kashmir.* Harvard Oriental Series 94–95. Cambridge, MA: Harvard.

Intellectual History

Chomden Reldri on Dharmakīrti's *Examination of Relations*

Allison Aitken

I owe a debt of gratitude to Leonard van der Kuijp for bringing my attention to both of Chomden Reldri's commentaries on the *Sambandhaparīkṣā* upon learning of my interest in the subject. Leonard consistently models a spirit of collegial generosity, with the exchange of resources constituting a regular component of his seminars, as all his students can attest. Sharing these texts with me was just one of innumerable instances of his uncommon thoughtfulness.

Dharmakīrti's *Examination of Relations* (*Sambandhaparīkṣā*) is unique in the Indian Buddhist canon for being the only extant root text devoted entirely to the topic of the ontological status of relations. But the core thesis of this treatise—that relations are only nominally real—is in prima facie tension with another claim that is central to Dharmakīrti's epistemology: that there exists some kind of natural relation (*svabhāvapratibandha*)[1] that comes in two varieties—an identity relation (*tādātmya*) and a causal relation (*tadutpatti*)[2]—which can reliably underwrite inferences. Understanding how Dharmakīrti can consistently rely on natural relations to prop up his presentation of inferential reasoning while at the same time advancing an antirealist account of relations is critical for making sense of his system of logic and epistemology, which came to be nearly universally adopted in Tibetan Buddhism, cutting across traditions.

Despite the importance of the *Examination of Relations* to understanding Dharmakīrti's thought, Chomden Rikpé Reldri (Bcom ldan rig[s] pa'i ral gri,

I am grateful as well to Ernst Steinkellner for generously making available his edition of the SP and SPV in advance of its official publication, together with his working English translation of both these texts. Finally, I thank Pascale Hugon for helpful comments on an earlier draft of this paper.

1. PVSV 12.4

2. PV I.31=PVin 2.37.23–26: *kāryakārarṇabhavad vā svabhāvād vā niyāmakāt / avinābhāvaniyamo 'darśanān na na darśanāt //.*

1227–1305)[3] and Gyeltsap Darma Rinchen (Rgyal tshab Dar ma rin chen, 1364–1432) are the only Tibetan philosophers known to have written independent commentaries on this work. Chomden Reldri, the great scholar, prolific author, and canon cataloger of Nartang (Snar thang) Monastery, in fact, composed two texts commenting on the *Examination of Relations*, which are the subject of the present chapter: (1) *Flower to Ornament the Examination of Relations* (*'Brel pa brtag pa rgyan gyi me tog*, hereafter *Flower*),[4] which is a summary of the text identifying the subject of each stanza, and (2) *Annotations and Topical Outline of the Examination of Relations* (*'Brel pa brtag pa'i mchan dang sa bcad gnyis*,[5] hereafter *Annotations*), a reproduction of Dharmakīrti's root text interspersed with explanatory annotations with a topical outline appended at the end, for which we have a *dbu med* manuscript in the *Collected Works of the Kadampas* (*Bka' gdams gsung 'bum*).[6] In this chapter, I offer introductory remarks on Dharmakīrti's *Examination of Relations* and Chomden Reldri's two commentaries, followed by a translation of Dharmakīrti's *Examination of Relations* and Chomden Reldri's *Annotations* together with subject headings for each stanza of the root text based on *Flower*.

3. On Chomden Reldri's life and work, see Samten Zangpo's (Bsam gtan bzang po) biography ($BSAM_1$), which was requested by Chomden Reldri's nephew; see also Schaeffer and van der Kuijp 2009, 3–8; and van der Kuijp 2003, 406ff. Chomden Reldri is known also by his name in religion, Darma Gyeltsen (Dar ma rgyal mtshan) ($BSAM_1$, 3a). On Chomden Reldri's names and dates, see van der Kuijp 2003, 406–7.

4. It would seem that Chomden Reldri regarded "flower to ornament" or "ornamental flower" (*rgyan gyi me tog*) as a kind of signature, or at least a favored expression, for he composed no fewer than thirty-five texts that include this expression in their titles.

5. This is the title in the table of contents in the Kadam Sungbum, but the bibliographic title there and in the Lhasa (2006) typeset edition of Chomden Reldri's collected works is listed as *'Brel pa brtag pa'i rab tu byed pa*. This, however, is the longer title of the root text, not Chomden Reldri's commentary, as is clear from the manuscript.

6. Among the three editions of the collected works of Chomden Reldri available on BDRC, only the Lhasa (2006) typeset edition includes his commentaries on the SP. Many handwritten manuscripts of his writings are known to have circulated; as Schaeffer and van der Kuijp note, "The library of 'Bras spungs monastery's Gnas bcu lha khang contained some seventy-five texts that issued from his fertile pen" (2009, 51). And indeed, the Lhasa typeset editions of *Flower* and *Annotations* were based on manuscripts found at Drepung, as stated in their colophons. As Pascale Hugon pointed out (in personal correspondence), the source manuscript for the typeset edition of *Flower* is likely no. 19262 (four folios, misspelled *'Grel pa rtag pa rgyan gyi me tog*) in the Drepung catalogue (*'Bras spungs dpe rnying dkar chag*), while there appear to be two manuscripts of *Annotations* in this catologue, nos. 16382 (nine folios) and 19282 (four folios). Unfortunately, the manuscript of *Flower* is not available, which is particularly regrettable given the number of typos evident in the Lhasa typeset editions of both works.

I begin with a few observations on Dharmakīrti's account of relations. Nominalism about relations follows from Dharmakīrti's basic twofold ontology of ultimately real particulars (*svalakṣaṇa*) and conventionally real, conceptually constructed universals (*sāmānyalakṣaṇa*). As Dharmakīrti explains, ultimately real particulars are each momentary, radically distinct entities (SP 25). As the basic building blocks of the world, particulars are mereologically simple and conceptually primitive. Relations, on the other hand, are necessarily conceptually complex. Dharmakīrti remarks, "A relation is something that is founded in two things" (SP 11a). While a given relation may denominate actual particulars among its relata, it is a mental act that brings the relata together, as it were, into the complex conceptual construct that we call a relation, which is purely a creature of the mind (SP 5, 17). Between the two sources of knowledge in Dharmakīrti's system of epistemology, perception (*pratyakṣa*) yields knowledge of particulars, while inferential cognition (*anumāṇa*) yields knowledge of conceptual constructs on the basis of what is given in perception by means of the process of the exclusion of what is contrary (*anyāpoha*) (SPV *ad* SP 6). It is inferential cognition, then, that provides structure to the world as we experience it, and it is thus at this second stage of the cognitive process that relations are conceived.

But if relations are only nominally real, what does Dharmakīrti intend by advancing a theory of "natural relations" to underwrite inferences? Although an adequate response to this question lies beyond the scope of this chapter, it is evident from the *Examination of Relations* that *svabhāvapratibandha* cannot be a "natural relation" in the sense of being a mind-independent entity that claims membership among the ultimate furniture of the world. Rather, such a relation is "natural" insofar as the relata that it denominates are (or bottom out in) real particulars that necessarily conform to the requisite pattern of invariable co-presence (*anvaya*) and co-absence (*vyatireka*),[7] either simultaneously as in the case of an identity relation or sequentially as in the case of a causal relation.[8] What's more, it is a natural, or essential, property of some particular that necessarily conforms to this pattern. Thus, purported relations like contact (*saṃyoga*), which involve extrinsic properties such as spatiotemporal location, do not count as the kind of natural relation that *necessarily* obtains and can thereby reliably underwrite inferences.

It seems very likely that, as Steinkellner (2022, xviii) argues, Dharmakīrti composed the *Examination on Relations* subsequent to his *Explanation*

7. PVSV 2.19–20=PVin 10.14–15. Cf. NB 2.19: *svabhāvapratibandhe hi sati artho 'rthaṃ na vyabhicarati* |; "For it is due to a natural relation that one thing invariably attends another."

8. On Dharmakīrti's account of *svabhāvapratibandha*, see, for instance, Oetke 1991; Katsura 1992; Steinkellner 1997, 627–29, and 2021, xv–xxi; and Dunne 2004, 42–45.

of the Sources of Knowledge (*Pramāṇavārttika*) and autocommentary (*Pramāṇavārttikasvavṛtti*), wherein he introduces his theory of "natural relations" in order to clarify that this theory does not commit him to the existence of real, mind-independent relations. And in the *Examination of Relations*, he is specifically concerned with clarifying his account of causal relations, for curiously the identity relation receives no mention whatsoever in this text. Although causal relations garner the most attention in the *Examination of Relations*, Dharmakīrti devotes a number of stanzas to rejecting various species of relations defended by non-Buddhist schools of thought, such as the inherence relation (*samāvaya*), which Naiyāyikas and Vaiśeṣikas take to link properties with substances, universals with particulars, and wholes with parts, and a blending relation (*śleṣa*), which (according to Dharmakīrti) Mīmāṃsakas take to link words with their meanings.[9] According to these systems, real, mind-independent relations are responsible for structuring reality. Yet, for Dharmakīrti, we occupy a world without structure. All relations—and accordingly all structure—are superimposed by the mind.

The *Examination of Relations* has a negative and a positive agenda: (1) to reject real, mind-independent relations, and (2) to explain how relations are conceptually constructed with a focus on how we know when conceptually constructed *causal* relations are well founded. This agenda is stated explicitly at the outset of the *Commentary on the Examination of Relations* (*Sambandhaparīkṣāvṛtti*), which the Tengyur editions identify as Dharmakīrti's autocommentary, and indeed, Chomden Reldri refers to it as such. However, a Sanskrit manuscript of the *Sambandhaparīkṣāvṛtti* discovered at Drepung ('Bras spungs) Monastery, an edition of which was recently published by Steinkellner (2022), attributes the text instead to Dharmakīrti's student Devendrabuddhi (ca. 630–90).[10] In addition to the *Sambandhaparīkṣāvṛtti*, the Tengyur includes two additional

9. As Eltschinger (2021, 101) notes, despite the fact that the Mīmāṃsā explicitly reject the blending relation ((*saṃ*)*śleṣa*), Dharmakīrti critiques this kind of relation in the context of rejecting the Mīmāṃsaka claim that a permanent and uncreated relation between words and their meaning (*śabdārthasambandha*) supports their belief that the Vedas lack a human author (PV 1.213–268, PVSV 113.23–25, 118.27–119.1). For a discussion of this dispute, see Eltschinger 2007, 115–28, 134–43. As Steinkellner (2022, xvii–xviii) points out, the SP and SPV elaborate on this argument from the PV.

10. Steinkellner (2022, xiv–xv) conjectures that the SPV was recorded by Devendrabuddhi after receiving a teaching on the SP from Dharmakīrti, noting that the SPV is markedly simple when compared with Dharmakīrti's sophisticated commentarial work in, for instance, his PVSV. See Tauscher 1994 for an edition of precanonical Tibetan translations of the SPV and SPṬ based on fragments discovered at Tabo (Ta pho).

commentaries on the *Examination of Relations*, the *Sambandhaparīkṣāṭīkā* by Vinītadeva (ca. 710–70) and the *Sambandhaparīkṣānusāra* by Śaṅkaranandana (ca. ninth–tenth century). Aside from these canonical commentaries, two Jaina commentaries survive, Prabhācandra's (980–1065) *Sambandhaparīkṣāvyākhyā* and Vādidevasūri's (1080–1170) *Syādvādaratnākara*.[11]

That Chomden Reldri is one of only two known Tibetans to author commentaries on the *Examination of Relations*—one of the so-called seven epistemological treatises of Dharmakīrti (*tshad ma sde bdun*)[12]—should not come as a surprise. As van der Kuijp (2003, 407) remarks, "In terms of quantity, the sheer volume of his literary output in this area [i.e., logic and epistemology] strongly suggests the likelihood that he was the most prolific and versatile Tibetan writer on *tshad ma* of his or, for that matter, of any other age." Indeed, in this genre, Chomden Reldri also composed commentaries on texts including Dignāga's *Compendium on the Sources of Knowledge* (*Pramāṇasamuccaya*) as well as each of Dharmakīrti's seven epistemological treatises—the *Explanation of the Sources of Knowledge* (*Pramāṇavārttika*), the *Determination of the Sources of Knowledge* (*Pramāṇaviniścaya*), the *Essence of Logic* (*Nyāyabindu*), the *Essence of Reasoning* (*Hetubindu*), the *Proof of Other Minds* (*Santānāntarasiddhi*), the *Logic of Debate* (*Vādanyāya*), and the *Examination of Relations*—in addition to writing a collective commentary on all seven. While Chomden Reldri had a great many teachers,[13] in the fields of logic and epistemology[14] he received teachings on the *Examination of Relations* from two scholars who appear to be his primary teachers in this domain:

11. Both texts are extant in Sanskrit and comment only on the first twenty-two stanzas of the SP. For editions of Prabhācandra's commentary, see Shastri 1972 and Jha 1990; the latter includes English translation and analysis. See Eltschinger 2021 for a detailed survey of Indian commentaries on the SP.

12. The SP is arguably more a metaphysical treatise than an epistemological one, though it does take up the question of how we come to know when (nominally real) causal relations obtain and the process by which we form conceptual constructs of relations.

13. See BSAM$_1$, 2aff, for a detailed record of the teachings and teachers of Chomden Reldri, accounts of which comprise most of the text. It is also worth noting that Chomden Reldri studied Sanskrit from Śīlaśrī (BSAM$_1$, 5b), which he makes a point to demonstrate. For instance, he provides Sanskrit translations of his own text title of *Flower* (*Saṃbandhaparīkṣālaṃkārapuṣpa*) and provides the Sanskrit etymology for the title of the root text.

14. For instance, Chomden Reldri studied "various texts" in this genre with Dānaśīla, a junior paṇḍita who accompanied the famed Kaśmīri scholar Śākyaśrībhadra (1127–1225) on his travels in Tibet (BSAM$_1$, 4b–5a); Kyeldrakpa Senggé (Skyel grags pa Seng ge) taught him the PVin and PV with numerous commentaries (BSAM$_1$, 9b); and Kyitön Drakbum (Kyi ston Grags 'bum) taught him the PVin (BSAM$_1$, 9a).

Tönshak (Ston śāk)[15] of Putang (Phu thang)[16] and Uyukpa Sönam Senggé ('U yug pa Bsod nams seng ge, or Rigs pa'i seng ge,[17] ca. 1200–after 1267).[18] Chomden Reldri also received teachings from Sakya Paṇḍita Künga Gyeltsen (Sa skya paṇḍita Kun dga' rgyal mtshan, 1182–1251) on his own *Treasury of Epistemology and Logic* (*Tshad ma rigs gter*),[19] the sixth chapter of which cites numerous verses from the *Examination of Relations.*

Chomden Reldri is remarkable not only for the volume of his output, but also for his original thought,[20] and there are several unique features of his commentaries on the *Examination of Relations* that bear noting. Although Chomden Reldri comments in the concluding section of *Flower* that he follows (what he takes to be) Dharmakīrti's as well as Vinītadeva's commentaries in his explanation, there are nevertheless several ways in which he deviates from these earlier commentaries. For example, Eltschinger observes that when it comes to the various kinds of relations that Dharmakīrti rejects, "None of Dharmakīrti's commentators . . . attempt to identify the advocates of these different models" (2021, 101). Yet Chomden Reldri's commentaries explicitly name the oppo-

15. From Tönshak, Chomden Reldri received instruction on the PVin with Dharmottara's short and long commentaries (*-ṭīkā*), NB, SS, SP, HB, VN, long and short versions of Dharmottara's *Examination of the Sources of Knowledge* (*Pramāṇaparīkṣā*), PS, and Dharmottara's *Explanation of Exclusion* (*Apohaprakaraṇa*) ($BSAM_1$, 5a). The final syllable of Tönshak's name is rendered *shag* in $BSAM_2$, 7; van der Kuijp (2003, 411) suggests that *śāk* stands for Śākya, prompting Hugon (2011, 129–130) to conjecture that this figure is Śākya brtson 'grus, who is mentioned in the colophon of Chomden Reldri's commentary on Dharmakīrti's *Vādanyāya* titled *Rtsod rigs rgyan gyi me tog*, which is the earliest known Tibetan commentary on this work.

16. Putang in Ü (Dbus) is also Chomden Reldri's birthplace ($BSAM_1$, 1b).

17. From Uyukpa, he received teachings on the PV, NB, SS, SP, HB, VN, PS, and the *Treasury of Epistemology and Logic* together with Uyukpa's commentary ($BSAM_1$, 9b–10a).

18. Dates follow Schaeffer and van der Kuijp 2009, 75. Uyukpa was one of the so-called nine principal students, or "sons" (*gnyal zhig gi bu dgu*), of Nyelzhik Jampel Dorjé (Gnyal zhig 'Jam dpal rdo rje, ca. 1150–1230), who was the abbot of Lingtö (Gling stod) from 1199 to 1207. His nine principal students founded many satellite institutes (*bshad grwa*), assisting in the diffusion of the teachings associated with Sangpu; on the history of Sangpu and the spread of its influence, see van der Kuijp 1987 and Hugon 2016. Uyukpa later converted to Sakya (Sa skya), becoming a disciple of Sakya Paṇḍita. As the story goes, Uyukpa is said to have gone to Sakya to engage Sakya Paṇḍita in debate, only to end up becoming Sapaṇ's disciple (van der Kuijp 2003, 401).

19. $BSAM_1$, 7b–8a.

20. As van der Kuijp (2003, 408) observes, Chomden Reldri is unhesitating in criticizing the views of his fellow Kadampa philosophers and even his own teachers, including Sakya Paṇḍita.

nent systems defending the various relations that Dharmakīrti's critique targets. For the present purposes, I will leave aside the questions of (1) whether these ascriptions are in fact Dharmakīrti's intended opponents (though there are certainly instances where they are not)[21] and (2) whether these systems are rightly characterized as advancing these kinds of relations (though there are certainly cases where they are not).[22] Nevertheless, in connection to the first question of Dharmakīrti's intent, it bears noting that Chomden Reldri identifies Yogācārins as proponents of real dependence relations[23] and Sautrāntikas, Vaibhāṣikas, and Yogācārins as proponents of real causal relations,[24] and given that Dharmakīrti himself defends claims associated with both Sautrāntika and Yogācāra systems at various places in his corpus, these are curious ascriptions.

In addition to identifying these non-Madhyamaka Buddhist schools as realists about certain relations, there are several places in *Flower* that are suggestive of a Madhyamaka reading of the *Examination of Relations*. For instance, Chomden Reldri uses characteristically Madhyamaka language when identifying the purpose of the text, stating that Dharmakīrti intends to explain that (1) all the kinds of relations that he surveys ultimately lack an intrinsic nature (*svabhāva*),[25] and yet (2) two kinds of relations (i.e., identity and causal relations) do exist conventionally.[26] Similarly, Chomden Reldri later comments that "the conventional mode of existence of things is distinct things arising anew in each moment,"[27] when this is how Dharmakīrti famously describes

21. For example, in *Flower* (2a.1–2), Chomden Reldri claims that even some Tibetans maintain that a real causal relation exists between cause and effect sequentially.

22. For instance, Chomden Reldri identifies one of the opponents targeted in Dharmakīrti's critique of the "blending" relation in SP 2 as the Mīmāṃsā. See note 9 above.

23. He seems to be drawing a connection between dependence (*paratantra, gzhan dbang*) and the nature of the same name from the Yogācāra three-nature theory.

24. *Flower* points to Śrāvakas and Yogācārins as proponents of real causal relations, while *Annotations* instead identifies the Sautrāntika and Vaibhāṣika, omitting Yogācārins.

25. Cf. SPV *ad* SP 1, according to which the purpose of the text is to reject relations as real entities (*vastubhūta*). Gyaltsap sticks closer to the Indian commentaries and to Dharmakīrti's own text by phrasing the negative program as rejecting the existence of substantially real relations (RGYAL 2a2: *'brel pa rdzas grub bkag pa . . .*) and the rejection of relations as particulars (RGYAL 2b1: *'brel pa rang mtshan pa med . . .*). Unfortunately, a comparison of Chomden Reldri's and Gyaltsap's commentaries is not possible here, but see Nishizawa (1997, 224–25) for Gyaltsap's outline of the SP.

26. *Flower* 1a.2: *'khor 'das 'brel ba don dam du // rang gzhan* [em: *bzhin*] *med kyang kun rdzob tu // 'brel gnyis bstan pas . . .*

27. *Flower* 3b.4: *skad cig so sor skye ba'i da ltar gyi dngos po tha dad 'di tsam zhig kun rdzob kyi gnas tshul yin . . .*

the mode of existence of *ultimately* real particulars. Finally, in identifying the purpose of the text, Chomden Reldri mentions Śaṅkaranandana's claim that Dharmakīrti rejects relations in order to establish the two kinds of selflessness: (1) the selflessness of persons is established by the rejection of agency relations, inherence relations, etc., since in the absence of such relations, neither can there be a real person qua agent, experiencer, etc., and (2) in the absence of any real subject in dependence upon which real phenomena qua objects of experience might exist, the selflessness of phenomena is established, where it is understood in the Yogācāra sense of the absence of subject-object dualism. Yet Chomden Reldri insists that rejecting real agential relations in fact establishes *both* kinds of selflessness, apparently reconceiving the selflessness of phenomena in a Madhyamaka framework.[28]

The following translation of Dharmakīrti's *Examination of Relations* is based on Steinkellner's (2022) Sanskrit edition, and the translation of Chomden Reldri's *Annotations* follows the *dbu med* manuscript from the *Collected Works of the Kadampas*.[29] Since this commentary takes the form of annotations to the root text, the root text embedded in the commentary is bolded. I follow the Sanskrit translation of the root text except when the Tibetan differs to the extent that a translation of the Sanskrit would be incompatible with Chomden Reldri's paraphrase; these instances are indicated in the apparatus. It was sometimes necessary to change the order of ideas of the root text as quoted in the commentary due to the grammatical structure of the annotations.

The enumerated and italicized subject headings are paraphrases (rather than strict translations) of the subjects of each verse as identified in Chomden Reldri's *Flower*. Nevertheless, significant editorial remarks about this text are noted. To assist with the comprehensibility of these texts, implied ideas that are elided for the sake of meter, etc., are included in the translation, but in the interest of readability, brackets are omitted; parentheses denote Chomden Reldri's own parenthetical remarks.

28. *Flower* 4a.2–5.

29. The Lhasa (2006) typeset edition of *Annotations* that was based on this manuscript was consulted, but it includes a number of typos and misplaces certain annotations while omitting others.

Dharmakīrti's *Examination of Relations* and Chomden Reldri's *Annotations and Topical Outline of the Examination of Relations* with subject headings according to Chomden Reldri's *Flower to Ornament the Examination of Relations*

In Sanskrit, *Sambandhaparīkṣāprakaraṇa;*[30] in Tibetan, *Explanation of the Examination of Relations.*
Homage to Mañjuśrī Kumārabhūta!
The following is stated in order to reject real relations maintained by our own and other schools of thought.

1. Dependence Relations: Established-or-Unestablished Dilemma

Rejecting real dependence relations maintained by Yogācārins

> Suppose there is a dependence relation. If the relata were already established, then what dependence is there? Thus, in reality, there are no relations between anything. [SP 1]

Suppose, as some followers of the mind-only system claim, **there is a dependence relation. If** that other thing, i.e., **the** dependent **relatum, were already established, then what dependence is there?** Its being unestablished or both established and unestablished are also untenable. **Thus, in reality,** viz., ultimately, **there are no** dependence **relations between anything.**

2. Blending Relations: Identical-or-Distinct Dilemma

Rejecting real blending relations that (1) Sāṃkhyas claim obtain between all things and prime matter[31] *and (2) other non-Buddhist systems claim obtain between words and their meanings*[32]

> Suppose there is a relation that is a blending of natures. But how could that be if there are two distinct things? Thus, there does not actually exist a relation between essentially distinct things. [SP 2]

30. *Annotations* 1b.1: *saṃbandhaparikṣāprakaraṇa*; em. *sambandhaparīkṣāprakaraṇa.*

31. *Flower* 1b.1: *rang gzhan*; em. *rang bzhin.*

32. Chomden Reldri presumably has the Mīmāṃsakas in view here; see note 9 above.

Suppose, as the Sāṃkhya claim, **there is a relation that is a blending of natures** into one, i.e., the causal foundation of all things, prime matter (*prakṛti*). But in that case, it is said: **how could that be** tenable that they are one **if there are two distinct things** in which the relation resides? **Thus, there does not actually exist a** blending **relation between essentially distinct things.**

3. Reliance Relations: Real-or-Unreal Dilemma

Rejecting real reliance relations maintained by Buddhist and non-Buddhist schools of thought

> Suppose there is a relation of reliance on another. How could that non-existent relatum rely on anything else? Or else, how could an existent entity, being completely independent, rely on anything else? [SP 3]

Moreover, **suppose**, as some others claim, **there is a relation of reliance on another.** But **if that relatum were non-existent** like the horns of a rabbit, **how could it rely on anything else? Or else, if it were existent** like a vase, **being completely independent, how could** it be tenable for **such an entity** to stand in a relation of **relying on anything else?**[33]

4. Relations Cannot Exist between Two Things Like Glue:[34] *Relation Regress*

Rejecting relations that Vaiśeṣikas claim exist between two things like glue

> If there were a relation due to two relata being related with a single thing, then what is that relation between the two and that thing? Moreover, an infinite regress would ensue. Thus, there is no admissible view of a relation. [SP 4]

The Vaiśeṣika claim that there is a relation located between the two relata, like glue. As for that, **if** one took it that **there were a relation due to two relata being related with a single thing, then what is that relation between the two** relata **and that** relation, which is a third element? **Moreover, an infinite regress would ensue. Thus,** i.e., therefore, **it should be understood that**[35] **there is no relation** whatsoever between any of these things.

33. The Tibetan translations of SP 3 includes the hypothetical grammatical particle *na* (n.e. Skt.) in articulating both alternatives of this "existent or nonexistent" dilemma.

34. *Annotations* 4b.3 alternatively describes the fourth topic as rejecting a relation that is distinct from its relata.

35. Here, I translate the Tibetan *shes par bya* instead of the Sanskrit *matis.*

How the mind apprehends relations

> These two things and everything that is distinct from them exist only in themselves. Thus, things themselves are not merged but are brought together by conceptual construction.[36] [SP 5]

These two things, i.e., the relata, **and everything that is distinct from them exist only in themselves**, i.e., their own nature. **Thus, things themselves are not merged** with other things, i.e., they are not related, **but are brought together by conceptual construction**[37] as though they were reliant.

How the terms "action" and "agent" are established despite the fact that a distinct action and agent do not actually exist

> In accordance with just that conceptual construction, for the purpose of bringing about the understanding of things as conceptually distinct,[38] speakers utter words like "action" and "agent." [SP 6]

In accordance with just that conceptual construction, for the purpose of bringing about the understanding of things as conceptually distinct from other things, **speakers utter words**[39] **like** this is the **"action,"** or effect, of that **"agent,"** or cause, despite the fact that there exists no relation between action and agent.

5. Causal Relations[40]

Simultaneous-or-Sequential Dilemma

36. Cf. PVSV 113.23–25 *ad* PV 1.227cd and PVSV 115.24–116.2 *ad* PV 1.231cd; for English translations of relevant passages, see Steinkellner 2022, xviii note 29; and Eltschinger 2007, 248 and 259.

37. *Annotations* 2a.3 accords with the Tabo variant *rtog* in SP 5d; canonical translations read *rtogs*. As Steinkellner (2022, xiii note 20) points out, the precanonical manuscript of the Tibetan translation of the SP (ed. Tauscher 1994) found at Tabo Monastery (together with manuscripts of the SPV and SPṬ) includes numerous preferable variants to the canonical versions indicating mistakes introduced during revision.

38. SPV *ad* SP 6 clarifies that distinctions of this kind are merely conceptual constructions formed by the process of the exclusion of what is other (*anyāpoha*).

39. *Annotations* 2a.4: *tshog*; em. *tshig*.

40. *Flower* only explicitly enumerates these first five topics; cf. *Annotations* outline.

Rejecting the Simultaneous Lemma: Rejecting real relations that Śrāvakas and Yogācārins claim exist between cause and effect simultaneously

> How could even a relation between cause and effect be established as founded in two things, since these two do not exist simultaneously? And if it is not founded in two things, how is it a relation? [SP 7]

Although the Sautrāntika and Vaibhāṣika[41] claim that there is **a relation between cause and effect**, it is conveyed that **even** this does not exist. As for that, **how could** such a relation **be established as founded in two things, since these two do not exist simultaneously**, one ceasing when the other arises? **And if it is not founded in two things, how is it a relation?**

Rejecting the Sequential Lemma: Rejecting real relations that even some Tibetans claim exist between cause and effect sequentially[42],[43]

> Suppose there were a real relation that existed sequentially in one relatum at a time, without requiring the simultaneous existence of the other relatum. There is no relation that exists in only one of the relata, since it would absurdly exist even in the absence of that other relatum. [SP 8]

Even if one were to **suppose there were a real relation that existed sequentially in one** of the two relata **at a time**, one prior and the other subsequently, if that were established, then it follows that it would not **require**, i.e., rely on, **the simultaneous existence of the other relatum,** since **it would absurdly exist even in the absence of that other relatum.** Thus, **there is no relation that exists** sequentially **in only one of the relata.**

> If, in dependence upon one of those two relata, a relation proceeded to the other relatum, what it depends on should be an assisting factor, but how can that relatum assist when it does not exist? [SP 9]

If this relation gradually **proceeded to the other relatum** at one time, that could not be a relation either. **If, in dependence upon** one, i.e., by requiring

41. Note that Yogācārins are omitted in *Annotations*.

42. *Flower* 2a.1 cites SP 8a1 as *rim gyis* rather than *rim las* as found in all extant Tibetan translations of the SP.

43. Obviously, Chomden Reldri can't mean that Dharmakīrti intended to engage a Tibetan view here but is instead observing that this position found defenders in his own intellectual context.

one of those two relata, what it depends on should be an assisting factor, but how can that relatum assist when that on which it depends **does not exist?**

Rejecting a real causal relation as a single thing

> If two things were related as cause and effect because they are both related to a single thing, then it follows that this same state of affairs would obtain for right and left horns since they are both related with "being a pair," etc. [SP 10]

If two things, like the pair of fire and smoke, **were related as cause and effect because they are both related to a single thing, then it follows that this same state of affairs**, i.e., being related as cause and effect, **would obtain for right and left horns since they are both related with "being a pair," etc.** Given that those two could not become cause and effect in that manner, nor could fire and smoke.

> For a relation is something that is founded in two things. Its defining characteristic is none other than this. [SP 11ab]

For a relation is something, i.e., an object, **that is founded in two things**, and **its**, i.e., a relation's, **defining characteristic is none other than this**, i.e., being founded in two things.

In the expression "a relation between cause and effect is founded in distinct things," the word "distinct" is simply a term that is dependent on what the speaker intends to express and does not reflect reality.

> If being a cause and effect is just the combination of the determining conditions (*upādhi*) of a specific sequence of presence and absence, [SP 11cd] then why is it not the case that a relation between cause and effect simply consists in these two combined determining conditions, i.e., presence and absence? One may say that it is because they are distinct, but does this term "distinct" not depend on the one who uses it?[44] [SP 12]

If it is maintained that **being a** relation between **cause and effect**, such as fire and smoke, etc., **is just the combination of the determining conditions of**

44. As Steinkellner (2022, xvii) points out, see PVSV 38.17–24 *ad* PV 1.68–69 (translated in Dunne 2004, 136; Eltschinger 2014, 262ff.; and Eltschinger et al. 2018, 76ff.) and PVSV 118.27ff. *ad* PV 1.327 for Dharmakīrti's explanation of how the fact that real entities are distinct (*bheda*) is concealed by the superimposition of relations.

a specific sequence of presence, i.e., existence, **and absence,** i.e., nonexistence, **then why is it not the case that a relation between cause and effect simply consists in these two combined determining conditions, i.e., presence and absence,** like both horns? Which is to say, this follows. **Does this term "distinct"**—and "identical"—**not depend on** what **the speaker** intends to convey?[45] Which is to say, it does. Thus, many things could be conveyed by the same words "cause and effect" without contradiction.

How the meaning of cause and effect is ascertained even though real causal relations do not exist

> If, upon seeing x at t_1, one sees y at t_2, which was not seen at t_1, and when one does not see x, one does not then see y, a person makes the connection that y is an effect without even having been told. [SP 13][46]

If, upon seeing x at t_1, e.g., fire, **one sees y,** e.g., smoke, **at t_2, which was not seen** previously **at t_1, and when one does not see x** (fire)**, one does not then see** y (smoke) either, **a person understands**[47] all by themselves **that y is an effect** of x **without even having been told,** i.e., taught.

How terms are applied after having been learned

> Since, in the absence of this special sequence of observation and non-observation, the idea of an effect does not occur, words like "effect" are also applied for the sake of convenience. [SP 14]

Since, in the absence of this special sequence of observation and non-observation, the idea of an effect does not occur, words like "effect" are also applied for the sake of convenience by those knowledgeable about linguistic conventions speaking to other individuals who apprehend such brief expressions as "the vase that has a cause is a product."

45. The Tibetan of SP 12c differs from the Sanskrit. Since the Sanskrit reads *bhedāc cen*, one would expect something like *tha dad [phyir] zhe na*, but the Tibetan instead reads *tha dad ces bya'i*. Thus, the phrase translated here as "One may say that it is because they are distinct" is omitted from the Tibetan translation.

46. On the three- or fivefold examination (*trikapañcakacintā*), the process by which we know causal relations to obtain based on a series of observations and non-observations, see, for example, Gillon 1991; Inami 1999; and Lasic 1999 and 2003.

47. Tib. *shes*; cf. Skt. *anveti* "makes the connection."

Example to illustrate the previous point

> From the successive presence of *x* followed by *y*, the understanding that *y* is the result of *x* is conveyed. That is called "the referent of that convention," just as when understanding "cow" from a dewlap, etc. [SP 15]

From the reason of the **successive** (i.e., prior) **presence of *x* followed by *y*,** if there is **the understanding that *y* is the result of *x*,** a knowledgeable individual may subsequently **convey** the fact that what was understood is **called "the referent of that convention"** to communicate that an effect is present *when* it is present, by virtue of which an ignorant individual will call this fact to mind. This is **just as when,** for example, someone knowledgeable about linguistic conventions causes an individual who is ignorant of linguistic conventions to **understand "cow" from** the sign of **a dewlap, etc.**

Explaining how relations are superimposed by conceptual thought

> When *y* is about to come into being, *x* is present, and only when *x* is present will *y* come into being—these two are commonly known as "cause" and "effect" from this sequence of perception and non-observation. [SP 16]

When *y* (i.e., the effect) **is about to come into being, *x*** (i.e., the cause) that will bring it about **is present, and only when *x*** (i.e., the cause) **is present,** i.e., only after the cause is present, **will *y*** (i.e., the effect) **come into being—these two** things **are commonly known as,** i.e., called, **"cause" and "effect" from this sequence of perception and non-observation.**

> Conceptual constructions that have false content, whose referents—cause and result—are real objects to just that extent, make things appear as though they were connected. [SP 17]

Conceptual constructions that have false content, whose referents—cause and result—are real objects to just that extent,[48] only as conceptual constructions, **make things appear** in that manner **as though they were connected.**[49]

48. *Annotations* 3a.4: *re shig*; em. *re zhig.*

49. Skt. *ghaṭitān*; n.e. Tib.; *Annotations* supplies an equivalent with *'brel par.*

Cognition falsely establishes relations[50]

> If two things are distinct, what is it for them to be connected? Even if the two are non-distinct, what is it for them to stand in a relation of cause and effect? For if something else exists, then how could these two unconnected things be connected? [SP 18]

One may ask, "Why is this content false?" **If two things are distinct,** each existing in its own nature, **what is it for them to be connected? Even**[51] **if the two are non-distinct, what is it for them to stand in a relation**[52] **of cause and effect? For if some other** thing **exists** between them, **then how could these two unconnected things be connected,** since the absurd consequence would follow that fire and water too would be connected as cause and effect?

Rejecting other kinds of relations imagined by non-Buddhist systems such as contact, inherence, and possession relations maintained by Naiyāyikas

> All this—what is in contact and what is inhered in, etc.—has been investigated by this, since there is no mutual support or any such relatum. [SP 19]

Naiyāyikas claim that there are five relations, such as **contact, inherence,**[53] possession, **etc. All this has also**[54] **been investigated by this** general refutation, **since there is no mutual support,** e.g., the inherence of the properties white and shiny in a cushion,[55] **or any such relatum.**

Denying that an inherence relation obtains between wholes and their basic parts, since this would absurdly entail that all causes and effects stand in an inherence relation because of the fact that parts "produce" wholes

> For even if an effect were produced by something that it inheres in, that cause would not be inhered in then, nor would it be inhered in

50. *Flower* 2b.1 cites SP 18a1 *tha snyad* . . . ; em. *tha dad.*

51. Skt. *api*; n.e. Tib.

52. While the abstract nominalization of the compound *kāryakāraṇatā* conveys the meaning of a relation, there is no corresponding nominalization or term for "relation" in the Tibetan translations.

53. While the Sanskrit refers (by way of the *-in* suffix) to the relata that stand in relations of contact and inherence, the Tibetan refers simply to contact and inherence.

54. Tib. +*kyang*; n.e. Skt.

55. *Flower* 2b.3 gives a similar example, though in place of *gdan* it reads *gnal*[*snal*] *ma.*

> on account of that production[56] since absurd consequences would follow. [SP 20]

For even if an effect, e.g., a whole, **were produced by something that it inheres in**, e.g., atoms, **those two do not**[57] stand in an inherence relation since **the cause would not be inhered in then**, i.e., when the result has already arisen, and **since the absurd consequence would follow** that the same would apply to the case of a potter and a pot, i.e., the potter would absurdly inhere in the pot.

Rejecting inherence relations between relata that do not support one another since this would absurdly entail that anything could stand in an inherence relation with anything else

> If there could be a relation, either in the case of inherence or otherwise, even between two things that did not support each other while inhering or otherwise, then everything could be mutually inherent. [SP 21]

If there could be a relation due to inherence **even between two** relata of inherence (or it could be said those two that inhere)[58] **that did not support each other while inhering or otherwise, then everything** in the world **could also**[59] **stand in mutual** inherence **relations.**[60]

Rejecting contact relations

> Even if two things bring about a contact relation, it cannot on that account be accepted that the two are conjoined, since it would then follow that action, etc., would enter into a contact relation. And remaining (*sthiti*) has been explained in detail. [SP 22]

Here, it is claimed that the contact relation is brought about from the action of one member of a pair as in the case of a tree and a bird, or by the action of

56. Skt. *na tato*; cf. Tib. *de gnyis min.*

57. See previous note.

58. Deviating from the remainder of the manuscript, this annotation (*de dag gnyis ni 'du ba'am zer*) is written in *dbu can* rather than *dbu med*, indicating that it may have been added by a different hand. The only other *dbu can* annotations in the manuscript are editorial: the addition of a missing syllable (*Annotations* 3a.4, SP 16a: *'gyur*) and missing suffix (*Annotations* 4a.1, SP 22d: +*-r*) from the root text.

59. Tib. +*kyang*; n.e. Skt.

60. Tib. SP 21 reads *phan tshun <u>'brel ba</u>* ("mutually *related*") rather than Skt. *<u>samavāyi</u> parasparam* ("mutually *inherent*").

both members as in the case of individuals involved in a quarrel with each other. **Even if two things**, i.e., relata, **bring about a contact relation, it cannot** on that account **be accepted** as a Buddhist commitment **that the two are conjoined since it would then follow that action,**[61] **etc.**, by virtue of which contact is brought about, **would enter into a contact relation. And remaining has** already **been explained in detail** in the texts, *Pramāṇavārttika* and *Pramāṇaviniścaya.*

Rejecting relations of contact, inherence, etc., between permanent entities

> Based on contact, etc., whatever was previously unfit to stand in that relation becomes fit, because for something that has a nature that is permanently fit to stand in a relation, the lack of this fitness would be contradictory. [SP 23]

If it is claimed that **based on contact,** possession, **action, etc.,**[62] separation, etc., **whatever was previously unfit to stand in that relation**, such as a vase, **becomes fit, because for something**, e.g., an effect that has been produced, **that has a nature that is permanently fit to stand in a given relation, the lack of this fitness would** furthermore **be contradictory.**

Relations like possession, separation, going, remaining, etc., all qualify only impermanent things and are wholly reducible to the things that they qualify

> Thus, let something's nature that is referred to as its fitness be spoken of as "separation," "connection," or "motion." What is the use of imagining some other real motion, etc.? [SP 24]

Thus, let this nature,[63] e.g., of an impermanent vase, **that is referred to as its fitness, be spoken of as "separation," "connection," or "motion,"** etc.[64] **What is the use of imagining**[65] **some other real motion, etc.?**

61. *Annotations* 3b.4, SP 22a agrees with the Tabo variant *las sogs*; canonical translations read *la sogs.*

62. Tib. SP 23: *las sogs* rather than *la sogs* as expected; n.e. Skt. for *las.*

63. Tib. *ngo bo 'di*; cf. Skt. *svabhāva 'sya.*

64. Tib. SP 24b +*sogs*; n.e. Skt.

65. *Annotations* 4a.3 SP 24d: *brtags* in accord with Tib. of SPV. Canonical translations of SP: *rtags*

Distinct things arising anew in each moment is the conventional mode of existence[66]

> Even if these relations did exist, since the relation "of this" is not commonly accepted, it is reasonable that things that arise in each moment have distinct natures. [SP 25]

Even if these substantial **relations**, such as motion, etc., **did exist** as distinct things, **since the relation** "the motion **of this** person" **is not** even **commonly accepted, it is** therefore **reasonable**—and it should be added that it is "established"—**that** the conventional mode of existence of **things** is **that** they **arise in each moment as distinct entities,**[67] i.e., they exist with their own natures. These annotations have thus been appended.

Here, since all phenomena exist with their own natures, an agential relation is rejected for established and unestablished things. However, a necessary connection is not rejected,[68] as has been established above. Thus, since all things ultimately lack any agential relation, it has been demonstrated that they are primordially pacified. These annotations[69] to the *Examination of Relations* have been set out by Chomden Reldri.[70]

The *Examination of Relations* by the great master and scholar Dharmakīrti is concluded. It was translated by the Indian scholar Jñānagarbha and the translator Bandé Namkha (Bande Gnam mkha').

This was edited and finalized by the chief editor-translator, the monk Tingedzin Zangpo (Ting nge 'dzin Bzang po), under the guidance of the Indian scholar Śrī Subhūtiśānti.

Homage to the Buddha! The eight topics of the *Examination of Relations* are as follows:[71]

66. *Flower* 3b.4: the quotative *zhes* follows *rigs shing grub bo*, although only *rigs* is included in Tib. SP 25d.

67. Tib. *dngos po tha dad*; cf. Skt. *svabhāvabhedha*.

68. Necessary connection (*avinābhāva, med na mi 'byung ba*) refers to the invariable connection that obtains between the relata in the two kinds of natural relation (*svabhāvapratibandha*) that underwrite inferences: an identity relation (*tādātmya*) and a causal relation (*tadutpatti*).

69. *Annotations ad* 4a.4: *chan*; typeset edition: em. *mchan.*

70. *Annotations ad* 4a.4: *dpal ldan*; typeset edition: em. *bcom ldan.*

71. The following topical outline (which is rendered in the same size as the SP root text that it follows) also includes several annotations, which denote the first few words of stanzas falling under each topic, and which are indicated by parentheses in the translation. For ease of reference, I supply the verse numbers here in square brackets. All annotations to the topical outline are omitted in the Lhasa (2006) typeset edition.

1. Rejecting dependence relations ("Suppose there is a dependence..." [SP 1])
2. Rejecting blending relations ("Suppose there is a blending of natures..." [SP 2])
3. Rejecting reliance relations ("Suppose there is a relation of reliance on another..." [SP 3])
4. Rejecting a relation that is distinct from its relata ("If there were a relation due to two..." [SP 4–6])
5. Rejecting causal relations [SP 7–18]
6. Rejecting inherence relations ("... what is in contact and..." [SP 19–21])
7. Rejecting contact relations ("... action, etc...." [SP 22–25ab])
8. Explaining the point of what was established by these refutations ("... in each moment..." [SP 25cd])

The rejection of causal relations has four subtopics:

5.1 Rejecting causal relations by examining them as simultaneous and sequential ("... between cause and effect..." [SP 7–9])
5.2 Stating the absurd consequences that would follow if a causal relation arose from being connected to a single thing and if a real causal relation consisted in co-presence and co-absence ("If..." [SP 10–12])
5.3 The meaning of cause and effect and the way in which these conventions are ascertained ("... *x*..." [SP 13–15])
5.4 Based on several lines of reasoning, establishing that it is an erroneous cognition that apprehends relations ("When *y* is about to come into being..." [SP 16–18])

The meaning of the *Examination of Relations* has thus been properly summarized by Chomden Reldri.[72]

Editorial Abbreviations and Symbols

+	add
*	unintelligible
em.	emended
n.e.	no equivalent in

72. An annotation at the end of the text appears to read: 2 *zhus yang* * *zhus yang zhus* ("This has been proofread twice").

Abbreviations of Primary Sources

BSAM$_1$	Bsam gtan bzang po. 2006. *Bcom ldan rigs pa'i ral gri'i rnam thar dad pa'i ljon shing*. In *Gsung 'bum Bcom ldan rig pa'i ral gri*, vol. 1, 41–94. Lhasa: Khams sprul bsod nams don grub.
BSAM$_2$	Bsam gtan bzang po. 2007. *Bcom ldan rigs ral pa'i rnam thar*. In *Gsung 'bum Bcom ldan rig pa'i ral gri*, vol. 1, 1–30. Kathmandu: Sa skya rgyal yongs gsung rab slob gnyer khang.
Annotations	Bcom ldan rig pa'i ral gri. 2006. *'Brel pa brtag pa'i mchan dang sa bcas gnyis*. In *Bka' gdams gsung 'bum*, vol. 55, 5–12. *'Brel pa brtag pa'i rab tu byed pa*. In *Gsung 'bum Bcom ldan rig pa'i ral gri*, vol. 10, 57–68. Lhasa: Khams sprul bsod nams don grub.
Flower	Bcom ldan rig pa'i ral gri. 2006. *'Brel pa brtag pa rgyan gyi me tog*. In *Gsung 'bum Bcom ldan rig pa'i ral gri*, vol. 10, 48–56. Lhasa: Khams sprul bsod nams don grub.
HB	*Hetubindu* (Dharmakīrti).
NB	*Nyāyabindu* (Dharmakīrti).
PV	*Pramāṇavārttika* (Dharmakīrti). 1971/72. Yusho Miyasaka, ed., *Pramāṇavārttika-kārikā* (Sanskrit and Tibetan). *Acta Indologica* (Narita: Naritasan Shinshoji) 2: 1–206.
PVin	*Pramāṇaviniścaya* (Dharmakīrti).
PVSV	*Pramāṇavārttikasvavṛtti* (Dharmakīrti). 1960. Raniero Gnoli, ed., *The Pramāṇavārttikam of Dharmakīrti. The First Chapter with the Autocommentary* (Text and critical notes). Serie Orientale Roma 23. Rome: Istituto Italiano per Il Medio ed Estremo Oriente.
PS	*Pramāṇasamuccaya* (Dignāga).
RGYAL	Rgyal tshab Dar ma rin chen. 1982. *'Brel ba brtag pa'i rnam bshad nyi ma'i snying po*. In *Gsung 'bum Rgyal tshab rje*. New Delhi: Zhol par khang. (Block prints reproduced from 1897 set of prints from Lhasa zhol blocks, Dga' ldan phun tshogs gling.)
Skt.	Sanskrit of SP.
SP	*Sambandhaparīkṣā* (Dharmakīrti), in Steinkellner 2022.
SPṬ	*Sambandhaparīkṣāṭīkā* (Vinītadeva).
SPV	*Sambandhaparīkṣāvṛtti* (Devendrabuddhi), in Steinkellner 2022.
SS	*Santānāntarasiddhi* (Dharmakīrti).
Tib.	Tibetan translations of SP.
VN	*Vādanyāya* (Dharmakīrti).

References

Bka' gdams gsung 'bum phyogs bsgrigs thengs dang po/gnyis pa/gsum pa/bzhi pa, vols. 1–30, 2006; vols. 31–60, 2007; vols. 61–90, 2009; vols. 91–120, 2015. Edited by Dpal brtsegs. Chengdu: Si khron mi rigs dpe skrun khang.

'Bras spungs dpe rnying dkar chag. 2004. 2 vols. Beijing: Mi rigs dpe skrun khang.

Dunne, John. 2004. *Foundations of Dharmakīrti's Philosophy*. Boston: Wisdom Publications.

Eltschinger, Vincent. 2007. *Penser l'autorité des Écritures. La polémique de Dharmakīrti contre la notion brahmanique orthodoxe d'un Veda sans auteur. Autour de Pramāṇavārttika I.213–268 et Svavṛtti*. Vienna: Verlag der Österreichischen Akademie der Wissenschaften.

———. 2014. *Buddhist Epistemology as Apologetics. Studies on the History, Self-understanding and Dogmatic Foundations of Late Indian Buddhist Philosophy*. Vienna: Verlag der Österreichischen Akademie der Wissenschaften.

———. 2021. "A Note on Śaṅkaranandana's *Sambandhaparīkṣānusāriṇī*." In *Illuminating the Dharma: Buddhist Studies in Honour of Venerable Professor K. L. Dhammajoti*, edited by T. Endo, 99–119. Hong Kong: Centre of Buddhist Studies, The University of Hong Kong.

Eltschinger, Vincent, John Taber, Michael Torsten Much, and Isabelle Ratié. 2018. *Dharmakīrti's Theory of Exclusion (apoha). Part I, On Concealing: An Annotated Translation of Pramāṇavārttikasvavṛtti 24, 16–45, 20 (Pramāṇavārttika I.40–91)*. Studia Philologica Buddhica 36. Tokyo: The International Institute for Buddhist Studies.

Frauwallner, Erich. 1934. "Dharmakīrtis Sambandhaparīkṣā: Text und Übersetzung." *Wiener Zeitschrift für die Kunde des Morgenlandes* 41: 261–300.

Gillon, Brendan. 1991. "Dharmakīrti and the Problem of Induction." In Steinkellner, *Studies in the Buddhist Epistemological Tradition*, 53–58.

Hugon, Pascale. 2011. "Argumentation Theory in the Early Tibetan Epistemological Tradition." *Journal of the International Association of Buddhist Studies* 34.1–2: 97–148.

———. 2016. "Enclaves of Learning, Religious and Intellectual Communities in Tibet: The Monastery of gSang phu Ne'u thog in the Early Centuries of the Later Diffusion of Buddhism." In *Meanings of Community across Medieval Eurasia: Comparative Approaches*, edited by Eirik Hovden, Christina Lutter, and Walter Pohl, 289–308. Brill's Series on the Early Middle Ages 25. Leiden: Brill

Inami, Masahiro. 1999. "On the Determination of Causality." In Katsura, *Dharmakīrti's Thought*, 131–54.

Jha, V. N. 1990. *The Philosophy of Relations (Containing the Sanskrit Text and English Translation of Dharma Kīrti's Sambandhaparīkṣā with Prabhācandra's Commentary)*. Delhi: Sri Satguru Publications.

Katsura, Shōryū. 1992. "*Pramāṇavārttika* IV.202–206—Towards the Correct Understanding of *Svabhāvapratibandha*." *Indogaku Bukkyōgaku Kenkyū / The Journal of Indian and Buddhist Studies* 40: 1047–52.

———, ed. 1999. *Dharmakīrti's Thought and Its Impact on Indian and Tibetan Philosophy: Proceedings of the Third International Dharmakīrti Conference, Hiroshima, November 4–6, 1997*. Vienna: Verlag der Österreichischen Akademie der Wissenschaften.

van der Kuijp, Leonard W. J. 1987. "The Monastery of Gsang-phu Ne'u-thog and Its Abbatial Succession from ca. 1073 to 1250." *Berliner Indologische Studien* 3: 103–27.

———. 2003. "A Treatise on Buddhist Epistemology and Logic Attributed to Klong chen Rab 'byams pa (1308–1364) and Its Place in Indo-Tibetan Intellectual History." *Journal of Indian Philosophy* 31: 381–437.

Lasic, Horst. 1999. "Dharmakīrti and His Successors on the Determination of Causality." In Katsura, *Dharmakīrti's Thought*, 233–42.

———. 2003. "On the Utilization of Causality as a Basis of Inference: Dharmakīrti's Statements and Their Interpretation." *Journal of Indian Philosophy* 31: 185–97.

Nishizawa, Fumihito. 1997. "*Sa bcad* of rGyal tshab rje's *'Brel pa brtag pa'i rnam bśad ñi ma'i sñiṅ po*." In *Basic Studies for Tibetan Buddhism: The Collected Sabcad of rJe yab sras gsung 'bum*, vol. 2, edited by Shojiro Nomura, Nishizawa Fumihito, Yumiko Ishihama, and Fukuda Yoichi, 224–25. Studia Tibetica 34. Tokyo: The Toyo Bunko.

Oetke, Claus. 1991. "*Svabhāvapratibandha* and the Types of Reasons in Dharmakīrti's Theory of Inference." In Steinkellner, *Studies in the Buddhist Epistemological Tradition*, 243–68.

Schaeffer, Kurtis R., and Leonard W. J. van der Kuijp. 2009. *An Early Tibetan Survey of Buddhist Literature: The Bstan pa rgyas pa rgyan gyi nyi 'od of Bcom ldan ral gri*. Harvard Oriental Series 64. Cambridge, MA: Harvard University Press.

Shastri, Dwarikadas. 1972. *Vadanyayaprakaraṇa of Acharya Dharmakirtti with the Commentary Vipañchitārthā of Acharya Śāntirakṣita, and Sambandhaparīkṣā with the Commentary of Prabhāchandra*. Varanasi: Bauddha Bharati.

Steinkellner, Ernst, ed. 1991. *Studies in the Buddhist Epistemological Tradition: Proceedings of the Second International Dharmakīrti Conference (Vienna, June 11–16, 1989)*. Vienna: Verlag der Österreichischen Akademie der Wissenschaften.

———. 1997. "Kumārila, Īśvarasena, and Dharmakīrti in Dialogue. A New Interpretation of *Pramāṇavārttika* I 33." In *Bauddhavidyāsudhākaraḥ. Studies in Honour of Heinz Bechert on the Occasion of His 65th Birthday*, edited by Petra Kiepper-Pülz and Jens-Uwe Hartmann, 625–46. Indica et Tibetica 30. Swisttal-Odendorf: Indica et Tibetica Verlag.

———. 2022. *Dharmakīrti's Sambandhaparīkṣākārikā and Devendrabuddhi's Sambandhaparīkṣāvṛtti*. Beijing and Vienna: China Tibetology Publishing House and Austrian Academy of Sciences Press.

Tauscher, Helmut. 1994. "Tanjur Fragments from the Manuscript Collection at Ta pho Monastery. *Sambandhaparīkṣā* with Its Commentaries *Vṛtti* and *Ṭīkā*." *East and West* 44.1: 173–84.

Maintaining Identification with a Buddha: Divine Identity or Simply False?

Yael Bentor

Introduction

THE "JERUSALEM Syndrome" is a well-known phenomenon among mental-health practitioners who treat tourists and pilgrims to Jerusalem. According to Kalian and Witztum, "Forty percent [of those diagnosed with Jerusalem Syndrome] reported mystical experiences, and many identified with religious figures; twenty-five percent thought they were the Messiah."[1] These individuals are often admitted to psychiatric hospitals but tend to recover quickly upon return to their home countries. Yogis, who engage in tantric visualization in accordance with the guidelines of their gurus and sādhana manuals, visualize themselves as buddhas, and act and speak accordingly. While they are altruistically motivated to lead all sentient beings to enlightenment, how can they know if they have formed a false identity for themselves or, put differently, engaged in self-deception? Here, I will explore the soteriological and ethical status of such an identity. The focus will be the practice of deity yoga (Tib. *lha'i rnal 'byor*, Skt. *devatāyoga*) within the twofold tantric practice of the creation[2] (Tib. *bskyed rim*, Skt. *utpattikrama*) and completion stages (Tib. *rdzogs rim*, Skt. *niṣpannakrama* or *utpannakrama*), according to the unexcelled tantra (*bla med kyi rgyud sde*).

Deity Yoga

In deity yoga, yogis visualize themselves as the principal deity of a maṇḍala at the center of a celestial mansion or divine palace. This visualization is basic to the first stage of the tantric path, known as the "creation stage." In the second or "completion stage" of the tantric path, the idea of the yogi as a deity remains important. Deity yoga is part of the tantric method known as "taking the fruit in the path." In this method, the agent is equivalent to its object and the path is

1. Kalian and Witztum 1998, 322.

2. Translated also as *generation*, *development*, or *visualization stage*.

analogous to the fruit, as in order to become buddhas, yogis meditate on themselves as buddhas already during the path toward that goal.

Prominent figures within the Indo-Tibetan tradition hold various views about the soteriological value of deity yoga. Generally speaking, the tradition regards the experience of a yogi, who imagines being a deity and acting like one, to have a definite effect on this yogi's advance toward buddhahood. Furthermore, the visions the yogi sees are considered more real than any other saṃsāric appearance. These visions of awakened beings dwelling in the maṇḍala are the realm of buddhahood; they are the transformed reality that is the goal of the tantric practice.

On the other hand, certain Indian and Tibetan scholars have identified particular problems with deity visualization. They argue that deities created through mental fabrication alone cannot be real, and that yogis who are not deities, but meditate as if they were, have wrong cognitions. False cognitions, they point out, are not only unsuitable causes for buddhahood—they can even create obstacles to attaining it.[3]

Buddha Nature and Purity

Two theoretical approaches support the practice of deity yoga—namely, *tathāgatagarbha* and "purity" (Tib. *rnam par dag pa*, Skt. *viśuddhi*). According to the former, sentient beings are in fact pure deities, but due to saṃsāric habitual tendencies without beginning, these beings arise as the aggregates, sense bases, and so forth. The purpose of deity yoga is to recognize the tathāgata family that is already present. From this perspective, when yogis meditate on themselves as deities, these deities are real and the yogis' cognitions are not false. However, such an interpretation of the *tathāgatagarbha* theory is not universally accepted by Indian and Tibetan scholars.

The notion of "purity"[4] is found in several major tantras, including the *Guhyasamāja* and *Hevajra* tantras.[5] Analogies are drawn in these tantras between psychophysical elements of the body and the deities of the maṇḍala that are their pure aspects. These may be described as actual equivalences

3. See, for example, the opinion of an opponent presented by Mkhas grub rje (1385–1438): "If you are not a deity, but meditate as if you were a deity, your cognition will be false and thus will not be suitable as a cause for buddhahood." Mkhas grub rje, *Bskyed rim dngos grub rgya mtsho*, 117b3.

4. On this subject, see Sferra 1999.

5. *Guhyasamāja Tantra* 17.50–51 in Matsunaga 1978, 109; and the *Hevajra Tantra* in Snellgrove 1959, 1.9. See also the *Saṃvarodaya Tantra*, chap. 4, in Tsuda 1974.

between male and female buddhas and bodhisattvas on the one hand, and the five aggregates, sense bases, afflictive emotions, and so forth on the other. Alternatively, as in the *Guhyasamāja Tantra*, these are described as affinities. In both cases, these special links between elements of the human body and their purified aspects as the deities of the maṇḍala are said to allow transformations into deities.

Notably, the *Hevajra Tantra*[6] speaks about the purification of the aggregates and so forth during the creation stage. This is important for the current discussion, as various treatises[7] suggest that while visualizations during the creation stage are conceptualized and the deities are not real, the actual transformation occurs in the completion stage. Let us consider another example from the *Hevajra Tantra*: "By means of the yoga of the *creation stage*, yogis must meditate on the proliferations of mental constructs. Once they have made the proliferations dream-like, they should use this very proliferation to de-proliferate."[8] This verse speaks explicitly about the creation stage, implying that this stage itself can bring the yogis to de-proliferate. However, some Indian and Tibetan scholars take this to mean that the creation stage consists of conceptualizations, while the completion stage brings yogis to nonconceptual realization.[9]

In the current context, I wish to examine especially the nature and the modes of the transformation from the impure to the pure states during the visualizations of the creation stage. These topics have attracted considerable debate among Indian and Tibetan scholars.

Is the Visualization Contrived?

We find this question in Indrabhūti's *Jñānasiddhi*,[10] dated to the eighth or ninth centuries.[11] In chapter 2 of this treatise, entitled "Refuting Meditation on Forms" (Skt. *rūpabhāvanāniṣedha*, Tib. *gzugs su bsgom pa dgag pa*), Indrabhūti[12] argues that when yogis visualize themselves in the form of Vajrasattva, they engage in a fruitless practice. This is because such a Vajrasattva is

6. Snellgrove 1959, 1.9.18cd–19ab.

7. Including some of the texts that will be mentioned below.

8. Snellgrove 1959, 2.2.29; my translation.

9. See, for example, Ratnarakṣita, *Padminī*, in Tanemura, Kano, and Kuranishi 2019, §13.2.6.4, 59–64; Tōh. 1420, 45a2–3. Tsong kha pa, for his part, understands this verse in both ways according to the context. See Tsong kha pa, *Sngags rim chen mo*, 459 and 493.

10. *Ye shes grub pa*, Tōh. 2219.

11. Gerloff and Schott 2020, 241.

12. *Jñānasiddhi*, 2.13–18. See also Krug 2018a, 241–42.

constructed (Skt. *kṛtaka*, Tib. *byas pa*) or compounded (Skt. *saṃskṛta*, Tib. *'dus byas*) and therefore is as impermanent as a pot. What is the utility, asks Indrabhūti, of meditating on a mentally created form that will disappear soon after it appears?

There are further objections to deity yoga in the same chapter of the *Jñānasiddhi*, but before continuing our discussion we must look at the entire context. These lines in Indrabhūti's work present the positions of his opponents, though they are not marked as such, for later on in the work he replies to them.

Puṇḍarīka's *Stainless Light*,[13] dated to the eleventh century,[14] raises the same issue. It maintains that yogis practicing deity yoga engage in a conceptual meditation,[15] because they must visualize numerous detailed colors, shapes, numbers, and more.[16] In order to demonstrate the impermanent nature of this meditation, the *Stainless Light* asserts that when one face of the deity appears, all other faces disappear.[17] Since this meditation is conceptual or constructed and thus its outcome is impermanent, the *Stainless Light* concludes here that conceptual meditation on the maṇḍala and the deities dwelling in it, while cultivating identification (Skt. *ahaṃkāra*, Tib. *nga rgyal*) with Vajrasattva, will not lead yogis to buddhahood.[18]

Similar discussions are found also in Ratnarakṣita's *Padminī*,[19] dated to the twelfth or thirteenth centuries, which clearly recognizes the potential of the creation stage to carry the yogis toward awakening. Here[20] the opponent maintains that contrived thoughts are false because they arise from clinging to unreal objects and thus are impermanent. In addition, the opponent[21] argues that meditating on the creation stage, which consists of mental elaboration, not only cannot lead to buddhahood but cannot even achieve a single pointed samādhi, because meditators are overburdened by numerous thoughts. In

13. Puṇḍarīka, *Vimalaprabhā*, in Dwivedi and Bahulkar 1994, 68.28–69.2; Tōh. 1347, *da*, 229b6–230a1. See also Wallace 2001, 199.

14. The relevant lines are found in the commentary on the *Kālacakra Tantra*, 5.127, which "probably existed as a separate and complete didactic text." Sferra 2005, 266.

15. Tib. *rnal par rtog pa'i sgom pa*, Skt. *vikalpabhāvanā*.

16. Dwivedi and Bahulkar 1994, 67.31, *da*, 228b4–5.

17. Dwivedi and Bahulkar 1994, 63.6–11, *da*, 223b2–4.

18. Dwivedi and Bahulkar 1994, 68.8–9, *da*, 229a1–2.

19. *Padminī*, chap. 13, commenting on the chapter on the creation stage in the *Saṃvarodaya Tantra*. See Tanemura, Kano, and Kuranishi 2017; Tōh. 1420.

20. Tanemura, Kano, and Kuranishi 2017, §13.2.1.1.2, 22–23; Tōh. 1420, 41b2–3.

21. Tanemura, Kano, and Kuranishi 2017, §13.2.1, 3–4; Tōh. 1420, 41a4–5.

reply, Ratnarakṣita[22] refers to the Buddhist epistemological tradition, which, it should be stressed,[23] is not always ignored in tantric literature. According to Dharmakīrti:[24]

> Therefore, whatever is very intensely meditated on, whether it is real or unreal, will give rise to clear non-conceptual cognition when the meditation becomes powerful.[25]

Therefore Ratnarakṣita concludes that even if the object consists of various aspects, yogis can see all of them simultaneously and nonconceptually.

The opponent in Ratnarakṣita's *Padminī*[26] argues that not only do visualized forms not endure but they are limited to a particular place and time, just like a pot, while deities are pervasive (Skt. *vyāpti* or *vyāpitva*, Tib. *khyab pa [nyid]*) and omnipresent. Clearly the *Padminī* follows the *Jñānasiddhi*[27] on this point. We know that Ratnarakṣita was familiar with the *Jñānasiddhi*, since he cites it in other contexts in the same chapter. Moreover, says the opponent in the *Padminī*, echoing the *Stainless Light*,[28] visualized deities are lacking qualities such as the super-knowledges and do not act for the sake of people.

Ratnarakṣita's position[29] is that when yogis visualize the deities, they do not meditate merely on their forms. Because the maṇḍala wheel is not separate from *dharmatā*, yogis in fact meditate on the nature of the Blessed One, which is a nondual union (Skt. *yuganaddha*, Tib. *zung 'jug gnyis su med pa*) of forms and suchness, emptiness and great bliss, grasped and grasper. Ratnarakṣita[30] continues to explain that a pot is indeed neither pervasive nor omnipresent, but this is not because it has a form but because it arises through bifurcation into subject and object. Deities, on the other hand, arise from aspiration

22. Tanemura, Kano, and Kuranishi 2017, §13.2.2.1.2, 86–96; Tōh. 1420, 42b5–43a1.

23. See also Krug 2018b.

24. *Pramāṇavarttika, Pratyakṣa*, in Miyasaka, 1971–1972, v. 285, translated by Isaacson and Sferra 2014, 267.

25. Likewise, Birgit Kellner (2020) has recently shown how in his works on the *Stages of Meditation* (*Bhāvanākrama, Bsgom pa'i rim pa*), Kamalaśīla, who lived in the eighth century, the period in which higher tantras evolved, uses concepts to eliminate conceptualization.

26. Tanemura, Kano, and Kuranishi 2017, §13.2.1.1.3, 27–29; Tōh. 1420, 41b4–5.

27. Indrabhūti, *Jñānasiddhi*, 12.1–6. See also Krug 2018b, 161–62.

28. Dwivedi and Bahulkar 1994, 70.27–29, *da*, 232a1–2.

29. Tanemura, Kano, and Kuranishi 2017, §13.2.2.1.1, 73–85; Tōh. 1420, 42b1–5.

30. Tanemura, Kano, and Kuranishi 2017, §13.2.2.1.5, 129–135; Tōh. 1420, 43b3–5.

prayers based on great compassion inseparable from emptiness. Therefore they can take every form and act to benefit others.

These discussions continued among Tibetan scholars as well. Barawa Gyeltsen Pelzangpo (1310–91)[31] opens his treatise *The Profound Meaning of the Creation Stage Free of Contradiction*[32] with the question:[33] "Is the creation stage contrived (*kun brtags*) or not?" His own position is: "There is no contradiction in maintaining both." To demonstrate that the creation stage is contrived, Barawa refers to the position of the *Stainless Light* mentioned above. Ultimately, however, Barawa does not accept the view that the meditation on deity yoga is merely contrived, because, he says, it has the potential for actualizing its goal. In this sense, for him this meditation is different from grasping an object as something that it is not. He brings the example of someone meditating on a small stone pile at the top of a mountain as a human being. No matter how long this person persists in this meditation, the stone pile will not become a human being. The indication that this yogi's cognition is wrong is that the meditation cannot bear fruit. On the other hand, says Barawa,[34] the visualization of oneself as a deity is not contrived, because it does yield its fruit. In other words, since yogis can attain buddhahood, their meditation on the deity during the path is uncontrived.[35] Furthermore, just like Ratnarakṣita, Barawa[36] maintains that when yogis meditate on themselves as deities and their minds are focused single-pointedly on these deities, a nonconceptual wisdom arises. Hence Barawa concludes that the creation stage is both contrived and uncontrived, without any contradiction between the two.

"I Am a King"

Yet another argument against the validity of deity visualization is found in the *Jñānasiddhi*,[37] where the opponent uses the example of a destitute man who meditates on the thought "I am a king." Even if this person meditates for a billion eons, he will never become a king, because his meditation is based on a mistaken thought (Skt. *mithyākalpana*, Tib. *log pa'i rtog pa*). Likewise, yogis

31. 'Ba' ra ba Rgyal mtshan dpal bzang po.

32. *Bskyed rim zab don 'gal du skyon med* = *Bskyed rim zab don*.

33. *Bskyed rim zab don*, 2a3–b5.

34. *Bskyed rim zab don*, 2b5–6.

35. *Bskyed rim zab don*, 7b5–8a1.

36. *Bskyed rim zab don*, 6a4–5 and 7b3–4.

37. Indrabhūti, *Jñānasiddhi*, 2.8–9.

will not become buddhas through wrong meditation. Indrabhūti's[38] own position, however, is that through meditative absorption, "may I be such," the yogis' concentrations become lucid and the deities are seen as clearly as if they were in paintings in front of them.

This matter is elaborated in the parallel discussion in the *Stainless Light*,[39] which emphasizes that the destitute man lacks any possessions (Skt. *dravyahīna*, Tib. *bsod nams dman pa*),[40] while the yogis lack the possessions of merit and wisdom, in addition to their wrong thoughts. Hence, the argument here is not against the practice of deity yoga as such, but in favor of the need for prior accumulation of merit and wisdom. The opponent in the *Padminī* further develops the argument by asking:[41] While yogis must accumulate merit and wisdom for attaining buddhahood, how can they do so through meditation alone? Now the opponent presents the example of the king: If this were possible, then a destitute man who meditates on the thought "I am a cakravartin king" would attain cakravartihood, regardless of his karma or whether his deeds were virtuous or not.

Ratnarakṣita's reply[42] is based on the Yogācāra approach, which holds that reality is fundamentally mental in nature and therefore even cakravartihood can be eventually achieved, though perhaps only in compliance with karmic causality and so forth. Furthermore, merit and wisdom can certainly be accumulated through meditation, because the six perfections do not depend on external objects but are mental attitudes, while wisdom undoubtedly can be accumulated through meditation alone.

Barawa[43] stresses that the meditation through which merit and wisdom are accumulated is no other than the creation stage itself. By meditating on themselves as deities, yogis clear away the habitual tendencies of their ordinary bodies and accumulate wisdom. Additionally,[44] when their minds are focused single-pointedly on the deities that, while lacking intrinsic nature, do appear, the accumulation of wisdom is actualized. Likewise, by making offerings to themselves as deities and by meditating on loving kindness, compassion, and bodhicitta, these yogis cleanse their wrongdoings and purify their obscurations,

38. Indrabhūti, *Jñānasiddhi*, 2.20–21.

39. Dwivedi and Bahulkar 1994, 68.28–69.2, *da*, 229b6–230a1. See also Wallace 2001, 200.

40. Note that according to the Tibetan this person possesses only inferior merit.

41. Tanemura, Kano, and Kuranishi 2017, §13.2.1.1.2, 15–20; Tōh. 1420, 41a7–b2.

42. Tanemura, Kano, and Kuranishi 2017, §13.2.2.1.3, 96–97; Tōh. 1420, 43a1–2.

43. *Bskyed rim zab don*, 2b4–6 and 3b6–4a1.

44. *Bskyed rim zab don*, 7b3–5.

thereby completing the accumulation of merit. As a result, the *dharmakāya* and *rūpakāya* of the fruit are actualized.

Thus in elaborating on lines from the *Stainless Light* that liken yogis lacking merit and wisdom who meditate on themselves as deities to a poor vagabond who habituates to the thought "I am a king," Barawa shows how by their very meditation these yogis can gain resources for becoming deities.

Contaminated Body

According to the *Stainless Light*,[45] it is impossible to say that the present contaminated body of the yogi is the divine body of the deity. Barawa[46] agrees with this position. For him,[47] unless yogis abandon their ordinary and impure bodies, they cannot reach awakening. Therefore,[48] he says, yogis should visualize their minds as deities, but not their bodies.

Similar to other proponents of the *tathāgatagarbha* theory, Barawa[49] maintains that as long as the Buddha essence is not recognized, a distinction must be made between the ground of purification (*sbyang gzhi*) and the object to be purified (*sbyang bya*). The object to be purified is not the ordinary body, but the arising of the bodily constituents, such as the aggregates and sensory spheres, as the grasped and grasper. The remedy that purifies this is the meditation on the aggregates and sensory spheres as deities. When the deity arises clearly and steadily, the taints that should be purified—the habitual tendencies of holding the aggregates and sensory spheres as ordinary—are purified. Since the yogis' minds are focused on the deity, they abide in a nonconceptual continuum and the taints of the dualistic perceiving mind are thus purified. Thereby, the *dharmakāya* and *rūpakāya* of the fruit are eventually actualized. However, as long as the fruit is not reached, yogis meditate on the aggregates and sensory spheres as deities, while these bodily constituents in their ordinary forms are not deities; instead, they are the object to be purified.

Conversely, as far as the true nature of things is concerned, the ground of purification and the object to be purified are indivisible. The ground is the *tathāgatagarbha* that, due to saṃsāric habitual tendencies since beginningless time, arises as the aggregates and so forth, but in fact is no different from these

45. Dwivedi and Bahulkar 1994, 69.17–18, *da*, 230b1.

46. *Bskyed rim zab don*, 6a5–b1.

47. *Bskyed rim zab don*, 5b6.

48. *Bskyed rim zab don*, 7b2.

49. *Bskyed rim zab don*, 2b6–3a6.

bodily constituents. From this perspective, the aggregates are taught as deities. Thus, once more, Barawa bridges between apparent contradictions.

Concurrently, Barawa[50] maintains that the ordinary contaminated body as such cannot become a deity's body but must be transformed before buddhahood can be attained. The transformation takes place when, during deity yoga, the yogi's mind is focused on the deity, thus giving rise to a nonconceptual wisdom. At that time, all the winds enter into the central channel of the subtle body, the bodily constituents are purified, and the body becomes rainbow body (*'ja' lus*) while the mind is awakened into the *dharmakāya*. Thus, to become a deity's body, the ordinary impure body must be abandoned and the rainbow body must arise. This accords with the classic notion of nirvāṇa with and without remainder (Skt. *sopadhiśeṣanirvāṇa*, and *nirupadhiśeṣanirvāṇa*). While the mind of Buddha Śākyamuni was capable of transformation during his life, it was only upon his death, when his impure constituents ceased to exist, that he attained nirvāṇa without remainder. On the other hand, according to the tantric tradition, buddhahood can be attained in the present lifetime. But this leaves the question: If awakening in the present body is not possible, how can yogis attain buddhahood in one lifetime?[51]

Tsongkhapa (1357–1419), who met Barawa when the latter was a renowned scholar and teacher,[52] shares the position that yogis can be awakened only after changing their bodies. In his works[53] we find an explanation for this conundrum. Yogis do attain buddhahood in their present life, because they do not undergo ordinary death and rebirth. For Tsongkhapa, the transformed body is not the rainbow body but the pure illusory body (Tib. *sgyu lus*, Skt. *māyādeha*) formed of mere-wind-and-mind. Nevertheless, on a par with Barawa, Tsongkhapa explains that the mind of innate great bliss, which directly realizes emptiness, results in the *dharmakāya*; the illusory bodies purified by the actual clear light likewise result in the *rūpakāya*.

We may add that, just like Ratnarakṣita and Barawa, Tsongkhapa[54] maintains that already during the creation stage yogis attain a union of appearances and emptiness through the yoga of nondual profundity and manifestation. Likewise, according to Tsongkhapa,[55] by meditating on the principal deity of

50. *Bskyed rim zab don*, 6a4–b1.

51. See also Bentor 2020.

52. Blo bzang 'phrin las rnam rgyal, *Tsong kha pa'i rnam thar*, 485–86.

53. See, for example, his *Rnam gzhag rim pa'i rnam bshad*, 19a–b.

54. *Sngags rim chen mo*, 493.

55. *Rnam gzhag rim pa'i rnam bshad*, 44b6–45a1.

the maṇḍala with the contrived resolve "I am that deity," yogis will gain the capacity to achieve an uncontrived mode of divine identification.

Barawa raises another question about the above statement that yogis should visualize their minds as deities, but not their bodies. If so, he asks, how do they meditate on themselves as deities? Barawa[56] replies that in fact yogis do not meditate on their bodies as deities, because prior to the visualization of the deities, they dissolve all bodies and appearances into emptiness through the mantra *svabhāva* or *śūnyatā*.[57] Only then, from within the continuum of emptiness, do they visualize the deities arising from their seed syllables and so forth. Hence, according to Barawa, the mind is visualized as a deity but the body is not. In this way, while yogis do not meditate on their bodies as deities, when they meditate on their minds as deities, the habitual tendencies of the present ordinary body are naturally purified.

Wrong Cognition

This brings us back to the question of whether yogis meditating on themselves as deities do so with wrong cognitions.[58] To the above discussion, we may add the example found in the *Stainless Light*[59] of yogis overcome by wrong identification with the deity (Skt. *mithyāhaṅkāra*, Tib. *log pa'i nga rgyal*) who think: "I am Vajrasattva endowed with the ten powers." The *Stainless Light* tells us that it would be astounding if such yogis attained buddhahood, since they are endowed with every obscuration.

Geluk lamas who investigate the meditating cognition by means of epistemological methods are especially concerned with the question of mistaken cognitions. Their reply to the claim that the cognition of the yogis is wrong is similar to that of Barawa. They argue that the meditating mind is not wrong; rather, the claim that yogis meditate on their ordinary existence as deities is wrong. For example, in his public talks, the Fourteenth Dalai Lama emphasizes that yogis do not meditate on themselves as deities while they are not deities, because first they dissolve, on the level of their minds, the ordinary existence of themselves and their environment into emptiness with the *śūnyatā* mantra. In doing so they change the bases of imputation, because when they

56. *Bskyed rim zab don*, 7a5–b2.

57. *Oṃ svabhāva śuddhāḥ sarvadharmāḥ svabhāva śuddho 'haṃ* and *Oṃ śūnyatā jñāna vajra svabhāva ātmako 'haṃ*.

58. On wrong cognitions or wrong conceptualization, *mithyāvikalpa*, see Yamabe 2021, 476–77.

59. Dwivedi and Bahulkar 1994, 67.31–68.3, *da*, 228b4–7; see also Wallace 2001, 200.

habituate to the thought "I am a deity," the referent for "I" is not their ordinary selves, but the deity that has arisen from emptiness. Therefore their cognitions are not wrong.

The issue of the mind meditating on deity yoga being a wrong cognition is not only philosophical in nature but psychological as well. If, while meditating on themselves as Vajradhara, the yogis' experience confirms that their bodies are in no way adorned with the major and minor marks of the Buddha and their minds are unable to realize the nature of all phenomena, they surely feel that they are pretending to be someone other than who they are. Those who accept the *tathāgatagarbha* view might explain that this feeling results from the yogis' habituation to conceive themselves and their environment as impure, while their true nature is pure. Yet these yogis still require a method to dissolve the discrepancy. One remedy offered to yogis engaged in deity yoga is to invite the real deity in the form of the *jñānasattva* into themselves, visualized as the *samayasattva*. This visualization is included in a large variety of sādhanas.

Self-Deception

Another way to address the uneasiness yogis experience while "pretending" to be something they are not is to point out that self-deception is part of the tantric approach called "taking the goal in the path." In order to become buddhas, yogis purposely meditate on themselves as buddhas already during the path. Various Tibetan lamas take into consideration that intentional self-deception is found in both Mahāyāna and Vajrayāna. For example, Drakpa Shedrup (1675–1748)[60] maintains that as long as yogis are aware of being self-deceived—though they meditate on something not present as if it were present—their cognitions are not mistaken.

Drakpa Shedrup offers a relevant example. Yogis know that during the sādhana, their offerings to buddhas and bodhisattvas are not real, since they themselves are mentally emanating these offerings. Likewise, they are aware that there are no actual buddhas and bodhisattvas before them to accept these offerings. However, they intensely wish the buddhas and bodhisattvas to be there and the offerings they make to be real. In the same way, says Drakpa Shedrup, yogis who meditate on themselves as deities maintain divine identification with the resolution: "At this time it is real." For Drakpa Shedrup, although the deities are not real, it is not inconsistent to identify with the deities as if they are real for a short time. This is because if yogis block their clinging to ordinary appearances in this way, they will focus on the supreme

60. Grags pa bshad sgrub, "Rdo rje 'jigs byed kyi rim pa dang po," 151–53.

appearances of the celestial mansion and the deities dwelling there, and thereby attain extraordinary goals. But if they hold the deities as actually real, their cognition will be mistaken because, overcome by delusion, they will cling to something that is not a deity as a deity.

Of even greater significance is the second reason Drakpa Shedrup offers to resolve the contradiction, a reason that, he says, has wider implications. This special wish for the deity to be real, just like the reality of interdependent origination, is inconceivable, that is to say, beyond the reach of human intellect; hence, it cannot be refuted by mere rational reasoning.

Relinquishing Ordinary Appearances and Attitudes

In the previous section of this article, Drakpa Shedrup refers to another important goal of the creation stage, which is accepted by most Tibetan yogi-scholars. This is blocking, even for a short time, one's clinging to ordinary identification, while attaining the divine pride of the deity, accompanied by a temporary renunciation of ordinary appearances, while attaining the supreme appearances of the maṇḍala. This goal can be achieved on the *path* itself—that is to say, even long before yogis undergo a substantial transformation and reach the ultimate *goal* of buddhahood. Barawa offers an interesting explanation for the effects of the shift of identities while on the path:[61]

> As a remedy for your habitual tendency of clinging to the color of your body, meditate on a deity in multiple various colors. As a remedy for your attachment to your male body, meditate on yourself as a female deity. . . . As a remedy for your attachment to having one face, meditate on yourself with many faces. As a remedy for your attachment to your attractive human form, meditate on yourself with animal faces, such as a buffalo, horse, pig, and crow. As a remedy for your attachment to having two arms, meditate on yourself with many arms, four, and more. . . . As a remedy for your attachment to pure and tasty food, such as the three whites, the three sweets, and so forth, meditate on the impure and repulsive five nectars and on the five meats, such as human meat and dog meat. As a remedy for your attachment to nice eating vessels made of precious substances such as gold, meditate on having vessels such as skull cups.

61. *Bskyed rim zab don*, 4b4–5b2.

By multiplying their possible identities, yogis reduce their attachment to their ordinary identities. Furthermore, by rendering their identities relative or conditional, they are on the way to realizing selflessness.

Conclusions

We have encountered a large variety of views on the working of deity yoga. Those who have spoken against its soteriological value, whether they were hypothetical opponents or actual individuals, raised claims such as: conceptual visualizations cannot produce real and enduring results; cognitions holding unreal objects as real are wrong and hence cannot bear fruit; and the contaminated body of the yogi cannot become the divine body of the deity. Several defenders of the capabilities of deity yoga find support in the Buddhist epistemological tradition, which maintains that nondual and nonconceptual mind can arise through a powerful meditation. They extend this position to the tantric meditation on deity yoga during the creation stage, in which yogis maintain a single-pointed concentration on themselves as deities. Hence, they argue that the creation stage is capable of carrying yogis to buddhahood.

Additionally, as certain masters argue, yogis can complete the accumulation of merit and wisdom not as a prior meditation but in the course of practicing the creation stage. Some scholars emphasize that the deities do not arise from the impure and conventional reality, but from emptiness, which enables all changes. Moreover, this emptiness is nondual, with great compassion toward all sentient beings and the aspiration to lead them to enlightenment. Therefore deities born from nondual wisdom realizing emptiness and great compassion cannot but achieve true and nondual results and are capable of appearing as *nirmāṇakāyas* guiding sentient beings to awakening. Some of the scholars who often engage in philosophical debates are all the same eager to stress the limitations of logical reasoning with regard to yogic experiences.[62]

None of the scholars surveyed accept that the ordinary contaminated body can transform into a deity's body, yet some find ways to purify the yogi's body during deity yoga itself. Another important goal that is achieved by those already on the path itself is a temporary blocking of ordinary identification and appearances. Replying to the claim that the cognition of yogis meditating on themselves as deities is wrong, certain scholars say that self-deception is part of the tantric approach called "taking the goal in the path." Others say that when the vision of the celestial mansion, along with the awakened beings dwelling in

62. On this point, see also A khu ching, *Mi bskyod mgon po'i zhal lung*, 76b; English, Jinpa 1999, 141

it, is regarded as more real than ordinary reality, it cannot be wrong. This is the position of Muniśrībhadra in his commentary on a *Guhyasamāja* sādhana:[63] When you know all the variety of the ordinary world to be in fact the maṇḍala wheel, how could your mind be wrong?

Yet many fascinating subjects are beyond the scope of the present article. For example, a closer examination of variations among the texts we have mentioned would likely be a fruitful line of research. Furthermore, the influence of Kagyü scholars on Tsongkhapa's thought on the working of the sādhana is a promising avenue of investigation. Tsongkhapa's views on this matter, primarily vis-à-vis Sakya scholars, have received some scholarly attention, but the inspiration Tsongkhapa drew from Kagyü scholars still awaits due consideration.

References

Tantras

Matsunaga, Yukei. 1978. *The Guhyasamāja Tantra: A New Critical Edition*. Osaka: Toho Shuppan.

Snellgrove, David L. 1959. *Hevajra Tantra: A Critical Study*. London: Oxford University Press.

Tsuda, Shinichi. 1974. *The Saṃvarodaya-Tantra: Selected Chapters*. Tokyo: Hokuseido Press.

Indic Works

Dharmakīrti (Chos kyi grags pa). *Pramāṇavārttikakārikā* (*Tshad ma rnam 'grel gyi tshig le'ur byas pa*). Tōh. 4210, *tshad ma, ce*, 94b1–151a7. Sanskrit and Tibetan: Yūsho Miyasaka. 1971–72. "*Pramāṇavārttika-kārikā*" *Acta Indologica* 2: 1–206.

Indrabhūti, *Jñānasiddhi* (*Ye shes grub pa*). Tōh. 2219, D. *rgyud, wi*, 36b7–60b6. Sanskrit and Tibetan: Samdhong Rinpoche, Dwivedi Vrajvallabh, et al., eds. 1987. *Guhyādiaṣṭasiddhisaṅgraha*. Sarnath: Central Institute for Higher Tibetan Studies.

Muniśrībhadra (Thub pa dpal bzang po). *Pañcakramārthaṭippaṇi* (*Rim pa lnga'i don mdor bshad pa*). Tōh. 1813, D. *rgyud, ngi*, 148b4–195b6. Sanskrit: Zhongxin Jiang and Tōru Tomabechi. 1996. *The Pañcakramaṭippanī of Muniśrībhadra: Introduction and Romanized Sanskrit Text*. Bern: Peter Lang.

63. *Pañcakramaṭippaṇī*, Jiang and Tomabechi 1996, 34; Tōh. 1813, D. 167b1. The first part of this work is a commentary on Nāgārjuna's *Piṇḍīkrama Sādhana*.

Nāgārjuna (Klu sgrub). *Piṇḍīkrama Sādhana* or *Piṇḍīkṛta Sādhana* (*Sgrub pa'i thabs mdor byas pa*). Tōh. 1796, D. *ngi*, 1b1–11a2. Sanskrit: de La Vallée Poussin, Louis. 1896. *Études et textes tantriques: Pañcakrama*. Ghent: Ghent University.

Puṇḍarīka. *Vimalaprabhā* (*Dri ma med pa'i 'od*). Tōh. 1347, *rgyud, tha*, 107b1–277a7 and *rgyud, da*, 1b2–297b7. Sanskrit and Tibetan: Vrajavallabha Dwivedi, and S. S. Bahulkar, eds. 1994. *Vimalaprabhāṭīkā of Kalkin ŚrīPuṇḍarīka on ŚrīLaghukālacakratantrarāja*, vol. 3. Sarnath, Varanasi: Central Institute of Higher Tibetan Studies.

Ratnarakṣita (Rin chen 'tsho). *Padminī = Saṃvarodayapadminīpañjikā* (*Sdom pa 'byung ba'i dka' 'grel padma can*). Tōh. 1420, D. *rgyud, wa*, 1b1–101b3. Sanskrit and Japanese of chap. 13, part 2: Tanemura, Ryugen, Kazuo Kano, and Kenichi Kuranishi. 2017, 2019, 2020, 2021.

Tibetan Works

A khu ching Shes rab rgya mtsho (1803–75). *'Dus pa 'phags lugs lha so gnyis pa'i lam rim pa dang po'i khrid dmigs kyi brjed byang mi bskyod mgon po'i zhal lung*. In *Collected Works, kha*, 101 folios. New Delhi: Ngawang Sopa, 1973. English: Jinpa 1999.

'Ba' ra ba Rgyal mtshan dpal bzang po (1310–91). *Bskyed rim zab don 'gal du skyon med*. In *Rtsib ri spar ma, tsha*, 68 folios. Darjeeling: Kargyud Sungrab Nyamso, 1985.

Blo bzang 'phrin las rnam rgyal (19th century). *Tsong kha pa chen po'i rnam par thar ba thub bstan mdzes pa'i rgyan gcig ngo mtshar nor bu'i phreng ba*. Mtsho sngon: Mtsho sngon mi rigs dpe skrun khang, 1981/1984.

Grags pa bshad sgrub (1675–1748). "Rdo rje 'jigs byed kyi rim pa dang po'i khrid rgyun man ngag snang brnyan kun 'char gsal ba'i me long." In *Gsangs bde 'jig gsum gyi rim gnyis kyi 'khri*, 147–223. Bylakuppe: Sera-Mey Computer Project Centre, 1998.

Mkhas grub rje Dge legs dpal bzang po (1385–1438). *Bskyed rim dngos grub rgya mtsho*. *Collected Works, ja*, 190 folios. New Delhi: Gurudeva, 1982 [Old Zhol].

Tsong kha pa Blo bzang grags pa (1357–1419). *Sngags rim chen mo*. Xining: Mtsho sngon mi rigs dpe skrun khang, 1995.

——. *Rnam gzhag rim pa'i rnam bshad [Don gsal]*. *Collected Works, ca*, work 4, 90 folios. New Delhi: Ngawang Gelek Demo, 1975–79 [Old Bkra shis lhun po].

Secondary Literature

Bentor, Yael. 2020. "The Body in Enlightenment: Purification According to dGe lugs' Works on the *Guhyasamāja Tantra*." In *Archaeologies of the Written: Indian, Tibetan, and Buddhist Studies in Honour of Cristina Scherrer-Schaub*, edited by Vincent Tournier, Vincent Eltschinger, and Marta Sernesi, 77–94. Naples: UniorPress.

Gerloff, Torsten, and Julian Schott. 2020. "Towards a Reassessment of Indrabhūti's *Jñānasiddhi*." *Buddhist Studies Review* 37.2: 241–60.

Isaacson, Harunaga, and Francesco Sferra. 2014. *The Sekanirdeśa of Maitreyanātha (Advayavajra) with the Sekanirdeśapañjikā of Rāmapāla*. Naples: Universitá degli studi di Napoli "L'Orientale."

Jinpa, Thupten. 1999. *Sacred Words of Lord Akshobya*. New York: Unpublished.

Kalian, Moshe, and Eliezer Witztum. 1998. "Facing a Holy Space: Psychiatric Hospitalization of Tourists in Jerusalem." In *Sacred Space: Shrine, City, Land*, edited by Benjamin Z. Kedar and R. J. Zwi Werblowsky, 316–30. London: MacMillan; Jerusalem: The Israel Academy of Sciences and Humanities.

Kellner, Birgit. 2020. "Using Concepts to Eliminate Conceptualization: Kamalaśīla on Non-Conceptual Gnosis (*nirvikalpajñāna*)." *Journal of the International Association of Buddhist Studies* 43: 39–80.

Krug, Adam. 2018a. "The Seven Siddhi Texts: The Oḍiyāna Mahāmudrā Lineage in Its Indic and Tibetan Contexts." PhD diss., University of California, Santa Barbara.

———. 2018b. "Tantric Epistemology and the Problem of Ineffability in *The Seven Siddhi Texts*." In *Buddhism and Linguistics: Theory and Philosophy*, edited by Manel Herat, 149–84. Cham: Palgrave.

Sferra, Francesco. 1999. "The Concept of Purification in Some Texts of Late Indian Buddhism." *Journal of Indian Philosophy* 27: 83–103.

———. 2005. "Constructing the Wheel of Time: Strategies for Establishing a Tradition." In *Boundaries, Dynamics and Construction of Traditions in South Asia*, edited by Federico Squarcini, 253–85. Florence: Firenze University Press.

Tanemura, Ryugen, Kazuo Kano, and Kenichi Kuranishi. 2017. "Ratnarakṣita's *Padminī*: A Preliminary Edition of the Excurses in Chapter 13, Part 1." *Journal of Kawasaki Daishi Institute for Buddhist Studies* 2: 1–34.

———. 2019. "——— Part 2." *Journal of Kawasaki Daishi Institute for Buddhist Studies* 4: 1–42.

———. 2020. "Why Is Awakening Brought by Visualisation of Buddha? Part 1: An Annotated Japanese Translation of the First Half of the Excurses in Chapter 13 of Ratnarakṣita's *Padminī*." *Journal of Kawasaki Daishi Institute for Buddhist Studies* 5: 1–25.

———. 2021. "——— Part 2." *Journal of Kawasaki Daishi Institute for Buddhist Studies* 6: 1–32.

Tsuda, Shinichi. 1974. *The Saṃvarodaya-Tantra: Selected Chapters*. Tokyo: Hokuseido Press.

Wallace, Vesna. 2001. *The Inner Kālacakratantra: A Buddhist Tantric View of the Individual*. New York: Oxford University Press.

Yamabe, Nobuyoshi. 2021. "The Position of Conceptualization in the Context of the Yogācāra Bīja Theory." In *Illuminating the Dharma: Buddhist Studies in Honour of Venerable Professor K. L. Dhammajoti*, edited by Endo Toshiichi, 463–86. Hong Kong: Centre of Buddhist Studies, The University of Hong Kong.

Rumblings of *Thunder*: Notes on the Identity and Intellectual Milieu of the Nyingma School Critic Peldzin

James Gentry

Introduction

LEONARD VAN DER KUIJP has consistently shown through his scholarship and teaching the productive capacity of reasoned argumentation, not only to prove or defend one's thesis against an opponent with whom one disagrees but also to bring to the surface assumptions and rationales—shared and unshared—that tend to otherwise remain tacit or unsystematically articulated. Tibetan arguments concerning the finer points of Buddhist doctrine have been amply discussed in Tibetological and Buddhalogical circles for some time now. A major focal point of Leonard van der Kuijp's work that has received somewhat less sustained attention is Tibetan literary arguments about the more fundamental question of what counts as authentic Buddhism and what the appropriate criteria should be for making this determination.[1] Apologia (*brgal lan*, *dgag lan*, *rtsod lan*, *rtsod bzlog*, *rtsod spong*, etc.) composed to defend the foundational scriptures, histories, practices, doctrines, and sacra of the Nyingma school (Rnying ma) of Tibetan Buddhism against charges of non-Buddhist inauthenticity—in terms of both out-and-out forgery and the inappropriate admixture of Tibetan or Indian non-Buddhist elements—stands out as a particularly stark example of how arguments over authenticity can bring into view a range of competing conceptions.[2]

1. Lopez 1996, for instance, disregards writings in this genre that are not devoted exclusively to doctrinal issues. For discussion of such arguments, see Kapstein 2000, 121–37; Wangchuk 2002; Schaeffer and van der Kuijp 2009; van der Kuijp 2018a and 2018b; and Almogi 2019 and 2020.

2. Lopez 1996, 218n2, prefers "polemics" for this genre label. Citing Schleiermacher's distinction between polemics and apologia, he argues that polemics refers to doctrinal disputes within a community, whereas apologia concerns itself with more general faith claims directed to redress criticisms coming from outside a community. Raudsepp 2009, 292n2, follows suit. However, "apologia" has the advantage of including both objections and rebuttals,

As a modest homage to Leonard van der Kuijp's contribution to my knowledge and thinking about this body of literature and the research potentials it presents, this paper considers Sokdokpa Lodrö Gyeltsen's (Sog bzlog pa Blo gros rgyal mtshan, 1552–1624) encyclopedic masterpiece of Nyingma school apologia titled *Thunder of Definitive Meaning*.[3] *Thunder*, as I will henceforth call it, together with its addendum, probably constitutes the most renowned instance of this literary subgenre ever written. In defending the Nyingma school against criticisms in the early years of the seventeenth century, Sokdokpa reproduced in *Thunder* several rare and/or historically important texts.[4] For decades scholars of Buddhism in Tibet have thus mined it to glean insights into controversies over the Indian pedigree and Tibetan reception of several Buddhist textual and practice traditions.[5] But fundamental questions about

whereas "polemics" concerns only objections. Moreover, as Onians 2003, 63–65, argues, several important early Christian apologias were written for readerships that included fellow Christians within a community, not just pagans and Jews outside it, and, more pointedly, the term "apologia" need not be confined to its historical Judeo-Christian usages. A final apology for the rendering of these Tibetan genre labels as "apologia" is precisely the presence of the important subcategory of this genre concerned not with arcane doctrinal points but with the more fundamental issue of what constitutes authentic Buddhism. Dudjom 1991, 887–942, offers in English translation a relatively recent and particularly rich example of this body of literature based on several earlier sources, including Sokdokpa's *Thunder* discussed here. The Tibetan is in Bdud 'joms 1967, 695–776. For a general introduction to this body of literature, see Raudsepp 2009, 281–85. For a discussion of this literature as it pertains to the authenticity of treasure revelation in particular, see Doctor 2005, 31–51.

3. *Nges don 'brug sgra* is its abbreviated title, which is commonly used in the living tradition. The full title appears variously as *Gsang sngags snga 'gyur la bod du rtsod pa snga phyir byung ba rnams kyi lan du brjod pa nges don 'brug sgra*, in Sog bzlog pa 1975, or simply as *Dris lan nges don 'brug sgra*, in Sog bzlog pa 1982. There are multiple versions of *Thunder* and its addendum available today, the details of which are presented in Gentry 2021. For the present article, I consulted Sog bzlog pa 1975, 1982, 1985, and 1999. For more on the life and writings of Sokdokpa, see Gentry 2017.

4. Sokdokpa records in the colophon of *Thunder* that he completed its composition on the first day of the month of *śrāvaṇa* (*gro bzhin*) in the wood-dragon year, which corresponds to July 27, 1604 (Sog bzlog pa 1975, 544.1; 1982, 285.3; and 1999, 620.3: *khro mo zhes pa shing pho[D mo, DA -] 'brug[D sbrul] gyi lo gro bzhin[em. zhun] gyi[K-] zla ba'i tshes gcig*). Cf. Smith 1969, 5n13; and Schaeffer and van der Kuijp 2009, 49n99. This calculation is based on Schuh 1973, 147. About ten months later, on May 31 or June 1 of 1605, he completed his composition of an addendum to the text entitled *An Eloquent Feast of Ambrosia* (Sog bzlog pa 1975, 601.1–.2; 1982, 341.6–342.1; 1985, 242.7; and 1999, 699.2–3: *sna tshogs dbyig ces pa shing mo sbrul gyi lo snron [D, K snon] gyis[D, DA gyi] nya ba'i dga' ba dang po'i tshes*). This calculation is based on Schuh 1973, 147. For a discussion of the texts Sokdokpa reproduced in *Thunder*, see Gentry 2021.

5. Examples include Achard 2015; Almogi 2020; Bajetta 2019; Davidson 2003 and 2005;

the composition and reception of *Thunder*, and the texts and passages it reproduces, must be addressed before scholars can fully appreciate the contributions it can make to our knowledge of the history of Buddhism in Tibet.

One question that has yet to be sufficiently examined since E. Gene Smith first introduced this seminal work to the Tibetological world in 1969 is what, precisely, is the identity and intellectual milieu of the figure known primarily as Peldzin (Dpal 'dzin), the putative author of perhaps the most elaborate and full-throated polemical attack ever waged against the authenticity of the Nyingma school.[6] Peldzin's critique of the Nyingma school, together with Sokdokpa's rebuttal, constitutes the first section of *Thunder*, and the lengthiest by far, measuring around half its total volume, including the addendum.[7] Moreover, it is abundantly clear elsewhere in *Thunder* that addressing Peldzin's polemic and its subsequent reception, specifically in the writings of Śākya Chokden (Shā kya mchog ldan, 1428–1507), was the principal impetus behind Sokdokpa's composition.[8] Thus inquiring into precisely who Peldzin was, the context he wrote in, and how his polemic was received prior to Sokdokpa's time is an important step in understanding Sokdokpa's *Thunder* as well.

Peldzin and the Context of His Literary Production

Peldzin's polemic against the Nyingma school, *A Treatise That Distinguishes Dharma and Non-Dharma*, is a rare document at present.[9] Aside from its complete citation in *Thunder*, today the text, with very minor variations, is available only through BDRC as a unique thirty-eight-folio manuscript, although a few verses from the text are also cited by figures other than Sokdokpa, such as Śākya Chokden.[10] Sokdokpa reproduces Peldzin's versified text by dividing

---

Higgins 2013; Kapstein 2000; Karmay 1975, 1980a, 1980b, and 1988; van der Kuijp 2004 and 2016a; Makidono 2011; Martin 2001; Raudsepp 2009 and 2011; Schaeffer and van der Kuijp 2009; Wangchuk 2002; and Wedemeyer 2014. This is by no means an exhaustive list.

6. Smith 1969, 5n13.

7. Sog bzlog pa 1975, 262.1–435.6 (86.5ff.); 1982, 1–178.3 (87/88ff.); and 1999, 225–467.3 (121ff.).

8. Sog bzlog pa 1975, 434.1–434.3, 599.5–600.3. Śākya Chokden cites and discusses Peldzin in Śākya mchog ldan 2006, 515–99, and 2013, 387–408. The composition, revision, and reception of *Thunder* are discussed in Gentry 2021.

9. *Chos dang chos ma yin pa rnam par dbye ba'i rab tu byed pa*. For more on Peldzin's polemical treatise, see van der Kuijp 2018a, 446, and 2018b, 97–100.

10. To peruse this version, see W1CZ885 on the Buddhist Digital Resource Center. Comparison reveals this manuscript to be nearly identical to what we find reproduced in Sok-

it into roughly 160 thematic units and interspersing these with his rebuttals of each issue, almost always following the Peldzin passages to which they pertain. Peldzin's text is composed in seven-syllable meter. Aside from the opening folios, which Sokdokpa writes in prose, Sokdokpa mimics Peldzin's metrical form in his replies. Despite Sokdokpa's attentiveness to formal considerations, he divides Peldzin's text based on topical grounds, thus allowing him to represent Peldzin's detailed criticisms as coherently as possible before delivering his own metrical point-for-point rebuttals. In all editions consulted, interlinear notes (*mchan bu*) are also interspersed throughout Peldzin's text, rendered in smaller print or handwriting. *Thunder* takes stock of these remarks as well, again matching the prose style of these interlinear notes with prose interlinear notes of its own. Who or how many authors were responsible for these notes remains an open question, which in the interest of space must be left aside for now. In Sokdokpa's replies, however, it is evident that at least some of the interlinear notes were integral sections of Peldzin's text when Sokdokpa received it in the early seventeenth century.[11]

The precise identity of Peldzin and the circumstances surrounding his presumed authorship of such a thoroughgoing rejection of the Nyingma school have remained something of a mystery. Sokdokpa refers to this figure primarily just as Peldzin, and only a few times as Drikung Peldzin.[12] Bryan Cuevas recently observed that a figure by the name of Peldzin was active in the latter half of the fourteenth century in the monastic centers of Tsurpu (Mtshur phu), Shambhara, Tangkya (Thang skya), Lhündrup Dzong (Lhun grub rdzong), and other institutions situated in the areas of Tsangrong (Gtsang rong), Meldro (Mal gro), and elsewhere throughout Ü and Tsang. Several extant texts related to the deity Vajrabhairava attribute authorship to him, forming a collection known as the Book of Pel.[13] Cuevas leaves open the question of whether this figure can be identified with certainty as the author of the anti-Nyingma polemic.[14] In a slightly earlier article cited by Cuevas, Leonard van der Kuijp

dokpa's text, aside from anonymous interlinear notes adorning its first five folios and its final folio.

11. Sog bzlog pa 1975, 381.3

12. Sog bzlog pa 1975.

13. Cuevas 2021a; Cuevas 2021b, 283–84, 284n14.

14. Cuevas 2021b, 284n14. As this article was going to press, Cuevas (2021a, 105–7) presented a few further pieces of circumstantial evidence suggestive of this identification, based primarily on analysis of Peldzin's Vajrabhairava writings. Unfortunately, this most recent of Cuevas's considerations of the issue was published too late to adequately address in the pres-

presents them as identical but elects to remain silent on how he reached this conclusion.[15]

Assessing the colophons of these Vajrabhairava texts, comparing them to clues in the Nyingma school polemic, and tracing these leads in other sources provides enough evidence to positively corroborate van der Kuijp's identification and conclude that the Vajrabhairava master Peldzin and the Nyingma school critic Peldzin are in fact one and the same person. More importantly, this body of evidence also allows us to begin drawing a rough sketch of Peldzin's intellectual milieu and thereby propose how he came to compose his critique of the Nyingma school.

Starting with the identity of this figure, the colophons of the forty-nine or so Vajrabhairava texts in the Book of Pel record several details about the author and the circumstances of his textual production. The author's name variously appears there as Peldzin, "the Tibetan Śrīdhara" (Bod kyi dpal 'dzin), Peldzin Zangpo (Dpal 'dzin bzang po), Peldzin Nyima Ö Zangpo (Dpal 'dzin nyi ma 'od bzang po), and Düdé Raptuchompa Barwé Ziji Pelzangpo (Bdud sde rab tu 'jom pa 'bar ba'i gzi brjid dpal bzang po), among others.[16] Most important for the present analysis, in the colophon of a writing entitled *Conqueror over the Triple-World System: The Procedure for Yantra according to the Glorious Vajrabhairava*, which was probably composed in the fire-rat year of 1396, the author's name is given as "Gyatso Tringyi Drukdra, the Śākya monk, yogin of the Supreme Vehicle, hailing from the stretches of the northern land."[17] The unusual name of Gyatso Tringyi Drukdra, but with Zangpo added to the end, also appears with the detail of his "hailing from the stretches of the northern land" in the authorial colophon of Peldzin's Nyingma school criticism.[18]

Another important detail in this regard is that authorial colophons in the Book of Pel make repeated reference to the author's Vajrabhairava guru, Zhang Rinchenpel Sönam Drakpa, otherwise known as Zhangtön Sönam Drakpa Pel Zangpo (Zhang ston Bsod nams grags pa dpal bzang po, 1292–1370), or Zhantön/Zhingtön Gyawo Sönam Drakpa (Zhang/Zhing ston Rgya bo Bsod nams grags pa). He was a famed Jonangpa lama, *Kālacakratantra* master, and

ent paper. Many thanks to Bryan Cuevas for drawing my attention to and sharing his excellent research prior to its publication.

15. van der Kuijp 2018a, 446.

16. *Rdo rje 'jigs byed kyi man ngag gi chos skor* (W3CN2615); Cuevas 2021a.

17. Rgya mtsho'i sprin gyi 'brug sgra, *Dpal ldan rdo rje 'jigs byed 'khrul 'khor kyi cho ga 'jig rten gsum las rnam par rgyal ba*, 7b.5–7b.6, pdf page 173 (Dpal 'dzin, *rDo rje 'jigs byed kyi man ngag gi chos skor*); Cuevas 2021a (text # 2086), 359–60.

18. Sog bzlog pa 1975, 433.3.

transmitter of the Ra tradition of Vajrabhairava practice.[19] Interestingly, in his rejection of the Nyingma school's Great Perfection tradition, Peldzin makes explicit reference to a figure who was closely associated with Zhangtön Sönam Drakpa. This is "the Omniscient Künga, the sole lord of the teaching," whom Peldzin approvingly cites as having "removed the Great Perfection from the fold of the Dharma."[20] In response, Sokdokpa fills out this name to be Nyawön Künga and identifies him as one of Peldzin's own gurus. In so doing, Sokdokpa counters that Nyawön Künga "abandoned the true Dharma from the depths of his heart by alleging that 'the authentic Indian texts belonging to the Nyingma school are Landza and Sanskrit script written by Tibetan mantrins on Indian tree bark paper.'"[21] Nyawön Künga happens to be none other than the renowned tenth hierarch of Jonang Monastery, Prajñāpāramitā expert, and *Kālacakratantra* master Nyawön Künga Pelzango (Nya dbon Kun dga' dpal bzang po, 1285–1379). He figures in Jonang lineage records alongside Peldzin's Vajrabhairava guru, Zhangtön Sönam Drakpa, as among the fourteen great heart disciples of the famed Jonang master Dölpopa Sherap Gyeltsen (Dol po pa Shes rab rgyal mtshan, 1292–1361) and holders of the combined Jonang lineage of sūtra and tantra.[22] Short biographies of these two figures appear directly adjacent to one another—Sönam Drakpa's first, followed immediately by that of Künga Pel—in a number of Jonang and *Kālacakratantra* lineage histories. Neither biography mentions the other figure, but details concerning when they each trained under Dölpopa's tutelage, and where they were active before and after their training, strongly suggest that these two figures were active in the same circles and likely familiar with each other.[23]

Künga Pel's rejection of the authenticity of the Great Perfection teachings no doubt refers to his scathing criticisms of the Nyingma school embedded in his broader polemical treatise on the finer points of Jonang theory and practice entitled *Dispelling Mental Darkness: Responses to Questions Departing from*

19. For a brief biography of this figure, otherwise known as Zhangtön Gyawo, see Stearns 2008a. For more details on his life, writings, and milieu, see van der Kuijp 2016b.

20. Sog bzlog pa 1975, 395.1–395.2.

21. Sog bzlog pa 1975, 395.2–395.3.

22. See, for instance, Blo gros grags pa 199?, 460.3–6; Rigs ldan rgyal ba jo bzang dpal bzang po 199?, 593.7–602.7; Phun tshogs tshe ring 2003, 471–73; and Rgyal ba ye shes 2004, 175–83.

23. Ibid. Mtshur phu, Sa skya, and Jo nang figure prominently as bases of activity for both figures. Moreover, their dates of interaction with Dol po pa Shes rab rgyal mtshan overlap significantly.

the Rubric of Ground, Path, and Fruition.[24] Künga Pel records no date in the colophon of this text, but he does mention that he composed it at a hermitage in Tsechen Chödé Monastery (Rtse chen chos sde), which he founded some time shortly before Dölpopa's passing in 1361.[25] Künga Pel also makes reference in the text to his extensive commentary on the *Prajñāpāramitā*, composed in 1371.[26] This suggests a date of composition for *Dispelling Mental Darkness* between 1371 and Künga Pel's passing in 1379. These details enable us to propose the window of time between the years of 1372 and 1380 as the *terminus post quem* for the composition of Peldzin's Nyingma school critique. As Dan Martin has pointed out, the date of the year of Wangpo (*dbang po'i lo*) given in the colophon of Peldzin's treatise suggests more specifically the earth-horse year of 1378, although the *Great Tibetan-Tibetan-Chinese Dictionary* gives the iron-dragon year of 1400 as its date of composition.[27] Whatever the case, comparing the content of Künga Pel's criticisms of the Nyingma school with Peldzin's only slightly later writing strongly suggests that Peldzin took Künga Pel's passages as the template for his more elaborate critique. In the interest of space, however, these commonalities will have to be presented in a future paper.

Sokdokpa's *Thunder* also provides another important clue about the context of production of Peldzin's polemical treatise. In the opening preamble and closing verses of *Thunder*'s addendum there are two references cast in the first-person voice of Sokdokpa to an earlier rebuttal of Peldzin's critique composed by a figure whom he calls Karmapa Könzhön (Karmapa Dkon gzhon).[28] This rebuttal, Sokdokpa adds, was written in reply to a letter drafted and delivered to him by Peldzin himself.[29] Karmapa Könzhön was surely the Karma Kagyü lama known as Karma Könchok Zhönnu (Karma Dkon mchog gzhon

24. *Gzhi lam 'bras bu gsum las brtsams pa'i dris lan yid kyi mun sel* (Kun dga' dpal 2010, 135–293).

25. This is evinced by Nyawön's invitation to the elderly Dölpopa to consecrate the new monastery, an invitation he had to refuse due to his failing health. See Stearns 2008b.

26. Kun dga' dpal 2010, 203; Kun dga' dpal 1978, vol. 2, 589.5, states that he wrote this *Prajñāpāramitā* commentary at Sakya over the course of about two months, during the spring of the iron-female-pig year (1371).

27. See the entry for 'Bri gung Dpal 'dzin in Martin 2016.

28. For the opening reference, see Sog bzlog pa 1975, 599.2–3. The reference in the closing verses only appears in Sog bzlog pa 1985, 188.4–5. I discuss this variation in Gentry 2021.

29. This might be identical to the text listed in the *Bka' brgyud pa'i gsung 'bum dkar chag* 2007, 241. Perhaps Karma(pa) Könchok Zhönnu was Peldzin's addressee rather than the third Karmapa, Rangjung Dorjé, as claimed in the catalogue.

nu). Situ Chökyi Jungné's Karma Kagyü lineage history, the *Golden Rosary*, describes Karma Könchok Zhönnu as a student of the Fourth Karmapa Rölpé Dorjé (1340–83), who lived primarily at Tsurpu and was just old enough to have met the Third Karmapa Rangjung Dorjé (1284–1339).[30] Situ also mentions that Karma Könchok Zhönnu famously served as "presider" (*gral dpon*) over the Namtsedeng Dharma teaching sessions (*gnam rtse ldeng gi chos 'khor*), named after the old Kadampa (Bka' gdams pa) monastic institution of Namtsedeng that played host to them.[31] These sessions were also attended by other high-profile scholars, including Rendawa Zhönnu Lodrö (Re mda' ba Gzhon nu blo gros, 1349–1412), Lochen Kyapchok Zangpo (Lo chen Skyabs mchog bzang po, fourteenth century), and Tsongkhapa Lozang Drakpa (Tsong kha pa Blo bzang grags pa, 1357–1419). Mangtö Ludrup Gyatso (Mang thos Klu sgrub rgya mtsho, 1523–96), in his *Chronology of the Teaching*, additionally describes Karma Könchok Zhönnu as one of the "six scholars of Glorious Sakya" who toured throughout Ü and Tsang to study and debate the Dharma at the various monastic centers of learning scattered throughout these regions.[32] This exclusive group, according to the *Chronology*, also included none other than Peldzin's own guru, Künga Pel.

It is also noteworthy that Peldzin's Vajrabhairava guru, Sönam Drakpa, and Künga Pel were both regular visitors to Sakya and Tsurpu during the same period, when Könchok Zhönnu would have also likely been present at these two locations. The colophons of Peldzin's Vajrabhairava texts record that he was also closely connected with Tsurpu Monastery, among other places where he could have easily encountered all three figures. We can therefore probably rule out that Peldzin was primarily of Drikung Kagyü sectarian affiliation. Evidence suggests that Peldzin's connection with Drikung might stem from his place of birth or his place of scholastic training rather than from his sectarian affiliation. Also listed alongside Künga Pel and Sönam Drakpa among the fourteen great heart disciples of Dölpopa Sherap Gyeltsen is a figure by the name of Drikung Lotsāwa Maṇikaśrījñāna, otherwise known in Tibetan as Norbu Pel Yeshé (Nor bu dpal ye shes, 1289–1363).[33] He was so nicknamed because he became learned in Sanskrit when studying at Drikung at the age of fifteen.[34] This figure was older than the other two, so cannot be identified as

30. Si tu paṇ chen Chos kyi 'byung gnas 2013, vol. 1, 416.

31. The name of this old Kadampa monastery variously appears as Gnam rtse/rtsi/btsib ldang/lding/ldeng/steng, etc.

32. Mang thos Klu sgrub rgya mtsho 1999, 465.5–466.2.

33. Blo gros grags pa 199?, 460.4.

34. Phun tshogs tshe ring 2003, 470.

Peldzin, but their mutual association with Drikung, even to the point of taking on the toponym as a personal nickname, additionally implies that Peldzin too was probably not a Drikungpa but rather primarily a Jonangpa, but with strong Sakya and Kagyü affiliations and Vajrabhairava practice specialization, like Zhangtön Sönam Drakpa. Peldzin was therefore likely similar to Norbu Pel Yeshé in taking on the nickname of Driking due to his personal association with the place through birth, education, or some other factor.

There are several other details in Peldzin's Nyingma school critique that help fill out a picture of who he was and what his associations were. In the opening section of his treatise, for instance, Peldzin mentions the *Kālacakratantra*, revered among the Jonangpa in particular as the "supreme among all tantra classes." More telling still is that Peldzin also lists the Indian master Śrīdhara as the final figure in a short lineage of authentic Indian Buddhist masters. Śrīdhara, who may have flourished in the late tenth century, was famous as a prolific writer of texts related to the fierce tantric deity Yamāri, closely associated with Vajrabhairava.[35] The name Peldzin, moreover, is Tibetan for Śrīdhara. The Vajrabhairava master Peldzin likely earned or assumed this name—sometimes calling himself the Tibetan Śrīdhara—from his association with these fierce tantric deities and their practices.

Further evidence indicative of Peldzin's milieu is his invocation of the authority of the great Jonang master Dölpopa Sherap Gyeltsen, the founder and first abbot of Jonang Monastery Künpang Tukjé Tsöndrü (Kun spangs Thugs rje brtson grus, 1243–1313), the Sakya master Butön Rinchendrup (Bu ston Rin chen grub, 1290–1364), and the Third Karmapa Rangjung Dorjé.[36] These details, coupled with the absence of any meaningful reference to important Drikung lineage holders, additionally point to a mixture of connections with various Sakya, Karma Kagyü, and especially Jonang lineage holders rather than a Drikung Kagyü lineage affiliation. There is ample additional evidence from Peldzin's Nyingma school critique to help fill out the picture further, but in the interest of space, its presentation must be left aside for now.

Concluding Remarks

All this suffices to begin providing a rough picture of the intellectual community in which Peldzin wrote his critique of the Nyingma school. This community consisted of some of the leading Jonang, Sakya, and Kagyü scholars active between the middle of the fourteenth century and the early decades of

35. Kuranishi 2008.

36. Sog bzlog pa 1975, 391.6–392.1, 396.2–3.

the fifteenth century, such as the Dölpopa Sherap Gyeltsen, his close students Künga Pel and Sönam Drakpa, the Sakya master Rendawa Zhönnu Lodrö, his student Tsongkhapa Lozang Drakpa, the Fourth Karmapa Rolpé Dorjé, and his student Karma Könchok Zhönnu. This was a period of particularly robust intellectual interaction, when these and other Buddhist scholars would commonly tour the major monastic centers of learning situated throughout Ü and Tsang for study and debate on a range of scholastic topics.

Topics of debate within this circle of scholars at times extended well beyond the abstract minutiae of Pramāṇa, Prajñāpāramitā, or Madhyamaka doctrinal points to probe the foundations and question the viewpoints and practices of some of Tibet's most hallowed Buddhist scriptural traditions. It was in this climate of fierce argumentation, for instance, that Rendawa first broached his infamous criticisms of the Buddhist pedigree of the *Kālacakratantra* and that Tsongkhapa developed his reformist agenda that would lead eventually to the inception of the Geluk school.[37] It was also in this milieu that Künga Pel composed his *Dispelling Mental Darkness*, which targets not just the Nyingma school but also a range of other issues of New School (Gsar ma) provenance, such as proper understanding of the view, path, and conduct of Mahāmudrā.

That rich intersectarian intellectual exchange and debate were such common features of this group suggests that the boundaries between the so-called schools or sects of Tibetan Buddhism were not as rigidly drawn during this time as has often been assumed from the vantage point of later periods. Other allegiances, such as monastic college affiliation and practice lineage affiliation, for instance, balanced with a pronounced penchant for their critical appraisal, were perhaps more defining then than rigid identification with the New School sectarian formations of Sakya, Jonang, or Kagyü. Nonetheless, the Nyingma school was largely left out of the conversation. By the late fourteenth century, the centuries-long process of compiling scriptural translations and forming them into the canonical Kangyur and Tengyur collections culminated with the exclusion of many of the scriptures belonging to the Nyingma school under suspicion of apocryphal authorship. Such suspicions were nothing new. As Sokdokpa's *Thunder* amply attests, Tibetans had been voicing them since the eleventh-century beginnings of the Later Dissemination period (Phyi dar). But the lively exchange across New School sectarian boundaries typical of the late fourteenth century seems to

37. For details on Rendawa's critique, see Khedrup Norsang Gyatso 2004, 16, 148, 235–36, 252. For the life and legacy of Tsongkhapa, see Jinpa 2019.

have given fresh impetus for the greatest intellectuals of the time to reevaluate the fundamentals of their own traditions and those of others, thus bringing renewed critical attention to the issue of Nyingma authenticity. Seen in this light, Peldzin's elaborate polemic against the Nyingma school, patterned after his guru Künga Pel's slightly earlier attempt to differentiate between authentic and inauthentic Buddhism, was one among many critical intellectual projects developed during this period that would have a lasting impact on Tibetan intellectual and spiritual life.

References

Achard, Jean-Luc. 2015. "The View of sPyi-ti Yoga." *Revue d'Etudes Tibétaines* 31: 1–20.

Almogi, Orna. 2019. "The Human behind the Divine: An Investigation into the Evolution of Scriptures with Special Reference to the Ancient Tantras of Tibetan Buddhism." In *Unearthing Himalayan Treasures: Festschrift for Franz-Karl Ehrhard*, edited by Volker Caumanns, Marta Sernesi, and Nikolai Solmsdorf, 1–26. Indica et Tibetica 59. Marburg: Indica et Tibetica Verlag.

———. 2020. *Authenticity and Authentication: Glimpses behind the Scenes of the Formation of the Tibetan Buddhist Canon*. Indian and Tibetan Studies 9. Hamburg: Department of Indian and Tibetan Studies, Universität Hamburg.

Bajetta, Nicolas. 2019. *The Clear Realisation of the Quintessential Instructions on All Dharma Practices: A Critical Edition and Annotated Translation of the *Sarvadharmacaryopadeśābhisamayatantra (Chos spyod thams cad kyi man ngag mngon par rtogs pa'i rgyud)*. Indian and Tibetan Studies 6. Hamburg: Department of Indian and Tibetan Studies, Universität Hamburg.

Bdud 'joms 'Jigs bral ye shes rdo rje. 1967. *Gangs ljongs rgyal bstan yongs rdzogs kyi phyi mo snga 'gyur rdo rje theg pa'i bstan pa rin po che ji ltar byung ba'i tshul dag cing gsal bar brjod pa lha dbang g.yul las rgyal ba'i rnga bo che'i sgra dbyangs*. Kalimpong: Dudjom Tulku Rinpoche.

Bka' brgyud pa'i gsung 'bum dkar chag. 2007. Lhasa: Bod ljongs mi dmangs dpe skrun khang.

Blo gros grags pa. 199?. *Bstan 'dzin skyes chen rim par byon pa'i lo rgyus mdor bsdus rin po che'i nor bu'i phreng ba*. In *'Dzam thang ba blo gros grags pa'i gsung 'bum*, vol. 11, 417–505. 'Dzam thang, 'Bar thang: 'Dzam thang bsam 'grub nor bu'i gling gi par khang.

Cuevas, Bryan. 2021a. *The* Rwa Pod *and Other 'Lost' Works of Rwa lo tsā ba's Vajrabhairava Tradition: A Catalogue of Recently Acquired Tibetan Manuscripts from Mongolia and their Significance*. Vienna: Arbeitskreis für Tibetische und Buddhistische Studien Universität Wien.

———. 2021b. "Four Syllable for Slaying and Repelling: A Tibetan Vajrabhairava Practice. From Recently Recovered Manuscripts of the 'Lost' *Book of Rwa* (*Rwa pod*)." In *Beyond Boundaries: Religion, Region, Language and the State*, edited by Michael Willis, Sam van Schaik, and Lewis Doney, 278–307. Berlin: Walter de Gruyter GmbH.

Davidson, Ronald. 2003. "gSar ma Apocrypha: The Creation of Orthodoxy, Gray Texts, and the New Revelation." In *The Many Canons of Tibetan Buddhism*, edited by Helmut Eimer and David Germano, 203–24. Leiden: Brill.

———. 2005. *Tibetan Renaissance: Tantric Buddhism in the Rebirth of Tibetan Culture.* New York: Columbia University Press.

Doctor, Andreas. 2005. *Tibetan Treasure Literature: Revelation, Tradition, and Accomplishment in Visionary Buddhism*. Ithaca, NY: Snow Lion Publications.

Dpal 'dzin. *Chos dang chos ma yin pa rnam par dbye ba'i rab tu byed pa*. Buddhist Digital Resource Center, W1CZ885. https://library.bdrc.io/show/bdr:W1CZ885.

Dpal 'dzin. *Rdo rje 'jigs byed kyi man ngag gi chos skor*. Buddhist Digital Resource Center, WA3CN2615. https://library.bdrc.io/show/bdr:WA3CN2615.

Dudjom Rinpoche, Jikdrel Yeshe Dorje. 1991. *The Nyingma School of Tibetan Buddhism: Its Fundamentals and History*. Translated and edited by Gyurme Dorje and Matthew Kapstein. Boston: Wisdom Publications.

Gentry, James Duncan. 2017. *Power Objects in Tibetan Buddhism: The Life, Writings, and Legacy of Sokdokpa Lodrö Gyeltsen*. Brill's Tibetan Studies Library 40. Leiden: Brill.

———. 2021. "Tracing the Life of a Buddhist Literary Apologia: Steps in Preparation for the Study and Translation of Sokdokpa's *Thunder of Definitive Meaning*." *Religions* 12.11: 933. https://doi.org/10.3390/rel12110933.

Higgins, David. 2013. *The Philosophical Foundations of Classical rDzogs chen in Tibet: Investigating the Distinction between Dualistic Mind (sems) and Primordial Knowing (ye shes)*. Vienna: Arbeitskreis für Tibetische und Buddhistische Studien Universität Wien.

Jinpa, Thupten. 2019. *Tsongkhapa: A Buddha in the Land of Snows*. Boulder, CO: Shambhala.

Kapstein, Matthew. 2000. *The Tibetan Assimilation of Buddhism: Conversion, Contestation, and Memory*. Oxford: Oxford University Press.

Karmay, Samten. 1975. "The Doctrinal Position of rDzogs chen from the Tenth to the Thirteenth Centuries." *Journal Asiatique* 263.1–2: 147–56.

———. 1980a. "The Ordinance of lHa Bla-ma Ye-shes-'od." In *Tibetan Studies in Honour of Hugh Richardson*, edited by Michael Aris and S. Aung San, 150–60. Warminster: Aris and Phillips.

———. 1980b. "An Open Letter by Pho-brang Zh- ba-'od." *The Tibet Journal* 3: 1–28.

———. 1988. *The Great Perfection: A Philosophical and Meditative Teaching of Tibetan Buddhism*. Leiden: Brill.

Khedrup Norsang Gyatso. 2004. *Ornament of Stainless Light: An Exposition of the Kālacakra Tantra*. Translated by Gavin Kilty. Boston: Wisdom Publications.

van der Kuijp, Leonard W. J. 2004. *The Kālacakra and the Patronage of Tibetan Buddhism by the Mongol Imperial Family*. Bloomington: Department of Central Eurasian Studies, Indiana University.

———. 2016a. "The Lives of Bu ston Rin chen grub and the Date and Sources of His *Chos 'byung*, a Chronicle of Buddhism in India and Tibet." *Revue d'Etudes Tibétaines* 35: 203–308.

———. 2016b. "On the Life and Ouvre of the Jo nang pa Scholar Zhang ston Rgya bo Bsod nams grags pa (1292–1370)." *Journal of Tibetan and Himalayan Studies* 1.1 (June): 17–31.

———. 2018a. "The Bird-Faced Monk and the Beginnings of the New Tantric Tradition, Part One." In *Tibetan Genealogies: Studies in Memoriam of Guge Tsering Gyalpo (1961–2015)*, edited by Guntram Hazod and Shen Weirong, 403–50. Beijing: China Tibetology Publishing House.

———. 2018b. "The Bird-Faced Monk and the Beginnings of the New Tantric Tradition, Part Two." *Journal of Tibetology* 19: 86–127.

Kun dga' dpal. 1978. *Bstan bcos mngon par rtogs pa'i rgyan 'grel pa dang bcas pa'i rgyas 'grel bshad sbyar yid kyi mun sel*. 2 vols. New Delhi: Ngawang Sopa.

———. 2010. *Gzhi lam 'bras bu gsum las brtsams pa'i dris lan yid kyi mun sel*. In *'Od gsal rgyan gyi bshad*. Beijing: Mi rigs dpe skrun khang.

Kuranishi, Ken'ichi. 2008. "Śridhara and His Works on the Yamāri Cycle." In *Esoteric Buddhist Studies: Identity in Diversity, Proceedings of the International Conference on Esoteric Buddhist Studies, Koyasan University, 5 Sept.–8 Sept. 2006*, 179–83. Koyasan: Koyasan University.

Lopez, Donald. 1996. "Polemical Literature (*dGag lan*)." In *Tibetan Literature: Studies in Genre*, edited by José Cabézon and Roger Jackson, 217–29. Ithaca, NY: Snow Lion Publications.

Makidono, Tomoko. 2011. "An Entrance to the Practice Lineage as Exemplified in Kaḥ thog Dge rtse Mahāpaṇḍita's Commentary on Sa skya Paṇḍita's *Sdom gsum rab dbye*." *Revue d'Etudes Tibétaines* 22: 215–42.

Mang thos Klu sgrub rgya mtsho. 1999. *Bstan rtsis chos 'byung gsal ba'i nyin byed lhag bsam rab dkar zhes bya ba'i bstan* bcos. In *Mang thos klu sgrub rgya mtsho'i gsung sko*, vol. 6, 281–525. Kathmandu: Sa skya rgyal yongs gsung rab slob gnyer khang.

Martin, Dan. 2001. *Unearthing Bon Treasures: Life and Contested Legacy of a Tibetan Scripture Revealer, with a General Bibliography of Bon*. Leiden: Brill.

———. 2016. *Tibskrit*. Unpublished.

Onians, Isabelle. 2003. *Tantric Buddhist Apologetics or Antinomianism as a Norm*. PhD diss., Oxford University.

Phun tshogs tshe ring. 2003. *Chos 'byung mkhas pa'i dgongs rgyan*. Lhasa: Bod ljongs mi dmangs dpe skrun khang.

Ra Lotsāwa Dorje Drakpa, Rwa chos rab, et al. *Rwa pod*. 3 vols. BDRC W4CZ302660, vol. 1, 270–79 (pdf).

Raudsepp, Kadri. 2009. "Dating and Authorship Problems in the Sngags log sun 'byin Attributed to Chag lo tsā ba Chos rje dpal." In *Contemporary Visions in Tibetan*

Studies, edited by Brandon Dotson, Kalsang Norbu Gurung, Georgios Halkias, and Tim Myatt, 281–97. Chicago: Serindia Publications.

———. 2011. "Rnying ma and Gsar ma: First Appearances of the Terms During the Early *Phyi dar* (Later Spread of the Doctrine)." *Revue d'Etudes Tibétaines*, 22, November: 25–46.

Rgyal ba ye shes. 2004. *Dus 'khor jo nang lugs gyi bla ma brgyud pa'i rnam thar*. Beijing: Mi rigs dpe skrun khang.

Rigs ldan Rgyal ba jo bzang dpal bzang po. 199?. *Chos kyi rje kun mkhyen chen po yab sras bco lnga'i rnam thar nye bar bsdus pa ngo mtshar rab gsal*. In *The 'Dzam-thang Edition of the Collected Works (Gsung-'bum) of Kun-mkhyen Dol-po-pa Shes-rab-rgyal-mtshan*, collected and presented by Matthew Kapstein, vol. 1, 559–630. 'Dzam thang: 'Dzam thang bsam 'grub nor bu'i gling gi par khang.

Śākya mchog ldan. 2006. *Mkha' spyod dbang po'i spyan drung du 'bul ba'i mol mchid sogs*. In *Śākya mchog ldan gsung 'bum*, vol. 17, 515–99. Kathmandu: Sachen International, Guru Lama.

———. 2013. *Gser gyi thur ma las brtsams pa'i dogs gcod kyi 'bel gtam rab gsal rnam nges sam nges don rab gsal*. In *Gser mdog paṇ chen Śākya mchog ldan gyi gsung 'bum*, vol. 17, 375–408. Beijing: Krung go'i bod rig pa dpe skrun khang.

Schaeffer, Kurtis R., and Leonard W. J. van der Kuijp. 2009. *An Early Tibetan Survey of Buddhist Literature: The Bstan pa rgyas pa rgyan gyi nyi 'od of Bcom ldan ral gri*. Harvard Oriental Series 73. Cambridge, MA: Department of Sanskrit and Indian Studies, Harvard University.

Schuh, Dieter. 1973. *Untersuchungen zur Geschichte der tibetischen Kalenderrechnung, Verzeichnis der Orientalischen Handschriften in Deutschland*, vol. 16. Wiesbaden: Franz Steiner Verlag.

Si tu paṇ chen Chos kyi 'byung gnas. 2013. *Bka' brgyud gser phreng*. 2 vols. Beijing: Mi rigs dpe bskrun khang.

Smith, E. Gene. 1969. "Preface." *The Autobiographical Reminiscences of Ngag-dbang-dpal-bzang, Late Abbot of Kaḥ-thog Monastery*. The Ngagyur Nyingma Sungrab Publication Series 1. New Delhi: Sonam T. Kazi.

Sog bzlog pa Blo gros rgyal mtshan (Sokdokpa). 1975. *Nges don 'brug sgra*. In *Collected Writings of Sog-bzlog-pa Blo-gros-rgyal-mtshan*, vol. 1, 261–601. New Delhi: Sanji Dorji (version D).

———. 1982. *Dris lan nges don 'brug sgra*. Dalhousie: Damchoe Sangpo (version DA).

———. 1985. *Several Hitherto Undiscovered Writings of the Rñiṅ-ma-pa Master, Sog-bzlog-pa Blo-gros-rgyal-mtshan* (*Sog bzlog pa blo gros rgyal mtshan gsung thor bu*). Sikkim: Dzongsar Khyentse Labrang, Palace Monastery (Version K).

———. 1999. *Nges don 'brug sgra*. In *Bka' ma shin tu rgyas pa* (*Kaḥ thog*), vol. 116 (*le*), 225–702. Chengdu: Kaḥ thog mkhan po 'jam dbyangs (version K).

Stearns, Cyrus. 2008a. "Zhangton Gyawo Sonam Drakpa." *Treasury of Lives*. https://treasuryoflives.org/biographies/view/Shangton-Gyawo-Sonam-Drakpa/3937.

———. 2008b. "Nyawon Kunga Pel." *Treasury of Lives*. https://treasuryoflives.org/biographies/view/Nyawon-Kunga-Pel/3673.

Wangchuk, Dorji. 2002. "An Eleventh-Century Defence of the Authenticity of the *Guhyagarbha Tantra*." In *The Many Canons of Tibetan Buddhism. PIATS 2000:*

Proceedings of the Ninth Seminar of the International Association for Tibetan Studies, Leiden 2000, edited by Helmut Eimer and David Germano, 265–91. Leiden: Brill.

Wedemeyer, Christian. 2014. "Sex, Death, and 'Reform' in Eleventh-Century Tibetan Buddhist Esoterism: 'Gos Khug pa Lhas btsas, *spyod pa* (*caryā*), *and mngon par spyod pa* (*abhicāra*)." In *Sucāruvādadeśika. A Festschrift Honoring Professor Theodore Riccardi*, edited by Todd Lewis and Bruce McCoy Owens, 240–60. Kathmandu: Himal Books.

“Thunderbolt Blaze” or “Armless Hero”? On the Authorship of the *Essence of Debate*

Pascale Hugon

Introduction

LIKE A MAGICIAN, Leonard van der Kuijp always surprised me by pulling out of his hat the rarest Tibetan works. Recently he entrusted me with an early work on debate of an unusual style. In anticipation of my forthcoming critical edition and translation of this text, the present essay is a small token of gratitude to Leonard’s immense kindness and generosity in sharing both fascinating texts and his expertise and enthusiasm.

Leonard van der Kuijp located a copy of *The Essence of Debate* (*Brtsod pa’i de nyid*, hereafter *Rtsod*) at the China Nationalities Library of the Cultural Palace of Nationalities in Beijing in 1993. Based on the colophon of *Rtsod* that names “the monk-logician Tsöndrü Senggé (Brtson ’grus seng ge)” as the author,[1] he ascribed the work to Tsangnakpa Tsöndrü Senggé (Gtsang nag pa Brtson ’grus seng ge, ?–after 1195), the foremost of the Eight Great Lions—the group of Chapa Chökyi Senggé’s (Phya pa Chos kyi seng ge, 1109–69) leading students in epistemology (*tshad ma*).[2] This paper puts the proposed authorship of *Rtsod* to the test through a comparison with the excursus on debate in Tsangnakpa’s extensive commentary on Dharmakīrti’s *Ascertainment of Valid Cognition* (*Pramāṇaviniścaya*; hereafter *Bsdus*).[3] The issue of its dating and

This paper was written under the auspices of the research project “The Dawn of Tibetan Buddhist Scholasticism (11th–13th centuries)” (TibSchol). This project has received funding from the European Research Council (ERC) under the European Union’s Horizon 2020 research and innovation program (grant agreement no. 101001002).

1. *Rtsod* 3a8: *rigs par smra ba’i dge slong brtson ’grus seng ges sbyar ba’o*. The colophon is followed by a topical outline of *Rtsod* (fols. 3a7–3b1) ascribed to “the monk Tsöndrü Senggé.” The cover page reports the latter ascription.

2. See van der Kuijp 1994, 7, and 2016, 240n124. On Chapa’s contribution and that of his successors, see van der Kuijp 1978 and 1983.

3. See van der Kuijp 1989 for an introduction to the publication of the facsimile of *Bsdus* preserved at the Tōyō Bunko. Ten other works have appeared so far. Nine were published in 2006 in vol. 13 of the *Bka’ gdams gsung ’bum* collection (hereafter KDSB), in which the

authorship is further addressed by exploring specific nicknames for arguments by consequence (*thal 'gyur*) mentioned in *Rtsod*.

Rtsod *and* Bsdus *on Debate*

Rtsod is a short treatise in verses available in a unique three-folio manuscript (nine lines per folio) in cursive *'bru tsha* script bearing a few interlinear glosses. This work on debate stands apart from discussions on the topic typical of early epistemological summaries and commentaries. Indeed, the greatest part of *Rtsod* is devoted to exposing the cause and result of vulgar and superior debate, providing compelling motives for rejecting bad debate (such as to avoid being reborn in hell) and giving a general exposition of the path to enlightenment. The central portion of the work (fols. 1b7–2b5) more specifically addresses topics constituting the "essence of debate" (*brtsod pa'i de nyid*), an expression that gives the work its name.[4] The programmatic verse of this section announces nineteen topics but actually lists twenty-seven notions, which are subsequently explained in thirty verses (notions 15, 16, and 17 being divided into two verses each). It is not obvious how these notions should be grouped to arrive at the number nineteen.[5]

Bsdus facsimile was also reprinted. One more appeared in 2010 in the collection *Bod kyi lo rgyus rnam thar phyogs bsgrigs* (BDRC W1KG10687; van der Kuijp 2016, 251). Nine of these ten works name Tsöndrü Senggé as author in their colophons, with the addition of various specifications—e.g., *shag kya'i dge slong, dbu ma smra ba'i dge slong, mang du thos pa'i dge slong*. The commentary on the difficult points of the *Bodhisattva's Way of Life* (*Bodhicaryāvatāra*) in KDSB, vol. 13, 647–742, names instead "the learned Tsangnakpa" (*mkhas pa rtsang* [=*gtsang*] *nag pa*). The colophon of *Bsdus* (fol. 201a4), like that of *Rtsod*, ascribes the work to "the monk-logician Tsöndrü Senggé." The authorship of *Bsdus* is confirmed by external evidence.

4. According to the topical outline, this is the third subsection of the section on the determination of the nature of debate (*brtsod pa'i rang bzhin nges par bya ba*). The preceding two subsections deal respectively with the cause and effect of vulgar and superior debate. The title of the third subsection, *spyi'i de nyid*, can be understood to mean "the essence of [debate] in general" (i.e., without the specification "vulgar" or "superior").

5. A reader—maybe the same person who wrote a few interlinear glosses on fol. 1—unsuccessfully attempted to make sense of this, writing numbers next to the verses in the explanatory section. The reader used "9" twice, regrouped several notions under "16," and gave up after "17," leaving the explanation of the last notions unnumbered.

1. participants in the debate
2. occasions that are improper for debating
3. occasions in which one engages in debate
4. points of defeat when questioning
5. points of defeat when pointing out faults
6. points of defeat when setting forth a state of affairs
7. points of defeat when presenting a proof
8. points of defeat of the referee
9. status of the object [about which one debates]
10. way to argue
11. questions
12. answers
13. causes [of expertise in disputation]
14. the ornaments [embellishing the disputation]
15. the motivations (inferior and superior)
16. the result (pure and impure)
17. similes [of good and bad debate]
18. philosophical positions
19. property possessors
20. characteristics of the logical reason
21. the divisions of logical reasons
22. fallacious reasons
23. modes of expression
24. autonomous arguments
25. arguments by consequence
26. fallacious consequences
27. elimination [of the conclusion]

In *Bsdus*, Tsangnakpa's excursus on debate (fols. 155b8–164b8) prefaces the word explanation of the third chapter of the *Ascertainment of Valid Cognition* on "inference for others." The author distinguishes three points: the determination of the participants in debate, the statements associated with each, and the division of these statements.[6] The last division is done according to the speaker (this includes a discussion of points of defeat), to what the statements achieve (proof or refutation), and to the mode of presentation (autonomous argument or consequence).

Many of the twenty-seven points presented in *Rtsod* simply do not appear in *Bsdus*—for instance, the ornaments, the causes for being an expert, or the similes for good and bad debate. These points are not discussed in Dharmakīrti's treatment of debate in the context of inference for others in the *Ascertainment of Valid Cognition* and the *Commentary on Valid Cognition* (*Pramāṇavārttika*), nor in the *Science of Debate* (*Vādanyāya*). Their nature recalls, rather, the kind of

6. These points are different from the three points the author identifies to be the main items in the *Ascertainment of Valid Cognition*: the way of proving a thesis to an opponent, stating the faults in the proof, and points of defeat (*Bsdus* fol. 156a4).

topics addressed in the sections on debate in Asaṅga's *Stages of Spiritual Practice* (*Yogācārabhūmi*) and *Compendium of Abhidharma* (*Abhidharmasamuccaya*).[7] However, the terminology in the Tibetan translation of the section of the *Stages of Spiritual Practice* devoted to the science of reasoning differs, and there is no specific match regarding the contents, details that would suggest a direct source of influence.[8] Mention of such "non-technical" elements of debate are not commonly found in early Tibetan epistemological works. Parallels may be located in Sakya Paṇḍita's (Sa skya Paṇḍita, 1182–1251) *Entrance Gate for the Wise* (*Mkhas pa 'jug pa'i sgo*), where the author highlights the features of "debate in accordance with the Dharma" and of a "noble debater" (building on Dharmakīrti's remark to this effect in the *Science of Debate*) and also points out that improper debating practices cause rebirth in evil realms.[9]

Regarding the more "technical" elements of disputation, the comparison between *Rtsod* and *Bsdus* is challenged by the format and style of *Rtsod*. Not only is *Rtsod* composed in verses, but it explains each notion (or subdivision in the case of nos. 15–17) in the form of a triad. A triad is actually expected in several cases, such as the three kinds of logical reasons (no. 21) or the three characteristics of the logical reason (no. 20). In other cases, the triad is artificial. For instance, for number 23, the modes of expression of arguments, the author adds to the standard pair (homogeneous and heterogeneous) the "fallacious statements with a residue" to arrive at three.

While the two texts agree on standard issues of Dharmakīrtian logic, there are notable differences regarding some notions, in particular *Rtsod*'s nos. 1, 4–8, and 25–26.

The Debate Participants (No. 1)

Both texts posit three participants—proponent (*rgol ba*), respondent (*phyir rgol*), and referee (*dpang po*)—but define the first two differently. The proponent is "he who takes up the defense of a thesis" in *Rtsod*, but "he who takes

7. See Wayman 1958 and the more recent study in Todeschini 2011.

8. See *Stages of Spiritual Practice*, Dergé Tengyur 187a7–199b2. Compare notably: *Rtsod* no. 13 *brtsod pa mkhas pa'i rgyu* ≈ *smra ba la gces spras byed pa'i chos rnams* (Skt. *vāde bahukarā dharmāḥ*); no. 14 *brtsod pa mdzes pa'i rgyan* ≈ *smra ba'i rgyan* (Skt. *vādālaṃkāra*); no. 15 *brtsod pa'i bsam pa* ≈ *smra ba las nges par 'byung ba* (Skt. *vādaniḥsaraṇa*).

9. See *Mkhas 'jug* 3.12–13 and 3.69, translated in Jackson 1987, 329, 364. One may also note that *Mkhas 'jug* 3.72 uses the same image as *Rtsod* in its introductory verse of homage—namely, the Buddha's speech defeating bad views is compared to the lion's roar scaring wild beasts.

up[10] the proof of his own position" in *Bsdus*. The respondent is "he who takes up the refutation of the thesis" in *Rtsod*, but "he who takes up pointing out the faults of the proponent" in *Bsdus*.[11]

The Points of Defeat (Nos. 4–8)

Tibetan scholars differ in their count of the points of defeat, as well as on the number of contexts associated with each participant.[12] *Rtsod* and *Bsdus* uphold two different models:

- *Rtsod* counts *fifteen* points of defeat, organized into five triads (nos. 4–8) that correspond to five contexts in which the participants are individually involved. The first two triads are associated with two contexts of the debate in which the respondent is involved (asking questions and stating faults), and the next two with contexts in which the proponent is involved (setting forth a state of affairs and presenting a proof). The last triad concerns the referee.
- *Bsdus* counts instead *nine* points of defeat distributed over three contexts: two contexts involving the respondent (asking question and refuting), but only one involving the proponent (setting forth a state of affairs);[13] it does not include points of defeat pertaining to the referee. One point of defeat linked with both the proponent and respondent is mentioned but not counted when the total number of points of defeat is stated.

Important differences of phrasing are found for the points of defeat common to the two works. For instance, regarding the faults for the proponent stating the object of debate:

10. *Bsdus* (fol. 156b1) makes clear that the mention of "accepting" or "taking up" (*khas len*) is part of each definition. It guarantees that the persons agree on the role they are to fulfill and are therefore liable to incur defeat if they do not fulfill it.

11. *Rtsod* (fol. 1b8): *brtsod pa'i skabs kyi gang zag gsum yin te / dam bca' skyong par khas len rgol ba dang // dam bca' sun 'byin khas len phyir rgol dang // brtsod pa'i shags 'byed khas len dpang po'o //*. *Bsdus* (fol. 156a7–8): *gang zag gsum gyi mtshan nyid ni rang gi 'dod pa bsgrub pa dang rgol ba'i skyon brjod pa dang de dag gi gshag 'byed* [156a8] *par khas blangs pa nyid yin te khas ma blangs kyang de dag du 'gyur na ha cang thal ba'i phyir ro //*

12. See Hugon 2011, 125.

13. A second context involving the proponent, "rejecting faults," is mentioned in *Bsdus* fol. 156b2, but no point of defeat is associated with it.

Rtsod no. 6	*Bsdus* fol. 156b3
- *gzhan gyis dris dang lan la mi 'bad* - *dam bcar mi 'os chos rnams sgrub pa* - *skabs las 'das pa sgrub byar byed pa*	- *pha rol gyis dris pa'i don mi brjod pa* - *skyon can brjod pa* - *ma dris pa'i don brjod pa*

Arguments by Consequence (Nos. 25–26)

Rtsod's discussion of consequences (*thal 'gyur*) is limited to the distinction between correct and fallacious consequences, while *Bsdus* (fols. 158b6–159a4) further distinguishes between correct consequences that prove a thesis and correct consequences that only refute the opponent.

Rtsod and *Bsdus* agree on a threefold division of fallacious arguments by consequence that corresponds to three possible retorts by the respondent—namely, "logical reason not established," "entailment not established," and "I accept (what follows from the premises)!"[14] Their phrasing of the first two cases differs:

Rtsod no. 26	*Bsdus* fol. 158b1 and 158b5–6
- *phyogs chos med pa* - *khyab pa med pa* - *bsal pa med pa*	- *rtan (=gtan) tshigs ma grub* - *khyab pa ma grub* - *bsal ba med pa*

A difference in genre (one work being an independent composition, the other a commentary) cannot be invoked to explain the above discrepancies, since the passage considered in *Bsdus* is an excursus in which Tsangnakpa presents his own model. One could invoke instead a difference of scope: *Rtsod*'s emphasis being on "moral" criteria for distinguishing proper and improper debate, *Bsdus*'s focus being on logical criteria. But this distinction does not warrant discrepancies pertaining to technical notions explained in both works.[15]

14. This model, shared by a number of early epistemological works and which found its way into Gelukpa textbooks, was criticized by Sakya Paṇḍita, who argued in favor of four possible answers. See Jackson 1987, 457n216 and 459n220.

15. Sakya Paṇḍita's discussions of debate in the third chapter of the *Entrance Gate for the Wise*

Nicknames for Consequences

A feature of *Rtsod*'s verses on arguments by consequence (that does not find an equivalent in *Bsdus*) deserving additional attention are nicknames given to correct consequences and to the three types of fallacious consequences:

a.	Correct consequence	*Thunderbolt blaze*	*rnam* [=*gnam*] *lcags 'bar ba*
b.	Fallacious consequence lacking qualification of the subject	*Catapult weapon*[16]	*mtshon cha khri sgyogs*
c.	Fallacious consequence lacking pervasion	*Armless hero*	*dpa'o lag rdum*
d.	Fallacious consequence lacking elimination	*Poison-destroying peacock*	*rma bya dug 'joms*

"Poison-destroying peacock" and "catapult weapon" are reminiscent of the titles of two works on mind training (*blo sbyong*) attributed to Dharmarakṣita, the teacher of Atiśa who translated the works into Tibetan with Dromtön ('Brom ston, 1008–64). The first work has this very title, *Poison-Destroying Peacock*, and the second is entitled the *Wheel Weapon* (*mtshon cha 'khor lo*, an expression not so different from *Rtsod*'s *mtshon cha khri sgyogs*).[17] It is likely that the inventor of these nicknames was acquainted with these works.

Searching Tibetan epistemological works for other occurrences of these terms, I discovered several concurring models. The three main ones are represented in the following table:

---

and in the eleventh chapter of the *Treasure of Reasoning* (*Tshad ma rigs pa'i gter*) illustrate a distinction of scope in this sense, but no divergence on technical points can be observed.

16. The term is also used for cannon, but it may refer here to a type of stone-slinger rather than a firearm.

17. These two works are translated in Geshe Lhundub Sopa 2001. The first verse of the *Wheel Weapon* and the *Poison-Destroying Peacock* refer to the peacocks that prefer the jungles' poisonous plants to the medicine gardens (bodhisattvas are later compared to them). See 59: "When the peacocks roam the jungle of virulent poison, the flocks take no delight in gardens of medicinal plants, no matter how beautiful they may be, for peacocks thrive on the essence of virulent poison." Peacocks supposedly are able to kill poisonous snakes and to eat poisonous plants without being affected by their toxins.

	A	B	C	A	B/C	A	B'
	Rtsod	***Rnam rgyal*** *Chu mig pa*	***Me tog*** *Ral gri*	***Mtshon cha*** *Ral gri "kha cig"*	***Tshad don bsdus*** *Blo gros mtshungs med "bod rnams"*	***Rigs rgyan*** *Dge 'dun grub*	***Rol mtsho*** *Śākya mchog ldan "Rtsang nag pa"*
a.	*rnam lcags 'bar ba*	*gnam/ rnam lcags 'bar ba*	*gnam lcags 'bar ba*		*gnam lcags 'bar ba*	*gnam lcags 'bar ba*	*gnam lcags* ***thog***
b.	*mtshon cha khri sgyogs*	*dpa' bo lag rdum*	*dpa' bo lag rdum*	*mtshon cha khri sgyogs*	*dpa' bo lag rdum*	*mtshon cha khri sgyogs*	*dpa' bo lag rdum*
c.	*dpa'o lag rdum*	*mtshon cha khri sgyogs*	*gzhu mo rgyud chad*	*dpa' bo lag rdum*	*mtshon cha khri sgyogs* *gzhu mo rgyud chad*	*dpa' bo lag rdum*	*mtshon bya'i khri sgyogs*
d.	*rma bya dug 'joms*	*rma bya dug 'joms*	*rma bya dug 'joms*	*rma byas (em. to bya) dug 'joms*	*rma bya dug 'joms*	*rma bya dug 'joms*	*rma bya dug 'joms*

Model A, the version found in *Rtsod*, is identical with the one reported by Chomden Reldri (Bcom ldan ral gri, 1227–1305) in *Mtshon cha* (fol. 152a3–4), where it is ascribed to "some people" (*kha cig*). It is found as well in *Rigs rgyan* (pp. 327 and 333) of Gendün Drup (Dge 'dun grub, 1391–1475), on which more will be said in the section "Gendün Drup's *Rigs rgyan*" below.

Model B is found in *Rnam rgyal* (A 67b8–68a2; B 77a1–2), an epistemological summary by Chumikpa Senggé Pel (Chu mig pa Seng ge dpal, ca. 1200–1270), which is also the earliest datable evidence for these nicknames.[18] In *Rnam rgyal*, the focus is on the expression, "thunderbolt blaze," that illustrates the function of "defeating others" (*gzhan tshar gcod pa*) common both to consequences that induce a proof and to those that do not. The four nicknames and corresponding specification appear after the statement on proof-inducing consequences; it may originally have been an insert. Model B is also found, for instance, in Séra Jétsün Chökyi Gyeltsen's (Se ra rje btsun Chos kyi rgyal mtshan, 1469–1544/46) commentary on the difficult points of the *Commentary on Valid Cognition*.[19]

Model B': Model B, with a slightly different phrasing for *a* (*gnam lcags **thog*** instead of *gnam lcags **'bar***) and a phonetic variant for *c* (*mtshon bya* for *mtshon cha*), is reported in *Rol mtsho* (fol. 127a7) by Serdok Panchen Śākya Chokden (Gser mdog Paṇ chen Śākya mchog ldan, 1428–1507), who names the "Learned Tsangnakpa" (Mkhas pa rtsang [=gtsang] nag pa) as the inventor of the four nicknames.[20] This passage (with the reference to Tsangnakpa) is repeated by Namgyel Drakpa (Rnam rgyal grags pa, b. sixteenth century), a student of the ninth Karmapa.[21]

Model C is attested in Chomden Reldri's *Me tog* (126). It gives to *c* the name "cut-off bow" (*gzhu mo rgyud chad*) instead of, as in B, "catapult weapon."

The other occurrences of this terminology I could trace are repetitions of, or variations on, one of these models. For instance, Lodrö Tsungmé (Blo gros mtshungs med, active between 1330 and 1371)[22] was aware of both models B and C, which he ascribes to unidentified "Tibetans" in *Tshad don bsdus* (fol. 58a4–5, *bod rnams*). As he frequently mentions the views of Chumikpa and Chomden Reldri in this epistemological summary, one can suppose that he learned these models from their works. Identifications of the source of this terminology in later works do not go beyond the vague mention of "previous scholars" (*mkhas pa snga ma rnams*).

A variant (maybe involving some confusion of terms from different models) is found in an early Kadampa work ascribed to "Nyak" (Gnyag), as yet

18. The two manuscripts of *Rnam rgyal* have different spelling. For *a*: A 67b8 *gnas lcags* [*sic*], 67b9, and 68a1 *gnam lcags*; B 77a1 and 77a2 *rnam lcags*. For *c*: A 67b8 *khri sgyogs*; B 77a2 *khri rgyogs*.

19. *Gsung 'bum* (BDRC W1AC364), vol. 2, 337.

20. This was noted in Jackson 1987, 456n216.

21. *Rtags rig rigs lam gsal byed* (BDRC W22314).

22. Hugon 2018, 867n36.

undated.[23] The author reports two terms for *a*, "peacock catapult" (*rma bya khri sgyogs*) and "lightning on the head" (*spyi bor thog bcas*), follows model C for *b* and *c*, and terms *d* "big castle with an escort of ants" (? *'khar che grog skyel*). Another alternative version is found in the work of a fourteenth-century Bön scholar, Nyammé Shérap Gyeltsen (Mnyam med Shes rab rgyal mtshan, 1356–1415), who uses the terms "cut-off bow" for *b*, and a terminological variant of "catapult weapon" (*mtshon cha 'phrul 'khor*) for *c*.[24]

Gendün Drup's Rigs rgyan

The plot thickens when taking a closer look at Gendün Drup's *Rigs rgyan*. First, the passage mentioning the "thunderbolt blaze" (327) is a quasi-literal repeat of Chumikpa's *Rnam rgyal*, but without the sentence mentioning the four nicknames together. As for the passage in which the nicknames of the three fallacious consequences occur, it is part of a section entitled "Presentation of the Three, Proponent, Respondent, and Referee" (329–35), which includes a short section providing definitions and divisions and a longer discussion of their respective role in debate.[25] This second subsection (*rtsod pa byed pa'i rnam gzhag*, 330–35) amounts to a prose version of the discussion of the twenty-seven notions addressed in *Rtsod*! The items appear in a different order and are arranged in a nested hierarchical structure. The only notable differences in contents between the two texts is that *Rtsod*'s nos. 3 and 24 are omitted in *Rigs rgyan* and that *Rigs rgyan* counts an additional point of defeat for the proponent in the first context (no. 6 in *Rtsod*), bringing the total number of points of defeat to sixteen. The following examples will suffice to demonstrate the extent of the terminological match (differences are marked in bold):

23. *Tshad ma'i spyi skad cung zad bsdus pa*, in KDSB, vol. 44, fols. 7b6–8a8.

24. See *Tshad ma'i rnam 'byed 'phrul gyi sgron me'i rang 'grel*, in *Bon po'i yig cha las tshad ma'i skor* (BDRC W23427), 220–21 and 374–75. This passage is cited in *Mu stegs kyi grub mtha' tshar gcod gtan tshigs thigs pa'i rigs pa smra ba'i mdo 'grel*, in *Gsung 'bum* of Shérapgyeltsen (BDRC W8LS16918), vol. 1, 273.

25. One can note that the shorter and the longer account offer different definitions of proponent and respondent, and that three types of referee are distinguished in the shorter section (as in *Rnam rgyal*) but not in the longer section. Note, in the first section, the division between correct and incorrect proponent and respondent (330), for which no details are provided. This part is reused by Purbuchok (see Nemoto 2013, 159n14).

Rtsod no. 1	*Rigs rgyan*, 330–31
brtsod pa'i skabs kyi gang zag gsum yin te / dam bca' skyong par khas len rgol ba dang // dam bca' sun 'byin khas len phyir rgol dang // brtsod pa'i ***shags 'byed*** *khas len dpang po'o //*	*rtsod pa'i dus kyi gang zag la gsum yod de / dam bca' skyong bar khas len pa'i snga rgol dang / dam bca' sun 'byin par khas len pa'i phyi rgol dang / rtsod pa'i* ***shan 'byed*** *par khas len pa'i dpang po gsum yod pa'i phyir /*
Rtsod no. 15a	*Rigs rgyan*, 334'
brtsod pa'i bsam pa tha shal gsum yin te // pha rol ***smad*** *par 'dod pa'i zhe sdang dang //* ***bdag*** *nyid* ***che*** *bar 'dod pa'i chags pa dang // rigs lam 'dor bar 'dod pa'i g.yo sgyu'o //*	*pha rol po* ***dma'*** *bar 'dod pa'i zhe sdang dang /* ***rang*** *nyid* ***mtho*** *bar 'dod pa'i* ***'dod*** *chags dang / rigs lam 'dor bar 'dod pa'i g.yo sgyu rnams ni rtsod pa'i bsam pa tha shal yin la /*

A prose presentation similar to that of Gendün Drup—and likely borrowed from him —is found in a number of monastic manuals, including the well-known *Magic Key of the Path of Reasoning* (*Rigs lam 'phrul gyi lde mig*) of Purbuchok Lozang Jampa Gyatso (Phur bu lcog Blo bzang byams pa rgya mtsho, 1825–1901).[26] Yet complicating the matter, some of them additionally cite verses for the notions corresponding to *Rtsod*'s nos. 13 to 17 (without mentioning a source), verses that, however, differ from the versified version of *Rtsod*, as illustrated on the next page in the third column:[27]

26. BDRC WA1KG22610. Other instances include: *Gangs ljongs dgon sde'i slob dep dpe tshogs* (BDRC W1KG16581) and *Dga' ldan shar rtse'i chos spyod mdzad rim ngo mtshar bstan pa'i mdzes rgyan nyin byed snang ba'i yang gsal* (BDRC WA1KG24220).

27. These verses are found, for instance, in *Dga' ldan shar rtse'i chos spyod mdzad rim ngo mtshar bstan pa'i mdzes rgyan nyin byed snang ba'i yang gsal* (BDRC WA1KG24220), *Bsdus grwar thog mar 'jug byed skyabs khrid dang 'brel ba'i man ngag gser gyi lde mig* of Dzötsang Lozang Tsöndrü (Mdzod tshang Blo bzang brtson 'grus, twentieth century) (BDRC WA20471), and in a text reproduced in several volumes of the compilation *Gangs ljongs rig bcu'i snying bcud chen mo* (BDRC WA1PD95727).

Rtsod no. 17b	*Rigs rgyan*	
rnam dag brtsod pa'i dpe ni gsum yin te // gti mug gcod pas 'khor lo 'dra ba dang // sun 'byin rlung gis mi g.yo lhun po 'dra // don la ma rmongs thub dbang 'dra ba'o //	*rang dang gzhan gyis gti mug gcod pa 'khor lo lta bu dang / sun 'byin pa'i rlung gis mi g.yo ba lhun po lta bu dang / tshig dang don la ma rmongs pa thub pa'i dbang po'i sras lta bu ni rnam par dag pa'i rtsod pa'i dpe yin no //*	*ji skad du/ rang gzhan gti mug gcod pa 'khor lo bzhin // sun 'byin rlung gis mi g.yo lhun po bzhin // tshig dang don la ma rmongs thub pa'i sras // 'di rnams rnam dag rtsod pa'i dpe ru bshad // ces pa'o //*

These five verses corresponding to *Rtsod*'s nos. 13–17 all appear together, in an order reflecting Gendün Drup's presentation, in a text by Kirti Lozang Tendzin (Kirti blo bzang bstan 'dzin, b. 1942) entitled *Precepts on Debate* (*Rtsod pa byed tshul gyi bslab bya*).[28] This is, however, not an original composition, as some of the verses are quoted by earlier scholars (the earliest I could find being a work by Yongdzin Paṇḍita Lozang Penden [Yongs 'dzin Paṇḍita Blo bzang dpal ldan, 1880–1944]). These verses are likely to be based on Gendün Drup's prose presentation or a later reuse and are as such not directly related to *Rtsod*.

The direction of the relationship between the versified version attested in *Rtsod* and the prose version attested in *Rigs rgyan*—assuming they would be directly related—is difficult to ascertain. It seems slightly more likely that the verses would be based on the prose, but it is also possible that the prose represents the unfolding of a versified text. Given Gendün Drup's reuse of previous material in other parts of *Rigs rgyan* (see above on the passage common to Chumikpa's *Rnam rgyal*), one can suspect that his presentation of debate is also not original. As no precedent could be traced so far, the dating of the prose version itself can at best be established with the first half of the fifteenth century as *terminus ante quem*.

28. It is published as part of *Legs bshad dpe tshogs nor bu'i phreng ba* (BDRC WA1GS54156).

Conclusion

The above considerations left unresolved the questions of the origin of the nicknames used for consequences. The main clues are the earliest datable occurrence in Chumikpa's *Rnam rgyal* (model B), followed by Chomden Reldri's secondary reference to model A and mention of model C, and the ascription by Serdok Panchen (and scholars reusing his presentation) of model B' to Tsangnakpa.

Chumikpa and Reldri have in common that they both studied under Kyelnak Drakpa Senggé (Skyel nag Grags pa seng ge), a student of the Sangpu (Gsang phu) abbot Nyelzhik Jampé Dorjé (Gnyal zhig 'Jam pa'i rdo rje)[29] and a disciple of Dānaśīla, who had founded a seminary of philosophical study in Nartang (Snar thang). Nyelzhik himself was a student of Denbakpa Mawé Senggé (Dan bag pa Smra ba'i seng ge)—another of Chapa's Eight Great Lions. Reldri studied with Chumikpa, but not in the field of epistemology. For this, his teachers were notably Kyelnak, Kyitön Drakbum (Kyi ston grags 'bum), Dānaśīla, and Uyukpa ('U yug pa). Uyukpa (d. 1253) mentions the "thunderbolt blaze" as the name for *a*, but not the other three terms, in his epistemological summary.[30] No epistemological work by Nyelzhik or Kyelnak is available. Extant epistemological summaries by two students of Nyelzhik—Tsangdruk Dorjé (Gtsang drug rdo rje), whose works bears many similarities with *Rnam rgyal*, and Dharmaratna—do not mention this terminology. The terms are also absent from the epistemological summary of Tsangnakpa's student Tsurtön Zhönnu Senggé (Mtshur ston Gzhon nu seng ge) and do not appear in Chapa's epistemological works or, earlier, in the extant ones by Ngok Loden Sherap (Rngog Blo ldan shes rab, 1059–1109).

The argument "from silence" would hint to the terminology emerging shortly before Chumikpa but not before nor with Nyelzhik. Such type of argument has some weight in a context of composition where extensive reuse of previous material is common practice. It cannot, however, be taken as conclusive: in addition to the limited range of extant sources, nothing speaks against the possibility that scholars knew this terminology but did not mention it in all their own compositions or did not mention it in *all* of their compositions (indeed, for instance, Chumikpa mentions the four nicknames in *Rnam rgyal* but not in his commentary on the *Ascertainment of Valid Cognition*).[31]

29. See Sparham 1996.

30. See *Rigs grub*, 352.

31. The absence of these nicknames in *Bsdus* whereas they are present in *Rtsod* is thus not a strong argument against identical authorship of *Bsdus* and *Rtsod*.

What does this say about the authorship of *Rtsod*? If the colophon of *Rtsod* is genuine and "Tsöndrü Senggé" refers to Tsangnakpa Tsöndrü Senggé,[32] there would be, against the argument "from silence," an instance of the use of the four nicknames predating Chumikpa. We would, however, have to conclude that Serdok Panchen is mistaken with regard to the model he ascribes to Tsangnakpa (since *Rtsod* exemplifies model A, and not model B'), or is mistaken about the nominal reference to the inventor of model B' (which would not be a unique case).[33] Should Serdok Panchen's claim be correct, it would be an argument against Tsangnakpa being the author of *Rtsod*, as it is unlikely that the same author would adopt different models in different works.[34]

I could not find compelling arguments for dating *Rtsod* in relation to other works, in particular other works by Tsangnakpa, the future study of which might still reveal pertinent similarities of phrasing or stylistic features comparable to *Rtsod*.

The colophon is, at this point, the only argument in favor of Tsangnakpa's authorship of *Rtsod*, whereas the divergences in *Rtsod* and *Bsdus* pointed out here—although one may argue whether it constitutes a genuine "thunderbolt blaze"—point to the authors of the respective works being different.

References

Primary Sources

BDRC, Buddhist Digital Resource Center (https://library.bdrc.io/). See this resource for full bibliographical references to the works mentioned only once, for which the BDRC work ID number is provided.

Bka' gdams gsung 'bum (KDSB). *Bka' gdams gsung 'bum phyogs sgrig thengs dang po/gnyis pa/gsum pa/bzhi pa*. 120 vols. Edited by Dpal brtsegs bod yig dpe rnying zhib 'jug khang. Chengdu: Si khron mi rigs dpe skrun khang, 2006 (vols. 1–30), 2007 (31–60), 2009 (61–90), and 2015 (91–120).

32. Although there are several other scholars named Tsöndrü Senggé, I am not aware of another candidate as "the monk-logician Tsöndrü Senggé" besides Tsangnakpa.

33. See van der Kuijp 1989, 22, on Serdok Panchen's misidentification of an opponent in the *Treasure of Reasoning* as Tsangnakpa, whereas it was actually Tsurtön (who held a different position than Tsangnakpa on this point).

34. The case of Chomden Reldri is unalike, as *Me tog* presents the model adopted by the author, while *Mtshon cha* is reporting someone else's model.

Bsdus. Gtsang nag pa Brtson 'grus seng ge. *Tshad ma rnam par nges pa'i ṭi ka legs bshad bsdus pa*. Otani University Tibetan Works Series 2. Kyoto: Rinsen Book Co, 1989.

Me tog. Bcom ldan rigs pa'i ral gri. *Tshad ma'i bstan bcos sde bdun rgyan gyi me tog*. In *Tshad ma sde bdun rgyan gyi me tog*. Edited by Rdo rje rgyal po. Xining: Krung go'i bod kyi shes rig dpe skrun khang, 1991.

Mtshon cha. Bcom ldan rigs pa'i ral gri. *Tshad ma bsdus pa rigs pa'i mtshon cha*. Sa skya'i dpe rnying bsdus sgrig khang. BDRC W3CN4042.

Rigs grub. 'U yug pa Rigs pa'i seng ge. *Bstan bcos tshad ma rigs pa'i gter gyi rgyan rigs pa grub pa*. In *'U yug pa rigs pa'i seng ge'i gsung 'bum*, vol. 1. Beijing, 2007. BDRC W2DB25060.

Rigs rgyan. Dge 'dun grub. *Tshad ma'i bstan bcos chen po rigs pa'i rgyan*. In *Rgyal dbang dang po dge 'dun grub kyi gsung 'bum*, vol. 7. Lha sa: Ser gtsug nang bstan dpe rnying 'tshol bsdu phyogs sgrig khang, 2011.

Rnam rgyal. Chu mig pa Seng ge dpal. *Gzhan gyi phyogs thams cad las rnam par rgyal ba*. A = In *Bka' gdams gsung 'bum*, edited by Dpal brtsegs bod yig dpe rnying zhib 'jug khang, vol. 87, 315–448. Chengdu: Si khron mi rigs dpe skrun khang, 2009; B = In *Bka' gdams gsung 'bum*, edited by Dpal brtsegs bod yig dpe rnying zhib 'jug khang, vol. 45, 11–163. Chengdu: Si khron mi rigs dpe skrun khang, 2007.

Rol mtsho. Gser mdog Paṇ chen Śākya mchog ldan, *Tshad ma rigs pa'i gter gyi rnam par bshad pa sde bdun ngag gi rol mtsho*. In *The Complete Works (Gsung 'bum) of Gser mdog paṇ chen Śākya mchog ldan*, vol. 19 (*dza*). Edited by Kunzang Tobgey. Timphu, 1975. Reprint, Delhi: Nagwang Topgyal, 1988.

Rtsod. Rigs par smra ba Brtson 'grus seng ge. *Brtsod pa'i de nyid*. Photocopy of a three-folio *dbu med* manuscript preserved at the China Nationalities Library of the Cultural Palace of Nationalities in Beijing, no. 004900(7).

Stages of Spiritual Practice. Asaṅga. *Rnal 'byor spyod pa'i sa* (Skt. *Yogācārabhūmi*). In *Bstan 'gyur (sde dge)*, vol. 127, 4–567 (=Tohoku No. 4035, tshi 1b1–283a7). Edited by Zhu chen tshul khrims rin chen. Reproduced by Delhi Karmapae Choedhey. Sde dge: Sde dge par khang, 1982–1985. BDRC W23703_4035.

Works in European Languages

Geshe Lhundub Sopa, with Leonard Zwilling and Michael J. Sweet. 2001. *Peacock in the Poison Grove: Two Buddhist Texts on Training the Mind*. Boston: Wisdom Publications.

Hugon, Pascale. 2011. "Argumentation Theory in the Early Tibetan Epistemological Tradition." *Journal of the International Association of Buddhist Studies* 34.1–2: 97–148.

———. 2018. "Sa skya Paṇḍita's Classification of Arguments by Consequence Based on the Type of the Logical Reason: Editorial Conundrum and Mathematics for Commentators." *Journal of Indian Philosophy* 46.5: 845–87.

Jackson, David. 1987. *The Entrance Gate for the Wise (Section III): Sa-skya Paṇḍita on Indian and Tibetan Traditions of Pramāṇa and Philosophical Debate*. Wiener Studien zur Tibetologie und Buddhismuskunde 17.1 and 17.2. Vienna: Arbeitskreis für Tibetische und Buddhistische Studien.

van der Kuijp, Leonard W. J. 1978. "Phya-pa Chos-kyi Seng-ge's Impact on Tibetan Epistemological Theory." *Journal of Indian Philosophy* 5: 355–69.

———. 1983. *Contributions to the Development of Tibetan Buddhist Epistemology*. Wiesbaden: Franz Steiner.

———. 1989. "An Introduction to Gtsang-nag-pa's *Tshad-ma rnam-par nges-pa'i ṭi-ka legs-bshad bsdus-pa*: An Ancient Commentary on Dharmakīrti's *Pramāṇaviniścaya*, Otani University Collection No. 13971." In Gtsang nag pa Brtson 'grus seng ge, *Tshad ma rnam par nges pa'i ṭi ka legs bshad bsdus pa*, 1–39. Otani University Tibetan Works Series 2. Kyoto: Rinsen Book Co.

———. 1994. "On Some Early Tibetan *Pramāṇavāda* Texts of the China Nationalities Library of the Cultural Palace of Nationalities in Beijing." *Journal of Buddhist and Tibetan Studies* 1: 1–30.

———. 2016. "The Lives of Bu ston Rin chen grub and the Date and Sources of His *Chos 'byung*, a Chronicle of Buddhism in India and Tibet." *Revue d'Etudes Tibétaines* 35: 203–308.

Nemoto, Hiroshi. 2013. "Who Is a Proper Opponent? The Tibetan Buddhist Concept of *phyi rgol yang dag*." *Journal of Indian Philosophy* 41: 151–65.

Sparham, Gareth. 1996. "A Note on Gnyal zhig 'Jam pa'i rdo rje, the Author of a Handwritten *Sher phyin* Commentary from about 1200." *The Tibet Journal* 21: 19–29.

Todeschini, Alberto. 2011. "On the Ideal Debater: *Yogācārabhūmi*, *Abhidharmasamuccaya* and *Abhidharmasamuccayabhāṣya*." *Journal of Indian and Tibetan Studies* 15: 244–72.

Wayman, Alex. 1958. "The Rules of Debate according to Asaṅga." *Journal of the American Oriental Society* 78.1: 29–40.

Eclipsing the Great Paṇḍita: Śākyaśrībhadra in the Later Biographies of Jetsün Drakpa Gyeltsen

Rory Lindsay

In 2011 I had a meeting with Leonard before heading to Nepal for a year. The plan was to prepare for my PhD exams there, and I asked him what Tibetan-language works I should read for my exam on the history of the Sakya lineage. He replied that I should read Amezhap's *Treasury of Wonders: The Sakya Lineage*, Taktsangpa Penjor Zangpo's *Archives of China and Tibet*, the first five volumes of the *Explanation of the Path and Result for Disciples*, and the first five volumes of the *Explanation of the Path and Result for Assemblies*—approximately eight thousand pages of Tibetan in total. Facing this daunting new reading list, I spent my days in my room at the International Buddhist Academy taking notes on these texts, but by the time I returned to Cambridge I had only gotten through about half of them. When Leonard and I met, I wanted to emphasize what I *had* read and not what I hadn't. I started by saying I had really enjoyed Amezhap's text. Seeming to have forgotten what he had assigned, Leonard stopped me and said, "You read the whole thing?! Good for you, lad!" He was so pleased that I just left it at that. Thank you for always pushing us to reach for the stars, Leonard!

EARLY SOURCES on the life of the Sakya patriarch Jetsün Drakpa Gyeltsen (Rje btsun Grags pa rgyal mtshan, 1147–1216) are lamentably succinct. His sole autobiographical work is *The Lord's Dreams* (*Rje btsun pa'i mnal lam*), a short but fascinating account of significant dreams he had during his lifetime. The other main source of early biographical data is the *Biography of My Lama, the Great Lord* (*Bla ma rje btsun chen po'i rnam thar*) composed by his nephew and chief disciple, Sakya Paṇḍita Künga Gyeltsen (Sa skya Paṇḍita Kun dga' rgyal mtshan, 1182–1251). This text is also somewhat sparing in detail, declaring at multiple junctures that there is simply too much to say, before moving on to a new topic. In keeping with the hagiographic conventions of the time, its focus is the miraculous and the visionary, which Ronald Davidson speculates "may in fact be a direct reflection of the values espoused by Drakpa Gyeltsen himself,"[1] given his choice to produce nothing else in the autobiographical medium. Rather than recording details about his life at Sakya, Drakpa Gyeltsen appears to have been keener on exploring the multiplicity of Buddhist topics to which he was dedicated, writing as he did some 150 treatises varying widely in length and concern.

It became the task of later writers, then, to fill out Drakpa Gyeltsen's life story, perhaps drawing on unwritten lore or documents emerging in the centuries following his death, or possibly even authoring new stories about him. We find in later sources, for example, accounts of alleged interactions between Drakpa Gyeltsen and the Kashmiri scholar Śākyaśrībhadra (1127–1225) that expand Drakpa Gyeltsen's life story and paint him in a decidedly favorable light, though such narratives are absent from his early biographies. Indeed, Sapaṇ's own disciple Martön Chökyi Gyelpo (Dmar ston Chos kyi rgyal po, 1198–ca. 1259) includes only a short summary of Drakpa Gyeltsen's life in his *Incisive Vajra* (*Zhib mo rdo rje*)—a text discussing Tibet's early Lamdré (Lam 'bras) masters—before directing his readers to Sapaṇ's work: "How could I explain his extensive life story? One should consult the composition of the honorable Bzang po, the great being who is of the same family line and is his close and sublime Dharma son."[2] If we compare the detail with which Martön writes about Sachen or Sapaṇ, we find Drakpa Gyeltsen dramatically overshadowed, and even in the little information that he does offer on Drakpa Gyeltsen, the spotlight remains almost entirely on his father and brother. For instance, Martön begins by explaining that Drakpa Gyeltsen received all the tantras and their branch transmissions from his father, Sachen Künga Nyingpo (Sa chen Kun dga' snying po, 1092–1158), and his elder brother Loppön Sönam Tsemo (Slob dpon Bsod nams rtse mo, 1142–82), among other teachers, before noting that on multiple occasions he sought guidance from his deceased father through dreams, asking about difficult topics and receiving answers that alleviated his doubts. Martön continues, "He also met both the great master and Loppön Rinpoché again and again in dreams, and when he asked about several points, they replied. Because the web of unknowing was completely removed, he possessed a great matchless intelligence."[3] This remark is noteworthy for its

1. Davidson 2005, 344.

2. Stearns 2001, 156–57: *'di'i rnam par thar pa rgyas par kho bos bshad par ga la nus/ de nyid kyi gdung dang nye ba'i chos sras mchog du gyur pa'i bdag nyid chen po bzang po'i zhabs kyis mdzad par blta'o/.*

3. Stearns 2001, 156–57: *bla chen dang slob dpon rin po che gnyis las kyang rnal lam du zhal yang yang 'byal zhing don 'ga' zhig zhus pas gnang te/ mi shes pa'i dra ba rnam par bsal bas na mi mtshungs pa'i blo gros chen po de/.*

emphasis on Drakpa Gyeltsen's continued reliance on his father and brother. Martön avoids undermining Drakpa Gyeltsen, of course, explaining that he "acquired control over infinite qualities"[4] and died amid miraculous signs. But the overall sense is that he was eclipsed by his elders, even after their deaths.

This pattern continues in several historical works that discuss the Khön ('Khon) family and the history of the Sakya line. Tselpa Künga Dorjé's (Tshal pa Kun dga' rdo rje) *Red Book* (*Deb ther dmar po*), written in 1346, lists only a few details about each of Sakya's early founders but provides comparatively richer detail about Sachen, Sapaṇ, and Sapaṇ's nephew Chögyal Pakpa Lodrö Gyeltsen (Chos rgyal 'Phags pa Blo gros rgyal mtshan, 1235–80). On the life of Drakpa Gyeltsen, Künga Dorjé states only that he was the third of Sachen's four sons, he was born in 1147, he built the Utsé Nyingma (Dbu rtse rnying ma) temple at Sakya,[5] and he died at the age of sixty-nine, in the year 1216.[6] Künga Dorjé provides more inspiring details about Sachen, including references to visions he had of the mahāsiddha Virūpa and the bodhisattva Mañjuśrī, his studies, and his capacity to emanate a miraculously lightweight body.[7] For Sapaṇ, moreover, Künga Dorjé emphasizes his ordination as a monk under Śākyaśrībhadra and his invitation to the court of the Mongol ruler Godan Khan (1206–51). Notably, Künga Dorjé states that Sapaṇ's influence among the Mongols was prophesied by Drakpa Gyeltsen, a move that at least elevates Drakpa Gyeltsen's visionary standing.[8] He then offers details about Sapaṇ's journey from Sakya to Godan's court, proclaiming that he spread the Dharma widely among the Mongols before his death. He likewise discusses Pakpa's life in comparable detail.

We find similar restraint regarding the life of the Jetsün in the fifteenth-century master Taktsangpa Penjor Zangpo's (Stag tshang pa Dpal 'byor bzang po) *Archives of China and Tibet* (*Rgya bod yig tshang*), penned in 1434,[9] which

4. Stearns 2001, 156–57: *yon tan gyi cha dpag du med pa la mnga' brnyes so/.*

5. Schoening identifies Sachen as the figure responsible for the construction of this building, adding that Drakpa Gyeltsen arranged the construction of the Utsé Sarma (Dbu rtse gsar ma). See Schoening 1990, 32. Davidson follows Schoening in this attribution. See Davidson 2005, 335.

6. Tshal pa Kun dga' rdo rje 1981, 47. According to modern Western calculations, Drakpa Gyeltsen lived to the age of sixty-nine; in the text he is identified as having lived to the age of seventy by virtue of the Tibetan custom of identifying newborn children as being one year of age.

7. Tshal pa Kun dga' rdo rje 1981, 46: *lus yang por sprul bsgyur nus so/.*

8. Tshal pa Kun dga' rdo rje 1981, 47.

9. Macdonald 1963, 53–159.

hosts just a few short lines about him. It notes Sachen's age at the time of Drakpa Gyeltsen's birth, the latter's birthdate, his status as the "king of the attainment of patience,"[10] his construction of the Utsé Nyingma temple, his leadership of Sakya for forty-five years, and finally the date of his death. Meanwhile, it offers considerable detail on the lives of Sachen and Sapaṇ, just as we find in Martön's text. For example, regarding Sachen's early years, Taktsangpa explains that he exhibited exceptional qualities from infancy; requested and received the Hevajra initiation from his father, Khön Könchok Gyelpo ('Khon Dkon mchog rgyal po, 1034–1102); suffered the loss of his father when he was a child; received encouragement from his mother to do like his father and study with translators; studied with Bari Lotsāwa (Ba ri Lo tsā ba, 1040–1111), to whom the seat of Sakya had been entrusted given Sachen was too young to assume this role; left Sakya to study philosophy before returning when Bari Lotsāwa fell ill; and so on.[11] The section on Sapaṇ's life offers similar detail, including information about his ordination under Śākyaśrībhadra in the year 1206, his conversion of non-Buddhists to the Buddhist path, and his travels to and activities in the Mongol court. The discussion of Pakpa is also comparable in length.[12]

To give just one more example, the famous *Blue Book* (*Deb ther sngon po*), which is attributed to Gö Lotsāwa Zhönnu Pel ('Gos Lo tsā ba Gzhon nu dpal, 1392–1481) but was almost certainly compiled by his disciples,[13] references Drakpa Gyeltsen on several occasions but offers little detail about his life. In the section on the early masters of the Lamdré tradition in Tibet, we are informed only that he was the third of Sachen's sons, was born in 1147, and led Sakya until his death at the age of sixty-nine.[14] Even Sachen and Sapaṇ receive brief treatments in this section alongside occasional references to them elsewhere in the text, yet the life of Pakpa is described at some length.[15]

Given this pattern of passing over Drakpa Gyeltsen, it was up to the authors of Sakya-focused histories to preserve his memory. Taktsang Lotsāwa Sherap

10. Stag tshang pa Dpal 'byor bzang po 1979, vol. 2, 26: *bzod pa thob pa'i rgyal ba yin*. This possibly alludes to Drakpa Gyeltsen's mastery of one of the six perfections of the Mahāyāna path, which he prophesies for himself in *The Lord's Dreams*. It may also denote "acceptance of the unborn" (*ma skyes pa'i chos la bzod pa*), an achievement that entails direct insight into emptiness. See Grags pa rgyal mtshan 1993, 399.

11. Stag tshang pa Dpal 'byor bzang po 1979, vol. 2, 18–21.

12. Stag tshang pa Dpal 'byor bzang po 1979, vol. 2, 27–30.

13. van der Kuijp 2006, 24.

14. 'Gos Lo tsā ba Gzhon nu dpal 1984, vol. 1, 263. See also Roerich 1976, 211.

15. 'Gos Lo tsā ba Gzhon nu dpal 1984, vol. 1, 263–64. See also Roerich 1976, 211–12.

Rinchen's (Stag tshang Lo tsā ba Shes rab rin chen, 1405–77) *Ocean of All Desirables: The Glorious Sakya Lineage* (*Dpal ldan sa skya'i gdung rabs 'dod dgu'i rgya mtsho*), written in 1467, pays much greater attention to Drakpa Gyeltsen, recognizing his importance for the development of the Sakya lineage. Organizing the biography according to Drakpa Gyeltsen's great faith, ethics, learning, giving, and intelligence, Taktsang Lotsāwa draws heavily on Sapaṇ's text and *The Lord's Dreams*, and his tone is unsurprisingly adulatory.[16] Meanwhile, Müsepa Dorjé Gyeltsen's (Mus srad pa Rdo rje rgyal mtshan, 1424–98) *Precious Garland: The Glorious Sakya Lineage* (*Dpal dan sa skya'i gdung rabs rin po che'i phreng ba*) is similar to Taktsang Lotsāwa's text, again relying heavily on Sapaṇ's work and *The Lord's Dreams*. His focus remains on Drakpa Gyeltsen's remarkable characteristics and achievements, with some detours into his past lives as reported in his dream text, among other visions.[17] Notably, both works say little beyond what is found in the earliest sources on Drakpa Gyeltsen's life.

By contrast, the twenty-seventh Sakya throneholder and influential author, Amezhap Ngawang Künga Sönam (A mes zhabs Ngag dbang kun dga' bsod nams, 1597–1659), compiled an account of Drakpa Gyeltsen's story with far greater narrative flair. In his *Treasury of Wonders: The Sakya Lineage* (*Sa skya'i gdung rabs ngo mtshar bang mdzod*), completed in 1629, he includes stories about Drakpa Gyeltsen that are absent in the sources so far described, including three about the Jetsün's alleged interactions with Śākyaśrībhadra. Visiting Tibet from 1204 to 1214,[18] Śākyaśrī exerted extraordinary influence on Tibetan cultural and intellectual history, prompting van der Kuijp to remark that "Tibet's subsequent intellectual history is unthinkable without him."[19] Sakya tradition regards Śākyaśrī as a pivotal figure in its history: Sapaṇ took full ordination with Śākyaśrī in 1206, a departure from the precedent set by Sachen, Sönam Tsemo, and Drakpa Gyeltsen, none of whom were fully ordained. Śākyaśrī and Sapaṇ also together retranslated Dharmakīrti's *Commentary on Valid Cognition* (*Pramāṇavārttikā*), which they completed in 1210. Given Sapaṇ's stature in the Sakya tradition and Śākyaśrī's role as his *upadhyāya* in ordination and epistemology, Śākyaśrī has been respected by Sakyapas ever since.

It is thus rather striking to find Śākyaśrī repeatedly upstaged in Amezhap's biography of Drakpa Gyeltsen. The first episode concerns a meditator in India

16. Stag tshang Lo tsā ba Shes rab rin chen n.d., 14a–16a.

17. Mus srad pa Rdo rje rgyal mtshan 2018, 20–24.

18. van der Kuijp 1994, 599.

19. van der Kuijp 1994, 613.

who, practicing the creation stage of Vajrabhairava meditation, dies without experience in the completion stage, or the "superior intentions" (*lhag bsam*) critical to the Vajrayāna, such as the altruistic aspiration to obtain awakening for the sake of all beings. This results in his horrifying rebirth as a ghost with nine goiters, which are piled in place of what would have been Vajrabhairava's nine heads had he properly identified with the deity. This ghost haunts Śākyaśrī, and neither he nor his retinue of junior paṇḍitas can repel it. When they arrive at Sakya, however, Drakpa Gyeltsen immediately recognizes the specter, and having set his vajra scepter and bell into the air, he dispels it with ease. Since the ghost is unable to return to India (we are not given a reason why), it wanders eastward to China, where it pursues wealthy Kashmiris even to this day.[20]

Leaving aside questions about the historicity of this story, we can reflect on how it and the remaining narratives position Drakpa Gyeltsen vis-à-vis Śākyaśrī, which in turn may grant us some purchase on the work that these stories do. First, notice how neither the great Kashmiri master nor anyone in his entourage can exorcise the ghost, despite their extensive Buddhist training and mastery of the tantras' ritual technologies. Only Drakpa Gyeltsen, a lay practitioner who had rarely left Sakya, has the capacity to dispel it, and he does so immediately after performing a public miracle. What is more, rather than being an awe-inspiring guest welcomed with due pageantry—a scene famil-

20. The full passage reads: "Further, the story of his marvels: Someone in India gained clarity through practicing the creation stage of Vajrabhairava meditation. Having died without superior intentions and experience in the completion stage, he was reborn as a malevolent ghost with nine goiters stacked on top of each other in place of Vajrabhairava's nine heads. That very ghost followed the Great Kashmiri Paṇḍita who had arrived in Tibet. At that time, no one was able to repel it, and when the Great Paṇḍita arrived at Sakya, the Lord Drakpa Gyeltsen, holding his vajra scepter and bell, went out to welcome him. Having perceived the ghost that was covertly pursuing Śākyaśrī, Drakpa Gyeltsen set his vajra scepter and bell in the air and banished it. Hence, being unable to return to India, it went to China and nowadays wanders only after wealthy Kashmiris" (A mes zhabs 1975, 86–87; A mes zhabs 2009, 79; A mes zhabs n.d., 44b–45a (here abbreviated MS): *yang 'di'i ngo mtshar ba'i rnam thar ni/ rgya gar du 'jigs byed kyi bskyed rim* [MS = *rims*] *gsal zhing / rdzogs rim* [MS = *rims*] *dang lhag bsam dang bral ba zhig tshe'i dus byas nas/ dbu dgu'i dod lba ba dgu* [MS – *dgu*] *brtsegs byas pa'i 'dre gdug pa can cig tu skyes/ de nyid kha che paN chen bod du byon pa'i rjes la 'brangs te/ su gang gis* [MS = *gi*] *kyang* [MS = *yang*] *bzlog par ma nus pa'i tshe/ paN chen sa skyar phebs pa'i skabs su rje pas rdo dril bsnams nas bsu ba la byon/ 'gab 'brangs* [MS = *'brang*] *de mkhyen* [MS = *mkhyin*; 1975 = *mkhyan*] *nas rdo dril nas mkhar* [MS = *khar*] *bzhag nas bskrad* [MS = *bkrad*] *pas/ rgya gar la yang ldog ma nus pa rgya nag la song bas/ deng sang rgya nor kham che* [MS = *khams che*; read *kha che*] *tsam gyi rjes la myul ba de'o/*). Note that Amezhap abbreviates Rje btsun Grags pa rgyal mtshan simply as Rje pa here and elsewhere.

iar from the autobiography of Tropu Lotsāwa Jampa Pel (Khro phu Lo tsā ba Byams pa['i] dpal, 1172–1236), the figure responsible for Śākyaśrī's visit to Tibet[21]—here Śākyaśrī arrives in a state of paranormal trouble, without even a hint of pomp. His prowess rhetorically diminished, he assumes the role of a foil—that is, a master whose alleged inabilities foreground Drakpa Gyeltsen's greatness.

The second narrative is similar. Here we find Śākyaśrī asking after Drakpa Gyeltsen, to which Sapaṇ replies that his uncle is meditating at the Zimchil Karpo temple, which was built by Sachen's father, Khön Könchok Gyelpo.[22] Śākyaśrī suggests that they visit him immediately, and when Sapaṇ recommends that he go first to notify his uncle of Śākyaśrī's visit, the Kashmiri paṇḍita insists that they go together. When they arrive, Drakpa Gyeltsen rises to offer prostrations, thinking to place his vajra scepter and bell on the table. In the bustle of the moment, however, he rests them in the air, amazing Śākyaśrī. The modest Jetsün remarks that he had not intended to perform a miracle, after which Śākyaśrī prostrates to him, angering his retinue of junior paṇḍitas, who had previously asked him to agree that, as a fully ordained monk, he never prostrate to lay practitioners. Śākyaśrī retorts that Drakpa Gyeltsen is the real *mahāvajra*—that is, an authentic tantric master—and he describes having perceived him in the Guhyasamāja maṇḍala.[23]

21. See, for example, Khro phu Lo tsā ba Byams pa dpal n.d., 56a.

22. This was the earliest temple established at Sakya. It later became known as Sgo rum, also spelled Dgu rum. Heimbel 2017, 136n370.

23. The full passage reads: "On another occasion, when the Lord Drakpa Gyeltsen was sitting in meditation at Zimchil Karpo temple, the Great Paṇḍita asked the Dharma Lord Sapaṇ, 'What's your uncle doing?' Since Sapaṇ replied that his uncle was meditating, the Great Paṇḍita said, 'Let's go see him!' Sapaṇ answered, 'I'll go first,' but the Great Paṇḍita replied, 'We'll go together!' They arrived before the Lord Drakpa Gyeltsen who had finished the self-visualization of the Guhyasamāja and was performing the offerings and praises of the front visualization. The Lord got up, having thought to offer prostrations. When he went to place his vajra scepter and bell on the table, it rested freely in the air, and since the Great Paṇḍita said, 'Just he possesses such vast marvels,' the Lord said, 'I didn't do that in hopes of a marvel!' Then, since the Great Paṇḍita offered prostrations in return to the Lord, the junior paṇḍitas petitioned the Great Paṇḍita, 'It's inappropriate to offer prostrations in return to him, an *upāsaka*! We have already asked you not to offer prostrations in return. Didn't we have an agreement?' Thus, the Great Paṇḍita said, 'This is so, but he is the actual *mahāvajra*,' and he explained that he had perceived him residing in the Guhyasamāja maṇḍala." (A mes zhabs 1975, 87–88; A mes zhabs 2009, 79–80; A mes zhabs n.d., 45a–45b (here abbreviated MS): *yang skabs shig* [MS = *gcig*] *tu rje btsun gzims spyil dkar por thugs dam la bzhugs dus/ chos rje la paN chen gyis* [MS = *gyi*] *khyod kyi khu bo ci byed kyin yod gsungs/ thugs dam la zhugs zhus pas/ rang re bltar 'gro gsungs/ bdag gi sngon la phyin lags*

Given Śākyaśrī's status as a bonafide South Asian Buddhist paṇḍita, the very fact that he inquires about Drakpa Gyeltsen promotes the latter's importance; we do not find Drakpa Gyeltsen seeking an audience with Śākyaśrī but rather the inverse. Noteworthy is Śākayśrī's insistence that he and Sapaṇ visit Drakpa Gyeltsen unannounced. It is as though he wants to see the great master in action, his practice being an attraction in itself. Drakpa Gyeltsen repeats his miracle of resting his vajra scepter and bell in the air, and Śākyaśrī's shock underscores the significance of the feat. Further, Śākyaśrī's willingness to prostrate before Drakpa Gyeltsen upraises the latter, and Amezhap pushes this point further by having the junior paṇḍitas challenge their own master on such behavior. The message is clear: Śākyaśrī respects Drakpa Gyeltsen so highly that he is willing to break protocol and bend his elderly body down before him. Moreover, his justification of this act becomes his first explicit praise of Drakpa Gyeltsen. He knows him to be an authentic master because he perceived him residing in the Guhyasamāja maṇḍala, which situates Drakpa Gyeltsen among the highest of tantric personas.

In the third narrative, Śākyaśrī's role qua foil becomes even more transparent. Here he predicts the time of an eclipse, only to have Drakpa Gyeltsen caution that he is mistaken and should not publicize his forecast. Drakpa Gyeltsen's warning is met with concern even among Śākyaśrī's retinue, and when the eclipse fails to occur at the designated time, Śākyaśrī acknowledges to Sapaṇ that Drakpa Gyeltsen was correct, saying, "Just he got it right! A senior *upāsaka* is proud up there!" Drakpa Gyeltsen's triumph issues a strong statement, elevating him beyond Śākyaśrī in his visionary capacities.[24]

---

kyis zhus pas/ mnyam du 'gro gsungs nas rje pas gsang ba 'dus pa'i bdag bskyed tshar nas mdun bskyed kyi mchod bstod mdzad pa'i thad du phebs rje pas phyag mdzad snyam bzhengs/ rdor [MS = *rdo*] *dril cog tse khar bzhag dgongs tsa na bar snang la khrol le bzhag 'dug* [MS + *pa*] *la/ paN chen na re/ de tsam la ngo mtshar rgya tsam yang yod de gsungs pas/ rje btsun gyis ngo mtshar du re nas byas pa ma lags* [1975 = *legs*] *gsungs/ de'i tshe rje pa la paN chen pas* [MS = *gyi*] *phyag lan mdzad pas/ paN chung rnams kyis khong dge bsnyen cig* [MS = *gcig*] *la phyag lan* [MS = *len*] *mdzad bar* [MS = *par*] *mi 'os/ snga gong nas kyang phyag lan mi mdzad bar* [MS = *par*] *zhu phul bar gda'/ zhal chad yod pa ma lags sam zhus pas/ de yin te khong ma hA badz+ra dngos su 'dug pa gsungs te/ gsang ba 'dus pa'i dkyil 'khor du gzigs pa yin gsungs/*).

24. "Further, on one occasion at Sakya, the Great Paṇḍita set in writing, 'At this time there will be a solar eclipse.' Since the Lord Drakpa Gyeltsen requested that he not announce this given there would certainly be no eclipse at that time, even the junior paṇḍitas were concerned. Then, the Great Paṇḍita went with the Dharma Lord Sapaṇ to Shang Sekshing. Since the solar eclipse did not occur at the designated time, the Great Paṇḍita said, 'Just he got it right! A senior *upāsaka* is proud up there!'" (A mes zhabs 1975, 88; A mes zhabs 2009, 80; A mes zhabs n.d., 45b (here abbreviated MS): *yang skabs shig* [MS = *gcig*] *tu sa skyar paN chen pas dus 'di la nyi ma gzas 'dzin zhes yi ge btab/ rje pas de skad mi gsung ba* [MS = *gsungs*

All this is especially striking given we find a very different presentation of Śākyaśrī in Amezhap's section on Sapaṇ. There Śākyaśrī is first cast as a trailblazer, aiding Sapaṇ in his ambitions to elevate the study of Buddhist epistemology.[25] Later, Śākyaśrī's teachings on the *Treasury of Abhidharma* (*Abhidharmakośa*) validate one of Sapaṇ's dreams, in which he studied this seminal work under a pale-blue Vasubandhu. Śākyaśrī says nothing different from what Vasubandhu had taught in Sapaṇ's dream, which affirms not only Sapaṇ's visionary qualities but also Śākyaśrī's mastery of the text's details.[26] Finally, after Sapaṇ describes a dream in which he memorizes some tantric songs, Śākyaśrī reports that he had the same dream on the very same night.[27] Notably, in none of these cases do we find Śākyaśrī cast in a negative light; nowhere does Sapaṇ rival him.

This more flattering treatment is perhaps unsurprising given the precedent of stories concerning Śākyaśrī and Sapaṇ's interactions. For example, in Martön's *Incisive Vajra*, we find multiple episodes involving Śākyaśrī and Sapaṇ, but none that downplay the abilities of the former. On one occasion while teaching, Śākyaśrī asks Sapaṇ why he is reading from a Tibetan text rather than from the Sanskrit, and Sapaṇ amazes everyone by back-translating into Sanskrit from the Tibetan. At this Śākyaśrī is extremely pleased, and he scolds the junior paṇḍitas who had laughed at Sapaṇ's methods.[28] In this case, Śākyaśrī's authority remains intact while Sapaṇ's abilities are underscored—a rather different narrative arc than what we have seen with Śākyaśrī and Drakpa Gyeltsen.

Interestingly, Drakpa Gyeltsen's overshadowing of Śākyaśrī recurs in sources subsequent to Amezhap's *Treasury of Wonders*. The Great Fifth Dalai Lama Ngawang Lozang Gyatso's (Ngag dbang blo bzang rgya mtsho, 1617–82) *Song of the Queen of Spring: The Book of Tibetan History* (*Bod kyi deb ther dpyid kyi rgyal mo'i glu dbyangs*), written in 1643, includes a short discussion of Drakpa

bar] *zhu da lan cis kyang mi 'dzin pa* [MS = *par*] *'dug zhus pas/ paN chung rnams kyang thugs khrel gyi* [MS = *gyis*] *rnam pa mdzad/ de nas paN chen chos rje pa dang bcas pa shang sreg* [MS = *bsreg*] *shing du phebs/ nyi ma gza' 'dzin dus btab bzhin ma byung bas/ paN chen pa na re/ de tsam dag kho rang shes te stod ya gi* [MS = *ki*] *na dge bsnyen rgan po cig* [MS = *gcig*] *nga rgyal* [MS + *byed gyin*] *yod gsungs so/*). As in the passages from Amezhap cited above, it is important to recognize Paṇ chen as referring to Śākyaśrī (not Sapaṇ), Rje pa as referring to Jetsün Drakpa Gyeltsen, and Chos rje pa (elsewhere simply Chos rje) as denoting Sapaṇ. Note also that Shang Sekshing (Shang sreg shing) is the name of one of Sapaṇ's "middling residences," his "great residences" being Sakya and Liangzhou. See Jackson 1987, 36.

25. A mes zhabs 1975, 114; A mes zhabs 2009, 101–2; A mes zhabs n.d., 59a.

26. A mes zhabs 1975, 124–25; A mes zhabs 2009, 110; A mes zhabs n.d., 64b–65a.

27. A mes zhabs 1975, 125; A mes zhabs 2009, 110; A mes zhabs n.d., 65a.

28. Stearns 2001, 163.

Gyeltsen and an alternate version of the eclipse story. This brief telling reads: "The Great Kashmiri Paṇḍita prophesied that there would be an eclipse. Since the Lord Drakpa focused intently on his channels and winds, the eclipse did not occur."[29] Here the story has a different arc: rather than simply warning Śākyaśrī that his prediction about the eclipse is wrong, Drakpa Gyeltsen uses his yogic power to prevent the eclipse from happening. Why he would do this is unclear, but the message is that Drakpa Gyeltsen outshone Śākyaśrī in his miraculous abilities as a tantric master.

Expansions of this second version of the eclipse episode appear in later Sakya histories. In the renowned Sakya master Chogyé Trichen Tupten Lekshé Gyatso's (Bco brgyad Khri chen Thub bstan legs bshad rgya mtsho, 1919–2007) *History of Sakya* (*Sa skya chos 'byung*), composed in 1969, we find this narrative relayed in greater detail. It begins with Śākyaśrī producing a written notice about a coming eclipse, which prompts Drakpa Gyeltsen to stop the movement of breath and mind (*rlung sems*) in the right and left channels (*ro rkyang gnyis*) of his subtle body and cause the red and white elements in the central channel to mix. This yogic feat halts the eclipse, and in response, Śākyaśrī declares, "That old *upāsaka* went through every difficulty to frame me as a liar!"[30] He then goes to confront Drakpa Gyeltsen, but when he arrives, the Jetsün stands to greet him and leaves his vajra scepter and bell floating in midair. With the sight of this marvel, Śākyaśrī proclaims "Mahāvajradhara Guhyasamāja!" and requests teachings from Drakpa Gyeltsen, which affirms his status as the "crown ornament of vajradharas."[31] Notably, an almost identical telling of this story appears in Dongtok Tenpé Gyeltsen's (Gdong thog Bstan pa'i rgyal mtshan, 1933–2015) *History of the Precious Teachings of Glorious Sakya* (*Dpal ldan sa skya pa'i bstan pa rin po che ji ltar byung ba'i lo rgyus*), which he completed in 1976, seven years after Chogyé Trichen Rinpoché's text was published.[32] Presumably Dongtok Rinpoché reproduced this from Chogyé Trichen Rinpoché's *History*, or perhaps they both copied it from a common source. Whatever the case, what is striking about this version of the eclipse story is Śākyaśrī's dramatic claim that Drakpa Gyeltsen is attempting

29. Ngag dbang blo bzang rgya mtsho 1980, 94: *kha che paN chen gyis nyi zla gza' 'dzin 'byung bar lung bstan pa/ rje grags pas rtsa rlung la gzir bas ma byung ba*. See also Tucci 1999, 625.

30. Bco brgyad Khri chen 1969, 30: *nga brdzun mar btang ba'i ched dge bsnyen bgres po de la dka' las ci yang byung song zhes gsungs pa*. See also Chogyé Trichen Rinpoche 2003, 13.

31. Bco brgyad Khri chen 1969, 30. See also Chogyé Trichen Rinpoche 2003, 14.

32. Gdong thog Bstan pa'i rgyal mtshan 1977, 90–91. See also Dhongthog Rinpoche 2016, 61.

to cast him as a liar, which is followed by an equally dramatic change of heart that ultimately stations him as Drakpa Gyeltsen's student.

What might we conclude from these developments in Drakpa Gyeltsen's life story? First, it should be noted that we do not know the origins of the three episodes about him and Śākyaśrī that appear in Amezhap's history. I have not yet located them in any earlier biographies, so it is possible that they were originally recorded in documents now lost, were transmitted orally, or were composed by Amezhap or some other author to expand Drakpa Gyeltsen's story. But regardless of these stories' roots, their use of Śākyaśrī as a foil reflects a movement among the Sakyapas to reinforce Drakpa Gyeltsen's authority through narrative. He is frequently overshadowed in earlier accounts, and while Sapaṇ's biography of him is laudatory, Sachen's, Sapaṇ's, and Pakpa's stories ultimately dominate the historical record. Thus, by setting Drakpa Gyeltsen beside a rhetorically diminished Śākyaśrī, later biographies frame the Jetsün as a grand master, one whose virtuosity surpassed even that of a great Kashmiri paṇḍita.

References

A mes zhabs Ngag dbang kun dga' bsod nams. 1975. *Sa skya'i gdung rabs ngo mtshar bang mdzod.* Delhi: Tashi Dorji.

———. 2009. *Sa skya'i gdung rabs ngo mtshar bang mdzod.* Dehradun: Sakya Dolma Phodrang.

———. n.d. *Sa skya'i gdung rabs ngo mtshar bang mdzod.* Unpublished *dbu med* manuscript. BDRC W4CZ307408.

Bco brgyad Khri chen Thub bstan legs bshad rgya mtsho. 1969. *Sa skya chos 'byung.* Dharamsala: Shes rig par khang.

Chogyé Trichen Rinpoche. 2003. *Parting from the Four Attachments: A Commentary on Jetsun Drakpa Gyaltsen's Song of Experience on Mind Training and the View.* Boston: Snow Lion Publications.

Davidson, Ronald M. 2005. *Tibetan Renaissance: Tantric Buddhism in the Rebirth of Tibetan Culture.* New York: Columbia University Press.

Dhongthog Rinpoche. 2016. *The Sakya School of Tibetan Buddhism: A History.* Translated by Sam van Schaik. Somerville, MA: Wisdom Publications.

Gdong thog Bstan pa'i rgyal mtshan. 1977. *Dpal ldan sa skya pa'i bstan pa rin po che ji ltar byung ba'i lo rgyus.* New Delhi: T. G. Dhongthog Rinpoche.

'Gos Lo tsā ba Gzhon nu dpal. 1984. *Deb ther sngon po*, vol. 1. Chengdu: Si khron mi rigs dpe skrun khang.

Grags pa rgyal mtshan. 1993. *Rje btsun pa'i mnal lam.* In *Sa skya bka' 'bum*, vol. 8, 394–401. Dehradun: Sakya Centre.

Heimbel, Jörg. 2017. *Vajradhara in Human Form: The Life and Times of Ngor chen Kun dga' bzang po.* Lumbini: Lumbini International Research Institute.

Jackson, David P. 1987. *The Entrance Gate for the Wise (Section III): Sa-skya Paṇḍita on Indian and Tibetan Traditions of Pramāṇa and Philosophical Debate*, vol. 1. Vienna: Arbeitskreis für Tibetische und Buddhistische Studien.

Jetsun Dragpa Gyaltsan. 2014. *Sakya Kongma Series: Jetsun Dragpa Gyaltsan: The Hermit King.* Translated by Christopher Wilkinson. Cambridge, MA: CreateSpace.

Khro phu Lo tsā ba Byams pa dpal. n.d. *Paṇ grub gsum gyi rnam thar dpag bsam 'khri shing.* Unpublished xylograph. BDRC W1KG13616.

van der Kuijp, Leonard W. J. 1994. "On the Lives of Śākyaśrībhadra (?–?1225)." *Journal of the American Oriental Society* 114.4: 599–616.

———. 2006. "On the Composition and Printings of the *Deb gter sngon po* by 'Gos lo tsā ba gzhon nu dpal (1392–1481)." *Journal of the International Association of Tibetan Studies* 2: 1–46.

Macdonald, Ariane. 1963. "Préambule à la lecture d'un *rGya-Bod yig-chan*." *Journal Asiatique* 251: 83–159.

Mus srad pa Rdo rje rgyal mtshan. 2018. *Dpal dan sa skya'i gdung rabs rin po che'i phreng ba.* In *Sa skya rdzong lugs kyi chos skor phyogs bsdus chen mo*, vol. 19. Lhasa: Bod ljongs bod yig dpe rnying dpe skrun khang.

Ngag dbang blo bzang rgya mtsho. 1980. *Bod kyi deb ther dpyid kyi rgyal mo'i glu dbyangs.* Beijing: Mi rigs dpe skrun khang.

Roerich, George N., trans. 1976. *The Blue Annals.* Delhi: Motilal Banarsidass.

Sa skya Paṇḍita Kun dga' rgyal mtshan. 1993. *Bla ma rje btsun chen po'i rnam thar.* In *Sa skya bka' 'bum*, vol. 10, 576–98. Dehradun: Sakya Centre.

Schoening, Jeffrey D. 1990. "The Religious Structures at Sa-skya." In *Reflections on Tibetan Culture: Essays in Memory of Turrell V. Wylie*, edited by Lawrence Epstein and Richard F. Sherburne, 11–47. Lewiston, NY: Edwin Mellen Press.

Stag tshang Lo tsā ba Shes rab rin chen. n.d. *Dpal ldan sa skya'i gdung rabs 'dod dgu'i rgya mtsho.* Unpublished *dbu med* manuscript. BDRC W1CZ1883.

Stag tshang pa Dpal 'byor bzang po. 1979. *Rgya bod yig tshang chen mo*, vol 2. Thimphu: Kunsang Topgyel and Mani Dorji.

Stearns, Cyrus. 2001. *Luminous Lives: The Story of the Early Masters of the Lam 'bras Tradition in Tibet.* Boston: Wisdom Publications.

Tshal pa Kun dga' rdo rje. 1981. *Deb ther dmar po.* Beijing: Mi rigs dpe skrung khang.

Tucci, Giuseppe. 1999. *Tibetan Painted Scrolls*, vol. 2. Bangkok: SDI Publications.

Flower Garland: The Transmission of the *Vinayakārikā Mālākāra* in Tibet

Cuilan Liu

I studied with Leonard as my PhD supervisor at Harvard from 2006 to 2014. His attention to the details of texts and manuscripts shows me what fine scholarship is, and his intellectual prowess continues to inspire me in my scholarly pursuits. The unconditional supports I have received from him as a mentor not only prepared and trained me to be who I am today as a scholar, but also allowed me to expand my scholarly pursuits into religion, law, music, and filmmaking. As an educator, he sets the bar of good mentorship so high that I can only aspire to keep becoming better in my own teaching career.[1]

On May 19, 1934, the Indian scholar Rāhula Sāṅkṛtyāyana (1893–1963) arrived in Tibet's capital city, Lhasa, where he would visit again in 1936 and 1938. The sole purpose of his visit was to search for Sanskrit manuscripts written on palm leaves. While visiting various monasteries in Central Tibet, he was accompanied by a Tibetan assistant, the famous Amdo scholar Gendün Chömpel (Dge 'dun chos 'phel, 1903–51).[2] At the Gorrum (Sgor rum) temple of Sakya Monastery, they found a manuscript titled *Flower Garland: Buddhist Monastic Law in Verse* (*Vinayakārikā Mālākāra*, hereafter, *Flower Garland*).[3]

1. I presented earlier versions of this chapter at the International Conference on "Tibet: Culture, Buddhist Thought, and Society" at Harvard University and the seventeenth IABS in Vienna in 2014. Comments from participants helped improve this chapter. I thank Leonard van der Kuijp for generously sharing the unpublished version of his 2013 article. I am also grateful to Shayne Clarke for many insightful conversations about this text since 2013, and for sharing his forthcoming article that identifies the Tibetan and Chinese translations that correspond to its surviving Sanskrit verses. I also thank Ernst Steinkellner and Hong Luo for helping me locate the Sanskrit manuscript of the *Flower Garland*.

2. Dge 'dun chos 'phel 2014, 3.

3. Sāṅkṛtyāyana 1937, 23–24, stated this manuscript's discovery was from the Phyag dpe temple at Sa skya Monastery's Lha khang chen mo. Dge 'dun chos 'phel reported seeing it in the Sgo rum temple at Sa skya Monastery (2009, 25–26, and 2014, 51–53).

In 1934, however, Sāṅkṛtyāyana did not photograph or copy this manuscript by hand, as he did not list this text in the descriptive catalog of his 1934 acquisition from Tibet published in 1935.[4] Two years later, Sāṅkṛtyāyana returned to Tibet and photographed this manuscript.[5] These photographs are now housed at the Bihar Research Society in Patna and Göttingen University.[6]

Sāṅkṛtyāyana was not the only who had attempted to survey, collect, and catalogue Tibet's Sanskrit manuscripts. During his trips to India, Nepal, and Tibet in 1933, 1935, 1939, and 1949, Giuseppe Tucci photographed or had other people manually copy some Sanskrit palm-leaf manuscripts. Some of these photographs and manuscripts became part of the library collections in India and Nepal, some are lost, and some others are now preserved in the Oriental Section of the Library of the Istituto Italiano per l'Africa e l'Oriente in Rome. Francesco Sferra, who curates the Tucci collection in Rome, has reproduced Tucci's photographs of the Sanskrit manuscript of the *Flower Garland* found in Tibet.[7] This manuscript is incomplete.[8] It is written double-sided on fourteen leaves, with four or five lines per side of each leaf in the Kuṭilā script.[9] Numerous interlinear notes written in cursive Tibetan are found on each leaf. Of these fourteen leaves, Sāṅkṛtyāyana transliterated the two sides of leaf 62 and the beginning lines of leaf 41.[10]

The original Sanskrit manuscript is still in Tibet, but it might have had a not-so-short sojourn in Beijing. In 1960, a number of Sanskrit and Tibetan manuscripts from Central Tibet were brought to the library of the Cultural Palace

4. Sāṅkṛtyāyana 1935.

5. Sāṅkṛtyāyana listed the *Flower Garland* in his 1937 catalog of the manuscripts he acquired in 1936.

6. Frank Bandurski published his catalogue of the collection at Göttingen in 1994. His description of this text in German in Bandurski 1994, 100, is based on Sāṅkṛtyāyana 1937, 23–24. The texts of some manuscripts from the Sāṅkṛtyāyana collection preserved at Göttingen are published online through the Göttingen Register of Electronic Texts in India and Related Indological Materials from Central and Southeast Asia.

7. I visited this Tucci collection in Rome in 2004 but was unable to locate Tucci's photographs of this manuscript or a reference to it in Francesco Sferra's catalogue of this collection in Rome (Sferra 2000, 397–413). Clarke, forthcoming, brought to my attention Tucci's photographs of the Sanskrit *Flower Garland* included in Sferra 2008.

8. The following description comes from Sāṅkṛtyāyana 1937, 23–24.

9. Sāṅkṛtyāyana 1937, 23, gave the page numbers as 41, 44, 47, 50–54, 56–59, 60, and 62. Clarke 2021 corrects that page 60 is indeed page 46 and that each folio had four or five lines rather than three to five lines described by Sāṅkṛtyāyana.

10. Sāṅkṛtyāyana 1937, 23.

of Nationalities in Beijing, where they remained for the next thirty-three years. While these manuscripts were in Beijing, Peking University acquired microfilms of the Sanskrit collection, but lost two rolls of film later.[11] In April 1985 Wang Sen completed an unpublished catalog of 259 manuscripts from these Peking University microfilms.[12] This catalogue, however, did not mention the Sanskrit manuscript of the *Flower Garland*. If this manuscript was sent to Beijing, its microfilm copy was likely lost among those two missing rolls when Wang produced his catalogue.

In 1993 these Sanskrit and Tibetan manuscripts were returned to Tibet, where they remained inaccessible to scholars for decades. After six years of surveying, photographing, and cataloguing, in 2006 the Committee for the Preservation of Palm Leaf Manuscripts in Tibet (Xizang beiyejing baohu xiaozu 西藏贝叶经保护小组) began to publish the Sanskrit palm-leaf manuscripts. To date they have published a one-volume concise catalog, a four-volume detailed catalog, and sixty-one volumes of color fascicles of all extant palm-leaf Sanskrit manuscripts found in Tibet.[13] On December 11, 2013, the Institute for the Study of Palm Leaf Manuscripts (Beiyejing yanjiusuo 贝叶经研究所) was established to study these manuscripts. Their publications, however, were printed in a small quantity, and only authorized readers have access to them.

The corpus of Buddhist legal texts has been a major source for the study of Indian monasticism as well as its practice in East and Central Asia. Today only a handful of them have survived in more than two Buddhist languages. What makes it more challenging is that those surviving texts transmitted from six different traditions—Mahāsāṃghika, Mahīśāsaka, Dharmaguptaka, Sarvāstivāda, Mūlasarvāstivāda, and Pāli—do not always agree with one another. The *Flower Garland* preserves a summary of the monastic rules and thus provides an additional source to crosscheck established understandings of Buddhist monasticism. The discovery of its incomplete Sanskrit manuscript in Tibet in the early twentieth century made this text even more valuable, as it is now preserved in the three major Buddhist languages of Sanskrit, Chinese, and Tibetan.

11. Saerji 2011, 374–77.

12. For Wang's catalog, see Wang 1965 and its reproduction in Hu-von Hinüber 2006, 283–337.

13. Without access to these publications, I can only see their titles shown in a TV documentary as 西藏自治区珍藏贝叶经影印大全简目， 西藏自治区珍藏贝叶经写本总目录, *Bod rang skyong ljongs su nyar tshags byas pa'i ta la'i lo ma'i dpe cha bris ma'i rtsa ba'i dkar chag*, and 西藏自治区珍藏贝叶经影印大全, *Bod rang skyong ljongs su nyar tshags byas pa'i ta la'i lo ma'i dpe cha kun btus par ma*. For an introduction of this project, see Ciwang Junmei 2013, 22–23.

In recent years the *Flower Garland* has attracted increasing scholarly attention. Apart from its translations in Chinese and Tibetan, at least two scholars have been working on a critically edited transliteration of the Sanskrit manuscript of the *Flower Garland*.[14] In particular, we can expect a critically edited version from Shayne Clarke soon. My research in this chapter is built on the long footnote discussing the Tibetan translators of the *Flower Garland* in Leonard's 2013 article.[15] My interest in this text began while taking my last course with Leonard, reading the biography of the Kashmiri Paṇḍita Śākyaśrībhadra (1127–1225) in spring 2013. The passage describing Śākyaśrībhadra teaching and translating the *Flower Garland* immediately caught my attention due to my obsession with any reference to Buddhist monastic law.

This chapter's goal is to understand the dissemination and reception of the *Flower Garland* in Tibet: How did Tibetan scholars and monastic institutions engage with this text? Who translated it into Tibetan, and who wrote commentaries on it? I will show how central the *Flower Garland* was in Tibetan monastic education, as Tibetan scholars actively engaged in translating, writing commentaries for, and integrating this text in the monastic curriculum. Today, only one Tibetan translation of the *Flower Garland* has survived in the Tibetan Buddhist canon. It was first translated in the late tenth or early eleventh century and later revised in the fifteenth century. This is also the version that has been widely cited in writings of Tibetan scholars. This chapter reveals the history of another alternative translation produced in the thirteenth century but now lost and little known, which Tibetan scholars have continuously cited in writings from the thirteenth to the seventeenth centuries.

Translations

The earliest documented, and also the only surviving, Tibetan translation of the *Flower Garland* came from the Newar scholar Jayākara and the Tibetan translator Dro Lotsāwa Sherap Drakpa ('Bro lo tsā ba Shes rab grags pa, Skt. Prajñakīrti).[16] A verse in the colophon of a fifteenth-century commentary on the *Flower Garland* suggests that this initial translation was produced during the time of Podrang Zhiwa Ö (Pho brang Zhi ba 'od, 1016–1111) from the royal

14. Bandurski 1994, 100, mentions that R. N. Pandey was working to edit the *Flower Garland*, but nothing has been published yet.

15. van der Kuijp 2013, 186–89.

16. For a most recent critical edition of the Tibetan translation of the *Flower Garland*, see Viśākhadeva 2002. Jayākara had also collaborated with the Tibetan translator Mar pa lo tsā ba Chos kyi blo gros (1002/1012–1097/1100).

family in western Tibet.[17] Van der Kuijp unpacks the verse further and suggests that this translation was produced most likely in the eleventh century at the behest of Zhiwa Ö.[18]

In the fifteenth century, the Tibetan scholar Rongtön Sheja Künrik (Rong ston Shes bya kun rig, 1367–1449) revised that first translation with Vanaratna (1384–1468).[19] Rongtön was the founding abbot of Nālendra Monastery in Penyül ('Phan yul), located to the north of Lhasa. In his study on the earlier abbots of this monastery, David Jackson described Rongtön as "indisputably one of the greatest scholastic luminaries of Tibetan Buddhism."[20] Born in a Bönpo family in Gyelmorong (Rgyal mo rong) district, Rongtön received his birth name Sherap Özer (Shes rab 'od zer) from his father.[21] In 1385 at age eighteen, he went to study at Neutok (Ne'u thog) Monastery in Sangpu (Gsang phu). He took full monkhood ordination in the Tongmön (Mthong smon) temple in Penyül with Drosa Khetsün Künga Gyelpo (Gro sa mkhas btsun Kun dga' rgyal po) as the preceptor, the Drosa abbot Martön Pelden Rinchen (Dmar ston Dpal ldan rin chen) as the sponsoring instructor, and the Vinaya master Yönten Ö Zangwa (Yon tan 'od bzang ba) as the private instructor. At this ordination, Rongtön obtained his religious name Śākya Gyentsen Pelzangpo (Śākya rgyal mtshan dpal bzang po). In Tibetan writings he is also known as Sheja Künrik (Shes bya kun rig) or Mawé Senggé (Smra ba'i seng ge).

Rongtön's collaborator in revising the *Flower Garland*, the Bengalese scholar Vanaratna, first visited Tibet in the male fire-horse year in 1426, again in the male fire-dragon year in 1436, and a third time in the female water-chicken year in 1453.[22] Vanaratna went to Gyantsé (Rgyal rtse) during his first trip to Tibet in 1426 upon the invitation of the Gyantsé king Rapten Pak (Rab brtan

17. Rong ston 1985, 514. For an English translation of this verse, see van der Kuijp 2013, 187–88.

18. van der Kuijp 2013, 182.

19. 'Gos lo 1988, 804, wrote that Vanaratna was eighty-five in the male earth-mouse year (1468); he died in the eleventh month of this year. This indicates that Vanaratna was born in 1384.

20. Jackson 1989, 6. For discussion on the life of Rong ston in English, see Jackson and Onoda 1988.

21. Śākya mchog ldan 2008, 82. For another edition of this biography, see Śākya mchog ldan 2008. In 1982 Jackson discovered a xylograph of a ten-folio biography of Rong ston at the Bihar Research Society in Patna titled *Bla ma dam pa rong ston chos kyi rje'i rnam thar thar pa 'phrin las rgyas shing rgyun mi 'chad pa'i rten 'brel bzang po*, written by a certain Nam mkha' dpal bzang. Jackson dated the printing blocks of this xylograph to ca. 1491 and argued that these blocks were carved under the urging of the author.

22. 'Gos lo 1988, 799, 800, 801.

'phags). In that year Rongtön traveled to the province of Tsang and received an invitation from the same patron to build a monastery and stay there permanently, an offer that Rongtön declined.[23] These connections convinced the fifteenth-century Tibetan historian Gö Lotsawa Zhönnupel ('Gos lo tsā ba Gzhon nu dpal) that the pair had met in 1426 in Gyantsé.[24] This was also their only encounter. During his second visit to Tibet, Vanaratna mostly stayed in Tsetang (Rtse thang) near the Pakmo Kagyü (Phag mo Bka' brgyud) center to the south of Lhasa. By that time Rongtön had left the region, two years earlier in 1434, when political disturbance occurred among the Pakmodrupa rulers.[25] When Vanaratna visited Tibet again in 1436, Rongtön was busy founding Nālendra Monastery in Penyül, located to the north of Lhasa. By the time of Vanaratna's third visit to Tibet in 1453, Rongtön had passed away. We can reasonably assume that their revised translation of the *Flower Garland* was produced after their meeting in 1426.

Rongtön played a key role in disseminating the *Flower Garland* in Tibet. Apart from producing the revised translation, he also wrote a commentary on it and offered teachings on the text to thousands of monks at different locations. One such teaching occurred during a debating tour in Central Tibet, during which he gave teachings on many Vinaya texts, including the *Vinayasūtra* and its commentary *'Od ldan*, and a text on the novice precepts (*Tshig le'ur byas pa lnga bcu pa*).[26]

The little-known alternative translation came from Śākyaśrībhadra and his Tibetan assistant Tropu Lotsawa Jampé Pel (Khro phu lo tsā ba Byams pa'i dpal, 1172–1237) in the early thirteenth century. Śākyaśrībhadra arrived in Tibet in 1204 and stayed until departing for Kashmir in 1214.[27] He arrived in Tibet accompanied by his students Vibhūticandra (Rnal 'byor zla ba) and Dānaśīla, who may have brought many Sanskrit Buddhist texts to Tibet, one of them being the Sanskrit palm-leaf manuscript *Garland Flower* found at Sakya.[28] In

23. Jackson 2007, 351.

24. 'Gos lo 1988, 799.

25. Jackson 1989, 7–8.

26. Śākya mchog ldan 2008, 90, 96–97.

27. For these dates, see van der Kuijp 1994, 599. For a summary of extant and nonextant biographical accounts of Śākyaśrībhadra and recent scholarship on the life of Śākyaśrībhadra, see Jackson 1990, 1–3. For the biography of Śākyaśrībhadra, see Bsod nams dpal bzang po 1990. Tucci 1949, 334–39, discussed a painting that portrayed the life of Śākyaśrībhadra.

28. Sāṅkṛtyāyana 1937, 11, identified a 215-folio incomplete manuscript of *Pramāṇāvāttikavṛtti-ṭīkā* written on paper from the same collection found at Sa skya Monastery. He identified it to be written in Vibhūticandra's own hand and also identified that a different

1205 Śākyaśrībhadra was working on a translation of the *Flower Garland* during a summer retreat at Lemoché (Glas mo che) in Nar (Snar).[29] At this retreat Śākyaśrībhadra gave lessons on the Vinaya texts such as the *Flower Garland* and Śākyaprabha's commentary on Guṇaprabha's *Vinayasūtra*.[30] In the morning he worked on translating the *Flower Garland*. In the afternoon he offered lessons on it.[31] Multiple Tibetan scholars, including Butön Rinchendrup (Bu ston Rin chen grub, 1290–1363),[32] Gö Lotsawa Zhönnupel,[33] Paṇchen Sönam Drakpa,[34] and the Fifth Dalai Lama Ngawang Lozang Gyatso (Ngag dbang blo bzang rgya mtsho, 1617–82),[35] would go on to write about Śākyaśrībhadra's translation of the *Flower Garland* on this occasion. Tibetans in the seventeenth century, for instance the Fifth Dalai Lama, were still acknowledging the learning on the *Flower Garland* transmitted from Śākyaśrībhadra.

Commentaries

The earliest recorded Tibetan commentaries on the *Flower Garland* were written in the thirteenth century by two students of Śākyaśrībhadra: Lhodrakpa Jangchup Pel (Lho brag pa Byang chub dpal, 1183–1264) and Senggé Zilnön (Seng ge zil gnon), who were both present at the summer retreat at

complete palm-leaf manuscript of the *Pramāṇavārttika-Bhāṣya* (Vārttikālaṅkāra) belonged to Dānaśīa. For further discussion on Vibhūticandra, see Stearns 1996.

29. Khro phu lo tsā ba (TBRC W1KG13616, 56b, line 6). This stay at Glas mo che is also mentioned in a fifteenth-century Sa skya scholar's composition on the three Vinaya lineages in Tibet, which shows that Śākyaśrībhadra and his Tibetan attendant were spending the summer retreat of the female fire-ox year (1205) at the Snar Glas mo che. See Grags pa rdo rje, 11b. Note that the name of the place is spelled differently as Slas mo che in a certain Bsod nam dpal bzang po's biography of Śākyaśrībhadra entitled *Sa'i steng na 'gran zla dang bral ba kha che paṇḍi ta shākya shrī bhadra'i rnam thar*. Jackson 1990, 66, noted these spelling variations. Furthermore, Sāṅkṛtyāyana 1938, 139, writes that Śākyaśrībhadra's religious robe, alms bowl, and shoes were held at Spos khang Monastery, one of the sites where Sāṅkṛtyāyana found Sanskrit manuscripts.

30. Both Khro phu lo tsā ba and Bsod nams dpal bzang po mentioned the teaching of these two Vinaya texts. The title of the *Flower Garland* was given as *Dge slong gi tshig le'ur byas pa*. See Khro phu lo tsā ba, 57a, line 4–5; and Jackson 1990, 60. Yet Grags pa rdo rje, 11b, line 1, did not mention any teaching during this summer retreat at Glas mo che.

31. Paṇ chen 1982–1990, 383.

32. Bu ston 1988, 228, 205.

33. 'Gos lo 1984, 112.

34. Paṇ chen 1982–1990, 383.

35. Ngag dbang 2009a, 13.

Lemoché in 1205. Each of them had written a commentary on the *Flower Garland*. These two commentaries are now lost, but they had left an important imprint on Tibetan scholars' Vinaya education from the thirteenth to the seventeenth centuries. In the thirteenth century the monastic community in Chölung (Chos lung) used Lhodrakpa's commentary on the *Flower Garland* as a core text for Vinaya study. Both Khenchen Sönam Drakpa (Mkhan chen Bsod nams grags pa, 1273–1353) and Butön took lessons on the *Flower Garland* transmitted from this community. In the seventeenth century the Fifth Dalai Lama listed Senggé Zilnön as an important teacher, appearing right after Śākyaśrībhadra and the Tropu translator in his account on the transmission lineage of the *Flower Garland*.

Three commentaries on the *Flower Garland* have survived. The first came from a certain Kazhipa Sherap Senggé (Dka' bzhi pa Shes rab seng ge), who wrote the commentary at Nartang Monastery in a female water-chicken year, which van der Kuijp dates to 1333.[36] This commentator also wrote a summary of his commentary on the *Flower Garland*. In this summary he only acknowledged that his commentary on the *Flower Garland* relied on the oral teaching of an "all-knowing" teacher whose name contains Namkha (Nam mkha').[37] This "all-knowing" teacher is probably Nartang Monastery's seventh abbot, Chim Tamché Khyenpa Namkha Drakpa (Mchims thams cad mkhyen pa Nam mkha' grags pa, 1210–89). According to Mönlam Tsültrim's (Smon lam tshul khrims) biography of Namkha Drakpa written at Nartang Monastery,[38] Namkha Drakpa gave teachings on Vinaya texts, including Guṇaprabha's *Vinayasūtra* and Śākyaprabha's *Āryamūlasarvāstivādiśrāmaṇerakārikā*.[39]

The second surviving commentary came from Samten Zangpo (Bsam gtan bzang po), written at Nartang Monastery in the fire-monkey year, 3,493 years after the Buddha's passing away.[40] Because the Kadampa community calculated

36. The author self-identifies as Dka' bzhi 'dzin pa in his summary of the *Flower Garland*. For the commentary, see Dka' bzhi pa 1979a and 1977b; for the summary, see Dka' bzhi pa 1979b and 1977a. Van der Kuijp 2013, 187, suggests him to be a Snar thang scholar.

37. Dka' bzhi pa 1979b, 59–60.

38. Skyo ston, 738–39, 36b–37a. Yet this biography did not mention Shes rab seng ge as his student. It did not mention that Nam mkha' grags had taught *Flower Garland* either.

39. This is a 300-stanza text on novice rules. In Tibetan writings it is often referred to as *Sum brgya pa*.

40. The author only stated that the commentary was written in the year of *gdong ngan*, the fire-monkey year. This and the following information are given in the colophon of the *Flower Garland* commentary in Bsam gtan bzang po 2007, 381.

the Buddha's passing to circa 2133 BCE, van der Kuijp suggests reading the year of this commentary's composition to be 1356.[41]

The third surviving commentary came from the above-mentioned Rongtön.[42] Van der Kuijp proposes two theories concerning the date of this commentary. In one theory, he dates the composition to between 1449 and 1451. This is because Śākya Chokden wrote in his biography of Rongtön that between the first and the sixth Mongolian month (*hor zla*) in the male earth-dragon year (1448), Rongtön wrote the commentary on the *Flower Garland*, shortly before his death in 1449.[43] Yet Namkha Pelzang (Nam mkha' dpal bzang), the author of another biography of Rongtön, mentioned that Rongtön wrote this commentary on the *Flower Garland* at age eighty-five in 1451.[44] These two sources led van der Kuijp to date the composition of the commentary to between 1448 and 1451.[45] The second theory from van der Kuijp is that Rongtön wrote this commentary before his meeting with Vanaratna, because the colophon of the commentary did not mention Vanaratna. If they had already collaborated on revising the translation of this text when Rongtön wrote the commentary, it would have been odd for Rongtön not to mention the influence of Vanaratna.[46]

Rongtön's study on the *Flower Garland* benefited from multiple teachers. From the Nartang abbot Druppa Sherap (Grub pa shes rab, 1357–1423), Rongtön studied the *Flower Garland* in the Kadampa tradition.[47] He also studied this text with Martön Gyatso Rinchen (Dmar ston Rgya mtsho rin chen, fourteenth century) from Penyül, who was teaching Vinaya in Drosa until his death at the age of seventy-six.[48] One teacher who was particularly influential on Rongtön's education on the *Flower Garland* was a certain scholar by the name of Losel. In the colophon of his commentary on the *Flower Garland*, Rongtön acknowledged a certain Khenpo Losel (Mkhan po Blo gsal). Van

41. van der Kuijp 2013, 187.

42. Rong ston 1985.

43. According to Śākya mchog ldan 2008, 137–38, Rong ston reached age eighty in the female fire-rabbit year (1447). A certain Nyer gnas chen mo wanted to erect a golden statue of Rong ston and requested Rong ston to stay with them for three years. Jackson 1989, 8, indicates that various sources differ on the year of Rong ston's death, from 1449 to 1451.

44. Jackson 1989, 74.

45. van der Kuijp 2013, 188–89.

46. van der Kuijp 2013, 188.

47. Śākya mchog ldan 2008, 87.

48. Śākya mchog ldan 2008, 84. Śākya mchog ldan only described him as a Gro sa scholar Dmar ston from 'Phan yul.

der Kuijp suggests that this Losel refers to the Nartang abbot Druppa Sherap, because Śākya Chokden speculated in his biography of Rongtön that Rongtön studied the *Flower Garland* and many Kadampa texts from this Druppa Sherap.[49] Here, I am suggesting a different possibility, that this Losel could be the Kyormolung (Skyor mo lung) scholar Khenchen Kazhipa Losel (Mkhan chen Dka' bzhi pa Blo gsal, 1326–1409), who was the abbot of Kyormolung Monastery from age thirty-two to sixty-one. I will discuss this possibility in detail in the section below.

The Flower Garland *in Tibetan Monastic Education*

Shortly after the *Flower Garland* was translated into Tibetan, it quickly became a core text in the Tibetan Buddhist monastic curriculum on Vinaya. In the early twelfth century, Chumiklung (Chu mig lung) Monastery, located in the upper Nyang (Myang) valley in Tsang, was one of the first centers offering lessons on the *Flower Garland*. This monastery is also where Butön had stayed and taught for a month in the female iron-rabbit year of 1351.[50] It is important to not confuse this Chumiklung Monastery with another Chumik monastery near Nartang Monastery.[51]

The primary teacher on the *Flower Garland* at Chumiklung Monastery was the Vinaya master Gya Wangchuk Tsültrim Bar (Rgya Dbang phyug tshul khrims 'bar, 1047–1131), who offered intensive lessons on many Vinaya texts, including the *Flower Garland*, at this monastery between 1126 and 1131. Gya had an unfortunate childhood but managed to become one of the greatest Vinaya masters of his time. In the female fire-pig year of 1047, he was born in Gya Mangra (Rgya mang ra) in the upper Nyang valley.[52] Having lost his parents in his youth, he spent some time at Jarok (Bya rog tshang) Monastery in the lower Nyang valley, but his inauspiciously unpleasant look soon forced him to leave. In the next few years, he learned to read at Gawa (Dga' ba; also spelled Kawa) Monastery by listening to monks reciting. He first studied Vinaya with a Sok (Sog) master and later visited every Vinaya scholar he could find in Ü

49. van der Kuijp 2013, 188.

50. Tāranatha 2002, 38.

51. Tāranatha 2002, 37–38.

52. The following biographical sketch of Rgya is extracted from 'Gos lo 1984, 107–8; and Paṇ chen 1982–1990, 352–53. For an English translation of the relevant passage from the *Blue Annals*, see 'Gos lo 1988, 78–79. Rgya's birth in 1047 also accords with Paṇ chen Bsod nams grags pa's description that Rgya Vinaya master was forty-five when Bya Vinaya master Brtson 'grus 'bar was born in 1091. See Paṇ chen 1982–1990, 370.

and Tsang. Sok, Nyangtsam (Myang mtshams), and Kokhyimpa (Ko khyim pa) became his three main Vinaya teachers. In 1080 Gya perfected his Vinaya education, and he received the title of *geshé* (*dge bshes*) in 1081.

Gya's teaching on the *Flower Garland* occurred in the last five years of his life. Having left his regular residence at Gawa Monastery, Gya took charge of Chumiklung Monastery at age eighty in 1126. During the five years from 1126 to 1131, Gya offered extensive courses on Vinaya. Aided by an assistant preacher (*zur chos pa*), Gya lectured on the *Prātimokṣa* texts, the *Vinayasūtraṭīkā*, and the *Flower Garland* three times a day for five years.[53] By this time, Jayākara and Dro Lotsawa Sherap Drakpa would have completed their translation of the *Flower Garland*. Since Gya studied Vinaya with scholars of the Lower Vinaya tradition in Tibet and had no recorded study-abroad experience, Gya's teaching probably relied on this earlier translation of the *Flower Garland*.

In the beginning of the thirteenth century, Lemoché became an influential center for disseminating the *Flower Garland* in Tibet. Śākyaśrībhadra's sojourn at Lemoché between 1204 and 1214 had a significant impact on the revitalization of Buddhist monasticism in Tibet. Before Śākyaśrībhadra's arrival in Tibet in 1204, Vinaya education in Tibet focused on texts such as the Guṇaprabha's *Vinayasūtra* and its commentaries. Śākyaśrībhadra's translation and teaching on the *Flower Garland* at Lemoché sparked renewed interest in this text among Tibetans. A few students who were present at Lemoché during this summer retreat later became instrumental in the further dissemination of the *Flower Garland*. The first is Tsangsowa Sönamdzé (Gtsang so ba Bsod nams mdzes), who met Śākyaśrībhadra at Lemoché of Nar in 1205 and worked as Śākyaśrībhadra's attendant during his sojourn in Tibet.[54] The second important student at Lemoché in 1205 was Shangpa Joten (Shangs pa jo stan).[55] He had invited Śākyaśrībhadra to Central Tibet, where he worked as Śākyaśrībhadra's personal attendant for eight years.[56] During this period, Shangpa Joten earnestly attended teachings on the *Flower Garland* and became a Vinaya expert.

53. 'Gos lo 1984, 108, and 1988, 79; Paṇ chen 1982–1990, 353.

54. Heimbel 2013, 191.

55. Heimbel 2013, 193–94, identifies this Shangs pa jo stan as Byang ston Rin chen grags, who was the sponsoring instructor at the full monkhood ordination ceremony of Lho brag pa Byang chub dpal at Khro phu in 1204. Heimbel's source on this event was a five-folio *dbu med* text on the abbatial lineage of the Dge 'dun sgang monastic community. Yet the author of this text only mentioned Shangs pa jo stan as the sponsoring instructor. Śākyaśrībhadra was the preceptor and Rgyang rob a Gzhon nu rin chen was the private instructor. For a description of this ordination ceremony, see *Dge 'dun gsang pa'i mkhan brgyud* 2011, 338, line 7.

56. Paṇ chen 1982–1990, 383–84.

Two other Lemoché students of Śākyaśrībhadra were also said to have written commentaries on the *Flower Garland*, which I mentioned above. The first is Lhodrakpa Jangchup Pel (Lho brag pa Byang chub dpal).[57] In 1204 Lhodrakpa first met Śākyaśrībhadra at Pakri (Phag ri). He and Tsomda Dorjé Pel (Mtsho mda' Rdo rje dpal), another important student of Śākyaśrībhadra, unsuccessfully attempted to become Śākyaśrībhadra's attendants. Instead, Śākyaśrībhadra sent them to study Vinaya with the abbot of Zülpu (Zul phu) Monastery.[58] During their stay at Zülpu, they took Vinaya lessons with Tsangsowa Sönamdzé.[59] The second Lemoché student who was said to have written a commentary on the *Flower Garland* was Senggé Zilnön, who gave teaching on the *Flower Garland* to Sönam Gönpo (Bsod nams mgon po), from whom Butön studied the *Flower Garland*.[60]

A few decades after Śākyaśrībhadra's departure from Tibet in 1214, Lhodrakpa founded the Chölung (Chos lung) monastic community in the Nup (Snubs) valley of Rong, which rose to become an important center for studying the *Flower Garland*. Following Śākyaśrībhadra's departure, Lhodrakpa broke up with his longtime companion Tsomdawa (Mtsho mda' ba). Among the four monastic communities that they had established separately,[61] the Chölung monastic community established around the mid-1250s became a center for teaching the *Flower Garland*.[62] During the time of its third abbot Kazhipa Drakpa Zhönnu Pelzangpo (Bka' bzhi pa Grags pa gzhon nu dpal bzang po, 1257–1315), whose tenure lasted from 1294 to 1315, Lhodrakpa's now-lost commentary on the *Flower Garland* was one of the two core texts incorporated into its monastic curriculum on Vinaya. [63]

In the early fourteenth century, Lhodrakpa's commentary on the *Flower Garland* continued to be influential in Tibet. One of its most famous students was the Tibetan historian Butön, whose primary Vinaya teachers included Zhöngyel (Gzhon rgyal) of the Upper Vinaya tradition and Tsemapa Sönam

57. Grags pa rdo rje W1CZ1079, 12; Heimbel 2013, 193–94.

58. Heimbel 2013, 192.

59. Heimbel 2013, 192, quotes Ngag dbang 1991–1995, 35.1–5.

60. 'Gos lo 1988, 82.

61. For a detailed study on the four monastic communities, see Heimbel 2013.

62. Heimbel identifies the Chos lung monastic community as the monastery in the Snubs valley of Rong mentioned in *Mkhas pa'i dga' ston*. For further discussion on the location of Chos lung, see Heimbel 2013, 198; and Ferrari 1958, 124n231.

63. Heimbel 2013, 193, writes that Bka' bzhi pa acted as the abbot of both Chos lung and Zhwa lu. Therefore he might have taught the *Flower Garland* at either or both places.

Gön (Tshad ma pa Bsod nams mgon) of the Śākyaśrībhadra tradition.[64] While studying with Sönam Gön, Butön used Lhodrakpa's commentary on the *Flower Garland*. For that reason, Butön traced the teaching on the *Flower Garland* he received all the way to its author Viśākhadeva through the following lineage line:

Viśākhadeva
. . .
Śākyaśrībhadra
Jampé Pel (Byams pa'i dpal)
Senggé Zilnön (Seng ge zil gnon)
Druppa Senggé (Grub pa seng ge)
Tsemapa Sönam Gön

Butön's connection with the Śākyaśrībhadra tradition on the *Flower Garland* is also confirmed in the *Blue Annals*, which states that Butön's teacher Sönam Gön had studied the *Flower Garland* from Senggé Zilnön, who was also a student of Śākyaśrībhadra in 1205.[65]

Butön assigned the *Flower Garland* an important place in the Tibetan monastic curriculum on Vinaya. In his *Chos 'byung*, composed between 1322 and 1326,[66] Butön discussed how Buddhist monastic education should proceed in the three stages of early, intermediate, and final. In each stage, he further distinguished texts on views (*lta ba*) and texts on practices (*spyod pa*). He categorized the Vinaya texts as texts on behaviors that should be taught and learned in the early stage.[67] He recommended starting the Vinaya curriculum with the section on ordination in the *Vinayavastu*, followed by the detailed explanations of the Vinaya rules in the *Vinayavibhaṅga* for both monks and nuns, as well as the remainder of the *Vinayavastu*. Afterward, the curriculum should proceed to the *Flower Garland* and other texts such as the *Āryamūlasarvāstivādiśramaṇerakārikā*.

In the late fourteenth century Kyormolung Monastery in Central Tibet was an important place for studying the *Flower Garland*. The monastery's most

64. Bu ston 1965–1971, 36–37, for the record of his Vinaya education in his *gsan yig*.

65. 'Gos lo 1988, 82.

66. The dates from van der Kuijp 2013, 115.

67. This transliteration is based on the computerized *dbu can* edition in Bu ston 1988, 28. For the passage in the handwritten *dbu med* edition published in 2008, see Bu ston 2008, 895–96. For Guo Heqing's and Pu Wencheng's Chinese translation of this passage, see Bu ston 1988, 25, and 2007, 19.

influential teacher on the *Flower Garland* was its twelfth abbot, Khenchen Kazhipa Losel (Mkhan chen Dka' bzhi pa Blo gsal, 1326–1409). Losel was born the son of Belti Sönam Gyelpo (Sbal ti Bsod nams rgyal po) in the fire-tiger year (1326), when Butön was thirty-seven years old.[68] He studied Vinaya and Abhidharma with Sönam Tsültrim (Bsod nams tshul khrims). At age thirty-two, with the sponsorship of Gongma Tai Situ Jangchup Gyentsen (Gong ma ta'i si tu Byang chub rgyal mtshan, 1302–64), Losel was appointed the abbot of Kyormolung Monastery. Later he entrusted the abbatial seat to Wön Gongselwa (Dbon Dgongs gsal ba) and retired. In the female earth-ox year of 1409, he passed away at age eighty-four.

Rongtön, the author of a revision and a commentary on the *Flower Garland*, had likely studied it with this Losel at Kyormolung sometime around 1393. In 1393 Rongtön traveled as an attendant of Yaktön Sanggyé Pel (G.yag ston Sangs rgyas dpal, 1348–1414) to Tsang.[69] During this trip Rongtön went on a debating tour (*grwa skor*) to Sakya, Nartang, and other monasteries. At the end of the tour, Yaktön went to attend Khenpo Losel's teachings on Vinaya at Kyormolung. Rongtön also went there and studied Vinaya with Losel. In particular, Rongtön studied the four divisions of the Vinaya literature (*'dul ba lung sde bzhi*), as well as the *Vinayasūtra* and its commentaries, with Losel in the way the Vinaya master from Ja (Bya) had taught them.[70] Although the *Flower Garland* was absent from this list, Rongtön still acknowledged Losel in the colophon of his commentary on the *Flower Garland*. I must confess that my identification of Losel is challenged by the fact that while Kazhi Losel's Vinaya teachings had attracted many scholars, including Tsongkhapa and his disciples, Rongtön's name did not appear in Paṇchen Sönam Drakpa's list of scholars who had studied Vinaya with Kazhi Losel.

In the fifteenth century two students who had studied in the Kyormolung tradition further expanded the influence of the *Flower Garland* in Tibetan monastic education. One was Rongtön, who offered teachings on the *Flower Garland* at Nālendra Monastery. One most notable student of Rongtön at Nālendra was Trimkhang (or Trükhang) Lotsāwa Sönam Gyatso (Khrims khang [or Khrus khang] lo tsā ba Bsod nam rgya mtsho, 1424–82). Sönam Gyatso had previously attended Rongtön's teachings at Samyé Monastery.[71] At Sönam Gyatso's ordination ceremony, Rongtön was the preceptor. Later,

68. Paṇ chen 1982–1990, 363–64.

69. Śākya mchog ldan 2008, 108–9. Jackson 1989, 6, and 2007, 345, specified that Mkhan rin po che was G.yag ston Sangs rgyas dpal (1348–1414).

70. Śākya mchog ldan 2008, 84.

71. 'Gos lo 1988, 806.

Sönam Gyatso took lessons with Rongtön at Nālendra Monastery on many subjects, including the *Flower Garland*.[72] At twenty-one, Sönam Gyatso became a Vinaya teacher and offered courses at Pel Tsetang (Dpal Rtses thang) Monastery on texts such as the *Flower Garland* and the *Vinayasūtra*.[73]

Another student from the Kyormolung tradition brought the *Flower Garland* to Tsetang, south of Lhasa. At some time during the fifteenth century, a Kyormolung scholar, Loppön Küngyelpa (Slob dpon Kun rgyal pa [possibly Rin chen kun dga' rgyal mtshan]), was staying at Tsetang. He was a student of Neten Gelek Pel Zangpo (Gnas brtan Dge legs dpal bzang po), who was himself a student of the above-mentioned Khenchen Kazhipa Losel.[74] During his time in Tsetang, Küngyelpa had some ten religious friends surrounding him. One of them requested lessons on the *Vinayasūtra* and the *Flower Garland* from him. Paṇchen Sönam Drakpa (Bsod nams grags pa, 1478–1554) had also identified Künga Gyeltsen (Kun dga' rgyal mtshan, 1432–1506) as his teacher on the *Flower Garland*.[75]

In the seventeenth century the *Flower Garland* connected to the Śākyaśrībhadra tradition reached one of its most influential students, the Fifth Dalai Lama. Like many other Tibetan scholars, the Fifth Dalai Lama kept a record of the teachings he had received from various teachers (*thob yig*). In this record, the Fifth Dalai Lama traced his training on the *Flower Garland* beyond its purported author, Viśākhadeva, to the historical Buddha. In the following transmission lineage of the *Flower Garland* reconstructed by him, the Fifth Dalai Lama acknowledged the Zhalu scholar Rinchen Sönam Chokdrup (Rin chen bsod nams mchog grub) as his teacher on this text.

1. Buddha (Thub dbang)
2. Mahākāśyapa
3. Ānanda
4. Śāṇavāsika
5. Upagupta
6. Dhītika
7. Kṛṣṇa
8. Sudarśana
9. Saṅghadāsa

72. 'Gos lo 1988, 809.

73. 'Gos lo 1988, 808. A monastic regulation for the Dpal Rtses thang Monastery can be found in Ngag dbang 2009b, 24–29.

74. Paṇ chen 1982–1990, 386–88.

75. Paṇ chen 1975, 60.

10. Viśākhadeva
11. Ācārya Matiratna
12. Kashmiri Paṇḍita Śākyaśrībhadra (1127–1225)
13. Gnubs lo tsā ba Byas pa'i dpal (1173–1225)
14. Rong pa mkhan po Seng ge zil gnon
15. Khro phu pa Rin chen bsod nams seng ge
16. 'Um phug gnas rnying pa Kun dga' dbang phyug
17. Snar thang Mkhan chen Nyi ma rgyal mtshan (?1225–1305), the ninth abbot of Snar thang
18. Dka' bzhi pa Shes rab seng ge (1383–1445)
19. Dka' bzhi pa Shes rab rgyal mtshan
20. Ācārya Dge ba dpal
21. Mkhas btsun Skal bzang pa
22. The fourth Mkhan chen of Snar thang Grub pa shes rab (1357–1423)
23. 'Jam dbyangs chos rje
24. Chos rje Kun dga' dbang phyug (?Ngor mkhan chen 04 Kun dga' dbyang phyug 1424–78)
25. Ācārya Sangs rgyas dpal grub
26. The ninth Mkhan chen of Ngor Lha mchog seng ge (1468–1535)
27. The eleventh Mkhan chen of Ngor Sangs rgyas seng ge (1504–69)
28. Thar rtse Paṇ chen Nam mkha' dpal bzang (1532–1602)
29. Sgrub khang pa Dpal ldan don grub (1563–1636)
30. Khyab bdag bka' 'gyur ba Mgon po bsod nams mchog ldan (1603–59)
31. Mkhan chen Zha lu pa Rin chen bsod nams mchog grub (1602–81)
32. Ngag dbang blo bzang rgya mtsho (1617–82), the Fifth Dalai Lama[76]

This record is not just a testimony of the Fifth Dalai Lama's training on the *Flower Garland*. It also shows how the *Flower Garland* remained a key text in the Tibetan monastic curriculum across time, location, and school affiliations.

Concluding Remarks

In this chapter I introduced an alternative translation of the *Flower Garland* from Śākyaśrībhadra and Tropu Lotsawa Jampé Pel. This translation was never mentioned in any of the eight available canonical catalogs or the five redactions of the Tibetan canon (*Bstan 'gyur*). For this reason, it remains largely unknown among contemporary scholars. While it is no longer extant, or is not yet discovered if it has survived, its influence on the monastic education in Tibet was

76. Ngag dbang 2009a, 13–14.

far reaching. Śākyaśrībhadra's lessons on the *Flower Garland* during his summer retreat at Lemoché in 1205 had inspired many Tibetans to add this text to their monastic training on Vinaya. Many of his students founded new monastic centers, where they offered teachings on the *Flower Garland*, or received invitations to offer courses on the *Flower Garland*. From the eleventh century to the seventeenth century, Tibetans had uninterrupted access to such teachers. Along with the *Vinayasūtra* and the *Vinayavibhaṅga*, the *Flower Garland* became integrated into the Tibetan monastic curriculum at many important intellectual centers in Chumiklung, Kyormolung, Chölung, Nālendra Monastery in Penyül, Pel Tsetang Monastery, and Tsetang. These locations are by no means comprehensive, but they do highlight a few significant monastic centers in the lives of a few eminent individuals whose interests and efforts in teaching and studying the *Flower Garland* were documented between the eleventh and the seventeenth centuries.

References

Primary Sources

Bsam gtan bzang po. 2007. *Me tog phreng rgyud kyi ṭīkka legs bshad rgya mtsho*. In *Bka' gdams gsung 'bum phyogs sgrigs*, edited by Dpal brtsegs bod yig dpe rnying zhib 'jug khang, vol. 38, 177–381. Chengdu: Si khron mi rigs dpe skrun khang.

Bsod nams dpal bzang po. 1990. *Sa'i steng na 'gran zla dang bral ba kha che paṇḍi ta shākya shrī bhadra'i rnam thar.* In *Two Biographies of Śākyaśrībhadra: The Eulology by Khro phu Lo tsā ba and Its Commentary by Bsod nams dpal bzang po*, edited by David Jackson, 38–85. Stuttgart: Franz Steiner Verlag Stuttgart.

Bu ston Rin chen grub. 1965–1971. *Bla ma dam pa rnams kyis rjes su bzung ba'i tshul bka' drin rjes su dran par byed pa*. In *The Collected Works of Bu ston*, edited by Lokesh Chandra, vol. 26, 1–142. New Delhi: International Academy of Indian Culture.

———. 1988. *Bu ston chos 'byung*. Beijing: Krung go bod kyi shes rig dpe skrun khang.

———. 2007. *Bu Dun fojiao shi* 布頓佛教史. Translated by Pu Wencheng 蒲文成. Lanzhou: Gansu renmin chubanshe.

———. 2008. *Chos kyi 'byung gnas gsung rab rin po che'i mdzod*. In *Bu ston Rin chen grub kyi gsung 'bum*, edited by Dpal brtsegs bod yig dpe rnying zhib 'jug khang, vol. 24, 847–1414. Beijing: Krung go'i bod rig pa dpe skrun khang.

Dka' bzhi pa Shes rab seng ge. 1977a. *'Dul ba me tog phreng rgyud kyi ṭīkka sogs 'grel pa dkon rigs khag cig*. Delhi: Trayang and Jamyang Samten. TBRC W1KG9604.

———. 1977b. *'Dul ba me tog phreng ryud kyi ṭīkka legs bshad rgya mtsho*. Delhi: Trayang and Jamyang Samten. TBRC W1KG9604.

———. 1979a. *'Dul ba me tog phreng rgyud kyi ṭi ka legs bshad rgya mtsho*. In *'Dul ba me tog phreng rgyud kyi sa bcad dang tshig le'ur byas pa'i de'i 'grel pa legs bshad rgya mtsho*, 61–417. Thimphu: Kunsang Topygel and Mani Dorji. TBRC W26074.

———. 1979b. *'Dul ba me tog phreng rgyud kyi sa bcad*. In *'Dul ba me tog phreng rgyud kyi sa bcad dang tshig le'ur byas pa'i de'i 'grel pa legs bshad rgya mtsho*, 1–60.

Dpal brtsegs bod yig dpe rnying zhib 'jug khang, ed. 2011. *Dge 'dun gsang pa'i mkhan brgyud*. In *Bod kyi lo rgyus rnam thar phyogs bsgrigs thengs gnyis pa*, vol. 41, 337–41. Xining: Mtsho sngon mi rigs dpe skrun khang.

'Gos lo tsā ba Gzhon nu dpal. 1984. *Deb ther sngon po*. Chengdu: Si khron mi rigs dpe skrun khang.

———. 1988 [1949]. *The Blue Annals*. Translated by George Roerich. Delhi: Motilal Banarsidass.

Grags pa rdo rje. n.d. *Mkhan rgyud rnam gsum byon tshul*. TBRC W1CZ1079.

Khro phu lo tsā ba Byams pa'i dpal. n.d. *Paṇ grub gsum gyi rnam thar dpag bsam 'khril shing*. TBRC W1KG13616.

Ngag dbang blo bzang rgya mtsho. 1991–1995. *Bstan pa'i rtsa ba rab byung dang khyim pa la phan gdags pa'i las kyi cho ga mtha' gcod dang bcas pa 'khrul spong rnam rgyal gser mdog*. In *The Collected Works of the Fifth Dalai Lama Ngag dbang blo bzang rgya mtsho*, vol. 14 (*pha*), 3–530. Gangtok: Sikkim Research Institute of Tibetology.

———. 2009a. *Zab pa dang rgya che ba'i dam pa'i chos kyi thob yig dang gā'i chu rgyun las glegs bam dang po*. In *Gsung 'bum of Nnag dbang blo bzang rgya mtsho*, vol.1, 1–600. Beijing: Krung go'i bod rig pa dep skrun khang. W1PD107937.

———. 2009b. *Ser gtsug nang bstan dpe rnying 'tshol bsdu phyogs sgrig khang gis bsgrigs*. In *Gsung 'bum of Ngag dbang blo bzang rgya mtsho*, vol. 23, 24–29.

Paṇ chen Bsod nams grags pa. 1975. *'Dul ba'i chos 'byung*. Dharamasala: Library of Tibetan Works and Archives.

———. 1982–1990. *'Dul ba'i chos 'byung dad pa'i 'bab stegs*. In *Mdo sngags rab 'byams pa Paṇ chen Bsod nams grags pa'i gsung 'bum*, vol. 11, 333–88. Mundgod: Drepung Loseling Library Society. TBRC W23828.

Rong ston Shes bya kun rig. 1985. *'Dul ba me tog phreng rgyud kyi rnam 'grel tshig don rab gsal nyi 'od*. Manduwala: Pal ewan chodan ngorpa center. TBRC W8469.

Śākya mchog ldan. 2008. *Rje btsun thams cad mkhyen pa'i bshes gnyen Sh'a kya rgyal mtshan dpal bzang po'i zhal snga nas kyi rnam par thar pa ngo mthar dad pa'i rol mtsho*. In *Gsung 'bum of Rong ston Shes bya kun rig*, vol. 1, 76–158. Chengdu: Si khron mi rigs dpe skrun khang. TBRC W1PD83960

Skyo ston Smon lam tshul khrims. n.d. *Mchims Nam mkha' grags kyi rnam thar*. In *Snar thang gser phreng*, 665–764. TBRC W2CZ7888.

Tāranatha. 2002. *Myang yul stod smad bar gsum gyi ngo mtshar gtam gyi legs bshad mkhas pa'i 'jug ngogs*. Lhasa: Bod ljongs mi dmangs dpe skrun khang.

Viśākhadeva. 2002. *'Dul ba tshig le'ur byas pa [me tog phreng rgyud]*. In *Bstan 'gyur (Dpe bsdur ma)*, vol. 93, 3–166. Beijing: Krung go'i bod rig pa dpe skrun khang.

Secondary Sources

Bandurski, Frank. 1994. "Übersicht über die Göttinger Sammlungen der von Rāhula Sāṅkṛtyāyana in Tibet aufgefundenen buddhistischen Sanskrit-Texte." In *Untersuchungen zur buddhistischen Literatur*, edited by Frank Bandurski, Bhikkhu Pāsādika, Michael Schmidt, and Bangwei Wang, vol. 5, 9–126. Göttingen: Vandenhoeck und Ruprecht.

Ciwang Junmei 次旺俊美. 2013. "Xizang beiyejing 西藏贝叶经." *Zhongguo Xizang* 中国西藏 4: 22–23.

Clarke, Shayne. Forthcoming. "A Preliminary Survey of Viśakha(deva)'s Bhikṣuvinayakārika-kusuma-raj." In a ridiculously long-overdue and entirely top-secret publication celebrating the work of a very important person.

Dge 'dun chos 'phel. 2009. "Rgyal khams rig pas bskor ba'i gtam rgyud gser gyi thang ma." In *Mkhas dbyang Dge 'dun chos 'phel gyi gsung 'bum*, 1–480. Chengdu: Sichuan minzu chubanshe.

———. 2014. *Grains of Gold: Tales of a Cosmopolitan Traveler*. Translated by Thupten Jinpa and Donald S. Lopez Jr. Chicago: University of Chicago Press.

Ferrari, Alfonsa Ferrari (ed. and tr.). *Mk'yen brtse's Guide to the Holy Places of Central Tibet*. Completed and edited by Luciano Petech, with the collaboration of Hugh Richardson. Roma: Istituto Italiano per il Medio ed Estremo Oriente, 1958.

Heimbel, Jörg. 2013. "The Jo gdan tshogs sde bzhi: An Investigation into the History of the Four Monastic Communities in Śākyaśrībhadra's Vinaya Tradition." In *Nepalica-Tibetica: Festgabe for Christoph Cüpper*, edited by Franz-Karl Ehrhard and Petra Maurer, vol. 1, 187–242. Andiast: International Institute for Tibetan and Buddhist Studies GmbH.

Hu-von Hinüber, Haiyan. 2006. "Some Remarks on the Sanskrit Manuscripts of the Mūlasarvāstivāda-Prātimokṣasūtra Found in Tibet." In *Jaina-Itihāsa-Ratna: Festschrift für Gustav Roth zum 90. Geburtstag*, edited by Ute Hüsken, Petra Kieffer-Pülz, and Anne Peters, 283–337. Marburg: Indica et Tibetica Verlag.

Jackson, David P. 1989. *The Early Abbots of 'Phan po Na-lendra: The Vicissitudes of a Great Tibetan Monastery in the 15th Century*. Vienna: Arbeitskreis für tibetische und buddhistische Studien.

———. 1990. *Two Biographies of Śākyaśrībhadra: The Eulology by Khro phu Lo tsā ba and Its Commentary by Bsod nams dpal bzang po*. Stuttgart: Franz Steiner Verlag Stuttgart.

———. 2007. "Rong ston Bka' bcu pa: Notes on the Title and Travels of a Great Tibetan Scholastic." In *Pramāṇakīrtiḥ: Papers Dedicated to Ernst Steinkellner on the Occasion of His 70th Birthday*, edited by Birgit Kellner, 345–60. Vienna: Arbeitskreis für Tibetische und Buddhistische Studien Universität Wien.

Jackson, David P., and Onoda Shunzō, eds. 1988. *Rong ston on the Prajñāpāramitā Philosophy of the Abhisamayālaṃkāra: His Sub-commentary on Haribhadra's "Sphuṭārthā": A Fascicle Reproduction of the Earliest Known Blockprint Edition from an Examplar Preserved in the Tibet House, New Delhi*. Kyoto: Nagata Bunshodo.

van der Kuijp, Leonard W. J. 1994. "On the Lives of Śākyaśrībhadra (?–?1225)." *Journal of the American Oriental Society* 114.4: 599–616.

———. 2013. "Some Remarks on the Textual Transmission and Text of Bu ston Rin chen grub's *Chos 'byung*, a Chronicle of Buddhism in India and Tibet." *Revue d'Etudes Tibétaines* 25: 111–89.

Saerji 萨尔吉. 2011. "Xizang de beiyejing 西藏的贝叶经." In *Quanjiuhua xia de fojiao yu minzu: Disanjie liang'an sidi xueshu yantaohui lunwenji* 全球化下的佛教与民族: 第三届两岸四地学术研讨会论文集, edited by Liu Chengyou 刘成有 and Xue Yue 学愚, 374–77. Beijing: Guangming ribao chubanshe.

Sāṅkṛtyāyana, Rāhula. 1935. "Sanskrit Palm-Leaf Mss. in Tibet." *Journal of the Bihar and Orissa Research Society* 21: 21–43.

———. 1937. "Second Search of Sanskrit Palm-Leaf Mss. in Tibet." *Journal of the Bihar and Orissa Research Society* 23: 1–37.

———. 1938. "Search for Sanskrit Mss. In Tibet." *Journal of the Bihar and Orissa Research Society* 24.2: 137–63.

Sferra, Francesco. 2000. "Sanskrit Manuscripts and Photos of Sanskrit Manuscripts in Guiseppe Tucci's Collection: A Preliminary Report." In *On the Understanding of Other Cultures*, edited by Piotr Balcerowicz and Mark Major, 397–413. Warsaw: Oriental Institute of Warsaw University.

———. 2008. "Sanskrit Manuscripts and Photographs of Sanskrit Manuscripts in Guiseppe Tucci's Collection." In *Sanskrit Texts from Guiseppe Tucci's Collection: Part I*, edited by Francesco Sferra, 15–78. Manuscirpta Buddhica 1. Serie Orientale Roma 104. Rome: Instituto Italiano per l'Africa e l'Oriente.

Stearns, Cyrus. 1996. "The Life and Tibetan Legacy of the Indian Mahāpaṇḍita Vibhūticandra." *Journal of the International Association of Buddhist Studies* 19.1: 127–71.

Tucci, Giuseppe. 1949. *Tibetan Painted Scrolls*. 2 vols. Rome: Libreria Dello Stato.

Wang Sen 王森. 1965. *Zongkaba zhuan lun* 宗喀巴傳論. Beijing: Zhongguo kexueyuan minzu yanjiusuo.

Subhāṣākīrti's *Sarvabhāṣāpravartana* and Its Relevance to the *Smra sgo*

Zhouyang Ma

Introduction

AMONG THE COPIOUS works on linguistics in the Tibetan Buddhist canon, many have yet to be examined closely.[1] Most of these works have Indic origins and can be generally divided into two categories based on the object languages they deal with. The first category aims to describe Sanskrit grammar. These treatises include the *Kātantra* and the *Cāndra*, the two fundamental treatises used by the Tibetans to acquire knowledge of Sanskrit. In contrast, the object languages of the treatises in the second category are less specific. A typical work of this category is the *Sword-Like Entrance into Speech* (Skt. *Vacanamukhayudhopama*, Tib. *Smra ba'i sgo mtshon cha lta bu*, hereafter *Entrance into Speech*) composed by Smṛtijñānakīrti (eleventh century).[2] This treatise was structured on the derivative model of phoneme (*yi ge*), word (*ming*), and phrase (*tshig*). A remarkable feature of the text is that while the section on phoneme deals with Sanskrit phonology, the section on phrase discusses undoubtedly Tibetan particles such as the nominalizers *pa*, *ba*, and *po*. Other works from the second category do not elaborate specifically on Tibetan grammar, but whether they deal with Sanskrit grammar is not clear, as they describe language in a general way without going into such issues as conjugation. A work of this kind is the *Eight Great Subjects* (*Gnas brgyad chen po*), composed by Ché Khyidruk (Lce Khyi 'brug) in the Early Diffusion (Snga dar).[3]

While the need for studying Tibetan acceptance of the systems presented in works of the first category is apparent, there is also value in examining texts from the second category. The immediate question that arises is whether these texts have any shared characteristics, apart from being less Sanskrit-

1. Verhagen 1994 and 2001 provides a general survey of these works.

2. For scholarship on this text, see Inaba 1963; and Verhagen 2001, 37–57.

3. See Verhagen 2001, 6–28. Whether Ché Khyidruk is the author or translator of the text is under debate. This paper will nonetheless take him as the author.

specific. If so, what are the common features? In this paper, I will pursue these questions by investigating Subhāṣākīrti's *Introduction to All Speech* (Skt. *Sarvabhāṣāpravartana*, Tib. *Smra ba kun la 'jug pa*, D 4290). I will first provide some bibliographic information. Then I will briefly analyze the content. Next I will compare this work with *Entrance into Speech*, mainly based on the compounds these texts present. I will conclude the paper by presenting some preliminary observations about the connections between these two texts.

Author and Date

Verhagen has aptly delineated the content of the *Introduction to All Speech* as follows: "It describes semantic and syntactic phenomena in such general terms, without explicitly referring to Sanskrit and without including morphological elements from the object-language, that it is not self-evident whether or not it is dealing with classical Sanskrit per se."[4] Indeed, not only is the object language veiled, but its author and the circumstances through which it entered the Tibetan intellectual world are likewise elusive. While the colophon of the text unequivocally names the author as the "Great Master Subhāṣākīrti" (*slob dpon chen po su bhā ṣa kīrti*),[5] we do not know any more about this figure. The work has a commentary entitled *Commentary on the Linguistic Treatise: An Introduction to All Speech* (Skt. *Sarvabhāṣāpravartanavyākaraṇaśāstravṛtti*, Tib. *Smra ba kun la 'jug pa'i sgra'i bstan bcos 'grel pa*, D 4291; hereafter *Commentary*). The *Commentary* bears the same authorship statement in its colophon, indicating that this is an autocommentary also composed by Subhāṣākīrti. In the *Commentary* Subhāṣākīrti cites other sources three times. The first time, Subhāṣākīrti cites "previous masters" (*sngon gyi slob dpon rnams*), then "some masters" (*slob dpon kha cig*), and finally "previous master" (*sngon gyi slob dpon*).[6] Except for perhaps the first citation, which will be discussed below in the section on connections between *Introduction to All Speech* and *Entrance into Speech*, it is difficult to ascertain the outside sources he refers to. The only statement we can make is that Subhāṣākīrti was somehow building on existing thoughts rather than presenting an entirely new set of ideas.

No translator is named in either the basic text or the commentary, making the history of its encounter with the Tibetans unclear. That being said, the catalog put together by Wüpa Losel Tsöpé Senggé (Dbus pa Blo gsal Rtsod pa'i

4. Verhagen 1994, 72.

5. *Kun 'jug*, 1702.

6. *Kun 'jug 'grel pa*, 1706, 1709, 1722.

seng ge, ca. 1270–ca. 1355) for the Old Nartang Tengyur no later than the 1320s can aid us to a certain degree.[7] Toward the end of the catalog, an entry reads:

> The basic text and the commentary of the *Introduction to All Speech* composed by Master Subhāṣākīrti.[8]

Therefore the catalog establishes the *terminus ante quem* for the composition of the *Introduction to All Speech*. Further, it should be noted that the *Introduction to All Speech* is not included in chapter 17 of the catalog, in which Wüpa Losel lists grammatical literature such as the *Kātantra*, *Cāndra*, and *Entrance into Speech*.[9] Instead, it is located in chapter 19, where the included titles are all "very rare texts" (*shin du dkon pa'i dpe*) found by Wüpa Losel's colleague Gyangro Jangchupbum (Rgyang ro Byang chub 'bum) "with extraordinary effort" (*brtson pa mchog gis*) after the completion of the main body of the catalog. Hence, if we believe that the rareness of a text can somehow reflect its popularity, then we can conclude that the *Introduction to All Speech* was not widely studied when Wüpa Losel composed his catalog, at least compared with the other major works that are mentioned.

Content and Structure

The basic text of the *Introduction to All Speech* is a metrical treatise consisting of twenty verses. While the verses represent a rather encoded form of the work, the *Commentary* sheds light on its structure. After an homage to the Omniscient One, it contains a general survey (vv. 1–7) of sound (*sgra*). Subhāṣākīrti proposes (v. 2) that all sound can be categorized in three ways: a sound is either a man-made sound (*zin pa'i 'byung ba chen po'i rgyu las byung ba'i sgra*), or not, or both; it is either a sound that points to sentient beings (*sems can du ston pa*) or not; it is either an analyzable (*lung du ston pa*) sound or not. While Subhāṣākīrti does not clearly explain the distinction between a natural sound and a sound

7. The completion of this catalogue predates the catalog that Butön Rinchendrup (Bu ston Rin chen grub, 1290–1364) appended to his famous *Religious History*, composed in the period 1322–26. This is clear because Butön references the Nartang catalogue. For a detailed discussion of the date of the Nartang catalogue, see Almogi 2021, especially 188–89. The Nartang catalogue is currently available in two versions. This paper utilizes the longer version in 81 folios (see *Bstan bcos dkar chag*).

8. *Bstan bcos dkar chag*, 78b6: *slob dpon su bha sha kīrtis mdzad pa'i smra ba kun la 'jug pa rtsa 'grel* /. See also van der Kuijp 2009, 34, for the larger context of the influx of Indic grammatical works in Tibet.

9. *Bstan bcos dkar chag*, 58a–59b.

that has become language, he mentions that if there is no purpose (*dgos 'brel*) to make a sound, then it is meaningless and does not have the capacity of showing things (*don med cing nus pa med*).[10] It appears that in all subsequent verses he discusses only formulized sound (i.e., language). In verses 6 and 7, he uses two examples to demonstrate analyzable and unanalyzable sound in detail. An unanalyzable sound (v. 6), according to our author, is a sound for which we cannot explain why it must sound as it does. This kind of sound would include the sounds of water, fire, beasts,[11] and, as the example in the verse indicates, *gu lu gu lu*, the sound of a fish eating fruit in the water. An analyzable sound (v. 7), on the contrary, is a sound for which we can explain the internal logic of why it sounds like it does. The example "impermanent" (*mi rtag*) is an analyzable sound, because, in the process of reasoning, whether we label an entity permanent or not is conditioned by whether it is produced (*byas pa*).[12]

At first glance, this division looks like the division of a primordially established word (*thog mar grub pa'i ming*) from a subsequently established word (*rjes su bsgrub pa'i ming*), as seen in the *Entrance into Speech*.[13] However, since "suffering" (*sdug bsngal ba*), which is presumably a primordially established word, is classified as an analyzable word[14] in the *Introduction to All Speech*, Subhāṣākīrti's idea must be different. His division seems to be based on whether a sound can be semantically parsed.

The verses in between (vv. 3–5) put forward the central concept of this treatise, the four formulas (*sbyor ba*) of a formulized sound.[15] They are: (1) the exclusion of the assembly of categories (*rigs kyi 'dom pa sel ba*), (2) the exclusion of the assembly of compounds (*dus kyi 'dom pa sel ba*),[16] (3) the making of an object into a purpose (*ched du bya ba*), and (4) the designation of a word (*ming du btags pa*).

10. *Kun 'jug 'grel pa*, 1705.

11. *Kun 'jug 'grel pa*, 1706: *me sgra dang chu sgra dang byol song gi ngag gi sgra.*

12. *Kun 'jug 'grel pa*, 1707.

13. *Smra sgo*, 1831; *Smra sgo 'grel pa*, 1862–64. While a primordially established word does not have an etymology (*nges pa'i tshig*), a subsequently established word does.

14. *Kun 'jug 'grel pa*, 1707.

15. The Tibetan term *sbyor ba* (Skt. **prayoga*) certainly poses some difficulty for translation in this context. My translation "formula" is only tentative. "Formula" here is understood as a procedure to form a formulized sound.

16. The Tibetan term *dus* normally means "tense" in grammatical works (Verhagen 2001, 218). However, in this treatise it cannot bear such a meaning. Although it is unusual, it is reasonable to translate the *dus* here as "compound," not only because it fits the context but also because it is morphologically related to the verb *sdud* (past tense, *bsdus*), "to condense."

Of course, these obscure terms need further elaboration. For this, we may turn to Subhāṣākīrti's explanation of verse 4, in which the four formulas are defined:

> The sound expressed in the first place is one that excludes the categories that are not consistent with it, like "man." Or it is one that excludes the categories people do not know, like "teachings."[17] That one is just the object and is related to the first formula. A compound that is compounded [through two or more words] or endowed with inflection[18] is the second formula and is a particular phrase. The thing that is shown is the third formula. The sound consistent with it is the fourth formula. In that connection, the third formula is the thing expressed by the sound because it is the thing to be shown. The sound consistent with that is the sound that expresses the expressed because it is the thing that shows the shown. The expression is the relation because it is related to the understanding of the object.[19]

According to this passage, a category (*rigs*) is the substance to which a word refers. A compound (*dus*) is the object to which a word refers as a specific case—that is, a substance with a qualifier or a substance that plays a specific role in an action. A purpose (*ched*) stands for an object that has become a concept. A word (*ming*) is the sound image that expresses a concept. In any case, our author does not analyze a word within the domain of morphology, even though the first two formulas do look like descriptions of a word's lexical and inflected forms. This system is rather established on the functional level, in which each formula represents a function that a formulized sound provides. In particular, the first two formulas represent two steps in the cognitive process. Here, the verb "excludes" (*sel*)—meaning that a cognitive agent cognizes an object only through excluding all other possibilities—no doubt reminds us of the Dharmakīrtian tradition of Buddhist epistemology. The last

17. For more on these two types of exclusion, see discussion below.

18. "Inflection" here is a translation of *byed pa'i tshig*, the *kāraka* system. For an explanation of the *kāraka* system in the Tibetan grammatical tradition, see Verhagen 2001, 284–85.

19. *Kun 'jug 'grel pa*, 1707: *thog mar brjod pa'i sgra rigs mi mthun pa sel bar byed pa skyes bu zhes bya ba lta bu'am / rigs mi shes pa sel bar byed pa chos rnams zhes bya ba gang zhig go / gang zhig ni don tsam ste / sbyor ba dang po dang 'brel to / bsdus pa'i dus dang byed pa'i tshig dang ldan pa'i dus ni sbyor ba gnyis pa ste khyad par gyi tshig go / bya ba yongs su ston pa ni sbyor ba gsum pa'o / mthun pa'i sgra ni sbyor ba bzhi pa ste / de la sbyor ba gsum* [*pa*?] *ni bstan par bya ba yin pas sgra'i brjod bya'o / de dang mthun pa'i sgra ni ston par byed pa yin pas sgra'i rjod byed do / rjod byed ni don go ba dang 'brel pas 'brel pa'o /.*

two formulas show the way that language acts as a tool for communication. Surprisingly, both formulas echo Saussure's modern linguistic theory of the signified and the signifier. In fact, in verse 4 Subhāṣākīrti regards the two formulas exactly as dividing the signified (*mtshon bya*) and the signifier (*mtshon par byed*). Therefore it is obvious that Subhāṣākīrti's system diverges from the Pāṇinian tradition of explaining Sanskrit grammar, which is essentially morphologically based.

Following the general survey, *Introduction to All Speech* continues with a detailed explanation of the four formulas. This explanation is divided into four parts based on the order of the formulas. Verses 8 and 9 explain the first formula, the "exclusion of the assembly of categories" (*rigs kyi 'dom pa sel ba*). According to the *Commentary*, this formula has again two subtypes. The first subtype aims at "excluding the inconsistent categories" (*rigs mi mthun pa ni sel*). The *Commentary* reads:

> So, if one says "man," while one does not reject the inclusion of Devadatta, Nistṛṣṇa, and Īśvara, etc., one excludes the categories that are not man, such as woman, horse, and elephant.[20]

The second subtype is defined by verse 9ab as follows: "When one shows what is general, one excludes what is unknown."[21] The *Commentary* reads:

> If one says "teachings," some of the teachings are the teachings of the basis, some are the teachings of the path; some are the teachings of the result; some are the teachings of the ultimate truth; some are explanatory teachings. Although there is nothing that is not teaching, some people, being ignorant in all ways, do not know some; some do not regard some as teachings; some have doubts for some. The exclusion of those involves the exclusion of categories.[22]

20. *Kun 'jug 'grel pa*, 1705–6: *'di ltar skyes bu zhes smos na lhas byin dang sred med dang dbang phyug la sogs pa ni mi 'dor la / bud med dang rta dang glang po la sogs te skyes bu ma yin pa'i rigs ni sel lo /.*

21. *Kun 'jug*, 1701: */ spyi la 'jug pa bstan pa na / / mi shes pa ni sel bar byed /.*

22. *Kun 'jug 'grel pa*, 1707–8: *chos rnams zhes smos na kha cig ni gzhi'i chos / kha cig ni lam gyi chos / kha cig ni 'bras bu'i chos / kha cig ni don dam pa'i chos / kha cig ni bshad pa'i chos te / chos ma yin pa med kyang skyes bo kha cig ni kun du gti mug ste ma shes / kha cig ni ma yin par 'dod* [Derge: *'dor*; Peking: *'dod*] */ kha cig ni the tshom can te / de dag sel ba ni rigs sel ba'o /.*

The first subtype is easy to understand. It means that saying "*x*" involves the exclusion of non-*x*. However, it is a bit more difficult to know what Subhāṣākīrti means exactly with the second subtype. Most likely it refers to the following scenario: Substance *x* consists of subtypes *a*, *b*, *c*, and so forth. While some people do not know *c*, or do take *c* as a subtype, the potential for ignorance and misconception is eliminated if they say "*x*." If this is the case, then the first subtype prevents a concept from being too broad and the second prevents it from being too narrow.

The second part of the explanation, verses 10–17, discusses the second formula, the "exclusion of the assembly of compounds" (*dus kyi 'dom pa sel ba*). Since this will be examined in detail in the following section, I will describe it only briefly here. The compound (*dus*), as explained in the *Commentary* in verse 4, is further divided into two categories: the stem compound (*bsdus pa'i dus*, vv. 12–13) and the inflection compound (*byed pa'i dus*, vv. 14–17). Subhāṣākīrti defines the stem compound in verse 12: "A compound, in which inflection does not present between the two or more of its members, is compounded in abbreviation."[23] This definition indicates that, at least in theory, the stem compound is not so different from the nominal composition we are familiar with. It is difficult, however, to find an equivalent for the inflection compound in modern terminology. The definition of the inflection compound—"the stem compound is compounded for the purpose of eliminating doubts with regard to the identity"[24]— does not assist us much in this direction. Besides, among the thirty-five types of inflection compounds listed by our author (see appendix), while some (nos. 1–6, 15, 20–23) certainly concern inflection, others (nos. 8, 24, 25, etc.) cannot be said to do so. Some other types (nos. 16–17, etc.) are quite ambiguous and hard to make sense of. Further, the criteria for singling out these types of inflection compounds is not completely clear. For example, why is number (nos. 20–22) divided into three types while gender (no. 23) is not? In any case, the inflection compound will no doubt require more study in the future.

The explanations for the final two formulas are succinct. They basically repeat the definitions from verse 4. In short, a sound, in formula 3 (vv. 18–19), takes an object as its signified. And formula 4 (v. 20) makes a sound a meaningful signifier.

23. *Kun 'jug*, 1701: */ gnyis dang rnam grangs sogs rnams kyi / / gang du byed tshig mi gnas pa / / de ni mdo ru bsdus pa ste /*.

24. *Kun 'jug*, 1701: */ byed pa'i dus ni de nyid la / / the tshom gcod byed 'dus byas yin /*.

Connections between Introduction to All Speech *and* Entrance into Speech

Verhagen has already pointed out some connections between *Introduction to All Speech* and Ché Khyidruk's *Eight Great Subjects*. A major shared component of these two works is the verse (v. 6) that exemplifies the sound a fish makes when eating fruit in the water.[25] In *Eight Great Subjects*, this verse appears in the third subject, the subject of derivation (*bsgyur ba'i gnas*). It is used to account for the derivation based on continuation (*brgyud de bsgyur ba*), in which, by repeating the sound *gu lu*, the sound *gu lu gu lu* is formed.[26] Now, in *Introduction to All Speech*, Subhāṣākīrti cites "previous masters" (see Author and Date section) who explained the sound *gu lu* as being consistent with the fish-eating-fruit event. While it is possible that he had Ché Khyidruk in mind, this cannot be proven. Further, the purposes of quoting this verse are different in each text. In contrast to Ché Khyidruk, who cites this verse to explain a kind of derivation, Subhāṣākīrti employs it to exemplify an unanalyzable sound. Nevertheless, we notice that the verses in both texts are not just similar but completely identical in Tibetan, if we ignore a few minor variants. If we suppose *Introduction to All Speech* was at least translated after the imperial period, then either the translator knew very well the fixed Tibetan equivalent of the verse or Subhāṣākīrti quoted this verse from *Eight Great Subjects* in Tibetan. Therefore I assume that the identical wording indicates a relatively strong connection between the two texts.

Another connection between these two works suggested by Verhagen is a similarity between types of compounds.[27] According to Subhāṣākīrti, there are altogether fourteen types of stem compound. Most of their names can also be found in the second subject of *Eight Great Subjects*, the subject on compounds (*bsdu ba'i gnas*). We also find most of these names in the first part of the section on phrase in *Entrance into Speech*, where Smṛtijñānakīrti lists ten types of compounds. The following table provides the names of the fourteen types of stem compound from *Introduction to All Speech* and their equivalents in both *Entrance into Speech* and *Eight Great Subjects*. As the exact meanings of some types of compounds have yet to be decided, the translations for them are only tentative:

25. See Verhagen 2001, 11.

26. *Gnas brgyad*, 409.

27. See Verhagen 2001, 9–10.

No.	Tentative Translation	**Stem Compounds in *Introduction to All Speech* (14 in total)**	**Compounds in *Entrance into Speech* (10 in total)**	**Compounds in *Eight Great Subjects* (8 in total)**
1.	phrase of parallels	*tshig gnyis*	*tshig sdud: gnyis* [2.1]	*mdor bsdu: gnyis* [2.1]
2.	phrase that contains numbers	*rnam grangs*	*tshig sdud: rnams grangs* [2.2]	*mdor bsdu: rnams grangs* [2.2]
3.	phrase that indicates another object	*tshig don gzhan*	*tshig sdud: gzhan* [2.4]	*mdor bsdu: gzhan* [2.3]
4.	phrase that contains case relations	*byed [pa'i] tshig*	*tshig sdud: byed pa'i tshig* [2.5]	*mdor bsdu: byed pa'i tshig* [2.4]
5.	phrase that contains attributes	*khyad par*	*khyad par* [3]	*mdor bsdu: khyad par* [2.5]
6.	*bahuvrīhi*	*'bru mang po*	*'bru mang po* [1]	*'bru mang po* [1]
7.	phrase of instance	*bye brag*	*tshig sdud: bye brag* [2.3]	*bye brag* [3]
8.	phrase of collection	*gzhi*	*gzhi* [5]	*gzhi* [5]
9.	phrase of a predicated collection	*gzhi gcig*	*gzhi gcig* [6]	*gzhi gcig* [6]
10.	*dvandva*	*zlas dbye*	*zlas dbye* [9]	*zlas dbye* [8]
11.	*dvigu*	*ba gnyis*	*de'i skyes bu: ba gnyis* [8.3]	*de'i skyes bu: ba gnyis* [7.2]
12.	*tatpuruṣa*	*de'i skyes bu*	*de'i skyes bu: byed pa'i tshig* [8.1]	*de'i skyes bu: byed pa'i tshig* [7.3]
13.	inconclusive phrase	*zad par mi 'gyur*	*zlas dbye: *gzhan sdud pa?* [9]	*absent
14.	*karmadhāraya*	*las 'dzin*	*de'i skyes bu: las 'dzin* [8.2]	*de'i skyes bu: las 'dzin* [7.1]

First of all, numbers 5, 6, 8, 9, and 10 in *Introduction to All Speech* are found under the same names in *Entrance into Speech* (as numbers 3, 1, 5, 6, and 9). Further, while in the uppermost level some names from the former text do not correspond to the names of compounds in the latter text, the same names can be found in the sublevels. For example, the phrase of instance (no. 7) is found in *Introduction to All Speech* as the third subtype of the second type of compound, the compounded phrase (*tshig sdud*). Finally, we need to examine the "inconclusive phrase" (no. 13), whose name is not found in either *Eight Great Subjects* or *Introduction to All Speech*. The *Commentary* explains this type as follows: "Any phrase that does not express its end is an inconclusive phrase."[28] We do not know the precise meaning of this definition, since no example is given. However, it might refer to a phrase that implies more content. If this is the case, it can potentially match a subtype in the *dvandva*, discussed in *Entrance into Speech* as the "compound that contains others" (*gzhan sdud pa*). Smṛtijñānakīrti explains: "The compound that contains others contains other meanings that are not stated in the phrase."[29]

It should be noted that such a list of different types of compounds is quite uncommon if we take all linguistic treatises translated into Tibetan into consideration. Some types mentioned here have no equivalents in classical Sanskrit grammar, either in terms of their names or their formations. Examples of such unique types include the phrase of collection (no. 8) and the phrase of a predicated collection (no. 9). Others, such as the *dvandva*, have fairly different meanings in *Introduction to All Speech* than the meanings we understand from classical Sanskrit grammar. Most of the types are conceptualized based not on morphology but on certain cognitive processes, as we have seen in Subhāṣākīrti's definitions of his formulas. But this issue will unquestionably require separate study. It is sufficient to say here that the similar ways that these three works conceive of types of compounds are unique.

The section on the inflection compound in *Introduction to All Speech* is also connected to the section on particles in *Entrance into Speech* in many ways, although their subjects are ostensibly unconnected. The main evidence for this claim is that particles are by and large the catalysts used to make inflections. There are several examples worth mentioning here. To begin with, when *Entrance into Speech* discusses the semi-particle *ste* in Tibetan, it claims "the particle *ste* means there is something more."[30] In comparison with this state-

28. *Kun 'jug 'grel pa*, 1710: *gang mtha' mi brjod* [Derge: *'dzed*; Peking: *brjod*] *pa'i tshig ni zad par mi 'gyur ba'o* /.

29. *Smra sgo 'grel pa*, 1876–77: *gzhan sdud pa ni tshig tu ma smos pa'i don dag sdud pa'o* /.

30. *Smra sgo*, 1835: / *ste ni lhag ma yod pa ste* /.

ment, the *Commentary* explains the introductory phrase (*lhag bcas*), the eighth inflection compound, as follows:

> A phrase with something more is the introductory phrase. "Something more" is the supplement to the meaning. That which has something more is the introductory phrase. So, for example, it is like statements such as "Devadatta cuts the tree (*de*) . . .," which introduces something else.[31]

The Tibetan original of this passage puts *de* (allomorph of *ste*) at the end of the example, thus indicating there is something more that comes after "Devadatta cuts the tree." Therefore this inflection compound presented in *Introduction to All Speech* seems to be just the other side of the coin of the semi-final particle *ste* that is presented in *Entrance into Speech*.

Similarly, the discussion of the use of "only" (*kho na*) in *Entrance into Speech* is mirrored by the eighteenth inflection compound in *Introduction to All Speech*, which refers to the exclusion of others (*gzhan gcod*). Smṛtijñānakīrti gives six examples to demonstrate the six different uses of the particle. Among these, the first two examples annotate the two uses of the particle that express the restriction for possessive verbs. They read:

> *a*. The Tathāgata possesses *only* the perfect quality.[32]
> *b*. *Only* the Tathāgata possesses many perfect qualities.[33]

In comparison, among the three examples provided by Subhāṣākīrti for the exclusion of others, the first two read:

> *a'*. The blue lotus (*utpala*) has *only* the blue color.[34]
> *b'*. *Only* the blue lotus has the blue color.[35]

31. *Kun 'jug 'grel pa*, 1715: *tshig lhag ma can ni lhag bcas te / lhag ma ni don gyi kha skong ba'o / de gang la yod pa de ni lhag ma dang bcas pa ste / 'di ltar dper na lhas byin shing gcod de zhes bya ba gzhan 'dren pa lta bu dag go /.*

32. *Smra sgo 'grel pa*, 1884: *de bzhin gshegs pa ni yongs su rdzogs pa'i yon tan kho na dang ldan no.*

33. *Smra sgo 'grel pa*, 1884: *de bzhin gshegs pa kho no la yongs su rdzogs pa'i yon tan mang ngo.*

34. *Kun 'jug 'grel pa*, 1717: *sngon po kho na utpala yod.*

35. *Kun 'jug 'grel pa*, 1717: *sngon po utpala kho na la yod.*

Introduction to All Speech explains that the exclusion of others aims at expressing a restrictive relation between a substratum (*gzhi*) and its attribute (*khyad par*). However, examples *a* and *b* obviously showcase the same logic as *a'* and *b'*. The only difference is that while Smṛtijñānakīrti's discussion centers on the particle itself, Subhāṣākīrti puts more emphasis on the cognitive aspect.

A further crucial connection between these two texts can be found in the section on the demonstrative pronoun "this" (*'di*) in *Entrance into Speech*. Smṛtijñānakīrti points out that "this" can be applied to two kinds of entities, the entity in a short distance (*nye ba*) and the entity that is immediately perceivable (*mngon sum pa*). At the same time, "this" cannot be applied to the other two kinds of entities—the one in a long distance (*ring ba*) and the hidden one (*lkog tu gyur pa*).[36] The names of these four kinds of entities match exactly the names of four types (nos. 26–29) of inflection compound in *Introduction to All Speech*.

Apart from the three points elaborated here, several other instances from the section on particles in *Entrance into Speech* and the section on the inflection compound in *Introduction to All Speech* may help us establish connections between these works. But given the limited space, I will refrain from going further for now.

Let us now turn to the last trace of evidence that may potentially reveal intellectual ties between these works. We notice that a part of Subhāṣākīrti's name—"kīrti"— is identical with Smṛtijñānakīrti's. To be sure, "kīrti" is by no means an uncommon component in the religious names of Buddhists. But given the connections between the two texts that we have observed so far, it is not unreasonable to consider that both figures were from the same Vinaya lineage, in the same way that the disciples of Śākyaśrībhadra (1127–1225) concluded their names with "śrībhadra." A passage that can further support this hypothesis is the colophon of *Entrance into Speech*,[37] where Smṛtijñānakīrti specifies the persons from whom he received the teaching of linguistics and to whom he gave it. From this passage, we know his teacher's name is Norzang Drakpa (Tib. Nor bzang[s] grags pa, Skt. *Manibhadrakīrti) and his student's is Zhönnu Drakpa (Tib. Gzhon nu grags pa, Skt. *Kumārakīrti). As a result, it is not impossible that Subhāṣākīrti, whose treatise on linguistics—*Introduction to All Speech*—contains many elements seen in *Entrance into Speech*, was also from this lineage, though the chronology has yet to be decided.

36. See *Smra sgo 'grel pa*, 1879.

37. For a translation of the colophon, see Verhagen 2001, 44.

Conclusion

The general ideas presented in *Introduction to All Speech* suggest that its linguistic system disagrees with classical Sanskrit grammar in some major ways. Subhāṣākīrti analyzes the structure of the language mainly from a cognitive perspective. I established certain connections between *Introduction to All Speech* and Smṛtijñānakīrti's *Entrance into Speech*. First, most of the names of stem compounds in *Introduction to All Speech* are also found in *Entrance into Speech*. Further, many of the inflection compounds discussed in the former work are essentially similar to the concepts presented in the section on particles in the latter work. Lastly, Subhāṣākīrti was likely a figure in the linguistic tradition of Smṛtijñānakīrti, because "kīrti," as a component of a religious name, seems to associate with that linguistic tradition.

It is significant that we consider *Introduction to All Speech* and *Entrance into Speech*—and likely *Eight Great Subjects* as well—as belonging to the same linguistic tradition. For one, it may allow us to grasp more comprehensively the Tibetan assimilation of Indic linguistics. Sakya Paṇḍita Künga Gyeltsen (Sa skya paṇḍita Kun dga' rgyal mtshan, 1182–1251), in his *Introduction to Language* (*Sgra la 'jug pa*), articulated the systems of both *Eight Great Subjects* and *Entrance into Speech*,[38] though he did not mention Subhāṣākīrti's work. Nevertheless, *Introduction to All Speech* was cited by later figures such as Taktsang Lotsāwa Sherap Rinchen (Stag tsang lo tsā ba Shes rab rin chen, 1405–77).[39] In the future, having clarified the roles these canonical works played in subsequent Tibetan authors' compositions, we may attain an understanding of how this linguistic tradition shaped certain developments in Tibetan indigenous linguistics. In any event, it would be beneficial to hold these three texts as one group in subsequent studies.

38. See *Sgra 'jug*, 136, which discusses the system of *Eight Great Subjects*. The rest is based on the system of *Entrance into Speech*. See also Verhagen 2001, 64–65.

39. Verse 16bc of the text is quoted in Taktsang Lotsāwa's 1451 commentary on the *Kātantra* (*Sgron me*, 50).

Appendix

The Thirty-Five Inflection Compounds Listed by Subhāṣākīrti

No.	Tibetan	Tentative Translation	No.	Tibetan	Tentative Translation
1.	*las*	patient	19.	*gnyis pa*	pairs
2.	*byed pa*	agent	20.	*gcig gi tshig*	singular
3.	*ched*	purpose	21.	*gnyis kyi tshig*	duel
4.	*'byung khungs*	origin	22.	*mang po'i tshig*	plural
5.	*'brel pa*	possessive relation	23.	*rtags can*	gender inflection
6.	*gzhi*	location	24.	*mtha' yi tshig*	ending enumeration
7.	*zla bsdu*	pair-composition	25.	*dbus kyi tshig*	middle enumeration
8.	*lhag bcas*	introductory phrase	26.	*nye ba*	short distance
9.	*dgag*	negation	27.	*ring ba*	long distance
10.	*sgrub*	affirmation	28.	*mngon du ba*	directly perceivable
11.	*brnan*	emphasis	29.	*lkog*	hidden
12.	*bdag po*	synonym	30.	*shin tu lkog*	extremely hidden
13.	*rgyan*	ornament	31.	*'dri ba'i tshig*	phrase of question
14.	*kha skong*	supplement	32.	*lan gyi tshig*	phrase of answer
15.	*dus la 'jug*	tense conjugation	33.	*bdag gi tshig*	subject phrase
16.	*'byed*	separation	34.	*gzhan gyi tshig*	non-subject phrase
17.	*sdud*	condensation	35.	*sbyor ba'i tshig*	phrases of formula
18.	*gzhan gcod*	exclusion of others			

References

Primary Sources

Bstan bcos dkar chag	Wüpa Losel Tsöpé Senggé (Dbus pa Blo gsal Rtsod pa'i seng ge). *Bstan bcos gyi dkar chag*. CPN 002376(1). BDRC W2CZ7507.
Bstan 'gyur	Krung go'i bod kyi shes rig zhib 'jug lte gnas kyi bka' bstan dpe sdur khang, ed. *Bstan 'gyur dpe bsdur ma*. 120 vols. Beijing: Krung go'i bod rig pa'i dpe skrun khang, 1994–2008.
Gnas brgyad	Ché Khyidruk (Lce Khyi 'brug). *Gnas brgyad chen po'i rtsa ba*. In *Bstan 'gyur*, vol. 115, 407–15.
Kun 'jug	Subhāṣākīrti. *Smra ba kun la 'jug pa*. In *Bstan 'gyur*, vol. 109, 1700–1703.
Kun 'jug 'grel pa	Subhāṣākīrti. *Smra ba kun la 'jug pa*. In *Bstan 'gyur*, vol. 109, 1704–27.
Sgra 'jug	Sakya Paṇḍita Künga Gyeltsen (Sa skya paṇḍita Kun dga' rgyal mtshan). *Sgra la 'jug pa*. In *Sa skya bka' 'bum dpe bsdur ma las sa paṇ kun dga' rgyal mtshan gyi gsung 'bum*, vol. 4, edited by Dpal brtsegs bod yig dpe rnying zhib 'jug khang, 135–52. Beijing: Krung go'i bod rig pa'i dpe skrun khang, 2007.
Sgron me	Taktsang Lotsāwa Shérap Rinchen (Stag tsang lo tsā ba Shes rab rin chen). *Lung ston pa ka lā pa'i rnam par bshad pa legs sbyar snang ba'i sgron me*. In *Stag tshang lo tsā ba shes rab rin chen gyi gsung 'bum*, vol. 7, edited by Dpal brtsegs bod yig dpe rnying zhib 'jug khang, 1–394. Beijing: Krung go'i bod rig pa'i dpe skrun khang, 2007.
Smra sgo	Smṛtijñānakīrti (Dran pa'i ye shes grag pa). *Smra ba'i sgo mtshon cha lta bu*. In *Bstan 'gyur*, vol. 109, 1827–40.
Smra sgo 'grel pa	Smṛtijñānakīrti. *Smra ba'i sgo mtshon cha lta bu zhes bya ba'i 'grel pa*. In *Bstan 'gyur*, vol. 109, 1841–1903.

Secondary Sources

Almogi, Orna. 2021. "The Old sNar thang Tibetan Buddhist Canon Revisited, with Special Reference to dBus pa blo gsal's *bsTan 'gyur* Catalogue." *Revue d'Etudes Tibétaines*, no. 58: 165–207.

Inaba, Shōju 稲葉正就. 1963. "Sumuriti cho *Gengo no mon* ni toka reteiru Chibetto bunpōgaku" スムリティ著「言語の門」に説かれているチベット文法学 [Tibetan Grammar Exposited in Smṛti's *Entrance into Speech*]. In *Iwai Hakushi koki kinen tenseki ronshū* 岩井博士古稀紀念典籍論集, edited by Iwai Hakushi Koki Kinen Jigyōkai, 68–79. Tokyo: Iwai Hakushi Koki Kinen Jigyōkai.

van der Kuijp, Leonard W. J. 2009. "On the Vicissitudes of Subhūticandra's *Kāmadhenu*

Commentary on the *Amarakoṣa* in Tibet." *Journal of the International Association of Tibetan Studies*, no. 5: 1–105.

Verhagen, Pieter. 1994. *A History of Sanskrit Grammatical Literature in Tibet*, vol. 1, *Transmission of the Canonical Literature*. Leiden: Brill.

———. 2001. *A History of Sanskrit Grammatical Literature in Tibet*, vol. 2, *Assimilation into Indigenous Scholarship*. Leiden: Brill.

Some Interesting Passages from the *Noble Noose of Methods, the Lotus Garland Synopsis* and Its *Commentary*

Robert Mayer and Cathy Cantwell[1]

THE *Noble Noose of Methods, the Lotus Garland Synopsis* (*'Phags pa thabs kyi zhags pa pad ma 'phreng gi don bsdus pa*, henceforth the *Noose of Methods*) is a Nyingma Mahāyoga tantra, cited by such scholars as Longchenpa. Versions are preserved in all known editions of the *Ancient Tantra Collection* (*Rnying ma'i rgyud 'bum*) and in those Kangyur editions that contain a special Ancient Tantra (*Rnying rgyud*) section. The *Noose of Methods* has additionally surfaced in some local Kangyur editions, such as Hemis, Batang, and Orgyen Ling.

The Tibetan title of its commentary is simply a *Commentary on the Noble Noose of Methods, the Lotus Garland Synopsis* (*'Phags pa thabs kyi zhags pa padma 'phreng gi don bsdus pa'i 'grel pa*, henceforth the *Noose of Methods Commentary*). A version of the *Noose of Methods Commentary* is shared by the Golden, Peking, and Nartang Tengyurs. Unfortunately, this, the sole traditionally transmitted version of the *Noose of Methods Commentary*, has lost around 30 percent of its text, among other misfortunes. No other transmitted versions of the *Noose of Methods Commentary* appear to have survived, not even in Nyingma compilations.

Fortunately, however, a probably late-tenth-century manuscript in eighty-five folios preserving a *Noose of Methods Commentary* with the *Noose of Methods* embedded as highlighted lemmata was among the Dunhuang treasures brought to London in the early twentieth century, now held at the British Library (IOL Tib J 321). Although the Dunhuang version of the *Noose of Methods Commentary* is often even more corrupted through transmissional error than the Tengyur versions and incomplete, its lost portions are mainly different from

1. Much gratitude for sage advice from Peter Harvey, John Nemec, Francesco Sferra, Jonathan Silk, Péter-Dániel Szántó, Dorji Wangchuk, and Ben Williams.

those of the Tengyurs', so most (probably not all) of *Noose of Methods Commentary* can be recovered, albeit with transmissional corruptions.[2]

Published research on the *Noose of Methods* and the *Noose of Methods Commentary* remains limited. Responding to the unusual and very large discrepancies between the *Noose of Methods*'s surviving versions, we published a critical edition, not least to establish the boundaries of the original scripture, for confusions between which passages were commentarial and which were scriptural had produced conflicting conclusions over the centuries.[3] Textual analysis also dashed our naive hopes that the possibly late-tenth-to-early-eleventh-century Dunhuang manuscript's lemmata of the *Noose of Methods* would prove significantly closer to a plausibly late-eighth-to-ninth-century archetype: alas, this Dunhuang witness of the *Noose of Methods* not only has serious lacunae but also has complex transmissional corruptions, sharing major indicative errors with the equally problematic mainstream Kangyur and Ancient Tantra Collection versions. Indeed, it is only the regionally peripheral (and sometimes very ancient) local Kangyurs, such as Hemis from West Tibet, Batang from East Tibet, and above all the unique hybrid Orgyen Ling manuscript from Tawang, along with some Ancient Tantra Collection editions from the Nepalese borderlands, that preserve better versions, closer to the archetype. In the same work, we also reunited the surviving fragments of the *Noose of Methods Commentary* to present a nearly complete (albeit hybrid) diplomatic edition. However, we produced no English translation (which will follow, for the 84000 nonprofit translation initiative).

Other academic interest has focused on one mention of Padmasambhava in a passage of the *Noose of Methods Commentary* and three in the marginalia to the Dunhuang text, but unfortunately mainly analyzed in isolation, divorced from their textual embeddedness in the *Noose of Methods* and its *Commentary*. Mayer has also posted on academia.edu the unpublished draft of an explor-

2. Cantwell and Mayer 2012, 30–31.

3. Cantwell and Mayer 2012. The versions of the *Noose of Methods* shared by all mainstream Kangyurs (Peking, Derge, etc.), and the Derge *Ancient Tantra Collection*, have major lacunae and also gain substantial (but differing in different editions) accretions from the commentary. Similar problems also afflict the forty-six-volume Bhutanese *Ancient Tantra Collection* recension (Tsamdrak, etc). For those unused to navigating critical editions, only Orgyen Ling is close to the original *Noose of Methods* (very much closer than the corrupted Dunhuang manuscript!); next closest are Batang and Hemis, while some Nepal borderlands Ancient Tantra Collections (such as Tingkyé) at least preserve the earlier chapter structure and avoid adding commentarial text. Sadly, in this unusual case, if one requires any degree of fidelity to the historically original texts, it is viable to rely on neither the usual popular editions, such as Derge, Peking, Tsamdrak, nor the Dunhuang manuscript.

atory public lecture mentioning the winged heruka of the *Noose of Methods*, one of the earliest known references to the classic Nyingma winged heruka.

The *Noose of Methods* and its *Commentary* are remarkable texts, and it is regrettable that their contents remain so little studied. Preliminary to our translation of the *Noose of Methods* for the 84000 project, we present here a few interesting passages, an offering to Leonard van der Kuijp, without whose generous support our work on Nyingma tantrism would never have flourished.

The first passage is an etymology of the words *tshogs kyi dkyil 'khor* in chapter 6 of the *Noose of Methods Commentary*, which seems to have been authored in the Tibetan language rather than translated from Sanskrit. We read the passage as follows:

> The term "assembly" (*tshogs*): since everything is gathered together and assembled through the consecration of oneself, it is called "assembly." The reason it is called "center" (*dkyil*): since everything is emanated from one's own mind, and moreover, since all the primordial wisdom[s] are emanated from the pure *dharmatā*, and since, with pure awareness, dharmas and mind become the same, [everything is] said to be "centered" in the mind. The reason it is called "circle" (*'khor*): since primordial wisdom [is] within everything, without center or circumference, actively pervading and perfecting, it is called "circle." In this way, it is called the "assembled center [and] circle" (*tshogs kyi dkyil 'khor*).[4]

The analysis of *dkyil 'khor* seems telling. It glosses the Tibetan term for *maṇḍala*, *dkyil 'khor*, according to its two halves, giving first an explanation of "center" (*dkyil*), followed by an elaboration on "circle" (*'khor*). Yet it is unlikely that the Sanskrit word *maṇḍala* could have been similarly separated into two parts with exactly these implications, and a Sanskrit etymology should enlarge on the syllables of the original word, but this is not the case here. Were the text written in Sanskrit, we would expect the more usual explanation: "it takes [*lā*], i.e., grasps the essence [*maṇḍa*], thus it is a *maṇḍala*" (*maṇḍaṃ lāti gṛhṇātīti*

4. Cantwell and Mayer 2012, 253–54: *tshogs zhes bya ba ni bdag gyi byin rlabs las thams cad 'dus shing tshogs pa'i phyir tshogs shes bya/ dkyil zhes bya ba gang zhe na /thams cad bdag gi sems las sprul pa'i phyir / ye shes thaṃs cad kyang chos nyid dag pa las sprul pas/ chos dang sems rig pas mnyaṃ par gyur pa la dkyil te sems la bya 'o / 'khor gang zhe na / thams cad du dbung mtha' myed par ye shes kyis khyab cing rdzogs par spyod pa ni 'khor zhes bya / / de lta bu ni tshogs kyi dkyil 'khor zhes bya 'o /.*

maṇḍalam).[5] It seems, then, that this section of the *Noose of Methods Commentary* on chapter 6 was most likely composed in Tibetan rather than translated from Sanskrit. Might the whole commentary have been composed in Tibetan?

A second interesting but difficult passage occurs in the *Noose of Methods Commentary*'s discussion of the final chapter of the *Noose of Methods*, which shows Buddha Vairocana concluding his teachings by reemanating and reabsorbing his enlightened retinue, from whom he has never been separate. Vajrakumāra deities (another name for Vajrakīlaya deities), often associated with Padmasambhava but never appearing in the *Noose of Methods* until now, are described as rejoicing at this.

The *Noose of Methods Commentary* comments by describing the utterances of any person (*skyes bu gang gis*) who has achieved highest awareness as "tantra" (the word is given in Sanskrit) and by explaining that such a "protector great being turns the vajra wheel, in Akaniṣṭha, by extension of his tongue faculty." Such a form of words is normally only applied to the transcendent Buddha teaching such tantras, but the term used here, "person" (*skyes bu* = Skt. *puruṣa*), more generally implies an embodied noble person, often human, although it can also indicate a buddha. The next sentence refers to the sublime result of relying on the teachings of the flawless tantra, but the echo of its wording "flawless" (*ma nor*) in the marginal note might suggest a link to Padmasambhava. Next, the lotus king of great *siddhi*, Padmasambhava, is praised. Is he being connected in some way with the utterance of the tantra? Lexically speaking, this seems possible but uncertain. It might also partly depend on what weight one gives to a prior and ambiguous marginal note mentioning "noncontrivance," preserved only in the corrupted Dunhuang manuscript (without proof it was included in the original commentary), and on how one chooses to translate it. Where we remain undecided about meanings, we present alternative translations:

> Since they are emanated from evenness,
> {note beneath the line} [*the maṇḍalas described in the related root-*

5. Note that Tibetan commentarial traditions do sometimes break the Sanskrit word *maṇḍala* into two for the purpose of glossing its meaning, but the connotations would not correspond neatly to the Tibetan equivalent term. For instance, Mi pham glosses *maṇḍal* as "essence" or "vital juice," and *la* as taking or holding, so that *maṇḍala* would mean "to grasp the essence of enlightened qualities." He adds that if the word is taken as a whole, it can also mean completely circular or entirely surrounded, and hence is translated as *dkyil 'khor* (Mi pham rgya mtsho 1984–93, 136: *maṇḍal ni snying po'am/ bcud dang la ni len cing 'dzin pa ste snying po'i yon tan 'dzin pa'i gzhir gyur pa'am/ rnam pa gcig tu sgra 'brel mar thad kar bsgyur na kun nas zlum zhing yongs su bskor ba'i don du 'jug pas dkyil 'khor zhes bya ste/*).

text verses above] are taught by Padmasambhava without contrivance, OR, *Padmasambhava explains [the above maṇḍalas] as being uncontrived*

the significance of their arising [is that when] such a pure awareness [is produced] by any noble person (*skyes bu*) whatsoever, whatever sound is articulated by his speech, all without exception is called "tantra."

In the supreme incomparable place of Akaniṣṭha, the protector great being, turning the vajra wheel, speaks by "extending his tongue faculty."

By relying on that, because what will be realized is the accomplishment of the yoga of the protector's secrets of body, speech, and mind, [such utterances of tantra] can only be flawless (*ma nor*), it is said.

I prostrate to he who has attained the supreme *siddhi* of great wonder,

{note beneath the line} *the master Śāntigarbha, after examination finding [these utterances of tantra] flawless (ma nor), praises Sambhava*

the lotus king (*padma rgyal po*), who overpowers the world;[6] he who unravels from the expanse[7] the Tathāgata's great secret pith instructions (*upadeśa*).[8]

6. Btsan lha 1997, s.v. *ngam pa*. Alternatively, the Tengyurs' reading of "who is not worldly" (*'jig rten ma 'gyur*) might be more correct if Padmasambhava is intended as some kind of Buddhist equivalent to an avatāraka (see below). The Dunhuang manuscript's *ngam* may well be a scribal error, given the persistent similarity between the *tsheg* and the letter *nga* in these manuscripts.

7. We take *klung* here to indicate *klong*, for three reasons: IOL Tib J 321 repeatedly reads *klung* for *klong*; Peking, Golden, and Nartang Tengyurs descend from a separate stemmatic line, but read *klong*; ditto Nyangrel in his rendering of this praise (Cantwell and Mayer 2012, 93–94).

8. Transcription from IOL Tib J 321: $ = mgo yig; *** = blank spaces left by copyist; : = *visarga*

/mnyam las' 'phros te

{note beneath the line} *pad ma sam ba bhas rang gz[or?] byas pa ma yin bar ston*

[84r.1] *$/ /byung ba'-i don/ /skyes bu gang gis rig pa de / /ngag gis ci skad brjod pa'i sgra / /thams cad ma lus tan tra zhes /*

[2] *'og myin bla myed gnas mchog du / /mgon po bdag nyid chen po yis / /rdo rje 'khor lo bskor pa na / /ljags kyi dbang po*

[3] *bkram las gsungs / /de las brte* *** *n te mgon po 'i/ /sku gsung thugs* *** *kyi gsang ba rnams / /rnal 'byor*

"Extending his tongue faculty" (*ljags kyi dbang po bkram*) is classic Buddhist terminology to signal the Buddha preaching, or about to preach, Dharma. A supernormally large tongue (*prabhūtajihvaḥ*) is the twenty-seventh of the Buddha's thirty-two bodily marks (*lakṣaṇas*) of a great being (*mahāpuruṣa*), which physically establish and demonstrate his authority. Hence many scriptures describe the Buddha's preaching, or preparing to preach, in terms of covering his entire face, his entire assembly, as far as the Brahma worlds, or even the 1000^3-fold (i.e., billionfold) great chiliocosm with his tongue—for such a tongue cannot lie.[9] The exact form of Tibetan words found here occurs in numerous canonical sūtras and tantras, such as the *Perfection of Wisdom in 100,000 Lines* (*Mahāprajñāpāramitā*, Toh 8),[10] the *Jewel Cloud* (*Ratnamegha*, Toh 231), the *Questions of Ratnajālin* (*Ratnajāliparipṛcchā*, Toh 163), the *Shorter Tantra for the Practice of the King of Vajra Wrath* (*Vajrakrodharājakal palaghutantra*, Toh 632), and in the Ancient Tantras too, such as the *Blazing Lamp* (*Sgron ma 'bar ba'i rgyud*, *Mtshams brag*, vol. *na*, 467–91). The occurrence of this term is thus a powerful indicator that the preaching of Buddha's word (*buddhavacana* = Tib. *bka'*) is being signaled here.

The first interlinear note is ambiguous. If applying to Padmasambhava's

---

[4] *sgrub pas rtogs bya 'i phyir* / **** /*ma nor tsam du bshad pa yin* // ***** //

[5] *$/ /dngos grub mchog brnyes ya mtshan chen po 'i/ / 'jig rten ngam gyur pad ma rgyal po yis / /de bzhin gshegs pa'i man ngag*

{note beneath the line} *slobs dpon shan ting gar bas brtags nas ma nor nas/ sam ba bha la stod pa 'o/*

[6] *gsang chen rnams/* *** /*klung nas bkrol mdzad de la phyag 'tshal lo* // *****//

[84v.1] $/ // ***** // ***** // *****//

[3] // ***** // ***** // *****// ** //

[4] *$/ 'phags pa thabs kyis* ****** *zhags pa pad ma 'phreng las rtog pa'-i rgyal* ***** *po 'i don bsdus pa'i 'grel pa/*

[5] *rdzogs s.ho* // *** : *** //

{note beneath the line} **** **** *kam cu pa bo'u ko gis bris*// ***** // ***** //

The Dunhuang text—like those *Noose of Methods* versions with which it shares indicative errors—omits any chapter ending; however, the three Tengyur editions, descended from a separate stemmatic line, do include a chapter ending, after the praise and before the text ending: *le'u ste/ bzhi bcu rtsa gnyis pa'o*//.

9. Skilling 2013, 21–47.

10. Derge Kangyur, *'bum*, *ka*, vol. 14, 5b: *de nas bcom ldan 'das kyis zhal gyi sgo nas/ ljags kyi dbang po bkram ste/ stong gsum gyi stong chen po'i 'jig rten gyi khams 'di thams cad ljags kyi dbang pos khyab par mdzad nas/*. See also the *Mahāprajñāpāramitāśāstra* (*Da zhidu lun* 大智度論): "Now, wishing to preach with his mouth the *Mahāprajñāpāramitā*, which is profound (*gambhīra*), difficult to fathom (*durvigāhya*), difficult to understand (*duravabodha*), and difficult to believe (*durgrāhya*), he puts out his broad tongue as his witness (*sākṣin*), for the words pronounced by such a tongue are necessarily true" (Lamotte 1944, 457).

action rather than to the maṇḍalas, it would attribute to his teaching the related Buddhist terminology "uncontrived" (*rang bzor byas pa ma yin pa*),[11] meaning not fancifully contrived by ego or intellect. This term can apply more generally to egoless activities, but here in the context of "emanating maṇḍalas out of evenness," "turning of the vajra wheel," and "utterances of tantra," it would more likely indicate a scripturally authoritative voice (*pramāṇapuruṣa* = Tib. *tshad ma'i skyes bu*);[12] thus we find both major types of scriptural authority, *pramāṇapuruṣa* as well as *mahāpuruṣa*.[13] The term "uncontrived" is typically applied to buddhas and to compilers (*saṃgītikāra*), senior sangha members like Ānanda, who recited accurately (or organized the collective recitation of) the utterances of the Buddha at the great historic Buddhist councils (*saṅgīti*) with the words "Thus have I heard on one occasion," thereby compiling the scriptural canons.[14] In much tantric Buddhism, an equivalent function (and the term *rang bzor byas pa ma yin pa*) is typically attributed to the celestial bodhisattva Vajrapāṇi (often also identified as Vajrasattva or Vajradhara), who without contrivance compiles and transmits to humankind those secret tantric scriptures he previously heard from the Buddha but which the Buddha had temporarily secreted in various heavens.

The mention of the "supreme incomparable place of Akaniṣṭha" as the location where the "protector great being turns the vajra wheel" is likewise interesting. Akaniṣṭha (Pāli: Akaniṭṭha) has had a variety of interpretations in the many schools of Buddhism. Mahāyāna cosmologies often associate Akaniṣṭha with the highest level of the fourth *dhyāna*, an exalted meditative state achieved by superior beings cognizant of emptiness, immediately prior to full buddhahood. However, in the Ancient School's Mahāyoga class of scriptures to which the *Noose of Methods* belongs (and in many Great Perfection tantras too), Akaniṣṭha predominantly features as the inconceivable nondual expanse of total realization, where the vajra wheel of tantric scriptures is turned.[15]

11. *Rang bzor byas pa* = Sanskrit *kāvyaṃ*.

12. van der Kuijp 1999; Silk 2002, 116–20; and Skilling 2013.

13. Skilling 2013.

14. See, inter alia, passages from Jñānagarbha's *Anantamukhanirhāradhāraṇī-ṭīkā* cited in Silk 2002, 116: "What is to be established refers to . . . the compiler (**saṃgītikāra*) making himself an authority (**pramāṇīkṛta*?), so that his words may produce in others certainty with respect to this discourse on the Teaching, because when certainty is produced, people will obtain what they seek by firm practice, but when it is not they will not obtain it."

15. This is frequently described in their *nidānas*: see, for example, *Guhyagarbhatantra* (*Mtshams brag*, vol. 20 [*wa*], 153); *Phur bu myang 'das* (*Mtshams brag*, vol. 36 [*chi*], 229); *Phur pa bcu gnyis* (*Mtshams brag*, 19 [*dza*], 786); *Dbang rgyas rta mchog rol pa* (*Mtshams

Subsequent Ancient School exegetes continue to embrace this theme: Dudjom Rinpoche's *History of Nyingma*, for example, devotes a chapter to the "Turning of the Secret Mantra Wheel," which describes Great Akaniṣṭha as the realm of nondual realized mind, the buddhafield in which Samantabhadra manifests nondually as Vajradhara or Vajrasattva so he can turn the wheel of the nondual tantras.[16]

Perhaps it is no coincidence that another Dunhuang text, IOL Tib J 644, specifies Padmasambhava as the exemplar of the Mahāmudrā highest level of Mahāyoga awareness holder (*vidyādhara*), called a "Second Buddha" and equal to Vajarapāṇi, while IOL Tib J 464/1 explains that such a realized awareness holder is indistinguishable from Vajrasattva?[17] Might Padmasambhava then somehow be equated with the Vajrasattva interlocutor to whom Vairocana utters the *Noose of Methods*? For, prima facie, such appellations seem not inconsistent with the idea of a humanly embodied siddha, Padmasambhava, abiding as a realized Vajrasattva in the realm of Akaniṣṭha, where tantras resound.

The final verse finds a close parallel in the *Zangs gling ma* (twelfth century) of Nyangrel (Myang ral): "I prostrate to and praise the Buddha Body, who has attained the supreme siddhi, of great wonder, the body of incomparable realization, the Lotus King, you who unravel from the expanse the Tathāgata's great secret pith instructions!"[18] This final verse of the *Noose of Methods Commentary* was very likely present in its archetype, since it has persisted in all of the extant witnesses of the *Noose of Methods Commentary* across both lines of transmission. In the Dunhuang manuscript, but not in the three Tengyur versions, this praise is set on a new line, perhaps intended to draw attention to it[19] or otherwise merely to fill empty page space, as is the wont of this scribe.[20]

---

brag, vol. 30 [*a*], 520); *Buddhasamāyoga* (*Mtshams brag*, vol. 18 [*tsha*], 4); *Sgyu 'phrul bzhi bcu pa* (*Mtshams brag*, vol. 20 [*wa*], 219); *Gsang snying bla ma chen po* (*Mtshams brag*, vol. 20 [*wa*], 338); *Rdo sems rol chen* (*Mtshams brag*, vol. 21 [*zha*], 350); and scores of others.

16. Dudjom 1991, 447–50.

17. Dalton 2020, 34–35. In his 2003 publication on IOL Tib J 644, Dalton failed to notice that it mentioned Padmasasmbhava's name. Mayer 2007 compounded the error by accepting Dalton's report without reexamining the Dunhuang manuscript—unwarranted laziness since IOL Tib J 644 is only three folios!

18. Cantwell and Mayer 2012, 93–94: *dngos grub mchog brnyes ya mtshan chen po'i sku/ rtogs ba bla med padma rgyal po'i sku/ de bzin gshegs pa'i man ngag gsang chen rnams/ klong nas grol mdzad khyed la phag 'tshal bstod/*. See chapter 4 of the *Zangs gling ma*, when King Indrabodhi and his retinue experience a breakthrough realization and Indrabodhi praises the Guru's miraculous appearance.

19. IOL Tib J 321, 84 recto.

20. See, for example, similar spaces on the proximate folios: IOL Tib J 321, 83 recto and 84 verso.

Note that a few of the praise's words also occur in the famous *Seven Line Prayer* to Padmasambhava, popularized by Nyangrel's thirteenth-century Dharma heir, Guru Chöwang (Gu ru chos dbang). The sublinear note, in which "flawless" (*ma nor*) seems to echo the *ma nor* just above, specifically attributes this praise to Śāntigarbha, possibly suggesting it might have existed independently, to be reused in the *Noose of Methods Commentary*, although the mention of Śāntigarbha could also have other reasons.

What are we to make of such text, which is ambiguous and might simply be referring to Vairocana uttering the tantra to his interlocutor Vajrasattva in chapter 1, but which is also juxtaposed with references to Padmasambhava's supreme siddhi, great wonder, and his unraveling the Tathāgata's pith instructions from the expanse? To current Tibetological knowledge, any utterance of tantric scripture by a human siddha seems unusual and extraordinary. Thus there have been fully understandable attempts, some more plausible than others, to interpret this passage in accord with conventional expectations (which we will consider below).

But a further interpretive strategy is also available, never so far attempted. We can try locating the *Noose of Methods* and the *Noose of Methods Commentary* within *all* of their proper historical contexts—not only Tibet before the Later Dissemination period (Phyi dar) and not only Indian tantrism in general, but also, more specifically, the contemporaneous tantric culture of Padmasambhava's homeland, Uḍḍiyāna, the modern-day Swat Valley, from where he and many of his tantric traditions are said to have originated. The former two are already much discussed. Here we focus on the third, hitherto never considered at all.

For current Tibetology, our text has two unfamiliar aspects: (1) the apparent attribution of scriptural revelation to an embodied human siddha, and (2) the attendant characterizations of that siddha as a divine being, realized from the very start. How do these look if set against the contemporaneous tantric cultures of Uḍḍiyāna?

(1) It is generally recognized by scholars of the field (Sanderson, Nemec, Williams, et al.) that the nondual Śaiva traditions of Kashmir of that period introduced important innovations. While the revelations of previous Śaiva traditions were typically attributed to fabled interactions at mythical locations of intangible beings, such as divine *ṛṣis* and *devas*, a defining feature of these traditions was their ostensible projection of scriptural revelation out of the distant domains of myth into the plain view of recordable history and tangible geography. Correspondingly, the intense sanctity required for the act of scriptural revelation had to be transposed from distant heavens onto humanly embodied siddhas of the

here and now whose inseparability from the supreme reality rendered them at one with the divine sources of scripture.

To give some examples: Within the Krama tradition, and close to Padmasambhava's time, a named individual, Jñānanetra (a.k.a. Śrīnātha, ca. 850–900), while staying in Uḍḍiyāna, became the first in human form to reveal the *Kramasadbhāva* and *Kālīkulapañcaśataka* scriptures.[21] Another Krama scripture, the *Yonigahvaratantra*, was likewise revealed at Uḍḍiyāna's Karavīra cremation ground by Jñānanetra.[22] Similar narratives apply to Matsyendranātha (perhaps eighth century?), Niṣkriyānanda (dates uncertain), and Vasugupta (ca. 825–75), who discovered teachings engraved on a rock.[23] Such revelations, ostensibly situated within recordable history and the geographical landscape, rather than veiled behind myth, became a hallmark of the nondual Śaiva traditions of Kashmir, central to their theology of the historically existent but supremely exalted human-embodied siddha as source of revelation. Extant Indic traditions apparently record at least one approximate Buddhist equivalent: the *Vajramahābhairavatantra* was first revealed at Uḍḍiyāna to the eighth-century Indian siddha Lalitavajra.[24]

(2) If the Śaiva term *siddha* might seem familiar to Vajrayāna scholars, then appearances are deceptive, because *siddha* had differing implications in different genres of medieval Sanskrit literature. In earlier literature, such as epics, and in the Purāṇas and Kāvya, siddhas were mythic semidivine beings who lived in the sky (*antarikṣa*), comparable to *gandharvas*, *yakṣas*, and the like.

In later centuries, for most Buddhists, siddhas were ordinary human beings who achieved realization through the practice of Vajrayāna. An elite few among them, like Tilopa, might receive Vajrayāna transmissions direct from Vajradhara, the Buddha's *dharmakāya*, but were nevertheless terrestrial human beings: crucially, even if Buddhist siddhas might become privileged recipients of tantric scriptures, they were not the divine originators of them.

But in Kashmir's nondual Śaiva traditions, the term *siddha* was more complex. Some siddhas were accomplished humans approximately resembling the Buddhist definition, but many others were very much more: divine or semidivine nonhumans, realized from the very start, who adopted the guise of human siddhas to descend from their lofty abodes to specific geographical

21. Williams 2017, 147; and Sanderson 2007, 264 (for the Sanskrit colophons, see note 97).

22. Sanderson 2007, 264; for the Sanskrit colophon, see note 96.

23. See Williams 2017, 134–43, 143–46, 182–90.

24. The Sanskrit colophon specifies where it was revealed (*Śrī-oḍḍiyānayoginīpīṭhāt* . . .), while numerous Tibetan sources specify to whom. See Wenta 2020, 15–22; also Siklos 1996, 113–14.

locations in the Kashmir region for the express purpose of disseminating nondual tantric scriptures.

The term that came to be applied to such primordially realized siddhas descended from on high in human guise to disseminate tantric scriptures was *avatāraka*, which Sanderson translates as "promulgator" and Williams as "agents of revelation." Another term used was *avatīrṇa*, implying Śiva descended to earth. As Sanderson puts it, "the term *avatārakaḥ* is used to denote a divine or semi-divine promulgator of scripture."[25] Some avatāraka siddhas could be hugely significant as sources of the entire tantric dispensation. Jayaratha, for example, described the avatāraka siddha Matsyendranātha as the sole source of revelation of the entire Kaula tradition,[26] while Abhinavagupta describes the three avatāraka siddhas Tryambaka, Āmardaka, and Śrīnātha, respectively, as founders of the nondual, dual, and nondual-cum-dual teachings of Śiva.[27] Were such avatārakas in any sense historical figures? Certainly traditional historians, such as Kalhaṇa (twelfth century), envisaged them as such, and most Western scholars too believe that in most or at least many cases, beneath the dense mythology real humans had indeed existed.[28]

Much more can and will be said about avatāraka siddhas. Here, we merely wish to signal in outline their remarkable parallels with representations of Padmasambhava in Tibetan sources, such as the *Bka' thang* literature. Padmasambhava's unique and unusual representation is too well known to require elaboration here: emanated by Buddha Amitābha, Padmasambhava is a divine

25. Sanderson 2007, 264.

26. Williams 2017, 135–36; Sanderson 2007, 264n95.

27. Williams 2017, 166. *Tantrāloka* 36.12–14: *teṣāṃ krameṇa tanmadhye bhraṣṭaṃ kālāntarād yadā | tadā śrīkaṇṭhanāthājñāvaśāt siddhā avātaran || tryambakāmardakābhikhyaśrīnāthā advaye dvaye | dvayādvaye ca nipuṇāḥ krameṇa śivaśāsane || ādyasya cānvayo jajñe dvitīyo duhitṛkramāt | sa cārdhatryambakābhikhyaḥ saṃtānaḥ supratiṣṭhitaḥ || ataś cārdhacatasro 'tra maṭhikāḥ saṃtatikramāt | śiṣyapraśiṣyair vistīrṇāḥ śataśākhaṃ vyavasthitaiḥ.*

28. Sanderson 2007, 427: "Kalhaṇa speaks of the reign of Avantivarman (*c.* 855/56–883) as one that was marked by the descent of Siddhas among men for the benefit of the world. That this development had a major impact on Kashmirian society is evident in the fact that Kalhaṇa records it. For he is generally silent about the recent history of religion in the valley beyond noting the religious affiliations of certain kings and the temples and other religious foundations that they established. Such figures as Bhaṭṭa Rāmakaṇṭha, Abhinavagupta, and Kṣemarāja, who loom so large in the learned literature of the Śaivas of Kashmir and beyond, receive not even a passing mention." Of all avatārakas, Matsyendranātha seems the most densely mythologized and hence historically least probable; yet even regarding him, see Dyczkowski 2009, vol. 2, 273–74: "Matsyendranātha, who may well have been a historical figure, represents a major watershed in the development of Kaulism."

being, enlightened from the start.[29] Manifesting miraculously in Uḍḍiyāna, Padmasambhava descends onto a specific geographic location in Kashmir. Known as the "Buddha of Vajrayāna," Padmasambhava is the founder of tantric Buddhism, the first to reveal the Vajrayāna teachings in their entirety, which the historical Buddha Śākyamuni had not been able to do.[30] The Padmasambhava of the *Bka' thang* literature is thus very close to the avatāraka of Kashmir and Uḍḍiyāna yet altogether different from the better-known, more human Buddhist siddha models, such as Abhayadatta's *Caturaśītisiddhapravṛtti*, which describes Tilopa, Virūpa, Saraha, and so on. Why then measure the Padmasambhava of the *Noose of Methods* and the *Noose of Methods Commentary* exclusively by the latter and not also by the former, which is surely also appropriate? If we do look at the *Noose of Methods* and the *Noose of Methods Commentary* in the light of the contemporaneous tantric culture of Uḍḍiyāna, a reasonable thing to do, it appears quite possible that Padmasambhava might be envisaged as some kind of Buddhist avatāraka. If so, he might indeed be intended as an actual utterer of the *Noose of Methods* scripture itself, one who "unravels from the expanse the Tathāgata's great secret pith instructions." Moreover, the other Dunhuang references to Padmasambhava could support this interpretation in their various ways: Padmasambhava as a figure in ritual narratives (PT 307, PT 44), the redactor of *Phur pa* tantras (PT 44), equal to Vajrapāṇi and called a "Second Buddha" (IOL Tib J 644), and so forth.[31]

Knowledge of Kashmiri tantric influences has been slow to penetrate Tibetology, yet without such contextual understanding one cannot do justice to the *Noose of Methods Commentary* passage. Without this necessary contextual understanding, the traditional Tibetan idea of Padmasambhava revealing tantric scripture, and which we think might be prefigured in the *Noose of Methods* and the *Noose of Methods Commentary*, appears so far-fetched that an entirely understandable initial response is to seek ways to explain it away.

Thus Dalton suggests the final verse of praise attributed to Śāntigarbha (see above) is really a colophon,[32] somehow implying Padmasambhava as the

29. Even in the rarer "womb-birth" narratives, Padmasambhava is a divine being, enlightened from the start.

30. For a fine traditional explanation of Padmasambhava, see Palden Sherab 1992.

31. Cantwell and Mayer 2016; Mayer 2020; and Dalton 2020.

32. Dalton 2020, 48.

human author of the *Noose of Methods Commentary*. Yet it contains no recognizably colophonic material, certainly none spelling out Padmasambhava as the author of the *Noose of Methods Commentary*, and in all surviving witnesses Tibetan scholars have situated it within the main body of the final chapter, not the colophon. The editors of the Peking, Golden, and Nartang Tengyurs place the passage unambiguously within the main body of the final chapter, preceding all end matter, before the chapter-ending chapter title and number, before the text-ending text title, and before the text-terminating phrase "The End" (*rdzogs so*). The Dunhuang text—like those *Noose of Methods* versions with which it shares indicative errors—omits any chapter ending at all but nevertheless places the praise within the main body of the commentary, before the end matters of text title, text termination, and scribal colophon.

Second, Dalton seeks to reframe the entirety of the *Noose of Methods* and the *Noose of Methods Commentary* by construing a quite separate marginal note found only in the Dunhuang version as depicting the Buddha himself as *saṃgītikāra* of the tantra and Padmasambhava as the human author of the commentary.[33] Yet the Buddha acting as a *saṃgītikāra* is widely thought to be unprecedented in Buddhist literature, whether Śrāvakayāna, Mahāyāna, or Vajrayāna: as the compiler of words they had previously heard from the Buddha, a *saṃgītikāra* must be someone other than the Buddha by definition, so it makes little sense to call the Buddha himself a *saṃgītikāra*.[34] Logically this could only happen if the Buddha were repeating teachings he had "heard" from another buddha, which is not described here. The marginal note Dalton invokes is attached to the title of the Dunhuang document, at its very start. It appears as follows:

> {title} *'phags pa thabs kyi zhags pa zhes bya ba pad ma 'phreng gi don bsdus pa'i 'grel pa'*
> {note beneath the line} *do rje sems dpa'-i dngos grub thob par bya ba*

33. Dalton 2020, 48: "A note explains that the tantra's reciter (Skt. *saṃgītikāra*; Tib. *sdud pa po*) was the buddha (typically held to be Vajrapāṇi in most tantric works), while the commentary's author was Padmasambhava."

34. The closest one gets to the buddha as a *saṃgītikāra* is in those Rdzogs chen tantras with an 'uncommon' *nidāna* that emphasizes the non-duality of teacher, teaching, place, audience, and time; yet even in them, one could not single out the buddha as a separate *saṃgītikāra*, as would be required here. Moreover, this is a Mahāyoga tantra, not a Rdzogs chen tantra. Thanks to Peter Harvey, Jonathan Silk, and Dorji Wangchuk, for their advice on this issue.

dang/[35] *bsam ba la bgegs myi 'jug cing bsam ba mthar phyin par bya ba'i don/ /'bu tas bsdus sam ba bhas byas*

{title} *The Noble Noose of Methods the Lotus Garland Synopsis: Its Commentary*
{note beneath the line} *The meaning is that Vajrasattva's siddhis should be accomplished, no obstacles to [one's] aspirations will arise, and [one's] wishes should be perfected. Synopsized by the Buddha, produced by Sambhava.*

If Dalton's interpretation of *'bu tas bsdus* to indicate the Buddha as a "compiler" (*sdud pa po* = Skt. *saṃgītikāra*) is unlikely, we suggest that it is referring to the Buddha as synopsizer. Buddhist tantrism often claims the scriptures taught to humans are shortened summaries of vaster versions preserved in the heavens and pure lands. And indeed, all extant witnesses of the *Noose of Methods* that represent its earliest recension specify that our forty-two-chapters version is merely synopsized (*bsdus pa'i*) from a vast sixteen-thousand-chapters version (*le'u khri drug stong ba las*).[36] Likewise, the *Noose of Methods Commentary*'s analysis of the title explains that *bsdus pa'i* means it is summarized from "the twelve collections of the scriptures and the eighteen tantras and so on."[37] Thus *'bu tas bsdus* means the Buddha synopsized these conveniently short instructions, while *sam ba bha byas* might possibly mean that Padmasambhava subsequently manifested the synopsis into our world by "unraveling from the expanse the Tathāgata's great secret pith instructions," as the verse of praise describes him. Interestingly, John Nemec sees this scenario as "a perfect analog" of what he describes in his work on the nondual Śaivism of Kashmir.[38] Moreover, if this is indeed a tantra synopsis first revealed to the human

35. The positioning of this reference to Vajrasattva, its grammar, and perhaps also its meaning might make it a bit unlikely to be referring to the homage instead of to the title, as some have suggested.

36. Cantwell and Mayer 2012, 228: "From out of the *Noble Noose of Methods* in 16,000 Chapters, the Synopsised Tantra King of Ritual Manuals (*kalparāja*) known as the *Lotus Garland*, is here completed" (*'phags pa thabs kyi zhags pa le'u khri drug stong ba las/ pad ma 'phreng zhes bya ba rtog pa'i rgyal po bsdus pa'i rgyud/ rdzogs s.ho//*). With these words, the Batang, Hemis, Orgyen Ling, Tingkyé, Rigdzin, and Kathmandu editions all specify the root text is only a tiny synopsis of a huge sixteen-thousand-chapter version. For evidence that the above represent the earliest recensions, see Cantwell and Mayer 2012, 43–67.

37. Cantwell and Mayer 2012, 231: *don bsdus pa ni gsung rab bcu gnyis dang tan tra sde bco brgyad la stsogs pa la bsdus pa 'o.*

38. Personal communication, October 9, 2021. See Nemec 2020.

world by Padmasambhava, it might not be coincidental that in every one of its numerous extant witnessess, be they in Kangyurs, in Tengyurs (as lemmata), in Ancient Tantra Collections, or from Dunhuang, it is the title of the *Noose of Methods* tantra itself that includes both of the elements *padma* and *don bsdus pa*: these elements are definitely not, as Dalton suggests, linked to the title of the commentary alone.[39]

Finally, it must be emphasized that research into the *Noose of Methods* and the *Noose of Methods Commentary*, the mutual relationships between the non-dual Śaivism of Kashmir, Padmasambhava, and the wider Nyingma traditions of Tibet have barely begun. Much of what is suggested above is inevitably tentative and exploratory. Much still needs to be examined: for example, the relative chronologies of Padmasambhava, the early Padmasambhava school, and Kashmir's avatārakas; the relation (if any) between several other distinctive structural, organizational, and doctrinal features possibly shared by Kashmiri Śaivism and Nyingma Buddhism;[40] and, of course, full translations of the *Noose of Methods* and the *Noose of Methods Commentary*, and the still unresolved questions of their authorship. Intriguingly, might Padmasambhava be somehow equated with the Vajrasattva, to whom Vairocana utters the *Noose of Methods*? We look forward to forthcoming developments in the field.

39. Dalton 2020, 47.

40. Structurally speaking, for example, the Kaubjikā and Traipura Śaiva-Śākta traditions had three orders of lineage holders: "stream of divine masters" (*divyaugha*), "stream of siddhas" (*siddhaugha*), and "stream of human masters" (*mānavaugha*; Ben Williams, personal communication, September 25, 2021). How might that compare (if at all) with the three orders of Nyingma lineage holders, "mind direct transmission of the buddhas" (*rgyal ba dgongs brgyud*), "sign transmission of the awareness-holders" (*rig 'dzin* [=*vidyādhara*] *brda brgyud*), and "oral transmission from humans" (*gang zag snyan brgyud*)? Organizationally, Somānanda's *Śivadṛṣṭi* and descriptions of Matsyendranātha detail lineages that were patrilineal, hereditary, and ostensibly descended from a divine first ancestor (Williams 2017, 173–75): how might that compare (if at all) with the Nyingma "bones lineage" (*gdung rgyud*)? Doctrinally, how might *Pratyabhijñā* compare (if at all) with the Great Perfection (Rdzogs chen)?

References

Btsan lha, Ngag dbang tshul khrims. 1997. *Brda dkrol gser gyi me long.* Beijing: Mi rigs dpe skrun khang.

Cantwell, Cathy, and Robert Mayer. 2012. *A Noble Noose of Methods: The Lotus Garland Synopsis: A Mahāyoga Tantra and Its Commentary*. Vienna: Austrian Academy of Sciences Press.

———. 2016. "Representations of Padmasambhava in Early Post-Imperial Tibet." In *Zentralasiatische Studien 45*. Andiast: International Institute for Tibetan and Buddhist Studies.

Dalton, Jacob. 2020. "The Early Development of the Padmasambhava Legend in Tibet: A Second Look at the Evidence from Dunhuang." In Samuel and Oliphant, *About Padmasambhava*, 29–64.

Doney, Lewis. 2014. *The Zangs gling ma: The First Padmasambhava Biography. Two Exemplars of the Earliest Attested Recension.*Andiast: International Institute for Tibetan and Buddhist Studies.

Dudjom Rinpoche. 1991. *The Nyingma School of Tibetan Buddhism.* Translated by Gyurme Dorje and Matthew Kapstein. Boston: Wisdom Publications.

Dyczkowski, Mark S. G. 2009. *Manthānabhairavatantram: Kumārikākhaṇḍaḥ: The Section Concerning the Virgin Goddess of the Tantra of the Churning Bhairava.* 14 vols. New Delhi: Indira Gandhi National Centre for the Arts.

van der Kuijp, Leonard W. J. 1999. "Remarks on the 'Person of Authority' in the dGa' ldan pa / Dge lugs pa School of Tibetan Buddhism." *Journal of the American Oriental Society* 119.4: 646–72.

Lamotte, Étienne. 1944. *Le traité de la grande vertu de sagesse de Nāgārjuna (Mahāprajñāpāramitāśāstra).* Bibliothèque du Muséon 18. Louvain-la-Neuve: Institut orietaliste de Louvain.

Mayer, Robert. 2007. "The Importance of the Underworlds: Asuras' Caves in Buddhism, and Some Other Themes in Early Buddhist Tantras Reminiscent of the Later Padmasambhava Legends." *Journal of the International Association of Tibetan Studies*, no. 3: 1–31.

———. 2020. "Geographical and Other Borders in the Symbolism of Padmasambhava." In Samuel and Oliphant, *About Padmasambhava*, 65–96.

Mi pham rgya mtsho. 1984–93. *Gsang 'grel phyogs bcu'i mun sel gyi spyi don 'od gsal snying po.* In *'Jam mgon 'ju mi pham rgya mtsho'i gsung 'bum rgyas pa sde dge dgon chen par ma*, vol. 19, 1–272. Paro: Lama Ngodrup and Sherab Drimey.

Mtshams brag: *The mtshams brag Manuscript of the Rñiṅ ma rgyud 'bum* (*rgyud 'bum/ mtshams brag dgon pa*), forty-six volumes. Thimphu: National Library, Royal Government of Bhutan, 1982. [TBRC W21521].

Nemec, John. 2020. "Innovation and Social Change in the Vale of Kashmir, circa 900–1250 C.E." In *Śaivism and the Tantric Traditions: Essays in Honour of Alexis G. J. S.*

Sanderson, edited by Dominic Goodall, Shaman Hatley, Harunaga Isaacson, and Srilata Raman, 283–320. Leiden: Brill.

Palden Sherab. 1992. "The Eight Manifestations of Guru Padmasambhava." Translated by Tsewang Dongyal Rinpoche. https://welcomingbuddhist.org/wp-content/uploads/2011/03/The-Eight-Manifestations-of-Padmasambhava.pdf.

Samuel, Geoffrey, and Jamyang Oliphant, eds. 2020. *About Padmasambhava*. Schongau: Garuda.

Sanderson, Alexis. 2007. "The Śaiva Exegesis of Kashmir." In *Mélanges tantrique à la mémoire d'Hélène Brunner*, edited by Dominic Goodall and André Padoux, 231–442. Pondicherry: Institut Français d'Indologie / École Française d'Extreme-Orient.

Siklos, Bulcsu. 1996. *The Vajrabhairava Tantras: Tibetan and Mongolian Versions, English Translation and Annotations*. Tring: Institute of Buddhist Studies.

Silk, Jonathan. 2002. "Possible Indian Sources for the Term *Tshad ma'i skyes bu* as *Pramāṇapuruṣa*." *Journal of Indian Philosophy* 30: 111–60.

Skilling, Peter. 2013. "The Tathāgata and the Long Tongue of Truth: The Authority of the Buddha in *Sūtra* and Narrative Literature." In *Scriptural Authority, Reason and Action*, edited by Vincent Eltschinger and Helmut Krasser, 1–47. Vienna: Austrian Academy of Sciences Press.

Wenta, Aleksandra. 2020. "The *Vajramahābhairavatantra*: Its Origins, Intertextuality, and Transmission." DPhil thesis, Oxford University.

Williams, Benjamin. 2017. "Abhinavagupta's Portrait of a Guru: Revelation and Religious Authority in Kashmir." PhD diss., Harvard University.

Notes on the Tibetan Lexeme *lo rgyus*: Other Than "History"

Sun Penghao

IN MODERN literary and spoken Tibetan, *lo rgyus* is the most common equivalent for English "history," in both its senses, the past and accounts of the past. The modern sense of the word "history" is so engrained in the word *lo rgyus* that one finds it in many Tibetan calques for historical concepts from Chinese and other modern languages, including the "direction of history" (*lo rgyus kyi kha phyogs*), "historic opportunity" (*lo rgyus kyi go skabs*), and "historic mission" (*lo rgyus kyi las 'gan* = Chi. *lishi shiming* 歷史使命).[1] Employing *lo rgyus* to refer to the past per se is by no means the way in which the term *lo rgyus* was used in Old or Classical Tibetan, however. Nor does this modern usage of *lo rgyus* suggest that the Classical Tibetan language lacks vocabulary for "the past" (*byung ba*), "happenings" (*'byung ba*), "changes" (*'gyur ba*), or other concepts about temporality. Rather, the modern usage of *lo rgyus* appears to be the result of a two-step process: (1) the choice of *lo rgyus* for a secular conception of "history" (as an account of past events),[2] and (2) the subsequent accretion of other connotations of "history" and its derivative forms, such as "historic" and "historical."

I thank Tewo Naljor Tsering for his help with several Tibetan passages, Nathan Hill for his suggestions on etymological analysis, and Janet Gyatso and William McGrath for their advice on many points in an earlier draft. I am also grateful to Du Xuchu for providing a comparative perspective, Kiril Solonin for his help with Tangut texts, Hou Haoran for sending me materials during the pandemic, and Mekata Shoko for her help in Japanese. As always, I thank Leonard van der Kuijp for reading with me my several drafts and for the wide-ranging *lo rgyus* he disclosed.

1. Ma'o Tse tung 1965, 28. These uses are not limited to the mainland and are also found in articles and public speeches in Dharamsala and other Tibetan communities.

2. A similar example of word choice influenced by "a kind of modernist reflexivity" in the autobiographical writings of Tseten Zhabdrung (Tshe tan/brtan zhabs drung, 1910–85) and Mugé Samten (Dmu dge bsam gtan, 1914–93) is using "telling what happened" (*byung ba brjod pa*) to title their writings; see Willock 2021, 75–85.

As for the first step, it is not difficult to see the advantage of *lo rgyus*: it not only is among the oldest terms for historical writing in Old and Classical Tibetan,[3] but also has fewer "feudal" or religious connotations than other candidates, such as *rgyal rabs*, *deb ther*, *chos 'byung*, or *rtogs brjod*. This "secular" character, as we will see, is related to *lo rgyus*'s other and more fundamental meanings besides "narrative." This short essay will focus on these other meanings and propose a larger semantic range for *lo rgyus* in Classical Tibetan, which will help us better understand *lo rgyus*'s secular flavor and the value of this term for modern Tibetan language.

Let us begin with a few words on the lexeme's two stems. Heinrich Jäschke, followed by Helmut Eimer, already takes the first syllable *lo* in *lo rgyus* to be "speech," instead of the more intuitive "year."[4] Nathan Hill proposes **law* 謠 ("sing, song") as *lo*'s cognate.[5] Joanna Bialek compares *lo rgyus* to *ngag rjes* ("oral story") and *ngag rgyun* ("oral tradition"), suggesting that the first and the second stems of these three terms respectively denote speech and a duration of time.[6] The second syllable, *rgyus*, may derive from the verb *rgyu* ("to move") with the *-s* suffix, which, according to Guillaume Jacques, produced many derivations in the pre-Old Tibetan period.[7] Below I provide some Classical Tibetan examples that complement these understandings and, in particular, draw our attention to some of the neglected semantic aspects of *lo rgyus*: in some contexts, *lo rgyus* has nothing to do with narratives and simply refers to "words" or "familiarity."

1. Lo rgyus *as Speech*

1.1. Synonyms for *lo rgyus*

Several Tibetan translations of the Sanskrit thesaurus *Amarakośa* and its commentary, the *Kāmadhenu*, offer us valuable insights into the lexical relationships of Classical Tibetan. Lexicography is characteristically a conscious process

3. See van der Kuijp 1996, 43. For several Tibetan texts from the "intermediate period" (roughly, 850–1000 CE) that call themselves *lo rgyus*, see Dotson 2016.

4. Jäschke 1881, 552. Eimer 1979, 101–3, further applies this reading of *lo* on the textual criticism of Atiśa's early two biographies and gives "Reihe von Aussagen, Bericht" for *lo rgyus*. Hahn 1999 connects *lo* with the verb *zlo* "to speak."

5. See Hill 2019, 21.

6. Bialek 2018, vol. 1, 479–81. Bialek also suggests a word family that includes *rgyud* "string," *brgyud* "to transmit," *brgyud* "lineage," *rgyus pa* "sinew or thread," *rgyu ma* "intestines," and *rgyun* "flow" (vol. 1, 398).

7. Jacques 2016, 209.

of evaluating vocabulary. In the case of the *Amarakośa* and the *Kāmadhenu*, these evaluations belong to their Tibetan translators—Sapaṇ (Sa skya Paṇḍita, 1182–1251), Yarlung Lotsawa (Yar lungs Grags pa rgyal mtshan, active in late thirteenth century), Nyetang Lotsawa (Snye thang Blo gros brtan pa, ?– ca. 1460), Zhalu Lotsāwa (Zha lu Chos skyong bzang po, 1441–1527), and Situ Paṇchen (Si tu Chos kyi 'byung gnas, 1699/1700–1774). Based on the survey made by Leonard van der Kuijp,[8] the following table provides different renditions of Tibetan terms for "speech" found in the *Amarakośa*, where *lo rgyus* was used twice by Zhalu Lotsāwa.

TABLE 1. TIBETAN TRANSLATIONS OF SYNONYMS FOR "SPEECH" (*ŚABDA*) IN THE *AMARAKOŚA*.[9]

Amarakośa	Sapaṇ (and Nyetang)	Yarlung-Zhalu	Zhalu	Situ
vyāhāraḥ	*rnam brjod*	*tha snyad*	*gtam*	*tha snyad*
uktiḥ	*gleng ba*	*gsung*	*lo rgyus* or *tshig*	*smra ba*
lapitam	*smra*	*smra ba*	*smra ba*	[none given]
bhāṣitam	*'chad*	*gtam*	*bshad pa*	[none given]
vacanam	*bshad*	*lo rgyus*	*brjod pa*	*brjod pa*
vacaḥ	*lab*	*tshig*	*tshig*	*gleng ba*

Here, neither the Sanskrit equivalents for *lo rgyus*—*vacanam* and *uktiḥ*—nor their alternative Tibetan counterparts from other translations, such as *gleng ba* or *bshad*, indicate any meanings other than "speech." It is also clear that Zhalu Lotsāwa, one of the greatest Sanskritists of his era, renders *lo rgyus* and *tshig* ("expression") as interchangeable, both reflecting Sanskrit *uktiḥ* ("expression").

8. For the Tibetan reception of the corpus around the *Amarakośa* and the *Kāmadhenu*, see van der Kuijp 2009, 15–55.

9. Lines 1.6.11cd in the *Amarakośa*; see Deokar 2018. Readers are referred to van der Kuijp 2009 for a full bibliography of the Tibetan texts. Deokar 2018 provides an edited edition of Situ Paṇchen's translation, which is consulted here. Nyetang simply commented that all these words were about "explaining the meanings" (*don ston pa*) and gives *don rnam brjod pa*, *don gleng ba*, *don smra ba*, *don 'chad pa*, *don bshad pa*, and *don lab pa* (Snye thang 2003, 123), so I put him together with Sapaṇ.

This synonymity is also attested in the Tibetan translation of Vairocanarakṣita's running commentary on the *Bodhicaryāvatāra*:

> *bag yod pa'i lo rgyus ni byang chub kyi sems bag yod pa bstan pa'i le'ur brjod do* //[10]
>
> The phrase *bag yod pa'i lo rgyus* (**apramāda-kathā*) refers to the chapter on the "Heedfulness of the Awakening Mind."

The commented phrase appears in the chapter on strength (*vīrya*, *brtson 'grus*), referring back to a previous chapter on heedfulness (*apramāda*, *bag yod*). The phrase *bag yod pa'i lo rgyus* corresponds to *bag yod gtam*, "Discourse on Heedfulness," in other extant versions of the *Bodhicaryāvatāra*,[11] and both supposedly render Sanskrit *apramāda-kathā* (translated as "Sermon sur l'attention" by La Vallée Poussin). This variant corroborates the *Amarakośa* in the sense that *lo rgyus* and *gtam* are synonyms, meaning "speech/discourse."

1.2. *Lo rgyus* and *lo*

As shown in table 1, a great translator of the fifteenth and sixteenth centuries interpreted *lo rgyus* as equivalent to "words" (*tshig* = Skt. *uktiḥ*). But why did he choose *lo rgyus* rather than just *lo*, "speech," as a synonym for the spoken word? One possible reason is the grammaticalization of *lo* as a quotation marker, which happened rather early on, probably even before the ninth century. This is true in the examples from the western Tibetan dialects given by Jäschke, as well as in Eimer's examples taken from the early biographical traditions of Atiśa.[12] Another example is found in the ninth-century Tibetan translation of the *Abhidharmakośabhāṣya*, which alternatively uses *grag* and *lo*, without any noticeable distinctions, to render "some say" (Skt. *kila* = Chi. *tashuo*/*chuanshuo* 他說/傳說).[13]

10. Vairocanarakṣita, *Bodhicaryāvatārapañjikā* (*Byang chub kyi spyod pa la 'jug pa'i dka' 'grel*; Toh 3875), in *Bstan 'gyur dpe bsdur ma*, vol. 62, 324. For the identity of the author, see Ishida 2004.

11. For a full bibliography on the *Bodhicaryāvatāra*, including La Vallée Poussin's translation, see Braarvig et al. 2015, https://www2.hf.uio.no/polyglotta/index.php?page=volume&vid=1120.

12. Jäschke 1881, 552; Eimer 1979, 100–104.

[illegible] again, Braarvig et al. 2015, https://www2.hf.uio.no/polyglotta/index. [illegible]me&vid=511, for collated texts of the *Abhidharmakośabhāṣya* in Sanskrit, [illegible].

The sense of "some say" is also indicated by another usage of *lo*. In a short speech attributed to Jikten Gönpo ('Jig rten mgon po, 1143–1217), we learned that he said:

> *spyir ngas chos thos pa dang bsam pa ni ma byas/ shes rab che lo/ chos mkhas lo/ gang dang yang mi 'dra lo bya ba la sogs pa'i lo 'dod pa'i bsam pa yang ma mchis/*
>
> Generally, I have not really learned or contemplated the Dharma. And I also do not entertain any desire for such reputations as "he has great intelligence," "he is learned in the Dharma," "he is one of a kind," and so forth.[14]

Jikten Gönpo humbly tells his audience that he cares little about reputation (*lo*). The *Great Tibetan-Chinese Dictionary* (*Bod rgya tshig mdzod chen mo*) explains *lo 'dod* as "to seek fame" (*skad grags don gnyer*), and the example thereof indicates that this kind of fame has a negative connotation of vanity.[15]

Although examples given by Eimer indicate that *lo* can be neutral and simply means "it is said,"[16] Jikten Gönpo implies the sense of hearsay. Also, the above example and Eimer's examples show that it was on its way to losing its notional status and becoming an auxiliary similar to *zhes* and the semi-auxiliary *skad*. Perhaps this negative connotation of vanity or hearsay, as well as its common auxiliary function, was on later translators' minds when they were looking for Tibetan equivalents for "speech." Instead of *lo*, they chose *lo rgyus*.

2. Lo rgyus *as Empirical Knowledge*

2.1. *Lo rgyus* as cognitive source

In the Lamdré literature that developed around the central text of the *Vajra Lines* (*Rdo rje tshig rkang*),[17] we find further connotations for *lo rgyus*. There, the term *lo rgyus kyi tshad ma* constitutes one of the four valid cognitive sources (*tshad ma bzhi*). According to an early commentary by Pakmodrupa Dorjé Gyelpo (Phag mo gru pa Rdo rje rgyal po, 1110–70), the four are (1) Buddha's words, (2) instructions from the experience of a teacher, (3) the experience of

14. 'Jig rten mgon po 2001, 3–4.

15. Zhang 1993, 2809: *lo 'dod can gyis gnas lugs kyi don mi rtogs/*. See also 2805, and compare the entries on *skad* (105) and *zer lo* (2470).

16. Eimer 1979, 103.

17. See Stearns 2001 and Davidson 2005 for more information on the cycle.

a student, and (4) orally transmitted practical guidance.[18] Dorjé Gyelpo twice explains the fourth valid cognitive source, *lo rgyus kyi tshad ma*,[19] with metaphors that shed light on his understanding of *lo rgyus*:

> *de'ang dper na rdo rje gdan du 'gro ba la lam rgyus can gcig gis 'di skad bya ba nas 'di skad bya ba'i bar du 'jigs pa yod pas skyel ma dgos/ 'di skad bya bar 'gro ba'i dus su mi dgos zhes bshad pa dang 'dra'o//*[20]
>
> Further, for example, were one to go to Vajrāsana, someone who is familiar with the road (*lam rgyus can*) would give information, saying, "From this to that place, you will need escorts because there will be danger," and "The road to such place does not require escorts." [The fourth cognition, *lo rgyus kyi tshad ma,*] is just like this.
>
> *slob dpon gyis lo rgyus kyis bstan pa ste dper na rgya gar du 'gro ba la lam 'di nas 'dir 'gro zhes bstan pa dang 'dra'o//*[21]
>
> A master who teaches [his students] with *lo rgyus* is like someone who teaches another person who is going to India by saying, "From here, to here, via such a route."

As these examples demonstrate, the fourth cognitive source of *lo rgyus* is immediately applicable guidance. It is like a step-by-step road guide, which is, as we shall see below, very similar to the meaning of the monosyllabic lexeme *rgyus*.

18. Phag mo gru pa 2008, 121: [1] *dang po ni lung 'di nyid dang kye'i rdo rje la sogs pa dang/ lung gzhan mtshan yang dag par brjod pa la sogs pa'o//* [2] *gnyis pa'i bla ma nyid kyis nyams myong skyes pa rnams slob ma la bstan pa'o//* [3] *gsum pa ni rang gis bsgoms pas nyams myong skyes pa'o//* [4] *bzhi pa ni rdo rje 'chang nas bla ma'i bar du brgyud pa ma chad pa dang po 'di lta bu zhig bsgom/ des nyams myong ma skyes na 'di lta bu zhig bsgom/ bogs ma byung na 'di lta bus bogs dbyung 'di lta bus bogs 'don zhes pa la sogs pa ston pa ste/ mdor na lam 'bras gzhung chung 'di nyid do//.*

19. This usage of *lo rgyus* has caused Davidson (2005, 495–96) to reasonably suspect that the word *lo rgyus* might have "a greater semantic field [than just lineal hagiographies] in the tenth and eleventh century, which was excluded as the term became completely identified with the hagiographical genre."

20. Phag mo gru pa 2008, 121–22.

21. Phag mo gru pa 2008, 143.

2.2. *Lo rgyus* and *rgyus*

The practical knowledge of *lo rgyus* exemplified by the *Vajra Lines* literature can actually be expressed by *rgyus* alone in many contexts. As a noun, *rgyus* is used like the English terms "information" or "familiarity," which one can possess (*rgyus yod*), not possess (*rgyus med*), obtain (*rgyus lon*), and show to others (*rgyus ston*). It can also make up compounds, such as "internal information" (*nang rgyus*) and "familiarity with the road" (*lam rgyus*). Like the road-knowledge simile for explaining the cognitive source of *lo rgyus*, the connection between learning and road metaphor finds an echo in the ethos of the medical education of "familiarity" (*goms*) in the *Four Treatises* system. As shown by Janet Gyatso, the crucial virtue of familiarity is to be obtained only through firsthand observation (*mthong*) of how the teachers practice, and it accompanies but contrasts with verbal teaching and book learning.[22] Below is a simile used to emphasize the importance of this particular kind of training:

> *mthong goms med pa'i sman pa de// rgyus med lam du zhugs pa 'dra//*

> A physician who has not observed how the teachers practice is like one who sets out on a road with which he is not familiar.

This familiarity-through-observation (*mthong goms*) is similar to the status of empirical knowledge as a cognitive source (*lo rgyus kyi tshad ma*) in the *Vajra Lines*. One more example found in the *Supplemented Testimony of Ba* (*Sba bzhed zhabs btags ma*) confirms that *lo rgyus* can be used like *rgyus* to mean "familiarity."

> *chos bya bar 'chams nas/ da chos byed pa la mtha' nas 'ongs pa'i mi lo rgyus can su yod zhes glengs pa dang/ ba lam klag na sba gsal snang mang yul nas 'ongs pa rje'i spyan sngar bos mchi nas gsal snang rje'i spyan sngar mchis ste/*[23]

> Having agreed to practice Buddhism, [the council] said, "Now, in order to practice Buddhism, we need someone who comes from the

22. Gyatso 2015, 371–76 (the following example is on 372).

23. For the Tibetan, see Stein 1961, 15; and Tsumagari 2011, 427. Tong and Huang (1990, 17) correctly translate *lo rgyus can* as *shuxi* 熟悉, "having familiarity." Tsumagari, probably influenced by the rephrasing in the *Mkhas pa'i dga' ston* (*chos mkhas pa'i lo rgyus can su*), quoted in Tsumagari 2011, 422n2, inaccurately renders *mtha' nas 'ongs pa'i mi lo rgyus can* as 隣国から来る人で[仏法を修あた]経歴を有する者 ("a person who comes from the neighboring country and has a background [of learning Buddhism])."

> border area and possesses the knowledge (*lo rgyus can*) [of the situation in Nepal and India]. Who do we have?" "Ba Selnang of Balamlak is from Mangyül. Summon him to have an audience with the lord!" Selnang then came to have an audience with the lord.

Later on, the *Supplemented Testimony of Ba* tells us that the council was looking for someone who knew the situation in India and Nepal and thus knew which Buddhist masters should be invited to Tibet. In the sense of "knowledge," there seems to be no distinctions between *lo rgyus* and *rgyus*.[24]

Tangut and Chinese translators also seem to have had difficulty translating *lo rgyus* in the twelfth and thirteenth centuries. They rendered *lo rgyus* as *dạ nio̱w* [illegible] ("speech-cause")[25] and *zongshuo* 宗說 ("?-speech"),[26] for example, both of which seem to be ad hoc calques in their respective languages.

3. Lo rgyus *as Explanation*

Perhaps combining both senses of *lo rgyus* as "speech" and "knowledge," some authors use *lo rgyus* to mean "explanation." In the *Life of Milarepa*, for example, Tsangnyön Heruka (Gtsang smyon Heruka, 1452–1507) states that several hunters came to Milarepa's cave and found him to be a skeletal being with green hair, due to his diet of nettles:

> *thog mar 'dre 'dug zer bros song/ mi dang bsgrub pa po yin pa'i lo rgyus byas pas/ yin yin rang mi 'dra ste blta ru rung zer/*[27]
>
> At first they said, "A ghost!" and fled. Since I explained (*lo rgyus*

24. Another example is found in the wedding ceremony speech in today's Amdo, as recorded in Nyangchakja's ethnography (2016, 232): "Horse-owners have thorough knowledge of their horses, dzo-owners have thorough knowledge of their dzo" (*rta yi lo rgyus rta bdag la gsal// mdzo yi lo rgyus mdzo bdag la gsal//*). Naljor Tsering has also told me that a bride's father uses this metaphor to make the point that parents really know their children.

25. Characters no. 1045 and no. 2484 in Li 2008. For this reference, I thank Professor Kiril Solonin, who found this word in a Tangut version of Pa gor Vairocana's biography (catalogued as Tang 250), which roughly corresponds to the transmitted *'Dra 'bag chen mo*.

26. This appears in the Chinese translation of an unknown Tibetan commentary of the *Vajra Lines*. The Chinese translation also gives a road simile: "*zongshuo* . . . is like an experienced traveler guiding people through convoluted paths" (宗說者 . . . 如熟路人與群生作指迷者也). For the background of the tantric anthology in which this Chinese translation is included, see Shen 2017.

27. For the Tibetan text, see de Jong 1959, 127. For slightly different English translations, see Lhalungpa 1982, 119; and Tsangnyön Heruka 2010, 137.

byas) that I was a human and also a practitioner, they said, "It doesn't seem like he is, but let's take a look anyways."

In the *Life of Milarepa*, we find that Tsangnyön Heruka uses *lo rgyus* to mean "explanation" on multiple occasions.[28] A similar example is also found in one of the shorter autobiographical pieces of Tai Situ Jangchup Gyeltsen (Ta'i si tu Byang chub rgyal mtshan, 1302–64) concerning whether he needed a life-enhancing ritual.

mo rtsis pas/ sku rim spong thag che ba thams cad ngoms shing tshims pa cig dgos zer nas/ rgyal mtshan bzang po'i rna ba yang yang gtser 'dug pas sems kyis ma bzod par/ sku rim che ba zhig bsgrub na drag gi/ sku khams bzang na des chog/ zer nas lab kyin 'dug pas/ de'i khar med zer ba'i lo rgyus byas na'ang/ ldab kyin lab kyi 'dug pas/ . . . [29]

The astrologer said, "We need a big life-enhancing ritual to make all [deities and demons] satisfied and appeased." He again and again nagged [my steward] Gyeltsen Zangpo, so that Gyeltsen Zangpo could not resist and started to urge me, "If a big ceremony can help you recover and become healthy, it is worth a try." Even when I explained (*lo rgyus byas*), "His [= the astrologer's] words are nonsense,"[30] [Gyeltsen Zangpo] still insisted with repeated requests . . .

From this translation, we can see that *lo rgyus byas* denotes an explanatory speech act. In light of this, we may venture another try on a famous but difficult passage in the *Supplemented Testimony of Ba*. After Samyé Monastery was built and the monastic community established, the text tells us:

dus der blon po 'gos kyis mchid nas lha chos ni rgyas par mdzad/ da skye bo mi chos kyi lo rgyus ci gnang mchis nas rje'i gdung rabs dang/ 'bangs kyi sa bcad dang/ bla rabs dkon mchog gsum la phyag dang zhes sa dang/ gtam dang lo rgyus dang/ dge dang yig tshangs ji ltar yin lugs rgyas par gnang ngo/[31]

28. See, for example, de Jong 1959, 32 and 45.

29. Ta'i si tu 1986, 423.

30. Elsewhere in this same story (Ta'i si tu 1986, 423), Tibetan *khar* is used for "words." But the translation of *de'i khar med* is tentative.

31. Stein 1961, 53; Tong and Huang 1990, 158.

> At that time the minister Gö asked the emperor, "You have developed the divine religion. Now what instructions (*lo rgyus*) will you give on the secular ethics of the people?" Then the emperor gave in detail the proper conventions concerning the royal genealogy, classifications of the subjects, etiquette and courtesy toward the nobility and the Three Jewels, oral knowledge (*gtam dang lo rgyus*), and rewards and insignia.

The whole passage is difficult not only because of the numerous sociopolitical terms but also because of the obscure phrase *mi chos kyi lo rgyus*. Rolf Stein translates the minister's question as "what accounts of the religion of humans will you give to the people?"[32] By virtue of the above examples, I believe "words" or "instructions" fits better here than "account." The subcategories of *gtam* and *lo rgyus* are also not necessarily narratives but could simply be some form of "oral knowledge." This kind of oral text is illustrated by a *lo rgyus* told by a Drak-yap (Brag g.yab) native, which is translated and studied in Schwieger 2002. This Drak-yap's *lo rgyus* is an encyclopedic type of local knowledge, including local geographical features, fairy tales, and descriptions of public ceremonies. Therefore I suggest that this example of *lo rgyus gnang* denotes an explanatory act, similar to those that we have seen in the writings of Tsangnyön Heruka and Tai Situ.

Along with this hypothesis, let us now consider a tentative compound analysis. Both stems, "words" (*lo*) and "familiarity" (*rgyus*), convey some sense of "information," with the former emphasizing verbal sources and the latter emphasizing empirical knowledge. In fact, interpreting *lo rgyus* as "information" would be appropriate in most contexts.[33] If this were the case, *lo rgyus* would be a synonymous compound that is based on two seemingly redundant units, the typical English example of which is *subject matter*.[34] A common function of this repetition is to reduce ambiguity. In Old Tibetan we also

32. Stein 1981, 170: "que donnerez-vous aux hommes comme récits de la religion des hommes?" Stein also employs the fourteenth-century *Blon po bka' thang*, in which the subcategories of *mi chos* are followed by the verb *gleng*, which he translates as "récite" or "raconte." Actually, the rest of the chapter on *mi chos* is not narratives at all, but aphorisms and practical advice. See O rgyan gling pa 1986, 469–72.

33. The large corpus of Buddhist translations is only tangentially mentioned in this essay, and I leave the task of a more thorough study to better-equipped scholars. Suffice it to say that the expression *lung gi lo rgyus* in the sixth chapter of Candrakīrti's *Madhyamakāvatāra* seems to be a case in which *lo rgyus* simply means "information."

34. I thank Nathan Hill for pointing out to me the possibility of the term's being a synonymous compound. For a discussion of this phenomenon in English, see Benczes 2014.

see synonymic coordinate compounds, such as *so nam* ("abundance"), *nyes yo* ("mishap"), and *zla dpe* (or *dpe zla*, "exemplar").[35] In this way, the interpretation of *lo rgyus* as "history" is derivative; it is simply one kind of "discourse" (*lo rgyus*) that sometimes emphasizes chronology.

Conclusion

In both Classical and modern Tibetan, the term *lo rgyus* is most commonly used to mean "tale" or "account." However, as we have seen, it can also mean "speech, words" or "knowledge, familiarity, firsthand experience." These latter connotations do not necessarily indicate any aspect of temporality. Combining the senses of both speech and experiential knowledge, *lo rgyus* also can denote explanatory or instructional speech acts.

The wide semantic range may help us understand its secular flavor, which appeals to certain ideologies. In other words, it is perhaps not a coincidence that *lo rgyus* was chosen by both Buddhists and socialists,[36] roughly a millennium apart, as a broad label for "history." The general and nontechnical senses of *lo rgyus* have made it useful for the newly emerging political ideologies of the twentieth and twenty-first centuries.

35. See Bialek 2018, vol. 1, 185–87.

36. William McGrath informs me that Gendün Chömpel also used *lo rgyus* to mean "the past." So perhaps "modernists" is the more accurate term here.

References

Benczes, Réka. 2014. "Repetitions Which Are Not Repetitions: The Non-Redundant Nature of Tautological Compounds." *English Language and Linguistics* 18: 431–47.

Bialek, Joanna. 2018. *Compounds and Compounding in Old Tibetan: A Corpus Based Approach*. 2 vols. Marburg: Indica et Tibetica Verlag.

Braarvig, Jens, Dag T. Haug, Frode Helland, and Stephan Guth. 2015 [2007]. *Bibliotheca Polyglotta*. https://www2.hf.uio.no/polyglotta/.

Bstan 'gyur dpe bsdur ma. 1994–2008. Beijing: Krung go'i bod rig pa'i dpe skrun khang.

Davidson, Ronald. 2005. *Tibetan Renaissance: Tantric Buddhism in the Rebirth of Tibetan Culture*. New York: Columbia University Press.

Deokar, Lata Mahesh. 2018. *Subhūticandra's Kavikāmadhenu on Amarakośa 1.4.8 to 2.2.5 Together with Si tu Paṇ chen's Tibetan Translation*. Marburg: Indica et Tibetica Verlag.

Dotson, Brandon. 2016. "The Dead and Their Stories: Preliminary Remarks on the Place of Narrative in Tibetan Religion." *Zentralasiatische Studien* 45: 77–112.

Eimer, Helmut. 1979. *Rnam thar rgyas pa: Materialien zu einer Biographie des Atiśa (Dīpaṃkaraśrījñāna)*. Wiesbaden: Otto Harrassowitz.

Gyatso, Janet. 2015. *Being Human in a Buddhist World: An Intellectual History of Medicine in Early Modern Tibet*. New York: Columbia University Press.

Hahn, Michael. 1999. "Blags und Verwandtes (Miscellanea etymologica tibetica, vi)." In *Studia Tibetica et Mongolica (Festschrift Manfred Taube)*, edited by Eimer Helmut et al., 123–25. Swisttal-Odendorf: Indica et Tibetica Verlag.

Hill, Nathan. 2019. *The Historical Phonology of Tibetan, Burmese, and Chinese*. Cambridge: Cambridge University Press.

Ishida, Kidō 石田貴道. 2004. "Kōdenki niokeru Vairocanarakṣita no yakuwari nitsuite: Nyūbosatsugyōron ruden no ichidanmen 後伝期における Vairocanarakṣitaの役割について--『入菩薩行論』流伝の一断面." *Nihon chibetto gakkai kaihō* 日本西蔵学会会報 50: 31–48.

Jacques, Guillaume. 2016. "How Many *-s Suffixes in Old Chinese?" *Bulletin of Chinese Linguistics* 9.2: 205–17.

Jäschke, Heinrich. 1881. *A Tibetan-English Dictionary*. Berlin: Unger Bros.

'Jig rten mgon po. 2001. "Rdo rje ye shes kyi zhu chos." In *Khams gsum chos kyi rgyal po thub dbang ratna shrī'i phyi yi bka' 'bum nor bu'i bang mdzod*, vol. 3. Delhi: Drikung Kagyu Ratna Shri Sungrab Nyamso Khang.

de Jong, Jan Willem, ed. 1959. *Mi la ras pa'i rnam thar*. The Hague: Mouton.

van der Kuijp, Leonard. 1996. "Tibetan Historiography." In *Tibetan Literature: Studies in Genre*, edited by José Ignacio Cabezón and Roger R. Jackson, 39–56. Ithaca, NY: Snow Lion Publications.

———. 2009. "On the Vicissitudes of Subhūticandra's *Kāmadhenu* Commentary on the *Amarakoṣa* in Tibet." *Journal of the International Association of Tibetan Studies* 5: 1–105.

Lhalungpa, Lobsang Phuntshok, trans. 1982. *The Life of Milarepa*. Boulder, CO: Prajñā Press.

Li, Fanwen 李范文. 2008. *Xia Han zidian* 夏漢字典. Beijing: Zhongguo shehui kexue chubanshe.

Ma'o Tse tung. 1965. *Ma'o tse tung gi gsung rtsom gces bsgrigs klog deb*. Beijing: Mi rigs dpe skrun khang.

Nyangchakja (Snying lcags rgyal). 2016. "The Last Dragon Banquet? Changing Wedding Traditions in an Amdo Tibetan Community." *Asian Highlands Perspectives* 41: 1–523.

O rgyan gling pa. 1986. *Bka' thang sde lnga*. Beijing: Mi rigs dpe skrun khang.

Phag mo gru pa Rdo rje rgyal po. 2008. "*Gzhung rdo rje tshig rkang gi 'grel pa sa chen gyi slob ma rje phag grus mdzad pa'i bshad mdzod ma*." In *Sa skya lam 'bras*, vol. 42, 1–310. Kathmandu: Guru Lama, Sachen International.

Schwieger, Peter. 2002. "History as Oral Tradition: The Construction of Collective Identity in Brag g.yab (Khams)." In *Khams Pa Histories: Visions of People, Places, and Authority*, edited by Lawrence Epstein, 127–54. Leiden: Brill.

Shen, Weirong 沈衛榮. 2017. *Dasheng yaodao miji yanjiu chubian* 大乘要道密集研究初編. Beijing: Beijing shifan daxue chubanshe.

Snye thang Blo gros brtan pa. 2003. *Tshig gter gyi ṭik*. In *Dpal ldan sa skya pa'i gsung rab pod bzhi pa: Mngon brjod*, 27–176. Beijing: Mi rigs dpe skrun khang.

Stearns, Cyrus. 2001. *Luminous Lives: The Story of the Early Masters of the Lam 'Bras Tradition in Tibet*. Boston: Wisdom Publications.

Stein, Rolf, ed. 1961. *Une chronique ancienne de bSam-yas: sBa-bźed*. Paris: Adrien-Maisonneuve.

———. 1981. *La civilisation tibétaine*. Paris: le Sycomore: l'Asiathèque.

Ta'i si tu Byang chub rgyal mtshan. 1986. *Si tu zhal chems gsang ba yang chung*. In *Rlangs kyi po ti bse ru rgyas pa*, 422–31. Lhasa: Bod ljong mi dmangs dpe skrun khang.

Tong, Jinhua 佟錦華 and Bufan Huang 黄布凡. 1990. *Baxie (zengbu ben) yizhu* <拔協>（增補本）譯註. Chengdu: Sichuan minzu chubanshe.

Tsangnyön Heruka. 2010. *The Life of Milarepa*. Translated by Andrew Quintman. New York: Penguin Classics.

Tsumagari, Shin'ichi 津曲真一. 2011. "*Bashe* yakuchū (2): Fundosuru maki『バシェ』訳註 (2): 忿怒する魔鬼." *Shitennōji daigaku kiyō* 四天王寺大学紀要 51: 421–30.

Willock, Nicole. 2021. *Lineages of the Literary: Tibetan Buddhist Polymaths of Socialist China*. New York: Columbia University Press.

Zhang, Yisun 張怡蓀, ed. 1993. *Bod rgya tshig mdzod chen mo*. Beijing: Mi rigs dpe skrun khang.

Tibetan Expertise on Sanskrit Grammar (6): Dar Lotsāwa Ngawang Püntsok Lhündrup on Pāṇini

Pieter C. Verhagen

To Leonard: I fondly recall us circumambulating Walden Pond in Massachusetts together in the early 1990s, and slouching on your living-room couch watching David Letterman's *Late Night* show. Your great bear-like hug and our clumsy exchanges in a kind of Anglo-Dutch pidgin, honoring your Dutch roots, every time we meet. And I reflect on the many, many instances where you have magnanimously supplied materials and ideas to feed and fuel my investigations. To have a friend like that ranks among the greatest boons a man may wish for.

EVER SINCE the introduction of Buddhism into Tibet and—hand in hand with that—the influx of Buddhist scripture from India, starting from the mid-seventh century onward, it is clear that the competence to read and understand and translate these crucial "alien" sources, usually in Sanskrit, has been of paramount importance for the transmission of Buddhist doctrines and practices into and within Tibet. The extensive and extremely sophisticated world of indigenous Sanskrit grammar (*vyākaraṇa*) was an obvious option for Tibetans wishing to attain the language mastery needed for authentic translations. Indeed we find, as far as we have been able to ascertain so far, that almost all successful Tibetan translators based their knowledge of Sanskrit grammar on the two major Indian Buddhist systems of *vyākaraṇa*—namely, Kātantra (also known as Kalāpa) and Cāndra. I call these systems Buddhist as they were by far the most popular in the later Buddhist world of South and Central Asia. No wonder, as the Kātantra and Cāndra grammars were far more geared to a Buddhist readership than was the pinnacle and core of the indigenous Sanskrit grammar, Pāṇini's *Aṣṭādhyāyī* (fifth century BCE). Pāṇini quite often dwells on abstruse idiosyncrasies of Vedic and classical Sanskrit that were irrelevant for Buddhist scripture and that were therefore omitted by both Kātantra and Cāndra.

Not surprisingly, quite a number of treatises belonging to the Kātantra and Cāndra traditions were translated into Tibetan and added to the Tengyur

(Bstan 'gyur) canon between the eleventh and sixteenth centuries.[1] But we have to wait until the seventeenth century before we see the first Tibetan translations of Pāṇinian treatises. In the middle of that century, under the patronage of the Great Fifth Dalai Lama Ngawang Lozang Gyatso (Ngag dbang blo bzang rgya mtsho, 1617–82), a Tibetan translator joined forces with two Indian master grammarians who were residing in Lhasa. The translator was known as Dar Lotsāwa ('Dar lo tsā ba), the "translator from Dar." His common ordination name was Ngawang Püntsok Lhündrup (Ngag dbang phun tshogs lhun grub), but he was also occasionally designated Tsewang Rapten Dorjé (Tshe dbang rab brtan rdo rje, 1633?–after 1665).[2] He hailed from the Sekar (Se dkar) clan, from the Dar region in Upper Tsang, hence his appellation "translator from Dar." Under the tutelage of and in cooperation with two brahman scholars from northern India, probably Benares—the brothers Gokulanāthamiśra and Balabhadra—he produced the first integral translation of Pāṇini's corpus of rules into Tibetan in the late 1650s in Drepung Monastery.[3] It was not, strictly speaking, a translation of the *Aṣṭādhyāyī* as such but of the reordering of the Pāṇinian rules (*sūtra*) in the *Prakriyākaumudī* commentary by Rāmacandra (fourteenth–fifteenth century). This type of reordering became a standard in the important Kaumudī tradition of Pāṇinian exegesis flourishing in the seventeenth and eighteenth centuries in India.

In the same period, between the years 1658 and 1660, the same team of scholars coauthored—I find this would be the appropriate term here—the *Chariot Carrying Jewels [in the Form of] Aphorisms* (*Legs bshad nor bu 'dren pa'i shing rta*). This extensive commentary on the Pāṇinian sūtra corpus was based on the *Prakriyākaumudī* but is not really a translation of that Indian commentary.[4] It consists of what one might call a synoptic rendering or reading of *Prakriyākaumudī* based on the notes[5] that Dar Lotsāwa took from the teachings given by the two Indian paṇḍitas on *Prakriyākaumudī*, expanding where further clarification was needed and omitting parts that were considered redundant. It ranks among the most voluminous of premodern Tibetan

1. Verhagen 1994, CG 1–6, 8–9, 21, 24–25, 27, 35–38, and 40 belong to the Cāndra system (and possibly CG 18, 26, 32, and 39 as well), and CG 7, 10–15, 22–23, 28, 30, and 33–34 are Kātantra treatises.

2. BDRC P2947; Verhagen 1994, 135–37.

3. Verhagen 1994, CG 46, 133–35, 314–17.

4. Verhagen 1994, CG 47, 135–37, 317–22.

5. I can only concur with Luo's (2016, 122) critique of my initial rendering (Verhagen 1994, 135) of *zin bris* as "synopsis." Indeed a better interpretation is "notes"—i.e., the "written documentation" (*bris*) of "what was received" (*zin*), namely from the teacher.

writings on Sanskrit grammar, its size ranging from approximately 425 to 520 folios in the various xylograph editions of the Tengyur.

The team also collaborated on translations of two basic treatises belonging to the Sārasvata system of Sanskrit grammar—namely, the *Sārasvata sūtra* text and its *Prakriyācaturā* commentary, the latter translation dated 1665.[6] These were not the first Tibetan translations of Sārasvata. The famed erudite Tāranātha Künga Nyingpo (Kun dga' snying po, 1575–1634?) had in collaboration with his Indian expert Kṛṣṇabhaṭṭa translated only the first section on sandhi; this translation too has found its way into the Tengyur canon, and it is particularly significant as it is bilingual, recording the Sanskrit and the Tibetan translation.[7] Sārasvata-vyākaraṇa was, again, not unlike Kātantra and Cāndra, a simplified version of Pāṇinian grammar more specifically aimed at a Buddhist audience. It too, like the Pāṇinian Kaumudī tradition, had gained great popularity in northern India, particularly in Bihar and Bengal, in the sixteenth and seventeenth centuries.

Some twenty-five years later, in 1685, again under the aegis of the Great Fifth Dalai Lama, a translation of the Pāṇinian *Dhātupāṭha*, "lexicon of verbal roots," was made by Könchok Chödrak (Dkon mchog chos grags) and his Indian assistant Kṛṣṇodaya.[8] This is the latest addition to the Tengyur corpus of works on Sanskrit grammar recorded. All three Pāṇinian works belong to the very last accretions to the Tengyur canon,[9] attested only in eighteenth-century block print editions, some four centuries after the first redaction by Butön Rinchendrup (Bu ston Rin chen grub, 1290–1364).

Although they never achieved the level of popularity of the Cāndra and Kātantra systems, we do see a continuation of Pāṇinian studies in Tibetan since their inception at the hands of Dar Lotsāwa. First of all we see that extracanonical xylograph editions of Dar Lotsāwa's writings on Pāṇini were produced in subsequent centuries,[10] for instance, in the collected works (*gsung 'bum*) of Desi Sanggyé Gyatso (Sde srid Sangs rgyas rgya mtsho, 1653–1705), which famously also contains works authored by protégés of the Dalai Lama's court.[11] Tsering Wangyel (Tshe ring dbang rgyal, 1697–1763) mentions Dar Lotsāwa's commentary as one of the sources that he used for his Sanskrit-Tibetan

6. Verhagen 1994, CG 43–44, 129–31, 304–12.

7. Verhagen 1994, CG 31, 117–18, 285–86.

8. Verhagen 1994, 131–33, 139–40, 157–58.

9. Note that the *Dhātupāṭha* translation (Verhagen 1994, CG 45) is preserved only in the Peking and Snar thang *Bstan 'gyur* editions, but not in Sde dge and Co ne.

10. Verhagen 1994, 137nn111–12.

11. Verhagen 1994, 137n113; Smith 2001, 243, 331.

dictionary.[12] About a century after Dar Lotsāwa, the grand linguist Situ Paṇchen Chökyi Jungné (Si tu paṇ chen Chos kyi 'byung gnas, 1699/1700–1774) translated the *Vaidika-prakriyā*, "Formation of Vedic [Sanskrit forms]," a chapter of *Prakriyākaumudī* that had not been included in Dar Lotsāwa's translation.[13] Even among the current diaspora of Tibetans we see examples, such as the translation of Varadarāja's epitome of the *Siddhāntakaumudī* entitled *Laghu-siddhāntakaumudī* by Lozang Noṛbu Śāstrī (Blo bzang Nor bu Śāstrī), which was published in Sarnath in 1989.[14]

Earlier Research

A mere few "modern" scholars have investigated—some more critically, some less so—the corpus of *vyākaraṇa* translations by Dar Lotsāwa, in particular his Pāṇinian work. The earliest I could trace was Sujit Kumar Mukhopadhyaya (1944), who gave a first evaluation of Dar Lotsāwa's translation of the sūtra text and the commentary. He noted a number of erroneous translations, the insertion of *vārttikas* into the sūtra corpus (which is not uncommon in the Kaumudī tradition), and readings of sūtras stemming from the *Siddhāntakaumudī*. Mukhopadhyaya also reflects on the mention of Bhaṭṭojī Dīkṣita's *Siddhāntakaumudī* (ca. 1630) in the introductory part of the commentary (see below). This reference need not surprise us, as by the time the Tibetan versions were created, mid-seventeenth century, the *Siddhāntakaumudī* had already—and very quickly after its composition—risen to enormous popularity in Indian *vyākaraṇa* didactics, and it makes perfect sense that the paṇḍita brothers would use it in their work with Dar Lotsāwa. After all, the *Siddhāntakaumudī* was a sort of culmination of the Kaumudī tradition of Pāṇinian exegesis that started with the commentary at hand, Rāmacandra's *Prakriyākaumudī* (fourteenth/fifteenth centuries). It should be noted, though, that the *Siddhāntakaumudī* is emphatically critical of *Prakriyākaumudī* at several occasions.

In a 1986 paper two Mongolian scholars, Shagdaryn Bira and O. Sukhbaatar, repeat much of what had been said by Mukhopadhyaya and in other early investigations of the Tibetan canon and its grammatical contents.[15] They also discuss the Mongolian translation, which is of course based on the

12. Verhagen 1994, 137n114.

13. Verhagen 2001, 112–17; *Si tu paṇ chen chos kyi 'byung gnas kyi bka' 'bum*, vol. 8, 382–89; also see below.

14. Blo bzang 1989.

15. For example, Liebich 1895; Liebich 1919; and Ghosh 1970.

Tibetan. Their evaluation of the quality of the Tibetan as well as the Mongolian translation is very positive. This, as Hong Luo rightly observes,[16] is an opinion in need of some revision. We can pass by the 1994 article by Narendra Kumar Dash, which is actually a plagiarism of Mukhopadhyaya (1944), adding some random comparisons.[17]

The most recent significant progress in this specific area is being made by Hong Luo. He has looked critically at Dar Lotsāwa's translation of the sūtras on the *kārakas* (syntactic-semantic underlying case relations) and is about to publish a collation of the Sanskrit and Tibetan Pāṇinian sūtras.[18] It is for this reason that I will not focus on the sūtra text here but rather make a few observations on the *Chariot Carrying Jewels* commentary.

Pāṇini Commentary, the Chariot Carrying Jewels

Let us have a closer look at this impressive commentary on Pāṇini that Dar Lotsāwa and associates have contributed to Tibetan scholarship.[19] Its full title is—somewhat surprisingly—not given at the beginning of the text but only in the intermediate colophons: the *Chariot Carrying Jewels [in the Form] of Aphorisms, Consisting of the Notes Taken on the Interpretation, Rules, Examples, and so on of the Commentary on the Basic Text of the Great Grammatical Treatise Pāṇini-vyākaraṇa* (*Brda sprod pa'i bstan bcos chen po pā ṇi ni byā ka ra ṇa gzhung 'grel gyi go don cho ga dper brjod sogs zin bris su bkod pa legs bshad nor bu 'dren pa'i shing rta*). So this work reflects—it may even primarily consist of—the notes taken by Dar Lotsāwa when he received instruction on *Prakriyākaumudī* from the two Indian brothers.

The colophon[20] informs us that the work was written in the years 1658 to 1660 in Drepung Monastery by Dar Lotsāwa and his two paṇḍita tutors, the project taking place *sub aegide* of the Fifth Dalai Lama, and the Indian scholars being generously remunerated with "many hundreds of *zho* of gold and

16. Luo 2016, 122.

17. Of course this is not the only occasion when Narendra Kumar Dash was culpable for plagiarism. In 1993 he published a book entitled *A Survey on Sanskrit Grammar in Tibetan Language* (Delhi: Agam Kala Prakashan), a blatant verbatim plagiarism of two chapters from my PhD thesis (1991). For more details on this sordid affair, see Verhagen 1994, 7.

18. Luo 2016.

19. Verhagen 1994, CG 47, 135–37, 317–22 (containing an index of chapters and subchapters, as well as a translation of the colophon). I will base my readings on the *Gser 'bris Bstan 'gyur*, vols. 223 and 224, BDRC W23702.

20. The full text and a translation of the colophon is given in Verhagen 1994, 318–20.

silver" (*gser dngul zho grangs brgya phrag du ma*). It specifies that Rāmacandra's *Prakriyākaumudī* "served as the basis" (*gzhir bzhag/gzhag*) of the work, but that especially in the chapters on verbal morphology, "sections that are hard to understand have been amended and slightly extended in accordance with the stream of instructions given by the learned masters [namely, Balabhadra and Gokulanāthamiśra], while those [sections] that are easy to understand have been somewhat reduced" (*kun bshad sogs cho ga rtogs dka' ba rnams la slob dpon mkhas pa'i gsung rgyun gyis zur brgyan te cung zad rgyas par byas / rtogs sla ba rnams nyung ngur byas te*).

After a number of introductory dedicatory verses in various meters at the very beginning of the text,[21] there follows a brief preface on Sanskrit grammatical studies in India and on the paramount place of Pāṇini in that cosmos of *vyākaraṇa*. Maitreyanātha's *Mahāyānasūtrālaṃkāra locus classicus* admonition to study the five "fields of knowledge" (*vidyāsthāna*) is cited initially.[22]

21. *Gser 'bris Bstan 'gyur*, vol. 223, f. 39v1–40r2: */ phul byung mkhyen pa'i chu gter klong du grang yas shes bya'i gzhol 'gro'i tshegs / mtha' dag nyer 'bab brtse ba'i nor ldan dag* [= *ngag*?] *dbang tshangs sras bzhad pa'i blo / skal bzang klu dbang rgya mtsho'i gnyen gyur dge legs rin cen* [sic] *'byung ba'i gnas / rigs kun khyab bdag rdo rje 'chang dbang srid gsum 'gro ba'i mgon por 'dud /*
ma smad dam bca'i rtsa ba rab brtan snying rje'i 'dab ma phyogs brgyar g'yo / phan bde'i 'bras ldan ro bda' ma phabs [?] *'chi med 'gro kun skyong la brtson / rgyal ba'i myu gu dang ga bsam ljon shing kun bzod tsha gdung sel ba'i lha / rnam 'dren gsang ba kun 'dus yid bzhin nor bu pad dkar 'dzin des skyongs /*
gang thugs zla ba'i ma ma las 'ongs rnam dpyod 'od 'phreng khar yug can / yid can mi shes smag rum drung 'byin bcu phrag rig pa'i chum thong mtha' / mngon gyur 'jig rten mgon po pā ṇi ni zhes bnyis [= *gnyis*] *med gsung des lung bstan pa'i / 'phags yul mkhas mchog gnyis skyes yongs kyi gtsug gi rgyan gyur khyod gcig bsngags /*
bgrod bya 'chi med lam du rgyu min nyin dang / mtshan mor gsal 'grib bral / 'degs byed bsir bus ma bskul bar yang 'jig rten mun pa sel bya'i phyir / lnga rig snang ba 'bum gyis bsil ldan 'gengs mdzad 'phags yul paṇḍi ta / stobs bzang ma [?] *tshang kyi bka' drin bsams na lag pad snying khar cis mi 'dzum /*
/ gang de'i zhal sgo las brgyud rin cen [sic] *dbyig / tshul min rdul gyi dri mas mi gos pa / brda sprod rgyan 'phreng kun gyi mchog / blo gsal don gnyer sgeg mo'i zur phud du / mdzes byed legs bshad nor bu'i do shal gang / 'dren pa'i shing rta mchog 'dir zhugs tsam gyis / bgrod dka' gzhung lugs rin chen gling yangs por / thogs med 'jug pa'i lugs bzang 'di na spro /*.

22. *Gser 'bris Bstan 'gyur*, vol. 223, f. 40r3–40r6: *de yang 'dir mgon po byams pas rig pa'i gnas lnga dag la brtson par byas na / 'phags mchog gis kyang thams cad mkhyen nyid mi 'gyur te / de bas gzhan dag tshar bcad rjesu bzung phyir dang / rang nyid kun shes bya phyir de la de brtson byed / ces shes bya rigs* [sic] *pa'i gnas che ba lngar gsungs pa de rnams kyi nang nas kyang thog mar gang la slob par bya ba'i gnas ni / / thog mar sgra la mkhas pa yis / tshig don rnam par phyed ste bstan / de nas don la mkhas pa yis / lhag chad 'khrul pa med par bshad / / ces sgra pa* [?] *shes na don la mi rmongs shing rjod byed kun gyi gzhir gyur pa gzhung lugs thams cad la dang por 'jug pa'i sgo lta bu rig pa'i gnas 'di nyid yin pas /*.

Then follows a listing of the major "eight grammatical treatises" in India:[23]

1. *Indra-vyākaraṇa*
2. *Cāndra-vyākaraṇa*
3. **Piśali-vyākaraṇa*
4. *Śākaṭāyana-vyākaraṇa*
5. *Pāṇini-vyākaraṇa*
6. *Samantabhadra-vyākaraṇa*
7. *Patañjali-vyākaraṇa*
8. *Manujendra-vyākaraṇa*

The list is actually quite a motley collection. The *Indra-vyākaraṇa* appears to be the mythical primordial Sanskrit grammar but could also trace back to a now lost pre-Pāṇinian treatise.[24] The grammars of *Piśali, Śākaṭāyana, Samantabhadra, and Manujendra have thus far defied unquestionable identification. It has been suggested that the *Piśali/Paiśala-vyākaraṇa* could reflect Sanskrit *Vaiśala-vyākaraṇa*,[25] but I think it far more likely that we have here a reference to the (pre-Pāṇini) grammarian Āpiśali.[26] In the Vedic period we know of a grammarian/etymologist named Śākaṭāyana who is mentioned by Yāska in his *Nirukta* (fifth century BCE), but there is also a ninth-century (?) CE Jain grammarian of the same name who composed his *Śabdānuśāna* rule system to rival Pāṇini's grammar.[27] Samantabhadra may also be a Jain scholar, *inter alia* author of a grammatical treatise entitled *Cintāmaṇiṭippanī*.[28] Pāṇini and Patañjali (author of *Mahābhāṣya*, the paramount commentary on *Aṣṭādhyāyī*) bring us to the solid attestation of historicity. It is especially noteworthy that the *Cāndra* grammar, written by "the divine/royal son Candra"—that is,

23. *Gser 'bris Bstan 'gyur*, vol. 223, f. 40r6–40v2: *de la yang rgya gar 'phags pa'i yul du sgra mdo chen po brgyad ces grags pa ni / lha'i dbang pos mdzad pa'i indra byā ka ra ṇa / lha'i bu zla bas mdzad pa'i tsandra byā ka ra ṇa / slob dpon pi sha lis mdzad pa'i pi sha li byā ka ra ṇa / drang srong shā ka ṭa ya nas mdzad pa'i shā ka ṭa na byā ka ra ṇa / drang srong pā ṇi nis mdzad pa'i pā ṇi ni byā ka ra ṇa / drang srong su manta bha dras mdzad pa'i su manta bha dra byā ka ra ṇa / drang srong pa tānydza lis mdzad pa'i pa tānydza li byā ka ra ṇa / rgyal po ma nu dzendras mdzad pa'i ma nu dzendra byā ka ra ṇa ste 'di brgyad la sgra mdo chen po brgyad ces grags pa.*

24. Verhagen 1994, 168–69, 178–80; Cardona 1976, 150–51.

25. Smith 2001, 191.

26. Cardona 1976, 148–49; Abhyankar and Shukla 1977, 62.

27. Cardona 1976, 149; Abhyankar and Shukla 1977, 388; Verhagen 1994, 183–84.

28. Abhyankar and Shukla 1977, 414.

Candragomin—is represented in this list, but oddly enough not the grammar of the Kātantra tradition.

We find the same eight grammars, albeit in a slightly different order and in a more corrupted nomenclature, listed about a century later by Longdöl Lama Ngawang Lozang (Klong rdol bla ma Ngag dbang blo bzang, 1719–94) in his reasoned lexicon of terminology in the secular fields of knowledge.[29] Longdöl Lama was apparently also well aware of the blatant omission of the Kātantra and hastened to rectify it. After the listing of eight he deftly introduces the Kātantra and the Sārasvata-vyākaraṇa.[30]

Dar Lotsāwa follows this with two citations of prophesies regarding Pāṇini recorded in the *Mañjuśrīmūlatantra* and the *Laṅkāvatārasūtra*, respectively, that are often quoted in justification of this grammarian's prestige in a later Buddhist context,[31] and with a brief description of some major works in the Pāṇinian tradition, stressing that their transmission was still continuing unabated in India at the time. The author mentions—in a non-chronological order—the *Mahābhāṣya* (mid-second century BCE), *Prakriyākaumudī* (late fourteenth/early fifteenth centuries CE), *Siddhāntakaumudī* (late sixteenth/early seventeenth centuries CE), and *Kāśikāvṛtti* (late sixth/early seventh centuries CE). From these, the commentary at hand, the *Prakriyākaumudī* by Rāmacandra, was selected, as it was "easy to understand and light to carry" (*go sla zhing 'khyer bde ba*).[32]

29. Smith 2001, 191; Chandra 1975, 721–61: *Rig gnas thun mong ba* [var.: *che ba*] *sgra rig pa / snyan ngag / sdeb sbyor / zlos gar / mngon brjod / brda gsar rnying gi khyad par las byung ba'i ming gi rnam grangs*, 723–24: *gzhan yang sgra mdo chen po brgyad yod de / brgya byin gyis mdzad pa'i indra byā ka ra ṇa / bram ze pā ṇis mdzad pa'i pā ṇi byā ka ra ṇa / slob dpon tsantra go mis mdzad pa rtogs dka' ba paṇḍi ta'i lugs kyi bstan bcos tsandra bya ka ra ṇa / pi sha li byā ka ra ṇa / sha kau ṭa ya na byā ka ra ṇa / su mantra byā ka ra ṇa / pa ta nydza li bya ka ra ṇa / ma nu dzentra byā ka ra ṇa te brgyad.*

30. Chandra 1975, 724: *gzhon nu gdong drug gis slob dpon dbang phyug go cha la gsungs pa rtogs sla ba rgyal po lugs kyi bstan bcos ka lā pa / de'i 'grel pa jo bo grags 'byor gyi mdzad pa'i slob phan sogs dang / dbyangs can byā ka ra ṇa ni / lha mthong lo tsā ba dang / jo nang ta ra nā thas bsgyur ba dang / rgyal ba lnga pa chen po'i skabs su 'dar pa ngag dbang phun tshogs kyis a tsarya go kū la nā tha sogs la brten nas bsgur ba dbyangs can sgra mdo dang / de'i 'grel pa slob dpon a nu bhu tas mdzad pa rab tu bya ba gsal ldan 'dar pa rang gi bsgyur ba rnams so.*

31. *Gser 'bris Bstan 'gyur*, vol. 223, f. 40v2–40v4: *de rnams kyi nang nas kyang go don cho ga sogs phul du phyin pa mdor na sgra'i gtsug lag thams cad kyi phyi mo lta bur gyur pa 'o skol gyi ston pa mnyam med shākya'i rgyal pos 'jam dpal rtsa ba'i rgyud las / bram ze khye'u pā ṇi ni / nges par nyan thos byang chub tu / nga yis lung bstan byas pa yin / 'jig rten dbang phyug bdag nyid che / de yang de yi sngags grub pa'o / langkar gshegs pa las / sgra byed pa ni pa ṇi ni zhes sogs kyis lung bstan pa'i bram ze khye'u pā ṇi la / 'phags pa 'jig rten dbang phyug gis dngos su bstsal ba'i bstan bcos chen po pā ṇi ni byā ka ra ṇa zhes bya ba.* Verhagen 1994, 170, 181.

32. *Gser 'bris Bstan 'gyur*, vol. 223, f. 40v4–41r2: *bstan bcos chen po pā ṇi ni byā ka ra ṇa zhes*

It is at this point that the actual commentary commences with the title of the sūtra text and an opening verse of homage, both also given in Sanskrit.[33] The homage to Viṭṭhala, the author of a commentary on *Prakriyākaumudī*, is transposed to a dedication to "those who thoroughly understand" (*rnam mkhyen rnams*).

The reader immediately notices that key phrases of the Sanskrit original, including the basic rules (the sūtras), are given in transcription along with their translation. This of course makes the work especially precious, as it conserves the Sanskrit of the sūtras (and of some key passages of the *Prakriyākaumudī* commentary) as transmitted in Tibet in the seventeenth century juxtaposed with Dar Lotsāwa's translation. His canonized rendering of the sūtra text, I should note here, contains only his translation of the sūtras.

At times one wonders how much Dar Lotsāwa actually understood of Pāṇini's rules. For instance, in the very first sūtra of the first chapter (*upadeśe 'J anunāsika it*, Pāṇini 1.3.2), he opts for an all-too-mechanical translation of *upadeśe* as "in the subregion" (*nye ba'i yul la*; from the combination of the preposition *upa* with the noun *deśa*, "region"), instead of the correct analysis as "in the (primary) instruction/introduction" (something like *nye bar bstan pa la*?) *in casu* in the *Dhātupāṭha* lexicon of verbal roots. Granted, his commentary shows that he understood the gist of the matter—namely, that the nasalized final vowel in the primary introduction of a verbal root is a metalinguistic marker technically termed *it*.[34] Nonetheless, his translation of the sūtra as it stands is incomprehensible to any Tibetan reader unless he or she

---

bya bas shlo ka nyis stong yod pa 'di nyis la klu'i rgyal po nor rgyas bu [?] *she ṣa zhes bya bas mdzad pa'i 'grel pa mā hā ṣa* [sic] *shlo ka 'bum yod pa dang / slob dpon rā ma tsandras mdzad pa'i 'grel pa pra kri ya zhes pa shlo ka stong phrag drug yod pa 'di nyid dang / slob dpon bha ṭo dzi bha dras mdzad pa'i siddhānta kau mu dī zhes pa shlo ka stong phrag bcu yod pa dang / slob dpon kā shi ka ras mdzad pa'i kā shi ka zhes pa shlo ka stong phrag bco brgyad yod pa rnams da lta 'ang 'phags pa'i yul na 'chad nyan rgyun ma nub par yod gsungs shing / de rnams kyi nang nas kyang go sla zhing 'khyer bde ba slob dpon rā ma tsandras mdzad pa'i 'grel pa pra kri ya ste rab tu bya ba zhes pa bzhir* [= *gzhir*?] *bzhag pa'i gzhung 'grel gyi cho ga'i rnam gzhag cung zad bshad par bya ba.*

33. *Gser 'bris Bstan 'gyur*, vol. 223, f. 41r2–41r4: *dang po mtshan don ni / rgya gar skad du / pā ṇi ni byā ka ra ṇa sū tra / bod skad du / brda sprod pa pā ṇi'i mdo zhes pa'o / / gnyis pa 'grel pa'i thog mar ji skad du / shrī ma dwi ṣṣa* [?] *la mā na mya pā ṇi nyā di mu nīn gu rūn / pra kri ya kau mu dīng kurmaḥ pā ṇi ni yā nu sā ri ṇāṃ / de bod skad du / thub pa pā ṇi ni sogs bla ma dang / dpal ldan rnam mkhyen rnams la kun btud de / pā ṇi ni yi rjes 'brangs nas ni / rab tu bya ba shin tu rgyas par bya / zhes pa'o.*

34. *Gser 'bris Bstan 'gyur*, vol. 223, f. 41r6–42r2: *u pa de she 'dza nu nā si ka it / nye ba'i yul la ats dang rjes su sna ldan 'gro ba'o / / nye ba'i yul te byings dang rkyen sogs kyi mtha'i rjes su sna ldan gyi yi ge nga nya ṇa na ma srog med rnams dang mtha' na yi ge gzhan med pa'i ats rnams ni dgos pa dang bcas pa'i 'gro ba'i ming can zhes ming dgos byed do.*

was well versed in Pāṇinian grammar in the first place. However, he immediately follows this up with clever translations for the next two sūtras: *de dbyi'o* for *tasya lopaḥ* (Pāṇini 1.3.9)[35] and *mtha'i hal 'o* for *haL antyam* (Pāṇini 1.3.3).[36] So it is immediately clear that the accuracy and adroitness of his translations vary considerably. This is a tendency destined to continue throughout Dar Lotsāwa's Pāṇinian oeuvre—namely, a qualitative inconsistency and instability of his work.

Generally speaking, the first half of the work follows quite closely the Sanskrit text that we have for the *Prakriyākaumudī*. For instance, if we compare the brief section on *dvirukta* (Tib. *gnyis su brjod pa*, "repetition") formations in Sanskrit in the *Prakriyākaumudī* at the end of the first part of the work[37] with that in Dar Lotsāwa's commentary, we see that our Tibetan translator faithfully follows the Sanskrit original.[38]

However, as stated in the colophon (see above), it is particularly in the latter half of the commentary, devoted to verbal formations, that Dar Lotsāwa deviates from the Sanskrit original and introduces additions and changes that were based on the oral tuition by the two paṇḍita brothers.

The Peking and Nartang block print editions of the Tengyur as well as the Golden Tengyur (*Gser 'bris ma*) commence the second volume of this commentary apparently somewhat randomly—in the approximate mathematical middle of this text—namely, at the beginning of the section on medial (*ātmanepadin*) verbs of the first conjugational class, whereas the natural cutoff point for a bipartition would have been the beginning of the chapter on verbal morphology (some sixty folios in xylograph before), which would have corresponded to the traditional Indian *Kaumudī* subdivision into a *pūrvārdha* ("first section," comprising the sections on sandhi and nominal morphology) and an *uttarārdha* ("latter section," on verbal morphology and primary nominal derivation).

If we compare the *Chariot Carrying Jewels* commentary with Rāmacandra's *Prakriyākaumudī* at this particular point in the texts, it becomes abundantly clear that the Tibetan work we have here is nothing like a translation of that Sanskrit original. On the one hand, Rāmacandra, at the beginning of the *ātmanepadin* (i.e., medial) verbs of the first conjugational class for the first root

35. *Gser 'bris Bstan 'gyur*, vol. 223, f. 42r2: */ ta sya lo paḥ (/) de dbyi'o / bshad ma thag pa'i rjes su sna ldan sogs 'gro ba'i ming can de rnams ni dbyi'o.*

36. *Gser 'bris Bstan 'gyur*, vol. 223, f. 42r2–3: *ha lantyaṃ / mtha'i hal 'o / / rjes su sna ldan dang atsar ma zad gzhan yang rkyen sogs kyi mtha'i hal mang po'ang 'gro ba'i ming can no.*

37. *Dvirukta-prakriyā*, Trivedi 1925–1931, 257–66.

38. *Gser 'bris Bstan 'gyur*, vol. 223, f. 260r6–261v6.

in that sequence (*edh* in the sense of "growth")—admittedly quite laconically—only introduces the examples *edhate* (third-person medial singular present tense), *aidhiṣṭa* (third-person medial singular aorist), and *aidhiḍhvam* (second-person medial plural aorist) before coming to the first Pāṇinian sūtra in this chapter (*āmpratyayavat kṛÑo 'nuprayogasya*, Pāṇini 1.3.63, which deals with perfect tense formation).[39] Dar Lotsāwa, however, elaborates on the *prakriyā* (the technical systematic derivation) of each and every form of the root *edh* in the present, optative, imperative, imperfect, and aorist tenses/moods before reaching the perfective tense, taking more than almost four folios in the Golden Tengyur to do so (Pāṇini 1.3.63 is introduced at f. 4v3),[40] as compared to the single line in the Sanskrit. Not even Viṭṭhala's *Vivaraṇa*, a *Ṭīkā* commentary on his uncle's (?) *Prakriyākaumudī*, goes into that much detail on these *prakriyās*, nor even Bhaṭṭojī Dīkṣita's *Siddhāntakaumudī* or its many epigons. But this is exactly the kind of approach one would choose when introducing a novice, such as the Tibetan Dar Lotsāwa, to the intricacies of Pāṇinian grammar. It seems to become more and more likely—if not evident—therefore that the *Chariot Carrying Jewels* not only is based on a scriptural source but in fact reflects also (in certain parts largely) the lecture dictation or notes taken down by Dar Lotsāwa from the oral instruction he received from the two Indian paṇḍitas.

A second random example from the chapter on medial and active-voice verbs of the first conjugation group is the treatment of the root *paṇ* ("to negotiate/discuss" or "to praise"). In Trivedi's edition of the *Prakriyākaumudī* it occupies five lines in the Western-style reproduction, giving seven example forms,[41] whereas Dar Lotsāwa devotes more than an entire folio side to this segment in the Golden Tengyur, offering no less than forty-one example forms.[42]

It is therefore evident that this work is not by any means a translation of Rāmacandra's *Prakriyākaumudī*. It is very much the registration of the tutelage provided by the two Indian paṇḍitas to their eager Tibetan pupil. This tuition obviously also involved (usually unspecified) reference to and application of *Kaumudī* types of exemplification and analysis.

39. Trivedi 1925–1931, 133, line 2.

40. *Gser 'bris Bstan 'gyur*, vol. 224, f. 1v2–4v3.

41. Trivedi 1925–1931, 139–40.

42. *Gser 'bris Bstan 'gyur*, vol. 224, f. 10r1–10v1.

Historical Circumstances

How can we explain this relatively late and rather sudden upsurge of interest in Sanskrit grammar in Tibet in the seventeenth century?[43] It seems that the prestige of the Tibetan government may have played a role. And it may relate to the flourishing of the Kaumudī school of traditional grammar in India. Was there perhaps a greater influx of Indian intelligentsia, in particular residual Indian Buddhists, into Tibet at the time? Let us therefore consider briefly the historical backdrop to this latter-day, peculiar Pāṇini peak in Tibet.

The establishment of the Ganden Podrang (Dga' ldan pho brang) government under the Fifth Dalai Lama in the seventeenth century entailed a strong efflorescence of many fields of secular (at least not specifically religious) expertise, many of which were founded on Indian antecedents. One branch of the political agenda of the Ganden Podrang government lies in the confirmation of the direct link of Gelukpa orthodoxy to the authentic Indian roots of Buddhism. It stands to reason, therefore, that two Indian experts on Sanskrit grammar, Gokulanāthamiśra and later his brother Balabhadra, were welcomed at the court of the Dalai Lama and were granted considerable stipends to ply their trade in Tibet. Under the auspices of the "Great Fifth" in the latter years of the 1650s, they collaborated with Dar Lotsāwa to produce his translation of Pāṇini's sūtra text and his *Chariot Carrying Jewels* commentary. Such projects certainly contributed to the prestige of Gelukpa rule, to its status as curator and continuator of the Indian traditions of old.

It is interesting that in the Degé and Choné editions of the Tengyur, Pāṇini and Balabhadra were singled out for portraits on the opening pages of the commentary. Obviously, in the eyes of the redactors of the Degé (and Choné) Tengyur xylograph, Balabhadra was responsible for this work more than Gokulanāthamiśra, or even more than Dar Lotsāwa. Indeed, Gokulanāthamiśra requested his brother Balabhadra to come to Tibet, as he found he was out of his depth in the teaching of Pāṇinian grammar, so we may infer that Balabhadra was indeed the greater expert of *vyākaraṇa* of the two brothers. But it is all the more striking that the Tibetan translator, Dar Lotsāwa, was not chosen here for portraiture. Does this suggest that the xylograph redactors regarded the Indian paṇḍita(s) more as the "creator(s)" of this work than the Tibetan *lotsāwa*?

The popularity of the Kaumudī type of Pāṇinian grammar and the more Buddhist-oriented Sārasvata-vyākaraṇa in northern India, in particular Bengal, in the seventeenth century may have contributed also to their warm recep-

43. Snellgrove and Richardson 1968, 201; Huber 2003, 174.

tion in Tibet. In addition to the canonical Tengyur editions, for instance, we find separate xylograph editions of Dar Lotsāwa's Pāṇinian and Sārasvata grammatical works published in the well-famed printing houses of Zhöl (Zhol par khang) and Ganden Püntsokling (Dga' ldan phun tshogs gling) in the nineteenth or early twentieth century that clearly attest to their prominence.[44]

The seventeenth century may have witnessed an increased influx of Buddhist, or more generally non-Muslim Indian, intellectuals into Tibet. Further research would be required to establish whether this was a contributing factor in this latter-day blooming of Sanskrit studies in Tibet.

The role of the Indian experts Balabhadra and Gokulanāthamiśra can hardly be overestimated. It makes sense that they would have stressed the importance of adding Pāṇini to the Tibetan canon, being brahmin paṇḍitas from Varaṇāsī, one of the major centers of *vyākaraṇa* studies in India, where Pāṇini's grammar reigned supreme. They were also involved in Dar Lotsāwa's work on Sārasvata grammar, so they contributed significantly to the dispersion in Tibet of the two predominant traditions of *vyākaraṇa* in northern India at the time—namely, the Pāṇinian Kaumudī and the Sārasvata-vyākaraṇa schools. In doing so they left an indelible stamp on Dar Lotsāwa's efforts in the field of Sanskrit grammar and established their own role in Indo-Tibetan grammatical studies from the mid-seventeenth century.

Giuseppe Tucci, in the mid 1950s, was the first Western scholar to draw attention to the dubious quality of Dar Lotsāwa's skills as a Sanskrit scholar, specifically as the author of Sanskrit verses.[45] Critical voices were also raised within the indigenous Tibetan scholastic traditions, and not just with regard to his command of Sanskrit versification, most notably perhaps by the eighteenth-century master-grammarian Situ Paṇchen Chökyi Jungné (1699/1700–1774). Situ Paṇchen translated the *Vaidika-prakriyā* chapter of the *Prakriyākaumudī* that had been omitted in Dar Lotsāwa's rendering.[46] This chapter deals with morphology specific to Vedic Sanskrit and was therefore not deemed relevant to the Tibetan Buddhist readership. This may very well have been the reason why Dar Lotsāwa did not include the chapter in the *Chariot Carrying Jewels*. In the brief colophon to his translation, Situ Paṇchen was dismissive of the translator from Dar's efforts.[47] Situ does not rate the *Chariot Carrying Jewels* as

44. Verhagen 1994, CG 43–44; Verhagen 1994, 130–31; *Dbyangs can sgra mdo'i rtsa 'grel dang mtshams sbyor lnga pa sogs*. Verhagen 1994, CG 46–47; Verhagen 1994, 137.

45. Tucci 1957.

46. Verhagen 2001, 112–17; *Si tu paṇ chen chos kyi 'byung gnas kyi bka' 'bum*, vol. 8, 382–89.

47. The colophon, *Si tu paṇ chen chos kyi 'byung gnas kyi bka' 'bum*, vol. 8, 388–89: *zhes pa pā ṇi pa'i rab byed zla zer 'di sngon lha ldan du 'dar los bsgyur bar bsgrags mod don la brtags pa'i*

a translation in the true sense of the word (*don la brtags pa'i tshe ji bzhin 'gyur ba'ang mi 'dug*), and he adds a somewhat abrasive pun on the title, saying that "in the *Chariot Carrying Jewels* errors and incorrect forms abound" (*legs bshad nor shing der yang nor 'khrul dang ma tshang ba mang ba*), playing on the double entendre of Tibetan *nor* that can mean "treasure" (or *nor bu* "jewel," as in the title) as well as "error" or "mistake" (*nor 'khrul*). Situ Paṇchen was often quite severe in his judgment of the work of his predecessors, so this critique of Dar Lotsāwa should probably not come as a surprise.

We see this imputed lack of competence attested in Dar Lotsāwa's rendering of Pāṇini's sūtras and in his commentary. His interpretations are of varying quality and precision. One may wonder therefore if he leaned (too) heavily on the skills of Balabhadra and Gokulanāthamiśra? Were his own skills perhaps rather limited? Was it indeed Dar Lotsāwa who gained the Fifth Dalai Lama a bad reputation as a composer of Sanskrit poetry, as Tucci would have it?[48]

It seems likely that Dar Lotsāwa was an ambitious young scholar who was propelled into fame and glory at a tender age owing to the patronage by the Dalai Lama's court. We should not overlook the fact that he translated the Pāṇinian sūtras and wrote his commentary of Pāṇini between his twenty-fifth and twenty-seventh year.[49] So, owing to the relative immaturity of his own scholarship as well as the extreme complexity of Pāṇinian grammar, it stands to reason that he would need to depend largely on the instructions offered by the paṇḍita brothers.

We should also keep in mind that he was the first Tibetan to venture into this veritable cosmos of Pāṇinian grammar. Until then the sporadic encounters with Pāṇini's *vyākaraṇa* within Tibetan scholasticism had been restricted to the reference to specific Pāṇinian rules in Buddhist exegesis and to broad outlines of its principles among authors like Smṛtijñānakīrti (eleventh century) and Pang Lodrö Tenpa (Dpang Blo gros brtan pa, 1276–1342). Dar Lotsāwa was the first to make a valiant attempt to tackle the entirety of the Pāṇinian rule system, translating it into Tibetan and making it accessible to a Tibetan readership. No mean feat, by any standard.[50] Even if his published Pāṇinian works are by no means flawless, we should tip our hat to this brave young

---

tshe ji bzhin 'gyur ba'ang mi 'dug cing / legs bshad nor shing der yang nor 'khrul dang ma tshang ba mang ba dang lhag par rig byed las 'byung ba'i nges tshig gi sgrub pa 'di rnams kyi gzhung 'grel gsham du yod pa'i don ma shes nas sgros tsam yang mi 'dug par tshe dbang kun khyab kyis bskul nas bstan pa'i nyin byed kyis bsgyur ba'o / / mangga laṃ / gu ṇas zhus so.

48. See also Smith 2001, 331n826.

49. Verhagen 1994, 320.

50. See also Mukhopadhyaya 1944, 69.

scholar, Dar Lotsāwa Ngawang Püntsok Lhündrup, for opening the portal to the palace of Pāṇini's grammar for Tibetan scholastics.

In this spirit, Leonard van der Kuijp, the honoree of this splendid volume, has throughout his career been a formidable force in opening portals, granting his students and colleagues access to many venues and documents of interest and importance in their research. A *kalyāṇamitra* if ever there was one.

References

Abhyankar, K. V., and J. M. Shukla. 1977 [1961]. *A Dictionary of Sanskrit Grammar.* 2nd rev. ed. Gaekwad's Oriental Series 134. Baroda: Oriental Institute.

Bira, S., and O. Sukhbaatar. 1986. "On the Tibetan and Mongolian Translations of Sanskrit Grammatical Works." In *Sanskrit and World Culture: Proceedings of the Fourth World Sanskrit Conference of the International Association of Sanskrit Studies, Weimar, May 23–30, 1979*, edited by W. Morgenroth, 153–61. Schriften zur Geschichte und Kultur des Alten Orients 18. Berlin: Akademie-Verlag.

Blo bzang Nor bu Śāstrī. 1989. *Mchog sbyin rgyal gis mdzad pa'i dga' byed zla zer* [Lokacakṣu-granthamālā 1]. Sarnath: n.p.

Cardona, G. 1976. *Pāṇini: A Survey of Research.* The Hague: Mouton.

Chandra, Lokesh, ed. 1975. *The Collected Works of Longdol Lama: Parts 1, 2.* New Delhi: International Academy of Indian Culture.

Dash, N. K. 1993. *A Survey on Sanskrit Grammar in Tibetan Language.* Delhi: Agam Kala Prakashan.

———. 1994. "Tibetan Translation of *Pāṇini–Vyākaraṇa Sūtras, Mahābhāṣya, Kāśikā, Prakriyā-Kaumudī* and *Siddhānta-Kaumudī*: A Comparative Study." *The Tibet Journal* 19.1: 24–47.

Dbyangs can sgra mdo'i rtsa 'grel dang mtshams sbyor lnga pa sogs. Zhol par ma. BDRC W12419.

Ghosh, B. 1970. "Study of Sanskrit Grammar in Tibet." *Bulletin of Tibetology* 7.2: 21–41.

Gser 'bris Bstan 'gyur. Unpublished manuscript. BDRC W23702.

Huber, T. 2008. *The Holy Land Reborn: Pilgrimage and the Tibetan Reinvention of Buddhist India.* Buddhism and Modernity 3. Chicago: The University of Chicago Press.

Liebich, B. 1895. "Das *Cāndra-Vyākaraṇa.*" *Nachrichten der Königlichen Gesellschaft der Wissenschaften zu Göttingen, Philologisch-historische Klasse* 3: 272–321.

———. 1919. *Zur Einführung in die indische einheimische Sprachwissenschaft*, vol. 1, *Das Kātantra.* Heidelberg: Sitzungsberichte der Heidelberger Akademie der Wissenschaften.

Luo, Hong. 2016. "The *Kāraka* Section of Rāmacandra's *Prakriyākaumudī*: A Comparative Study of the Sanskrit Original and the Tibetan and Mongolian Translations." In *Cross-Cultural Transmission of Buddhist Texts: Theories and Practices of Translation*, edited by Dorji Wangchuk, 119–38. Indian and Tibetan Studies 5. Hamburg: Department of Indian and Tibetan Studies.

Mukhopadhyaya, S. K. 1944. "Tibetan Translation of *Prakriyā-Kaumudī* and the Mention of *Siddhānta-Kaumudī* Therein." *Indian Historical Quarterly* 20: 63–69.

Si tu paṇ chen chos kyi 'byung gnas kyi bka' 'bum. 2014. Chengdu: Si khron mi rigs dpe skrun khang. BDRC W2PD17429.

Smith, E. G. 2001. *Among Tibetan Texts: History and Literature of the Himalayan Plateau*. Boston: Wisdom Publications.

Snellgrove, D. L., and H. E. Richardson. 1968. *A Cultural History of Tibet*. London: Weidenfeld and Nicolson.

Trivedi, K. P., ed. 1925–1931. *The Prakriyākaumudī of Rāmachandra (in Two Parts), with the Commentary Prasāda of Viṭṭhala and with a Critical Notice of Manuscripts and an Exhaustive and Critical Introduction*. Bombay Sanskrit and Prakrit 78 and 82. Poona: V. G. Paranjpe.

Tucci, G. 1957. "The Fifth Dalai Lama as a Sanskrit Scholar." *Sino-Indian Studies* 5: 235–40.

Verhagen, Pieter C. 1994. *A History of Sanskrit Grammatical Literature in Tibet*, vol. 1, *Transmission of the Canonical Literature*. Leiden: Brill.

———. 2001. *A History of Sanskrit Grammatical Literature in Tibet*, vol. 2, *Assimilation into Indigenous Scholarship*. Leiden: Brill.

Institutional History

All in the Dudjom Family: Overlapping Modes of Authority and Transmission in the Golok Treasure Scene

Holly Gayley

Religious life in the Tibetan region of Golok and neighboring Serta has historically synthesized a variety of local, regional, and pan-Tibetan modes of religious authority and networks of affiliation. These include clan configurations cemented through local mountain deity cults, teacher-student relationships established through tantric ritual, reincarnation schemas connecting people and places across lifetimes, and networks of monastic affiliation. Its local Nyingma monasteries are typically linked to monastic seats in neighboring Kham, primarily Katok, Dzogchen, and Payül. The revelation of treasures, or *terma* (*gter ma*), has operated within these dense and overlapping networks. Charismatic *tertöns* or "revealers of treasures" (*gter ston*) often founded new monasteries and ritual systems that gradually became integrated into existing networks of affiliation while maintaining a distinct line of transmission, frequently passed through the family and/or incarnation lines.

This chapter considers a towering figure in the Golok treasure scene, the visionary Dudjom Lingpa (1835–1904), and his scions across four generations—all formidable religious figures in their own right. I turn to a local genealogy of the Dudjom line that I stumbled on during field research. The find was based on an impulse to collect noteworthy texts that was inculcated in me by Leonard van der Kuijp and Gene Smith. In their estimation, contemporary Tibetan publications are ephemera, published once and difficult to locate thereafter. During the early years when the Tibetan Buddhist Resource Center (TBRC, now BDRC) was located in Gene's house in Cambridge, Leonard encouraged all the Tibetan studies graduate students at Harvard to volunteer there. Some of the seemingly mundane tasks of sorting Tibetan works by genre, organizing new acquisitions by topic, and cataloguing collections proved to be invaluable skills for scouring bookstores for intriguing works. Since then, whenever I visit Tibetan and Himalayan areas, I am always on the lookout for new and unusual publications, and a number of research projects were born out of that impulse. This chapter is one such project; it is a revision of a series of blog posts originally published on the TBRC website.[1]

Four generations of the Dudjom line are presented in a genealogical work published in 2003 titled *Wondrous Golden Ears of Grain* (*Ngo mtshar gser gyi snye ma*). It takes up seventy-four pages in *A Literary Cornucopia of Myrobalan* (*Deb chung a ru ra'i dga' tshal*), an anthology dedicated to the biographies of local religious figures in and around Golok. This genealogy by the Serta-based historian Pema Ösel Tayé traces the family and religious lineage of Dudjom Lingpa down to the present, constructed from the vantage point of the current holder of its transmission, his great-grandson Pema Tekchok Gyeltsen (b. 1937), whose name is found in the subtitle, *An Abbreviated Chronicle of a Vidyādhara Lineage, the Ancestors of the Supreme Lord of Refuge, Pema Tekchok Tenpé Gyeltsen.* In this way, *Wondrous Golden Ears of Grain* is part of a wider trend in Tibetan areas of China to recover local histories in the interest of cultural continuity after the ravages of the Maoist period.

From the eighteenth century forward, Golok has been a hub for treasure revelation in line with the Nyingma predominance in the region, particularly at the nexus of the Ser, Do, and Mar river valleys in present-day Serta and Padma counties, Sichuan and Qinghai provinces respectively.[2] This chapter examines overlapping modes of religious authority and transmission in Golok through the terma lineage of Dudjom Lingpa. I discuss the synthesis of distinct types of lineage transmission and reincarnations schemas, linking people and places across time and space in line with the relational personhood described by Wen-shing Chou and Nancy Lin as a "layering and sharing of multiple identities" in Tibetan contexts.[3] The impact of Dudjom Lingpa and his scions on the Nyingma milieu of Golok is a social history that remains to be written.[4]

1. The posts, published in 2010 and 2011 on www.tbrc.org, made it through at least one website revamp but not subsequent ones. Since I still receive periodic requests for the genealogical information and analysis contained therein, it felt fitting to revise the posts as a chapter in this volume.

2. These counties are predominantly Nyingma. Today in Serta all of the thirty-some monasteries are Nyingma, and in Padma twenty out of twenty-three monasteries are Nyingma. Prior to their forcible incorporation into the People's Republic of China (PRC), there was tremendous mobility and exchange between Serta and Padma as parts of Golok, culturally construed.

3. Chou and Lin 2021, 160.

4. Note that I use the term "scions" here to include three generations of his descendants who have played key roles in Buddhist institutions and lineages in Golok and more broadly in eastern Tibet.

This chapter attempts the more modest task of inquiring into the details of his family genealogy as intertwined with modes of transmission specific to the Nyingma school of Tibetan Buddhism.

The Scions of Dudjom Lingpa

The scions of the nineteenth-century tertön Dudjom Lingpa had a significant impact on the religious history of Golok and environs. The eldest, Jikmé Tenpé Nyima (1865–1926), became a scholar of great acclaim and served as the third in a line of Dodrupchen incarnations. Another son, Drimé Özer (1881–1924), became a leading tertön of his generation and was considered an emanation of the fourteenth-century Nyingma master Longchenpa. As a family treasure lineage *par excellence*, each generation in the Dudjom line has produced prominent tertöns: among his sons, Drimé Özer, Namkha Jikmé, and Dorjé Dradül; among his grandsons, Künzang Nyima, Sönam Detsen, and Tendzin Nyima; and among his great-grandsons, Doli Nyima. In the late nineteenth and early twentieth centuries in Golok, the treasure lineage of Dudjom Lingpa flourished while overlapping with others, particularly Jikmé Lingpa's legacy through the First Dodrupchen Jikmé Trinlé Özer (1745–1821), whose associated monasteries—Yarlung Pemakö and, later, Dodrupchen Gön—became important hubs for the practice and study of the *Longchen Nyingtik* cycle in eastern Tibet.[5] Not only was his eldest son recognized as a reincarnation of Dodrupchen, but other sons and grandsons were linked to Jikmé Lingpa's legacy in the region in various ways, including student-teacher relationships and reincarnation lines.

The Dudjom line has synthesized distinct processes for the transmission of esoteric Nyingma teachings and ritual cycles, including family succession, reincarnation schemas, and the revelation of treasures. One can see this synthesis through three variants of reincarnation found in his family line. First and foremost, Jikmé Tenpé Nyima as the Third Dodrupchen exemplifies the normative schema for reincarnate lamas in Tibet, consisting of a line of successive tulkus (*sprul sku*) associated with a monastic seat, each recognized and enthroned after the death of the previous one. The tulku system developed in central Tibet from the thirteenth century onward and later spread to eastern Tibet.[6] According to Gray Tuttle's statistical analysis, the eighteenth century

5. According to Tulku Thondup (1996), the First Dodrupchen established his seat in 1810 at Yarulung Pemakö in Serta and the Second Dodrupchen had to relocate his community to present-day Dodrupchen Gön in neighboring Padma in 1862 during the Nyarong War.

6. The Karmapa line is often depicted as the oldest existing line of tulkus or reincarnate

witnessed a flourishing of tulku lines among the Geluk in Amdo, followed by a rise in tulku recognition among the Nyingma in eastern Tibet during the nineteenth to early twentieth centuries.[7] This came about, in part, through their proclivity for recognizing multiple reincarnations of a single figure. For example, Jikmé Lingpa had three incarnations in eastern Tibet,[8] and one of those, Jamyang Khyentsé Wangpo, had another five plus.[9] Needless to say, the Third Dodrupchen himself had three recognized incarnations.[10] In its more classic one-to-one style of succession, the tulku system allowed for a "concentration of charismatic, economic, and social power"[11] that provided administrative continuity for monastic succession and in Central Tibet facilitated the hierocratic form of government under the Dalai Lamas.[12]

Early on, the Nyingma formulated its own reincarnation schema in the emergent treasure tradition, though not without contention. As a case in point, the famed twelfth-century tertön Nyangrel Nyima Özer claimed to be the rebirth of the emperor Tri Songdetsen, augmenting his family genealogical connections to the imperial period (seventh to ninth centuries) when Buddhism first became established in Tibet.[13] Dan Hirshberg traces the "confrontation between patrilineal and reincarnate inheritance" when Guru Chöwang staked a claim as Nyangrel's reincarnation, thereby promoting his own stature while challenging the primacy of family succession.[14] In the Dudjom line, the tertön Drimé Özer traced his past lives through Longchenpa to the eighth-century princess Pemasel who, according to treasure lore, was temporarily revived by

---

lamas; see Wylie 1978, and Manson 2009, 31–32. Cabezon 2017 traces the phenomenon of Tibetans identifying the "incarnations of previous masters" to the eleventh and twelfth century. Yet it is important to distinguish between claims of emanation (*sprul pa*) status that provide one or more authoritative antecedents for a living master, male or female, and a tulku (*sprul sku*) line with an associated monastic seat and material assets.

7. Tuttle 2017.

8. These are characterized as body, speech, and mind emanations: Do Khyentsé Yeshé Dorjé (1800–66), Dza Patrül Rinpoché (1808–87), and Jamyang Khyentsé Wangpo (1820–92), respectively.

9. See Smith 2001, 268–9; and Tuttle 2017, 49–50. Tulku Thondup 1996 provides biographical information for a number of these figures as holders of the *Longchen Nyingtik*.

10. These were Yarlung Tenpai Nyima, Rigdzin Jalü Dorjé, and Thubten Trinlé Palzangpo.

11. Tuttle 2017, 29.

12. On the system of incarnate lamas, as it evolved into the succession of Dalai Lamas, see van der Kuijp 2005.

13. See Hirshberg 2016.

14. Hirshberg 2017, 65.

Padmasambhava in order to pass on esoteric knowledge, later hidden as treasures. This form of reincarnation, particular to the treasure tradition, traces the past lives of tertöns to the imperial period in order to legitimate their revelations as the teachings of early tantric masters in Tibet, foremost among them the eight-century Indian master Padmasambhava.

The treasure traditions' version of reincarnation does not demand a linear succession of incarnations, and the past-life genealogy of Dudjom Lingpa illustrates this point well. After a timeless reference to his identity as the emanation of Vajradhara, the first on the list of Dudjom Lingpa's past lives is Śāriputra, linking him to the historical Buddha as a prominent disciple, and next is the Indian siddha Hūṃ(chen)kara, locating him in the tantric milieu of medieval India. Never mind the gap of more than a millennium. His past life in Tibet during the eighth century, which is crucial to his capacity to reveal treasures, is reckoned as the translator Khyeuchung of the Drok clan, situating him as a direct disciple of Padmasambhava. Rather than emphasizing linear succession, a tertön's past lives routinely skip across the centuries with a focus on linking them to seminal times and places in the history of Buddhism and its transmission to Tibet. In addition, tertöns often count previous tertöns among their past lives. In this vein, Dudjom Lingpa is referred to as the Third Düdül, an emanation of the seventeenth-century tertön Düdül Dorjé (1615–72) and a lesser-known figure Düdül Rölpatsel.

Next and perhaps most interestingly, in the Dudjom line one finds reincarnation schemas articulated within the family. Rather than the confrontation noted by Hirshberg early in the treasure tradition,[15] in this case we see a synthesis between patrilineal decent and reincarnation schemas in a way that was mutually reinforcing. Dudjom Lingpa spawned a line of three emanations, the most famous of which was Dudjom Rinpoché Jikdrel Yeshé Dorjé (1904–87), who was based in Kongpo and left Tibet in the 1950s to become the head of the Nyingma lineage in exile. Notably, Dudjom Lingpa's other two emanations were his own grandsons, Dzongter Künzang Nyima (1904–58) and Sönam Detsen (1910–58), who both remained in Golok and became tertöns in their own right. The latter also served as the steward of Dudjom Lingpa's monastic seat, Dartsang Kelzang Gön. In Künzang Nyima and Sönam Detsen, one sees several processes of transmission intertwined: family succession, reincarnation schemas, and the revelation of treasures.

Alongside the tertöns in the family, all of the scions of Dudjom Lingpa's were recognized as reincarnate lamas. It is not uncommon for the children of a Nyingma master to be identified as emanations of prominent religious figures

15. Hirshberg 2017.

from the previous generation. Two of his sons, Khyentrül Dzamling Wangyal (1869–1907) and Drupwang Namkha Jikmé (1888–1960) were regarded as emanations of no less figures than Do Khyentsé Yeshé Dorjé and Patrül Rinpoché respectively, themselves considered emanations of Jikmé Lingpa. While the male heirs of Nyingma masters, when recognized as such, can become high-ranking lamas at area monasteries, female heirs are more likely to be identified as ḍākinīs or emanations of Yeshé Tsogyal, and thereby have no proximate antecedent or associated monastic seat. Unusually the female tertön Sera Khandro, a teacher in her own right and consort to Drimé Özer, provided a proximate antecedent for at least one of Dudjom Lingpa's great-granddaughters, Lhacam Chökyi Drönma, as well as for the female tertön Khandro Tāré Lhamo (1938–2002). Khandro Tāré Lhamo was the daughter of a tertön of local renown and married into the Dudjom line through one of Künzang Nyima's sons, Mingyur Dorjé.[16]

Articulating Lineage in Golok

In its broad contours, *Wondrous Golden Ears of Grain* chronicles the "vidyādhara lineage of the great tertön father and sons" (*gter chen yab sras rig 'dzin brgyud pa*), whereby *yab sras* refers to the progenitor Dudjom Lingpa and his successors in both familial and religious senses. Here it might be more appropriate to use "scions," since it can refer to descendants of more than one generation. In addition, several figures such as Dudjom Lingpa and Drimé Özer have reincarnations in subsequent generations within the family. In this fashion, the work establishes generational continuity through male figures in the family line through which the treasures of Dudjom Lingpa and other tertöns among his scions have passed. Again we can discern the emphasis on lineage transmission and continuity from the subtitle, which labels the text as "a chronicle of the ancestors of Pema Tekchok Tenpé Gyeltsen." As this suggests, lineage is constructed from the vantage point of the contemporary holder of its transmission, affirming his legitimacy. This assertion of continuity takes place against the historical backdrop of rupture, with the imprisonment of elites including religious figures in the late 1950s in Golok, the closure of Buddhist monasteries, and the nearly twenty-year hiatus in public religious observances through the end of the Cultural Revolution and death of Mao.

Thus *Wondrous Golden Ears of Grain* forges continuity across that rupture as a family genealogy and history of the transmission for Dudjom Lingpa's corpus

16. See Gayley 2016. Tragically, he and two of his brothers were imprisoned in the late 1950s and died in prison, as discussed later in this chapter.

of revelations. It is somewhat of a hybrid between genres. In line with a family genealogy (*gdung rabs*), it is concerned with family succession in patrilineal terms—the bone (*gdung*) being related to the male. For this reason, unfortunately the daughters, granddaughters, and great-granddaughters of Dudjom Lingpa are relegated to the footnotes of history, a line or two at the end of each generation. Similar to "golden rosary" (*gser phreng*) collections, it traces the transmission for a specific set of teaching through its lineage holders and features a collection of abbreviated biographies for each of the male lineage successors. This is clear from the colophon, which refers to its contents as *Brief Biographies through the Fourth Generation of Terchen Dudjom Lingpa* (*Gter chen bdud 'joms gling pa'i mi rabs bzhi pa yan chod kyi rnam thar mdor bsdus*).

In line with this, several distinct modes of religious authority and lineage transmission are highlighted. Structurally, family is most prominent, with the text arranged according to four generations (*mi rabs*): biographies for Dudjom Lingpa himself being first, his eight sons second, his seven of nine grandsons third, and his eight great-grandsons fourth. His four daughters, five granddaughters, and two great-granddaughters are also mentioned, but unlike their male counterparts, they are not accorded actual biographies. This is despite the fact that one granddaughter, Kunzang Wangmo,[17] is listed as an emanation of Yeshé Tsogyal and a lineage holder of Dudjom Lingpa's treasures, while others are named as mothers to local lamas of some prominence. Within the biographies for the male descendants, incarnation status is also accorded prominence and given at the outset. Only for Dudjom Lingpa and two of his sons is a past life genealogy provided; otherwise the focus is on one or two main figures for whom the individual serves as tulku or emanation. (A range of terms are used: *yang srid*, *rnam sprul*, *rol gar*, and variants.) Next the father is listed, and often but not always the mother; then the birth year is given, according to Tibetan and Western calendars. This indicates the importance of reincarnation schema to religious authority in Golok and environs, even in a lineage concerned with transmission primarily through the family.

Rather than a chronology of each of their lives, only a skeleton account is provided, for the most part in just one or several paragraphs. As an exception to this pattern, more detailed narratives are provided for four figures, one in each generation: Dudjom Lingpa himself, his son Drimé Özer, his grandson Dzongter Künzang Nyima, and his great-grandson Pema Tekchok Gyeltsen. The first three were charismatic figures and prominent tertöns of their respective generations, whose life stories are compiled in another work by the same

17. Kunzang Wangmo is featured in the documentary *Sky Dancer* (2010), directed by Jody Kemmerer (http://www.skydancermovie.com/about-2/).

author, *Liberation of the Great Tertön Dudjom, Father and Scions* (*Gter chen bdud 'joms yab sras kyi rnam thar*).[18] As for Pema Tekchok Gyeltsen, that his biography is more extensive than those of his brothers and cousins is another way (in addition to the title) that the text foregrounds him as the main lineage holder of his generation.

Given the brevity of biographical sketches, it is easy to discern what is considered the most important information to convey. After incarnation status and family ties, the teacher-student relationship is the other mode of lineage transmission highlighted in this collection. Not surprisingly, the teacher-student relationship overlaps with family relations such that many in the Dudjom line served as teachers to their sons and nephews. Each brief account also provides dates of birth and death, a list of teachers and disciples—in the case of tertöns, the trustees (*chos bdag*) for their treasure corpus are also named—and any textual compositions and building projects. See the appendix for a list of each figure, with several of these features duly noted.

While the family members in Dudjom Lingpa's lineage served as teachers and students to one another, over time fewer are singled out in *Wondrous Golden Ears of Grain* as having received and propagated Dudjom Lingpa's treasure corpus. In the second generation, six are highlighted as lineage holders for his treasures: Mipam Dorjé, Drimé Özer, Lhachen Tobgyel, Namkha Jikmé, Dorjé Dradül, and Dzamling Wangyal, who is also credited with managing Dudjom Lingpa's seat, Dartsang Kelzang Gön. Notably his first two sons, affiliated with Dodrupchen Monastery, which is the monastic seat established by the Second Dodrupchen Jikmé Püntsok Jungné, do not. In the third generation, his incarnations Künzang Nyima and Sönam Detsen (who managed Dudjom Lingpa's seat in Dartsang) were holders of his treasures, as was his grandson Choktrül Dampa and granddaughter Kunzang Wangmo, who is said to have distinguished herself in protecting the succession of Dudjom Lingpa's teachings. In large part due to historical circumstances, in the fourth generation of patrilineal succession, Pema Tekchok Gyeltsen is centered as the one carrying forward Dudjom Lingpa's treasures in addition to the revelations of his own father, Dzongter Kunzang Nyima. Yet in an interview (Serta, June 2006) Pema Tekchok Gyeltsen also named his cousin Tamdrin Wanggyel as an important lineage holder as head of Dartsang Kelzang Gön.

18. Pad ma 'od gsal mtha' yas 2000. This work in 188 pages features a secret autobiography by Dudjom Lingpa in roughly sixty pages (3–64), an abbreviated biography of his son Drimé Özer in thirty pages (73–102), and a biography of his grandson Künzang Nyima in eighty pages (105–86). The latter two were composed by Pema Ösel Tayé.

Vagaries of Transmission

The assertion of lineage continuity in *Wondrous Golden Ears of Grain* participates in a larger literary trend to recapture local history against the historical backdrop of rupture during the years leading up to and including the Cultural Revolution. Broadly speaking, Ban Wang notes how across China in the post-Mao era the impulse to rearticulate the past informs the Chinese writing of history, personal memories, family sagas, and regional lore.[19] Similarly, in Tibetan areas under Chinese rule, the publication of family genealogies (*gdung rabs*), monastic succession (*gdan rabs*), and sacred biographies (*rnam thar*) is part of a movement to recover local history since economic and cultural liberalization became possible from the 1980s forward. The author of this work, Pema Ösel Tayé,[20] is an important contributor to this movement in the Golok region as the publisher, author, and editor of numerous biographies, histories, and edited volumes dedicated to preserving local history and culture.

Through the scions of Dudjom Lingpa, we can see both the strength and vulnerability of densely woven modes of religious authority concentrated within the family. On the one hand, family members served as teachers and students to one another across the generations, providing a strong sense of continuity. On the other hand, the transmission of Dudjom Lingpa's treasures within the family has been precarious for several reasons. For the scions of Dudjom Lingpa who were themselves tertöns, it is not clear to what extent they propagated Dudjom Lingpa's treasures versus their own revelations. For those recognized as incarnations outside the family, with seats at local monasteries, none are listed as receiving or propagating his treasures. To the extent that these same figures were generally ordained, they also could not contribute to the growth of the family line. Among Dudjom Lingpa's grandsons, only two had children, Künzang Nyima and Sönam Detsen, and both were tertöns in their own right. What this means is that the number of sons through patrilineal descent remained rather constant over the generations (eight, seven, and eight), and not all of them propagated his treasures. These small numbers left the family line vulnerable to the vagaries of recent Tibetan history.

Dudjom Lingpa's family line was nearly wiped out during the socialist transformation of Golok in the late 1950s. One can measure the enormous damage to Buddhist lineages and their continuity into the present in the loss of human

19. Ban Wang 2004.

20. Pema Ösel Tayé is a monk affiliated with Dungkar Gompa who works at the Bureau of Culture, History, Education and Health (Rig gnas lo rgyus tshan slob 'phrod rten mthun tshogs su u yon ltan khang) at the county seat in Serta, Sichuan Province.

life, including lineage holders. In Tibetan Buddhism, even if textual collections are preserved, a direct transmission is necessary for their practice. When we look at a single family, as we have been, it vividly illustrates the Paṇchen Lama's criticism of Communist rule in his 7,000 Character Petition, submitted to Chinese Communist Party leadership, in which he complained about the "endangering of Tibetan people as a nationality" due to the decline in population, the imprisonment of young men, and the repression of Buddhism.[21] While the Cultural Revolution (1966–76) involved the destruction and looting of buildings on the grounds of Buddhist monasteries, in the late 1950s the target was Tibetan elites: landowners, wealthy traders, and prominent religious figures, who were imprisoned, subjected to struggle sessions, and/or condemned to hard labor in an attempt to eradicate the so-called evils of the old society. On top of that there was widespread famine throughout China, precipitated by the failed policy of the Great Leap Forward. Between 1958 and 1960, Dudjom Lingpa's two youngest sons, four of his grandsons, and three of his great-grandsons died. Few details are given in *Wondrous Golden Ears of Grain* for the fourth generation, although Pema Tekchok Gyeltsen indicated to me in an interview that his three brothers all died in prison,[22] including Mingyur Dorjé, the first husband of Khandro Tāré Lhamo.

Within the patrilineal family, the transmission for Dudjom Lingpa's treasure corpus continues mainly through Pema Tekchok Gyeltsen, the only surviving son of Künzang Nyima. According to *Wondrous Golden Ears of Grain*, he received the transmission for Dudjom Lingpa's treasures as well as his father's in his youth directly from his father before the age of twenty. Nonetheless his focus has been on preserving and propagating his father Dzongter Künzang Nyima's treasure corpus, much of which was lost during the Cultural Revolution. In the early 2000s Pema Tekchok Gyeltsen republished what could be recovered from his father's treasure corpus in twenty-seven volumes,[23] and following that, at the request of Gyatrul Rinpoché, he traveled to the United States in 2008 to transmit the collection in Oregon, Texas, and California.[24] As for the sons of Sönam Detsen, one was a tertön named Doli Nyima, whose mother was Chöying Drölma, the daughter of Sera Khandro. Tragically, he disappeared sometime in the mid-1960s. The other surviving sons of Sönam

21. Tibet Information Network 1997.

22. Interview in Serta, June 2006.

23. According to Pema Tekchok Gyeltsen, only twenty-seven volumes from Dzongter Künzang Nyima's treasure corpus survive of the original collection of sixty volumes. Drimé Özer's treasure corpus appears to have been lost.

24. Personal communication from Lama Chönam.

Detsen were too young to have received meaningful teachings and transmissions prior to the persecution of religion that took place during their childhoods. Yet they played a major role in reconstructing Dartsang Kelzang Gön,[25] the seat of Dudjom Lingpa that had been in their father's care before being destroyed in the Cultural Revolution.

Conclusion

With its emphasis on the patrilineal line, *Wondrous Golden Ears of Grain* leaves out important parts of the story regarding the transmission for Dudjom Lingpa's teachings and treasure corpus. When the matrilineal line is taken into account, lineage succession broadens and appears more resilient. Notably, a daughter of Dorje Dradül had three accomplished sons, Gönpa Kyab, Tsedrub Kyab, and Sönam Drakpa, one of whom I met in Golok in 2004 and received the *lung* for Dudjom Lingpa's celebrated Chöd practice.[26] Transmission through the Dudjom family line continues up to the present through these figures and also descendants of Kunzang Wangmo, such as Chakung Jigmé Wangdrak who teaches in the United States and founded the Abhaya Fellowship in 2014 in El Cerrito, California. Thus, while overlapping modes of authority enhance the prestige of tertöns and their successors, the diffusion of authority through multiple avenues of transmission increases the chances for the survival and continuity of a lineage of teachings.

Outside the family, Dudjom Lingpa's renowned incarnation, Dudjom Rinpoché Jikdrel Yeshé Dorjé, has been the most dynamic in spreading the transmission for his treasures. Under the banner of the *Dudjom Tersar*, or the "new revelations" of Dudjom (*Bdud 'joms gter gsar*), he published Dudjom Lingpa's treasure corpus in twenty volumes in Kalimpong in 1978 and complemented it with his own writings and revelations.[27] As head of the Nyingma lineage in exile, Dudjom Rinpoché spread the *Dudjom Tersar* far and wide internationally, making it one of the most widely practiced treasure cycles alongside the *Longchen Nyingtik*. Back in Golok, Dujdom Rinpoché's own son Dola Tulku Jikmé Chökyi Nyima is a prominent holder of the *Dudjom*

25. Krung go'i bod rig pa zhib 'jug lte gnas kyi chos lugs lo rgyus zhib 'jug 1995.

26. This was an auspicious meeting with Gönpa Kyab during preliminary research on a trip with Sarah Jacoby to Dartsang Kelzang Gön and its surrounding area.

27. See Bdud 'joms gling pa 1978. See Cathy Cantwell 2020 on how Dudjom Rinpoché augmented and integrated revelations from his predecessors, Dudjom Lingpa and Düdül Dorjé.

Tersar, and he empowered others, including Khandro Tāré Lhamo and her second husband, Namtrül Rinpoche, to disseminate it.

There is a final twist in the fate of the Dudjom line. After the passing of Dudjom Rinpoché in 1987, one of his reincarnations was discovered in Golok, identified by Khandro Tāré Lhamo in the early 1990s as his own grandson, Sangyé Pema Shepa, the child of Dola Tulku Jikmé Chökyi Nyima. Notably, one of Dudjom Rinpoché's other sons, Thinley Norbu (1931–2011), was recognized as an emanation of Drimé Özer. Once again, family and reincarnation schemes overlap as the Dudjom reincarnation line has migrated over to the family of Dudjom Rinpoché Jikdrel Yeshé Dorjé. Yet, with the sudden passing of Sangyé Pema Shepa on February 15, 2022, at the young age of thirty-two, the vagaries of lineage transmission remain as salient as ever.

Appendix

The following biographical notes on the scions of Dudjom Lingpa are derived from *Wondrous Golden Ears of Grain: An Abbreviated Chronicle of a Vidyādhara Lineage, the Ancestors of the Supreme Lord of Refuge, Pema Tekchok Tenpé Gyeltsen* (Pad ma 'od gsal mtha' yas 2003). Only details relevant to the discussion of overlapping modes of religious authority and lineage transmission are included.

First Generation

Terchen Dudjom Lingpa (Gter chen Bdud 'joms gling pa, 1835–1904)
Alias: Khrag thung Bdud 'joms rdo rje, Lcags skong Gter chen Bdud 'joms rdo rje khro lod rtsal
Parents: Rje lcags skong A bstan (*yab*) and Dmu tsha lga yi rigs kyi Bo rdzogs (*yum*)
Past Lives: Rnal byor dbang phyug Nus ldan rdo rje, Nyan thos Śāri'i bu, Rig dzin Hūṃ chen ka ra, Brog ban Khye'u chung lo tsa, Kaḥ thog Dam pa bde gshegs, Grum gyi mkhar nag pa, He pa chos 'byung, Rig 'dzin Bdud 'dul rdo rje, and Bdud 'dul rol pa rtsal
Consorts: Khra bza' Bsod nams mtsho, Ske bza' Sangs rgyas mtsho, and A skyabs bza' Skal bzang sgron ma
Emanations: 'Jigs bral ye shes rdo rje, alias: Gter chen 'Gro 'dul gling pa (*sku sprul*); Kun bzang nyi ma, alias: Rig 'dzin Nus ldan rdo rje (*gsung sprul*); and Bsod nams lde'u btsan, alias: Rdo rje drag po rtsal (*thugs sprul*)

Second Generation

1. Dodrup Rinpoché Jikmé Tenpé Nyima (Rdo grub rin po che 'Jigs med bstan pa'i nyi ma, 1865–1926)
Parents: Gter chen Bdud 'joms gling pa (*yab*) and Khra bza' Bsod nams mtsho (*yum*)
Incarnation Status: Rdo grup rin po che'i yang srid
Past Lives: Rgyal po Dza, Chos rgyal Mu khri btsan po, and Gter chen Sangs rgyas gling pa
Teachers: Mkhan chen Padmavajra, Dpal sprul rin po che O rgyan 'jigs med chos kyi dbang po, Mu ru sprul sku, Rdzogs sprul bzhi pa Mi gyur nam mkha'i rdo rje, Ju Mi pham phyogs las rnam rgyal, Kong sprul Yon tan rgya mtsho, Dznyā ba dge bshes, and 'Jam dbyangs Mkhyen brtse'i dbang po
Students: Mgar ra mkhan po 'Jigs med 'od gsal, A mye mkhan po Dam chos 'od zer, Ser shul mkhan po Ngag dbang rgya mtsho, Glu shul mkhan po Dkon mchog bstan pa'i sgron me, 'Jam dbyangs Chos kyi blo gros, and Gter chen Las rab gling pa

2. Choktrül Pema Dorjé (Mchog sprul Pad ma rdo rje, 1867–1934)
Parents: Gter chen Bdud 'joms gling pa (*yab*) and Khra bza' Bsod nams mtsho (*yum*)
Incarnation Status: Sgra bsgyur Mar pa'i skyes mtha' mchog sprul and Rdo grub chen dgon pa'i Tsha tsha sprul sku'i yang srid
Teachers: Dpal sprul rin po che O rgyan 'jigs med chos kyi dbang po and Rdo grub rin po che 'Jigs med bstan pa'i nyi ma

3. Khyentrül Dzamling Wanggyel (Mkhyen sprul Dzam gling dbang rgyal, 1869–1907)
Parents: Gter chen Bdud 'joms gling pa (*yab*) and Ske bza' Sangs rgyas mtsho (*yum*)
Incarnation Status: Mdo mkhyen brtse Ye shes rdo rje'i yang srid
Teachers: Dpal sprul rin po che O rgyan 'jigs med chos kyi dbang po, Mtshams sprul rin po che Kun bzang bde chen rdo rje, and Gter chen Bdud 'joms gling pa

4. Namtrül Mipam Dorjé (Rnam sprul Mi pham rdo rje, b. 1879)
Parents: Gter chen Bdud 'joms gling pa (*yab*) and Ske bza Sangs rgyas mtsho (*yum*)
Incarnation Status: Gong smyon sbas pa'i rnal byor and Rigs 'dzin chen po'i rnam sprul
Teachers: Dpal sprul rin po che O rgyan 'jigs med chos kyi dbang po and Gter chen Bdud 'joms gling pa

5. Tulku Drimé Özer (Sprul sku Dri med 'od zer, 1881–1924)
Alias: Rig 'dzin chen po Pad ma 'gro 'dul Gsang sngags gling pa
Parents: Gter chen Bdud 'joms gling pa (*yab*) and Ske bza' Sangs rgyas mtsho (*yum*)
Past Lives: Dge slong Kun dga' bo, Grub pa'i dbang phyug Dharmālakṣipa, Rgya gar mkhan po Vimamitra, Lha lcam Pad ma gsal, G.yu sgra snying po, Dar phyar ba, Pad ma las 'brel rtsal, Klong chen Rdo rje gzi brjid, Pad ma gling pa, O rgyan bsam gtan gling pa, Nam mkha rdo rje, Bzhad pa rdo rje, 'Gro 'dul gling pa, Hūṃ nag me 'bar, Nam mkha 'jigs med, Klong gsal snying po, Bde chen gling pa, Chos nyid rang grol, Mkhan po Śākyadeva, and Bla ma 'Jam dbyangs
Teachers: Rdo grub rin po che 'Jigs med bstan pa'i nyi ma and Gter chen Bdud 'joms gling pa
Consort: Mkha' 'gro Bde ba'i rdo rje (1892–1940), alias: Kun bzang bde skyong chos nyid dbang mo, Dbus bza' mkha' 'gro, or Se ra mkha' 'gro

6. Lhachen Topgyel (Lha chen stobs kyi rgyal po, 1884–1942)
Parents: Gter chen Bdud 'joms gling pa (*yab*) and A skyabs bza' Skal bzang sgron ma (*yum*)
Incarnation Status: Gnubs chen Nam mkha'i snying po'i sprul ba'i rol gar and Gzhi chen A phang sku chen gyi yang srid
Teachers: Gter chen Bdud 'joms gling pa and Sprul sku Dri med 'od zer

7. Drupwang Namkha Jikmé (Grub dbang Nam mkha 'jigs med, 1888–1960)
Alias: Pad ma mkha' klong yangs pa rtsal
Parents: Gter chen Bdud 'joms gling pa (*yab*) and A skyabs bza' Skal bzang sgron ma (*yum*)
Incarnation Status: Dpal sprul rin po che O rgyan 'jigs med chos kyi dbang po'i yang srid
Teachers: Gter chen Bdud 'joms gling pa and Dge ming mkhan po Kun dpal

8. Sechung Dorjé Dradül (Sras chung Rdo rje dgra 'dul, 1891–1959)
Parents: Gter chen Bdud 'joms gling pa (*yab*) and A skyabs bza' Skal bzang sgron ma (*yum*)
Incarnation Status: Gsang bdag dngos snang gnam chos Mi 'gyur rdo rje'i yang sprul
Teachers: Gter chen Bdud 'joms gling pa, Gter chen Las rab gling pa, Rdo grub rin po che 'Jigs med bstan pa'i nyi ma, and Phyag chung dge bshes Dge legs dpal bzang

Daughters of Dudjom Lingpa
Four daughters are identified as ḍākinīs but go unnamed.

Third Generation

1. Dzongter Künzang Nyima (Rdzong gter Kun bzang nyi ma, 1904–58)
Alias: Rig 'dzin Nus ldan rdo rje or Khrag 'thung Nus ldan rdo rje
Parent: Mkhyen sprul Dzam gling dbang rgyal (*yab*)
Incarnation Status: Gter chen Bdud 'joms gling pa'i gsung sprul
Teachers: Gter chen Las rab gling pa and Mkha' 'gro Bde ba'i rdo rje

2. Gyelsé Sönam Detsen (Rgyal sras Bsod nams lde'u btsan (1910–58)
Parent: Sprul sku Dri med 'od zer (*yab*)
Incarnation Status: Gter chen Bdud 'joms gling pa'i thugs sprul
Teachers: Rdo rje dgra 'dul, Kaḥ thog phyag tsha Pad ma phrin las rgya mtsho, Gter chen Las rab gling pa, and Sprul sku Dri med 'od zer

3. Choktrül Tendzin Nyima (Mchog sprul Bstan 'dzin nyi ma, 1918–59)
Parents: Rdo rje dgra 'dul (*yab*) and A skyong bza' Dbang sgron (*yum*)
Incarnation Status: Gzhu chen Bstan pa'i rgyal mtshan gyi yang srid
Teachers: Kaḥ thog phyag tsha Pad ma phrin las rgya mtsho, Rdo rje dgra 'dul, Lung zin Śīlavajra, and Gter chen Las rab gling pa

4. Tulku Tendzin Zangpo (Sprul sku Bstan dzin bzang po, d. 1984)
Parent: Lha chen stobs kyi rgyal po (*yab*)
Teacher: Rdo rje dgra 'dul

5. Choktrül Tashi Topgyel (Mchog sprul Bkra shis stobs rgyal, 1925–59)
Parents: Lha chen stobs kyi rgyal po (*yab*) and Dpa' ri bza' Byang chub sgron ma (*yum*)
Incarnation Status: Pad ma 'gro 'dul Gsang sngags gling pa'i yang srid
Teachers: Gyang sprul Don grub rdo rje, Rdo rje dgra 'dul, Nam mkha 'jigs med, and Kaḥ thog Rmog tsha

6. Choktrül Dampa (Mchog sprul Dam pa, 1928–83)
Parent: Lha chen stobs kyi rgyal po (*yab*)
Incarnation Status: Pha dam pa Rgya gar and Rdza khra ma bla ma 'Jigs med rgyal ba'i myu gu rnam gnyis kyi sprul ba
Teachers: Nam mkha 'jigs med, Rdo rje dgra 'dul, Gyang sprul Don grub rdo

rje, Kaḥ thog Rmog tsha, Lung zin Śīlavajra, and Dpal yul mchog sprul Chos kyi zla ba

7. Tulku Nyida (Sprul sku Nyi zla, 1929–85)
Parent: Lha chen stobs kyi rgyal po (*yab*)
Incarnation Status: Rdo grub rin po che 'Jigs med bstan pa'i nyi ma'i yang srid
Teachers: Nam mkha 'jigs med, Rdo rje dgra 'dul, Lung zin Śīlavajra, and Kaḥ thog Rmog tsha

Granddaughters (and Remaining Grandsons) of Dudjom Lingpa
Sprul sku Nyi zla had three sisters, stated to be ḍākinīs who intentionally took female form, named Dbang mo, Mtsho rgyal, and Bsod nams chos sgron. The former, Dbang mo, had a son who resides in Padma county, named Gter ston Mi 'gyur rin po che. A daughter of Rdo rje dgra 'dul had three accomplished sons—namely, Dgon pa skyabs (alias: Chos nyid gling pa), Tshe sgrub skyabs, and Bsod nams grags pa. Two other grandsons existed, but not enough is known about them to include biographies: Kun bzang lung rtogs 'phel rgyas dpal bzang po and Mchog sprul Bstan pa'i gsal byed. One granddaughter, Kun bzang dbang mo, who appears to be the daughter of Nam mkha 'jigs med, was recognized as an emanation of Ye shes mtsho rgyal. She distinguished herself in protecting the succession of Dudjom Lingpa's teachings and resided at Zla rgyal dgon.

Fourth Generation

1. Choktrül Sherab Tokmé (Mchog sprul Shes rab thogs med, 1925–59)
Parents: Rdzong gter Kun bzang nyi ma (*yab*) and Stug rgya bza' Rin chen mtsho (*yum*)
Incarnation Status: Sprul sku Dri med od zer gyi yang srid
Teachers: Rdo rje dgra 'dul and Rdzong gter Kun bzang nyi ma

2. Tulku Mingyur Dorjé (Sprul sku Mi gyur rdo rje, 1934–59)
Alias: Padma 'od gsal snying po
Parent: Rdzong gter Kun bzang nyi ma (*yab*)
Incarnation Status: Vairocana'i yang srid
Teachers: Rdo rje dgra 'dul, Mkhan po Gang rnam, and Rdzong gter Kun bzang nyi ma
Consort: Mkha' 'gro Tā re lha mo (1938–2002)

3. Choktrül Pema Tekchok Tenpé Gyeltsen (Mchog sprul Pad ma theg mchog bstan pa'i rgyal mtshan, b. 1937)
Parents: Rdzong gter Kun bzang nyi ma (*yab*) and Stug rgya bza' Rin chen mtsho (*yum*)
Incarnation Status: Pad ma rdo rje'i yang sprul
Teachers: Dge rgyan Phyag lo, Mkhan Shes rab grags pa, Grub chen bla ma Lha ri, Rdo grub rin po che Thub bstan phrin las dpal bzang po, Rdo grub rin po che Rig 'dzin Bstan pa'i rgyal mtshan, Dung dkar mchog sprul Nges don rgya mtsho, Rdzong gter Kun bzang nyi ma, Grub chen sprul sku Pad ma rnam rgyal, G.yung shul Pad ma rgya mtsho, and Stag bla Nor bu

4. Choktrül Lhündrup Dorjé (Mchog sprul Lhun grub rdo rje, 1940–60)
Parent: Rdzong gter Kun bzang nyi ma (*yab*)
Incarnation Status: Dbal shul Bsod rgan sprul sku Sna tshogs rang grol gyi yang srid
Teachers: Se ra sprul sku Rin chen phreng ba and Rdzong gter Kun bzang nyi ma

5. Choktrül Doli Nyima (Mchog sprul Mdo li nyi ma, b. 1946)
Alias: Dpal don grub phrin las rnam rgyal
Parents: Gter chen Bsod nams lde'u btsan (*yab*) and Mgar bza' Chos dbyings sgrol ma (*yum*)
Incarnation Status: Dgra lha rtse rgyal gyi sprul ba'i rnam rol
Teachers: Rig 'dzin Stag sham rdo rje, Mkhan Ngag dbang bstan 'dzin, and Bla ma Chos mdzod

6. Tulku Tamdrin Wanggyel (Sprul sku Rta mgrin dbang rgyal, b. 1952)
Parent: Gter chen Bsod nams lde'u btsan (*yab*)
Incarnation Status: Bla ma Che mchog gi yang srid
Teachers: Se ra yang sprul Tshul khrims rgya mtsho, Mkhan chen 'Jigs med phun tshogs, Mchog sprul Nyi zla, and Mchog sprul Dam pa

7. Tulku Pema Wanggyel (Sprul sku Pad ma dbang rgyal, 1953–90)
Parent: Gter chen Bsod nams lde'u btsan (*yab*)
Teachers: Se ra yang sprul Tshul khrims rgya mtsho, Lung rig smra ba'i nyi ma, Sprul sku Nyi zla, and Mchog sprul Dam pa

8. Choktrül Zhenpen Nyima (Mchog sprul Gzhan phan nyi ma, b. 1954)
Parent: Gter chen Bsod nams lde'u btsan (*yab*)
Teacher: Do grub rin po che Thub bstan phrin las dpal bzang po

Great-granddaughters of Dudjom Lingpa

Rdzong gter Kun bzang nyi ma had two daughters, Lha lcam Chos kyi sgron ma and Tshe dzin lha mo. The former is considered to be the reincarnation (*yang srid*) of Mkha' 'gro Bde ba'i rdo rje, alias Se ra mkha' 'gro.

References

Bdud 'joms gling pa. 1978. *The Collected Gter-ma Rediscoveries of Gter chen Bdud-'joms-gliṅ-pa*, edited by Bdud 'joms rin po che 'Jigs bral ye shes rdo rje, 20 vols. Kalimpong, India: Dupjung Lama.

Cabezón, José. 2017. "On Tulku Lineages." *Revue d'Etudes Tibétaines* 38: 1–28.

Cantwell, Cathy. 2020 "Reincarnation and Personal Identity in the Lives of Tibetan Masters: Linking the Revelations of Three Lamas in the Dudjom Tradition." *Life Writing* 17.2: 239–57.

Chou, Wen-shing, and Nancy Lin. 2021. "Karmic Affinities: Rethinking Relations among Tibetan Lamas and the Qing Emperor." In *Water Moon Reflections: Essays in Honor of Patricia Berger*, edited by Ellen Huang, Nancy Lin, Michelle McCoy, and Michelle Wang, 158–213. Berkeley: Institute of East Asian Studies.

Gayley, Holly. 2016. *Love Letters from Golok: A Tantric Couple in Modern Tibet*. New York: Columbia University Press.

Hirshberg, Daniel A. 2016. *Remembering the Lotus-Born: Padmasambhava in the History of Tibet's Golden Age.* Boston: Wisdom Publications.

———. 2017. "A Post-Incarnate Usurper? Inheritance at the Dawn of Catenate Reincarnation in Tibet." *Revue d'Etudes Tibétaines* 38: 65–83.

Krung go'i bod rig pa zhib 'jug lte gnas kyi chos lugs lo rgyus zhib 'jug so'o, Krung go bod brgyud nang bstan mtho rim slob gling, Zi khron zhing chen dkar mdzes khul chos lugs cud, and Dkar mdzes khul yig bsgyur cud. 1995. *Khams phyogs dkar mdzes khul gyi dgon sde so so'i lo rgyus gsal bar bshad pa thub bstan gsal ba'i me long*. Beijing: Krung go'i bod kyi shes rig dpe skrun khang.

van der Kuijp, Leonard W. J. 2005. "The Dalai Lamas and the Origins of Reincarnate Lamas." In *The Dalai Lamas: A Virtual History*, edited by Martin Brauen, 14–31. Chicago: Serindia.

Manson, Charles. 2009. "An Introduction to the Life of Karma Pakshi (1204/6–1283). *Bulletin of Tibetology* 45.1: 25–52.

Pad ma 'od gsal mtha' yas. 2000. *Gter chen bdud joms yab sras kyi rnam thar.* Chengdu: Si khron mi rigs dpe skrun khang.

———. 2003. *Skyabs rje mchog sprul rin po che padma theg mchog bstan pa'i rgyal mtshan gyi yab mes rig 'dzin brgyud pa'i byung ba mdor bsdus tsam brjod pa ngo mtshar gser gyi snye ma.* In *Deb chung a ru ra'i dga' tshal*, 1–74. Chengdu: Si khron mi rigs dpe skrun khang.

Smith, E. Gene. 2001. *Among Tibetan Texts: History and Literature of the Himalayan Plateau*. Boston: Wisdom Publications.
Thondup, Tulku. 1996. *Masters of Meditation and Miracles: The Longchen Nyingthik Lineage of Tibetan Buddhism*. Boston: Shambhala Publications.
Tibet Information Network. 1997. *A Poisoned Arrow: The Secret Report of the 10th Panchen Lama*. London: Tibet Information Network.
Tuttle, Gray. 2017. "Pattern Recognition: Tracking the Spread of the Incarnation Institution through Time and Space across Tibetan Territory." *Revue d'Etudes Tibétaines* 38: 29–64.
Wang Ban. 2004. *Illuminations from the Past: Trauma, Memory, and History in Modern China*. Stanford, CA: Stanford University Press.
Wylie, Turrell. 1978. "Reincarnation: A Political Innovation in Tibetan Buddhism." In *Proceedings of the Csoma de Körös Memorial Symposium*, edited by Louis Ligeti, 579–86. Budapest: Akadémiai Kiadó.

Conflicting Views on Kingship between the Tibetan Buddhist World and the Qing Dynasty: The Fifth Dalai Lama's Visit to Beijing

Ishihama Yumiko

AT THE END of the ninth year of the Shunzhi era (January 1653), the Fifth Dalai Lama (1617–82) visited Beijing, the capital of the Qing dynasty in its infancy. At the time, the Buddhist Khalkha Mongols had not yet become part of the Qing, and the Dalai Lama's visit was regarded as a sign of whether the Khalkha would join. Due to the political importance of this event, many studies have already been conducted on the Dalai Lama's visit to Beijing.[1] Focusing on their epistolary correspondence, this article will examine the political relationships between Tibetan lamas, Khalkha Mongols, and the Qing court in the mid-seventeenth century.

Documents from the Inner Secretarial Office (Nei mishu yuan) include correspondence between the Manchu Khan and Tibeto-Mongol Buddhist clergy and princes, written and translated in the Mongolian language, and are some of the most valuable sources on this subject.[2] Thanks to these letters, even when veritable records (*shilu*) state only that an envoy from Tibet has arrived, we can understand the content of the letter the envoy brought to the Manchu Khan.

Generally, there are two honorific hierarchical language styles for Inner Secretarial Office documents: the pompous style, in which the sender looks down on the recipient; and the polite style, in which the sender treats the recipient respectfully. Specifically, the pompous style is structured as follows: "the

1. Suzuki 1962 revealed the details of the Dalai Lama's visit to Beijing using *Shizu shilu* and analyzed the significance of the event. Ahmad 1970 analyzed this visit from the perspectives of both the Manchu and Tibetan courts, linking *Shizu shilu* with the Fifth Dalai Lama's autobiography. Guo 1997 used the Inner Secretarial Office archive to clarify Qing history. Dalizhabu 2011, Qimudedaoerji 1998, and Sekine 2017 referred to the Dalai Lama's visit to Beijing from the viewpoint of Khalkha-Qing relations.

2. Since there is incorrect collation as well as missing pages in the facsimile edition, the original text housed in the First Historical Archives of China (Zhongguo diyi lishi dang'anguan) should be consulted.

sender's edict [space] is sent to the recipient" (*A-u/yin ǰarliγ bicig* [space] *B du ilegebe*). The sender can adjust the level of respect for the recipient by switching verbs—for example, by replacing "sent" with "submitted" (*bariba*), "gave" (*ögbe*), or "proclaimed" (*baγulγaba).* On the other hand, the polite style states, "In the presence of the recipient, the sender submitted the letter" (*B - ü/ yin emüne, A bicig erügbe*). The sender could adjust the level of respect for the recipient by omitting "in the presence of" and using modest expressions.

In addition to Mongol-Manchu style letters, the Inner Secretarial Office archive also includes Tibetan style letters. After the sender gives his or her name, Tibetan style letters usually lay out the contents in the following order: words of congratulation for the recipient's good health based on the preceding correspondence, the sender's current status, the main topic, a request for a reply, a list of gifts, and the date and place of sending.[3] Tibetan high lamas, the family of Gushi Khan (1582–1654), and some Khalkha princes usually use this format.

It is noteworthy that most of the Dalai Lama's letters included in the Inner Secretarial Office archive are written in syntactically complex sentences making full use of Sanskrit rhetoric. Since it is unlikely that the Manchu court, with their limited understanding of Tibetan Buddhism, would have been able to understand these letters accurately,[4] we should assume that the Dalai Lama's purpose in sending them was to show the Qing emperor the depths of Indo-Tibetan culture and to bring Tibetan Buddhist monks closer to the emperor in order to decipher the rhyming letters. In contrast to the Dalai Lama's letters, in the letters sent from the Qing court there is no sophisticated rhetorical style and no formalized confirmation of safety or thanks for the recipient.

This study presents the conflicting views of kingship between the Manchu Khan and the Tibetan clergy, the Qing's change in attitude toward Tibetan Buddhism, and the significance of the Dalai Lama's visit to Beijing by examining the Inner Secretarial Office archive's contents. I follow the Tibetan and Chinese lunar calendar in the original text, replacing the original expression of months in each text with the Arabic number. As there are many ways to render names, I use common names. When the original text has no sender name—for example, a respected figure like the Dalai Lama would not identify himself in a

3. For the format of Tibetan letters, see Ishihama 2001, 170–73. See also Kilby 2022 in the present volume.

4. For example, in the First Dalai Lama's letter to the Qing, the name of Tsongkhapa Lozang Drakpa (Tsong kha pa Blo bzang grags pa), the founder of the Dalai Lama's sect, was translated literally and is not recognized as a proper noun (Zhongguo diyi lishi dang'anguan 2003, vol. 2, 146; Ngag dbang blo bzang rgya mtsho 1975, 19b2–21b3).

letter—I consulted notes added to the translated text by the Inner Secretarial Office that identify the senders and the recipients of letters.

Initial Plans for the Dalai Lama's Invitation

In 1635 Taizong Hongtaiji (1543–1643) brought the Cahar Mongols, the direct descendants of Genghis Khan, under control and took from them the state seal, a symbol of political importance from the Yuan era. The next year, after Hongtaiji received the protector Mahākāla's statue, a symbol of religious importance from the Yuan era, he changed his state's name to the Qing 清 and started to build a Buddhist temple named Shishengsi to enshrine the Mahākāla statue.

Just about this time, Hongtaiji apparently proposed that the Khalkha and Oirat together invite the Dalai Lama to their courts. In the letters received in August in the second year of the Chongde 崇德 era (1637) by Hongtaiji, the two khans of the Khalkha, Secen Khan and Tüsiyetü Khan, state, "We seven *khoshuun*, Khalkha and four Oirat, agree to invite the Dalai Lama. Let your envoy follow our envoys."[5] In these letters, Secen Khan demonstrates his superiority with a pompous style, whereas Tüsiyetü Khan uses the polite style.

In July of the third year of the Chongde era (1638), Shisheng temple was completed, and the history of the construction was inscribed in four scripts: Chinese, Tibetan, Mongolian, and Manchu. For the Chinese inscription, the words related to the Buddha were raised higher than those related to the Manchu kingship and the protector Mahākāla. Based on the spatial hierarchies established in such letters and inscriptions, the emperor may have regarded his position to be the same as that of the protector deity Mahākāla.[6]

On September 24 Hongtaiji wrote to Jasaγtu Khan, pressing the latter to surrender to the Qing, using the pompous style. In this letter Hongtaiji states, "Among religious (*sasin*) and secular (*törü*) reasons, from the viewpoint of the former, I invited the Dalai Lama in order for Buddhism to flourish. From the viewpoint of the latter, I destroyed the Cahar Mongols, which made people suffer." Subsequently, he states:

> Like this, [rising] Heaven deigns to love me, and I think [rising] Heaven gave me the throne of six *ulus* (Khalkha) and the other Mongol *ulus*.[7]

5. Zhongguo diyi lishi dang'anguan 2003, vol. 1, 190–92.

6. Ishihama 2011, 64, 271.

7. Zhongguo diyi lishi dang'anguan 2003, vol. 1, 256.

We do not know whether what Hongtaiji calls "Heaven" is the Confucian or the Shamanistic Heaven. In any case, in this letter he continues to insist that Heaven conferred on him the throne of the Mongol.

To counter Hongtaiji's highhanded attitude, in August 1640 an alliance was forged between the left-wing Khalkha and the Oirat, with Jasaγtu Khan as leader. On October 6 Hongtaiji sent Jasaγtu Khan a more coercive letter, from which we can observe that Jasaγtu Khan refused to surrender to the Qing, on the pretext that Buddhism preaches peace and harmony, and that Hongtaiji regarded himself as the representative of the Buddhist government.[8] Thus time passed without realizing Khalkha's subordination to the Qing and the Dalai Lama's invitation.

On October 2 in the seventh year of the Chongde era (1642), envoys of the Dalai Lama, Ilaγuγsan Khutugtu and Daicing Corj, arrived at Mukden, the Manchu capital, and were given a magnificent reception. On May 5 in the eighth year of the Chongde era (1643), in addition to the Dalai Lama and Paṇchen Lama, who might have already been invited, Hongtaiji sent letters to five other high lamas, namely, the Black Hat Karmapa, the Great Sakya, Tsedong (Rtse gdong) Khutuktu, Drukpa ('Brug pa) Khutuktu, and Taklung (Stag lung) Khutuktu, and letters to the two kings, Tsangpa Khan and Gushi Khan.[9] The schools of the invited lamas (the Kagyüpa, Sakyapa, and Gelukpa) were most likely chosen based on the Ming dynasty's politics. The three people on whom the Ming dynasty conferred the highest title, Dharma king (Fawang), were from these three schools, and the former part of the Dalai Lama's title later given by the Shunzhi emperor (Xitian dashan zizaifo suoling tianxia xujiao) was the same as the title of the Black Hat Karmapa given by the Yongle emperor in 1407.[10]

According to Sato, the reason that Ming emperors gave the Pakmodrupa, the king of Tibet, the title of king (*wang*), which is inferior to that of Dharma king, is that "ethnic groups in the western region only hear the Monks' advice . . . the Ming emperor expected high lamas to mediate political struggle."[11] The Qing emperor seems to have had the same idea as the Ming emperor, because the Qing court thought that the Khalkha, who antagonized the Qing, would listen only to the Dalai Lama.[12]

8. Zhongguo diyi lishi dang'anguan 2003, vol. 1, 280.

9. Zhongguo diyi lishi dang'anguan 2003, vol. 1, 367–79.

10. Ishihama et al. 2019, 84.

11. Sato 1986, 153–57.

12. *Shizu shilu*, vol. 68, 1a–2a, September 3, the ninth year of the Shunzhi era.

By examining these nine letters, we can see that Hongtaiji paid greater respect to the seven lamas than to the two lay kings. While the letters to the seven lamas were written in polite style, those to the two kings used the pompous style. Furthermore, while golden diplomas were presented to the seven lamas, less noble metal diplomas were sent to the two kings.[13] Three years after Hongtaiji sent these letters, he died.

Conflicting Views on Kingship

An invitation letter in pompous style dated January 15, the first year of the Shunzhi era (1644), was sent by the Khagan (*qaγan*) to the Dalai Lama.[14] It would have been a massive change if the Qing were to have treated the Dalai Lama like a subject. However, it is unclear whether this letter was actually sent to Tibet, because there was no "Khan" after Hongtaiji's death, no recipient name on this letter, and no relevant veritable record *(shilu)* articles.

On October 1 the accession to the throne of the infant emperor Shunzhi, the son of Hongtaiji, was widely announced, with his uncle Dorgon (1612–50) serving as regent. Two months later, on December 5, the young Shunzhi Emperor sent a letter to Tüsiyetü Khan of the left-wing Khalkha,[15] and in January of the following year, he sent a letter to Secen Khan. In both letters he states, "Now that I have taken the throne of China, the enemy, in order to bring peace to all the *ulus*, we (Khalkha and Manchu) must unite peacefully."[16]

In March, four temples with "All-Victorious Stūpas" (Rnam rgyal mchod rten) were completed in Mukden. In the inscriptions at these temples, the words related to Buddhism and Manchu kingship were elevated to the same level.[17] Compared with the spatial hierarchies in the inscription on the Shisheng temple, the Manchu court's respect for Buddhism seems to have declined.

Two letters from the Gushi Khan family received on April 3 reveal that the Manchu Khan called for an alliance with the Gushi Khan family, as he previously had had with the Khalkha.[18] Both letters (one is from the sixth son, Dorj Dalai Baatur, to Shunzhi and another is from Gushi Khan's two queens—jointly signed by the second son, [Secen] Hongtaiji, the grandson Danjin, and

13. Zhongguo diyi lishi dang'anguan 2003, vol. 1, 379.

14. Zhongguo diyi lishi dang'anguan 2003, vol. 2, 3–4. The first page of this letter in facsimile is missing.

15. Zhongguo diyi lishi dang'anguan 2003, vol. 2, 56.

16. Zhongguo diyi lishi dang'anguan 2003, vol. 2, 61.

17. Ishihama 2011, 54–57, 64.

18. Zhongguo diyi lishi dang'anguan 2003, vol. 2, 97–100.

the seventh son, Qorimasi Erdeni Daicing—to Dorgon)[19] refer to the Qing's conquest of China and the Manchu Khan's proposal for an alliance.

Their letters are interesting in four ways. First, the letter from Gushi Khan's two queens uses a pompous style that disrespects Dorgon. Second, the opening verses of refuge in lamas in the letterheads show the Gushi Khan family's deep dedication to Buddhism, while also criticizing the Manchu court. Third, they also belittle the court by calling Dorgon only "imperial prince" (*jinwang* 親王), calling Hongtaiji "Khan of the Jurchid," and referring to Shunzhi as "his son." Fourth, they describe the way of the bodhisattva king as follows:

> Your envoy's words do not seem to touch our people's hearts. A good politician is one who lets people get what they want, leads them to the Three Precious Jewels, achieves what they intended, and abandons an arrogant heart.[20]

Although they found Shunzhi's offer uncomfortable, the Gushi Khan family seems to have eventually reacted positively to the Manchu Khan's offer. This conclusion is derived from the veritable record article for December 14, which states that Dorj Dalai Baatur said that "if the Qing emperor and our Khan (Gushi Khan) have formed an alliance, we will follow your order."[21]

On August 25, in the third year of the Shunzhi era (1646), replies to the letters sent on May 5, in the eighth year of the Chongde era, were received. The letters from the Gelukpa lamas were written in 1645 and the ones from the Sakyapa lamas in 1644, when the Manchu conquest of China was confirmed.[22] The letter from the Dalai Lama contains all the elements found in his subsequent letters. First, in the section on rejoicing about the recipient's safety, the Dalai Lama praised Shunzhi as the one "empowered by Heaven." In this letter, Heaven refers to neither a Confucian heaven nor a Shamanistic one but to an Indo-Tibetan conception of heaven, which is one of the six realms of rebirth for sentient beings in saṃsāra and is transcended by Buddhist enlightenment. In this context, the gods in heaven are not necessarily admirable, but instead are spiritually immature beings expected to receive the Buddha's teachings.

Furthermore, the Dalai Lama rejoiced that the Manchu Khan would accept the present Buddha Śākyamuni as one of the thousand buddhas of this aus-

19. For the identification of Gushi Khan's queen and descendants, see Ishihama 2001, 152–54.

20. Zhongguo diyi lishi dang'anguan 2003, vol. 2, 99–100.

21. *Shizu shilu*, vol. 22, 3ab, December 14.

22. Zhongguo diyi lishi dang'anguan 2003, vol. 2, 146–72.

picious eon. The Dalai Lama sent these words in the expectation that the Manchu Khan really intended to become a Buddhist, and he preached the following way:

> Courageous bodhisattvas are born as powerful kings at will and then take control of politics and lead all their subjects to the right path by the imperial law of ten virtues,[23] which is the birthplace of short- and long-term good deeds. Please think about these marvelous [bodhisattva] deeds. The king empowered by Heaven has the power to enjoy the banquet of a golden new age and to open the endless doors of the two accumulations (*tshogs gnyis*) with the precious three collections of scripture as a witness. Because the Chorj Jinakarma has successfully shown you the new face of Śākyamuni's teachings,[24] I sent him to your palace to show all your subjects the high and good path of righteousness. Please turn your attention to him.[25]

The Paṇchen Lama's letter is much simpler than the Dalai Lama's, but the main points are the same. He requests that the Manchu Khan protect Buddhism, especially the Geluk school.[26] The Drukpa Khutuktu also recommends specific Buddhist practices, such as observing the eight precepts on auspicious days and remembering the six perfections.[27] The lamas of the Sakya school also preached the history of Pakpa and Khubilai Khan, who introduced Buddhism to Mongolia.[28] In other words, in these letters each school urges the Manchu Khan to allow Buddhism to flourish and to achieve peace for sentient beings.

As a result, the letters of the Dalai Lama and other Tibetan lamas continued to treat Manchu Khan as a devout Buddhist. "You have become the king of the world according to the good deeds in previous lives. The bodhisattva king should allow Buddhism to flourish and bring peace among sentient beings." Through these sermons, the Tibetan lamas seemingly seek to correct the emperor's entitled attitude and claim to rule all of East and Central Asia.

23. The concept of a "bodhisattva king" is based on the Perfection of Wisdom sūtras. See Ishihama 2001, 8–11.

24. Chorj Jinakarma (*chor rje rgyal ba'i 'phrin las pa*) in this context means *Secen chorj*, a.k.a. Ilaγuγsan qutuγtu (Ikejiri 2013, 51–54).

25. Ngag dbang blo bzang rgya mtsho 1975, 19b2–21b3.

26. Zhongguo diyi lishi dang'anguan 2003, vol. 2, 151–54.

27. Zhongguo diyi lishi dang'anguan 2003, vol. 2, 155–57.

28. Zhongguo diyi lishi dang'anguan 2003, vol. 2, 157–67.

Deterioration of Khalkha-Qing Relations

In the spring of the third year of the Shunzhi era (1646), Tinggis of the Sunid tribe, leading his clan, fled from the Qing and pledged his clan's allegiance to the Khalkha. This event caused Khalkha-Qing relations to deteriorate rapidly.[29] On February 15 in the fourth year of the Shunzhi era (1647), Shunzhi sent letters to Gushi Khan and high lamas in Tibet for the first time since his ascension to the throne. These letters have the same content—namely, brief messages confirming the safety of the recipient, using the polite style, with the recipient's name raised to the same level as the Manchu Khan's name, which is contrary to the arrogant letter written on January 15 in the first year of the Shunzhi era.[30]

In the letter received on November 25 in the fourth year of the Shunzhi era, Jasaγtu Khan tried to repair the relationship between the Khalkha and the Qing. He said, "Let us unite our governments, become family, and by inviting the Dalai Lama, dedicate ourselves to Buddhism."[31] This letter is composed in the pompous style and does not contain any posture of surrender. We should note that every time tensions between Jasaγtu Khan and Shunzhi eased, they reinitiated the Dalai Lama invitation project.

In the fourth year of the Shunzhi era (1647), letters from Tibet were limited to the high lamas of the Geluk school and the Gushi Khan family. In the following year, correspondence between Tibet and the Qing became more frequent. On March 10, letters from the Dalai Lama; Paṇchen Lama; Gushi Khan; his fifth son, Mergen Jinong; Gushi Khan's queen; and his sixth son, Dorj Dalai Baatur were received.[32] Among them, Mergen Jinong's letter is interesting because it shows the depth of the understanding of Buddhism by Gushi Khan's family and his views on Tibetan kingship. In the opening verse of the letter, Mergen Jinong takes refuge in "the six ornaments and two supreme ones" (*rgyan drug mchog gnyis*), eight Indian saints revered by all Tibetan Buddhist scholars,[33] and the leading Geluk monks (Tsongkhapa and the Paṇchen and Dalai Lamas). It should be noted that in the section on the main topic, Mergen Jinong describes China as the seat of the Dharmarāja of Bodhisattva

29. Sekine 2017, 3–5.

30. Zhongguo diyi lishi dang'anguan 2003, vol. 2, 308–18.

31. Zhongguo diyi lishi dang'anguan 2003, vol. 2, 367.

32. Zhongguo diyi lishi dang'anguan 2003, vol. 2, 407–22, vol. 3, 1–6.

33. The six ornaments (*rgyan drug*) are Nāgārjuna, Āryadeva, Asaṅga, Vasubhandu, Dignāga, and Dharmakīrti; and the two supreme ones (*mchog gnyis*) are Śākyaprabha and Guṇaprabha.

Mañjuśrī, ruled by Shunzhi, and Tibet as the seat of the Dharmarāja of Bodhisattva Avalokiteśvara, ruled by his father, Gushi Khan.[34] Jinong's juxtaposition of Shunzhi and Gushi Khan indicates that he, like the Khalkha, was not ready to surrender to the Qing, and his reference to Gushi Khan rather than the Dalai Lama as the ruler of Tibet indicates that a government of political and religious unity had not yet been established in Tibet.

Shunzhi's replies to these letters were written on May 20 for the Dalai Lama, Paṇchen Lama, and Gushi Khan, and on June 29 for Gushi Khan's descendants.[35] In the text of the reply to the Dalai Lama, Shunzhi clearly invites him to visit, and the invitation is reported in the text of the replies to the Paṇchen Lama and Gushi Khan. In Shunzhi's letters, he continues to use the pompous style to address Gushi Khan and his descendants, treating them as subjects:

> The Khagan's edict, which was sent to the Ombo Mergen Jinong, Ombo Secen Daicing, and Ombo Qorimasi Erdeni Daicing. It is very good that on hearing about the Muslim uprising, you brought your troops. I acknowledged [your contribution]. I knew later that you three supported our army. You never let your troops go beyond the city's walls. As soon as you receive this edict, go home.[36]

The Muslim rebellion mentioned in this letter may refer to the Muslim uprising that broke out in Shaanxi 陝西 in the leap month of April in the fifth year of the Shunzhi era.[37] Despite the pompous style, the army was clearly not under Qing's control, as Shunzhi instructed them not to go beyond the city walls.

At the end of the fifth year of the Shunzhi era, relations between the Qing and Khalkha again deteriorated. The right-wing Khalkha plundered the Tümed tribe under Qing rule, and in addition to this, as successive rebellions broke out in Shanxi 山西, Shaanxi 陝西, and Gansu 甘肅 provinces, the Qing court became exhausted by battles throughout the country. On August 8 in the sixth year of the Shunzhi era (1649), Dorgon and Shunzhi received letters from the Khalkha.[38] In these, the author does not mention his name (the Qing regarded

34. Zhongguo diyi lishi dang'anguan 2003, vol. 2, 417–18.

35. Zhongguo diyi lishi dang'anguan 2003, vol. 3, 11–14.

36. Zhongguo diyi lishi dang'anguan 2003, vol. 3, 14.

37. Ishihama 1998, 106–7.

38. Zhongguo diyi lishi dang'anguan 2003, vol. 3, 64–67.

unnamed letters as disrespectful) and states that he could accept a peace agreement but could not show them in the imperial court for several reasons.

> There are three reasons that we cannot show ourselves to your court. The first is the incarnate lama's edict. It states, "Because you have become acquainted with the patrons (*danapati*), settle [not at Beijing but] there for the benefit of politics of Manchu, Khalkha, and Oirat." The patrons work together for the benefit of political stability. The second reason involves the words of the khans, Dharma king (Danjin Lama), and nobles. Seven *otuγ* Khalkha are brothers who have one father. If the left wing and right wing conduct politics without asking the khans, internal strife will break out. Therefore, we would like to discuss this matter [in private].[39]

Showing themselves in the Qing court could have been interpreted as surrender, so the Khalkha chose not to do so. Since Shunzhi ostensibly expressed his reverence for Buddhism, it was difficult for him to refute the monk's edict. For this reason, the Khalkha referred to the monk's words first. The third reason cited was an outbreak of epidemic disease within the boundaries of the Great Wall.

Changes in the Attitude of the Qing

On August 10, two days after the Khalkha letter was received, Shunzhi received two letters from the Dalai Lama. One, written in February of the ox year of 1649 at the Potala Palace, contained an additional sentence at the end of the letter: "As for the meeting at the palace, it would be the summer of the dragon year (1652)."[40] The reason why the Dalai Lama accepted the Qing's invitation at this time requires an analysis of Tibet's internal affairs and the transition of power among the Dalai Lama, Gushi Khan, and the regent, which is not the theme of this paper. At this point, we can speculate as follows: the Qing's policy toward Tibet basically followed that of the Ming dynasty, as mentioned above, and the Ming dynasty conferred the highest title on the three representatives of three schools, who had showed themselves at the Ming palace. Because only the Dalai Lama accepted the Qing's invitation, his visit to Beijing may have represented the sovereignty of the Geluk school over the other sects of Tibetan Buddhism in the eyes of the Dalai Lama and the Qing court.

39. Zhongguo diyi lishi dang'anguan 2003, vol. 3, 64–65.

40. Zhongguo diyi lishi dang'anguan 2003, vol. 3, 73–75.

Replies to this letter were written on October 7. It is worth mentioning that, for the first time, Shunzhi used the expression "emperor's edict" (*quwangti yin jarliγ bicig*) in a letter to the Dalai Lama.[41] As soon as the Dalai Lama accepted his invitation, Shunzhi's attitude became more demanding, and the contents of the emperor's letters to Gushi Khan's family became more highhanded. In a letter to Gushi Khan, Shunzhi ordered him to turn against the Khalkha after providing a lengthy account of how much trouble the Khalkha had caused.[42] In a letter to Gushi Khan's descendants, he praised them for besieging the city of Xining during the Muslim uprising and gave them titles as if they were his subjects. In a letter to Mergen Jinong, for example, he stated:

> The Khagan's edict: You, Ombo-Mergen-Jinong, hearing that the Muslims within the city walls had rebelled [against the Qing], brought your subordinate troops and besieged the city of Xining, defeated its troops three times, and helped seize the city. In recognition of this, you are awarded the title of Joriγtu Baatur Jinong.[43]

As mentioned above, the siege of Xining was conducted not by order of the Manchu Khan but on the initiative of the Gushi Khan family. Conferring this title on them was tantamount to demanding their surrender.

On February 2 in the seventh year of the Shunzhi era (1650), the Qing court banned trade with the Khalkha,[44] and in a letter dated April 12, it requested Ochirt Taiji, a nephew of Gushi Khan, to break off relations with the Khalkha.[45] Perhaps as a result of the economic blockade, in a letter received on October 25, the Khalkha tried to ease the tension by stating that "two Khans of the left wing of the Khalkha and Danjin Lama sent their ministers . . . to swear allegiance, since there is no use arguing over past words and deeds."[46] On January 12 in the eighth year of the Shunzhi era (1651), Shunzhi refused to recognize Dorgon's reign,[47] listed his crimes, and proclaimed to all the imperial princes that he would take office himself.

41. Zhongguo diyi lishi dang'anguan 2003, vol. 3, 87–88.

42. Zhongguo diyi lishi dang'anguan 2003, vol. 3, 88–90; Sekine 2017, 14.

43. Zhongguo diyi lishi dang'anguan 2003, vol. 3, 92.

44. Sekine 2017, 16–17.

45. Zhongguo diyi lishi dang'anguan 2003, vol. 3, 120–25.

46. Zhongguo diyi lishi dang'anguan 2003, vol. 3, 165–66.

47. Zhongguo diyi lishi dang'anguan 2003, vol. 3, 183–93. Dorgon passed away at the end of 1650.

In a letter dated March 8, Shunzhi said that he sent an envoy named Donzang Gushi (Mon. Tobtsang Güsi = Tib. Don bzang gu shri) to welcome the Dalai Lama and stated, "I would like to see you in July of the dragon year." In this letter, despite using the pompous style, the words denoting the Dalai Lama and Shunzhi himself are raised to the same height, and he uses the polite expression "in the presence of."[48] Donzang Gushi translated the inscriptions of Shisheng temple and the All-Victorious Stūpa temples into the Tibetan language.[49]

In Ochirt Taiji's letter, received on October 11, he does not respond to the Qing's request to "oppose Khalkha together." Perhaps because of this, Shunzhi sent a letter to Baatur Taiji of Jungγar on October 17, threatening, "If you protect Jasaγtu Khan, when I invade Khalkha, our peace will be defeated, because we cannot distinguish between Khalkha and Oirat."[50] It seems that as soon as the Dalai Lama accepted the invitation, Shunzhi started to force the Dalai Lama's guardian, the Gushi Khan family, and the Jungγar to antagonize the Khalkha.

In November one stūpa and two temples were completed in Beijing to commemorate Shunzhi's direct rule. In three inscriptions in these shrines, unlike Shisheng temple and the All-Victorious Stūpa temples built in Mukden, the words related to Buddha were not raised according to the standards of spatial hierarchies.[51] This reveals that the Qing court's respect for Buddhism had declined further.

In the letter dated February 5 in the ninth year of the Shunzhi era (1652), Shunzhi states that Shajidara, an official of the Board for Managing the Frontiers (Lifan yuan 理藩院), and other officials from the Ministry of Rites (Libu 礼部), War (Bingbu 兵部), Revenue (Hubu 戸部), and Works (Gongbu 工部) would be sent to escort the Dalai Lama.[52] As for the protocol, Gushi Khan's following proposal in the letter dated August 11 seems to have been adopted:

> This meeting [between the Dalai Lama and Shunzhi] is not the same as the past meeting between the khans and the lama. If you order [space] the Dalai Lama to be respected as much as possible, that is very good. In my opinion, let the officials receive the Dalai Lama at

48. Zhongguo diyi lishi dang'anguan 2003, vol. 3, 242–43.

49. Ishihama 2011, 46, 48, 271.

50. Zhongguo diyi lishi dang'anguan 2003, vol. 3, 299–300.

51. Ishihama 2011, 57–63, 278–283.

52. Zhongguo diyi lishi dang'anguan 2003, vol. 3, 312–13.

> the border of the *ulus* [nation]. Then, let the imperial prince receive him. It would be very good if the emperor himself would welcome the Dalai Lama at Taiga.[53]

The fact that the Dalai Lama was escorted from Lhasa to Kokonor by Gushi Khan's descendants in shifts, and from Qinghai by Shajidara, indicates that the border between the Gushi Khan family and the Qing dynasty was in the Kokonor area.[54] Thereafter, the Dalai Lama's correspondence became less rhetorical and included more practical briefs, such as itinerary reports. Since the Dalai Lama's trip has been described in detail in previous studies, I focus here on the part related to the dignity of the reception.

The emperor's letter to the Dalai Lama, dated August 13, states that he would dispatch the imperial prince on behalf of himself owing to a lack of security outside the Great Wall and that he would show himself when the security situation improved.[55] In other words, up to this point, the procedure of receiving the Dalai Lama followed Gushi Khan's proposal. The Dalai Lama's letter, which arrived on August 29, states that he had arrived in Hohhot and that the meeting would take place in either Taiga or Hohhot outside the Great Wall, owing to the epidemic inside the boundaries of the Great Wall.[56]

The Emperor's Waning Enthusiasm for Meeting the Dalai Lama

On September 3 in the ninth year of the Shunzhi era (1652), a well-known debate took place in the palace about the reception of the Dalai Lama.[57] Shunzhi asked his subjects:

> The Dalai Lama has three thousand followers with him. Since there is a shortage of revenue this year, it would be disadvantageous to bring so many people into the country. However, if the Dalai Lama is not welcomed, he would become angry and return to his homeland, and then the Khalkha would not obey our rule. What are your thoughts on whether we should go outside the Great Wall?

53. Zhongguo diyi lishi dang'anguan 2003, vol. 3, 337. According to Guo (1997), Taiga is in present-day Liangcheng County 凉城县 in Inner Mongolia, near Shanxi Province 山西省.

54. Ngag dbang blo bzang rgya mtsho 1975, 183b4.

55. Zhongguo diyi lishi dang'anguan 2003, vol. 3, 338–39.

56. Zhongguo diyi lishi dang'anguan 2003, vol. 3, 341–42.

57. Ngag dbang blo bzang rgya mtsho 1991, 183b4.

While the Manchu subjects insisted on welcoming the Dalai Lama outside the Great Wall, the Han Chinese subjects replied: "The Lord of the Heavenly Kingdom would not receive a lama. The Dalai Lama should be given gold and silver by representatives outside the Great Wall." It is noteworthy that the Qing court was not willing to receive the Dalai Lama inside the Great Wall. Some Han officials even thought that the meeting did not need to take place. These debates show that the Qing court invited the Dalai Lama not to learn about Buddhism but to use the Dalai Lama for its own political purposes.

This issue was not settled immediately. In Shunzhi's letter dated September 11, he states that he still intended to go to Taiga,[58] while in the Dalai Lama's letter received on September 21, he confirms the location of the meeting as Taiga.[59] However, on September 29, the emperor's departure for Taiga was canceled because of a well-known warning from the Astronomy Office.[60] The decision to cancel the emperor's departure was communicated to the Dalai Lama in a letter dated October 13, much later, and the reason for the cancelation was attributed to the deteriorating security situation.[61] The Dalai Lama's letter, received on November 6, complained about this decision, urging them "to remove obstacles so that you can reach Taiga."[62]

Ten days later, on November 16, Shunzhi sent an edict to Tüsiyetü Khan, Secen Khan, and Danjin Lama, pressing for the return of stolen livestock and urging the leading nobles to show themselves to the Qing court.[63] However, the Khalkha never complied with the Qing's request, probably suspecting that China had relegated them to a vassal state. On December 15 the reception party was held at the Southern Garden (Nanyuan 南苑) in Beijing.[64] This decision raises interesting questions. Why did the Dalai Lama, who had been refused entry to China owing to the epidemic, agree to visit Beijing? Was the Dalai Lama's visit to Beijing related to Shunzhi's request for the two Khans of Khalkha to turn themselves in to the court in Beijing? Unfortunately, because of the lack of historical documents on this issue, this paper cannot provide answers to these questions.

On January 18 in the tenth year of the Shunzhi era (1653) the Dalai Lama

58. Zhongguo diyi lishi dang'anguan 2003, vol. 3, 343–44.

59. Zhongguo diyi lishi dang'anguan 2003, vol. 3, 344–45.

60. *Shizu shilu*, vol. 68, 21b–22a, September 29.

61. Zhongguo diyi lishi dang'anguan 2003, vol. 3, 349–50.

62. Zhongguo diyi lishi dang'anguan 2003, vol. 3, 354–55.

63. Zhongguo diyi lishi dang'anguan 2003, vol. 3, 356–59.

64. *Shizu shilu*, vol. 70, 13b, December 15.

announced his intention to return to Tibet. At this time, the Qing court again debated whether the Dalai Lama should be asked for his opinion on the situation. However, it was concluded: "Our dynasty accomplished this great deed with the help of Heaven. There were no lamas at that time. There was no need to ask for his opinion. Give him a title or something; that is enough."[65] Again, Shunzhi placed his self-esteem before his faith in Buddhism. On February 18 a farewell party was held at the Taihe 太和 hall for the Dalai Lama, and on April 22 official titles, golden seals, and diplomas were sent to the Dalai Lama and Gushi Khan on their return to Tibet.[66]

Conclusion

After Hongtaiji brought the Cahar under his control, he started to claim that "Heaven gave me the throne of Mongolia" and called on Khalkha to surrender. Furthermore, he initiated a plan to invite the Dalai Lama from Tibet together with the Khalkha and the Oirat. In the beginning, despite his limited understanding of Buddhism, the Manchu Khan humbled himself by raising Buddhism-related words higher than Qing-related words in the inscription of the Shisheng temple and wrote letters to Tibetan lamas using the polite style.

Meanwhile, the letters from Tibetan lamas to the Manchu Khans commonly refer to Buddhist kingship. "Bodhisattvas are born as wheel-turning kings (*cakravartin*) to make Buddhism flourish and bring happiness to people," one states, "and the fact that you have become the king of all is the result of your good deeds in your previous life." Through these letters, the Tibetan high lamas try to deepen Hongtaiji's understanding of Buddhism and to discourage his arrogant attitude toward neighboring nations. The Khalkha, using the Buddhist ideology of peace as a shield, continued to refuse the Qing's calls for surrender. Tinggis's escape to the Khalkha further worsened Qing-Khalkha relations.

In a letter dated February in the ox year (1649), the Dalai Lama announced that he would visit Beijing in the summer of the dragon year (1652), and the situation began to move quickly. Once the Dalai Lama had confirmed he would accept the invitation, it is interesting to note that the Qing court changed their letter style to the pompous one in their correspondence with Tibetan high lamas and began to force the Gushi Khan family and Jungγar to confront the Khalkha as if they were subjects. These styles of correspondence demonstrate

65. *Shizu shilu*, vol. 71, 13b–14a, January 18.

66. *Shizu shilu*, vol. 74, 12a–13a, April 22.

an increasingly confident and entitled attitude at the Qing court in the first decade of the Shunzhi era.

Furthermore, the Qing's enthusiasm for meeting the Dalai Lama declined over time. As the Dalai Lama approached Beijing without the confirmation of Khalkha presence, in compliance with the Qing's request, the Shunzhi emperor canceled the reception of the Dalai Lama outside the Great Wall. From this, it can be concluded that the Qing's purpose for inviting the Dalai Lama was not to promote Buddhism but to induce the Khalkha to surrender.[67] Minus the Khalkha presence during the Dalai Lama's visit to Beijing, the meeting was nothing more than a reception that would cost the Qing dynasty a great deal of money. In other words, the concept of the "bodhisattva king" preached by the Tibetan high lamas does not seem to have touched the Manchu Khan's heart.

Eventually the Dalai Lama visited Beijing and the Qing dynasty conferred titles on him, namely, "Buddha, Most Virtuously and Peacefully Residing in the Divine Realm in the West, Presiding over Buddhism in the World, Unchanging Vajradhāra, Dalai Lama" (Xitian dashan zizaifo suoling tianxia shijiao putong wachila danla Dalai Lama)—and on Gushi Khan, namely, "Learned Gushi Khan Obeying the Culture and Justice" (Zunxing wenyi minhui gushihan). While some regard this outcome as a victory for the Manchu empire, it is well known that conferring titles simply denotes a one-way conception of a hierarchical relationship and does not prove the recipient's obedience. Furthermore, the Fifth Dalai Lama and Gushi Khan never used these titles in their subsequent correspondence with the Qing. By contrast, Gushi Khan continued to use the title of the "Protector of Buddhism, Dharmarāja" (Śasin i bariγci nom un qaγan) conferred by the Dalai Lama in 1637.[68]

The Dalai Lama's visit to Beijing made his presence as the bodhisattva Avalokiteśvara felt among the peoples of Central Eurasia and strengthened his government.[69] However, the Qing's arrogant and entitled attitude at the reception of the Dalai Lama increasingly isolated the Qing from the Khalkha-Oirat, which led to future conflicts between these two sides.

67. *Shizu shilu*, vol. 68, 1a–2a, September 3; vol. 71, 13b–14a, January 18.

68. Examples include the Dalai Lama's letter to Shunzhi dated June 22 in the eleventh year of the Shunzhi era (1654), and Gushi Khan's letter to Shunzhi dated June 20 in the eleventh year of the Shunzhi era. Zhongguo diyi lishi dang'anguan 2003, vol. 4, 153–59.

69. Ishihama 1993.

References

Ahmad, Zahiruddin. 1970. *Sino-Tibetan Relations in the Seventeenth Century*. Serie Orientale Roma 40. Rome: Istituto Italiano per il Medio ed Estremo Oriente.

Dalizhabu 达力扎布. 2011. "Qing Taizong he Qing Shizu dui mobei kaerkabu zhaofu 清太宗和清世祖对漠北喀尔喀的招抚." *Lishi yanjiu* 历史研究 14: 50–62.

Guo Meilan 郭美兰. 1997. "Wushi Dalai Lama rujin shulun 五世达赖喇嘛入觐述论." *Zhongguo bianjiangshidi yanjiu* 中国边疆史地研究 2: 33–41.

Ikejiri Yōko. 2013. *Shinchō zenki no Chibetto Bukkyō seisaku: Jasaku rama seido no seiritsu to tenkai* 清朝前期のチベット仏教政策: 扎薩克喇嘛制度の成立と展開. Tōkyō: Kyūko shoin.

Ishihama, Yumiko. 1993. "On the Dissemination of the Belief in the Dalai Lama as a Manifestation of the Bodhisattva Avalokitesvara." *Acta Asiatica* 64: 38–56.

———. 1998. "Darairama shosei no haikei ni aru junchi gonen no shin mongoru kankei ni tsuite." *Shiteki* 20: 100–120.

———. 2001. *Chibetto bukkyosekai no rekishiteki kenkyu*. Tokyo: Tohoshoten.

———. 2011. *Shincho to chibetto bukky*. Tokyo: Waseda Daigaku Shuppanbu.

Ishihama, Yumiko, Makoto Tachibana, Ryosuke Kobayashi, and Takehiko Inoue. 2019. *The Resurgence of "Buddhist Government" Tibetan-Mongolian Relations in the Modern World*. Osaka: Union Press.

Ngag dbang blo bzang rgya mtsho, the Fifth Dalai Lama. 1975. *Rgya bod hor sog gi mchog dman bar pa rnams la 'phrin yig sñan ṅag tu bkod pa rab sñan rgyud maṅ: Letters to Various Notables of China, Tibet, and Mongolia Written by H. H. the Fifth Dalai Lama Ṅag-dbaṅ-blo-bzaṅ-rgya-mtsho*, edited by Kunsang Tobgay. Delhi: Jayyed Press.

———. 1991. *Za hor gyi ban de ngag dbang blo bzang rgya mtsho'i 'di snang 'khrul pa'i rol rtsed rtogs brjod kyi tshul du bkod pa du ku la'i gos bzang glegs bam dang po*. In *The Collected Works (Gsung-'bum) of the 5th Dalai Lama, Ngag-dbang blo-bzang rgya-mtsho*, vol. 6, 9–569. Gangtok: Sikkim Research Institute of Tibetology.

Qimudedaoerji 齐木德道尔吉. 1998. "1640 nian yihoude Qingchao yu Kaerkade guanxi 1640 年以后的清朝与喀尔喀的关系." *Neimenggu daxue xuebao* 内蒙古大学学报 4: 12–20.

Sato Hisashi 佐藤長. 1986. *Chusei chibettoshi kenkyu* 中世チベット史研究. Kyōto: Dōhōsha.

Sekine, Tomoyoshi. 2017. "Junchiki ni okeru shincho to haruha no koshokatei." *Manzokushikenkyu* 16: 1–28.

Shizu shilu 世祖實録 [Qianlong Edition]. 1985. 144 vols. Beijing: Zhonghua shuju.

Suzuki Chūsei 鈴木中正. 1962. *Chibetto o meguru Chū-In kankeishi : 18-seiki nakagoro kara 19-seiki nakagoro made* チベットをめぐる中印關係史; 十八世紀中頃から十九世紀中頃まで. Tōkyō: Hitotsubashi shobō.

Zhongguo diyi lishi dang'anguan 中国第一历史档案馆, ed. 2000. *Qingchu Wushi Dalai Lama dang'an shiliao xuanbian* 清初五世达赖喇嘛档案史料选编. Beijing: Zhongguo zangxue chubanshe.

———. 2003. *Cing ulus-un dotuġadu narin bicig-ün yamun-u Mongġol dangsa ebkemel-ün emkidkel*. 7 vols. Hohhot: Neimenggu renmin chubanshe.

Newar Merchants in Tibet: Observations on Frontiers of Trade and Buddhist Culture[1]

Todd Lewis

THE YOUNGHUSBAND INVASION of Tibet (December 1903–September 1904) and the ensuing Anglo-Tibetan Treaty of 1904 had ripple effects across the Himalayan region. It changed the geography of the trade and human migration networks that linked South Asia to Central Tibet, opening up a new route for trade and later agreements to establish mail/telegraph communication lines from British India to Central Tibetan cities. Scholars of Tibetan history have noted a variety of major effects this had on Tibetan society, political leaders, and Buddhist institutions, as new

1. Most of the information on Newar merchants who lived and worked in Tibet was gathered from oral histories collected from 1980 to 1982. All of these men were from Kathmandu, and all became friends: Donam Dorje Namgyal, Tej Ratna Tuladhar, Buddha Jiv Tuladhar, Sapta Bir Singh ("Cik Sau"), and Pratyek Man Tuladhar. I owe them and their descendants profound thanks for generously sharing their stories, photos, and records with me. The last was most significant for several reasons: Pratyek Man was the great-grandson of the great Lhasa trader "Dhamma Sau"; he was an inveterate collector of artifacts such as photos, negatives, letters, souvenirs from the business, and especially postage stamps. Present in the closing down of the Newar trading houses in the late 1950s, Pratyek Man rescued items being discarded by other Newar traders in their hasty clearing out from the Bakhor bazaar in Lhasa. In the early 1980s, I helped his son Sidhartha get hundreds of copy negatives made on acetate made from the large glass negatives, storing the latter so they were not fire hazards; some of these are found in this article. I do regret not being able to focus much more fully on these remarkable merchants, including some of the greatest Kathmandu families as well as the Dhakwa families native to Patan. Other ethnic groups from Nepal—Sherpas, Thakalis, and Mustangis from the Gandaki Valley—also traded in small numbers in Tibet. By now, all of these merchants have passed away. As I was a doctoral student and new to Nepal in 1979, my first priority was to study contemporary Newar Buddhism among the Urāy merchants of Kathmandu, and this I did. But it was often the case that research inquiries among this exceptional community led to my stumbling into extraordinary "side caverns" of great interest and historical significance, such as records of the Lhasa traders; the art masterworks in every medium possessed by affluent families, including thousand-year-old painted Sanskrit texts; and the modern literary or devotional writings by Urāy authors such as Chittadhar Hridaya, the greatest modern Newar poet. I did translate his masterpiece on the life of the Buddha, *Sugata Saurabha*, with Subarna Man Tuladhar (Lewis and

visitors and media brought in awareness of the world beyond the Tibetan plateau.[2] New possibilities and problems quickly emerged; merchants venturing north seeking new moneymaking opportunities were joined by adventurers in search of magic, mystery, and spiritual insight, and by pioneering scholars from India, Europe, China, and Japan, our academic predecessors, who crossed into Tibet through this new frontier gateway in search of art and texts.

For Newar merchants of the Kathmandu Valley, this newly opened route through the Sikkim mid-montane region enabled them to shift to a more favorable blueprint for organizing the centuries-old trade that flowed between their home region and Tibet's major cities.[3] Now goods made in South Asia (and more distant points) could be shipped to Calcutta, sent by land (train or lorry) to Darjeeling, then conveyed by horse/mule caravans and porters up onto the Tibetan plateau through the Chumbi Valley, Sikkim;[4] in eighteen to twenty days, goods could reach their shops in the major Tibetan cities, where individual and institutional customers would then purchase them. This new route cut the transit time and its cost greatly for Newar merchants by alleviating the need to bring goods up into the Kathmandu Valley; although they now had to pay taxes on goods imported from Tibet into British territory, a cost they didn't have when importing goods directly to Kathmandu, the net savings were well worth it. Most ordered much less from their wholesaler suppliers in Patna, as Calcutta (with its seaport) became the new and better supply hub. Trade no longer had to move through Kathmandu to begin the long-established one-month horse/porter trek to Lhasa moving north from Kathmandu either through mountain passes to Nyalam (northeast) or to Kyirong (north), followed by a long eastern leg to Shigatse, Gyantse, and Lhasa.

These old routes to the Tibetan plateau date back at least a millennium (and likely much earlier), as Newars for centuries exported metal tools, utensils, and

Tuladhar 2019). It is still possible that Newar families who are descendants of these traders have preserved photos, letters, diaries, and other materials and that well-sourced studies can be made from them. Several books published in Nepal (Lall 2001; Tuladhar 2004; Hilker 2005) as well as the Facebook group Lhasa Newah: Nepalese Traders on the Silk Road, created in 2016, are promising signs of cultural preservation. https://www.facebook.com/Lhasanewah/.

2. Goldstein 1989.

3. Newar trading houses are known to have been established in the major cities: Lhasa, Shigatse, Gyantse, and Tsetang/Samyé. Many had offices in the border-crossing towns Nyalan/Kuti and Kiyrong.

4. Bell 1924a estimated that half of the trade with Tibet through British India shifted to the Sikkim route, with merchants through Kashmir and Assam equal in accounting for the other half. Occasional caravans still left from Kathmandu on the old routes.

luxury goods made in India and Nepal and brought back wool, musk, salt, yak tails, silver, and gold. Especially important was the Newar export of artisan labor, a long-standing tie that contributed greatly to the development of Buddhist material culture in Tibet. This connection was a major source of income that added greatly to the aggregate wealth in the Kathmandu Valley. It was primarily patronage by Tibet's growing number of monastic schools in the "second introduction" of Buddhism from South Asia that benefitted the Newar artisans who traveled to the highlands, sometimes staying for long periods,[5] to complete major projects.

The scant studies to date on these projects[6] note that Newar masters (in architecture, painting, metalwork) brought crews from Nepal that built stūpas and major monasteries; they also created statues, metalwork decorations, and paintings for them. The Newar artistic diaspora spanned across the Tibetan plateau, at times extending beyond Tibet as far as Mongolia and even Beijing during the Yuan dynasty. Only recently have accounts of Tibetan art fully acknowledged the major role that Newar artists played in every medium of religious art that developed in Tibet.[7]

Newar projects in Tibet were at times so large in scale that artisan groups back in the Kathmandu Valley worked exclusively on filling orders of commonly needed monastery elements, which were then transported in caravans into Tibet. Newar metalworkers (working in repoussé and lost wax casting), especially those in Patan, were renowned for their craft[8] and in high demand

5. Stein 1972. While the older history of foreign resident artisans in the major Tibetan cities remains little documented, Abbé Huc, a missionary visitor to Lhasa, observed how by the middle of the nineteenth century a colony of Newar artisans had settled in Lhasa and had come to dominate in the metalworking there: "Only Newar metal workers are found in Lhasa: smiths, braziers, tin-men, plumbers, goldsmiths, silversmiths" (Bista 1978, 192). These gold workers, most from the Shākya caste, have always had steady employment in Nepal making religious images and ornaments for families, the latter especially for marriages. See, e.g., Riley-Smith 1989 and Slusser et al. 1999.

6. These records, as well as accounts of Tibetans visiting the Kathmandu Valley, can contribute greatly to understanding this cross-cultural connection and Nepal's history.

7. The contributions of Roberto Vitali 1990; David Jackson 2010; and Eberto Lo Bue 1985, 1988, and 1990, have signaled the need for this changing assessment, a scholarly perspective that was perhaps related to the marginalization of Newar traditions in the study of South Asian Buddhism.

8. As Sylvain Lévi once noted, quoting the missionary visitor to Lhasa Abbé Huc (1813–60): "Among the *Peboun* (one Tibetan name for Newars), one meets very distinguished metal workers. They manufacture vases in gold and silver for the benefit of the monasteries and ornaments of all kinds which would certainly not dishonor European artists" (Lévi 1905–8, vol. 2, 108). A recent major book has been devoted to this metalwork (Furger 2017). Patan

across the Himalayas; records show that Nepal's weavers and blacksmiths also supplied this market. The Newar kings, and their Shah successors (1768), profited greatly from taxes on this trade and so protected it.[9]

Of course it was on these same trails that Tibetan pilgrims and scholars came south to the Kathmandu Valley to acquire Sanskrit texts, receive initiations in esoteric teachings, and earn merit from pilgrimage. Some Tibetan masters likewise gave teachings and initiations to Kathmandu Valley residents. The history of these exchanges, though vitally important to understanding Buddhist history in the region and the Kathmandu Valley as well, has not yet been explored in depth.[10]

After peace returned following the Younghusband invasion, Newar merchants were quick to take advantage of the new circumstances. Already benefitting from their duty-free status and extraterritorial rights according to the Nepal-Tibet Treaty of 1856, more Nepali merchants with capital had begun trading there. Most of these Lhasa family trading houses now moved their main offices to Calcutta. As word spread of these new circumstances—that is, the lessened "friction of distance" involved in going to and from Tibet—the post-1905 period saw a steadily increasing number of additional Newars[11] living in Tibet. Relatives were also recruited to staff new offices that were located to oversee shipments and final sales, from Calcutta to Darjeeling, then in cities

artisans now attract international clients seeking images for temples and Buddhist supply businesses located across the globe. Some Patan artists are now major patrons sponsoring the revitalization of Newar Buddhism.

9. Rana Chandra Shamshere by treaty had a permanent Nepal ambassador stationed in Lhasa after 1856. This representative, appointed by the Nepal government, was designated the *vakil*; typically he was a high-caste Hindu civil servant tasked with advocating for the interests of the Newar merchants with the Tibetan government. He would also solve internal disputes among the Nepalis (Regmi 1971, 25). Other major cities had *adda*, "branch offices," where the *thakali* ("representative head") worked on instructions from the Lhasa *vakil* and, ultimately, Kathmandu. Over time, the most important *adda* was in Gyantse (Mishra 1989).

10. Lewis and Jamspal 1988. Several publications that begin to define the terms of analysis and articulate their importance are found in Lewis 1989 and 1996.

11. In 1904 one estimate of the number of Nepalese living in Lhasa at the time of the Younghusband expedition was eight hundred. The same source had two hundred Kashmiri/Ladakhi, fifty Mongols, and fifty Bhutanese (Waddell 1987, 345). Tucci 1987 estimates three thousand Nepalese in Lhasa.

across Tibet. Some additional branch shops were opened in new cities; as Newars extended this classic example of ethnic diaspora, trade expanded.[12]

The Newars were also aided in this business reconfiguration by the new postal and telegraph systems the British Indian government established, linking Lhasa to points along the trade routes, all the way to Calcutta. The Anglo-Tibetan Treaty allowed for British representatives with small troop garrisons to be located in major towns along this route through the Chumbi Valley and as far as Gyantse; while this made the route fairly secure, it was still true that brigands were an occasional problem in the isolated stretches of the trail, where robberies and murders were periodic.[13] For this reason, it was necessary to have a member of the business, and sometimes armed guards, accompany the caravans when they moved north or south.

The Newar merchant families that had been operating in Tibet for generations had the advantage over Hindu *sauji* since they spoke Tibetan; their long-standing Tibetan allies and partners also facilitated their adapting to the rising volume of business (especially in the main highland cities) after 1905. Some merchants had decades-long connections with traders from Kham who regularly visited their shops; lacking any similar institutions in their own region, the Kham traders would "bank" their money with the Newar trading houses, earning from 6 to 12 percent interest while providing additional capital for the merchants. Several Newars who accepted these deposits reported that many Khampas saw the Newars as fellow outsiders in Lhasa and therefore more trustworthy than the resident Tibetans.

Numerous Newar houses pursued a wool-cloth business that for decades was entirely based in Tibet: buyers would travel across the rural areas to collect the natural woolen cloth, *namba*, that was commonly woven by village and nomad women; these Newar enterprises would dye the wool in one of

12. Curtin 1984.

13. One oral account recorded this incident from sometime in the 1930s: "Ratna Man Singh Tuladhar was attacked by a gang of people while travelling back from Lhasa in the jungle, robbed, [and] thrown in a jute bag. A team of three Newar merchants, while travelling back, discovered the bag [and noticed] light movement. When they opened the bag they discovered Ratna Man Singh. Luckily one of the three knew minor [first aid] treatment and tried his best to save him. The three took turns carrying this injured body by foot . . . walking [back] for two days . . . [they] came across a Tibetan monastery. They handed over the body to the monks and the three returned [on the trail] back to Kathmandu. Ratna Man Singh returned to Kathmandu after he recovered. . . . (http://www.dharmaheera.com/all-stories, accessed September 6, 2021, with minor editing for clarity).

six colors back in the cities, where it would then be sold in shops, both to Tibetans as well as for export.[14]

Middleman trade in Tibet was, at times, a difficult and dangerous occupation. The transport entailed high costs and risky overland routes;[15] after 1800, political events in Tibet, conflicts with the Shah state of Nepal,[16] and local resentment for prosperous non-Tibetans led to periodic boycotts and riots that roiled the market.[17] Several episodes of looting of Newar stores seriously hurt some of the affected stores.[18] During the annual twenty-four-day Mönlam Chenpo festival, the custom, begun by the Fifth Dalai Lama, was to turn over civil and criminal administration to two monks, called *shengo*, who commanded a corps of *dabdab*, "warrior monks."[19] This was the one Tibetan festival that the Lhasa shopkeepers disliked; despite the Thirteenth Dalai Lama's attempted reform of the excesses of the *shengo*, there was no escaping the

14. The profit in this business was usually four times what was paid to the Tibetan village weavers. *Namba* trading was difficult, but for some Newar families entering the Tibet market it was a starting point to accumulate capital and expand their business.

15. Two of the five Newar families I studied had members die on the trade routes, one from illness in remote Phari above Sikkim, the other after falling off a horse five miles on the trail out of Lhasa. Narrowly averted disasters—from bandits, landslides, panicking horses, sudden illness—are common in Newar merchant lore. Dealing with danger was a common challenge for diaspora traders.

16. Modern Nepal was created by the Shahs of Gorkha in 1769, and the new aggressive state fought two wars with China-Tibet in 1788–92 and 1855–56. The latter war, won by Nepal, through treaty established tax-free residence for its citizens in Tibet, as well as their not being subject to Tibetan laws; Nepalese law governed residents in Tibet, and was administered by a government appointee, the *vakil*, who resided in Lhasa.

17. Charles Bell, reflecting the views filtered through the Lhasa diplomatic corps in the first decades of the twentieth century, reports Tibetan "jealousy and dislike" of resident Nepali due to incidents of their not respecting Tibetan customs (e.g., smoking near the Jokhang, fishing in and eating fish from the Lhasa River, unfairly cornering the yak dung market that was used for home heating!). It is hard to scale the frequency of such actions or the magnitude of these opinions among the resident Tibetan population at large. Clearly, while conflicts did occur (as seen in the next note), the businesses had many loyal customers, and Newar accounts of their working in Tibet did not center on constant troubles. See Bell 1924a, especially chapter 25.

18. According to Prem Uprety, there were violent incidents against Newar merchants in Lhasa in 1854, 1862, and 1871. In 1883, "all 84 Newar shops in Lhasa were looted" (1980, 97–98). Again in 1911–12, "rioters killed five Nepalese and burned thirty-eight shops" (132). The Tibeto-Nepal conflict of 1928–30 was another time of disorder in the Bakhor (Mishra 1989).

19. An apt alternative translation was offered by Georges Dreyfus at an NEH Institute event directed by the author and Leonard van der Kuijp in 2003.

dabdabs' unimpeded power to impose temporary and often arbitrary laws and punish anyone for breaking them, sometimes violently. Despite Lhasa being inundated by tens of thousands of pilgrims (and therefore customers) for this festival, Newar merchants often closed their shops.[20]

Fig. 1. Two *dabdabs*, "warrior monks," pose with a friend in a Newar photo studio for a portrait (ca. 1935). The latter shows off a revolver, while the monks' hands hold snuff and snuff bottles. Their large keys dangle from their waist belts. Photo used with permission from collection of Sidhartha Man Tuladhar.

As the twentieth century continued, the Newars were joined by a growing number of competitors in Lhasa and other cities: Indians, Kashmiri Muslims, and Chinese trading houses added to the economy's complexity.[21] Family fortunes could be lost in other ways besides competition, such as the men getting caught up in drinking, opium, gambling, or liaisons with Tibetan women

20. Bell 1924b, 96. When I showed former Lhasa traders photographs showing the *dabdab*, the typical reaction was to recoil upon seeing them and use the Newar word *hārān* ("wild") to describe them. The large keys characteristically worn on their belts were also swung as weapons to control crowds.

21. Chinese merchants after the fall of imperial China were free to set up shops that specialized in tea; Yunnan Chinese moved to Gangtok to enter into the wool trade (Bose 2013). For an account of opium trade in the Tibetan communities of Sichuan during this period, see Yudru Tsomu in this volume.

(prostitution or marriage). In addition to tales of downward mobility, there are stories of individuals starting out as servants in a trading house but eventually rising to become towering successes.[22] Most families with Lhasa trade businesses monitored the performance of their Tibetan enterprises, made strategic choices, and took action to remove family members who were not managing the work well. Family histories include memories of not being treated well by relatives for whom the person worked.[23]

The Newar trading houses that thrived most were those that adopted careful, modern business practices and cultivated good relations with Tibetan officials and customers. The Newar merchants brought all kinds of products available in Calcutta to sell in Tibet;[24] and many still shipped the usual items traditionally traded in Tibet from the Kathmandu Valley to sell to Central Tibet's local and international buyers.[25] They also sent caravans back to India and Nepal with raw wool, musk, borax, rock salt, and yak tails[26] for sale to Indian and international buyers. By 1949 the scope of middlemen trading in

22. It is common to hear rags-to-riches and riches-to-rags narratives used as examples of one's karma taking a sudden opposite turn.

23. Newars today, including the descendants of some of the most successful Lhasa traders, point to how the great wealth that families garnered had a common negative cost: in many of these families, the division of wealth and inheritance led to bitter disputes, some of them dividing families for decades.

24. From the records of one of the largest Newar houses: imports of turquoise from Iran, amber and luxury fabrics from Germany, coral from Italy, silk brocades from Benares, woolen goods from England, cultured pearls from Japan, and silk cloth from China and Japan. A few brought conch shells from India, as these were prized for use in Tibetan rituals and could be sold for their weight in gold; one trader noted that Tibetans felt that these shells retained the spirit of the storm inside them (Lévi 1905–8, n184). There was a large Chinese wholesaler centered in Calcutta, Quangling Yung, that supplied hundreds of goods, including carpets, that Newars bought wholesale for sale in Tibet.

25. Household goods made from copper and brass; raw and beaten rice; art objects in metal, stone, and wood; opium and other medicinal herbs; cooking spices; woven goods, sugar, and tobacco. Some merchant families had shops in the Kathmandu market, where they sold Tibetan goods and had trade connections with Tibetans residing in Kuti and Kiyrong who came in the winter to Kathmandu: "Moti Kaji [Kansakar], managed their shop at home [in Kel Tol], where he sold clothes to Tibetans from Kiyrong and the border areas who came to Kathmandu during the winter, who brought with them goats, sheep and blankets for sale in Kathmandu. For several months, these people were lodged in the ground floor of their home" (http://www.dharmaheera.com/all-stories, accessed September 6, 2021).

26. Yak tails, called *chauri*, have been used as ritual tools for centuries throughout South Asia to fan images in temples and homes.

Tibet had become so great that, according to one German visitor, "There is nothing one cannot buy, or at least order, in the Lhasa market."[27]

One extraordinarily lucrative Newar business was exchanging raw gold for currency or allowing customers to use gold to pay for the shop's goods. Nomads and many others would bring in gold nuggets or gold flakes that were still found in surprising abundance in streams and other localities across the Tibetan plateau. Newars who lived in Tibet recalled the common incident of being handed fist-size nuggets by customers and sometimes spending entire days doing nothing but gold exchange; they had to learn to recognize gold's purity, and a few frankly reported how easy it was to swindle the "country Tibetans," especially Khampas and indigenous peoples of the lower Tsangpo Valley,[28] who were "far too trusting." This raw gold was also taken back to the Kathmandu Valley.[29]

The Newars who became the most prosperous were those who secured individual contracts from the Tibetan government to have the exclusive, duty-free right to supply imported gems, motorcycles, automobiles, and other luxury items. Several Newar businesses had contracts to import special gold and silver plates used to mint money, a very profitable enterprise indeed. Major monasteries also contracted with businesses for supplying items needed for Buddhist sanctuaries and devotional practices. This is a modern Tibetan example of an ancient and universal phenomenon across the Buddhist world linking merchants and trade to monastery building and merit-making.[30]

Newars were quick to set up, even before the Younghusband invasion, some of the first photo studios in Tibet, where Tibetans who visited the major cities could pose for photographs shot on large-format cameras that used large glass negatives. The records of Tibetan life that these photographer entrepreneurs captured are now invaluable sociohistorical documents. The panoply of pilgrims visiting the Lhasa photo studios, for example, included aristocrats, commoners, and country folk, the clothing and jewelry reflecting the various regional material cultures of Tibet. Monks dropped in to pose as well, sometimes with family, resulting in remarkable portraits of the *dabdab* ("punk

27. One list of exotics included "Bing Crosby records, Elizabeth Arden perfumes, German clocks, Japanese watches, Australian butter . . . "

28. One merchant recalled tribal people, who "were jungli," wearing bear fur and yak skins showing up periodically.

29. Newar merchant lore includes tales of porters coming from Tibet with their packs filled with little else beside a Lhasa's *Sau*'s ("Merchant's") gold. Importing gold back for sale in Nepal was highly lucrative but also very risky.

30. Ray 1986; Liu 1988; Sen 2003.

monks") and of friends holding out their prized possessions, such as snuff containers, oversize keys, and even handguns! Some Newar photo-shop entrepreneurs also made and sold a variety of large composite photo prints featuring important religious figures that could be placed on Tibetan family altars.

Fig. 2. A group of young women pose in a Newar photo studio in front of a painted background (ca. 1935). Photo used with permission from collection of Sidhartha Man Tuladhar.

Venturing into India and then going up to the major cities of Tibet attracted young men from upper-caste Buddhist families, primarily the Urāy of Kathmandu and the Dhakwa of Patan. A few other Newar castes were noted in these regions as well, such as Shākya metal artisans and, in the 1940s, Shrestha and Manandhar importers and a Jyāpu who worked as a "handyman." Most of the Newar houses employed their own workers from the valley to serve as servants and salesmen; these workers outnumbered the business owners and were usually paid a salary. "Going off to Tibet" was a course of action open to young Newars with connections; it attracted a variety of individuals, from the ambitious to the desperate—young men in trouble with the law or escaping marriage or bad luck in the local family business.

Some Tibet traders were notable for their adventurousness. The photographs they took of their own lives in Tibet show them posing on horses and motorcycles, crossing the Tsangpo River in yak skin or wooden boats, wearing

Tibetan clothes, or just venturing out on picnics to see the sights. At times they took tourist-style photos of Tibetan festivals, processions, or historical events.[31]

A few of the Newar photographs from Lhasa show the Tibetan women that some merchants married, a practice that eased the loneliness of staying in Tibet for many years but could complicate or often poison family relations with kin back in the valley.[32] The prevalence of Newar men fathering children with Tibetan women is indicated by the number of male offspring known as *khacara* ("half breeds"), a number that grew to be over a thousand by 1910.[33] Any males having a Nepalese father or grandfather could claim Nepali citizenship. Being legally recognized as such gave them special status, though female children had no such right and were deemed "Tibetan." As guaranteed by the Tibet-Nepal Treaty of 1856, *khacara* had full tax-exempt privileges as well as extraterritorial legal rights. Some were known for abusing this status and flouting authority; Tibetan officials regularly complained about *khacara* ("high-handedness").[34]

Most Newars in Tibet practiced Buddhism and participated in the devotional life that mingled with trade, as the interplay of both was integral to old Lhasa's cityscape, where the innermost route circumambulating the central temple, the Jokhang, is also the city's main market, the Bakhor. Here is where most Newar trading houses, or *kothi*, had their Lhasa headquarters, in stone buildings with shops on the ground floor and living quarters behind and above. Tibetans and foreign visitors after 1904 provide vivid impressions of the Newar merchants residing in Lhasa. They are recalled wearing *topi* hats (still distinctive of modern Nepal male attire) and wool shawls over their shoulders, in a manner still

31. One family has photographs of the Chinese army arriving in Tibet in 1950.

32. Poor Tibetan families with beautiful daughters or a widowed or divorced young daughter sought marriage alliances that they hoped would benefit their family's prospects. Some observers estimated that "most" Newars had Tibetan wives. The male children of these marriages, according to Tibetan law, could not inherit their Newar father's estates unless they resided in Nepal. Only if a man returned to Nepal (as many did after 1959) could he claim a share of his Newar father's estate, alongside his Newar half brothers and sisters. This requirement led to many intra-family disputes. My article on a popular Buddhist merchant didactic story in the Kathmandu Valley relates its popularity to this contextual factor (Lewis 1993b). Recent studies of this enduring community in Kathmandu are found in Mishra 2003 and Ellingsen 2017.

33. Mishra 2003.

34. Uprety 1980, 146. These provisions for Nepali citizens in Tibet ended with the Sino-Nepali Treaty of 1958.

seen during cold months in the Kathmandu Valley. Observers also note that unlike the Tibetans, Newars could be recognized by *tika* dots on their foreheads that reflected their daily devotions. Their shops were very tidy, which some observers contrasted with the dirty shops of other groups. Multiple observers record that the Newars seemed happy and had a "jovial" nature and a special fondness for singing.

Although in some respects they competed with one another, Newar merchants in Tibet still joined together to form *guthi* ("endowed committees") to perform rituals, sing devotional songs, and lend money internally.[35] A Lhasa *guthi* with five divisions united all Newars for a variety of collective religious rituals; each had a leader (*pāla*) who changed yearly. The *guthi* provided support to any family experiencing a death, with each division expected to send as many of its section members as possible to help with funeral arrangements and other needs. This association also organized the observance of Newar Buddhism's holy month, Guṃlā, in Lhasa.[36] Throughout this late summer month (July–August), merchants display religious paintings and light butter lamps in their shops, and they make visits to temples around the city to present offerings. Every morning during Guṃlā, ten or more Newars formed a procession to the Jokhang as part of the traditional music ensemble (*Guṃlā bājan*), just as done by Newar Buddhists in the Kathmandu Valley: a leader keeping time with small cymbals, the dominant sound a chorus of drummers playing the same beat using over-the-shoulder drums, accompanied by a few playing larger cymbals.[37] As in Nepal, too, on a day during Guṃlā called "Pañca Dāna" they made merit-earning offerings to Tibetan monks.

Nepal's main national holidays, Dassain and Tihar (Newari: Mohani and Saunti), were also celebrated. The latter was observed in homes, with the Newar New Year's ritual that strengthens the body, *Mhaḥ Pūjā*, routinely done. But Mohani was observed in public and centered on the *vakil*'s residence. For it, the Buddhists formed a group that went around the outer circumambulatory route of the city, then back into their Bakhor neighborhood. At the *vakil*'s home, the *guthi* heads (*pāla*) would form a line and "sacrifice" long radishes with a demon face painted on them to the goddess Durgā.[38]

35. Bista 1978, 195. See Toffin 1975 for the definitive study of the Newar tradition that still relies on these institutions (Skt. *goṣṭhi*) known to have existed in ancient India.

36. For a summary of this tradition in Kathmandu, see Lewis 1993c.

37. One merchant recalled an unplanned encounter between the *Guṃlā bājan* and the young Fourteenth Dalai Lama, who is said to have enjoyed the music and praised the Newars for their devotion.

38. This is in the style of the non-animal "sacrifices" done by most Newar Buddhists on

Another public expression of Newar tradition was the festival of Bhimsen (Newari: Bhiṃ Dyaḥ). In the Newar bazaar shops of the valley, Bhimsen is honored daily as the protector of merchants and their businesses, whose image in the shop receives an incense offering before opening. Most Newars in Lhasa followed this practice. But in Lhasa, a larger celebration focusing on Bhimsen came around every twelve years: supported by several *guthi*, the Lhasa traders sponsored one man from the Kathmandu Valley to come up from Kathmandu to act as a *pūjāri* for this deity. After doing a ritual inside the large Bhimsen temple in Kathmandu, this man (not a professional priest) set out with a large trunk of flower *prasād* on the nearly one-month trek. Once at Lhasa's western gateway, he was welcomed by representatives from the Newar community and the *vakil*, then escorted to a house where he would stay almost a month. On the auspicious day, the resident Newars formed a musical procession and set up a Bhimsen image attended by the visiting ritualist in an open space in the Bakhor. All the Newars (and many others) would come to make offerings, with the *dakṣina* (honorarium) to the *pūjāri* amounting to many tens of thousands of rupees. The *sauji* also pooled funds to make the emissary a silver crown with the name Bhimsen on it (that he wore during the festival) and a set of heavy gold earrings (to honor his completing the mission), both as an additional form of payment. In 1942 one Tuladhar merchant traveled with the Bhimsen entourage and gave a detailed oral account of these events.[39] By the time the ad hoc priest returned to Nepal, he had accumulated tens of thousands of rupees in donations.

Some Newars living in Tibet were known for their strong Buddhist devotion. They routinely did full prostrations outside temples and before holy teachers, including the Dalai Lama; they regularly gave donations to monks, circumambulated the Jokhang temple, and turned hand-held prayer wheels in their leisure time. Many wore rosaries for regular meditation practice, having taken teachings from Tibetan lamas. In the 1940s and 1950s, there was a Newar *vajrācārya* priest residing in Lhasa; many of the merchants utilized him to

Vijayāṣṭami or Durgā Pūjā day in Kathmandu, where a pumpkin with a demon face painted on it is hacked up by clan leaders.

39. That year, amid the offerings on the main day, Tej Ratna Tuladhar described how the *pūjāri* suddenly acted as if possessed by Bhimsen. This keen and skeptical observer bluntly added: "Watching this man, I not believing. No god coming."

have rituals performed in Tibetan monastery temples and for their in-home ceremonies.

There were also a number of Newar men in Tibet who were known to have "gone native" in their devotional practices, and at least one merchant, Laxmi Bir Singh Kansakar, was so engaged with Tibetan Buddhism that he acquired the nickname Lama Sau. Some Newars in Lhasa even took vows and became Tibetan monks, adopting the monastic life in different *gompas*.[40] One famous Newar lama among them, whose Newar name was Jñāna Man Singh Tuladhar of Naradevi Tol, returned to Nepal and in 1954 established a *gompa* at Svayaṃbhū. Other members of its founding sangha were also Newars: three Tulādhars, two Shākyas, and one Shrestha[41] Jñāna Man was the resident teacher at Maitri Gompa (Sumati Maitri Śāsana Vihāra), located as of this writing just below the upper parking lot on Svayaṃbhū hill. He had acquired such a following that a commercial photographer with a shop in Kathmandu sold photographic prints of him for local, mostly Newar, devotees.

Both before and increasingly after the Younghusband invasion, the Newar merchants in Tibet brought their profits home, and in several dozen cases at least, these represented small fortunes. The most successful used these funds to invest in land, expand houses, and start family enterprises in Nepal, increasingly so when the country opened to the outside world after the restoration of the Shah monarchy in 1951. Since they had a head start in learning modern economic practices and had "seen the world" and gained experience in running business enterprises, most have flourished, several becoming among the wealthiest men in Nepal today.

Like householders throughout the history of Buddhism, the Newar Lhasa merchants also invested in merit-making, providing the funds to build new or restore old stūpas and monasteries back in the Kathmandu Valley. Svayaṃbhū

40. Bista 1978, 41, mentions knowing a Newar man who had been living for over twenty-one years in Drepang Monastery. Harrer 1976, 205, notes that "many Nepalis" were ordained monks, most of whom resided with other Newars in the large Lhasa monasteries (as did Tibetans from different regions), and that the Newars "were regarded as very apt pupils." A few Lhasa merchants had been so happy living in Tibet that upon returning to Nepal after 1959, they were unsettled in Kathmandu and longed to return to Lhasa.

41. The name of the monastery is Śri Sumati Maitri Śāsana Mahāvihāra, referred to colloquially as Maitri Gompa. This *gompa* was consecrated in 1954. The other founding monks were Devakul Singh Tuladhar, Mahācandra Śākya, Nhuche Śākya, Keśa Ratna Tulādhar, Jñānendra Śreṣṭha, and Gajānanda Śākya.

Fig. 3. Jñāna Man Singh Tuladhar of Naradevi Tol, a Newar merchant who was ordained as a Tibetan monk in Tibet and became abbot of the Tibetan-styled Maitri Gompa on Svayaṃbhū. Photo used with permission from collection of K. T. Tuladhar, Dagu Baha in Kathmandu.

and Bauddha were beneficiaries of Newar merchant largesse.[42] Many Lhasa mercantile families also sponsored special iterations of the two greatest Newar Buddhist donative festivals, Pañca Dāna[43] and Samyak.[44] For both, individual

42. See von Rospatt 2009 and 2018; Decleer 1998.

43. This big event is usually held during the holy month of Guṃlā.

44. This is certainly a cultural survival of the old Indic and Central Asian Buddhist *Pañcavārsika*. A *guthi* in Patan organizes its Samyak every five years; the Kathmandu

sponsors must invite the Kathmandu Valley's entire Newar sangha to receive food and other donations. In the former festival, the sponsor must offer as a gift a house and lands to one monastic; in the latter, basic rice and other offerings to each and every monastic must be made, along with a feast. On the second day, any woman wanting to come for a feast must be fed. In addition to these donations, the Samyak sponsor must make a large moveable image of a standing Dīpaṅkara Buddha, a metal stūpa, and other items used in processions through the old city. The sponsor must also invite all the previous Samyak sponsors to join in three days of processions to the royal palace, to a field at the eastern foot of Svayaṃbhū hill where the donations are bestowed for two days, and then back to their homes. It is no exaggeration to attribute the rich array of religious monuments in the Kathmandu Valley, and the vibrant cultural practices of Newar Buddhist communities, to the great profits derived from the Tibetan trade. Many of the remarkable array of monasteries, rest houses, *caityas*, and temples in Newar towns were created thanks to the strong religious sentiments of Lhasa merchant families.

Not only did most Newar merchants contribute to their own traditions, but some were also deeply impacted by Tibetan Buddhist traditions and teachers. They brought this devotion back to Nepal with them and found new outlets to continue some of these beloved Tibetan spiritual practices. Dating back to at least the nineteenth century, Newar patronage supported the living costs of prominent lamas coming on pilgrimage to Nepal. Some merchants provided funds to build Tibetan monasteries in the Kathmandu Valley; others added Tibetan prayer wheels to Newar monasteries (*bāhā*).

In the late 1920s several Newars were ordained as novices in the Tibetan Nyingma tradition after traveling to Kiyrong. They did so after their spiritual inclinations had been stirred by two lamas who had visited the Kathmandu Valley, and their travel expenses were supported by Lhasa trading families. Upon returning to Nepal, these Newar monks wearing Tibetan robes drew patrons and special attention when they went through the Kathmandu streets on traditional alms rounds and then gave Dharma talks. This brought them to the attention of the Rana government, which expelled them from Nepal. The group eventually became monks in the Theravāda tradition, which led to the introduction of the Theravāda modernist movement in the post-Rana period.

A few Lhasa traders have served as "cultural middlemen," advocating for, and often organizing, special events so that Newar kin and friends can practice

---

Samyak *guthi* holds its event only every twelve years. New sponsors can devote their donations and organize the event at any time. It is noteworthy that there have been very few new Samyak sponsors since the closing of the Lhasa trade.

Tibetan-style rituals (*homa*, healing, *nyungné* fasting retreats,[45] and meditation) and earn merit by donating to lamas and their *gompas*. Three generations after the last of the Newar traders returned to Kathmandu, many of these Tibetan merchant families continue their custom of calling resident lamas to do Tibetan Buddhist rituals in their homes.[46]

Historically in Newar-Tibetan relations, the pattern of frontier communities being incorporated into greater Tibet can be discerned in Nepal. Among Newars venturing to Tibet, there were several who "crossed over" to take ordination as monks. One early and famous example was an Urāy who took the name of Dharmalok and traveled to Tibet; but he later had a change of heart, and upon his return to Nepal he embraced the reformist Theravāda movement, becoming a monk.

Another kind of Newar connection to Tibetan tradition also built on this trans-regional Newar-Tibetan history: the practice of identifying Tibetan reincarnate lamas among Newar children in the Kathmandu Valley. At least two such cases have been recorded in the last four decades; one that I knew of in 1980 was found in a *khacara* family.[47]

It has long been my view that the cultural history of the Kathmandu Valley, and its Buddhist traditions, cannot be complete, or accurate, without incorporating the records of Tibetan visitors and the work of Tibetan teachers who at various points made a significant impact on local Newar traditions.[48]

45. Also popular among other Tibetan groups across Nepal. See Wangchen Rinpoche 2009.

46. A few wealthy families shifted their loyalty, and Tibet-derived fortunes, to support the valley's Theravāda movement (Levine and Gellner 2007).

47. The child was taken to Dharamsala and confirmed in 1981, after which I lost touch with his family. My interview with his father indicated that the boy had been identified as a *trülku* associated with Ganden, who was given the ordination name of Jikmé Tenpa Wangchuk and was destined to be educated in the rebuilt monastery in Karnataka, in India. After a new inquiry for this article, I received this response from Jangchup Choeden, Executive Director, Geluk International Foundation: "This young *trülku* has grown up and graduated as a *geshe* from the monastery and lately he has been spending most of his time in Taiwan giving Dharma teachings. I am informed his father passed away several years back. . . . The *trülku* is now known as Serkong Khentrul and I wish you good luck finding more information on him" (September 1, 2021).

48. These were summarized in an article (Lewis 1989) and in edited volumes (Lewis 1993a, Lewis 1995). Since then, additional *trülku* identifications in Newar families have come to light as well as ties (still unstudied) between the *vajrācāryas* of Kathmandu's Tache Bāhā and the Karmapa lineage. I recall with gratitude that Gene Smith encouraged the pursuit of this subject. He was attentive to Tibetan monks who visited the Kathmandu Valley and pointed this out in his introductions to the Tibetan texts he published.

Fig. 4. Donam Tsering (a descendent of a Newar merchant man and a Tibetan mother) with his son right after he was recognized as a *trülku* in 1980. Photo by Todd Lewis.

My first meeting with Leonard van der Kuijp, then also a young scholar of Buddhism, occurred when he heard that in the course of my research on the Newars of Kathmandu, I had formed friendships with prominent families with ties to Tibet. In 1981 we were both working on the frontier of Himalayan Buddhist studies, where one could make exciting discoveries about cultures still largely unknown in the West. He was looking for information about one lama and had heard that a family in Asan Tol knew him. And it was indeed true, upon inquiry, that his quest was for one very important family, the descendants of the aforementioned Dhamma Sau. After a few inquiries, Dhamma Sau's great-grandson met Leonard and shared what he knew about this lama, a *trülku* they called "Tuton Rinpoché." I had even once gone to meet this lama with Pratyek Man's family at his monastery behind Svayaṃbhū to get blessings, and on other occasions I watched him do prognostication rituals and observed his performing a Tibetan-style *homa* ritual in Asan Tol to appease the ghost of a troubled Newar teenager who had died from suicide.

Helping Leonard make this connection was the beginning of a personal and professional friendship that has flourished for over forty years. Leonard's interest in this hitherto little-explored link between Newars and Tibetans alerted me that this cultural connection between Newars and Tibetans should be

Fig. 5. A Newar woman devotee makes a donation to the Tibetan monk they knew as "Tuton Rinpoché" during a visit to his monastery in 1980. Photo by Todd Lewis.

explored further. This first meeting with Leonard also led me to see how Buddhist institutions must be imagined with permeable ethnic boundaries. Our meeting at the start of our careers laid the foundation for an academic friendship and, once Leonard moved to Harvard, our codirecting six NEH Institutes for K-12 teachers and higher education faculty on the cultures, arts, and religions of the Himalayan region.[49] Here we did some of the finest teaching of our careers. I came to see what a blessing it was for these teachers and his graduate students to have Leonard van der Kuijp as a mentor.

49. A website from one program that we curated as a scholarly resource can be found at: https://college.holycross.edu/projects/buddhists_traditions/.

References

Bell, Charles. 1924a. *Tibet: Past and Present*. Oxford: Clarendon Press.

———. 1924b. "A Year in Lhasa." *The Geographical Journal* 72.2: 89–101.

Bista, Dor. 1978. "Nepalis in Tibet." In *Himalayan Anthropology*, edited by James Fisher, 187–204. The Hague: Mouton.

Bose, Arpita. 2013. "Kolkata's Early Chinese Community and Their Economic Contributions." *South Asia Research* 33.2: 163–76.

Curtin, Philip. 1984. *Cross Cultural Trade in World History*. Cambridge: Cambridge University Press.

Decleer, Hubert. 1998. "Two Topics from the *Svayambhu Purana*: Who was Dharmashri-mitra? Who was Shantikara Acharya?" Paper presented at the Conference on the Buddhist Heritage of Nepal Mandala.

Ellingsen, Winfried. 2017. "The Khacchara of Kathmandu—Mobility, Situatedness and Ethnic Identification." *Journal of Ethnic and Migration Studies* 43.3 (March): 513–27.

Furger, Alex R. 2017. *The Gilded Buddha: The Traditional Art of the Newar Metal Casters in Nepal*. Basel: Librum.

Gellner, David N., and Declan Quigley, eds. 1995. *Contested Hierarchies: A Collaborative Ethnography of Caste among the Newars of the Kathmandu Valley, Nepal*. Oxford: Oxford University Press.

Goldstein, Melvyn C. 1989. *A History of Modern Tibet, 1913–1952*. Berkeley: University of California Press.

Harrer, Heinrich. 1976. *Seven Years in Tibet*. London: Hart Davis.

Hilker, D. S. Kansakar. 2005. *Syamukapu: The Lhasa Newars of Kalimpong and Kathmandu*. Kathmandu: Vajra Publications.

Jackson, David P. 2010. *The Nepalese Legacy in Tibetan Painting*. New York: Rubin Museum.

Lall, Kesar. 2001. *The Newar Merchants in Lhasa*. Kathmandu: Ratna Pustak Bhandar.

Lévi, Sylvain. 1905–8. *Le Nepal: Étude historique d'un royaume Hindou*. 3 vols. Paris: Ernest Leroux.

Levine, Sarah, and David Gellner. 2007. *Rebuilding Buddhism: The Theravada Movement in Twentieth-Century Nepal*. Cambridge, MA: Harvard University Press.

Lewis, Todd T. 1989. "Newars and Tibetans in the Kathmandu Valley: Ethnic Boundaries and Religious History." *Journal of Asian and African Studies* 38: 31–57.

_____. 1993a. "Himalayan Frontier Trade: Newar Diaspora Merchants and Buddhism." In *Anthropology of Tibet and the Himalayas*, edited by Charles Ramble and Martin Brauen, 130–45. Zurich: Volkerkundemuseum.

_____. 1993b. "Newar-Tibetan Trade and the Domestication of the *Simhalasārthabāhu Avadāna*." *History of Religions* 33.2: 135–60.

_____. 1993c. "Contributions to the Study of Popular Buddhism: The Newar Buddhist Festival of *Gumlā Dharma*." *Journal of the International Association of Buddhist Studies* 16: 7–52.

_____. 1995. "Buddhist Merchants in Kathmandu: The Asan Tol Market and *Urāy* Social Organization." In *Contested Hierarchies: A Collaborative Ethnography of Caste among the Newars of the Kathmandu Valley, Nepal*, edited by David Gellner and Declan Quigley, 38–79. Oxford: Oxford University Press.

_____. 1996. "A Chronology of Newar-Tibetan Relations in the Kathmandu Valley." In *Change and Continuity: Studies in the Nepalese Culture of the Kathmandu Valley*, edited by Siegfried Lienhard, 149–66. Torino: Edizioni Dell'orso.

Lewis, Todd T., and Lozang Jamspal. 1998. "Newars and Tibetans in the Kathmandu Valley: Three New Translations from Tibetan Sources." *Journal of Asian and African Studies* 36: 187–211.

Lewis, Todd T., and Subarna Man Tuladhar. 2019. *The Epic of the Buddha: His Life and Teachings by Chittadhar Hridaya*. Boulder, CO: Shambhala.

Liu, Xinru. 1988. *Ancient India and Ancient China*. Bombay: Oxford University Press.

Lo Bue, Erberto. 1985 and 1986. "The Newar Artists of the Nepal Valley: A Historical Account of Their Activities in Neighboring Areas with Particular Reference to Tibet." I and II. *Oriental Art* 21: 262–77, and 22: 409–20.

_____. 1988. "Cultural Exchange and Social Interaction between Tibetans and Newars from the Seventh to the Twentieth Century." *International Folklore Review* 6: 86–114.

_____. 1990. "Iconographic Sources and Iconometric Literature in Tibetan and Himalayan Art." In *Indo-Tibetan Studies: Papers in Honour and Appreciation of Professor David L. Snellgrove's Contribution to Indo-Tibetan Studies*, edited by Tadeusz Skorupski, 171–97. Tring, UK: The Institute of Buddhist Studies.

Mishra, Tirtha P. 1989. "Nepalese Thakali at Gyantse (1905–1938)." *Ancient Nepal* 114: 9–17.

_____. 2003. "Nepalese in Tibet: A Case Study of Nepalese Half-Breeds (1856–1956)." *Contributions to Nepalese Studies* 30: 1–16.

Pal, Pratapaditya. 1991. *Art of the Himalayas: Treasures from Nepal and Tibet*. New York: Hudson Hills Press.

Ray, Himanshu P. 1986. *Monastery and Guild*. Delhi: Oxford University Press.

Regmi, Chandra Mahesh. 1971. *A Study of Nepali Economic History 1768–1846*. New Delhi: Manjusri Publishing House.

Riley-Smith, Tristram. 1998. "Image, Status and Association: Aspects of Identity among Newar Gods and Men." *Kailash* 15.3–4: 223–42.

Slusser, Mary, Nutan Sharma, and James Giambrone. 1999. "Metamorphosis: Sheet Metal to Sacred Image in Nepal." *Artibus Asiae* 58.3–4: 215–52.

Stein, Rolf. A. 1972. *Tibetan Civilization*. Translated by J. E. Stapleton Driver. Stanford, CA: Stanford University Press.

Toffin, Gerard. 1975. "Etudes sur les Newars de la Vallee Kathmandou: *Guthi*, Funerailles et Castes." *L'Ethnographie* 2: 206–25.

Tucci, Giuseppe. 1987 [1956]. *To Lhasa and Beyond: A Diary of the 1948 Expedition*. Ithaca, NY: Snow Lion Publications.

Tuladhar, Kamal. 2004. *Caravan to Lhasa: Newar Merchants of Kathmandu in Traditional Tibet*. Kathmandu: Nepal Printing House.

Uprety, Prem R. 1980. *Nepal-Tibet Relations, 1850–1930*. Kathmandu: Puja Nara.
_____. 1996. "Treaties between Nepal and Her Neighbors: A Historical Perspective." *Tribhuvan University Journal* 19.1: 15–24.
Vitali, Roberto. 1990. *Early Temples of Central Tibet*. London: Serindia.
von Rospatt, Alexander. 2009. "Sacred Origins of the *Svayambhucaitya* and the Nepal Valley: Foreign Speculation and Local Myth." *Journal of the Nepal Research Centre* 13: 33–39.
_____. 2018. "The Collective Sponsorship of the Renovations of the *Svayambhūcaitya* in the Later Malla Era, and Its Documentation in Historical Records." In *Studies in Historical Documents from Nepal and India*, edited by S. Cubelic, A. Michaels, and A. Zotter, 163–91. Heidelberg: Heidelberg University Publishing.
Waddell, L. Austine. 1987 [1905]. *Lhasa and Its Mysteries*. New York: Dover.
Wangchen Rinpoche. 2009. *Buddhist Fasting Practice: The Nyungne Method of Thousand-Armed Chenrezig.* Boston: Shambhala.

A Discourse on Kingship from the Eighth Karmapa

Ian MacCormack

It was my learned Professor van der Kuijp who first brought this text to my attention many years ago, and patiently reminded me of it on several other occasions. I offer this short essay in thanks for his kindness.

SOMEWHAT RECENTLY, a *Collected Works* of the Eighth Karmapa Mikyö Dorjé (Mi bskyod rdo rje, 1507–54) was published by the Tsadra Foundation, redacted from two incomplete versions of his corpus from Drepung Monastery, plus texts from the Potala Palace, the Nationalities Cultural Palace (Minzu wenhua gong 民族文化宫), and collections in Tibet and India.[1] The collection includes roughly a dozen missives to the heads of noble houses in Ü and Tsang. One of the more substantial items is a discourse on kingship addressed to the Neudong king, which I translate below.

The text reads as an epideictic address, imparting a moral-historical lesson at a precarious juncture to sway the monarch toward a preferred course. The modern edition incorporates a title page closely matching the description in the Fifth Zhamarpa's catalog of the Karmapa's works, completed in 1555, which guided the organization of this edition.[2] Mikyö Dorjé lived during the tenure of the Neudong Gongma Ngawang Tashi Drakpa (Sne'u gdong gong ma Ngag dbang bkra shis grags pa, r. 1499–1564), but another plausible target is the king's grandson Ngawang Drakpa, who temporarily supplanted him in a minor coup in 1554. This discourse seems premised on an event of enthronement (*khri la gnas pa'i dus*) or investiture (*mnga' gsol ba*) of a divine prince (*lha gzhon nu*), more suggestive of a young upstart than someone already in power for decades. It is not in the list of compositions in Mikyö Dorjé's 1546 autobiography, which mentions several other letters in the new *Collected Works*.[3]

1. See Rheingans 2017, 43–53. It has since been reissued in an anthology of Karmapa works by Paltsek.

2. The full title is *Bod ryal po chen po'i rgyal thabs kyi mdzad pa gtam du byas pa ne'u gdong rgyal po la gnang ba rin po che'i phreng ba*; cf. Dkon mchog yan lag 2000, 4a.

3. *Mi bskyod rdo rje'i spyad pa'i rabs*, in Mi bskyod rdo rje 2000–2004, vol. 1, 362.

The tone and contents also lend themselves to the exacerbated circumstances of Mikyö Dorjé's last years. Granted, he was quite ill by this time and died only months later, but as Olaf Czaja notes, he wrote letters to the new ruler and his deposed grandfather, so a longer discourse is not implausible.[4]

Formally, we can parse the text into three movements: historical, diagnostic, and prescriptive. It starts with a survey of Tibet's political fortunes (1b–3b), setting up a contrast with the recent turmoil (4a–5b), together giving the advice to the king (5b–7b) a chiaroscuro shading of dire circumstances offset by fragile possibility. Rhetorically, the instructions gain their charge, so to speak, from the friction generated by rubbing Tibet's present predicaments against the memory of lost glory. This guidance ends on a utopian note, anticipating an imminent horizon where untold riches flow and neighboring kings tremble in awe, capped by fourteen stanzas of eulogistic verse.[5] The narrative can describe different trajectories depending on one's focus. Cosmologically, it evokes that most malleable trope of the decline of Dharma, lamenting the long descent from an unrecoverable golden age down to the disappearance of religion and even beyond, into a kind of zombie afterlife where pretenders stalk a barren spiritual landscape. From a political-historical vantage, the pattern is rather one of oscillation: plummeting from the heights of the *tsenpos* before sweeping up with the Sakya-Mongol partnership, then cresting twice more with Jangchup Gyeltsen (Byang chub rgyal mtshan) and Drakpa Gyeltsen (Grags pa rgyal mtshan) before the latest dip back into chaos. As a religious narrative of Kagyü origins, it has a more triumphant arc, recalling how the rise of this superior tradition ushered in a stable social order, now suddenly threatened by disturbing new factional tendencies.

Contemporary history adds some piquancy to these at-times conventional laments and blandishments. At the risk of oversimplification, Central Tibetan society in the late fifteenth and early sixteenth centuries was characterized by a shifting network of affinities and antagonisms between several noble houses under the *de jure* overlordship of the Pakmodru. The major modalities of power were marriage alliances, church-state relations, and occasionally outright conflict (or its mediation)—in other words, a politics of succession, patronage, and war. The royal throne at Neudong typically passed from uncle to nephew, with other brothers holding the seats at Densatil (Gdan sa mthil) and Tsetang (Rtse thang). Monastic leaders moved laterally across this field of

4. Czaja 2013, 269n98.

5. I have kept the enumeration seen in the modern edition, but also the frequent enjambment between stanzas.

power, cultivating multiple ties that could vary from one generation to the next according to the fortunes of each family.

Pakmodru rule did not end abruptly but was decentralized and eroded over time, ceding to an increasingly volatile distribution of power between noble houses and religious institutions. The Seventh Karmapa Chödrak Gyatso (Chos grags rgya mtsho, d. 1507) and the influential Fourth Zhamarpa Chödrak Yeshé (Chos grags ye shes, d. 1524) were contemporaries and allies of the Rinpungpa family, who made themselves the dominant force in Tsang while leveraging strategic marriages to assert influence behind the throne. Their ascent began with Norbu Zangpo (Nor bu bzang po, d. 1466), whose father and grandfather were ministers to Drakpa Gyeltsen (r. 1385–1432), sometimes considered the apogee of consolidated Pakmodru power. Norzang, whose sisters were married to the king's brother Sanggyé Gyeltsen (Sangs rgyas rgyal mtshan), took advantage of a succession crisis in 1433 to make himself *de facto* lord at Samdruptsé (Bsam 'grub rtse). Meanwhile the throne went to the king's nephew (Sanggyé Gyeltsen's son), Drakpa Jungné (Grags pa 'byung gnas, d. 1445), and then to his brother Kunga Lekpa (Kun dga' legs pa, r. 1448–81), whose contentious marriage to another Rinpungpa daughter fissured the court and compelled the major houses to line up behind one side or the other.[6]

Rinpung authority passed through Norzang's son Kunzang (Kun bzang) to his grandson Dönyö Dorjé (Don yod rdo rje, d. 1512), while another son by his second wife, Tsokyé Dorjé (Mtsho skyes rdo rje, d. 1510), established himself at Khartok in Yarlung (Yar klung Mkhar thog). Dönyö Dorjé was close with the Karma Kagyü leaders, with whom he shared designs on Lhasa. Chödrak Gyatso, recalling Neupa sponsorship of the Fifth Karmapa at Marpori (Dmar po ri), aimed to start a monastery nearby, but his encampment was stymied by opposition from about five hundred hastily armed Geluk monks.[7] (Later, in 1503, with Dönyö Dorjé's support, they established Yangpachen [Yangs pa can] for the Zhamarpa in Tölung [Stod lung] to the west, and Tupchen [Thub chen] for the Karmapa, east of Lhasa, laying the literal and metaphorical groundwork for future antagonism.)[8] Dönyö Dorjé brought forces into Kyishö (Skyid shod) in 1480, seizing several estates and prompting a council at which the Rinpungpas and their allies backed Drakpa Jungné's son Ngaki Wangpo (Ngag gi dbang po) for the throne. The Zhamarpa (patronized by the Yargyap [G.yar rgyab] family, who aided Dönyö Dorjé in those attacks) delivered the benediction at his enthronement in 1481; later he would be given

6. Tucci 1971, 222–23.

7. Gtsug lag 'phreng ba 1986, 1078–79; Chos kyi 'byung gnas 1972, vol. 1, 180b.

8. Gtsug lag 'phreng ba 1986, 1105–6.

the seat of Densatil. After Ngaki Wangpo's death in 1491, Tsokyé Dorjé was named regent to the young scion, Ngawang Tashi Drakpa, born in 1488. In 1498 Dönyö Dorjé invaded Lhasa, eliminating the regional power, the Neupa house, and spurring the child prince's promotion, again with the Zhamarpa's endorsement.

Yet as Ngawang Tashi Drakpa came into his own—and notwithstanding that Rinpung gains were a boon for their own fortunes—the Karma Kagyü leaders increasingly favored the reconsolidation of Pakmodru power away from the Rinpungpas. This shifting of the tides may have accelerated after 1510, which saw the death of Tsokyé Dorjé, followed by another military advance by his son, Ngawang Namgyel (Ngag dbang rnam rgyal), and a souring of relations with Dönyö Dorjé after his gift of territory to placate the Neudong Gongma and Zhamarpa (who tried to curtail these incursions) was deemed insufficient.[9] Recalling his great-granduncle's support of Tsongkhapa, the Gongma turned to the Gelukpas, promoting Gendün Gyatso (Dge 'dun rgya mtsho) at Drepung ('Bras spungs; establishing the Ganden Podrang [Dga' ldan pho brang] estate) and reinstituting Geluk control over the Lhasa Mönlam (Smon lam) ceremonies in 1517. (He still collaborated with the Zhamarpa, as to support the succession at Drigung ['Bri gung] in 1516.) In short, the Zhamarpa and Seventh Karmapa appear to have pursued a dynamic political strategy of negotiating the distribution of power to circumvent any undue concentration, although the effect seems to have been to undercut one of their staunchest supporters while opening the door for a potential adversary who did not necessarily share these same goals.[10]

Mikyö Dorjé, born in 1507, started paying attention to Central Tibetan politics in his late twenties. His student, the Second Pawo Tsuklak Trengwa (Dpa' bo Gtsug lag 'phreng ba), suggests it was around 1535, when he was then in Kongpo, that he recognized the importance of direct engagement:

> He realized that Ü-Tsang was now the religious epicenter and resolved to go there . . . for in Ü-Tsang, those who fancied themselves lords were rich in influence and wealth but poor in the currency of faith, unembraced by virtuous allies and lacking good judgment. Often he thought, "Many who are discerning and faithful, like parched men craving water, despair at how degenerate the religion has become; might they be restored if some leader were to come?" He would be one drop of fresh water in a salty ocean. How-

9. According to Sönam Drakpa; Tucci 1971, 229.

10. Czaja 2013, 249, 255, comments on their motivations and those of the king.

ever, a mother feels even more love for a mentally ill child, and likewise this was when he became convinced that he must absolutely go to Ü-Tsang.[11]

The Karmapa spent much of 1536 and 1537 at monasteries around Lhasa, such as Tsurpu (Mtshur phu), Yangpachen, and Taklung (Stag lung), receiving invitations from Gendün Gyatso and Paṇchen Sönam Drakpa (Paṇ chen Bsod nams grags pa) and visiting Radreng (Rwa sgreng). (There would be no such courtesy one decade later.) His efforts to placate unrest in 1538 earned him accolades from the throne.[12] In 1539 he went to Tsang on the invitation of Ngawang Namgyel and was feted with hundreds of dignitaries in attendance. He toured Tsang over the next year before returning to install the Fifth Zhamarpa at Yangpachen in 1541.

The next decade was one of retrenchment: Ngawang Tashi Drakpa remained unable to extend his authority over Rinpung-allied territories in Tsang and Yartö (Yar stod), and while the latter reaffirmed their support of the Karma Kagyü, the Gongma and his second wife, Sanggyé Peldzomma (Sangs rgyas dpal 'dzom ma)—a daughter of the fallen Neupa house, and a major backer of the Geluk cause—orchestrated the identification of the Third Dalai Lama and installed Sönam Drakpa at Kyormolung (Skyor mo lung).[13] This was now one of two centers of power bifurcating the royal family, the other being at Gongkar (Gong dkar), the seat of Drowé Gönpo ('Gro ba'i mgon po, d. 1548), the king's elder son by his first wife (Dönyö Dorjé's daughter). That split, exacerbated by another divide between the sons from Drowé Gönpo's own two wives, lay behind the effort to unseat the Gongma and put his grandson Ngawang Drakpa on the throne in 1554.[14]

Mikyö Dorjé had tried to remain politically aloof while staying in the Gongma's good graces and cultivating his own patronage relationships. In 1541 he turned down a request to be proprietor (*zhal bdag*) over Gyelkhartsé (Rgyal mkhar rtse), allegedly insisting "we Karmapas have no custom of exercising ownership of political estates or secular properties."[15] In 1543 he strengthened his ties in Yartö with a grant for a new monastery from the lady of the Samdé (Bsam sde) family, longtime adversaries of the Gongma. The king

11. Gtsug lag 'phreng ba 1986, 1281–82.

12. Gtsug lag 'phreng ba 1986, 1284; Chos kyi 'byung gnas 1972, vol. 2, 20b.

13. On the importance of this queen, see Sørensen and Hazod 2004, 515, 763n10.

14. Summarized in Czaja 2013, 256–71.

15. Chos kyi 'byung gnas 1972, vol. 2, 22a.

nevertheless remained beneficent in his patronage, for instance, offering the Karma Kagyüpas the old monastery at Zülpu (Zul phu), southwest of Lhasa, in 1545. That same year, the Karmapa wrote his *Madhyamakāvatāra* commentary, notorious for its critiques of Tsongkhapa and receptiveness to the "extrinsic emptiness" doctrine, anathema to Geluk exegetes. When the Karmapa and Zhamarpa tried to visit Lhasa again in 1546, they were brusquely driven off by Drepung and Sera monks.[16]

This unraveling of the power structure and hardening of sectarian lines can illuminate Mikyö Dorjé's missive to the Neudong king. He laments not just a turning away from Dharma but a deeper shift in the nature of the relationships binding clerical and secular spheres, on which point his invective is unsparing. We can acknowledge the Karmapa's demonstrable disinterest in realpolitik and reputation as an above-the-fray intellectual, while also appreciating the highly political character of this discourse. Of course, even an earnest appeal urging the king to eschew partisanship carries its own partisan subtext, thereby positioning its own side as the most deserving of all. But we can also read the author as making a larger point about the ideal political dynamics of Tibet's dualistic society. He advocates for ecumenical rule as an alternative and countermeasure to the factionalism increasingly pitting groups against one another, being both the effect and cause of increasing fragmentation. Insofar as this amounts to a tacit argument that the Kagyü are the more deserving beneficiaries of royal patronage, it is because this jeremiad against hyperpartisanship (whose intended target is not hard to guess) is itself a demonstration that their leaders have the better political vision for long-term stability. The real issue, our author seems to suggest, is not which party to associate with (choose us, not them!) but rather what sort of politics of association, so to speak, each embodies—as if to say, *they* are the sort who would make you choose (and that way lies hell). Better to forsake that style of politics altogether, beginning by heeding just these sage words. The reward? Heaven on earth.

16. Chos kyi 'byung gnas 1972, vol. 1, 22b; Gtsug lag 'phreng ba 1986, 1292–94.

A Precious Garland or, A Discourse on Tibet's Great Kings and Their Methods of Rule Addressed to the Neudong King[17]

Svasti! In olden times, those with the fortune to have amassed the good karma, tainted or untainted, to set other beings (mothers, elderly, destitute) on their way to perfect buddhahood, lived together in a land conducive to performing good works. Among them came a great king who was a refuge to others, spurring them to higher rebirths and guaranteed awakening. He betook himself to a palace where there was no fear of the great gulf between the two extremes of existence and escape and, turning the wheel that safeguards all vulnerable beings (limitless as the sky) from that vast gulf between those two extremes, presided in state as the *tsenpo*, one whose command is forceful, with vast dominion and in blazing splendor, and issued forth his lineage.

It should elicit great faith from the depths of your heart that there is a worthy source of refuge in the unfathomable kindness that these divine *tsenpos* of Tibet, projected human lords, showed to all potent, powerful masters—the projected *dharmarājas*, *lotsāwas*, and *paṇḍitas* who established the peerless tradition of the Three Jewels within this snowy country of Tibet, once populated by slow-witted beasts and human-like creatures and benighted as in a dark gloom. [2a] People like us, whom karma has brought together in this realm, have never at any time had even the tiniest part of a mere fragment of such bliss and virtue to proceed toward liberation and omniscience. If only we had some means to make ourselves capable of wishing to pursue such a course—oh, what marvelous fortune it would be!

Alas, out of all the base deeds of vile persons, it was a sinister king who tore down what the Buddha taught and so destroyed all peace and happiness in the nine regions of Tibet. In that fallen age, the descendants of those great religious kings began again to heed the documents and legends of that bygone era. They could not countenance the situation of their Tibetan subjects, one of extreme, everlasting suffering. They would not indulge in any pleasures of body and spirit, even to the tip of a blade of grass, troubling themselves not over things like food and drink, hot and cold, day and night, but did everything in their power to save all beings in general (numerous as the sky) and especially their own subjects, with the connections of good karma that foster higher rebirths and guaranteed awakening. To rejoin them with the Buddha's

17. The foliation follows the Tsadra edition (Mi bskyod rdo rje 2000–2004, vol. 3, 43–58); cf. Mi bskyod rdo rje 2013, vol. 43, 337–54.

teachings, the *tsenpos* of Ü fanned the embers of the teachings from Dokham and Domé; and in cooperation, the *tsenpos* of Ngari [2b] retrieved Buddhist teachings from eastern, western, and central India and from Kashmir.

And so once more they propagated these teachings throughout the snowy kingdom, until at last it became as the Buddha predicted in the *Mañjuśrīmūlatantra*: in the east, under the horizon, came an emanation of Mañjughoṣa in the royal line of Hor Chinggis Khan, and in the west, past the setting sun, an emanation of Venerable Mañjughoṣa, the glorious Sakyapa; and they formed a relationship as patron and beneficiary, sun and moon paired. Over Tibet and Greater Tibet they established laws for liberation and omniscience following the two systems, making the Buddha's teachings rise like the sun in a spotless sky. Concurrently, as the *Samādhirājasūtra* predicted, here in the north the bodhisattva Candraprabhakumāra took the name Pel Gampopa and became a monk.[18] His exclusive disciples, like Pakmodrupa, who was preeminent in methods of ascetic virtue, were distinguished for attaining miraculous powers of restraint, quiescence, bravery, meditation, and wisdom. In turn, their disciples and sub-disciples made this snowy country seem like the pure worldly realm Luminous Light.[19] Then, in another outgrowth of their teachings, Nāgārjuna himself returned as the Drigung Jikten Sumgyi Gönpo.

The radiance of the colored robes of the members of these three lineages, who are a match for Venerable Maitreya's own retinue, [3a] and of countless advocates of liberation, made a redness like the dawning sun in the sky. They made an exalted object of worship of His Eminence the All-Knowing One, that prince who was the holy guardian of our world, across Ü, Tsang, Ngari, Kham, India, China, Minyak, Hor, Sokpo, and Turushka. They made the Buddha's teachings in general and especially the teaching of the glorious Dakpo Kagyü, the Mahāmudrā transmission, spread over the whole vast horizon. They increased the stores of accumulations all over the endless sea that is the domain of the Three Jewels, including sites in India like the Vajrāsana, Śrī Nālandā, Odantapuri, and the Śrī Dhānyakaṭaka Stūpa, as well as Oḍḍiyāna to the west, the eight great stūpas, and so on. By their kindness, all in Jambudvīpa have found peace and happiness. This was especially so under the great magistrate Tai Situ, the adept Jang Gyel, who kept the fine legal system of the Eastern King and the glorious Sakyapa, tamed foreign foes who would harm the black-headed Tibetans while supporting our domestic brethren, and gave his services to all who upheld the Buddha's teachings through exposition and practice. He

18. This is the sūtra's interlocutor, identified with Gampopa by Potowa; see Roerich 1976, 451–52.

19. Tib. *dag pa'i 'jig rten gyi khams 'od zer can*; perhaps the Marīcika-lokadhātu?

shone as a sun, a haven for a fragmented Tibet, and thanks to his kindness it has been daylight up until recent times, when the Sakya, Kagyü, and the rest are but an abiding reflection of the Buddha's teachings. [3b]

Not long after, Mañjuśrī and Avalokiteśvara presented themselves in the form of patron and beneficiary as the Great Ming Emperor of China and the Karmapa Dezhin Shekpa, investing the Miwang Drakpa Gyeltsen as overlord of the thirteen myriarchies of Ü-Tsang, issuing an edict naming him "Propagator of the Buddha's Teachings in Snowy Tibet" and a jade seal.[20] He attracted the finest scholars from Ü, Tsang, Kham, and Ngari to come here to Central Tibet. He restored all the older traditions expounding the Buddha's teachings that had deteriorated and reinstituted those no longer extant, working to ensure that the lineages practicing them would rise to greater heights. He used skillful methods to tame all unruly persons who would obstruct this progress, putting them back onto the path of virtue. He labored with much effort to increase sponsorship of monastic establishments and, in the interest of purifying evil, reformed each discordant or corrupted doctrine and practice while promoting pure doctrines and practices that accorded with the Word of the Buddha. And so, peace and happiness returned to the people as the sun from behind clouds.

But the fact is that in these times our peace and happiness are crumbling; for originally, Tibet's demons and monsters could not abide the institution of the Buddha's teachings [4a] and unleashed all sorts of magic against them until the Orgyen Abbot, Padmasambhava, bound them to an oath, but their vows and promises have loosened their hold over time. Nurturing in their hearts resentment against these old oaths, they now strive to undermine the Buddha's teachings and ruin all peace and happiness in Tibet, deceiving all Tibet's powerful clerics and patrons so that ill will escalates and virtuous thoughts collapse, allowing these demons and spirits an opportunity to interfere. All those who would have upheld the Buddha's teachings are coaxed into worldly activities of merchants, idlers (?*bre mo*), soldiers, or farmers, or pressed into servitude or forced labor. When even renunciates are so susceptible to their sway, need we even mention the common folk?

Clerics and patrons are all amassing exclusively bad karma ripening in this same lifetime: throughout the kingdom are epidemics, crop failures, domestic strife within, foreign invaders without, everyone oppressed by suffering. This influence touches even supports of the Three Jewels: due to the decline of the teachings, which enable the faithful to accumulate merit and purify evil, in order that these excellent supports of the Buddha's activity might serve to

20. Tib. *sbel kha*, perhaps from Mon. *belge*; this was awarded in 1406.

tame foreigners, and so that temples, as a support of the projected Three Jewels, might bring accumulation and purification to other worldly realms, [4b] in the aim of better serving beings the great elements have caused them to be taken off to other lands. Here in this region, the faithful who yearn for liberation are like stars in the daytime. No more than a handful have the fortune to live where they can accumulate and purify, and to bear no delusions about how to do so. Even those willing to achieve this in some fraction face ever greater obstacles and fail to muster sufficient motivation to set that will in motion. The result is that all virtuous thoughts and deeds are sputtering out and commitments are being forsaken. Taking it all in, we can only despair of ever knowing how to achieve higher rebirths and guaranteed awakening.

In turn, that influence redoubles the strength of those blackened roots and branches to interfere. Even abbots who are worshipped by the people and monastic communities that are an influential refuge are all being summoned by the allied partisan factions who are their benefactors and pressed into subjection. They are made to compete, provoke, curse, and entrap one another, to try to kill one another, steal ritual objects, destroy one another's temples and courtyards, and commit base worldly behavior beneath that even of thieves and adulterers. These sorts of behaviors diminish the authority and weaken the influence of the Sangha Jewel, these precious places of refuge, which, increasingly bereft of necessities, are compelled to give themselves over to strongmen and local officials, [5a] body, speech, and mind, along with their hermitages, wealth, and power, as gifts to secure protection. Everything body and soul, including their attendants, influence, treasure, and military capacity, is being heedlessly wasted. The Buddha's dispensation now exists only in name. Even its reflection fades. In matters like monastic dress, too, out of a deluded attachment to wherever there is some link to the worldly wealth of whichever corrupt local official in the kingdom is the greater, ever so many different customs are being introduced from one moment to the next, like making dedications inspired by whatever comes to mind, changing the style of hats, or instead using garb never seen before. Even those with a reputation for being learned, dedicated, kind, and accomplished, hoping to secure ties with a patron for their food and clothing, get caught up in evil and immorality, with no recourse but to chase after them as dogs and crows flock behind men.

Then the greater part of our own religious traditions—all the *tormas*, offering rites, blessings, empowerments, instructions, and transmissions by famed scholars of teaching, debate, and composition, and by those formidable in deity meditation and spell-chanting—become no more than a religion of consumption, like a Bönpo's special meal, as the usual practice is to apply oneself to peaceful methods out of attachment to one's own side, or harmful methods only out of loathing for the other side. Such behavior could only ever be a cause for staggeringly many rebirths in saṃsāra, especially lower rebirths. [5b] Just this sort of ill fortune now suffuses our country. Woe! The Buddha's teachings have declined utterly, causing living beings to suffer fiercely and continuously, without interruption, not even an instant of peace.

You, however, by dint of just this sort of supreme power and wealth, have been born into a rich family. All subjects are called irrevocably by the commands you issue to them. All beings alike respect you as an object of the highest esteem. You do not partake of the animosity or vituperative rivalry of demons and spirits. And now you take your seat on the throne of the *tsenpo*, the ancestors whose soles are upon the crown of your head. All those projected lords, your forefathers of old, were motivated by an impartial love and compassion for all beings. They developed an aspiration for awakening as deep and unstirrable as the ocean, striving for others' benefit with a ferocity as incendiary as the world's end. You should feel a joyful, reverential attraction toward their accomplishments, acing just like those holy persons who perfected their faith. Taking them into your heart, generate a will for awakening so your thoughts do not stray even an instant from the singular goal of increasing the peace and happiness of all beings (numerous as the sky). Through the incontrovertible force of being born into the spiritual family, with the blessing of the Three Jewels, you have intentionally taken birth here in our current evil times. [6a] So, heeding what is right for this time of action, it behooves you to think in the following ways:

Work to expand the temples, supports of the Three Jewels, of the earlier, middle, and later transmissions of the Buddha's teachings. Restore what was destroyed and reinvigorate what is not, so the masses again have a way to accumulate and purify karma. Exhort the present-day Sangha Jewel, all those who serve as lama to living beings, to read, recite, and be renunciate meditators, with a view and practice unsullied by the ways of householders. They will furnish the conducive condition for secular workers like merchants, farmworkers, intellectuals, foremen, and so on, who may be swayed by evil deeds, to reach the elite station of all faithful and wealthy patrons, without having to be compelled. What is more, those who renounce in this way will not, even for an instant, act only for the enrichment in this lifetime of family, friends, servants, communities, or rulers and officials, excepting deeds that properly purify the three trainings in one's mindstream, like the ten dharmic activities, the two wheels, and so on. If they do not know how to accomplish the work of the right Dharma of these monastic communities, and cannot bring their body, speech, and mind under control, then you must seek well throughout Jambudvīpa for masters capable of love and wisdom, who are not contentious but rather spiritual allies of all, bearing instructions for study and practice potent enough to tame their three doors; [6b] and having brought them back with great difficulty, appease them with virtuous enjoyments of the three doors. Given the quality of this sort of virtuous ally, in order to engender faith in all beings, venerate them and sing their praises with utmost respect so everyone is inspired to achieve the same insatiable goodness as those exalted beings possess.

In the aim that your proclamations be realized as issued, if you disregard your own self-interest, this method will cause all the common subjects occupying this area to awaken into the good community of myriad faithful beings who have formerly cultivated virtue, taking the Three Jewels as guru, thereby establishing the precious dispensation just as the Buddha taught it. As his teachings flourish and spread, it will birth a state of universal peace and happiness like unto the Perfected Age. When this realm of the Three Jewels is so endowed, even ordinary folk will naturally develop virtuous intentions. They will venerate their superiors, including father and mother, the elderly, and the king and nobility. They will compassionately protect all inferiors, namely the poor and destitute, rescuing them from misery. They will be mutually friendly with their peers. The benefits of good karma will thereby be realized. Physically, they will no longer act or think criminally toward the lives and property of others. [7a] Verbally, defects like lying or divisive talk will spontaneously cease. Mentally, they will start to consider one another as father and son, mother and child.

So then: *the ruling line shall not be corrupted; the vassal lineages, not cut; the might of warriors, not wasted; the herds of method, not scattered; the gateways of positions, not shut; the magic of ministers, not contested; the wisdom of healing, not unraveled!*[21]

An unending font of jewels will spring from the ground. When this happens, the faithful and wealthy must offer their riches exclusively for the purpose of worshipping the Three Jewels. The merit accumulated will have effects in this lifetime: a cause for peace, without any harm from foes and demons, for your lineage, court, servants, subjects, horses and livestock, fields, houses, even insects. Everyone's lifespan and prosperity will increase. Faith in the good qualities of the Jewels will naturally transform the attitudes of all nonhuman, malevolent forces, who will take especial delight in the pursuit of good and benefit living beings in a way both pleasurable and in accord with Dharma. Human or livestock epidemics, crop failure, threats of foreign invasion—all such inauspicious, ill-omened things that bring stress and fear will be forestalled. The center of this realm will be flush with glory, the periphery enriched

21. I have added emphasis as the author shifts into an archaic idiom evoking the language of the old Tibetan kings.

with prosperity. On all sides word will spread of how this effort to protect Dharma has brought such fortune, [7b] rendering neighboring kings in India and China awestruck and reverential in the face of your superb qualities. They will offer up their riches, whatever is desired. In reply, you will unfurl the victorious banner of fame: the marvel of the Buddha's teachings is present here! Letters scribed in the fine language of right Dharma will be issued, stamped with the seal of your authority, and wrapped up on the head [i.e., put into action] of the jewel-studded turbans of foreign kings. Even when leaving behind this life, departing heavenward to the blissful, perfect mansion of gods and humans who are likewise inclined, nothing will be bereft of the Three Jewels. One will be able to navigate by one's own power through the vast ocean of the conduct of omniscience.

Now, if you do not adopt these methods at this very moment, in this era where one cannot survive but a few years given the short lifespan of the five degeneracies, then only indolence will remain and the leisures and freedoms will become worthless. So think well about being a divine lord, a king of humans!

Ema! Again, I pray to you, who have the superb character of a victor, who steals away the suffering of all living beings, that amid the down-curling petals of this fresh blossom of your princely elegance as a divine *vidyādhara*, the sweet syrup of just these fine deeds wells up within your innermost nectary!

> O glorious one, whose sublime face
> bears Songtsen Gampo's [8a] wondrous mark—
> when need there was to ward the dark
> from Snowlands, Victor, you were born
> within the manse of kings untold. //1//
> Immutable, your virtues ten
> are pure gold, crossed, a blessed gate
> whose splendor shining overhead
> fills hearts with clear-light ambrosia, //2//
> a sunshine ending birth and death,
> as rainclouds densed from wisdom's seas
> pour down a shower of riches, which
> your scholar's scattered rays refract, //3//
> that down here on mandalic earth
> what means is there to comprehend?
> Astride the porcine spirit, you

again produce the highest stage[22] //4//
as fanned by such expansive fame,
a freshing wind that gathers all,
your Buddha-face, the Jowo's kin,
by deeds superb from lives bygone //5//
bemarked, in all its beauty flames!
As forming self-emergent, scented
projections whose fragrant chambers
fructify like clustered jewels, //6//
you reject both of life's extremes,
what urge could there be your heart?
Your darting glance, the smiling mouth,
of Tri Songdetsen's sportive //7//
play, it is the mirror image, say!
O maker of the Buddha's truths,
may hoisted tellings of your fame
reach out to every living thing //8//
and may your proclamations, each
an Indian *garuḍa* great
confounding brains of *tīrthikas*,
swell in this land like summer lakes! //9// [8b]
So wondrous is your secret talk
for many reasons asserted,
admired by literary lords
like Ludrup, Losemtso and such.[23] //10//
Your way of ruling earth is like
the Lord of Aṭakāvatī
who will be born of Kalki line
with braided locks, the Forceful Wheel,[24] //11//
and when you wield the golden disc
then Indra, yes, and Brahmā too
must shed their puffed conceit and bow
as once at Śākya Prince's feet. //12//
So as your glory grows the more

22. The meaning of these two lines escapes me. Perhaps the pig (*brtan ma phag la zhon pa*) alludes to the Pakmodru.

23. Ludrup (Klu sgrub) is Nāgārjuna; Losemtso (Blo sems 'tsho) is Buddhirakṣita, here probably referring to *Śānta*rakṣita as per the *Blue Annals*.

24. That is, Rudracakrī, the future golden-age king foretold in the *Kālacakra*.

in clouds of blue that, thickly stacked,
upraise you to the firmament,
whose princely peals of church and state //13//
resound across the threefold world,
O lord supreme of Lhazik Lang
on high atop your Yartö peak—
are you not king on every side? //14//

Flustered by the rapturous delight of this thought—that you, who are decorated with the inestimable treasure of the gilded handprints imprinted onto posterity by the fine works of the Three Ancestors, Tibet's religious kings of old, may be stamped with the elite seal of the merit of your own person and invested with the authority of a great sovereign—and with body hairs quivering on end, this sage counsel is hereby bestowed upon the divine prince of the glorious Pakmodrupas, which the glorious Karmapa named Yangchen Zhepa put into words at the great monastic school Karma Zhungluk Ling.

References

Chos kyi 'byung gnas, Si tu paṇ chen. 1972. *Sgrub brgyud karma kaṃ tshang brgyud pa rin po che'i rnam par thar pa rab byams nor bu zla ba chu shel gyi phreng ba.* New Delhi: D. Gyaltshan and Keshang Legshay.

Czaja, Olaf. 2013. *Medieval Rule in Tibet.* 2 vols. Vienna: Verlag der Österreichischen Akademie der Wissenschaften.

Dkon mchog yan lag, Zhwa dmar pa V. 2000. *Karma pa mi bskyod rdo rje bzhad pa'i gsung 'bum gyi dkar chag.* In *Dpal rgyal ba karma pa sku 'phreng brgyad pa mi bskyod rdo rje'i gsung 'bum,* edited by Karma Bde legs, vol. 1, 1–28. Lhasa: Tsadra Foundation. BDRC W8039.

Gtsug lag 'phreng ba, Dpa' bo II. 1986. *Chos 'byung mkhas pa'i dga' ston.* Beijing: Mi rigs dpe skrun khang.

Mi bskyod rdo rje, Karma pa VIII. 2000–2004. *Dpal rgyal ba karma pa sku 'phreng brgyad pa mi bskyod rdo rje'i gsung 'bum,* edited by Karma Bde legs. Lhasa: Tsadra Foundation. BDRC W8039.

———. 2013. *Dpal rgyal dbang karma pa sku phreng brgyad pa'i gsung 'bum.* In *Karma pa sku phreng rim byon gyi gsung 'bum phyogs bsgrigs.* Lhasa: Dpal brtsegs bod yig dpe rnying zhib 'jug khang. BDRC W3PD1288.

Rheingans, Jim. 2017. *The Eighth Karmapa's Life and His Interpretation of the Great Seal.* Freiburg: Projekt Verlag.

Roerich, George N., trans. 1976. *The Blue Annals.* New Delhi: Motilal Banarsidass.

Sørensen, Per K., and Guntram Hazod. 2004. *Rulers on the Celestial Plain: Ecclesiastic and Secular Hegemony in Medieval Tibet.* Vienna: Verlag der Österreichischen Akademie der Wissenschaften.

Tucci, Giuseppe. 1971. *Deb t'er dmar po gsar ma: Tibetan Chronicles by bSod nams grags pa.* Rome: Istituto Italiano per il Medio ed Estremo Oriente.

Tibetan Medicine under the Mongols: The Emergence of Medical Houses and Official Physicians in Tibet

William A. McGrath

THIS ESSAY concerns the *Expanded Elucidation of Knowledge* (*Shes bya rab gsal rgyas pa*), a manuscript once held in Beijing. It is just one of the dozens of rare texts that Leonard van der Kuijp studied during his two visits to the Nationalities Cultural Palace (Minzu wenhua gong 民族文化宫) in the early 1990s. He was probably the first, and certainly one of the only, foreign scholars to examine this collection of rare texts. In an interview with Professor He Huanhuan 何欢欢, Professor van der Kuijp reflected, "There is no doubt that this experience helped shape my academic accomplishments and transformed my life."[1] Indeed, the fruits of Professor van der Kuijp's visits to the Nationalities Cultural Palace in Beijing have helped shape the field of Tibetan studies for the past thirty years.

In the first edition of his *Tibetan Histories*, Dan Martin mentions a *Shes bya rab gsal*, which subsequent scholars of Tibetan medicine dated to the thirteenth century.[2] In his review of the work, Kurtis Schaeffer, then a student of Professor van der Kuijp, alerted the world to the existence of the work in a forty-eight-folio manuscript,[3] the first nineteen folios of which are now missing. Professor van der Kuijp had copied the manuscript in Beijing and read it with Kurtis, who then kindly shared it with me. Despite the emergence of several alternative editions of the *Expanded Elucidation of Knowledge* in the intervening years, the Nationalities Cultural Palace manuscript still contains preferred spellings and passages that are missing from the other editions. Without the generosity of Professor van der Kuijp, my study of the *Expanded Elucidation of Knowledge* would lack the historical nuance offered by this rare and otherwise unpublished manuscript. This essay is dedicated to Leonard van

1. He 2016: 毫无疑问, 这段经历塑造并成就了我的学术, 改变了我的人生.

2. Martin and Bentor 1997, 37, no. 35. In his most recent edition, Martin dates the work to approximately 1375 (Martin and Bentor 2020, 143–44, no. 151). As explained below, I agree with this estimation.

3. Schaeffer 1998, 857.

der Kuijp, teacher of my own teacher, and inspiration to all who have had the good fortune of studying with him.

The Sakya Medical House

The Sakya Medical House was one of the first medical houses (*sman grong*) in Tibet. In his preliminary study of the Drangti family and their contributions to the history of Tibetan medicine, Professor van der Kuijp observed that their *Gold Measure* (*Gser bre*) collection was composed during the fifteenth century, "in the two-storied 'medical village' seminary (*nyi thog sman grong gi grwa tshang*) of Sa skya."[4] What was a "medical village" or "medical house" in the fifteenth century, and how did these institutions facilitate the study and practice of medicine in Tibet? As a humble response to these questions, this essay argues that the term "medical house" emerged in thirteenth- and fourteenth-century Tibet as part of the Mongol tax system, and that the Sakya Medical House expanded from the lineage of the Drangti family into one of the earliest and most influential medical schools in Tibet.

Before we continue exploring the medical houses of Tibetan history, let us first consider the role of medical houses in the present day. Theresia Hofer has interviewed representatives from the medical houses of Ngamring County (Ngam ring rdzong) in Tsang, for example, and analyzed these institutions through the lens of the "house society" theory developed by Claude Lévi-Strauss. According to this system, a house (*maison*) is a "corporate body holding an estate made up of both material and immaterial wealth, which perpetuates itself through the transmission of its name, its goods and its titles down a real or imaginary line considered legitimate as long as this continuity can express itself in the language of kinship or of affinity and, most often, of both."[5] In line with this interpretation, the medical house in Tibet refers to (1) material and immaterial assets, including therapeutic instruments, instructional texts, and practical knowledge; and (2) the transmission of these assets under a particular name or title. In other words, the formation of the medical house in Tibet marked the institutionalization of medical practice and knowledge within a named lineage or school.

Like the medical houses of present-day Tsang studied by Hofer, the Sakya Medical House first referred to a familial lineage. Indeed, the seventeenth-

4. van der Kuijp 2010, 37. Mkhan po kun dga' bzang po 2004, 296: *man ngag rin chen nor bu rin chen ni/ dpal ldan sa skya'i nyi thog sman grong gi grwa tshang du legs par bris pa'o/*. See also Tsering Paljor Emchi 1975, 515 (fol. 358a).

5. Lévi-Strauss 1990, 174; cited in Hofer 2018, 29.

century biographer of a Drangti scion used the language of the Sakya Medical House to describe the lineage of physicians within the latter's family.

> Ever since the Sakya Lama Daknyi Chenpo Zangpopel invited Drangti Jampel Zangpo to Sakya and he became initiated as an official physician (*bla sman*), this branch of the [Drangti] family has been known as the Sakya Medical House.[6]

In this passage, Ngaripa Sanggyé Püntsok (Mnga' ris pa Sangs rgyas phun tshogs, 1649–1705) reflects on the lineage of Drangti Paṇchen Namkha Pelzang (Brang ti paṇ chen Nam mkha' dpal bzang, 1535–1602), the Thirteenth Ngor Khenchen (Ngor mkhan chen). Drangti Paṇchen did study some medicine with his father but, in his own words, he chose to pursue the "sūtras and tantras" instead of medicine.[7] Even four centuries after Daknyi Chenpo Zangpopel and Drangti Jampel Zangpo, despite this later shift of the Drangti away from medicine and away from Sakya itself, Ngaripa still describes the lineage of physicians in the Drangti family as the Sakya Medical House.

As indicated by Ngaripa Sanggyé Püntsok, the Drangti lineage of medical practice first rose to prominence at the turn of the fourteenth century, during the reign of Daknyi Chenpo Zangpopel (Bdag nyid chen po Bzang po dpal, 1262–1323; r. 1298–1323). Daknyi Chenpo Zangpopel was the final remaining scion of the Khön clan when he was sent into exile by Khubilai Khan (1215–94; r. 1260–94). Following the latter's death in 1294, however, Temür Khan (1265–1307; r. 1294–1307) not only allowed Zangpopel to return to Sakya but also entrusted Princess Müdegen to him in marriage.[8] After his return in 1298, Zangpopel was enthroned as the Eleventh Sakya Throne Holder (Sa skya khri 'dzin), and around this time he summoned Drangti Jampel Zangpo to Sakya. Thus the institution of the Sakya Medical House began with the institutionalization of the Drangti medical lineage at Sakya Monastery around the year 1300, under the aegis of the Khön clan and during the period of Mongol-Sakya hegemony in Tibet (ca. 1250–1350).

6. Mnga' ris pa sangs rgyas phun tshogs 1985, 283 (fol. 17a): *sa skya'i bla ma bdag nyid chen po bzang po dpal gyis brang ti 'jam dpal bzang po sa skyar spyan drangs nas/ bla sman du dbang bskur ba nas bzung ste/ rje 'di sku mched yan sa skya sman grong par grags so/.*

7. Mnga' ris pa sangs rgyas phun tshogs 1985, 284 (fol. 17b): "I will not study to be a physician. By studying the sūtras and tantras, I will bring benefit to the teachings and to sentient beings" (*lha rje slob gnyer ma byed/ mdo rgyud la slob gnyer gyis/ bstan pa dang sems can la phan pa srid gsungs/*).

8. Petech 1990, 72–74.

Thanks to the historiographic efforts of Drangti Jampel Zangpo's son, Drangti Penden Tsojé (Brang ti Dpal ldan 'tsho byed, ca. 1310–80), we have some other details about the early history of the Drangti physicians. Penden Tsojé provides the year for neither the birth nor the death of his father but, in his *Expanded Elucidation of Knowledge* (*Shes bya rab gsal rgyas pa*, ca. 1372),[9] he does state that Jampel Zangpo lived for fifty-nine years.[10] As already noted by van der Kuijp,[11] the Second Karmapa Künkhyen Pakshi (1204–83) purportedly prophesied that the young Jampel Zangpo would be a "bodhisattva of benefit to beings."[12] Presuming that this statement does reflect some historical relationship between Karma Pakshi and Jampel Zangpo, we can determine that he was born no later than Karma Pakshi's death in 1283, and probably sometime after Karma Pakshi's return from exile in 1272.[13] In light of these details and his flourishing at Sakya around the turn of the fourteenth century, we can settle on the approximate dates of 1277–1335 for Drangti Jampel Zangpo. And based on his composition of the *Expanded Elucidation of Knowledge* in the early 1370s, we can also conclude that Penden Tsojé lived from approximately 1310 to 1380.

In the *Expanded Elucidation of Knowledge*, we also learn that Jampel Zangpo studied medicine with his father and with teachers from at least three other prominent medical traditions. After studying with his father, Drangti Sönam Bum (Brang ti Bsod nams 'bum), Jampel Zangpo reportedly traveled to Gozhi Retang (Sgo bzhi re thang) in the upper Nyang river valley to study the *Four Tantras* with Yutok Jampel (G.yu thog 'Jam dpal). Jampel Zangpo is also said to have studied with Master Yeshé Zangpo in Jang Mokhü, along with another

9. The first nineteen folios of the Beijing manuscript are missing, so I cite an alternative edition. Tashigang 2005, 25–26: "The Teacher [Śākyamuni] was born on a male earth-dragon year [2213 BCE], achieved enlightenment on a male water-tiger year [2179], and passed away on a male fire-pig year [2134]. In the male water-mouse year [1372 CE] of the system explicated by Sakya Paṇḍita—toward the end of the turning of the wheel of doctrine by Chöjé Sönam Gyentsen Pelzangpo in the year 3505 [1372]—1495 years [of the Dharma] remain" (*ston pa sa pho 'brug la bltams/ chu pho stag la sangs rgyas/ me pho phag la mya ngan las 'das par/ sa skya paṇ ḍi ta chen po bzhed pa'i lugs kyi chu pho byi ba'i lo/ chos rje bsod nams rgyal mtshan dpal bzang po chos 'khor mdzad pa yar spyad la/ lo sum stong lnga brgya dang lnga 'das la/ stong bzhi brgya dang dgu bcu rtsa lnga lhag par gnas so//*).

10. *Shes bya rab gsal rgyas pa*, 39a: "At the age of fifty-nine, during his summer teachings, he declared, 'This year shall be my final lecture'" (*dgung lo lnga bcu rtsa dgu bzhes pa'i dbyar chos kyi tshe da lo 'chad nyan gyi tha ma yin zhes pa dang . . .*).

11. van der Kuijp 2010, 35.

12. *Shes bya rab gsal rgyas pa*, 39a: *karma kun mkhyen dpag shis kyang / byang chub sems dpa' 'gro la phan pa 'byung ngo / zhes lung bstan cing /*.

13. For the life and times of Karma Pakshi, see van der Kuijp 1995.

teacher referred to as the "Tangut Mendicant." Although we know little else about these figures, Jampel Zangpo was reportedly a son born from their hearts.[14] Combining each of these narrative threads, Penden Tsojé depicts his father as a physician, scholar, and teacher who combined the Drangti, Yutok, Jang, and Minyak lineages of medicine in Tibet. As a result, by the end of the thirteenth century Jampel Zangpo had become known as a "physician's physician," and Daknyi Chenpo Zangpopel granted him the "rank and status of official physician" (*rgya mtsho phyed* [='*tsho byed*] *kyi go sa dang/ bla sman gyi mthil*) at the capital of Sakya.[15] We will return to the implications of these official titles in the next section.

In line with Karma Pakshi's prediction, Drangti Jampel Zangpo did indeed bring benefit to the sentient beings of Tibet. Drangti Penden Tsojé reports that his father generated the mind of awakening, donating food and medications to the poor and disenfranchised by day and dedicating the merit to all sentient beings by night. He is also said to have maintained his esoteric commitments, teaching the *Four Tantras*, the *Essence of the Eight Branches*, and the *Practical Manual* (*Lag len spu*[=*po*] *ti*) during his lectures. Even in the twilight of his life, he continued to selflessly work for the sake of others. He finally passed away at the age of fifty-nine while practicing guru yoga and the transference of consciousness. After his death, the people praised him as a "great bodhisattva."[16] Thus, in addition to his great learning, his official position, and his practical skill in medicine, it was Jampel Zangpo's compassionate service that secured his place in the hearts and memory of his community.

With this biography of Drangti Jampel Zangpo in mind, let us now turn to the question: What was the Sakya Medical House in the fourteenth and fifteenth centuries? To be clear, the term "Sakya Medical House" does not appear in the *Expanded Elucidation of Knowledge*, and it first appears in the fourteenth- and fifteenth-century *Gold Measure* (*Gser bre ma*) and *Silver Measure* (*Dngul bre ma*) collections. In addition to the example cited by Professor van der Kuijp in his initial study, a colophon for the *Treatment for Pediatric Lung Disease* presents itself as "the practice of the master doctor [of the Sakya

14. *Shes bya rab gsal rgyas pa*, 39a: *rtsis dus byang mo khud du ljang sman pa slob dpon ye shes bzang po yun ring du bsten nas/ bstan bcos brgyad pa rgyas par gsan/ mi nyag bandhe dang gnyis thugs las 'khrungs pa'i sras su grags/*.

15. *Shes bya rab gsal rgyas pa*, 39a–b: *sman pa'i sman par grags la/ bla ma* [39b] *bdag nyid chen pos gdan sar spyan drangs te/ brgyad pa'i 'chad nyan btsugs/ rgya mtsho phyed* [='*tsho byed*] *kyi go sa dang/ bla sman gyi mthil mdzad la/*.

16. *Shes bya rab gsal rgyas pa*, 39b: *de nyid skye bo thams cad kyi mthun par byang chub sems dpa' chen po yin/ zhes bsngags par brjod pa lags so/*.

Medical House]."[17] The *Special Jangpa Method for Subjugation* also begins with the following homage: "I bow with respect to the Sakyapa [Dorjé Pelgön Zangpo, physician of the Sakya Medical House]."[18] I have been unable to identify Dorjé Pelgön Zangpo, but he appears to have been a later scion of the Drangti lineage, indicating that the *Gold* and *Silver Measure* collections continued to grow even beyond the fourteenth century.

Based on this survey, we can conclude that the official title of the "Sakya Medical House" was established by Drangti physicians at Sakya in the fourteenth century. Later generations then used "Sakya Medical House" to simply refer to the lineage of Drangti physicians. This lineage did not remain limited to the members of the Drangti family, however. As initially noted by van der Kuijp, the Sakya Medical House also once referred to a two-storied medical college (*nyi thog sman grong gi grwa tshang*) at Sakya, for example. During the height of the Drangti at Sakya, Penden Tsojé, the younger son of Jampel Zangpo, also referred to himself as a monastic teacher of students from the Yutok and Jang schools of medicine, among others.[19] As this and other references to the Drangti school indicate,[20] the instructions of the Sakya Medical House had spread beyond the familial lineage of the Drangti to include interested students hailing from all over the Tibetan plateau. As we will see in the next section, the rise of the Sakya Medical House took place during a larger shift in the organization and regulation of medical institutions in Tibet.

17. *Bu chung gi glo nad bcos pa lha rje dpon po'i phyag len*, in Bod rang skyong ljongs sman rtsis khang 2005, 85: *lha phye* [=*rje*] [*sa skya sman grong*] *dpon po'i phyag len yin*. Here *sa skya sman grong* is an interlinear note.

18. *Byang pa 'dul thabs khyad par can*, in Bod rang skyong ljongs sman rtsis khang 2005, 126: *sa skya pa* [*sman grong pa 'tsho byed rdo rje dpal mgon bzang po*] *la gus btud nas/*. Here *sman grong pa* is also in an interlinear note.

19. *Shes bya rab gsal rgyas pa*, 47b: "At the request of Yutokpa Geshé Sherap Gyentsen, Yeshé Lekwang of Upper Jang, and Geshé Könchok Drak of Dokham, the Venerable Penden Tsojé redacted this *Expanded Elucidation of Knowledge* . . . " (*shes bya rab gsal rgyas pa* [*zhes bya ba 'di ni/ g.yu thog pa dge bshes shes rab rgyal mtshan*] *dang / byang stod pa ye shes legs dbang / mdo khams pa dge bshes dkon mchog grags rnams kyis bskul nas dge slong dpal ldan mtsho byed kyis sbyar ba dge legs su gyur cig/*). See also Tashigang 2005, 134.

20. See, for example, this short note from the *Eighteen Auxiliary Branches* (*Cha lag bco brgyad*) of the Yutok school (A ru ra 2005, 257): "These days here in the Snowy Land of Tibet, there are many people who claim to be physicians. Other than Master Drangti and his students, however, there are no others that I would consider to be healers" (*ding sang kha ba can gyi ljongs 'di na// sman par rlom pa'i skye bo rab mang yod// brang ti mkhas pa slob mar bcas ma gtogs// 'tsho byed yin snyam bdag gi sems la med//*).

The Medical Houses and Official Physicians of the Mongol Empire

In the previous section, we learned that the Sakya Medical House was an official title for the familial medical lineage of Drangti Jampel Zangpo, which eventually grew into a medical school. In Penden Tsojé's biography of his father, however, we also learned that Jampel Zangpo studied with representatives from the Yutok, Jang, and Minyak schools of medicine. How did the title of "official physician" (*bla sman*) granted by Daknyi Chenpo Zangpopel differentiate the Sakya Medical House from other Tibetan medical schools? In a second article on the history of medicine in Tibet, Professor van der Kuijp notes that Drangti Penden Tsojé uses the term, "official physician," in reference to "a certain Lha rje Nyi ma dpal. Brang ti Dpal ldan 'tsho byed mentions him in his history of medicine as one who had received an edict (*'ja' sa* < Mon. *ǰasar* [=*ǰasaγ*]) from the Mongol court with which the inhabitants of Lha ri sgrol lung were given a tax-exempt status (*dar rgan* < Mon. *darqan*)."[21] Building on these observations, below I argue that the title of "Sakya Medical House" and the status of "official physician" both emerged in thirteenth- and fourteenth-century Tibet under the tax system of the Mongol empire. More than mere economic designations, however, these official titles took on unique institutional connotations in Tibetan history.

In 1979 Christopher Beckwith introduced readers to Galen in Tibet and told of his status as a "royal physician" (*bla sman*).[22] Since that time, scholars have continued to analyze these stories and puzzle over the term *bla sman*.[23] In her preliminary analysis of the *Expanded Elucidation of Knowledge* and other derivative works, for example, Frances Garrett has shown that Songtsen Gampo grants the title of "official physician" (*bla sman*) to Tsen Pashilaha (Btsan Pa shi la ha) of Byzantium (Khrom).[24] Building on the analysis of Dan Martin, I propose that we interpret the latter figure as a legendary emperor basileus.[25] Martin has also proposed a Greek equivalent for the title of "royal physician" (Grk. *archiatros*),[26] but has failed to find examples of the term in Tibet prior to the thirteenth or fourteenth century. Thus it is entirely possible

21. van der Kuijp 2016, 73.

22. Beckwith 1979, 301.

23. On later legends of Galen as a royal physician in Tibet, see Yoeli-Tlalim 2012, 356.

24. Garrett 2007, 372.

25. Martin 2011, 129–30, proposes Tsan Basileos (Btsan Pa shi la ha), interpreting Tsan as a surname. Here I interpret *btsan* as "emperor" (*bstan po*), equivalent to the title of basileus in the Byzantine empire.

26. Martin 2017.

that Central Eurasian precedents inspired the emergence of the term "official physician" in Tibet, but these tales of legendary physicians serving at the court of Songtsen Gampo are best understood as Mongol-era compositions. The better question, then, is what thirteenth- and fourteenth-century institutions may have inspired these legends?

Throughout the period of Mongol-Sakya hegemony, medical institutions in Tibet expanded from familial lineages to larger schools of unrelated students. This trend is most obvious in Drangti Penden Tsojé's bifurcation of the student (*slob brgyud*) and familial lineages (*sras brgyud*) of the Yutok school. "Master Yutok Yönten Gönpo had both a familial lineage and a student lineage," he explains in the *Expanded Elucidation of Knowledge*.[27] From here, Drangti Penden Tsojé traces the student lineage of Yutok from Dza Yeshé Zung (Rdza Ye shes gzungs), through his relatives and students, and finally back to himself. Drangti also cites Yeshé Zung's own *Indispensable Account of Transmission* (*Brgyud pa'i rnam thar med thabs med pa*, ca. 1234), wherein Yeshé Zung describes his studies with Yutok at an institution called Gyaché Kendrong (Rgya che rkan grong). Unfortunately, even in an early manuscript of the *Indispensable Account of Transmission* the title of this institution remains unclear (Rgya phyed kan [= sman?] grong),[28] but the parallel wording of the official status cited above (*rgya mtsho phyed* [='*tsho byed*] *kyi go sa*) may indicate that Yeshé Zung studied with Yutok at an official medical house. If the Gyaché Kendrong was actually an official medical house, then the Yutok school would have also established one of the first official medical houses in Tibet.

According to Drangti Penden Tsojé, the familial lineage of the Yutok school first passed through the young son of Yutok Yönten Gönpo, Yutok Bumseng ('Bum seng). Somewhat confusingly, though, the familial lineage then passes on to a classmate and teacher of Bumseng, a mostly forgotten figure named Shakrampa Belmen Nyimapel (Shag ram pa 'Bal sman nyi ma dpal) of Nyemo (Snye mo), then back to Bumseng's son, Yutok Jampel, and, as noted above, on to Drangti Jampel Zangpo. Thus, despite the fact that he was related to neither Yutok Bumseng nor Yutok Jampel, Shakrampa was a central figure in the development of the Yutok familial lineage.

> [Shakrampa] founded the institutional seat of Yutok Gönpo and, evoking the water goddess, he entrusted the sealed teachings of the master to Yutok Bumseng. After he became a supreme master,

27. *Shes bya rab gsal rgyas pa*, 37a: *g.yu thog mkhas pa yon tan mgon po la/ sras brgyud slob brgyud gnyis byung zhing* / . . . .

28. See McGrath 2017, 301.

> [Shakrampa] acted as the official physician for Khubilai Khan. In the valley of Lharidro, [the Great Khan] sent an ordinance appointing [Shakrampa] to the rank of *dargen*. [Shakrampa] created many temples and stupas, copied many scriptures, and composed many medical commentaries, anthologies, and tutorials. By examining the channels and fluids of a patient, [Shakrampa] was able to know their lifespan within seven years, as well as their virtuous and sinful deeds. With his attainments in alchemy, he performed lectures and made extensive contributions until the age of fifty-five for the sake of beings.[29]

While it is unlikely that a single figure both studied with Yutok Yönten Gönpo (twelfth century) and served Khubilai Khan (Bse[=Se] chen, r. 1260–94), it is entirely possible that Shakrampa Belmen Nyimapel attained a prominent position in the Yutok school and attracted the official recognition of the Mongol court. Regardless of whether it was a medical house or not, Penden Tsojé states that Shakrampa established the institutional seat of the Yutok school and composed works of medical scholasticism that are now lost or no longer identified as his. Most important for our purposes, though, Khubilai Khan granted to Shakrampa Belmen Nyimapel the title of official physician (*bla sman*), the same title that Daknyi Chenpo Zangpopel granted to Drangti Jampel Zangpo one generation later. Implicit in the latter case and explicit in the former is the status of *dargen* (*dar rgan* < Mon. *darqan*), which indicates that official physicians in Tibet could avoid the usual fees associated with medical houses under the Mongol tax system.[30]

Shortly after taking command of the eastern Mongol sphere of influence, and before even establishing the Yuan dynasty (1271–1368), Khubilai Khan began directly regulating the medical institutions of his empire. In an apparent attempt to regulate the sale and taxation of medicine, in 1262 Khubilai Khan

29. *Shes bya rab gsal rgyas pa*, 38b: *g.yu thog mgon po'i gdan sa lta bu mdzad cing / chu'i lha mo'i grub pa/ slob dpon gyi bka' rgya ltar g.yu thog 'bum seng la gtad cing / mkhas pa'i mchog tu gyur pas/ bse chen gyi bla sman mdzad/ lha ri sgro'i lung pa la dar rgan gyi 'ja' sa gnang / gtsug lag khang dang rten gsung rab mang du bzhengs shing / sman dpyad kyi 'grel pa gces bsdus stong mthun [=thun] yig cha mang du mdzad/ rtsa chu gzigs pa'i mi rnams kyis tshe'i tshad lo bdun tshun chad kyi dge sdig ji lta ba bzhin mkhyen cing / bcud len grub pas dgung lo lnga bcu rtsa lnga'i bar du/ 'chad nyan dang 'gro don rgya cher mdzad de/*. The Tashigang edition (2005, 108) indicates that Shakrampa lived for ninety-five years rather than fifty-five.

30. See, for example, the 1254 ordinance in which the Sakya were exempted from taxation, in Petech 1990, 14–15.

issued the following ordinance in regard to the role of "medical houses" (*yirenmeihu* 醫人每戶 or *yihu* 醫戶) as institutional centers throughout the empire:

> Regarding the taxes and labor service that medical houses owe, they should pay silk, cotton, and dye taxes. Also, if they produce rice, they shall pay rice tax, and if they trade, they owe trade taxes. However, they shall be exempt from all miscellaneous service duties, such as providing military supplies, raising horses, taking care of messengers in the postal relay system, and taking care of cows and personnel. When officials in appanages buy medicines from physicians, they should pay reasonable prices and should never just take it by force. Following annual practice, medical houses under the jurisdiction of the government should pay three taels of silver tax, and they should pay with our paper money. While determining the taxes [of medical houses], Wang Zijun and other officials should consider their wealth and status, and they should pay according to the requirements of the Imperial Academy of Medicine members who serve the court.[31]

In line with other specialized household registers (*huji* 戶籍) that developed during this period, here the Mongol court explains the regulations for levying taxes on the physicians of medical houses according to the requirements of the Imperial Academy of Medicine (Taiyiyuan 太醫院). Like most other subjects of the Mongol empire, physicians would have paid taxes for goods, agriculture, and trade, but they were exempted from corvée labor. According to this ordinance, the Mongol court also promised to protect physicians from extortion but required an annual fee of three taels of silver. Unlike the Sakya Medical House, then, physicians of most other medical houses under the Mongol empire had to pay taxes in order to practice medicine.

Despite its appearance in the legends of the Tibetan empire, the title of "official physician" (*bla sman*) first emerged in Tibet in the thirteenth century under the tax system of the Mongol empire. As previously noted by Professor van der Kuijp, Shakrampa Belmen Nyimapel was one of the first Tibetan physicians that the Mongol court promoted to the rank of a tax-exempt official physician in an official edict. This implies, of course, that the physicians of Tibet would have paid taxes to the Mongol court. In addition to this edict, Professor van der Kuijp also notes that the Mongol court sent a Pakpa-script ordinance in an ox year (probably 1277 or 1289), which exempted an otherwise

31. Guoli Gugong bowuyuan 1976, 32.1b; translated in conversation with Shinno 2016, 31.

unknown Tibetan physician, Lharjé Senggepel (Lha rje Seng ge dpal), from tax responsibilities.[32] Like Shakrampa Belmen Nyimapel and Lharjé Senggepel before him, Drangti Jampel Zangpo received the title of official physician at the turn of the fourteenth century. Combining the titles of official physician and medical house, the Sakya Medical House was a lineage of physicians who did not necessarily have to pay taxes but who were presumably still protected as part of the Imperial Academy of Medicine network.

Medical Houses and Official Physicians beyond the Mongol Empire

The medical house and the official physician were titles that emerged in Tibet during the period of Mongol-Sakya hegemony (ca. 1250–1350). The former title initially referred to a familial lineage of physicians in the household registration system of the Mongol-Sakya government. Under the status of the medical house, these familial lineages were afforded protections from exploitation and coercion and, in turn, were expected to follow the centralized tax regulations set out by the Yuan government and the Imperial Academy of Medicine. While many families undoubtedly took on the status of medical house throughout Tsang, the Sakya Medical House specifically referred to the lineage of physicians within the Drangti family.

While the title of medical house was primarily limited to Tsang, the title of the official physician (*bla sman*) spread throughout the Tibetan plateau.[33] In addition to this relatively vast geographic spread, during the period of Mongol-Sakya hegemony, historians also began projecting the term "official physician" back into Tibetan history. In his biography of Drangti Paṇchen, for example, Ngaripa Sanggyé Püntsok states that scions of the Drangti family have acted as official physicians for Tibetan kings ever since the time of Tri Songdetsen.[34] Unsurprisingly, the first account of Drangti physicians serving at the courts of

32. See van der Kuijp 2016, 73; citing Sgrolkar 1995, 1.1–1.3. Karl-Heinz Everding (2006) argues that this Lharjé Senggepel is Urgyenpa Rinchenpel (U rgyan pa Rin chen dpal, 1229–1309). I would like to thank Jue Liang and Penghao Sun for this information.

33. For official physicians in early modern Lhasa, for example, see van Vleet 2018.

34. Mnga' ris pa sangs rgyas phun tshogs 1985, 283 (fol. 17a): "Beginning in the time of the Dharma King, Tri Songdetsen, the Drangti lineage has served as official physicians for the Dharma kings of Tibet, including Drangti Gyelnyen Kharpuk, Drangti Sepo, and Drangti Jayarakṣitā. They were born in Jang Raptentsé in Central Tibet, among other [places]" (*brang ti'i brgyud te/ chos rgyal khris srong lde btsan nas bzung / bod chos rgyal rnams bla sman/ brang ti rgyal bsnyen khar phug dang / brang ti sras po dang / dza ya rakṣi ta sogs dbus ljang rab brtan rtse sogs su byung /*).

imperial Tibet found expression in the Drangti works of the thirteenth and fourteenth centuries, including the Drangti family's *Red Register* and Penden Tsojé's *Expanded Elucidation of Knowledge*. According to these two sources, it was during the reign of Jé Tri Dhé Aktsom (Rje Khri Dhe ag tsom), also known as Tri Detsuktsen (Khri Lde gtsug brtsan, ca. 704–54), that their illustrious ancestor, Drangti Gyelnyé Kharbu (Brang ti Rgyal mnyes mkhar bu), gained the title of "official physician."[35] Adding further confusion to this story, a colophon in the *Gold Measure* collection describes Gyelnyé Kharbu not as an imperial physician but as a post-imperial treasure revealer.[36] Regardless of Drangti Gyelnyé Kharbu's true role in the buried past of Tibetan medicine, here we find a fourteenth-century legend grounding the official status of Drangti physicians not in the contested authority of Sakya hierarchs but in the perennial glory of Tibetan emperors.

Taken together, the institution of the medical house and the title of "official physician" emerged under the auspices of Yuan and Sakya hierarchs and then expanded beyond the Mongol tax system to designate the elite physicians of Tibet. Like the early hospitals and medical colleges of medieval Europe, the Sakya Medical House represents the institutionalization of medical practice and education beyond personal reputation and familial lineages in Tibet. With the official support of the Khön clan at Sakya, Drangti Jampel Zangpo could care for the most vulnerable members of his community and Penden Tsojé could establish a centralized institution for the study of medicine in Tibet. Indeed, this confluence of state support, bodhisattva ethics, and scholastic learning at the Sakya Medical House set a precedent for the rise of Geluk medical colleges and the subsequent spread of Tibetan medicine throughout Central Eurasia. In other words, the emergence of medical houses and official physicians in fourteenth-century Tibet helped establish the educational and institutional norms of Sowa Rigpa, a medical tradition that continues to flourish throughout the world today.

35. A ru ra 2014, 206: *smad la dmar byang 'phrul gyi me long gnang / bla sman byas pas mkhas par byung bas rje dges so// 'di gnang bas zhal la dris thams cad rang grol du go'o// lo rgyus so// [rgyal mnyes kyi rgyud (=brgyud) pa thams cad kyis bla sman bya bar byas so]*.

36. Bod ljongs bod lugs gso rig slob grwa chen mo 2014, 54 (fol. 4a): *gu ru nā gā rdzu nas shin tu zab par dgongs nas pad ma 'byung gnas la/ des mnga' bdag khri srong lde btsan la/ des gnam steng bcu gsum ka gzhu'i nang du sbas/ de brang ti rgyal mnyes mkhar bus ston nas sgrub pas grub cing rtags thon pa'o// de nas rim par brgyud de/ brang ti 'jam dpal bzang po/ des brang ti rgyal ba bzang po// des brang ti dpal ldan 'tsho byed/ de la brang ti dpal ldan rgyal mtshan bdag gis zhus nas// bu dang slob ma'i don du gab sbas ser sna spangs nas yi ger bkod pa// ithi//.*

References

Primary Sources

A ru ra, ed. 2005. *Cha lag bco brgyad. Bod kyi gso ba rig pa'i gna' dpe phyogs bsgrigs dpe tshogs*, vol. 25. Beijing: Mi rigs dpe skrun khang.

———, ed. 2014. *Byang khog dmar byang gsal ba'i sgron me. Bod kyi gso ba rig pa'i gna' dpe phyogs bsgrigs dpe tshogs*, vol. 101. Beijing: Mi rigs dpe skrun khang.

Bod ljongs bod lugs gso rig slob grwa chen mo, ed. 2014. *Reg pa rtsa'i spra sgrub klu sgrub gyis mdzad pa bzhugs s.ho*. In *Krung go'i bod lugs gso rig rtsa che'i dpe rnying kun btus* [Zhongguo zangyiyao yingyin guji zhenben 中国藏医药影印古籍珍本], vol. 1, text 10. Lhasa: Bod ljongs mi dmangs dpe skrun khang.

Bod rang skyong ljongs sman rtsis khang, ed. 2005. *Sa skya sman grong pa'i man ngag dngul bre ma*. Lhasa: Bod ljongs mi dmangs dpe skrun khang.

Guoli Gugong bowuyuan, ed. 1976. *Da Yuan shengzheng guochao dianzhang* 大元聖政國朝典章. Taipei: Guoli Gugong bowuyuan.

Mkhan po kun dga' bzang po, ed. 2004. *Brang ti lha rje'i rim brgyud kyi man ngag gser bre chen mo*. In *Dpal ldan sa skya pa'i gsung rab*, vol. 9, 33–296. Beijing: Mi rigs dpe skrun khang.

Mnga' ris pa sangs rgyas phun tshogs. 1985. *Dpal e waṃ chos ldan gyi gdan rabs nor bu'i phreng ba*. In *Lam 'bras Tshogs bśad: The Sa-skya-pa Teachings of the Path and the Fruit, According to the Ṅor-pa Transmission*, vol. 27 (*sha*), 251–313 (fols. 1a–32a). Dehra Dun: Sakya Centre.

Sgrolkar et al., eds. 1995. *A Collection of Historical Archives of Tibet* [Xizang lishi dang'an huicui 西藏历史档案荟萃]. Lhasa: Wenwu chubanshe.

Shes bya rab gsal rgyas pa = Gsang ba man ngag gis [*sic*] *rgyud kyi spyi don shes bya rab gsal rgyas pa*. n.d. Unpublished manuscript, catalog no. 002291. Beijing: Nationalities Cultural Palace Museum.

Tashigang, Tashi Y., ed. 2005. *Rgyud bzhi'i spyi don shes bya rab gsal rgyas pa*. Delhi: TY Tashigang.

Tsering Paljor Emchi, ed. 1975. *Gser bre chen mo: A Collection of Medical Formulae and Incantations of the Branti*. Leh: T. Paljor Emchi.

Secondary Sources

Beckwith, Christopher I. 1979. "The Introduction of Greek Medicine into Tibet in the Seventh and Eighth Centuries." *Journal of the American Oriental Society* 99.2: 297–313.

Everding, Karl-Heinz. 2006. *Herrscherurkunden aus der Zeit des mongolischen Grossreiches für tibetische Adelshauser, Geistliche und Kloster*. Halle: International Institute for Tibetan and Buddhist Studies GmbH.

Garrett, Frances. 2007. "Critical Methods in Tibetan Medical Histories." *Journal of Asian Studies* 66.2: 363–87.

He Huanhuan 何欢欢. 2016. "Fan Dekang tan Zangxue yanjiu de fazhan 范德康谈藏学研究的发展" [Leonard van der Kuijp Discusses the Development of Tibetology].

Dongfang zaobao: Shanghai shuping 东方早报：上海书评 [Oriental Morning Post: Shanghai Review of Books]. July 24. https://www.thepaper.cn/newsDetail_forward_1502535.

Hofer, Theresia. 2018. *Medicine and Memory in Tibet: Amchi Physicians in an Age of Reform*. Seattle: University of Washington Press.

van der Kuijp, Leonard W. J. 1995. "'Baγši' and Baγši-s in Tibetan Historical, Biographical and Lexicographical Texts." *Central Asiatic Journal* 39.2: 280–86.

———. 2010. "Za hor and Its Contribution to Tibetan Medicine, Part One: Some Names, Places, and Texts." *Bod rig pa'i dus deb* [Zangxue xuekan 藏学学刊] 6: 21–50.

———. 2016. "Za hor and Its Contribution to Tibetan Medicine, Part Two: Sources of the Tibetan Medical Tradition." *Bod rig pa'i dus deb* [Zangxue xuekan 藏学学刊] 12: 63–108.

Lévi-Strauss, Claude. 1990 [1975]. *The Way of Masks* [*La voie des masques*]. Translated by Sylvia Modelski. Seattle: University of Washington Press.

Martin, Dan. 2011. "Greek and Islamic Medicines' Historical Contact with Tibet." In *Islam and Tibet: Interactions along the Musk Routes*, edited by Anna Akasoy, Charles S. F. Burnett, and Ronit Yoeli-Tlalim, 117–44. Burlington, VT: Ashgate Publishing Company.

———. 2017. "Foreign Doctors in Tibet? An Old Zhijé Source Shows Up." *Tibetologic*. http://tibeto-logic.blogspot.com/2017/12/foreign-doctors-in-tibet-old-zhije.html.

Martin, Dan, and Yael Bentor. 2020 [1997]. *Tibetan Histories: A Bibliography of Tibetan-Language Historical Works*. London: Serindia Publications.

McGrath, William A. 2017. "Origin Narratives of the Tibetan Medical Tradition: History, Legend, and Myth." *Asian Medicine* 12.1–2: 295–316.

Petech, Luciano. 1990. *Central Tibet and the Mongols: The Yüan-Sa-skya Period of Tibetan History*. Rome: Instituto Italiano per il Medio ed Estermo Oriente.

Schaeffer, Kurtis R. 1998. "Review of *Tibetan Histories: A Bibliography of Tibetan-Language Historical Works* by Dan Martin in collaboration with Yael Bentor." *Journal of Asian Studies* 57.3: 856–58.

Shinno, Reiko. 2016. *The Politics of Chinese Medicine under Mongol Rule*. New York: Routledge.

van Vleet, Stacey. 2018. "Strength, Defence, and Victory in Battle: Tibetan Medical Institutions and the Ganden Phodrang Army, 1897–1938." *Cahiers d'Extrême-Asie* 27: 173–210.

Yoeli-Tlalim, Ronit. 2012. "Re-visiting 'Galen in Tibet.'" *Medical History* 56.3: 355–65.

Some Remarks on the *Genealogy of the Sakya* (Sa skya gdung rabs) by Taktsang Lotsāwa (Stag tshang lo tsā ba, 1405–77)

Shoko Mekata

I sincerely thank Prof. van der Kuijp, who introduced this text to me and guided me through reading it. I started attending his classes at Harvard shortly after finishing my PhD in Japan in 2011. He has always been welcoming and has helped me tremendously over the past decade. I am very grateful for the opportunity to participate in this Festschrift. Thank you so much, Leonard.

Introduction

GENEALOGY (*gdung rabs*) is one of the genres commonly found in Tibetan texts.[1] Since the list of Sakya school abbots has been transmitted by the Khön family, we know that numerous genealogical writings on the Sakya or the Khön family exist, whether or not they are available to us.[2] One of them is the *Genealogy of the Glorious Sakyapa: The Ocean of All Wishes* (*Dpal ldan sa skya pa'i gdung rabs 'dod dgu'i rgya mtsho*; hereafter, *Taktsang Genealogy*) by Taktsang Lotsāwa Sherap Rinchen (Stag tshang lo tsā ba Shes rab rin chen, 1405–77). This work is not very long, but it contains plenty of valuable chronological information.

This essay will describe the *Taktsang Genealogy* (*Stag tshang gdung rabs*) by discussing its general contents and its relationship with other Sakya genealogical documents. In so doing, this article will address a lacuna in the scholarly literature on Sakya and will elucidate an underappreciated but important

1. Dung dkar 1997, 146; Dge shis Chos grags 2001, 94. The general understanding is that *gdung* of the Sakya clan is Khön, and Sakya is not their *gdung*, but the name of the sect and the name of their philosophical system. Also, see Wang 1991 for a general survey on Tibetan names.

2. Dbus phrug and Fermer 2018 gives us the detailed list of various Sakya genealogies and their different editions, including manuscripts privately owned.

Tibetan document originally brought to light by Professor van der Kuijp after decades of obscurity.

The Life of Taktsang Lotsāwa

According to his autobiography, composed in 1470,[3] Taktsang Lotsāwa's grandfather was Sönam Gyelpo (Bsod nams rgyal po), an official of Khangmar (Khang dmar) and also a secretary (*yig dpon*) of Wang Namsé Gyentsen (Dbang Rnam sras rgyal mtshan, 1360–1408). Sönam Gyelpo had two sons, Döndrup Gyelpo (Don grub rgyal po), who was an official and was Taktsang Lotsāwa's father, and Peljor Zangpo (Dpal 'byor bzang po), who was a secretary (*dpon yig*) and the author of the *Rgya bod yig tshang*.[4]

When Taktsang Lotsāwa was younger, he traveled and studied in many places with eminent teachers. He studied at Drepung with Jamyang Chöjé Trashi Pelden ('Jam dbyangs chos rje Bkra shis dpal ldan, 1379–1449), for example, who was the first throneholder of the monastery; at Sangpu Neutok (Gsang phu ne'u thog) with Rongtön Sheja Künrik (Rong ston Shes bya kun rig, 1367–1449), who was the founder of Nālendra in Penpo ('Phan po) and who stayed at Sangpu at that time; and at Zhalu with Rinchen Sönam Pelwa (Rin chen bsod nams 'phel ba, b. fourteenth century), and so forth.[5] It is obvious, when we examine his various writings, that those experiences greatly

3. *Stag tshang rang rnam* 52.18–19: *rnam 'gyur zhes bya ba lcag pho stag hor zla dgu pa tha skar gyi zla ba'i yar ngo'i tshes bzhi la sbyar ba re zhig rdzozgs so//*. As for his biography, the Potala Palace has the collected works of Taktsang Lotsāwa, including his biography. See 'Jad pa 2015, 83, no. 01858–9. It is entitled *Rje tsham cad mkhyen pa stag tshang lo tsā ba shes rab rin chen rgyal mtshan dpal bzang po'i rnam par thar pa dad pa'i nor 'phel zhes bya ba dgos 'dod 'byung ba'i rin po che gngos grub kun 'byung* (38 fols., 5 lines; *Dbu can* manuscript, folio 35 missing). The author of this work is listed as Taktsang Lotsāwa himself. The title is different from his autobiography published by Krung go'i bod rig pa dpe skrun khang in 2007. It seems that this work does not appear in his other collected works. Unfortunately, I cannot identify whether this is the same as the one published in 2007.

4. *Stag tshang rang rnam*, 12.15–13.4: *de yang kho bo'i mes po khang dmar ba dpon bsod nams rgyal po ni/ dbang rnam sras rgyal mtshan pa'i yig dpon byas/ . . . de la bu dpon don grub rgyal po dang/ dpon yig dpal 'byor bzang po gnyis byung ba kho bo ni/*. Namsé Gyentsen was a son of Bailanwang Drakpa Gyentsen (Grags pa rgyal mtshan, 1336–78). See van der Kuijp 2018, 37n68. For the relationship between the Mongol court and both Taktsang Lotsāwa and his uncle Peljor Zangpo, see van der Kuijp 2004, 40–41.

5. *Stag tshang rang rnam*, 24.1–27.20. He left Chökhor and arrived in Drepung in the winter of 1431 and moved to Tsangpu in the summer of 1432. He went to Zhalu in the autumn of 1436. In the summer of 1437 he studied with Tukjé Pelzangpo (Thugs rje dpal bzang po, b. fourteenth century) in Shap (Shabs) and went back to Chökhor in the winter.

affected his life and productivity. For instance, he devoted a lot of space to explaining the *Kālacakra* and its system in his genealogy, as we will see. This is understandable, since he learned the *Kālacakra* in Zhalu and wrote the *General Meaning of the Kālacakra: The Ocean of Teachings* (*Dus 'khor spyi don bstan pa'i rgya mtsho*).[6]

One of his writings, the *Taktsang Genealogy* was mentioned in the *Sa skya gdung rabs chen mo* (hereafter *Amezhap Genealogy* [*A mes zhabs gdung rabs*], 1629) by Amezhap Ngawang Künga Sönam (A mes zhabs Ngag dbang kun dga' bsod nams, 1597–1659) as one of the sources he used. Also, the *Mdo smad chos 'byung*, composed in 1865, mentions the *Taktsang Genealogy* as one of its sources. The *Taktsang Genealogy* is listed as a rare text by Akhu Ching Sherap Gyatso (A khu ching Shes rab rgya mtsho, 1803–75).[7]

The Taktsang Genealogy *and Its Outline*

Currently there are two editions of the *Taktsang Genealogy* available to us. (There is one more typed edition published in 2018 from 西藏藏文古籍出版社 Xizang zangwen guji chubanshe. Unfortunately, I have not been able to view this edition yet.) *Dbu med* manuscript A was kept in the Tibetan Library of the Cultural Palace of Nationalities in Beijing (CPN no. 002437) and was located and introduced by Professor van der Kuijp.[8] Each folio has seven lines. Edition B is a computer-typed edition in Tibetan book (*dpe cha*) format. It is clear that edition B was made based on edition A, since there are no significant variants between them, and notes that were added in edition

6. Taktsang Lotsāwa is also known as having opposed the interpretation of the Madhyamaka philosophy by Tsongkhapa Lozang Drakpa (Tsong kha pa Blo bzang grags pa, 1357–1419). See Cabezón 1995.

7. *A mes zhabs gdung rabs*, 548–49; *Mdo smad chos 'byung*, 6.15–16; *A khu ching*, 509. Amezhap lists seven genealogies: Jetsün Drakpa Gyentsen (Rje btsun Grags pa rgyal mtshan, 1147–1216); Dampa Künga Drak (Dam pa Kun dga' grags [i.e., Sga A gnyan dam pa], 1230–1303); Sherap Dorjé (Shes rab rdo rje, fourteenth century), a direct student of Lama Dampa Sönam Gyentsen (Bla ma dam pa Bsod nams rgyal mtshan, 1312–75); Müsepa Tsang Jampa Dorjé Gyentsen (Mus srad pa Gtsang Byams pa Rdo rje rgyal mtshan, 1424–98); Chöjé Nyidewa (Chos rje Nyi lde ba, fourteenth century); Taktsang Lotsāwa; and Ngorchen Könchok Lhündrup (Ngor chen Dkon mchog lhun grub, 1497–1557). Akhu Ching lists six among them, except one by Drakpa Gyentsen, as rare texts. See Vostrikov 1994, 84–85; Khams sprul 2000, 388, no. 1964; and Martin 2000, 189, entry 218. According to recent numerous publications, many of them are available to us now. For instance, some *dbu med* manuscripts of genealogies by Müsepa have been identified. See Dbus phrug and Fermer 2018, 44–46.

8. van der Kuijp 1993, 114n14.

A are typed in small letters in edition B.[9] According to the colophon, Taktsang Lotsāwa completed this text at the Dzongkar Norbuling (Rdzong dkar nor bu gling) Palace in 1467.[10]

Here is the brief outline. Folio and line numbers in [ ] are according to editions A and B. Roman numbers in < > show the succession number of the abbots of Sakya Monastery. The names and spellings follow the *Taktsang Genealogy*.

1. Title page [A1a; B1]
2. Verses of praise [A1b1–2a4; B2.1–3.3]
3. History of Buddhism in India [A2a4–5a5; B3.3–9.6]
   3.1. The Buddha's teaching [A2a4–b6; B3.3–4.5]
   3.2. The *Kālacakra* [A2b6–5a5; B4.5–9.6]
4. Translators during the early and later spread of teaching [A5a5–6a2; B9.6–11.3]
5. Genealogy of Sakya [A6a2–33b3; B11.3–69.4]
   5.1. Genealogy of deities [A6a2–7a5; B11.3–14.1]
   5.2. Genealogy of the Khön family [A7a5–8b5; B14.1–17.4]
   5.3. Genealogy of the Sakya Khön family [A8b5–33b3; B17.4–69.4]
      'Khon rog Shes rab tshul khrims [A8b5–9a2; B17.4–18.1]
      <I> Dkon mchog rgyal po [A9a3–10b1; B18.1–21.1]
      <III> Sa chen Kun dga' snying po [A10b1–13b6; B21.1–28.3]
         <II> Ba ri lo tsā ba [A11b6–12a2; B24.1–4]
      <IV> Bsod nams rtse mo [A13b6–14a5; B28.3–29.2]
      <V> Grags pa rgyal mtshan [A14a5–16a5; B29.2–33.4]
      Dpal chen 'od po [A16a5–7; B33.4–34.1]
      <VI> Sa skya Paṇḍita Kun dga' rgyal mtshan [A16a7–19a7; B34.1–40.6]
      Zangs thsa Bsod nams rgyal mtshan [A19a7–b6; B40.6–41.5]
      <VII> 'Phags pa Blo gros rgyal mtshan [A19b6–23a1; B41.5–48.3]
      Phyag na rdo rje [A23a1–6; B48.3–49.1]
      <VIII> Rin chen rgyal mtshan and his siblings [A23a6–b4; B49.1–5]

9. For instance, compare notes in the *Stag tshang gdung rabs* A19a2–3 and small letters in *Stag tshang gdung rabs* B40.1–2.

10. *Stag tshang gdung rabs*, A34a5–6; B70.5–6: *dpal ldan sa skya pa'i gdung rabs 'dod dgu'i rgya mtsho zhes bya ba/ gtsang stag tshang gi lo tsā ba shes rab rin chen rgyal mtshan dpal bzang pos thams cad 'dul zhes bya ba/ me mo phag gi lo'i nag nya'i tshes gsum la/ rdzong dkar nor bu gling gi pho brang du sbyar ba'o//.*

<IX> Dharmapālarakṣita [A23b4–24a1; B49.5–50. 3]
<X> Shar pa 'Jam dbyangs rin chen rgyal mtshan [A24a1–4; B50.3–5]
<XI> Bdag nyid chen po Bzang po dpal [A24a4–25a6; B50.5–53.2]
Bailanwang Bsod nams bzang po [A25a7–b1; B53.2–3]
Dishi Kun dga' blo gros rgyal mtshan [A25b1–5; B53.3–6]
Dishi Kun dga' legs 'byung [A25b5–7; B53.6–54.2]
<XII> Guoshi Mkhas btsun Nam legs [A25b7–26a3; B54.2–4]
Bailanwang Kun dga' legs [A26a3–5; B54.4–6]
Guoshi Kun dga' nyi ma [A26a5–6; B54.6–55.2]
<XIII> 'Jam dbyangs Don yod rgyal mtshan [A26a7–b1; B55.2–4]
<XIV> Bla ma dam pa Bsod nams rgyal mtshan [A26b1–27b1; B55.4–57.4]
Summary of Bdag nyid chen po Bzang po dpal's descendants and [XV] Blo gros rgyal mtshan [A27b1–6; B57.4–58.3]
Theg chen chos rje Kun dga' bkra shis [A27b6–28a7; B58.3–59.4]
Bdag po Bsod nams bkra shis [A28a7–b4; B59.4–60.1]
<XVI> Bzhi thog pa Bdag chen Kun rin [A28b4–6; B60.1–3]
<XVII> Guoshi Blo gros rgyal mtshan and his son <XIX> Dbang phyug rgyal mtshan [A28b6–29a1; B60.3–4]
Grags pa blo gros and his son Chu mig pa Blo gros dbang phyug [A29a1–4; B60.4–61.1]
<XVIII> Dge sdings pa Nam mkha' rgyal mtshan and his sons <XX> Rgya gar ba and <XXI> Blo gros pa; Dge sdings pa's brother Bdag po Zha lu ba Bsod nams rgyal ba and his son [A29a4–6; B61.1–3][11]
Dishi Bsod nams blo gros [A29a6–29b4; B61.3–62.1]
Dbang Grags pa rgyal mtshan and his children [A29b4–30a2; B62.1–5]
Ta dben Kun legs [A30a2–3; B62.5–6]

11. *Stag tshang gdung rabs*, A29a5–6; B61.2–3: *sras* [B *shab*] *dge sdings pa nam mkha' rgyal mtshan pa dang/ bdag po zha lu ba bsod rgyal ba gnyis byon/ snga ma'i sras rgya gar pa dang blo gros pa/ phyi ma'i sras rgya nag pa grags rgyal ba rnams da lta bzhugs so//*. Here, Taktsang Lotsāwa mentions that the twentieth abbot, Gyagarwa Sherap Gyentsen (Rgya gar ba Shes rab rgyal mtshan, 1436–94, r. 1463–72), and the twenty-first abbot, Lodrö Gyentsen (Blo gros rgyal mtshan, 1444–95, r. 1473–95), who are sons of the eighteenth abbot, Gedingpa Namkha Gyentsenpa (Dge sdings pa Nam mkha' rgyal mtshan pa [i.e., 'Jam dbyangs Nam mkha' rgyal mtshan], 1398–1472, r. 1421–41), and Gyanakpa (Rgya nag pa) [and] Drak Gyelwa (Grags rgyal ba), who are sons of Dakpo Zhalu Sögyelwa (Bdag po Zha lu ba Bsod rgyal ba), are all alive.

Bdag chen Rnams sras rgyal mtshan [A30a3–b4; B62.6–63.6]
Bdag chen 'Jam dbyangs chos kyi rgyal mtshan [A30b4–31a3; B63.6–64.6]
Bdag po Kun blo, son of Bdag chen Rnams sras rgyal mtshan [A31a3–4; B64.6–65.1]
Dbang Nam legs pa [A31a4–b5; B65.1–66.1]
Dbang Nam mkha' rgyal mtshan dpal bzang po [A31b5–32b3; B66. 1–67.5]
Nam mkha' rin chen rgyal tshab dpal bzang po [A32b3–33a3; B67.5–68.4]
Nam mkha' bkra shis rgyal mtshan dpal bzang po [A33a3–7; B68.4–69.2][12]
5.4. Summary [A33a7–b3; B69.2–4]
6. Verses of praise [A33b3–34a5; B69.4–70.5]
7. Colophon [A34a5–7; B70.5–6]

We know that Taktsang Lotsāwa started writing the *Taktsang Genealogy* in 1466 from the section in which he explains the *Kālacakra* system.[13] He allocates portions of his text for the *Kālacakra*, which is reasonable since he studied it and wrote a book on it, as mentioned above. In the genealogy of Sakya, the main part of the *Taktsang Genealogy*, many sections describe the five Sakya forefathers (Sa skya gong ma rnam lnga) and give their biographies. Undoubtedly, Taktsang Lotsāwa adopted most of his descriptions from the *Rgya bod yig tshang*, of which I will give an example in the next section. After that, the succession of Sakya Monastery, Dishi 帝師, Guoshi 国師, and Bailanwang 白蘭王 are listed with the abbots' years of birth and death.

12. Both Namkha Rinchen Gyeltsap Pelzangpo (Nam mkha' rin chen rgyal tshab dpal bzang po, b. 1453) and his brother, Namkha Trashi Gyentsen Pelzangpo (Nam mkha' bkra shis rgyal mtshan dpal bzang po, b. 1458), who was the father of the twenty-second abbot, Sakya Lotsawa Künga Sönam (Sa skya lo tsā ba Kun dga' bsod nams, 1485–1533), are mentioned as being alive. *Stag tshang gdung rabs*, A33a4; B68.5–6: *da lta'i sku gsung thugs kyi gnas tshul yang yab ji lta ba bzhin du ngo mtshar bar bzhugs so//*. Especially, it is mentioned about Namkha Rinchen Gyeltsap Pelzangpo (Nam mkha' rin chen rgyal tshab dpal bzang po) that he went to Sakya with his sibling(s) when he was fifteen years old, which should be 1467, the year of the completion of the *Taktsang Genealogy*. *Stag tshang gdung rabs* A32b7; B68.2: *dgung lo bcwo lnga pa la sku mched thabs gcig tu gdan sar phebs/*.

13. *Stag tshang gdung rabs*, A4a2–3; B7.2–3: *de nas da lan gyi me pho khyi'i bar la lo brgya dang nyi shu rtsa gcig/ . . .*

Comparison with Other Sources

In the *Taktsang Genealogy*, Taktsang Lotsāwa does not mention the sources he used for writing his *gdung rabs*. To begin, here is a well-known narrative of Khön Könchok Gyelpo ('Khon Dkon mchog rgyal po, 1034–1102),[14] the founder of the Sakya school, composed to explain how he chose the site for building a temple while looking down from a mountain in Sakya. Let us compare this narrative from the *Taktsang Genealogy* with the same narrative in four other sources.

> [1.] *de'i tshe dpon slob rnams kyis skyo bsang la byon/ ri kha nas gzigs pas/ dpon po ri glang po che nyal ba 'dra ba'i mkhal khung g.yon pa'i thad na sa dkar zhing snum pa chu g.yas su 'bab pa la sogs pa bkra shis dang dge mtshan du ma dang ldan par gzigs nas/ 'dir dgon pa gcig btab na bstan pa dang sems can la phan pa rgya cher 'byung bar dgongs te/ de skor gyi sa cha spyi'i bdag po jo bo gdong nag pa la zhus pas kyang gnang/ dgos [sic B: sgos] kyi bdag po zhang zhung gu ra ba dang ban dhe grong bzhi lha mi grong bdun bya ba yod pa la/ nga 'dir dgon chung gcig byed 'dod pas/ khyed rnams la 'gal ba mi yong na khyed rnams la rin gcig kyang 'jal gsungs pas/ rin ye mi 'tshal cis kyang mdzad par zhu zer/*[15]
>
> At that time, the teacher and students came for recreation. Having looked from the mountain, Pönpori, the left side of which was like an elephant lying down, he saw there were many auspicious signs, such as white and shiny soil and flowing water to the right side. He thought that benefit would arise extensively for the teaching and for sentient beings if he built a monastery there. He also requested the lands around there from the official owner, Jowo

14. As for the birth year of Könchok Gyelpo, the typed edition of the *A mes zhabs gdung rabs* (18.7) published in Beijing has the male wood-mouse year (i.e., 1024). However, this seems to be a typo or mistake, since other block prints and *dbu med* manuscripts of the *Amezhap Genealogy* (as well as other chronological sources) have the male wood-dog year. Also, the *Stag tshang gdung rabs* says (A10a7–b1; B21.1) that he passed away "on the fourteenth day of the ninth [*dbyug gu*] month of the male iron-horse year [i.e., 1090] at the age of sixty-nine" (*re dgu pa lcags pho rta'i dbyug gu zla ba'i tshes bcu bzhi la*). However, the correct year of his death is the male water-horse year (i.e., 1102). See *Yar lung chos 'byung*, A141.20; *Yar lung chos 'byung*, B88b3; *Rgya bod yig tshang*, 315.14–15; and *A mes zhabs gdung rabs*, 24.20. These discrepancies are understandable, since the year system by gender and animal became popular much later and years were often reexamined.

15. *Stag tshang gdung rabs* (1467) A9b7–10a3; B19.6–20.3.

> Dong Nakpa. There were also private owners named Zhangzhung Gurawa, Bandhé Drongzhi, and Lhami Drongdün. Then he said, "I will pay you the price if you have an objection, because I want to build a small monastery here." So [the private owners] said, "We don't need any money. Please do anything."

Here is the same narrative from the *Yar lung chos 'byung*:

> [2.] *de'i tshe ri rtse nas gzigs pas/ dpon po ri'i ngos 'gram na sa dkar po*[16] *snum pa/ chu g.yas su 'bab pa/ bkra shis pa'i dge mtshan mang po gzigs nas/ dgon pa gcig der btab na sangs rgyas kyi bstan pa dang 'gro ba mang po la phan par dgongs te/ jo bo gdong nag ma*[17] *la zhus pas gnang/ sa de'i bdag po zhang zhung gu ra ba dang/ bande grong bzhi/ lha mi grong bdun du grags pa yod pa rnams la 'dir dgon chung gcig byas na khyed rnams la 'gal ba med las che/*[18] *rin gcig 'jal byas pas/ khong rnams na re/ rin ye mi 'tshal/ dgon pa mdzad par zhu zer ba la/ . . . .*[19]

Much of the terminology is very similar to that of the *Taktsang Genealogy*. For instance, there are similar terms, such as "many" (*du ma*) and "sentient being" (*sems can*) in the *Taktsang Genealogy* and "many" (*mang po*) and "[sentient] being" (*'gro ba*) in the *Yar lung chos 'byung*. By comparing descriptions in both texts, we notice that they have similar wordings, although the *Taktsang Genealogy* is slightly longer than the *Yar lung chos 'byung*. The author of the *Yar lung chos 'byung* sometimes mentions "the old document(s) in Khön" (*'khon gyi yig tshang rnying pa*),[20] meaning he was using Sakya Khön family documents for writing his genealogy.

The *Rgya bod yig tshang* has the same narrative:

16. *Dbu med* manuscript B has slightly different variants from the typed edition A. If B has the same terminology as the *Stag tshang gdung rabs*, it should correspond with the terms in the *Stag tshang gdung rabs*. po: zhing *Yar lung chos 'byung* B.

17. ma: pa *Yar lung chos 'byung* B.

18. khyed rnams la gal ba med las che/: khyed la 'gal ba med la che/ *Yar lung chos 'byung* B.

19. *Yar lung chos 'byung* (1376), A141.3–12; B88a2–5.

20. For instance, *Yar lung chos 'byung*, A136.7–8; B84b4: "It does not appear like this in the old document of Khön that exists in the great monastic seat" (*gdan sa chen po na yod pa'i 'khon gyi yig tshang rnying pa na 'di ltar snang ste/*). *Yar lung chos 'byung*, A138.17; B86b1: "That is not the case in the old document of Khön" (*'Khon gyi yig tshang rnying pa na de min/*).

[3.] *de'i tshe/ dpon slob 'ga' zung gis/ skyo bsangs la byon/ ri rtse nas gzigs pas/ spon po ri'i ngos 'gram na/ sa dkar zhing snum pa/ chu g.yas su 'bab pa/ bkra shis pa'i dge mtshan mang po tshang bar gzigs nas/ 'dir dgon pa gcig btab na/ sangs rgyas kyi bstan pa dang/ 'gro ba mang po la phan par 'dug dgongs pa byung nas/ jo bo gdong nag pa la zhus pas gnang/ sa de'i sgos kyi bdag po/ zhang zhung gu ra ba dang/ bandhe grong bzhi/ lha mi grong bdun bya ba 'dug pa la/ sa cha 'dir/ nged dgon chung gcig byed pa la/ khyed rnams la 'gal med na/ rin cig yang 'jal gsungs pas/ rin ye mi 'tshal/ dgon pa mdzad par zhu zer ba la/. . .*[21]

The terminology of both the *Taktsang Genealogy* and the *Rgya bod yig tshang* is quite similar, though the *Rgya bod yig tshang* is a bit shorter than the *Taktsang Genealogy*. It is possible that the *Taktsang Genealogy* lengthened the descriptions of the *Rgya bod yig tshang*. When we compare the *Yar lung chos 'byung* and the *Rgya bod yig tshang*, it is clear that some terms in the *Rgya bod yig tshang* follow terms in the *Yar lung chos 'byung*—for instance, "on the side of the Pönpori" (*spon po ri'i ngos 'gram na*) in the *Rgya bod yig tshang* and "on the side of the Pönpori" (*dpon po ri'i ngos 'gram na*) in the *Yar lung chos 'byung*. Whereas in the *Taktsang Genealogy*, the description is "in Pönpori, the left side of which was like an elephant lying down" (*dpon po ri glang po che nyal ba 'dra ba'i mkhal khung g.yon pa'i thad na*), which the *Yar lung chos 'byung* and the *Rgya bod yig tshang* do not have.

Peljor Zangpo, the author of the *Rgya bod yig tshang* and the paternal uncle of Taktsang Lotsāwa, was a secretary of Düchö Labrang (Dus mchod bla brang) of Sakya Monastery.[22] It might be possible that Peljor Zangpo used "the old document of Khön in Sakya," which the *Yar lung chos 'byung* mentions in accordance with the relation between him and the Sakya family, or he used the *Yar lung chos 'byung* as one of the sources for writing this narrative. Since the *Taktsang Genealogy* is less similar to the *Yar lung chos 'byung* than it is to the *Rgya bod yig tshang*, Taktsang Lotsāwa probably relied on the *Rgya bod yig tshang*, his uncle's text.

Here is the same narrative from the *Amezhap Genealogy*. Amezhap mentioned the *Taktsang Genealogy* as one of his sources, as noted above.

21. *Rgya bod yig tshang* (1434), 314.10–315.2.

22. Interesting aspects of the relation between Peljor Zangpo and the Sakya Khön family are described by Sarat Chandra Das, who apparently had access to a manuscript roll of the *Rgya bod yig tshang* that contains the seal of Pönchen Śākya Zangpo (Dpon chen Śākya bzang po, d. 1270) in the archives of Sakya Monastery. See Das 1904, 100. See also Macdonald 1963, 53–55.

> [4.] *de'i tshe dpon slob rnams kyis skyo bsangs la byon te ri kha nas gzigs pas/ dpon po ri glang po che nyal ba 'dra ba'i mkhal khung g.yas pa'i thad nas dkar zhing snum pa/ chu g.yas su 'bab pa la sogs pa bkra shis dang dge mtshan du ma dang ldan par gzigs nas/ 'dir dgon pa cig btab na bstan pa dang sems can la phan pa rgya chen po 'byung ba 'dug snyam du dgongs te/ de skor gyi sa cha spyi'i bdag po jo bo gdong nag pa bya ba yod pa de la zhus pas kyang gnang/ sgos kyi bdag po zhang gzhung gu ra ba dang/ bande grong bzhi/ lha mi grong bdun bya ba yod pa de rnams la/ nga 'dir dgon pa cig byed 'dod pas khyed rnams la 'gal ba mi 'ong na khyed rnams la rin cig kyang 'jal bas sa cha 'di nga la byin na ji ltar legs gsung pas/ rin ye mi 'tshal cis kyang mdzad par zhu zer nas phul ba la/ . . .*[23]

It seems quite likely that this narrative of the *Amezhap Genealogy* was taken from the *Taktsang Genealogy*, since they are significantly similar except for some terms, such as "left" in the *Taktsang Genealogy* is "right" in the *Amezhap Genealogy*. Amezhap was quite young, only thirty, when he completed the *Amezhap Genealogy*. So let us take a look the *Mgon po chos 'byung* by Amezhap, written thirteen years later.

> [5.] *de'i tshe dpon slob rnams kyis skyo bsang la byon/ ri kha nas gzigs pas/ dpon po ri glang po che nyal ba 'dra ba'i mkhal khung g.yas pa'i thad na/ sa dkar zhing snum pa chu g.yas su 'bab pa la sogs pa bkra shis ba'i dge mtshan du ma dang ldan pa gzigs nas 'dir dgon pa gcig btab na bstan pa dang sems can la phan pa rgya cher 'byung bar dgongs te de skor gyi sa cha spyi'i bdag po jo bo gdong nag pa la zhus pas kyang gnang/ sgos kyi bdag po zhang zhung gu ra ba dang/ bandhe grong gcig lha mi grong bdun*[24] *bya ba yod pa la nga 'dir dgon chung gcig byed 'dod pas khyed rnams la 'gal ba mi yongs na khyed rnams la rin cig*[25] *'jal gsungs pas/ rin ye mi 'tshal cis kyang mdzad par zhu zer/.*[26]

Interestingly, the *Mgon po chos 'byung* quotes almost exactly from the *Taktsang Genealogy*. Furthermore, in light of the close similarities of all the texts

23. *A mes zhabs gdung rabs* (1629), 19.16–20. 3.

24. Editions A and B have some minor variants. Interestingly, this part of B is exactly the same as the *Stag tshang gdung rabs*. bandhe grong gcig lha mi grong bdun: ban dhe grong bzhi lha yi grong bdun B.

25. cig: gcig kyang B.

26. *Mgon po chos 'byung* (1641), A311.6–312.4; B181.3–6.

just considered about this same passage, the likelihood of a closely dependent relationship among these texts is quite strong.

Concluding Remarks

In his *Genealogy*, Taktsang Lotsāwa adopted numerous sections from the *Rgya bod yig tshang*, especially the parts about the five Sakya forefathers. The *Taktsang Genealogy* provides detailed information about the birth and death years of major Khön family members, as well as the names of wives and sisters that other sources sometimes do not provide. However, a few details (such as names or years) do not correspond with other sources. Finally, it is evident that Amezhap quotes this text a lot, especially in his later writings. Further research could provide a clearer view on the Sakya genealogy by comparing and analyzing the *Taktsang Genealogy* with other sources.[27]

References

A khu ching = A khu ching Shes rab rgya mtsho. *Dpe rgyun dkon pa 'ga' zhig gi tho yig*. In *Materials for a History of Tibetan Literature*, edited by Lokesh Chandra, part 3, 503–601. Śata-Piṭaka Series, Indo-Asian Literatures 30. New Delhi: International Academy of Indian Culture, 1963.

A mes zhabs gdung rabs = A mes zhabs Ngag dbang kun dga' bsod nams. *Sa skya'i gdung rabs ngo mtshar bang mdzod*. Beijing: Mi rigs dpe skrun khang, 1986.

Mdo smad chos 'byung = Brag dgon Dkon mchog bstan pa rab rgyas. *Mdo smad chos 'byung*. Lanzhou: Kan su'u mi dmangs dpe skrun khang, 1982.

Mgon po chos 'byung A = A mes zhabs Ngag dbang kun dga' bsod nams. *Dpal rdo rje nag po chen po'i zab mo'i chos skor rnams byung ba'i tshul legs par bshad pa bstan srung chos kun gsal ba'i nyin byed*. New Delhi: T. G. Dhongthog, 1979. Also in *Bod kyi lo rgyus rnam thar phyogs bsgrigs*, vol. 20, 143–556, and vol. 21, 1–427. Xining: Mtsho sngon mi rigs dpe skrun khang, 2010.

Mgon po chos 'byung B = A mes zhabs Ngag dbang kun dga' bsod nams. *Dpal rdo rje nag po chen po'i zab mo'i chos skor rnams byung ba'i tshul legs par bshad pa bstan srung chos kun gsal ba'i nyin byed*. In *Dpal sa skya pa chen po sngags 'chang thams cad mkhyen pa*

27. One final point to be emphasized is that Tibetan texts must be checked across as many editions as are available, even though some editions might not be reliable in terms of spelling, since multiple editions of many texts—including typed, block print, and manuscripts—have recently become available.

ngag dbang kun dga' bsod nams kyi gsung 'bum, vol. 25, 1–491. Kathmandu: Sa skya rgyal yongs gsung rab slob gnyer khang, 2000.

Rgya bod yig tshang = Stag tshang Rdzong pa Dpal 'byor bzang po. *Rgya bod yig tshang chen mo*. Chengdu: Si khron mi rigs dpe skrun khang, 1985.

Stag tshang gdung rabs A = Stag tshang lo tsā ba Shes rab rin chen. *Dpal ldan sa skya pa'i gdung rab 'dod dgu'i rgya mtsho*. CPN 002437. BDRC W1CZ1883. Also in *Bod kyi lo rgyus rnam thar phyogs bsgrigs*, vol. 93, 369–435. Xining: Mtsho sngon mi rigs dpe skrun khang, 2015.

Stag tshang gdung rabs B = Stag tshang lo tsā ba Shes rab rin chen. *Dpal ldan sa skya'i gdung rab 'dod dgu'i rgya mtsho*. In *Stag tshang lo tsā ba shes rab rin chen gyi gsung 'bum*, vol. 2, 1–70. Kathmandu: Sa skya rgyal yongs gsung rab slob gnyer khang, 2007.

Stag tshang rang rnam = Stag tshang lo tsā ba Shes rab rin chen. *Lo chen thams cad mkhyen pa shes rab rin chen rgyal mtshan dpal bzang po'i zhabs kyi rnam par thar pa*. In *Stag tshang lo tsā ba shes rab rin chen gyi gsung 'bum*, vol. 2, 1–52. Beijing: Krung go'i bod rig pa dpe skrun khang, 2007.

Yar lung chos 'byung A = Yar lung jo bo Śākya rin chen sde. *Yar lung jo bo'i chos 'byung*. Lhasa: Bod ljongs mi dmangs dpe skrun khang, 1988.

Yar lung chos 'byung B = Yar lung jo bo Śākya rin chen sde. *Yar lung jo bo'i chos 'byung*. CPN 002446 (2). BDRC W25583. Also in *Bod kyi lo rgyus rnam thar phyogs bsgrigs*, vol. 11, 1–231. Xining: Mtsho sngon mi rigs dpe skrun khang, 2010.

Cabezón, José. 1995. "On the sGra pa Shes rab rin chen pa'i rtsod lan of Pan chen bLo bzang chos rgyan." *Asiatische Studien: Zeitschrift der Schweizerischen Asiengesellschaft* 49.4: 643–69.

Das, Sarat Chandra. 1904. "Tibet under the Tartar Emperors of China in the 13th Century A.D." *Journal of the Asiatic Society of Bengal* 73.1 (extra): 94–102.

Dge shis Chos grags, et al. 2001. *Bod kyi gdung rus zhib 'jug*. Beijing: Mi rigs dpe skrun khang.

Drongshar Tsering [Dbus phrug, Tshe ring], and Mathias Fermer. 2018. "Dpal ldan sa skya pa'i gdung rabs yig rnying khag gi ngo sprod." *Chos dung dkar po* 14: 33–59.

Dung dkar Blo bzang 'phrin las. 1997. *Bod kyi rig gnas dang lo rgyus kyi re'u mig*. Chengdu: Si khron mi rigs dpe skrun khang.

'Jad pa Dpal ldan tshe ring, ed. 2015. *Pho brang po ta lar bzhugs su gsol ba'i dpal ldan sa skya'i gsung rab rnams kyi dkar chag*. Lhasa: Bod ljongs mi dmangs dpe skrun khang.

Khams sprul Bsod nams don grub. 2000. *Bod kyi lo rgyus dpe tho*. Lhasa: Bod ljongs mi dmangs dpe skrun khang.

van der Kuijp, Leonard W. J. 1993. "Fourteenth Century Tibetan Cultural History III: The Oeuvre of Bla ma dam pa Bsod nams rgyal mtshan (1312–1375), Part One." *Berliner Indologische Studien* 7: 109–47.

———. 1994. "Apropos of Some Recently Recovered Texts Belonging to the *Lam 'bras* Teachings of the Sa skya pa and Ko brag pa." *Journal of the International Association of Buddhist Studies* 17.2: 175–201.

———. 2004. *The Kālacakra and the Patronage of Tibetan Buddhism by the Mongol Imperial Family*. Central Eurasian Studies Lectures 4. Bloomington: Department of Central Eurasian Studies, Indiana University.

———. 2018. "Fourteenth-Century Tibetan Cultural History III: The Oeuvre of Bla ma dam pa Bsod nams rgyal mtshan (1312–1375), Part Two." *Revue d'Etudes Tibétaines* 46: 5–89.

Macdonald, Ariane. 1963. "Préambule à la lecture d'un Rgya-Bod yig-chaṅ." *Journal Asiatique* 251: 53–159.

Martin, Dan, in collaboration with Yael Bentor. 2020 [1997]. *Tibetan Histories: A Bibliography of Tibetan-Language Historical Works.* Revised electronic edition. London: Serindia Publications.

Vostrikov, A. I. 1994. *Tibetan Historical Literature.* Translated by Harish Chandra Gupta. London: Curzon Press.

Wang Gui 王贵. 1991. Zangzu renming yanjiu 藏族人名研究. *Bod rigs kyi rus ming dpyad pa*. Beijing: Minzu chubanshe.

Who Owned the Land in Tibet?

Peter Schwieger

"IN TIBET all land is considered to belong to the ruler." This statement made by Pedro Carrasco in 1959,[1] and later repeated by others,[2] is the background of my present paper. On the one hand, the consequences of this situation have been strictly underlined. Rolf A. Stein stated: "The land 'given' or rather lent by the overlord . . . is essentially indivisible and non-transferable."[3] On the other hand, it has been acknowledged that there apparently existed some exceptions.[4] In this paper, I will help clarify the issue of landownership in traditional Tibetan societies on the basis of primary sources. In particular, I focus on legal documents that were created not only to testify and prove a change of ownership but also to perform such a change.

In Tibetan society, land was the most important source for increasing prosperity, and economically exploitable land was a scarce resource. The rights to and usage of farmed land reflected the hierarchic-seigneurial structure of Tibetan society. Similar to the *dominium directum*, the doctrine of primary or direct ownership in the late Middle Ages of Europe,[5] land—besides a few exceptions addressed later—belonged to the ruler as the uppermost lord: the Dalai Lama or, in the periphery, a local ruler. Land for farming and stockbreeding was partitioned into estates. The ruler could either have the estates cultivated directly by farmers and stockbreeders paying taxes and rendering corvée labor, or he could also convey beneficial ownership to a noble landlord in exchange for government services or to a clerical institution as a basis for sustenance and for financing religious services. The clerical institutions were either monasteries or households of reincarnated clerics, the so-called *trülkus* (*sprul sku*). The respective landlord did not manage his estates himself but

1. Carrasco 1959, 209.

2. See, for example, Kapstein 2006, 176: "The land was the property of the ruler . . . ."

3. Stein 1972, 128.

4. Stein 1972, 129; Kapstein 2006, 184.

5. See, for example, Volkert 1991, 87–89.

delegated this task to a specially chosen custodian. The right to use land was not conveyed by the ruler *ad personam*, and in the case of noble landlords, it did not end at his death but was handed down to his descendants with all the obligations attached to it. The ruler had the authority to confiscate the land when one defaulted on obligations, when a noble house became extinct, or in the case of legal misconduct. The Tibetan government kept precise records of the estates and their associated tax liabilities, classified by district. The lands controlled by an individual landlord were not usually all in one place but were often far apart and frequently even scattered over several districts. A noble landlord's name and identity were derived from the name of his ancestral family estate, which commonly had been in the family for generations. According to a survey carried out by the Chinese occupants in 1959, at the end of the Ganden Podrang (Dga' ldan pho brang) government's rule, within their jurisdiction 24 percent of farmland was owned by the aristocracy, 37 percent was owned by the clergy, and 39 percent was managed directly by the Tibetan government.[6] Strictly speaking, the percentages do not refer to the farming area but to the yield capacity of the soil, which was the basis for tax collection. In Tibet, farmland was assessed by the bushels of seed that a field could carry. The number of bushels was dependent on both the surface area of the field and the fertility of the soil, which varied substantially depending on the quality of the location. The information that fifteen bushels would have corresponded to one hectare and that, consequently, about 220,000 hectares of farming land was available in Tibet is therefore only a rough estimate.[7]

In Tibetan law, land was always conceived of in unity with the inhabitants cultivating it. They—and therefore also their labor—were bound to the land, and they could only leave the land with the landlord's permission. Any reduction of the labor force in this way had to be compensated, either through an annual, albeit low, fee or—in cases of a marriage outside the estate—through a labor exchange. Dependents who left the land without permission had to be returned when they were caught. As the factors of production, land and labor formed an indissoluble unit.

Aristocrats and clerical landlords were in principle liable to taxation. They also had to provide laborers for government services, such as the transport and postal services, road construction, and the construction and maintenance of government and district buildings. In practice, such obligations were frequently reduced or even completely waived for clerical landlords.

The landlords left their land and cattle herds to be cultivated by their depen-

6. Jin Hui, Ren Yinong, and Ma Naihui 1995, 65.

7. Jin Hui, Ren Yinong, and Ma Naihui 1995, 65.

dents. Farmers and nomadic stockbreeders carried the actual burdens through tax payments and corvée labor. In cases where estates were not directly subordinated to the ruler or the government, additional dues and service obligations were owed to the respective landlord. Since clerical landlords in many cases had reduced tax burdens or none at all thanks to attested privileges, the highest burdens usually fell on dependents living on noble estates.

Tax farmers were not without rights. As long as they fulfilled their obligations, they had a right to the land they cultivated. This right was, just like for aristocratic and clerical landlords, heritable but not alienable. Tax farmers were allowed to lease out individual plots in exchange for help with the fieldwork. Capable members of households without land, who were also bound to the landlord's estate, hired themselves out as workers to the tax farmers or directly to their landlord. They were compensated by having necessities, including accommodation, provided.

If the landlord was no longer able to fulfill his tax and service obligations toward the ruler, the estate was not necessarily always confiscated as a consequence. For instance, a case from 1889 records that the Tibetan government expressly agreed to lease out an entire estate for forty years.[8] The noble landlord saw himself unable to continue fulfilling his obligations toward the government due to his farming community being impoverished in the aftermath of war, the lack of a suitable custodian, a high tax burden on his family estate, a fire, and accumulated debts. Subsequently, he leased out the entire estate. The leasing contract was confirmed in a note added by the Tibetan government.

In Tibet the land remained first and foremost the property of the ruler. For him, land was primarily a political resource, and only second was it seen as an economic resource. It was used predominantly to stabilize the hierarchy within Tibetan society. By being bound to the ruler and because property rights were divided between the ruler, the landlords, and the tax farmers, the land could not be "liquefied" and used as capital for commercial transactions. The property was not a commodity that one could simply have or, alternatively, not have. Without freedom of disposal, a price could not be attributed to a tract of land. Thus no property market developed. The same is true for the labor force. As a means of production, the laborers were generally bound to the land. Wage labor existed only in a few exceptions, such as traveling craftspeople. As the main beneficiaries, the Tibetan upper class, and notably the clergy who supported the political domination, had little interest in seeing that changed. The close connection between land, domination, and the Tibetan upper class's

8. Schuh 1981, no. 13.

focus on land ownership is the main reason why the development of trade and a monetary economy lagged in Tibetan society.

However, there were first signs for such a development. The beginnings date back before the establishment of Ganden Podrang domination and were, therefore, not a result of late-developing trade relations with Tibet's neighbors. Such exceptions led to labor and land ownership being assessed in monetary terms and becoming operable with this medium. Statistically and economically, they are insignificant. However, it is interesting to observe how a legal structure developed in Tibet's society in conjunction with land not bound to lordship allowed such land to become a commodity for economic transactions.

It has been noted that, at times and in different places in Tibet, a small amount of land existed that was not bound by lordship and could be managed at the discretion of its local proprietor.[9] Indications of this can be found in early Tibetan hagiographies. The dispute over property as narrated by Tsangnyön Heruka (Gtsang smyon He ru ka, 1452–1507) at the beginning of Milarepa's biography (Mi la ras pa, 1052–1139) is well known.[10] The story suggests that Milarepa's family was initially a full proprietor of houses, fields, cattle, and all kinds of valuables. Prior to his death, his father decreed that this property should not be managed by his wife but by his relatives until his son was old enough to take on the responsibility himself. When his son turned fourteen, his mother demanded the inheritance back for him. However, his uncle and aunt refused, insisting that the property always belonged to them and that they had loaned it before to Milarepa's deceased father. It is noteworthy that the last will of the father is mentioned in this dispute but no legal authority is named to examine and enforce legal claims. In order to make her claim against the uncle and aunt public, his mother simply organized a party for the neighbors. But as the uncle and aunt publicly rejected her claim, she was left powerless. The revenge carried out later through black magic was also not legally but only morally evaluated in the narrative. There was no legal ruling.

The narrative took place when Tibet's society was largely segmented, with no central power to enforce the law. This changed with the increasing centralization of rule and the attendant stratification of society, which also played out in the division of property rights.

But as before, some small plots remained not bound to a lordship. These plots could be freely traded, but in order to change hands, it was necessary to determine in each case who was the former and the later proprietor. This requirement "has a legal name, namely 'contract.' In the economy, it is called

9. Kapstein 2006, 184.

10. Gtsan-smyon He-ru-ka 1982, 17–21.

exchange."[11] Such contracts are already known from the domination of the rulers of Tsang (Gtsang) in central Tibet, dating from the second half of the sixteenth century to the first half of the seventeenth. The following document is about the descendants of a man named Khangtak Gongmapa (Khang stag gong ma pa), who purchased a field.[12] The price was thirty-eight *zho*. The *zho* was a unit of weight used predominantly for gold and silver. Ten *zho* amounted to one *sang* (*srang*). In addition to the purchase price paid directly upon concluding the contract, a life annuity was agreed upon, which had to be paid annually to two persons at harvest time. The amount for the second person was only six-twentieths of a Tibetan bushel of grain.

The content of the document that was executed on the eighteenth calendar day in the tenth month of the hare year was the following:

> When *pön* Guru Peljor (*dpon* Gu ru Dpal 'byor) passed away, a field was, together with a small field north of Jemalung (Bye ma lung), permanently purchased by Khangtak Gongmapa's descendants. Concerning the price, thirty-eight *zho* were paid immediately without deceit or reduction. Later, as an obligation for subsistence, Zhangdrong Gyakpön (Zhang grong rgyag dpon) was offered a bushel [of grain] and a pot of beer as life annuity, and Ratsangpa (Ra tshang pa) was offered six *dré* (*bre*) [of grain].
>
> If later somebody comes along saying, "Now I am the main proprietor of this field," I, Samdrup (Bsam 'grub), will accept responsibility and settle any doubts. Should the doubts not be removed, I will reimburse the price of the field in double.
>
> Seal stamped by me, Samdrup.
>
> As mediators and witnesses, *zimpön* Zanggyam (*gzim dpon* Bzang rgyam) and Apo Lerap (A po Las rab) were present. [May there be] auspiciousness![13]

11. Luhmann 2004, 393.

12. The name appears with variant spellings in different documents: Khang stag gong pa, Khang brtag gong ma pa, etc.

13. Digitized Tibetan Archives Bonn, Kundeling Archives, ID 1021: *yos lo zla ba bcu pa'i tshes cwo {bco} rgyad {brgyad} gi nyin (yi ge) byas pa'i don la/ dpon ('gu ru) dpal 'byor 'das dus/ zhing byi {bye} ma lung gi byang kyi zhing chung dang sbrags pa/ mkhang brtag gong ma pa mi rgyud kyi {kyis}/ bstan rtsa ba nas nyos pa'i rin la dmar {rma} med snyong {snyung} med gi {gis} zho sum bcu so rgyad {brgyad} kyi rin bstan {stan} thog gcig du sprad bting {rting} lto khral zhang grong rgyag dpon la bogs khal gcig dang chang rdze {rdza} ma gcig/ ra tshang pa la bogs bre drug sprad bting {rting}/ da zhing steng 'dir rtsa ba'i bdag po nga yin zer mi byung na nga bsam 'grub gi khag mkhur cing dogs sel ba byas/ gal te ma sol {bsal} na/ zhing [ri]n phyir*

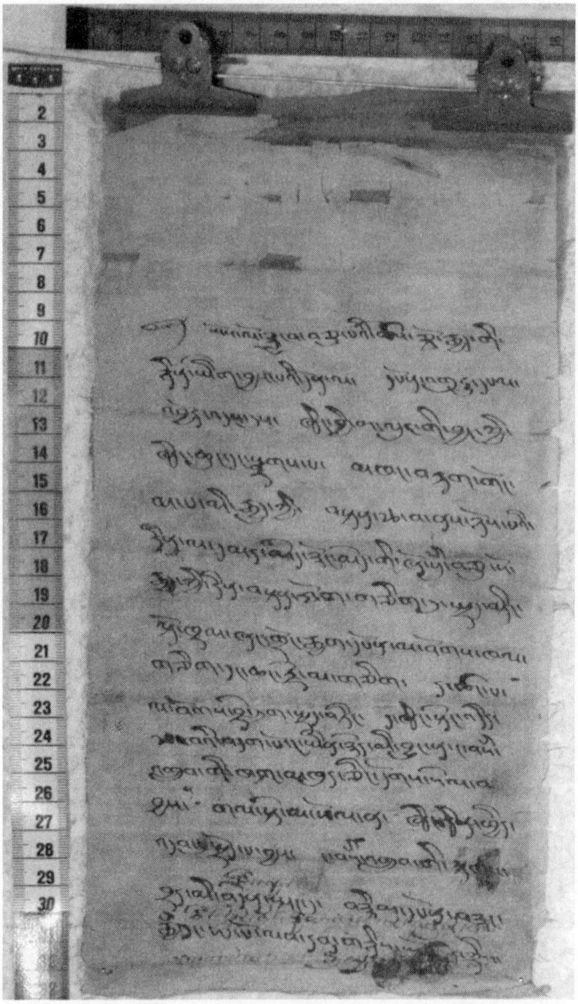

Document about land purchase.

Already at this time, the ruler could additionally confirm the legal force of such a contract. That is proven by a charter from the same bunch of documents:

> Here is what I have sent to the strong and the weak, the custodian of Nangtsé (Snang rtse), and those commissioned as headmen for civil and military affairs:
>
> It is said that for [financing] the religious ceremony for Tseten

'dab [su] sprod pa byas/ nga bsam 'grub gi stags brar [bar] mi bden spang {dpang} du/ bskim {gzim} dpon bzang rgyam dang a po las rab gnyis yod/ (bkra shis)/.

> Dorjé (Tshe brtan rdo rje), a field was sold to Khangtak Gongpa from Jemalung. In agreement with that, Abar (A bar) has granted a confirmation for the document regarding [the purchase of] his field. You, [above-mentioned persons] whoever you are, let Khangtak Gongpa and his descendants keep the document [of the purchase] of the field, together with the confirmation document, without behaving even slightly in a way that would lead to accusation or nuisance, such as [the demand for] rent or taxes.
>
> The fourth month of the female wood-bird year [1585] . . . [in part illegible][14]

Contracts documenting the purchase and sale of smaller plots have also survived from the kingdom of Ladakh.[15] Such documents are known also from Gyeltang (Rgyal thang), the southeastern periphery of the Tibetan settlement area. The local archives preserve the following contract document issued at the time when Gyeltang already belonged to the jurisdiction of the governor-general of the Chinese province of Yunnan. The date given presumably corresponds to May 22, 1749.[16] The document is remarkable in three ways: First, the contract was concluded between a Tibetan household and a traveling Chinese merchant. Second, the location and size of the plot were specified in more detail than in the previously mentioned case, and the contract expressly considered the possibility of land development. Third, the contract included the threat of interrogation under torture and a severe financial penalty should the contract be violated—that is, contravening the property relations arranged in the contract:

> As far as the persons are concerned who, on the sixth calendar day in the fourth month of the earth-serpent year, have concluded the irrevocable agreement, the brothers Tsabo (Tsha bo), Bokmen ('Bog

14. Digitized Tibetan Archives Bonn, Kundeling Archives, ID 1001: *nged rang gis drag zhan du/ snangs tshe'i {snang rtse'i} gnyer las 'dzin zhi drag gi sna mor sngags {mngags} slebs dang bcas pa rnams la springs pa/ tshe rtan rdo rje'i rims 'dro la zhing bye ma lung khang stag gong par tshongs {btsongs} lugs byas pa'i/ kho rang gi zhing yig la Za bar gyis rgyam mnon mthun grub tu gnang 'dug pa bzhin/ khyod sus kyang bogs thon khral rigs sogs snyad rtser za 'dod du 'gro ba spu rtsam ma byed par/ khang stag gong pa mi brgyud bcas dang zhing yig rgyab mnon dang bcas pa 'dzin chug/ shing mo bya lo zla ba bzhi pa'i [gnam . . . pas] dbar don rgyal kyi yi ge yod 'dug pa'i* [. . .]/.

15. Schuh 2008, nos. 26, 43, 44, 46a, 51, 53, 54, 57, 61, 65, 66.

16. The Tibetan publisher of the document (see note 17) mentions the year 1749 in his Chinese translation. Without additional information, a later date is, of course, also possible because the text itself does not reveal which sexagenarian cycle applies.

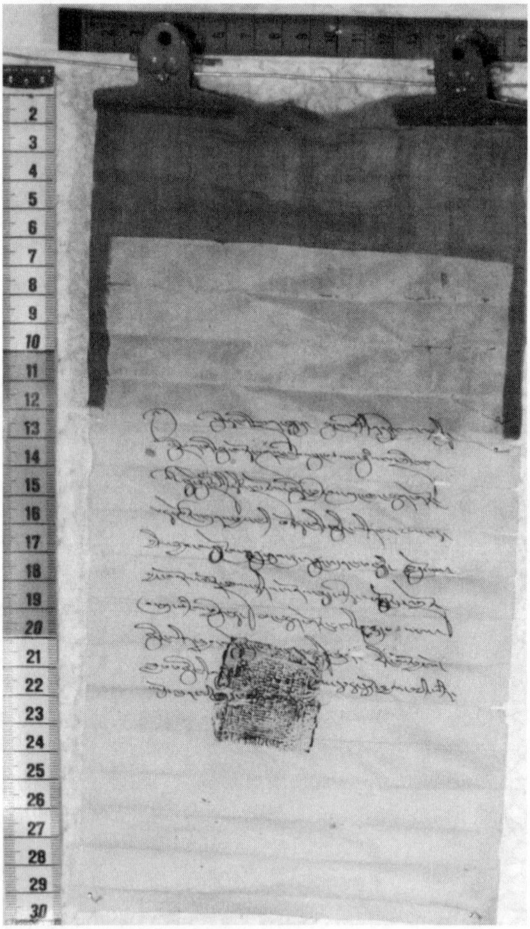

Confirmation of a land purchase.

sman), and Trashi (bKra shis), and [their common] wife, four [persons], have sold the building ground at the foot of the fortress, [bordering] the alleyway in the east, next to Orgyan's (O rgyan) house in the west, to Ahor's (A hor) house in the south, and to the shop at the northern side—thirty cubits long and twenty cubits wide—to the traveling merchant from Yunnan, Huang Weizhong, for however long.

Thirty *sang* of good-quality silver was offered and received as the agreed price. Should a house be built on the plot, the buyer is the proprietor. Other than that, there is no deceit or deduction on the part of the seller and his family.

> Should any infringements take place later [against the contract] in that [unjustified] contestations are filed, it was agreed that an investigation should proceed using torture and that three *sang* gold should be charged as a penalty.
>
> For the irreversibility of the contract: Tsabo's, Bokmen's, Trashi's, and [their common] wife's seal imprint, the seal imprint of the witness *ding* (*lding*) Orgyan, the seal imprint of the headman Gelong Zang (Dge slong Bzang), the seal imprint of [the Chinese clerk] Zhang Santing who prepared the written agreement, the seal imprint of the buyer, the traveling merchant Huang [Weizhong], . . .[additional seal imprints of four Chinese and one Tibetan witness].[17]

Concerning the area that belonged directly to the jurisdiction of the Ganden Podrang government under the Dalai Lama, there are also indications of small plots not bound to a lordship. The land registry of the Trashi Samtenling (Bkra shis bsam gtan gling) Monastery, near the border of Nepal, lists a great number of plots that were bequeathed by private persons as gifts.[18] Copies of two contracts regarding the purchase and sale of plots in the nineteenth and twentieth centuries exist in the archives of Kündeling (Kun bde gling) Monastery.[19] They differ from the above-mentioned contracts in that the addressee at the beginning of the text was explicitly called "precious lord over the law"—that is, the ruler who guarantees legal enforcement in the case of conflict—as was frequently common in private contracts within the Ganden Podrang's jurisdiction. This demonstrates that the basis for the functional differentiation of a subsystem "economy" existed in Tibetan society by which law and

17. Sems kyi nyi zla rdzong mi dmangs srid gzhung gi khun sdod don gcod khang 2003, no. 032: *sa sbrul zla ba bzhi pa'i tshes drug la/ 'gyur med yig dan bzhag mi tsha bo/ 'bog sman/ bkra shis spun bza' mad bzhis rdzong zhabs khyim sa/ shar khram {phran} lam/ nub o rgyan khang rtsa/ lho a hor khang rtsa/ byang sa tshong khang rtsa/ dkyus la cam so (khru dang 'dra) sum cu thams {tham} pa/ zhing {zheng} la cam so nyi shu rtsa lnga yul {yun} nan er khas byan hrang 'ol cung la ji srid bar btsong {btsongs} pa'i rin dngul spus bzang srang sum cu thams {tham} pa sprad len byas nas khyim 'gebs bzo ci byed kyang / nyos mis {nyo mis} dbang ba ma gtogs/ sa tshong mi dang nye rigs nas phar bslu chad med/ gal srid rjes bshad lab gleng gi 'gal cha'i rigs byed tshe/ khrims rtsa ra dang 'ba' gser srang gsum bka' gnang sgrub chad/ 'di mi 'gyur ba tsha ba {bo}/ 'bog sman/ bkra shis spun bcas bza' mi bzhi'i rtags/ bar mi lding o rgyan gyi rtags/ mgo pa dge slong bzang gi rtags/ yig dan bzo cang bsan 'thin gyi rtags/ ngo ya khas cang dbang gi rtags/ gying bzhung gyas kyi rtags/ cang khyil lor gyi rtags/ yos yon yong gi rtags/ yang rtsas khyil gyi rtags/ tshe ring gi rtags/.*

18. Schuh 1988, 14, 15, 168.

19. Digitized Tibetan Archives Bonn, Kundeling Archives, ID 1825, 2065.

economy, through property and contract, could be structurally coupled. When political domination acquires the monopoly on physical violence as a means of sanction, it can threaten this as a way to enforce legal regulations that allow, for example, system formation in the economy without that process being repeatedly disturbed by intruding physical violence.[20]

Overall, though, trade with plots of land remained a marginal phenomenon in the Tibetan economy. Therefore it comes as no surprise that no indications of something like a land transfer tax have been identified. At the beginning of the twentieth century, the Qing government in Gyeltang (Zhongdian 中甸) and Nyinak (Nyi nag = Chi. Weixi 維西) in the modern province of Yunnan evidently tried to introduce a tax on real-estate transactions. In a decree issued in 1903,[21] the local officials were exhorted to enforce this tax—in conjunction with the complaint that so far apparently nobody had been paying this tax. Given this circumstance, a sort of desperation is expressed in this decree: "How can it be that in this large valley, under the paymaster of Gyeltang, no business transactions with plots, farmland, and houses are carried out?!"[22] As we have seen in Gyeltang, landed property was indeed traded, yet real-estate taxes were apparently never paid.

Conclusion

Based on the findings from Tibetan legal documents, we are now able to answer a bit more precisely the fundamental question, who owned land and houses in traditional Tibetan societies? Most of the land was indeed owned by the ruler. It was organized in large estates that were either controlled directly by the ruler's government and administrated with the help of deputed stewards or given in feudal-like relationships to loyal subjects of the aristocratic and clerical elite.

However, since political domination in Tibetan society ensured law enforcement through its superior power, legal regulation in principle could have been used to enable the functional differentiation of a subsystem "economy" without the constant danger of violent interference. The necessary components were already extant: property rights that were legally bound and protected by

20. See Luhmann 2000, 56–58.

21. Sems kyi nyi zla rdzong mi dmangs srid gzhung gi khun sdod don gcod khang 2003, no. 055.

22. Sems kyi nyi zla rdzong mi dmangs srid gzhung gi khun sdod don gcod khang 2003, no. 055: *rgyal thang phogs dpon 'og tu lung chen po 'di nang sa zhing gdan gsum nyo tshong mi byed pa'i {pa} ga la srid kyang/.*

contract, enabling the use of property "as an aggregate state of money"[23] for economic operations. However, the amount of land bound by such legal agreements was small. Most farmable land was used by the ruler to ensure the loyalty of the upper class "from the perspective of a moderate balance of giving and taking."[24] Land also constituted the economic means of existence for numerous monasteries. Consequently, most land was not available to be entered into a profit-oriented economic cycle.

Nevertheless, beyond the large estates that constituted the ruler's economic base, it was common throughout Tibet for people and households not belonging to the aristocracy to own private property on a small scale—plots of land and houses that they could trade or donate at will without asking their chiefs for permission. The best evidence for this widespread kind of private ownership are the standardized property sales contracts found all over the Tibetan plateau.

References

Carrasco, Pedro. 1959. *Land and Polity in Tibet.* Seattle: University of Washington Press.

Digitized Tibetan Archives Bonn: Kundeling Archives [Results of a research project under the direction of Peter Schwieger in collaboration with the Archives of the Tibet Autonomous Region, Lhasa, 1999–2001]. https://dtab.crossasia.org.

Gtsan-smyon He-ru-ka (Gtsang smyon He ru ka). 1982 [1977]. *The Life of Milarepa.* Translated by Lobsang P. Lhalungpa. Boulder, CO: Prajñā Press.

Jin Hui, Ren Yinong, and Ma Naihui, eds. 1995. *Social History of Tibet, China: Documented and Illustrated.* Beijing: China Intercontinental Press.

Kapstein, Matthew T. 2006. *The Tibetans.* Oxford: Blackwell.

Luhmann, Niklas. 1988. *Die Wirtschaft der Gesellschaft.* Frankfurt am Main: Suhrkamp.

———. 1989. *Gesellschaftsstruktur und Semantik: Studien zur Wissenssoziologie der modernen Gesellschaft*, vol. 3. Frankfurt am Main: Suhrkamp.

———. 2000. *Die Politik der Gesellschaft.* Edited by André Kieserling. Frankfurt am Main: Suhrkamp.

———. 2004. *Law as a Social System.* Translated by Klaus A. Ziegert. Edited by Fatima Kastner, Richard Nobles, David Schiff, and Rosamund Ziegert. Oxford: Oxford University Press.

23. Luhmann 1988, 197: "als einen Aggregatzustand von Geld."

24. Luhmann 1989, 104: "unter dem Gesichtspunkt eines maßvollen Ausgleichs von Geben und Nehmen."

Schuh, Dieter. 1981. *Tibetische Handschriften und Blockdrucke*, part 8: *Sammlung Waddell der Staatsbibliothek Preussischer Kulturbesitz Berlin.* Verzeichnis der Orientalischen Handschriften in Deutschland 11. Wiesbaden: Franz Steiner Verlag.

———. 1988. *Das Archiv des Klosters bKra-sis-bsam-gtan-gliṅ von sKyid-groṅ*, part 1, *Urkunden zur Klosterordnung, grundlegende Rechtsdokumente und demographisch bedeutsame Dokumente, Findbücher*. Bonn: Vereinigung für Geschichtswissenschaft Hochasiens Wissenschaftsverlag.

———. 2008. *Herrscherurkunden und Privaturkunden aus Westtibet (Ladakh)*. Halle: International Institute for Tibetan and Buddhist Studies.

Sems kyi nyi zla rdzong mi dmangs srid gzhung gi khun sdod don gcod khang, ed. 2003. *Rgyal thang gi lo rgyus yig tshags dpyad gzhi phyogs bsgrigs* [Edition of Tibetan documents from Gyeltang together with translations into Chinese by Sönam Gyatso (Bsod nams rgya mtsho) and Sherap Gyatso (Shes rab rgya mtsho)]. Kunming: Yun nan mi rigs dpe skrun khang.

Stein, Rolf A. 1972. *Tibetan Civilization*. Translated by J. E. Stapleton Driver. London: Faber and Faber.

Volkert, Wilhelm. 1991. *Adel bis Zunft: Ein Lexikon des Mittelalters*. Munich: C. H. Beck.

The Institution of the Qinghai Amban

Gray Tuttle

When thinking of the time I spent with Leonard, my fondest memories are at his pond-side house in rural Massachusetts, where he and Ning hosted many wonderful parties with such a wide range of interesting people and where he carefully went over my dissertation with me page by page. And his love of books is infectious! I remember well that he warned that getting the books was easy but having the time to read them was quite another challenge. All too true, alas.

EXPLORING AN INSTITUTION as poorly documented in the secondary literature as the Qinghai Amban is a challenging task with rich rewards. Though the scholarly literature has mostly been restricted to brief mentions within larger treatments of the Qing government as a whole or the Board for Managing the Frontiers (Lifan yuan 理藩院) in particular, combining these studies with the copious accounts of travelers and residents in the region yields a complex picture of a hitherto little-understood institution. The institution of the Qinghai Amban started in 1725, in the aftermath of the Lobjang Danjin conflict with the Manchu forces. This essay will outline its origins and administrative structure and will summarize the various duties of the Amban that can be discovered in various narrative accounts and imperial documents.

The Origins of the Institution of the Qinghai Amban

The Manchus' conception of universal emperorship had ideological space for a diversity of forms of government under its sway and in relation to the emperor.[1] As far as the Mongols and the Tibetans were concerned, the applicability of the Manchu emperor's universal rule over their particular forms of government had a precedent in Mongol imperial rule, especially because the Manchus embraced Tibetan Buddhism. The special nature of this relationship was not lost on the Manchu emperors, and they were careful to maintain a respectful

1. Chia 1992, 96.

relationship with the Mongol noble families who submitted to them and to the Tibetan Buddhist hierarchs who acknowledged their dominion.[2]

To deal with the more exceptional relations with Inner Asians, the Manchu emperors developed some unique institutions never seen in previous dynasties. Before the Manchus invaded China, they had demonstrated a unique ability to work with the Mongols, as embodied in the institution of the Mongolian Office (Menggu yamen 蒙古衙門), which became the Board for Managing the Frontiers (Lifan yuan) in 1638. This high-level institution served the court's needs for normal bureaucratic administration and relations with Inner Asian peoples throughout the dynasty.[3] Another novel institution developed by the Qing was that of the Amban, which took the temporary position of an envoy (*amban*) of the court and made it into a permanent official bureaucratic position. The first Qing Amban to be appointed anywhere in the empire was the Qinghai Amban, in 1725, in the aftermath of the Lobjang Danjin conflict. The need for such a permanent appointment, it is clear, was at least partly linked to smoothing over the brutality which General Nian Gengyao 年羹堯 meted out during the conflict.

The Yongzheng emperor's disappointment with the men who handled the conflict in 1725 led to the permanent disgrace of Generals Funinggan 富寧安, Yanxin 延信, and Nian Gengyao (only Yue Zhongqi 岳鍾琪 escaped punishment).[4] In addition to the expanded network of imperial officialdom, the emperor had access to the councils of the Tibetan Buddhist hierarchs who were from the region in question.[5] Thus the emperor understood and punished the mismanagement of these important border regions.[6] The appointment of a permanent high-level Manchu official to oversee relations with the Kokonor Mongols and neighboring Tibetans was an appropriate, and apparently effective, response to dealing with these strategically and ideologically important elements of Inner Asian society that existed outside the borders (*bianwai* 邊外) of China proper.

An examination of the historical context of this new appointment is helpful

2. Farquhar 1978.

3. Chia 1992, 28–29.

4. This seems to have been largely as a result of the special favor of the emperor's brother, Prince Yi. See Bartlett 1991, 70.

5. Thu'u bkwan 1989, 89. Translated and cited as "p. 88" in Wang 1995, 69.

6. Hummel 1970, 589, 908: These crimes include "taking daughters of Mongolian princes as concubines; ordering high officials to kneel in his presence" [this may refer to offenses against the ranked Tibetan Buddhist clergy; for another example of such a breach in protocol, see Wang 1995, 163] . . . and "illegally appropriat[ing] 100,000 teals in Tibet in 1720."

in understanding how and why this institution came into existence. Because the Qoshot Mongols lived between the two centers of Asian authority in the seventeenth century, the Manchu Qing dynasty and the Tibetan Geluk regime, certain conflicts over territory arose as the Manchu forces took over and expanded the Ming dynasty's territory. Frequently in the seventeenth century, the Qing requested the aid of the Dalai Lama in managing the Kokonor Mongols. To do so, the Dalai Lama would send a commissioner to the region.[7] In 1686, making an effort to resolve these territorial disputes peacefully, the Qing court and the regent of Tibet (in the name of the Fifth Dalai Lama) discussed "settling the nomadic Ch'ing-hai Mongols." In 1693 the Dalai Lama replied that basically he could tell the Mongols to settle, but if they refused, the Tibetan forces in the region could not enforce his order.[8]

To resolve the problem, high-level representatives were sent by both governments to work together on the issue. The Kangxi emperor sent Ladugu, a Board for Managing the Frontiers vice-minister, and Wendaer, a first-degree imperial guard.[9] The regent Sanggyé Gyatso (again in the name of the Fifth Dalai Lama) sent Jampaling Khenpo (Byams pa gling Mkhan po) as the Administrator of Qinghai Affairs (Guanli Qinghai shi 管理青海師).[10] The likely Tibetan title for this position was the [A]mdo Garpön (Mdo sgar dpon), and the Garpön title is often glossed as "high commissioner," though it literally means "camp commander."[11] The holder of this title was a "representative of the [Tibetan] central government in the northern part of [Mdo] Khams."[12] The functions of this officerholder "were infinite, but possibly more on the lines of a resident in vassal states." Petech notes that this position also existed in the territory of Ngari, which had been annexed to Tibet in 1684 and was "still considered as a territory enjoying a special status."[13] Here then, from the Tibetan administrator of the Qinghai region, is the model for the Manchu Ambans: a specially appointed resident of a territory of special status. The presence of this

7. Ahmad 1970, 68–69, 196–97.

8. Ahmad 1970, 71. This problem arose from Qing incursions into Qoshot Mongol territory. In 1694 the territory of the lower valleys of the Huangshui (Tsong chu) and Datong River ('Ju lag) was annexed, against Mongol protest, to the Qing empire (Ahmad 1970, 198).

9. Chia 1992, 276.

10. Ahmad 1970, 71–72.

11. As late as 1824 there are references to a Xining Garpön (Zi ling sgar dpon) who was accompanying a caravan from Lhasa to Xining. See Shabkar 1994, 486.

12. Petech 1972, 254, citing the *Life of the Seventh Dalai Lama*, written after 1757 by Changkya Rölpé Dorjé.

13. Petech 1972, 254.

figure undermines Farquhar's suggestion that "the residents [Ambans] appear to be purely Chinese solutions to the new conditions prevailing" in Inner Asia.[14] Instead, it appears that this Central Tibetan envoy sent to supervise the Qoshot Mongols became a model for the later Qing efforts to establish their own special representative in this area.

The first mention we have of a high Manchu official receiving an official post in the Qinghai area is not until 1717, possibly because Central Tibetan influence was waning in the region given the chaos in Central Tibet. In that year, the Kangxi emperor appointed a Board for Managing the Frontiers vice-minister, Changshou, as what Chia Ning calls the "Grand Minister Superintendency of Xining."[15] This seems to be a precursor to the Qinghai Amban position that started only in 1725, after which its authority grew.[16] According to the *Annals of Xining* (*Xiningfu xinzhi* 西寧府新志; first compiled between 1755 and 1762), "the tribal jurisdiction of the Amban derived from a meeting that had been held in 1732 between the provinces of Szech'uan and Shen[hsi]-Kan[su]."[17] This meeting solidified the position of the Qinghai Amban as a broker with the "tribes" of Mongols and Tibetans in relation to the neighboring Chinese provinces.

The misunderstanding of a temporary envoy for a permanent Amban position has been treated at length by Petech with regard to the Tibetan Amban. Petech took some pains to clarify that the ambans who came to Tibet between 1723 and 1727 were "as expressly stated by Chinese texts . . . no permanent residents, had no administrative power and were without [a staff of] colleagues." Only after the Tibetan civil war and the approval of the emperor did the envoys (*amban*) present in Tibet become the official Ambans in Tibet with a supporting staff.[18] As an aside, the last Ambanship to be created was that of the Urga Amban. As with the Qinghai and Central Tibet Ambanships, the Urga Ambanship was created after rebellious political leaders in the Tibetan Buddhist world of the Mongols had almost succeeded in pulling away from the influence of the Manchu empire. Thus these official positions all handled

14. Farquhar 1978, 297.

15. Chia 1992, 123. Although she does not give the Chinese, this should be the translation of Xining Banshi dachen 西寧辦事大臣, which is a combination of the common title (Xining Amban) encountered in travel literature and the official title (Qinghai Banshi dachen 青海辦事大臣). See Rockhill 1891, 51. For the Manchu translation, see Farquhar 1960, 310.

16. See Wenfu 1993, 1.

17. Schram 1954, 21. See also Rockhill 1891, 187–88, for the effect this had on the people of Yushu 玉樹 (Khams).

18. Petech 1972, 86, 156, 255; for a list of Ambans to 1752, 284.

the delicate relations with Tibetan Buddhist hierarchs and their neighboring adherents, especially in the aftermath of Mongol-Tibetan Buddhist alliances that the Qing perceived as rebellious.[19]

The Administrative Structure of the Qinghai Amban

The relationship between the Qinghai Amban and the Qing court is ambiguous in nearly all secondary literature on the topic. The institution of the Qinghai Amban received passing notice in the Western-language works that document the government of the late Qing empire—Mayers and Playfair's *The Chinese Government: A Manual of Chinese Titles* as well as Brunnert and Hagelstrom's *Present Day Political Organization of China*—each of which gives a few details on this peculiar institution. Mayers lists the title of this official as the "Imperial Controller-General of Kokonor" (Zongli Qinghai shiwu dachen 總理青海事務大臣) and defines this official as being "invested with control of the Mongol and Tangutian (*fan* 番) tribes of the Ch'ing-Hai or Kokonor region."[20] Brunnert and Hagelstrom clarify that the Mongol and Tangut tribes were ruled directly by their own chieftains, who were only "under the sway of the Chinese Amban at Xining." The Tangut leaders of the forty Tibetan tribes in this area were called *tusi* 土司, and it was noted that they were under the Amban.[21] As for the Qinghai Mongol tribes, like the Khalkha, their government was described as being in their own hands, "with almost no interference from the Chinese higher authorities."[22]

In his treatment of Mongolia, Tibet, and Chinese Turkestan, Hsieh Pao Chao opens his discussion of the governance of these regions with the assertion that "organizations like the six departments [of the central government] . . . had nothing to do with the governments" of these outer regions. He also clearly places the Ministry for Managing the Frontiers (Lifan bu 理藩部) in charge of all these regions.[23] Given the concurrence of the Amban's control of Qinghai and the Lifan yuan's control of all frontier dependencies (which

19. When the Qinghai Amban post was created, the Kokonor Mongols were strong supporters of the Seventh Dalai Lama, on whom the Manchu were pinning their hopes for a stable regime in Tibet. See Katô 1993, 57–80; and Satô 1993.

20. Mayers and Playfair 1970, 103. Entry 524 (92) lists the Kokonor Mongols but not the Tibetan (Tangut/*fan*) tribes under the Amban's jurisdiction.

21. Brunnert and Hagelstrom 1912, 463–64. Almost as many tribes (thirty-nine) were under the Dalai Lama.

22. Brunnert and Hagelstrom 1912, 443, 464.

23. Hsieh 1925, 321–22.

explicitly include Qinghai), one might conclude from Hsieh's description that the Amban was under the Board for Managing the Frontiers.[24] Furthermore, the duties and scope of the Amban's powers were stipulated in the *Statutes of the Board for Managing the Frontiers* (*Lifan yuan zeli* 理藩院则例).[25]

In practice, however, the Qinghai Amban directly represented the emperor in this region. Farquhar, in the final paragraph of his chapter on the Qing "Central Control Apparatus," defines the relation between the high officials (Ambans) and the Qing court:

> Being imperial, not ministerial, officials, they linked the emperor directly to affairs in Mongolia, and they constitute a good example of the tendency of the absolutist Ming and Ch'ing rulers to bypass the ministries and assume personal control over important matters.[26]

As to how the office (*yamen* 衙門) of the Qinghai Amban was staffed, we are lucky to have Rockhill's own account, likely based on his time traveling in Qinghai, including time spent with one of the agents from the office. First, Rockhill explains that the Amban "represents the emperor in all matters relating to the administration of, or ceremonial relations with, the non-Chinese section of the population of this part of the empire." According to Rockhill, the Amban's staff consists of "a number of secretaries and clerks (*Pih-t'ieh-she*)." The more important group in the administrative structure of the Ambanship was the corps of thirty-two agents (*T'ung-shih*); on the latter devolve the primary duties of his office. They carry the orders of their head to the different chieftains, arbitrate quarrels between the tribes, collect the money tribute, and are practically the only representatives of the Chinese government among the remoter tribes.[27]

As a reminder, these thirty-two agents were all the Qing court had to do its business in Qinghai (a region the size of France), in contrast to a typical Chinese county, which had between one hundred and two thousand clerks to do the magistrate's business. As to what this business was, we are fortunate in pos-

24. Circumstantial evidence that this is not the case is available for the Urga Ambanship. Farquhar (1960, 289–90) demonstrates that the Amban, Grand Secretariat, Board of War, and Board for Managing the Frontiers each had their own offices in Urga. The implication is clearly that they were not subordinate but parallel organizations.

25. Chia 1992, 124, citing vols. 61–62 of the *Lifan yuan zeli*.

26. Farquhar 1960, 315.

27. Rockhill 1891, 52.

sessing a wealth of information about the daily functioning of the Ambanship to illuminate the practical functions of the Qinghai Amban.

Rights and Responsibilities of the Qinghai Amban

The expectations laid upon the Amban were, like those of the Tibetan Garpön and the Chinese magistrate, comprehensive. His duties included communication between the Qing court and the local leaders, confirmation of titles to the local leaders, participation in ritual activities, collection of tribute or taxes, monitoring of the economic life at the borders through the issuance of trade passes, maintaining peace and security of the borderlands through the suppression of banditry, as well as serving as a judge in some contexts. The principal right the Amban had in order to permit him and his staff to fulfill these responsibilities was access to *ulak*: corvée labor, use of animals, and a supply of food and shelter. Accurate population figures for Qinghai are difficult to find, but one estimate suggests between fifty thousand and seventy thousand Mongolians and Tibetans were under the authority of the Amban.[28] These tribal groups, many of them nomadic and therefore highly mobile, were spread over a huge area. Given the enormous range of his duties, the small size of his staff, and the dispersed and often hostile population that he was supposed to oversee, it is no surprise that the Amban failed to adequately fulfill many of these duties.

Communication

As with so much of the Chinese bureaucracy, probably the most important task of the Amban was communication. It appears that for routine matters of communication, such as the promotion or confirmation of native rulers, the emperor would relay these messages through the Board for Managing the Frontiers to the Qinghai Amban.[29] However, for more urgent matters, the emperor could communicate directly with the Amban. Around 1845, the emperor ordered both the Qinghai Amban and the Shaanxi-Gansu

28. Rockhill 1891, 82. This figure is based on the 1725 census of non-Chinese under the supervision of the Amban. See also Schram 1954, 21, which gives the results of the 1918 census of Tibetans in the region: roughly forty thousand Tibetans outside the borders and forty-two thousand inside the borders under subprefectural administration. Using Rockhill's 1891 ratio of two Amdo Tibetans to one Mongolian (as residents in the Buddhist monasteries), we can get a rough idea of the population for which the Amban was held responsible.

29. Chia 1992, 126.

governor-general to prevent rumors of rebellion from spreading within their jurisdictions in response to the dismissal of the Tibetan regent of the Dalai Lama, whose home region was south of Taozhou, Gansu.[30] When the Lhasa Ambans were killed after murdering the king of Tibet, Gyurmé Namgyel ('Gyur med rnam rgyal), the emperor took quick measures to prevent their murderers from escaping to the Dzungars by ordering the Qinghai Amban to be on his guard, in 1750. Interestingly, a separate circular letter was sent around to the leading monks in the Kokonor region, which may indicate that these men were not under the jurisdiction of the Amban, or at least not in good communication with the Amban.[31] These were all exceptionally important events, while the only demonstrable role in routine communication played by the Qinghai Amban was that mentioned by Rockhill in his discussion of the agents who carried the Amban's orders out to the various chieftains.[32]

Conferral of Titles

Related to his role as representative of the Qing court, the Qinghai Amban was responsible for conferring imperial titles upon "native" leaders. This role seems to have been more regularized with relation to the Mongolian tribes than with the Tibetans, as will be seen from the following examples. Once again, Rockhill is our primary source:

> Every year these princes [the Mori Wang and Chinghai Wang of the Koko-nor Mongols] are bound to repair to Tankar [modern Huangyuan, then a trading town on the border of Qinghai and Gansu] to visit the emperor's legate, the Amban, who confers on them gifts in the name of his master, and then they renew their oaths of fealty by doing obeisance before an imperial throne. . . . The Panak'a [Sba nag kha (gsum)] or Koko-nor Tibetans are not held to the accomplishment of these duties. . . .[33]

As for Tibetan leaders who did receive titles from the Qinghai Amban, Rockhill notes that the Amdowas, by which he means the Tibetans living within the borders of Gansu, were led by their own leaders under the supervision of the Amban, who "confers on them Chinese official rank, a button,

30. Zheng 1991.

31. Petech 1972, 222.

32. Rockhill 1891, 52. This may be linked to the league presidency, which the Amban seems to have acquired by the twentieth century, possibly as early as 1822.

33. Rockhill 1891, 263; see also 54.

and a title. Only one of the two Sba nag (Black) Tibetans leaders, the Konsa lama, is even nominally under the supervision of the Amban, and he has a blue button."[34]

Another instance of the Qinghai Amban making appointments is concerned more with his supervisory powers than his role as a representative of imperial commissions. Unfortunately, Rockhill's description is not specific as to the ethnicity of the appointee—the subject discussed here may well have been Mongol, Monguor, or even Chinese rather than a Tibetan. The passage deserves quoting in full:

> In a few of the larger monasteries there is an official appointed by the Amban who assists the lama officials (*seng-kuan*) in enforcing discipline, but whose principal duty consists in observing the spirit animating the convent, whether it is friendly or hostile to the Chinese government and keeping the Amban duly posted. This official is styled Erh-lao-yeh, or "the second old gentleman," by the Chinese.[35]

At present, we have little information with which to evaluate this position. How long had it been in existence? How regularly was the post filled and by whom? How effective was its information gathering? To judge by the fact that Huc and Gabet in the 1840s (as well as Rockhill several times some fifty years later) were able to avoid the Ambans while openly living at Kumbum Monastery for long periods suggests that these officials were either very lax in their duties or nonexistent.[36]

34. Prejevalsky 1876 says five banners of Tibetans living on the right bank of the Yellow River were directly under the Amban's authority without any mediating leader such as these two Mongol princes. Rockhill's more reliable account records that there were two leaders of the Sba nag kha gsum, the more influential of which lived north of Kokonor and is called the "Konsa lama." See Rockhill 1891, 260. It is interesting to note that only the Mongolian princes and apparently not the Tibetan leaders were expected to pay triennial tribute at the imperial capital.

35. Rockhill 1891, 87.

36. The case of Huc and Gabet is particularly interesting because they were openly proselytizing at the monastery at a time when it was still illegal to do so in China, yet according to their account, they lived for three months at the monastery "enjoying the friendly sympathy of the Buddhist monks and the protection of the authorities." See Huc and Gabet 1928, vol. 1, 77.

Ritual Duties

No doubt the Ambans had many ritual duties, but here I will mention only one noticed by Rockhill in his travels. The Qinghai Amban was based at Xining near Kumbum Monastery and was observed at one of the most important rituals of the religious year for Tibetan Buddhists in the region. When Rockhill was present at Kumbum Monastery's famous butter-sculpture festival at the new year, he observed that the Qinghai Amban and higher Chinese authorities visited the monastery on the fifteenth of the new year.[37]

Collection of Tribute/Taxation and *Ulak*

For all the importance that tax or tribute collection usually holds to indicate Chinese governance or dominion over a region, there is remarkably little information on the topic for Qinghai. All that we know from secondary sources is thanks to Rockhill, who encountered one of the Amban's agents on his tax-collection rounds. Apparently the division of territory between Qing and Central Tibetan zones of influence in 1732 resulted in the imposition of a token tribute for Tibetans. For every group of one hundred Tibetans (over which there was a leader, called a *depa* [*sde pa*]), the emperor was due one horse. At some later date, the horse tribute was changed to a poll tax.[38] The Banak Tibetans living north of Kokonor contributed a small poll tax, but their southern neighbors owed nothing at all to the Manchu authorities.[39] As for the Amdowa Tibetans living inside the borders, they also owed the Amban "the payment of the tribute money or poll tax."[40]

Related to this taxation, and making it possible to travel through this vast country without exhausting the government's resources, was the tradition of *ulak*. Those peoples who were liable to taxation were required to service those officials who presented them with an *ulak* order, which entitled the bearer to "a certain number of men, saddle and pack animals, food, etc., to be supplied at specified stations."[41] The burden of this *ulak* was very severe on the people in this sparsely populated country, so when they could, they tried to

37. Rockhill 1891, 255–57.

38. Rockhill 1891, 353; see also 187–88.

39. Rockhill 1891, 263; and Prejevalsky 1876, 153.

40. Rockhill 1891, 72–73.

41. Rockhill 1891, 52.

avoid rendering these services.[42] Rockhill describes how the service was prone to great abuse, yielding enormous profits for Manchu officials and impoverishing the countryside. This problem was well understood by Manchu authorities, as attested in Songyun's 松筠 *Illustrated Plan for Managing the West Xizhao tu lüe* 西招圖略, which illustrates "by numerous examples how the country has been depopulated by excessive demands of *ulak*."[43] Correspondingly, the tribes and districts that were not under the authority of the Amban did not provide these services without reimbursement.[44]

Economic Aspects of the Amban's Duties

The origin of the Qinghai Amban's economic role in the region is not clearly described in any of the secondary literature. However, combining the later travel accounts with Chia Ning's research into the Board for Managing the Frontiers, we have a rough idea of the Amban's place in the economy of the region. Chia says that after the Lobjang Danjin conflict was resolved, "when the court determined trade between China proper and Ch'ing-hai, the court also established marketplaces outside China proper and let the Chinese go *pien-wai* (beyond the border) for business." The "determination" of trade on the China-Qinghai border refers to the multiplication of the frequency and locations of market fairs. In 1723 an exchange fair was set up in Xining; shortly thereafter the annual number of fairs was doubled and additional exchange fairs were opened in Songpan and Hezhou. Finally, the Yongzheng emperor ordered fairs to remain open most of the year.[45]

Chia says that the exchange fairs set up on the borders in the Qing dynasty were under the control of the Board for Managing the Frontiers,[46] but Rockhill's experience suggests that this duty was actually exercised by the Qinghai Amban. First it should be noted that the trade restrictions seem to have applied entirely to the Chinese who wished to do business across the border. Tibetans and Mongols could probably trade at will in the exchange fairs in Xining, Hezhou, and Songpan, but could only go much further (into China proper) as part of lucrative tribute missions to the Manchu court. The regulations on the Chinese were as follows:

42. Rockhill 1891, 139.

43. Rockhill n.d., 53.

44. Rockhill 1891, 72–73, 141, 263.

45. Chia 1992, 326–27. Chia says that the order was that the "markets should remain open all the time after June every year."

46. Chia 1992, 321.

> All Chinese wishing to trade among the Mongols and Tibetans across the frontier must apply to the Amban for a pass (*piao*), for which they pay Tls. 2 for every man they intend taking with them. As this pass is only good for forty days, it almost invariably expires before they can return home, and they become liable to heavy fines and even confiscation of their goods. The T'ung shih [the Amban's agents] do their best to detect any traders they suspect of not having their passes in order, and the latter are obliged, if caught, to give the former presents, frequently of considerable value, for overlooking the irregularity.[47]

While in the district of Shang (the Central Tibetan fief in the Tsaidam Basin) Rockhill encountered some Chinese traders who were hiding there from the Amban's agent. One of their number had apparently been caught with an expired pass and fined by the agent the previous year, and they hid in the mountains to avoid the agent's exactions.[48]

By their own account, these traders were not able to make much profit even without running into the Amban's agent. Rather than damaging the indigenous traders and making the people dependent on the Chinese, the "system of forty-day passes has . . . practically killed legitimate trade between the Kan-su people and the Tibetans and Mongols, and has encouraged a large contraband trade carried on from Sung-p'an t'ing in northwestern Ssu-ch'uan."[49] The imperial economic policy in this region actually stimulated indigenous trade:

> The Sharba of Sung-p'an supply the Koko-nor and Ts'aidam at lower rates than the Kan-su traders can, and, their sojourn outside of China not being limited by any pass, they are free to go where they please and stay there as long as they see fit.[50]

Thus it seems these policies were mostly beneficial to the Tibetan peoples living outside the borders.

47. Rockhill 1891, 53. Tls. is short for *taels*, a Chinese unit of currency.

48. Rockhill 1891, 141.

49. Rockhill 1891, 112.

50. Rockhill 1891, 112. Rockhill lists tea (the principal commodity), leather boots, cotton goods, hardware, tobacco, and copper kettles as the goods they sell.

Border Duties

The Amban's responsibilities associated with managing the border were twofold: first, he was responsible for issuing passes that permitted people to travel beyond the borders, and second, he was supposed to maintain peace among the tribes and the settled peoples living under his jurisdiction. In both these respects, the Qinghai Amban was less than successful. However, it seems that the job did maintain stability—not in the region and for the people under his jurisdiction, but rather with regard to the maintenance of the border between China proper and the region beyond. Information about the passes required (or not) of travelers in this region are plentiful in the travelogues. The picture that these accounts give is that despite the importance with which the Amban's travel passes are treated, they were absolutely not essential for traveling in the area under the Amban's supposed jurisdiction.

Of course, most of the locals in any official capacity attached some weight to the Amban's travel passes, since they would be held responsible for anything that happened if they let people travel without them. However, none of the European travelers in the region actually got a pass from the Amban and yet they all moved successfully through the territory. With the exception of Prejevalsky, who traveled at a time when the Amban had been displaced from Xining by a Muslim rebellion, all of these travelers made long and public preparations for their trips into Qinghai in such a way that the Amban was sure to have been informed of their presence. These travelers were aware that they should avoid Qing authorities if at all possible.[51] Thus, although a headman in Qinghai might hesitate to help a traveler without the Amban's pass, as the *jasagh* of Baron did when Rockhill requested his aid in reaching Central Tibet, not everyone respected this rule. The *jasagh*'s steward readily agreed to the task.[52]

Interestingly, the Amban's pass was not the only such valuable document in the region. Prejevalsky had an introductory letter from a monastery he had helped defend from Muslim rebels that gained him access to the assistance of the Mori Wang, prince of the northern Mongols of the Kokonor region.[53] Likewise Rockhill was informed that one experienced trader "considered it necessary . . . to have a pass, if not the Amban's, at least one from the chief of

51. Huc and Gabet 1928, vol. 1, 376–87, and vol. 2, 77. Rockhill 1891, 17, 257, 880.

52. Rockhill 1891, 358.

53. Prejevalsky 1876, vol. 2, 155.

the north Koko-nor Panak'a, the Konsa lama, for it was respected throughout Tibet, and had the advantage of costing much less than the former."[54]

Border Security

The Amban utterly failed to keep peace among the people under his jurisdiction. Two examples of the Amban's failure to end interethnic strife in the region will suffice to demonstrate this. First, in both 1840 and 1841, the Dalai Lama's tribute mission to the Qing court had been attacked by Golok Tibetans who had managed to kidnap the Gyanak Khenpo (Rgya nag Mkhan po; literally "the China Abbot," the Dalai Lama's envoy to the Qing court) in the first year and kill the envoy the next year. The Amban was completely unable to do anything about these attacks, so the tribute missions from Tibet were reduced to once every three years.[55] Another example illustrates how the Ambans sought the intercession of Tibetan Buddhist lamas when they were unable to handle the security problems in their jurisdiction. When Changkya Rolpé Dorjé was in the area for the funeral of his father, he was called on to mediate between two Tibetan leaders. This was obviously a serious affair, as the emperor himself requested Rolpé Dorjé's aid, and the meeting took place with the Sichuan governor-general and the Qinghai Amban. Rolpé Dorjé was successful in resolving the problem.[56] For further evidence of constant warfare among Tibetan tribal groups, and the uselessness of appeals to the authority of the Amban, see Shabkar's biography.[57]

Conclusion

The shift from an Amban institution that largely mediated on behalf of the emperor with Tibetan and Mongol populations outside the border of China

54. Rockhill 1891, 113.

55. Huc and Gabet 1928, vol. 1, 124. When Huc and Gabet encountered some of these Golok "brigands" they were told that the Golok only attack the missions that travel from the Dalai Lama to the Qing court because the emperor does not deserve the tribute, and not in the other direction, as the Dalai Lama does deserve the gifts of the emperor (154). This was fortunate for the caravan, as the Chinese soldiers, who provided little security in the first place, had turned back at the edge of the Tsaidam Basin (125). For other examples of the Amban's incredible lack of ability when dealing with border security, see Huc and Gabet 1928, vol. 2, 12–13, 105–7; Prejevalsky 1876, vol. 2, 150–51; Rockhill n.d., 262; Rockhill 1891, 184–85; and Rockhill 1910, 70.

56. Wang 1995, 168.

57. Shabkar 1994, 501–2.

proper and was not well integrated into the Qing civil institutions came only in the twentieth century.[58] At the start of the twentieth century, as Han Chinese conceptions of China's territorial sovereignty changed, the 1906 administrative reforms changed the nature of the Qinghai Amban's position. The placement of the Ambans within the Department of War was part of the reorganization of the military according to Western standards (begun in 1903 under Yuan Shikai and put into effect in 1906). With Han Chinese control over much of the government that had traditionally been in Manchu control, the conception of the proper relations between the imperial representatives and the frontier dependencies naturally changed. As Chia Ning states so conclusively in her dissertation on the Board for Managing the Frontiers, "When the Manchus ruled China, imperial sovereignty was not the same as Chinese sovereignty."[59]

But after 1906, according to Hsieh, these imperial residents "represented the central government in a stricter governing sense; that is, [the Ambans] exercised more of the governing powers than they used to by taking more matters of importance in their own hands."[60] Hsieh clearly viewed the Ministry for Managing the Frontiers' modern innovations in 1907—described in Brunnert and Hagelstrom as the addition of a Department of Colonization, to exploit resources, and a Department of Frontier Defense, to control Mongol and Tibetan troops, etc.—as representative of the imperial efforts to increase governance of the frontier dependencies. Further support for associating the Amban's subordination to the Department of War with modernization is the fact that in 1915 Yuan Shikai officially terminated this institution and put Qinghai under the control of a Muslim general.[61] Despite this official termination of the post, the Amban was still performing functions related to *ulak* and Tibetan Buddhist lamas when the Paṇchen Lama came through this area in 1924.[62] It is in this enduring function, with the Amban representing a distant government to the east in the face of encounters with Tibetan lamas and local leaders, that we see the most crucial role of this official post for the three centuries it was in existence.

58. Hsieh 1925, 323. See also Kolmas, 1992, 545; and Kolmas 1994, 457.

59. Chia 1992, 17.

60. Hsieh 1925, 323.

61. Wylie 1962, 194n753.

62. Tuttle 2005, chap. 2.

References

Ahmad, Zahiruddin. 1970. *Sino-Tibetan Relations in the Seventeenth Century*. Serie Orientale Roma 40. Rome: Istituto Italiano per il Medio ed Estremo Oriente.

Bartlett, Beatrice S. 1991. *Monarchs and Ministers: The Grand Council in Mid-Ching China, 1723–1820*. Berkeley: University of California Press.

Brunnert, Īppolīt Semenovīch, and V. V. Hagelstrom. 1912. *Present Day Political Organization of China*. Shanghai: Kelly and Walsh.

Chia Ning. 1992. "The Li-fan Yuan in the Early Ch'ing Dynasty." PhD diss., Johns Hopkins University.

Farquhar, David Miller. 1960. "The Ch'ing Administration of Mongolia up to the Nineteenth Century." PhD diss., Harvard University.

———. 1978. "Emperor as Bodhisattva in the Governance of the Ch'ing Empire." *Harvard Journal of Asiatic Studies* 38.1: 5–34.

Hsieh Pao Chao. 1925. *The Government of China (1644–1911)*. Studies in Historical and Political Science. Baltimore: Johns Hopkins University Press.

Huc, Evariste Régis, and Joseph Gabet. 1928. *Travels in Tartary, Thibet and China, 1844–1846*. Translated by William Hazlitt. Edited by Paul Pelliot. London: Routledge.

Hummel, Arthur William, ed. 1970. *Eminent Chinese of the Ching Period (1644–1912)*. Taipei: Ch'eng Wen Publishing; New York: Paragon Book Gallery.

Katô Naoto. 1993. "Lobjang Danjin's Rebellion of 1723: With a Focus on the Eve of the Rebellion." *Acta Asiatica: Bulletin of the Institute of Eastern Culture* 64: 57–80.

Kolmas, Josef. 1992. "A Chronology of the Ambans of Tibet, Part I: The Ambans and Assistant Ambans in the Yongzheng and Qianlong Period (1727–1795)." In *Tibetan Studies: Proceedings of the 5th Seminar of the International Association for Tibetan Studies, Narita 1989*, edited by S. Ihara and Z. Yamaguchi, vol. 2, 541–58. Narita: Naritasan Shinshoji.

———. 1994. "The Ambans and Assistant Ambans of Tibet (1727–1912): Some Statistical Observations." In *Tibetan Studies: Proceedings of the 6th Seminar of the International Association for Tibetan Studies, Fagernes, 1992*, edited by P. Kvaerne, vol. 1, 454–67. Oslo: Institute for Comparative Research in Human Culture.

Mayers, William Frederick, and G. M. H. Playfair. 1970 [1896]. *The Chinese Government: A Manual of Chinese Titles, Categorically Arranged and Explained, with an Appendix*. Third ed., revised by G. M. H. Playfair. Taipei: Ch'eng-Wen Pub. Co.

Petech, Luciano. 1972 [1950]. *China and Tibet in the Early 18th Century: History of the Establishment of Chinese Protectorate in Tibet*. Monographies du T'oung Pao 1. Leiden: Brill.

Prejevalsky, Nikolai Mikhailovich. 1876. *Mongolia, the Tangut Country, and the Solitudes of Northern Tibet: Being a Narrative of Three Years' Travel in Eastern High Asia*. Translated by E. Delmar Morgan. Edited by Henry Yule. London: Sampson Low, Marston, Searle, and Rivington.

Rockhill, William Woodville. n.d. *Miscellaneous Papers Including Articles on Tibet and Mongolia*. Held at Harvard Yenching Library, Cambridge, MA.

———. 1891. *The Land of the Lamas: Notes of a Journey through China, Mongolia and Tibet*. London: Longmans, Green.

———. 1910. "The Dalai Lamas of Lhasa and Their Relations with the Manchu Emperors of China, 1644–1908." *T'oung Pao* 11: 1–104.

Satô Hisashi. 1993. "The Origins and Development of the Study of Tibetan History in Japan." *Acta Asiatica: Bulletin of the Institute of Eastern Culture* 64: 81–120.

Schram, Louis. 1954. *The Monguors of the Kansu-Tibetan Frontier: Their Origin, History, and Social Organization*. Introduction by Owen Lattimore. Philadelphia: The American Philosophical Society.

Shabkar Tsogdruk Rangdrol. 1994. *The Life of Shabkar: The Autobiography of a Tibetan Yogin*. Translated by Matthieu Ricard and Constance Wilkinson. Albany: State University of New York Press.

Thu'u bkwan (III) Blo bzang chos kyi nyi ma. 1989. *Zhangjia guoshi Ruobaidouojie zhuan* 章嘉国师若必多吉传. Lanzhou: Gansu minzu chubanshe.

Tuttle, Gray. 2005. *Tibetan Buddhists in the Making of Modern China*. New York: Columbia University Press.

Wang, Xiangyun. 1995. "Tibetan Buddhism at the Court of Qing: The Life and Work of lCang-skya Rol-pa'i-rdo-rje, 1717–86." PhD diss., Harvard University.

Wenfu 文孚. 1993. *Qinghai shiyi jielüe* 青海事宜节略 [Abbreviated Matters Concerned with Qinghai]. Xining: Qinghai renmin chubanshe.

Wylie, Turrell V. 1962. *The Geography of Tibet According to the 'Dzam gling rgyas bshad*. Edited by G. Tucci. Rome: Istituto Italiano per il Medio ed Estremo Oriente.

Zheng Qingyou. 1991. "Qishan and Tsemonling Nominhan." *Tibet Studies* 2.1: 151–61.

Poppy Cultivation, the Opium Trade, and Its Social Harm in Tibetan Regions of Sichuan Province during the Early Twentieth Century

Yudru Tsomu

THE IMPACT of the opium trade on state and national development in China has been an important research topic in modern Chinese history. Yet discussion rarely concerns minority regions, especially the Tibetan-speaking regions of Sichuan Province, such as Aba 阿坝 (Rnga ba) and Ganzi 甘孜 (Dkar mdzes). Drawing on recently opened archival sources and relevant social investigation reports, this paper explores the development and spread of opium cultivation and trade in those regions in the early twentieth century by addressing these questions: How did opium spread to Tibetan areas? How widespread was poppy cultivation in these regions? Who participated in these activities? What information is available to measure the economic impact of the opium trade on farmers, merchants, indigenous chieftains, headmen, warlords, soldiers, government officials, and secret societies, such as the Gowned Brotherhood (*gelaohui* 哥老會)?

Poppy Cultivation

Poppy cultivation likely started in Tibetan areas in Sichuan Province during the Guangxu 光绪 reign (1875–1908).[1] By 1831 poppy cultivation was already widespread in ethnic regions like Pingwu 平武, inhabited by Qiang 羌 and Tibetans, and in Huili 会理, where Yi 彝, Lisu 傈僳, and other minorities live. As explained below, in late Qing and Republican periods, opium production and consumption along with inland-Chinese anti-opium campaigns stimulated poppy cultivation and opium trade in Tibetan areas

By the turn of the twentieth century, Sichuan Province was the largest producer and consumer of domestic opium in China.[2] Consequently, poppy

1. Li Tao 1994, 39.

2. Wyman 2000, 212; Yao Xiguang 1908, vol. 2, 53.

cultivation gradually spread to Tibetan regions with suitable climate and soil. In Ganzi prefecture, poppy cultivation began in Danba 丹巴 (Rong brag) county in 1905.[3] In the late Qing period (i.e., 1900–1912), Yunnan traders transported opium to Kangding 康定 (Dar rtse mdo). Poppy cultivation existed in Tibetan townships such as Yutong 鱼通 (Mgo thang; Mgu thang), Kongyu 孔玉 ('Khob yul), and Jintang 金汤 (Mgo thang stod pa; Mgu thang stod pa) in Kangding county. In 1910, during the late Qing nationwide anti-opium campaign, Kangding county Magistrate Wang Dianzhang 王典章 announced a ban on poppy cultivation[4] because the scale of poppy cultivation in Kangding was so large. Similarly, Songpan subprefecture 松潘厅—comprising Songpan (Zungchu), Nanping 南坪 (present-day Jiuzhaigou 九寨沟; Tib. Gzi tsa sde dgu), Ruo'er gai 若尔盖 (Mdzo dge), and Hongyuan 红原(Dmar thang; Khyung chu) counties—was considered a poppy cultivation center.[5] In the Tibetan area of Aba, poppy cultivation initiated during the Guangxu reign in Maogong 懋功 county (present-day Xiaojin county 小金县; Tib. Btsan lha rdzong) had already been quite prevalent during the Xuantong 宣统 reign (1908–12).[6] Clearly, the late-Qing anti-opium campaign did not check poppy cultivation in Tibetan areas.

By 1915, due to efforts by the late Qing and Republican governments, poppy cultivation decreased substantially in the heartlands of Sichuan.[7] Yet, as Liu Jun 刘君 points out, with each anti-opium campaign from the late Qing period, opium cultivation moved to remote minority regions.[8] Because remote Tibetan areas and Yi regions were beyond the government's effective control, anti-opium efforts were ineffective there. Instead, suppression of poppy cultivation and opium trade in inland-Chinese regions provided minority regions with broader opium markets.[9] In the early years of the Republic of China poppies were grown on most land in Maogong county,[10] and poppy cultivation also started in Jiulong 九龙 county (Rgyad zur; Rgyad zil).[11]

3. Sichuan sheng Ganzi zangzu zizhizhou Danba xianzhi bianzuan weiyuanhui 1996, 496.

4. Liu Jun 2002, 51.

5. Wang Di 2001, 154.

6. Cao Shiyong 1992, 4.

7. Su Zhiliang 1997, 209, 228, 239.

8. Liu Jun 2002, 50.

9. For the relationship between suppression of poppy cultivation, opium trade, and opium consumption in inland-Chinese regions and poppy cultivation in Yi regions, see Qin Yi 2014, 31–32.

10. Sichuan sheng Aba zangzu qiangzu zizhizhou Xiaojin xian difangzhi bianzuan weiyuanhui 1995, 423.

11. Sichuan sheng Jiulong xian bianzuan weiyuanhui 1997, 374.

Under the area-garrison system (*fangqu zhi* 防区制) of management (1916–34), Sichuan warlords exploited the policy of "converting the ban into a tax levy" (*yujin yuzheng* 寓禁于征) in their garrison areas after 1921.[12] This led to rampant poppy farming across Sichuan. Sichuan warlords vigorously encouraged and even mandated poppy cultivation in order to receive exorbitant poppy taxes. Consequently, Sichuan "became the province with the largest opium production and most poppy fields in China."[13] There were five major poppy-growing regions corresponding to five garrison areas formed in Sichuan in the mid-1920s—each controlled by a different warlord. In the garrison area known as Chuanxi Circuit 川西道 under the control of warlord Deng Xihou 邓锡侯 from 1928 until 1935, poppies were actively farmed in the Tibetan counties of Songpan, Lifan 理番 (present-day Lixian county 理县; Tib. Bkra shis gling), Maoxian 茂县, Maogong, and Wenchuan 汶川.[14] There emerged the "opium regime" in the aforementioned Tibetan counties under warlord Deng Xihou's administration, which created a tax structure in these counties that effectively stifled other entrepreneurial pursuits in favor of poppy agriculture.[15] While poppy farming became more prevalent in Jiulong county,[16] it also expanded into Danba county in response to the magistrate's call.[17]

Between 1935 and 1940, the Nationalist government rigorously enforced eradication campaigns. "The plan to eradicate opium in six years" was quite effective in Han Chinese regions, but the geographical isolation and the lack of political control in Tibetan areas in western Sichuan allowed growers to avoid surveillance even after the policy to ban poppy cultivation.[18] As a result, Tibetan areas in western Sichuan and Yi regions had broader opium markets. Between 1936 and 1949, poppy-production regions included the entire territory of Maogong, one part of Jinghua 靖化 county (present-day Jinchuan county 金川县; Tib. Chu chen rdzong), as well as Heishui 黑水 (Khro chu), Baicao 百草,[19] Daxing 大姓, Xiaoxing 小姓,[20] and various minority regions

12. Li Longchang 1986, 117.

13. Xu Zhengxue 1936, 13–14.

14. Chen Mou 2021, 33.

15. For a detailed study of the opium regime in the Songpan region, refer to Jack Patrick Hayes 2014, 43–90.

16. Sichuan sheng Jiulong xian bianzuan weiyuanhui 1997, 374.

17. Sichuan sheng Ganzi zangzu zizhizhou Danba xianzhi bianzuan weiyuanhui 1996, 496.

18. Sichuan sheng Ganzi zangzu zizhizhou Danba xianzhi bianzuan weiyuanhui 1996, 496.

19. Baicao refers to Qiang-inhabited regions in present-day Pingwu county and Beichuan Qiang Autonomous county 北川羌族自治县 in Sichuan.

20. Daxing and Xiaoxing refer to townships in present-day Songpan 松潘 county.

under the jurisdiction of Lifan county. Other Tibetan regions also gradually started to grow poppies. The scale of poppy cultivation was the greatest in Maogong county.[21] Ma'erkang 马尔康 ('Bar khams) in western Sichuan began to grow poppy plants in 1935, and poppy farming there peaked between 1947 and 1949.[22] The Tibetan areas in the northwestern part of Sichuan named above became one of the two major opium production regions, the other being the southern part of Sichuan, including Leibo 雷波, Mabian 马边, Pingshan 屏山, and Ebian 峨边 Yi counties. Tibetan chieftains and headmen, together with Chinese strongmen—including secret-society leaders and opportunistic local despots—openly cultivated opium while also engaging in the large-scale purchase and sale of opium.

Claiming "poppy cultivation is the lifeline of our army," Liu Wenhui 刘文辉 implemented the policy of "converting the ban into a tax levy" in Xikang Province in 1942. Thus, poppy farming expanded further in Kangding, Jiulong, and Danba counties. In other Tibetan counties in present-day Ganzi prefecture, the climate and soil was not suitable for poppy farming.[23] Opium taxes were imposed on poppies cultivated in Xikang, and transit taxes were imposed on Yunnan opium passing through Kham. Also, people went to Yunnan to purchase opium and transported it with armed forces to markets in Chengdu. Thus Liu and his men reaped great profits from the opium trade in order to compensate for insufficient military provisions and funding during this time.[24]

Coercive Means and Gift Exchange

Poppy cultivation spread into Tibetan regions in Sichuan through peculiar exchange practices and other coercive means. By the beginning of the twentieth century, traditional trade and commodities exchanged by Tibetans with Chinese merchants were declining. Frontier trade was increasingly controlled by Chinese traders, especially by the Gowned Brotherhood, who were generally viewed as criminals. Tibetans in the region were becoming increasingly indebted to Chinese traders. As discussed below, these criminals colluded with local officials in forcing the local people to grow poppy plants.

Songpan is particularly representative of counties with poppy cultivation. The secret report submitted to the provincial government by Yang Zefu 杨泽

21. Sichuan sheng dang'an'guan cang 四川省档案馆藏, "Maogong sibian ji 懋功事变记," cited in Liu Jun 2002, 51.

22. Zhu Qingbao, 1995, 10.

23. Zhang Weijiong, 1979, 50.

24. Zhang Weijiong, 1979, 51–53.

孚, the head of the No. 1 township, describes how the rebel Li Ergang 李洱刚 forced local strongmen to levy opium taxes on local people.[25] Tang Decheng 唐德成, the local strongman in Longxi township 龙溪乡 of Lifan county and the leader of the Gowned Brotherhood secret society, and his son Tang Zhongren 唐忠仁, the county councilor, instigated local people to plant poppy seeds. According to the "Official Petition to the Provincial Anti-Opium Inspector's Office Submitted by all the People of Longxi Township, Lifan County":

> They took the initiative to distribute poppy seeds, coerced people to pay opium taxes, and extorted the local people. They also established checkpoints without permission, levying taxes from the merchants who passed though the checkpoints. In 1947 when the two Tangs, father and son, distributed poppy seeds, they stipulated that "each liter of poppy seeds should produce one thousand grams of opium . . . " After the poppy was harvested, they "ordered the people to hand in the required full amount . . . " They had "each household plant thirty to fifty liters of poppy seeds and set a deadline for completing the planting. Otherwise the father and son would fine people 20,000 yuan for being lazy, using the fine as bonuses for people who grew more poppy . . . "[26]

At the due date, the Tangs would forcibly detain anyone who had not paid what was required, or they would use illegal punishments to interrogate and torture them. The helpless people had to sell or pawn their houses, land, pigs, oxen, sheep, or goats to pay the required taxes. Otherwise the Tangs would then, at a discount price, buy the houses and land of those who had been punished forcibly separating families.[27]

A custom called "gift exchange" (*dazhuan* 打转), introduced by the Gowned Brotherhood, was common in Tibetan areas in northwestern Sichuan. Seeing the potential for profit from the custom, Tibetan chieftains and headmen adopted it in their dealings with their subordinates. Every spring in Songpan when the gift exchange started, senior members of the Gowned Brotherhood, like Li Ergang and his son, would give local Tibetans a pair of straw sandals, a pack of cigarettes, and a box of brown sugar. Local Tibetans viewed this as an honor. In the fall they would present several ounces of opium to these senior

25. "Yang Zefu kuaiyou daidian 杨泽孚快邮代电" (1943), cited in Liu Jun 2002, 51.

26. "Lifan xian Longxi xiang quanti renmin zhi sheng jinyan ducha chu chengwen 理番县龙溪乡全体人民致省禁烟督察处呈文," October 31, 1949, cited in Liu Jun 2002, 51.

27. Ibid.

Chinese members. Wang Kaiyuan 王开元, the senior leader of the Gowned Brotherhood in Nanping 南坪, forced opium loans on people that had to be repaid at five times the original amount. When Bumgyel ('Bum rgyal; Chi. Banjia 班加), a Tibetan in Daokouba 刀口坝, could not repay 2,500 grams of opium to Wang, his father was sent into exile.[28]

During the opium harvest, the Tibetan *shoubei* 守备 (second captain), *qianzong* 千总(lieutenant), *bazong* 把总 (sergeant), senior members of the Gowned Brotherhood, and public security personnel in the township would descend on the villages. As a method of extortion, they would require local farmers to repay each gift of liquor, meat, or candies with 500 grams of opium as a token of gratitude. Following this gift exchange, they forced approximately two hundred households in Xiameng township 下孟乡 (Tib. 'Bo tog shu do yul tsho) in Lixian county to repay the gifts with over 10,000 grams of opium.[29]

Malfeasance: Getting Rich Quick

Expertise in poppy cultivation and associated techniques came from inland China. When a few Han Chinese outsiders secretly entered Tibetan areas to grow poppies for profit, local Tibetan chieftains, headmen, and local Han Chinese strongmen initially gave them ample protections. Later, local Tibetans were enticed into large-scale poppy cultivation. As commented on in the "Opium Eradication Plan for Lifan County in the Thirty-Fifth Year of the Republic Period" (理番县民国35年烟毒肃清计划), "Baozuo 包座 (Bab bzo), the Xiaoxing valley, the Rewu valley 热雾沟, and other areas in Songpan bordering on Xigu 西固, Minxian 岷县, and Zhuoni 卓尼 (Co ne) counties in Gansu 甘肃 Province had always attracted 'evil people' to gather there; in the fall, they would be enticed to secretly cultivate poppies."[30] In the territories of the Chuchen River (the Great Jinchuan River), "in the fourth or fifth month of the lunar calendar, some 'bad' people, who were mostly armed businessmen, secretly went to the region to seek profit; in the ninth and tenth month, relying on the 'evil forces,' they formed groups to travel illicitly beyond the boundaries of the county and go directly to Wenchuan 汶川 and Guanxian 灌县 counties. Proximate areas had high mountains and dense forests crisscrossed with small paths that provided safe havens for rebels growing poppies."[31] In 1935 a

28. Xinan minzu xueyuan yanjiushi 1952, 21.

29. Zhonggong Lixian xianwei diaochazu 1955b, 385.

30. "Yijiu siwu nian Lifan xian minguo sanshi wunian yandu suqing jihua 年理番县民国三十五年烟毒肃清计划" (1945), cited in Liu Jun 2002, 51.

31. Ibid.

great number of officers and soldiers were no longer active in the army. Many became "opium bandits" who robbed people of their opium. In the spring and winter when people began to plant poppy seeds, increasing numbers of ex-officers and ex-soldiers travelled to these opium growing regions to settle with their families.[32]

In Zhuokeji 卓克基 (Cog tse), Han Chinese from northern Sichuan (Chuanbei 川北), Guanxian, and other counties continuously entered Tibetan regions. By reclaiming wasteland or renting land from Tibetan chieftains and headmen to grow poppies, the practice of "dividing the manor" and renting the land became increasingly popular.[33]

Administrative Orders to Grow Poppies on a Large Scale[34]

Levying opium taxes was commonly used to raise funds to purchase poppy seeds. In Songpan county, "among those who invested in growing poppy in the southern route, the participants who incited others to grow poppies the most were the greater and lesser tribes under the jurisdiction of the great local Yunchang 云昌 chief, and the various tribes of Rewu 热雾 under the rule of the local chief of Maoniu valley毛牛沟."[35] The chieftain of Qiudi 邱地 "forced everyone in the nine valleys" (*jiugou* 九沟) to grow poppy. The poppy seeds were transported from Heishui. Each household was levied fifty yuan in advance in opium taxes. The chieftain would exact a heavy fine if a household resisted.[36] For each *mu* (0.167 acre) of poppies in the four villages 四寨 under the jurisdiction of Zhuokeji, about 390 grams of opium was levied. Chieftains would collect a "lazy tax" from those who did not grow poppies or who did not grow enough.[37]

Around 1940, in the Biesiman 别斯满 colony (*tun* 屯) of Maogong county, the practice of randomly selecting land for poppy cultivation started. The *shoubei* forced each village to set aside a field of first-rate land big enough to grow 30 decaliter of poppy seeds. The common people were required to provide plow oxen, agricultural tools, manure, fodder, and manpower, but they had to

32. "Ma Renlong qiancheng 马人龙签呈," March 24, 1949, cited in Liu Jun 2002, 52.

33. Sichuan minzu diaochazu 1958a, 260–61.

34. Administrative orders directed Tibetan chieftains, headmen and *shoubei* to grow poppies in areas under their jurisdiction.

35. "Shengfu tepaiyuan Liu Ren mibao 省府特派员刘任密报" (1945), cited in Liu Jun 2002, 53.

36. "Lifan xianzang Mi Zhen chuxun situ baogaoshu," 1948.

37. Zhonggong Ma'erkang gongwei diaochazu 1954, 277.

hand over what they harvested to the *shoubei*. What is most unusual is that the *shoubei* would use the yield of the village that produced the greatest amount of opium as the standard for levying the opium tax. Villages blamed for inefficient poppy cultivation had to provide the full amount or be fined. In 1949 the lower village (*xiazhai* 下寨) of Dengchun valley 登春沟 (Tib. Tum chung) alone harvested as much as 1,571,500 grams of opium. Thus opium had become the main tax levied by the Tibetan headmen and *shoubei*.[38] The Tibetan *shoubei* extorted opium levies from the common people, without a set time or an established amount. They could levy the opium taxes any time they wished. Once, the local strongman Gu Longguang 古龙光 collected 15,000 grams of opium in Dazan valley 大咱沟 in Maogong county. Opium also became the source of income for the *shoubei* who handled local disputes. In addition to the court fee (75 grams of opium from the plaintiff and 90 grams from the defendant), the plaintiffs and defendants were required to hand over two bottles of liquor, a leg of pork, and 100 grams of opium to the commander as his compensation for being on duty. Each year the *shoubei* could collect 6,000 grams of opium just for handling disputes. In the 1940s the people in Zhuokeji surrounded and attacked the official residence of the Zhuokeji chieftain because "the opium taxes were too heavy and the corvée labor was too frequent."[39]

According to archival sources, with the increased poppy cultivation, opium profits began to account for a greater portion of the total income for *shoubei* and headmen. Yang Chunwu 杨纯武, the *shoubei* of Lixian county, is one such example. Each year his income included 636.49 *dan* 担 (equivalent to 50 kilograms) of grain, 1,300 silver dollars (equivalent to 43.33 *dan* of grain), and 2,650 *liang* 两 (about 50 grams) of opium (equivalent to 665 *dan* of grain). Half his total income was from opium. As for his sources, 750 *liang* of opium was supplied by opium traders, 400 grams were from opium levies, 1,200 *liang* were the profits from his opium business, and 300 *liang* were from other opium income.[40]

Local public security units such as *bao* 保 and *jia* 甲 also extorted opium from farmers. Two hundred farmer households in Xiameng township in Lixian county had to provide over 10,000 grams of opium to public security units; on average, each household had to provide 10 *liang* of opium.[41]

38. Sichuan minzu xueyuan diaochazu n.d., 219.

39. Sichuan minzu xueyuan diaochazu n.d., 219.

40. Zhonggong Lixian xianwei diaochazu 1954, 399.

41. Zhonggong Lixian xianwei diaochazu 1955b, 385.

Profits Motivating Opium Cultivation

In 1935 poppy growers in Zhuokeji could sell their opium for several silver dollars per *liang*. Later the price rose suddenly and sharply to over twenty silver dollars. Usually they could make at least ten silver dollars per *liang*. Each *mu* of land could produce approximately 70 *liang* of opium. Opium income was more profitable than grain and other cash crops.[42]

Tibetan chieftains and headmen cooperated with local Han Chinese strongmen and gentry to grow poppy plants for great profit. Tibetan people grew poppy plants not only for profit but also to pay their taxes, extra levies, and the cost of lawsuits. This led to the vicious expansion of poppy cultivation in Tibetan areas in northwestern Sichuan.

A notable feature in the history of poppy cultivation in China was that poppy cultivation gradually infiltrated from regions along transportation lines to the remote borderland and mountains. Similarly, in Tibetan areas in northwestern Sichuan, poppy cultivation spread from Lixian and the valleys of the Greater and Lesser Jinchuan Rivers into the inland regions of the four Tibetan regions under the rule of Gyarong Tibetan chieftains (commonly known as *situ* 四土).[43] In Lixian county, people tentatively started growing poppy in 1919. By 1935 poppy fields were all over the county. In the area of Wutun 五屯 alone, the annual opium yield reached 10,000 *liang*. At the beginning of the Republic period, Han Chinese fled from Xiaojin and Heshui to Ma'erkang to grow poppy. At first the scale was rather small. After the chieftain of Zhuokeji allowed Han Chinese to grow poppy and demanded 50 *liang* of opium in taxes, poppy cultivation rapidly expanded. By the 1940s the Zhuokeji region had become one of the major areas for poppy cultivation in the Tibetan areas of northwestern Sichuan.

Opium Trade

With the expansion of poppy cultivation in Tibetan areas, markets emerged specializing in opium trading. In a way, opium was increasingly a force for wider integration of aforementioned Tibetan areas into new markets and political networks. Opium-trading groups and opium traders flocked to Tibetan areas, bringing with them bolts of cloth, general merchandise, farm implements, grain, and firearms in exchange for opium. In Tibetan areas exchanging

42. Sichuan minzu diaochazu 1958a, 260.

43. The "four Tibetan regions" include Choktsé, Somang (So mang), Dzongga (Rdzong dga'), and Tenpa (Bstan pa) or Dampa (Dam pa).

guns for opium was popular.[44] Opium became the medium of barter and sometimes functioned as currency.[45] During the opium harvest, an exceptionally robust opium market would emerge in the Tibetan areas of Sichuan. Large-scale poppy cultivation in these areas—especially in Aba—led to a brisk opium trade in the region. Two main groups came to purchase opium in the poppy-growing regions. One group consisted of businessmen from Gansu and Qinghai in northwestern China who had a great amount of capital, were quite powerful, and generally had rather complicated political backgrounds. The other group was composed of Han Chinese traders from Chengdu, Guanxian, and various counties in northern Sichuan who formed opium-trading groups. These groups possessed weapons and means of transportation. They had very close relations with the local military and political powers, as well as with local forces along the transportation routes, like the Gowned Brotherhood. Local Tibetan chieftains and headmen, local Chinese strongmen and gentry, as well as opium-trading groups from other regions actively supported local Tibetans to grow poppy plants. They also vied with one another to monopolize control over the opium produced in the region. Buying low and selling high, they raked in huge profits.

The Ma 马氏 brothers, for example, were the only agents in Maogong who purchased and sold opium. For years they were involved in weighing the opium when it was traded. No outside opium sellers dared to sell opium on their own in Maogong. Weapons and ammunition brought by outside opium traders (to trade for opium) had to use the Ma brothers as agents. When weapons and ammunition were good and cheap, the Ma brothers would purchase the entire inventory. Ma Qishu 马麒书 also controlled all the grain transported from Danba and Baoxing 宝兴. The common people had to rely on him to survive, and he often exploited them with high interest rates. If one borrowed 1 *dou* 斗 of grain from Ma Qishu, one needed to return 3 *dou* (equivalent to 10 liters of grain); if one borrowed 1 *liang* of opium, one would have to return 3 *liang* of opium.[46]

44. 1941 内政部视察员蒋天锡视察禁政工作报告, cited in Liu Jun 2002, 54.

45. Four Tibetan regions under the rule of Gyarong Tibetan chieftains began growing poppy in 1938. Merchants from various regions brought goods to exchange for opium. Gradually opium functioned as currency; 1 *liang* of opium was equal to ten silver dollars.

46. "Maogong shibian ji 懋功事变记," n.d., cited in Liu Jun 2002, 53.

Opium Markets

Along with the cultivation of poppy plants, stable and concentrated opium markets emerged in the Tibetan areas in Sichuan. As early as the beginning of the Republican period (1912–49), Kangding had become the biggest public opium market within Tibetan areas of Sichuan. The Sichuan Borderland Department of Finance (Chuanbian Caizhengting 川边财政厅) specifically printed stamp-tax receipts for opium trading consisting of 10-, 5-, 3-, and 1-*liang* denominations. After opium was transported to Kangding, the tax-collecting agencies would issue stamp-tax receipts for the taxes paid by the trader. Opium sellers pasted stamps on packages according to the amount purchased. Opium with stamps on the package could be sold openly and could be transported freely between the various tax-office outposts.

In 1932 the Kangding market sold approximately 3 million *liang* of opium, valued at 1.5 million taels of silver. Opium accounted for about 10 percent of the total sales volume for Kangding that year—more than sales of borderland tea, gold, or musk. Except for a small amount supplied to opium shops and dens in Kangding and other towns, most was transported to be sold in Chengdu, Ya'an 雅安, and other regions.

Opium sold at the Kangding market consisted of Yunnan opium and local opium. Yunnan opium was of good quality, but expensive. Local opium was produced in Kangding, Danba, Maogong, and other regions. Yunnan merchants brought opium to be sold in Kangding and also established firms—for example, Xishunxing 翕顺兴 and Sanyitai 三益泰—in Kangding that specialized in selling opium. Fieldwork conducted in 1932 reported over 140 opium shops in Kangding that had exquisite furniture and interior decoration. These shops sold only high-quality Yunnan opium. They frequently changed the style of their shop signs and also had signage in Tibetan script to attract Tibetans to smoke opium. The sales volume for these shops averaged 20 to 30 *liang* of opium per day, and the monthly sales volume for the entire city was over 2,000 *liang*.[47]

After Xikang Province was established in 1939, to prevent opium consumption from proliferating among the people, the provincial government abolished stamp-tax receipts for opium and openly selling opium became illegal. The government also established the Office for Eliminating the Use of Opium (Suqing yandu shiwusuo 肃清烟毒事务所) in Kangding and appointed Liu Wenhui's trusted follower Hu Yulong 胡玉龙 as director. Opium transported to Kangding had to be reported and registered with this office. The office

47. You Shimin 1990, 37.

would purchase the opium for less than the current market price and seal it for safekeeping. If opium brought into Kangding was not reported or was sold without permission, the opium would be confiscated and the seller would be arrested and heavily fined. During this period, opium disappeared from Kangding. Yunnan firms that had brought opium to Kangding also closed their shops and returned to Yunnan. Once the confiscated opium reached over 10,000 *liang*, it was transported to Ya'an to be sold. Sometimes it was transferred to Chengdu 成都, where the headquarters of No. 24 army under Liu Wenhui would deal with it. In fact, this became a major source of finance for Liu Wenhui.[48]

According to statistics in the *Illustrated History of Danba County*, the annual sales of opium traded in Danba in 1942 and 1943 was approximately 800,000 silver dollars.[49] During opium harvesting season, merchants would gather in Danba to exchange general merchandise and grain for opium. The gathering, known as "attending the opium market" (*gan yanhui* 赶烟会), would last over a month. The *Illustrated History of Jiulong County* records that, since the Republican period, opium had become a luxury item.[50] At each fair in Jiulong county, merchants could purchase several hundred kilograms of opium. Buyers and sellers of opium all belonged to the military. Opium sold for half a Tibetan silver dollar per tael could be resold for five or six silver dollars per tael. Buyers of several thousand *dan* of opium or tens of thousands of *dan* would be escorted by the military.

Along with the large-scale cultivation of opium in the Aba region (northwestern Sichuan), opium-trading markets emerged that were more numerous and prosperous than those in the Ganzi region. Xiaojin, Heishui, Songpan, Zhagunao 杂谷脑, Matang 马塘, Ma'erkang, and other areas became well-known collecting and distribution centers for opium trading. Traders also sold weapons and ammunition. In opium-producing regions of Songpan county, local Tibetans purchased over two thousand guns in 1941 alone. Each Tibetan household owned seven or eight guns. Thus, opium contributed to social unrest in Tibetan regions.[51]

A report submitted to the provincial government by the Songpan county government lists the opium markets in Songpan. It states that transported opium was destined for Taozhou 洮州 and Zhongba 中坝 in Gansu, and

48. Feng Youzhi 1991, 61–62.

49. Liu Zanting 1961a, 21.

50. Liu Zanting 1961b, 13.

51. Liu Jun 2002, 54.

Chengdu in Sichuan, and identifies leaders of the Gowned Brotherhood as the primary transporters.[52] Vendors at the Songpan market were selling "opium from the western route" produced in Heishui. The top grade sold for 120 silver dollars per *liang*. "Opium of the southern route" was of lesser quality and sold for 90 silver dollars per *liang*.

The Ma'erkang market deserves special attention. In the four regions ruled by Tibetan chieftains, the first opium market that came into being was the Matang market in Suomo 梭磨. With the rapid expansion of poppy cultivation in Zhuokeji that had yields as high as tens of thousands of *liang* of opium, the great trading market for opium was formed in Ma'erkang. Since the end of 1930s Ma'erkang had replaced Matang as the opium-trading center in Aba. The Ma'erkang region was under the jurisdiction of the chieftain Suo Guanying 索观瀛. He actively advocated poppy cultivation and also promised to ensure the safety of opium-trading companies and opium traders. In contrast, the social forces in the Maogong and Jinghua regions were rather complicated: thieves and bandits made buying and selling opium too dangerous, the roads were not conducive for transporting goods, and these regions lacked pastureland for grazing livestock. But the road in Ma'erkang was comparatively flat, there were pasturelands for grazing, and Ma'erkang could provide many diversions for pleasure-seeking opium smokers.[53]

Since 1943 opium growers in areas such as Songgang 松岗, Dazang 大藏, Chapuhe 查铺河, Sidaba 四大坝, Dangba 党坝, and Suomo went directly to Ma'erkang to sell their opium. The concentration of sales in Ma'erkang enticed major opium-trading firms in the northwest to the region. Meanwhile, the opium purchased during the harvesting season in Xiaojin, Lixian, Heishui, Chuosijia, Laisugou 来苏沟, and Caodeng 草登 was also transported to Ma'erkang. The Ma'erkang market had mainly Chinese Muslim traders (from Gansu and Qinghai) and Han Chinese merchants (from Guanxian, Chengdu, and northern Sichuan). The Chinese Muslim traders brought cotton cloth, flour, copperware, guns, and ammunitions to exchange for opium on a large scale—some had capital amounting to 100,000 silver dollars. The Han Chinese merchants brought cotton cloth, grain, rice, candies, salt, rapeseed oil, tea, and ironware to exchange for opium and medicinal herbs.[54]

The opium harvesting season was during the eighth and ninth lunar months. Opium fairs thrived. Tibetan, Han Chinese, and Chinese Muslim traders all

52. "Songpan xian zhengfu zhi shengzhengfu chengwen 松潘县政府致省政府呈文," n.d., cited in Liu Jun 2002, 55.

53. Lu Zichang 1984, 131–36.

54. Sichuan minzu diaochazu 1958a, 260–61.

gathered in Ma'erkang, where they designated an area as the marketplace. This turned Ma'erkang from a valley of boulders and stones into a prosperous tent market. Several hundred households attended the fair, which had two or three thousand buyers and sellers in total. Gansu merchants usually set up eight hundred temporary tents. With Suo Guanying's support, Ma'erkang established not only teahouses, taverns, stalls, and shops, but also casinos, brothels, pharmacies, inns, and weapon-repair shops. In addition, the first central primary school was founded in Ma'erkang. Thus in a short period of time Ma'erkang became the greatest trading market for the Aba Tibetan region.

According to a fieldwork report, the annual amount of opium traded in Ma'erkang market was at one point as high as several million *liang*. Two powerful families bought and sold opium there. One family was headed by the Qinghai Chinese Muslim warlord Ma Bufang 马步芳. With as much as 100,000 silver dollars in capital, he usually stayed at the residence of the Tibetan chieftain. He even set up his trading firm in Ma'erkang, so he could do business for a long period of time. The other family was headed by the Gungtang Lama (Gung thang bla ma) from Gansu, whose capital was also 100,000 silver dollars. Opium-trading firms would gather in Ma'erkang, bringing silver dollars, gold, guns, ammunition, and daily necessities like cooking oil, grain, and cloth. The variety of goods at the bustling market was surely a feast for the eyes.[55]

The Social Impact of Opium

Poppy cultivation and opium trading caused serious consequences for Tibetan communities in Sichuan—especially those in Aba. I summarize these consequences here.

Destruction of the Rural Social Economy and the Decline of Agricultural Production

Because of the promise of opium profits, fertile land was used to cultivate poppy, fertilizers were set aside for growing poppy, and manpower was concentrated on trading opium, which directly caused a decline in agricultural production and yield so that the greater part of grain rations had to rely on importing. A fieldwork report conducted in 1958 states that Maogong county grew a total of 5,000 *mu* of poppy with an annual yield of 3 million *liang* of opium. Poppy cultivation accounted for one-third of the total cultivated land.

55. Ge Ai 1989.

In the past, the grain produced in the county would last for seven months; after poppy cultivation took over, Maogong had to rely on importing grain from other counties. In Chome (Kyo smad = Jiesi 结思) township, over 40 percent of the cultivated land was for poppies, and the grain yield was minimal. In 1949 forty-three people from seven Tibetan households in Mulong 木龙 village produced 3,870 kilograms of grain with an average of 90 kilograms per person.[56] In Manai 马奈 township, only nine households had enough to eat; the remaining 150 households had enough grain for only half a year.[57]

Songpan county had been a grain production region. After poppy cultivation began, its grain production provided rations for only four months. The sharp reduction of land used to grow grain forced people in Songpan county to import grain from Danba, Baoxing, Guanxian, and Taozhou in Gansu province, which inflated the prices for grain and other goods. The price of goods in these borderland regions was several times higher than in inland China. Because poppy cultivation had spread across Maogong county, the price of grain soared. Ten liters of rice cost fourteen yuan; 20 liters of other grains cost thirteen yuan—several times higher than in former times. The price of daily necessities was also ten times higher than in other regions.[58] Before poppy cultivation took over, collecting and selling medicinal herbs had been a major means of economic support for farmers.

Promotion of Usury and the Increased Poverty of Tibetans

Tibetan chieftains and headmen had practiced usury before the introduction of poppy cultivation. Widespread poppy cultivation and the opium trade simply replaced grain and silver dollars as the main goods for usury; sometimes it even became the standard for calculating usury. Since so many people smoked opium, when there was a temporary shortage of opium, addicts had to borrow from the local chieftains. They repaid the loan after harvesting their opium, typically 6 *liang* for 1 *liang* borrowed, and annual interest was as high as 500 percent.

In Xiameng township in Lixian county, the annual interest rate for buying grain on credit was 20 percent, and it was 40 percent for a tael of silver. The annual interest rate for buying 1 *liang* of opium on credit was from 4 *liang* to 8 *liang* of opium. In 1955 the eight rich households in the township loaned

56. Sichuan minzu diaochazu 1958c, 355.

57. Sichuan minzu xueyuan diaochazu n.d., 220.

58. "Maogong xian dangbu baogao" (1940), cited in Liu Jun 2002, 56.

out 15 *dan* of grain, eighty silver dollars, and 500 *liang* of opium.[59] Whenever there were grain shortages, local chieftains and headmen exploited the exchange of grain for opium. In Chuosijia, 10 liters of grain—or even 7 liters of grain—could be exchanged for 1 *liang* of opium. Each year in Songgang, the local chieftain would supply the headmen of the various villages with grain and opium, using them as intermediaries to engage in usury. The village headmen would force loans on people—whether loans were needed or not. The chieftain of Ciba 刺巴, in Minor Heishui, obtained 5,000 *liang* of opium in interest on loans. Although poppy cultivation caused a dramatic reduction in grain production, the rent for land increasingly rose, and rent arrears were also subject to usury. These practices placed even heavier burdens on farmers and sped up the descent into poverty of the common people.

The Unbalanced Prosperity of Trade and Commerce

Before poppy cultivation and opium trade spread unchecked, trade and commerce in Tibetan areas in Sichuan had been underdeveloped. Most traders and merchants were Han Chinese or Chinese Muslims from other regions; there were very few Tibetan traders. Opium sales from poppy cultivation brought great profit to some people. In 1897 poppy cultivated on 1 *mu* of land could produce 50 to 60 *liang* of opium, worth eight taels of silver. For 110 kilograms of corn, one could receive only 1.8 taels of silver.[60] The price of opium rose continuously. Profits prompted the growth of the opium trade. Whenever it was time to harvest opium, Han Chinese, Chinese Muslims, and Tibetan traders from Gansu, Qinghai, Sichuan, and other provinces participated in opium fairs. Thus many new markets emerged.

Profiteering enticed a great number of local chieftains, headmen, monks, and common Tibetan people to engage in opium trading. Among 252 households in the Zhuokeji chief's four villages, 92 households (or 36 percent) invested 393,200 yuan in opium trading. The primary practice in Aba was to exchange the opium they produced for daily necessities such as grain, cooking oil, cloth, and wool. Profits from this exchange more than doubled.[61]

Commerce driven by opium trading in Tibetan areas prospered in the 1930s and 1940s. Market towns emerged featuring such a variety of goods that the markets were feasts for the eyes. The capital invested in these markets, and their scale, expanded gradually. However, there was no solid economic base for this

59. Zhonggong Lixian xianwei diaochazu 1955b, 382–83.

60. Liu Jun 2002, 57.

61. Zhonggong Ma'erkang gongwei diaochazu 1954, 286.

prosperity. Indeed, the reliance on opium trade prevented national trade and commerce from developing normally.

Economic Stagnation and Impoverishment in Tibetan Households

The abnormal development of the household economy was the most disastrous result of poppy cultivation and opium trading. According to a report conducted in 1954, the households of two headmen in Ri'e'ya 日俄亚, one of the four villages under the rule of the Zhuokeji chieftain, had an annual income of 1,950 yuan from 7,180 kilograms of grain, 120 yuan from 60 kilograms of butter, 6,000 yuan from trade income, and 9,000 yuan from 1,500 *liang* of opium. Opium accounted for 52 percent of their total income. The household of Gepo Mönnyang (Rgas po mon nyang [?] = Chi. Geerbu Menniang 格尔布门娘), the head of Ri'e'ya village, had an annual income of 266 yuan from 950 kilograms of grain, 30 yuan from butter, 2,000 yuan from trade income, and 3,600 yuan from 600 *liang* of opium. Opium accounted for 61 percent of his total family income. The household of Dromo (Gro mo [?] = Chi. Geluomu 格洛木), a Tibetan commoner in Yudruk (G.yu 'brug = Chi. Yingboluo 英波罗) village, had an annual income of 357 yuan from 2,520 kilograms of grain. His 5,400 yuan in income from opium and other opium-related businesses accounted for 89 percent of his total income.[62]

As these statistics clearly indicate, both the Tibetan elite and the common people relied on their income from opium. Basing the rural economy on opium was very dangerous, however. Once opium was effectively banned, the rural population's source of income would evaporate. Meanwhile, poppy cultivation and opium trade had not raised the living standard of the common people. The chieftains, headmen, and major opium traders enjoyed huge profits, but common Tibetans were faced with rising costs, usury practices, heavy opium levies, and a breakdown of the social order. An investigation from 1951 noted that Manai township in Dajin 大金 county had only three quilts, three plow oxen, and a few horses.[63]

Impact on Socioeconomic Relations in the Tibetan Communities of Sichuan

As a commercial agricultural product, opium inevitably impacted local socioeconomic systems. For instance, primary opium markets emerged locally

62. Zhonggong Ma'erkang gongwei diaochazu 1954, 289–90.

63. Sichuan minzu xueyuan diaochazu n.d., 220.

and class differentiation also intensified. In Lifan county, poppy cultivation resulted in land concentration because farmers had to pawn their land in order to survive. Pawning land was particularly common in the flat regions of valleys where tenant-farmers and semi-self-cultivators also serving as tenant-farmers already accounted for 50 percent of the total number of farming households, thus decreasing further the amount of land owned by small farmers.[64] If households pawned their land in the spring, when the price of opium was high, they received silver dollars based on the value of opium. When the price of opium plummeted in the fall, they received a certain amount of opium converted from its current decreased worth in silver dollars. Many farming households would lose either money or their land.[65] Unlike grain, opium is not a common commodity. As such, it seriously damaged commercial production and the social cohesion of minority regions. The buying and selling of land did not lead to the development of a landlord economy or the corresponding improvement of the Tibetan people's life. Instead, the land lay wasted and people became destitute and homeless.

Population Reduction and Declining Physical Constitutions

The unchecked spread of opium resulted in many opium addicts. According to incomplete statistics, half of the adults in Maogong, Lifan, and Jinghua smoked opium. It was said that "every household has an opium lamp and every family has an opium smoker."[66] The disaster caused by opium meant that even most young children and white-haired men smoked opium. People treated their guests with opium and used opium to treat diseases. Even sick babies were fed opium. Lifan county had the greatest number of people who smoked opium. Among 213 people in eight villages in Xiongshan 雄山 in Kampuk (Kam phug = Chi. Ganpu 甘堡), 92 were addicts; among 240 people in Longxi Kuapo 龙溪跨坡 village, over 80 were addicts. Among the twenty-eight households in Maluo 马骡 village in Xinglong 兴隆 township, only one household did not smoke opium.[67] In Manai township in Dajin county, 90 percent of the villagers were opium addicts.[68] With increasing numbers of opium addicts, opium

64. Zhonggong Lixian xianwei diaochazu 1955a, 372.

65. Sichuan minzu xueyuan diaochazu n.d., 219–20.

66. Liu Jun 2002, 58.

67. Zhonggong Lixian xianwei diaochazu 1955a, 372.

68. Sichuan minzu xueyuan diaochazu n.d., 221.

dens became prevalent in both villages and cities. In the city, three out of ten shops were opium dens.

Opium smoking had a disastrous effect on the physical constitution of Tibetans. Since most men in Jiesi township in Xiaojin smoked opium, it was the women who worked primarily.[69] The resultant decline in health affected fertility and led to a continuous reduction in population numbers. Toward the end of the Qing dynasty (i.e., 1890–1912), the twenty-four villages of Songping 松坪 valley had 248 households and a total population of 1,900; by 1949 only 130 households totalling 470 people remained. The population had decreased by 75 percent.[70] Kampuk colony in Lifan originally had 630 households. On the eve of the Communist takeover, only 300 households remained.

Poppy cultivation, opium trade, and opium consumption in Tibetan areas of Sichuan thrust these areas into commercial and administrative integration with the emergent modern China. It led to several key socioeconomic and political transformations in these regions. First, the high value of opium and its use as a trade good, as currency, and as a pillar of a regional tax system shifted the nature of the local economy in these regions. Transforming the self-contained agropastoral economy into an economy mainly based on opium production, trade, and consumption integrated the local economy into wider regional markets. Second, poppy cultivation and opium trade had grave economic and social consequences for Tibetan areas: it was the leading cause of poverty and economic stagnation in Tibetan areas, it reduced the availability of land for grain production, and it led to usury that prompted the pawning and selling of farmer household plots. It also led to the unchecked spread of firearms, thereby exacerbating unrest in these regions. Third, local Tibetan elites exploited the new market conditions and opium production to support their social positions. Their cooperation with the Gowned Brotherhood and local Han Chinese strongmen and gentry created a new web of local authority in these regions.

69. Sichuan minzu diaochazu 1958c, 357.

70. Sichuan minzu diaochazu 1958b..

References

Cao Shiyong 曹世镛. 1992. "Maogong huihan guanxi shishang de buxing shijian—Ji minguoyuannian sanyue chuba xihui zhenxiang 懋功回、汉关系史上的不幸事件—记民国元年三月初八洗回真相." *Aba zangzu qiangzu zizhizhou Xiaojin wenshi ziliao xuanji* 阿坝藏族羌族自治州小金文史资料选辑, vol. 3, 1–46.

Chen Mou 陈谋. 2021. "Minguo shiqi Sichuan sheng yapian zhongzhi de shikong liubu jiqi shehui yxiang 民国时期四川省鸦片种植的时空流布及其社会影响." MA thesis, Xining: Qinghai minzu daxue.

Feng Youzhi 冯有志. 1991. *Xikang shi shiyi* 西康史拾遗. Kangding: Ganzi zhou wenshi ziliao weiyuanhui.

Ge Ai 葛艾. 1989. "Suo Guanying chuan 索观瀛传." In *Difang lishi wenji* 地方历史文集. Ma'erkang: Aba zhou fanzhi diming bangongshi.

Hayes, Jack Patrick. 2014. *A Change in Worlds on the Sino-Tibetan Borderlands: Politics, Economies, and Environments in Northern Sichuan*. Lanham: Lexington Books.

"Lifan xianzang Mi Zhen chuxun situ baogaoshu 理番县长米珍出巡四土报告书." June 28, 1948. Chengdu: Sichuan sheng dang'an'guan, 54-7656.

Li Longchang 李隆昌. 1986. "Fangqu zhi shiqi Sichuan de yapian yanhuo 防区制时期四川的雅片烟祸." *Xinan shifan daxue xuebao* 西南师范大学学报 4: 117–23.

Li Tao 李涛. 1994. "Yapain yan zai Jiarong zangqu de chuanbo 鸦片烟在嘉绒藏区的传播." *Xizang minsu* 西藏民俗 1: 39–40.

Liu Jun 刘君. 2002. "Jindai Sichuan zangqu yapian maoyi jiqi shehui weihai 近代四川藏区鸦片贸易及其社会危害." *Zhongguo zangxue* 中国藏学 3: 50–58.

Liu Zanting 刘赞廷. 1961a. *Danba xian tuzhi—fu Chuosijia* 丹巴县图志—绰斯甲. Beijing: Minzu wenhuagong tushuguan.

———. 1961b. *Jiulong xian tuzhi* 九龙县图志. Beijing: Minzu wenhuagong tushuguan.

Lu Zichang 路梓常, Narrator, 1984. "Wo suo zhidao de Ma'erkang yandu qingkuang 我所知道的马尔康烟毒情况," compiled by Wang Ankang. In *Aba zangzu zizhizhou wenshi ziliao xuanji* 阿坝藏族自治州文史资料选辑, vol. 1, edited by Sichuan sheng Aba zhou zhengxie wenshi ziliao weiyuanhui, 131–36. Ma'erkang: Aba Zangzu Zizhizhou Yishuachang.

Qin Yi 秦熠. 2014. "Yapian zhongzhi yu Liangshan yiqu shehui bianqian (1908–1949) 鸦片种植与凉山彝区社会变迁 (1908–1949)." *Zhongnan minzu daxue xuebao* 中南民族大学学报 34.3: 31–35.

Sichuan minzu diaochazu 四川民族调查组. Dec. 1958a. "Zhuokeji tusi tongzhi diqu diaocha 卓克基土司统治地区调查." In Sichuan sheng bianjizu, 258–70.

———. Dec. 1958b. "Lixian Ganbao tun shehui qingkuang diaocha 理县甘堡屯社会情况调查." In Sichuan sheng bianjizu, 403–8.

———. Dec. 1958c. "Xiaojin xian Jiesi xiang shehui diaocha 小金县结思乡社会调查." In Sichuan sheng bianjizu, 354–70.

Sichuan minzu xueyuan diaochazu 四川省编辑组. n.d. "Jiarong zangzu shehui qingkuang diaocha 嘉绒藏族社会情况调查." In Sichuan sheng bianjizu, 178–257

Sichuan sheng Aba zangzu qiangzu zizhizhou Xiaojin xian difangzhi bianzuan weiyuanhui 四川省阿坝藏族羌族自治州小金县地方志编纂委员会. 1995. *Xiaojin xianzhi* 小金县志. Chengdu: Sichuan cishu chubanshe.

Sichuan sheng bianjizu 四川省编辑组. 1985. *Sichuan sheng Aba zhou zangzu shehui lishi diaocha* 四川省阿坝州藏族社会历史调查. Chengdu: Sichuan sheng sheui kexueyuan chubanshe.

Sichuan sheng Ganzi zangzu zizhizhou Danba xianzhi bianzuan weiyuanhui 四川省甘孜藏族自治州丹巴县志编纂委员会. 1996. *Danba xianzhi* 丹巴县志. Beijing: Minzu chubanshe.

Sichuan sheng Jiulong xian bianzuan weiyuanhui 四川省九龙县编纂文员会. 1997. *Jiulong xianzhi* 九龙县志. Chengdu: Sichuan renmin chubanshe.

Su Zhiliang 苏智良. 1997. *Zhongguo dupin shi* 中国毒品史. Shanghai: Shanghai renmin chubanshe.

Wang Di. 2001. *Kuachu fengbi de shijie* 跨出封闭的世界 Beijing: Zhonghua shuju.

Wyman, Judith. 2000. "Opium and the State in Late Qing Sichuan." In *Opium Regimes: China, Britain, and Japan, 1839–1952*, edited by Timothy Brook and Bob Tadashi Wakabayashi, 212–27. Berkeley: University of California Press.

Xinan minzu xueyuan yanjiushi 西南民族学院研究室, ed. 1952. "Caodi shehui diaocha 草地社会调查." In Sichuan sheng bianjizu, *Sichuan sheng Aba zhou zangzu shehui lishi diaocha*, 1–74.

Xu Zhengxue 徐正学. 1936. *Nongcun wenti* 农村问题, vol. 2. Nanjing: Zhongguo nongcun fuxing yanjiuhui.

Yao Xiguang 姚锡光. 1908. *Chendu congchao* 尘牍丛钞, vol. 2. Jing Shi: [n.p.].

You Shimin 游时敏. 1990. *Sichuan jindai maoyi shiliao* 四川近代贸易史料. Chengdu: Sichuan daxue chubanshe.

Zhang Weijiong. 1979. "Xikang jiansheng ji liuwenhui de tongzhi 西康建省及刘文辉的统治." *Sichuan sheng wenshi ziliao xuanji* 四川文史资料选辑, vol. 16, 23–53. Chengdu: Sichuan renmin chubanshe.

Zhonggong Lixian xianwei diaochazu 中共理县县委调查组. 1954. "Lixian Xinglong xiang diaocha 理县兴隆乡调查." In Sichuan sheng bianjizu, 389–402.

———. 1955a. "Lixian shehui diaocha 理县社会调查." In Sichuan sheng bianjizu, 371–77.

———. 1955b. "Lixian Xiameng xiang jieji qingkuang diaocha 理县下孟乡阶级情况调查." In Sichuan sheng bianjizu, 378–88.

Zhonggong Ma'erkang gongwei diaochazu 中共马尔康工委调查组. 1954. "Zhuokeji dubu xia sizhai shehui diaocha 卓克基督部下四寨社会调查." In Sichuan sheng bianjizu, 271–300.

Zhu Qingbao 朱庆葆. 1995. *Yapian yu jindai zhongguo* 鸦片与近代中国. Nanjing: Jiangsu jiaoyu chubanshe.

About the Contributors

Allison Aitken is assistant professor of philosophy at Columbia University. She earned her PhD from Harvard University in a joint program bridging the Departments of South Asian Studies and Philosophy. Her publications include a forthcoming monograph entitled *Introduction to Reality: Śrīgupta's Tattvāvatāravṛtti*, and her articles on topics in Indian and Tibetan Buddhist philosophy as well as Early Modern European philosophy have appeared in such journals as *Philosophers' Imprint*, *Analysis*, *Philosophy East and West*, and the *Journal of South Asian Intellectual History*.

Christopher I. Beckwith is a distinguished professor in the Department of Central Eurasian Studies at Indiana University. He has received a MacArthur Fellowship and other awards. He works on the philology, linguistics, history, and thought of Central Eurasia and neighboring regions. His publications include *The Tibetan Empire in Central Asia* (1987/1993), *Koguryo* (2004/2007), *Phoronyms* (2007), *Empires of the Silk Road* (2009), *Warriors of the Cloisters* (2012), *Greek Buddha* (2015), *Imperial Biblical Aramaic* (forthcoming), *The Scythian Empire* (forthcoming), and over sixty articles.

Yael Bentor, professor emerita at the Hebrew University of Jerusalem, is a scholar of Tibetan tantric Buddhism. Her research work focuses on the crystallization of tantric traditions among Tibetan scholar-yogis and the different choices made by them that contribute to the individual identity of their schools or sub-schools. Currently she is researching the workings of tantric visualizations according to various Tibetan scholars and the special affinities between the cosmos, the individual, and the meditation, according to Tsongkhapa. Her forthcoming publication together with Penpa Dorjee is a study and translation of the creation stage of the *Guhyasamāja Tantra* according to Kedrupjé Gelek Pelzang (Mkhas grub rje Dge legs dpal bzang), to be published by Wisdom Publications.

Cathy Cantwell was a research officer at the University of Oxford from 2002 to 2015 and is now an associate member of the Faculty of Asian and Middle

Eastern Studies and an honorary research fellow at the School of Anthropology and Conservation, University of Kent. She has specialized in Tibetan and Himalayan tantric rituals of all periods from the tenth century CE to the present, especially the ritual texts and practices deriving from the "Early Transmissions" (Snga 'gyur rnying ma). This work has included the critical and historical analysis of texts and the ethnographic study of contemporary rituals. Her books include *Dudjom Rinpoche's Vajrakīlaya Works: A Study in Authoring, Compiling and Editing Texts in the Tibetan Revelatory Tradition* (2020, https://www.equinoxpub.com/home/dudjom-rinpoches/) and, with Robert Mayer, *A Noble Noose of Methods, the Lotus Garland Synopsis: A Mahāyoga Tantra and Its Commentary* (2012).

The late Hubert Decleer (1940–2021) wrote his final publication for this volume. Starting in the mid-1980s, he directed the School for International Training's program for Tibetan studies in Kathmandu, Nepal, for nearly thirty-five years. He is the author of many scholarly articles and book reviews, and the festschrift *Himalayan Passages* was published in his honor in 2014. He sadly passed away on August 25, 2021, and a traditional cremation ceremony was held for him at the Bijeśvarī Vajrayoginī temple near Swayambhū.

Franz-Karl Ehrhard (PhD, University of Hamburg, 1987) is professor emeritus of Tibetan and Buddhist studies, Ludwig Maximilian University, Munich. His research work centers on religious and literary traditions in Tibet and the Himalayas. Recent publications include the coedited volume *Tibetan Printing: Comparison, Continuities, and Change* (2016) and *A Mirror of Jewels Which Clears Away Errors: A Critical Guide to the Sacred Sites of the Nepal Valley* (2020).

Holly Gayley, associate professor in the Department of Religious Studies at the University of Colorado Boulder, is a scholar and translator of contemporary Buddhist literature in Tibet. Her research areas include gender and sexuality in Buddhist tantra, ethical reform in contemporary Tibet, and theorizing translation, both literary and cultural, in the transmission of Buddhist teachings to North America. She is the author of *Love Letters from Golok: A Tantric Couple in Modern Tibet* (2016), the coeditor of *A Gathering of Brilliant Moons: Practice Advice from the Rimé Masters of Tibet* (2017), the translator of *Inseparable across Lifetimes: The Lives and Love Letters of Namtrul Rinpoche and Khandro Tāre Lhamo* (2019), and the editor of *Voices from Larung Gar: Shaping Tibetan Buddhism for the Twenty-First Century* (2021). Her articles on contemporary Nyingma figures and communities in eastern Tibet have appeared in the *His-*

tory of Religions, the *Journal of Buddhist Ethics*, *Contemporary Buddhism*, *Religions*, the *Journal of Religious Ethics*, and the *Himalaya Journal*.

James Gentry is assistant professor of religious studies at Stanford University. He specializes in Tibetan Buddhism, with particular focus on the literature and history of its tantric traditions. He is the author of *Power Objects in Tibetan Buddhism: The Life, Writings, and Legacy of Sokdokpa Lodrö Gyeltsen* (2017), which examines the roles of tantric material and sensory objects in the lives and institutions of Tibetan and Himalayan Buddhists. His current projects include a study and translation of Sokdokpa Lodrö Gyeltsen's *Thunder of Definitive Meaning* (*Nges don 'brug sgra*) and a history of the *maṇi* pill and other pill traditions in Tibet that incorporate the flesh and bodily remains of the Buddhist special dead.

Jörg Heimbel is a lecturer in classical and colloquial Tibetan at the University of Hamburg, where he received his PhD in 2014. His research interest is in Tibetan cultural and religious history. He has published articles on the history of the Ngor and Sakya traditions, Buddhist ascetic traditions, vegetarianism, book culture, and Tibetan art. His recent publications are *Vajradhara in Human Form: The Life and Times of Ngor chen Kun dga' bzang po* (2017) and *The Ngor Branch Monastery of Go mig (sTeng rgyud) in Spiti* (2019). He is the founder of *Ngor's Textual Treasures*, an interactive web application presenting the results of an ongoing cataloguing project of a collection of manuscripts from Ngor Monastery.

Isabelle Henrion-Dourcy is professor of anthropology at Université Laval in Québec. She investigates Tibetan popular culture, looking at drama, pop music, dance, television, social media, cinema, and autobiographical writing. She seeks to understand the cultural and political dynamics running through High Asia—namely, the shifts in imaginaries and identity occurring in Tibetan societies since the takeover of the People's Republic of China, how tradition and modernity play out in ideology and practice, the uses of cultural heritage, and the emergence of contemporary Tibetan cultural forms—both official and popular. Her publications include *Le théâtre ache lhamo: Jeux et enjeux d'une tradition tibétaine* (2017), and she has edited three volumes on Tibetan performing arts and the anthropology of media.

Nathan W. Hill is the Sam Lam Professor in Chinese Studies and director of the Trinity Centre for Asian Studies at Trinity College, Dublin. He was educated at the Catlin Gabel School (1998) and Harvard University (AB 2003,

PhD 2009). Before coming to Ireland, he was a reader in Tibetan and Himalayan studies at SOAS University of London (2015–21), where he led the Department of East Asian Languages and Cultures (2017–19). He has had shorter term appointments at Tübingen, Munich, Berkeley, Renmin Daxue, and Zhongyang Minzu Daxue. His research focuses on the history of Tibetan and Sino-Tibetan comparative linguistics. His most recent book is *The Historical Phonology of Tibetan, Burmese, and Chinese* (2019).

Daniel A. Hirshberg is the founder and executive director of SŌTERIC Contemplative Training in Boulder, Colorado (www.soteric.org). Thanks to Leonard van der Kuijp's incomparable mentorship, he completed his PhD in Tibetan studies at Harvard University. The monograph based on his dissertation, *Remembering the Lotus-Born: Padmasambhava in the History of Tibet's Golden Age*, won Honorable Mention for the E. Gene Smith Book Prize from the Association for Asian Studies. Before moving to Boulder, Dan was an associate professor of religious studies at the University of Mary Washington, where he established one of the first contemplative studies programs, built a Japanese-style garden on campus, and led study-abroad programs to Nepal and Japan. He has held yearlong fellowships at the University of California Santa Barbara, LMU Munich, and the University of Virginia's Contemplative Sciences Center. He presently serves as visiting faculty for the University of Colorado Boulder's Tibet Himalaya Initiative and Naropa University's Psychedelic Studies program, and as the editor of the *Journal of the North American Japanese Garden Association.*

Pascale Hugon is a senior research associate at the Institute for the Cultural and Intellectual History of Asia at the Austrian Academy of Sciences. She studied Indology and Tibetology at the University of Lausanne (Switzerland). She was preparing a dissertation on Sa skya Paṇḍita when Leonard van der Kuijp entrusted her with copies of an epistemological summary by Mtshur ston Gzhon nu seng ge, which shaped the course of her subsequent research. Following the fortunate recovery of numerous additional significant texts by bKa' gdams pa scholars, her current research examines the early development of Tibetan scholasticism on a broader scale in the framework of the ERC-funded project "The Dawn of Tibetan Buddhist Scholasticism (eleventh–thirteenth centuries)" (TibSchol). Her publications include editions, translations, and thematic studies based on Sanskrit and Tibetan materials. Together with Jonathan Stoltz, she recently published the first monograph on Phya pa Chos kyi seng ge (*The Roar of a Tibetan Lion*, 2019).

Ishihama Yumiko is a professor in the School of Education at Waseda University. Her research primarily concerns the history of Qing-Tibet relations and of the age of the Fifth Dalai Lama. Her recent publications include *The Resurgence of "Buddhist Government": Tibetan-Mongolian Relations in the Modern World* (2019) and *The Early 20th Century Resurgence of the Tibetan Buddhist World* (edited with Alex McKay, 2021).

David P. Jackson received his PhD from the Department of Asian Languages and Literature at the University of Washington in 1985. He served for fourteen years as professor of Tibetan Studies at Hamburg University and is the author of several books and articles on Tibetan painting, including *Tibetan Thangka Painting: Method and Materials* (1984) and *A History of Tibetan Painting* (1996). He visited Tibet twice and the Himalayas a number of times, also living and working in both India and Japan for several years. He participated in a mural preservation project in Lhasa organized by Professor Knud Larsen in Norway. He was for ten years curator at the Rubin Museum of Art in New York, dedicated primarily to Himalayan pictorial art, producing a series of six catalogs including *The Nepalese Legacy in Tibetan Painting* (2010), *The Place of Provenance* (2012), and *A Revolutionary Artist of Tibet* (2016). His main biographical studies are *A Saint in Seattle* (2003) and *Lama of Lamas* (2020). He lives in the Pacific Northwest.

Matthew T. Kapstein is emeritus professor of Tibetan studies at the École Pratique des Hautes Études, Paris, and former Numata Visiting Professor of Buddhist Studies at the University of Chicago. His recent publications include *The Many Faces of King Gesar*, coedited with Charles Ramble. A major work on Tibetan codicology and paleography, *Tibetan Manuscripts and Early Printed Books*, in two volumes, is to be published shortly by Cornell University Press.

Christina Kilby is associate professor of religion at James Madison University. She earned her master's degree from Harvard Divinity School, where she had the pleasure of attending Leonard van der Kuijp's classes, and her doctoral degree in religious studies from the University of Virginia. She has published several articles on Tibetan epistolary literature. Her current work focuses on Buddhism and migration.

Todd Lewis is the Distinguished Professor of Arts and Humanities and a professor of religion at the College of the Holy Cross. His primary research since 1979 has been on Newar Buddhism in the Kathmandu Valley and the social history of Buddhism. Lewis has authored many articles on the Buddhist traditions of Nepal and the book *Popular Buddhist Texts from Nepal: Narratives and Rituals of Newar Buddhism* (2000). Recent books include the coedited *Teaching Buddhism: New Insights on Understanding and Presenting the Traditions* (2016), *Buddhists: Understanding Buddhism through the Lives of Practitioners* (2014), and the coauthored textbook *World Religions Today* (seventh edition, 2021). His translation *Sugata Saurabha: An Epic Poem from Nepal on the Life of the Buddha by Chittadhar Hridaya* (2010) received awards from the Khyentse Foundation and the Numata Foundation as the best book on Buddhism in 2011. His most recent publication, with Jinah Kim, is *Dharma and Puṇya: Buddhist Ritual Art of Nepal* (2019).

Jue Liang is assistant professor in the Department of Religion at Denison University. She received her PhD in religious studies from the University of Virginia in 2020. Her dissertation, "Conceiving the Mother of Tibet: The Life, Lives, and Afterlife of the Buddhist Saint Yeshe Tsogyel," examines the literary tradition surrounding the matron saint of Tibet, Yeshe Tsogyel, in the fourteenth and fifteenth centuries. She first met Leonard in 2010 in his literary Tibetan seminar at Renmin University of China in Beijing. Since then he has been a constant source of inspiration and wisdom, with his endless curiosity about everything that Tibetan texts have to offer.

Rory Lindsay is assistant professor in the Department for the Study of Religion at the University of Toronto and an editor at 84000: Translating the Words of the Buddha. He completed his PhD under Leonard's inimitable tutelage from 2009 to 2018.

Cuilan Liu is assistant professor of religious studies at the University of Pittsburgh. She received her PhD from Harvard University in 2014, where she made the documentary film *Young Jigme*, screened at the 2015 International Jean Rouch Film Festival in Paris. Her research focuses on the legal interaction between Buddhism and the state in China, Tibet, and India. Her publications have appeared in the *History of Religions*, the *Journal of Chinese Religions*, the *Journal of the International Association of Buddhist Studies*, the *Journal of the American Oriental Society*, and the *Journal of Indian Philosophy*.

Zhouyang Ma is a PhD candidate in Inner Asian and Altaic studies at Harvard University. His current project aims to delineate the history of the rise of Tibetan Buddhism in the Tangut Xia state (1038–1127) with a focus on Gsang phu ne'u thog scholasticism. Much of his side interest in Tibetan linguistics was inspired by the course "Sa skya Paṇḍita's Linguistics" taught by Professor van der Kuijp in spring 2019 and by working as a teaching fellow for his classical Tibetan courses. Zhouyang Ma is also a pianist and composer. Playing the piano at the professor's house parties is one of his best memories.

Ian MacCormack is the Khyentse Lecturer in Buddhist Studies at the Hebrew University of Jerusalem. He received his PhD from Harvard University in 2018. His research concerns relations of Buddhism and state in early modern Tibet. He is currently writing a book on the central Tibetan state in the late seventeenth century.

Robert Mayer left school intending to avoid an academic career. However, after befriending Michael Aris, he ended up doing a BA in religious studies at the University of Bristol in England. This was followed by a PhD at Leiden University in the Netherlands, where he enjoyed the immense good fortune of having Leonard van der Kuijp as his main PhD examiner. He spent most of his subsequent academic career in the Faculty of Oriental Studies (now the Faculty of Asian and Middle Eastern Studies) at the University of Oxford, enjoying visiting appointments at the Humboldt University in Berlin and at Ruhr-Universität Bochum. He has both British and German citizenship.

William A. McGrath is the Robert H. N. Ho Family Foundation Assistant Professor of Buddhist Studies at New York University, where he teaches in the Department of Religious Studies. His research primarily concerns the historical intersections of religion and medicine in Tibet, and he recently edited the volume *Knowledge and Context in Tibetan Medicine* (2019).

Shoko Mekata is an associate and Tibetan-language instructor in the Department of South Asian Studies at Harvard University. She received her PhD in intercultural studies (with a focus on Tibetan studies) in 2011 from Otani University, Kyoto. Her research focuses on the Sakya sect in the twelfth to fifteenth centuries.

Kurtis R. Schaeffer is the Frances Myers Ball Professor in the Department of Religious Studies at the University of Virginia, where he codirects the Tibetan Studies Program. He was a student of Leonard van der Kuijp at Harvard from 1991 to 2000. His books include *Himalayan Hermitess* (2004), *Dreaming the Great Brahmin* (2005; derived from his PhD dissertation, supervised by van der Kuijp), *The Culture of the Book in Tibet* (2009), *An Early Tibetan Survey of Buddhist Literature* (with Leonard van der Kuijp), and *The Life of the Buddha by Tenzin Chögyel* (2015). His edited volumes include *Among Tibetan Texts: History and Literature of the Tibetan Plateau* by E. Gene Smith (2000), *Power,*

Politics, and the Reinvention of Tradition with Bryan J. Cuevas (2006), *Sources of Tibetan Tradition* with Matthew T. Kapstein and Gray Tuttle (2013), and *The Tibetan History Reader* with Gray Tuttle (2013). His interests include the cultural and literary history of Tibet.

Peter Schwieger is professor emeritus of Tibetan studies at Bonn University in Germany. His publications cover the literature of the Tibetan Nyingma school, Tibetan diplomatics, Ladakhi and Tibetan history, Tibetan oral literature, and the grammar of Tibetan language. Among his key publications are *Conflict in a Buddhist Society: Tibet under the Dalai Lamas* (2021), *The Dalai Lama and the Emperor of China: A Political History of the Tibetan Institution of Reincarnation* (2015), *Handbuch zur Grammatik der klassischen tibetischen Schriftsprache* (2009), and *Teilung und Reintegration des Königreichs von Ladakh im 18. Jahrhundert. Der Staatsvertrag zwischen Ladakh und Purig aus dem Jahr 1753* (1999).

Michael R. Sheehy is a research assistant professor and the director of scholarship at the Contemplative Sciences Center at the University of Virginia. He first met Leonard van der Kuijp vicariously as a graduate student through stories told by Steven D. Goodman about taxi driving below the freezing point in Saskatoon, where they studied with the Tibetologist Herbert V. Guenther. While director of research at the Tibetan Buddhist Resource Center (renamed BDRC), he got to know Leonard via E. Gene Smith, and heard stories about their cocktail hours during the good ole days of Tibetology in Delhi. While living in Cambridge, and as a visiting scholar at Harvard University, he was fortunate to sit in on Professor van der Kuijp's Tibetan reading seminars and collaborate with him on text preservation efforts in Tibetan cultural regions of China. He is coeditor of *The Other Emptiness: Rethinking the Zhentong Buddhist Discourse in Tibet* (2019).

Victoria Sujata is an author, translator, annotator, photographer, and compiler of musical recordings she has made on the Tibetan plateau. She embarked upon her studies of Tibetan and Himalayan regions unexpectedly in her forties. Until then she had devoted herself to Physics (BA, 1969, Northwestern University), Classical Guitar (BM, 1978), and Theoretical Studies (MM, 1980, New England Conservatory of Music). Those paths seemed fulfilling enough for a lifetime, but a single trip to a Tibetan refugee camp in Nepal in the late 1980s inspired certainty in her that she had to be with Tibetan people and know about their culture. This led to studies at Harvard (MA, Sanskrit and Indian Studies, 1996; and PhD, Inner Asian and Altaic Studies, 2003), where she was fortunate to study with Professors Michael Aris and Leonard van der

Kuijp. For some four months a year since 1989 she has been visiting Amdo, Kham, and Himalayan regions, where she blends pilgrimage and scholarship, and specializes in a genre of Tibetan songs called *gur* (*mgur*), or songs of realization. Her publications include *Tibetan Songs of Realization: Echoes from a Seventeenth-Century Scholar and Siddha in Amdo* (2005); *Songs of Shabkar: The Path of a Tibetan Yogi Inspired by Nature* (2011); and *Journey to Distant Groves: Profound Songs of the Tibetan Siddha Kälden Gyatso* (2019).

Sun Penghao is a doctoral student at Harvard University. His dissertation asks how Tibetans presented the Mongols during the thirteenth to fourteenth centuries and how the etiquette concerns and the arrival of many official documents from the Yuan played a role in such presentations through the case of Orgyenpa and Qubilai. He has published an edition of the 1780 quadrilingual inscriptions and a study of several Kharakhoto documents related to Padampa Sanggyé.

Gray Tuttle, the Leila Hadley Luce Professor of Modern Tibetan Studies at Columbia University, studies the history of twentieth-century Sino-Tibetan relations as well as Tibet's relations with the China-based Manchu Qing empire. Since Leonard van der Kujip's arrival at Harvard, Gray has had the good fortune to work with him on many projects, from the first international Amdo conference to TBRC.

Ivette Vargas-O'Bryan is chair and professor of religious studies at Austin College. Among her notable publications is the edited volume with Zhou Xun, *Disease, Religion and Healing in Asia: Collaborations and Collisions* (2015), based on her long-term interest in the interface of religion and healing traditions in South and East Asia. She is best known for her innovative studies on the Dge slong ma Dpal mo legacy and disease deities in Tibetan medicine. Her book on the Dge slong ma legacy (*Dpal mo lugs*) is forthcoming in 2023. As a scholar of visual culture, she has curated several exhibitions on Indian and Tibetan Buddhist art and was a scholar-in-residence at the Trammell and Margaret Crow Collection of the Asian Art Museum in Dallas, Texas. Her second project on Newar Buddhist murals in Kathmandu, Nepal, with the art historian Naresh Shakya offers a provocative lens on the preservation of a critical cultural legacy after devastating earthquakes.

Pieter C. Verhagen is the University Lecturer of the Language and Culture of Tibet at the Leiden University Institute for Area Studies (LIAS), the Netherlands. The focus of his research lies in the area of indigenous (Sanskrit and

Tibetan) grammar in Tibet and the scriptural hermeneutics of Indo-Tibetan Buddhism.

Cameron David Warner is associate professor of anthropology and director of the Anthropology Research Program at Aarhus University. His research interests include material culture, social media, gender, music, migration, development, and of course Buddhism among Tibetans and Nepalis. From 2015 to 2022, he has been the principal investigator on *Precious Relics: Materiality and Value in the Practice of Ethnographic Collection*, a project funded by the Danish Council for Independent Research, as well as a contributing member to ongoing SSHRC- and ERC-funded research projects. In 2022 he edited *Impermanence: Exploring Continuous Change across Cultures*. He was extremely fortunate to study with Leonard from 1999 to 2008.

Michael Witzel, the Wales Professor of Sanskrit in the Department of South Asian Studies, Harvard University, studied at the University of Tübingen, the University of Erlangen-Nürnberg (PhD), and Tribhuvan University in Kathmandu. He has taught at Tübingen, Leiden, and Harvard (since 1986), and was director of the Nepal-German Manuscript Preservation Project and the Nepal Research Center at Kathmandu (1972–78). He has held six visiting positions in Paris, Kyoto, and Tokyo. He is the editor of the Harvard Oriental Series (since 1990) and Opera Minora (since 1995), and the founder and editor in chief of the *Electronic Journal for Vedic Studies* (since 1995). Some recent publications include *Inside the Texts—Beyond the Texts* (1997), *Das Alte Indien* (2003/2010), *The Origins of the World's Mythologies* (2012), *Der Rig-Veda* (2007, 2013), and *The Veda in Kashmir* (2020).

Yudru Tsomu is professor at the Center for Tibetan Studies, Sichuan University, People's Republic of China. A native of Kham, she received her PhD in Tibetan studies in 2006 from Harvard University and was a postdoctoral fellow at Stanford University in 2007. From 2007 to 2014 she served as assistant professor in the Department of History at Lawrence University. Her main academic interests are Tibetan history and culture from the late eighteenth century to the first half of the twentieth century and the history of Sino-Tibetan relations. She has a long and continuing interest in the historical continuity and disjuncture that marks the relationship between the center and the periphery, and between majority and minority discourse. Through her research she hopes to contribute to an understanding of Sino-Tibetan relations not only from a political perspective but also within the larger field of historical and cultural exchange and accommodation.

Tabula Gratulatoria

Orna Almogi
John Ardussi
Katia Buffetrille
Volker Caumanns
Christoph Cüppers
Hildegard Diemberger
Dragomir Dimitrov
Dorje Nyingcha
Dorji Wangchuk
Karl-Heinz Everding
Janet Gyatso
Paul Harrison
Jens-Uwe Hartmann
Sonam Kachru
Melissa Kerin
Suah Kim
Natalie Köhle
Per Kvaerne
Ruohong Li
Charles Manson
Petra Maurer
Eric Mortensen
Ulrich Pagel
Charles Ramble
Cristina Scherrer-Schaub
Weirong Shen
Jonathan Silk
Per K. Sørensen
Cyrus Stearns
Ernst Steinkellner
Dominique Townsend
Nicole Willock

Studies in Indian and Tibetan Buddhism
Titles Previously Published

Among Tibetan Texts
History and Literature of the Himalayan Plateau
E. Gene Smith

Approaching the Great Perfection
Simultaneous and Gradual Methods of Dzogchen Practice in the Longchen Nyingtig
Sam van Schaik

Authorized Lives
Biography and the Early Formation of Geluk Identity
Elijah S. Ary

Buddhism between Tibet and China
Edited by Matthew T. Kapstein

The Buddhist Philosophy of the Middle
Essays on Indian and Tibetan Madhyamaka
David Seyfort Ruegg

Buddhist Teaching in India
Johannes Bronkhorst

A Direct Path to the Buddha Within
Gö Lotsāwa's Mahāmudrā Interpretation of the Ratnagotravibhāga
Klaus-Dieter Mathes

The Essence of the Ocean of Attainments
The Creation Stage of the Guhyasamāja Tantra according to Panchen Losang Chökyi Gyaltsen
Yael Bentor and Penpa Dorjee

Foundations of Dharmakīrti's Philosophy
John D. Dunne

Freedom from Extremes
Gorampa's "Distinguishing the Views" and the Polemics of Emptiness
José Ignacio Cabezón and Geshe Lobsang Dargyay

Himalayan Passages
Tibetan and Newar Studies in Honor of Hubert Decleer
Benjamin Bogin and Andrew Quintman

How Do Mādhyamikas Think?
And Other Essays on the Buddhist Philosophy of the Middle
Tom J. F. Tillemans

Jewels of the Middle Way
The Madhyamaka Legacy of Atiśa and His Early Tibetan Followers
James B. Apple

Living Treasure
Buddhist and Tibetan Studies in Honor of Janet Gyatso
Edited by Holly Gayley and Andrew Quintman

Luminous Lives
The Story of the Early Masters of the Lam 'bras Tradition in Tibet
Cyrus Stearns

Mind Seeing Mind
Mahāmudrā and the Geluk Tradition of Tibetan Buddhism
Roger R. Jackson

Mipham's Beacon of Certainty
Illuminating the View of Dzogchen, the Great Perfection
John Whitney Pettit

Omniscience and the Rhetoric of Reason
Śāntarakṣita and Kamalaśīla on Rationality, Argumentation, and Religious Authority
Sara L. McClintock

Reasons and Lives in Buddhist Traditions
Studies in Honor of Matthew Kapstein
Edited by Dan Arnold, Cécile Ducher, and Pierre-Julien Harter

Reason's Traces
Identity and Interpretation in Indian and Tibetan Buddhist Thought
Matthew T. Kapstein

Remembering the Lotus-Born
Padmasambhava in the History of Tibet's Golden Age
Daniel A. Hirshberg

Resurrecting Candrakīrti
Disputes in the Tibetan Creation of Prāsaṅgika
Kevin A. Vose

Scripture, Logic, Language
Essays on Dharmakīrti and His Tibetan Successors
Tom J. F. Tillemans

Sexuality in Classical South Asian Buddhism
José I. Cabezón

The Svātantrika-Prāsaṅgika Distinction
What Difference Does a Difference Make?
Edited by Georges Dreyfus and Sara McClintock

Vajrayoginī
Her Visualizations, Rituals, and Forms
Elizabeth English

About Wisdom Publications

Wisdom Publications is the leading publisher of classic and contemporary Buddhist books and practical works on mindfulness. To learn more about us or to explore our other books, please visit our website at wisdomexperience.org or contact us at the address below.

Wisdom Publications
132 Perry Street
New York, NY 10014 USA

We are a 501(c)(3) organization, and donations in support of our mission are tax deductible.

Wisdom Publications is affiliated with the Foundation for the Preservation of the Mahayana Tradition (FPMT).